GUEVARA
ALSO KNOWN AS
CHE

Paco Ignacio
Taibo II

Translated by
Martin Michael Roberts

St. Martin's Griffin
New York

The photographs in this book are used with the permission of the Spanish editions of : AIN; *Revista Verde Oliva; Juventad Rebelde; Bohemia; El Universal; Rodrigo Moya;* and from *Archivo particular de Luis Adrian Betáncourt.*

Design by Bryanna Mills

Library of Congress Cataloging-in-Publication Data

Taibo, Paco Ignacio.
  [Ernesto Guevara. English]
  Guevara, also known as Che / Paco Ignacio Taibo II ; translated by
Martin Michael Roberts.
    p. cm.
  Includes bibliographical references.
  ISBN 0-312-15539-5 (hc)
  ISBN 0-312-20652-6 (pbk)
  1. Guevara, Ernesto, 1928-1967. 2. Guerillas—Latin America—
Biography. I. Title.
  F2849.22.G85T3313   1997
  980.03'3'092—dc21
  [B]

                                                  97-15343
                                                  CIP

First St. Martin's Griffin Edition: August 1999

10 9 8 7 6 5 4 3 2 1

This book is for my friends Miguel Bonasso and Juan Gelman, Argentines and Guevara buffs both, two things that are not well thought of these days.

Contents

Human beings are too important to be treated like mere symptoms of the past.

—*Lytton Strachey*

You have to love a lot to do something. To love passionately, you have to believe like crazy.

—*Régis Debray, talking about Che*

Author's Note

This is not an easy book, and doubtless the story it tells is caught between the point of view of those who came along afterward, the "forever after" generation, and their innocent children; nonetheless an effort must be made to read it as a story "from back then." There is no such thing as an innocent read. We now know that the second wave of the Latin American revolution washed up on the shore and quickly receded—that the industrial model set forth by Che worked in the short term and then wore itself out in the medium term without his style and supervision. We will read the book while knowing the final outcome of Che's operation in Bolivia.

Although we know all this, I would like to have the book read as a story "from back then," because only then may it be understood. The story cannot be told working back from the outcome to its origins, as then the perspective will be skewed. A biography is not an explanation of a dead man; as Lytton Strachey said in an inspired moment, human beings are too important to be treated like mere symptoms of the past. Characters are formed by acts whose consequences they will never learn. The story that interests me is not one that starts from the outcome and explains it, but one that is set in motion in the past, and whose leading players never had a crystal ball in which to see their future mapped out in our present.

It is amazing but true that Che's ghost, in a no-man's-land without visa or passport, is caught halfway across a generation gap. On one side, young people who do not know a lot about him but are dimly aware of him as the great utopian commander and red grandfather; on the other, the sixties generation who came late or whose plans failed (those of whom the Argentine poet Paco Urondo said, foreseeing his own fate: "We will lose our lives / badly") but who understand that Che is still the herald of a Latin American revolution that, as impossible as it might seem, is absolutely necessary.

Furthermore—in spite of his caustic wit and natural shyness—his ghost has been trapped in imagery, innocent or harmful machinery that tries to empty all contents from everything that comes its way, turning it into commercial goods—T-shirts, souvenirs, coffee mugs, posters, photographs. This is the fate of those who inspire nostalgia: to be trapped in the coffers of consumerism or in the shelter of innocence.

The list of acknowledgments is huge (I have not forgotten Miguel and his photocopier, nor my namesake Paco and his suitcase full of clippings, nor the old Guevara buffs, nor Justo who checked for errors in Cuban sayings and elsewhere, nor the Havana photographers, nor the management team at *Verde Olivo* magazine) but in an attempt to trim it, I wish to draw particular attention to the journalist Mariano Rodríguez (who helped me to write a book he deserved to write) and to the novelists Daniel Chevarría (who acted as my chauffeur in Havana out of sheer solidarity) and Luis Adrián Betancourt (who trusted me enormously in lending me his files), and to my colleague Jorge Castañeda, who, despite our different viewpoints concerning the leading player, became my most loyal competitor and confirmed my original idea that in history no one owns documents, just interpretations.

It helps the historian greatly to start from the premise that, try as he may, his book will be a failure in many ways. It helps to think of one's book as a first edition that will lead to clarifications and denials, corrections, the appearance of new documents, debates, and, maybe above all, the publication of Ernesto "Che" Guevara's copious unpublished writings. It is comforting to think of a book not as something dead, but as a provocative and mutant alien.

It would take someone more intelligent and with more historical and literary resources than I to be able to tell the story to two completely different generations of readers—to tell two versions of the story using the same material, and to two types of reader, those within and those without Latin America. For some, I would need to explain and describe the context—but I have cast that aside to concentrate more on the leading player; for others, I would need to devote more space to the political debate of the time. The omissions have been intentional, and due to the demands the alternatives would have made.

After all these years of reading and talking, some things, such as a phrase or an image, stick in the mind . . . for example, the half-laced-up boots. I found it strange to see in photo after photo of the National Bank manager, the minister of industry, and the revolutionary ambassador, that his boots were never quite properly laced up, maybe because he was in a hurry to live. This character, of whom Cuban novelist Edmundo Desnoes said "must have been blinding if the most opaque were lit up when he passed," was portrayed by Régis Debray as "the soberest practitioner of socialism."

The words in boldface belong to Che, and are fragments of private and public letters, diaries and handwritten notes, articles, poems, books, speeches, lectures, public or semipublic statements of which a record was made, replies to interviews, and even phrases of his recorded by reliable witnesses. He is this story's second narrator, the one who matters.

As this book goes to press, the announcement has just come that Guevara's body has been found buried in Bolivia and officially identified. His remains have been sent to Cuba, to be reburied there.

1. Little Guevara: Childhood Is Fate

The first of a lifelong series of photographs showing Guevara
with a donkey

PHOTOGRAPH TAKEN IN 1929 AT CARAGUATAY, IN THE PROVINCE OF MI- siones in Argentina, shows a fourteen-month-old Ernesto Guevara. He holds a small cup (possibly for *maté*), and he is wearing a little white overcoat and an awful colonial-style Filipino cap.

These clothes were the first of the sartorial disasters that were typical of Ernesto all his life. "Childhood is fate," the Mexican psychologist Santiago Ramírez said in one of his more inspired moments; impressions made on an individual's newly developing mind would shape his actions in the future. Was Ramírez right, or is childhood an accident, simply the prehistory of a person whose character will be molded by his own will and self-determination?

If childhood *is* fate, it is not simple to interpret the symbols of the future. There is a photograph from 1932, showing Ernesto on a little donkey. Our leading player is four years old. He sits very straight, wearing on his sleeve his love of that donkey—and of all donkeys, mules, horses, any four-legged mount, a love that would characterize him all his life. And if childhood really is des- tiny, then twenty-five years later, halfway through an air raid, leading Cuban rebels, the No. 4 Column commander, a certain Guevara known as Che, would advance mounted on a donkey called Balsana. He would look into the camera with the same perplexed expression: "Why am I the subject of history when the donkey deserves it more?"

The donkey is the ancestor of those providential mules that appeared dur- ing the invasion of the west of Cuba, and even of the little Bolivian horse he loved so much and ended up eating. It does seem evident that Ernesto Gue- vara was to be the last of our champions on horseback (or muleback, or don- keyback; it makes no difference to a man used to laughing at himself) in the heroic Latin American tradition.

In the Guevara's dim and distant past, there was a viceroy of New Spain, Don Pedro de Castro y Figueroa, whose stint, in the middle of the eighteenth century, lasted only a year and five days. He had a son called Joaquín, who fled with his wife to Louisiana and whose descendants joined the gold rush in San Francisco before their descendants ended up in Argentina a century later.

Relatives with absurd names turn up from the San Francisco period: Rosa- minda Perlasca; Uncle Gorgoño, who raised cattle to sell meat to the prospec- tors.

The Lynch branch of the family can be traced back to Argentina in the be- ginning of the eighteenth century, when they emigrated from Ireland. Is that how those ants got in Ernesto's pants, those wings on his feet? Anyway, they'd be there all his life.

There is not much more to say about the de la Serna side, apart from Grandfather Juan Martín de la Serna, a youth leader in the Argentine Radi- cal Party, whose militancy was shared by one of the Lynches, Great-Uncle Guillermo, and led both to take part in the failed 1890 revolution.

In any case, it seems that as time went by, Che no longer had much sym- pathy for the people he characterized as **my forebears . . . [who] were members of the great Argentine cattle-raising oligarchy.** As a child, though, Ernesto must have seen the exploits of his grandparents in the gold rush in California, the feats of his cattle-raising grandfather, as something out of a fascinating novel.

His father was a civil engineer who undertook a thousand projects and failed in most of them. His most notable act was slapping future writer Jorge Luis Borges in the face after the latter had reported him to a teacher, saying: "Sir, this boy will not let me study." For this he was expelled from the National College. Ernesto Guevara Lynch was a part-time adventurer, an architecture student who had dropped out to enter the small-business world and got really lucky, as he himself admitted, when he married Celia de la Serna, taking her away from numerous suitors in her native Córdoba.

Che's mother, Celia de la Serna, a devout Catholic converted to liberalism, carried the strength of her convictions over from her early religion. One of her nieces later remembered: "She was the first woman (according to my mama) who had her [hair bobbed] like a boy's, who smoked and crossed her legs in public. She led the feminist vanguard in Buenos Aires." She was underage when she became engaged, which caused a breach with her family; she had to move into her aunt's house.

Young Ernesto's parents were cultured, a little bohemian, embarrassed inheritors of an oligarchy they felt was spiritless and timid, and they imbued their children with a sense of adventure, a passion for books, and the poise that Ernesto Junior would nail to his mast years later.

There is a photo, also from 1929, that seems to foreshadow the true nature of the man the child was to become. Ernesto, big-eared and fluffy-haired, is sucking the index and little fingers of his left hand with great concentration, a pose that makes his remaining fingers seem to be offering an obscene gesture to anyone looking on.

The child's first two years were spent in Caraguatay, where his father had a *maté* plantation. Young Ernesto's sister Celia was born toward the end of 1929 in Buenos Aires, where the family had recently moved. They lived a roving life back then, propelled from place to place by Ernesto Senior's unfortunate business ventures, one of which resulted in the theft of his plantation's entire output.

When Ernesto was almost two, his father moved the family again—to San Isidro, almost on the border with Paraguay. Here he became a partner in a shipyard whose finances were not going very well, but he did succeed in getting the business back on its feet.

In his memoirs, Ernesto Senior, like many biographers gifted with hindsight, found suitable anecdotes to reinforce the image of the man his son became. He wrote:

> Little Ernesto was beginning to walk. As we liked to drink maté, we would send him to the kitchen, some twenty meters from the house, to have our glasses refilled. There was a small ditch between the house and the kitchen, with a drainpipe running through it. Almost invariably, the little boy would trip there and fall with the maté in his hands. And he'd always stand up annoyed, go back for a fresh glassful, trip over the pipe, and fall

down again. He'd fetch the maté time and time again until he learned to jump over the ditch.

This scene of the boy jumping over the ditch was like a film loop that would run repeatedly throughout the years, showing Ernesto and his dogged determination, his archetypal stubbornness, his firm belief in the importance of bring forceful. Was the image of the little boy, not quite two years old, a harbinger of things to come, or was it irrelevant?

As an infant, young Ernesto had fallen ill with a severe case of bronchial pneumonia. It almost killed him. His aunts Beatriz and Ercilia traveled up from Buenos Aires to help his young mother look after him, and there would always be ties of love between him and them.

In May 1931, the little boy began to cough as he emerged from a river where he and his mother had been bathing. When the cough persisted, a doctor diagnosed bronchitis; later, when the illness refused to go away, another decided he had chronic asthmatic bronchitis. Finally, one doctor identified the attack as asthma stemming from the pneumonia that Ernesto had suffered as a baby. All the doctors agreed they had never seen a child with such severe asthma attacks. Years later, his sister Ana María, salvaging a memory from the family storybook, said, "His asthma was so severe that our parents despaired. They thought he would die." They spent days and nights by his bedside, while the patient, mouth open and hands frantically waving in the air, gasped for breath. His breathing, as Don Ernesto recalled years later, sounded "like a cat mewing." One of the first words the boy learned to say was "injection," for when he felt an attack coming on.

Not only Don Ernesto's odd business ventures but also little Ernesto's asthma sent the family back to Buenos Aires in 1932, where the third child, Roberto, was born.

But, as Ernesto's mother said: "Ernesto could not bear the climate in the capital. His father regularly slept sitting up at our firstborn's bedside, so that he could take Ernesto in his arms when an attack came on to try and ease his distress." His father added, "I laid him on my body so he could breathe easier, so I hardly slept, if I did at all."

In 1933, the Guevaras moved yet again, to Argüello, in Córdoba province, still trying to find relief for Ernesto's asthma. But it returned. Following medical advice, they decided to try a dry mountain climate; in June, they moved to Alta Gracia, a small town also in Córdoba. Ernesto's condition seemed to improve there, but the asthma never left him again. He was five years old, and he stayed in Alta Gracia until he was fifteen. Here Ernesto made friends who would accompany him throughout his youth. The closest, Carlos Ferrer, nicknamed Calica, was the son of a doctor who treated Ernesto for his asthma attacks.

Since the asthma kept him from attending school regularly, Celia taught him to read. To while away the long hours Ernesto had to spend in bed, his father taught him to play chess. Ernesto became angry if they let him win. I don't play that way, he'd cry.

Ernesto's sister Ana María was born in 1934.

When he was nine, his asthma became seriously complicated by what the doctors diagnosed as "compulsive coughing." "When he felt an attack was coming on, he would lie still in bed and begin to bear up under the choking that asthmatics suffer from during coughing fits," his father remembered. "As the doctors advised, I had a large balloon full of oxygen at hand so I could give the boy a blast of the gas when the worst moment came. He did not want to depend on this treatment, and he tried to bear the attack as long as he could, but when he could no longer stand it and his face was turning purple from the choking, he would wriggle and point to his mouth to indicate that it was time. The oxygen relieved him immediately."

What sort of character was being forged by the disease? Enduring illness and reading books in bed is not a normal life for a nine-year-old. His personal war against the asthma's limitations began then. He developed a taste for danger. He would take walks without permission and play rough games.

To a certain extent he was like his mother in seeking risks and pushing things to the limit. There are dozens of anecdotes about the many times his mother came near drowning. Ernesto himself was present the time she plunged into the Paraná River and was dragged off by the current. Celia, an excellent swimmer, was attracted to danger. Her more placid husband recalls, "Ernesto inherited that tendency to face danger, but with one important difference: he weighed up the danger very carefully first." _irrational_

In 1936, the Education Ministry contacted Celia, asking why the boy had not been attending school. His parents decided that the time had come to send him, as he now enjoyed short breaks from the asthma attacks. He was enrolled at a public school, where he was surrounded by children whose parents were not well off. His brother said, "Our parents' friends were rich, and our own friends, the children who lived in the area, were poor, the children of campesinos and housekeepers."

Ernesto's asthma prevented him from being a normal pupil. "He attended only second and third grades with any regularity," his mother said. "He did what he could for the fourth, fifth, and sixth; his brother and sister copied down his work assignments so he could study at home."

Despite his illness, Ernesto did become the leader of a group of children who met in the backyard of his house. The group's greatest feat was setting fire to a canebrake while playing house.

Ernesto Senior worked on building a golf course. The family finances were rocky, and although the Guevaras were never penniless, they did suffer hardships. They were a middle-class family in crisis, living off the rent from a couple of plots of land. They had to use some of the money to pay for help with the children, as Celia could not cope with all four. Their money trickled out every which way—for schools, for clothes, for the exorbitant expense of Ernesto's medicine.

His father felt weighed down in Alta Gracia. Or, as he put it: "I felt as if I had fallen from grace and was imprisoned. I could not stand life among sick people or among those who treated them." He became more and more neurotic. Everything irritated him. His wife Celia showed greater strength in the face of adversity.

The family spent the summer of 1936 at the beach resort of Mar del Plata. The photographs from that holiday have a pathetic air. In one, Ernesto, doubtless suffering from an asthma attack, is wearing pants and a shirt. He is surrounded by children in swimsuits. Celia holds his hand as he dips his feet in the water he cannot enter. A family friend recalled that that summer people kept proffering infallible remedies for asthma, and Ernesto obediently accepted the most absurd advice his parents took—sleeping with sandbags, drinking all kinds of tea, and being plagued with inhalants and other medications. "We were so anxious over this disease that would not leave the child," his father said, "that we experimented with all kinds of ways to try and cure it. We followed the advice of doctors and laypeople. We used all kinds of homemade cures, and bought and tried out any panacea for asthma as soon as it was advertised in the newspapers. No sooner did I hear about this or that herbal or weed concoction than I was giving it to Ernesto."

In Alta Gracia in 1937, Ernesto listened wide-eyed as his father told afterdinner stories about the family, particularly about his grandfather, a geographer who traced the borders of the Chaco region of central South America, enduring terrible heat and Indian attacks. The latest newspapers, and broadcasts over the radio his father bought, reported on the Spanish Civil War, and the conflict made a strong impression on nine-year-old Ernesto. As well, the family took in the two sons of a Spanish Republican, a Dr. Aguilar, who had been forced to leave Spain.

For Ernesto, the victory of the Spanish Republic over the military and the Fascists became a personal matter. He began to follow events by sticking little flags on a map as the fronts moved. He also built a model of Madrid in the backyard and and re-created the siege of that city with his friends. They dug trenches in the dirt, where they held furious fights with slings, stones and rubble, and even nuts and bolts. Roberto almost broke his leg, and Ernesto limped for several days, but that did not stop him from learning the names of all the Republican generals by heart.

With the democracy of childhood, Ernesto, Calica Ferrer, and the Figueroa children found their friends among the children of porters at the summer villas, Decades later, a waiter at the Alta Gracia hotel would remember: "Ernesto was a kid from the neighborhood, he hung around with us rather than the preppy kids." A townsman, Juan Minguez, said, "If we were playing soccer and there were just five of us, Ernesto would want to play in goal against the other four." This seems to be a pre-Che myth, however; in the words of his friend César Díaz: "He played goalie because he couldn't run too much with his asthma."

What was clear is that he was active and always disheveled. His tenacity made up for the times his asthma held him back. For months on end he came in second in the table tennis competitions at the Alta Gracia hotel, behind the local champion, Rodolfo Ruarte. Then one day Ernesto told Ruarte that he was taking a short break from playing. He meanwhile built a Ping-Pong table in the privacy of his home and practiced on his own, then surfaced to challenge the champion—and beat him.

On Sundays, he would go with his father to target practice. He learned how to handle a pistol when he was five and he could shoot bricks to pieces. And he read and read, all the time—Jules Verne, Alexandre Dumas, Emilio Salgari,* Robert Louis Stevenson, and Miguel de Cervantes.

The family moved to another house in 1937, and Ernesto became enchanted with dressing up. He was, in turn, an Indian, an ancient Greek, a gaucho, or a marquis. He acted as a boxer in a school play. According to his sister Ana María, "everything was going very well until a fairy with a magic wand came on stage and the kids who were standing stiffly, like dolls, were supposed to come to life. Roberto and Ernesto were dressed as boxers and the fairy asked: 'Ye dolls, what can ye do?' to which they answered: 'Wait thou a moment, and thou wilt be astonished.'" The two boys began to playact, to shadow-box, until Ernesto hit Roberto harder than normal, and little brother hit back for real. "The teacher began to cry; even the fairy's magic wand couldn't stop them."

> The asthma persisted, on and on. Ernesto Senior recalled: Our despair was such that we even tried faith healing, and worse: I remember someone telling me that sleeping with a cat in bed could do a lot to help asthma. I didn't think twice. I fetched a stray cat and put it in bed with him. The outcome was that the cat was smothered and Ernesto was still laid low with asthma. We changed the stuffing in the mattresses and pillows, changed the cotton sheets for linen or nylon ones. We stripped all kinds of draperies and carpeting from the rooms. We cleaned dust from the walls, kept dogs, cats, and poultry out of the yard. But it was all useless, and all we got was disappointment and discouragement. The asthma persisted and all we knew was that it could be brought on by anything, at any time of the year, and by any type of food, and the sum total of all our efforts was the sure knowledge that the best thing for his illness was dry weather and altitude . . . and to do breathing exercises, especially while swimming.

Cold water, however, proved to be a powerful trigger of asthma attacks.

The Guevaras moved to a bungalow in Alta Gracia in 1939, when Ernesto was eleven. New friends entered his life. The Aguilar children introduced him to Fernando Barral, a Spanish orphan who had taken refuge in Argentina with his mother. Barral later remembered Ernesto well: "I must confess that I was somewhat envious of Ernesto. He was decisive, audacious, and self-assured, and above all, he was fearless. I remember that as being one of the most genuine of his character traits. . . . Danger held no fears for him, or at

---

*Emilio Salgari was an important nineteenth-century adventure novelist, better known in Spanish-speaking countries than in the U.S.

least not that you could tell." Ernesto would test himself. He'd jump from a third-floor attic room to make his friends blanch. His friend Dolores Moyano lucidly got to the real roots of Guevara's early adolescent behavior: "Ernesto's dicing with death and his Hemingway-style flirtations with danger were neither rash nor showing off. When he did something dangerous or forbidden, like eating chalk or walking along the edge of a fence, he was doing it to see if he could and, well, to see what was the best way. The underlying attitude was intellectual, the hidden motives were experimentation."

A year later, while World War II was raging, Ernesto Senior joined Acción Argentina ("Argentine Action"), an antifascist organization sympathetic to the Allies. The twelve-year-old Ernesto proudly showed off father's membership card and even volunteered to look into Nazi infiltration among the Germans living in the Alta Gracia area.

Reading remained the great passion of Ernesto's early adolescence, a comfort when he was laid low by asthma attacks. Ernesto Senior says that "when Ernesto turned twelve, he was as well read as a boy of eighteen. His shelves were piled high with all kinds of adventure stories and novels about travel." Years later, Ernesto filled up one of his many notebooks listing the books he had read, with written comments on some of them. He called it "Catalogue of Books Read in Alphabetical Order." Under the Jules Verne heading, he recorded twenty-three novels.

In 1942, at fourteen, Ernesto was admitted to the Colegio Nacional Dean Funes, in Córdoba. It was a liberal public school, as opposed to the private schools where the children of high society studied. He commuted twenty miles a day by train from Alta Gracia.

In Córdoba, he met the Granado brothers: Tomás, his classmate, and Alberto, who was six years older. Tomás, who was captivated by his new friend with the crew cut and unusual aggressiveness in sports, introduced him to his older brother so Ernesto could join the students' rugby team. Alberto, who was studying medicine, was not impressed. He noticed "his panting, which indicated some respiratory disorder."

They gave Guevara a test: he had to jump over a broom handle set between two chair backs four feet high, and land on his shoulder. "Skinhead" Guevara began to jump and had to be stopped before he made a hole in the yard. He began training several days later, and was playing shortly after. Sometimes he had to go to the sideline halfway through a game to use his inhaler.

He would run down the field scattering players and yelling **Out of the way, here's El Furibundo**—"Fu-ser" [mad Serna]! was to become his nickname. He played as if his life depended on it, but did not let the game take over his existence. He was still a teenager, switching between throwing himself body and soul into life by taking risks and pushing the limits, and warring against asthma.

And still with a passion for reading. His teammates often saw him opening a book and reading in his spare moments before a game, anywhere, under a lamppost or on the touch line. He would take a book out of his jacket and drift away. He read intensively and hastily, but doubtless he had some method, some sort of strange scenario. He enjoyed adventure and action stories, books on travel and Latin America, and books by Horacio Quiroga, Ingenieros, Pablo Neruda, and Jack London. He read Boccaccio's *Decameron* and, once his mother taught him French, Baudelaire in the original. He was particularly interested in psychology, and read Jung and Adler. José Aguilar's father, the exiled Spanish doctor, was surprised to see him reading Freud and commented on the fact to his children, suggesting that it was perhaps "he was a little young" to be reading the great doctor. Alberto Granado just could not believe Ernesto had read so much; they discussed Steinbeck and Faulkner. They were both very keen on Faulkner's "Sanctuary." Where did Mad Serna find the time?

Look, Mial ["my Alberto"], every time I have an asthma attack, or I have to stay indoors breathing in the incense they prescribe for me, I spend those two or three hours taking the opportunity to read what I can.

In 1943, when Ernesto was fifteen, the family moved into a large house in Córdoba, where his sister Celia had enrolled in a girls' school. Guevara Senior went into business with a Cordovan architect. On May 18, 1943, Juan Martín, the youngest of Ernesto's brothers, was born.

Ernesto's interest in literature continued; he read Mallarmé, Baudelaire, Marx and Engels, García Lorca, Verlaine, and Antonio Machado. He discovered Gandhi, who made a big impression on him. His friends remember him reciting poetry—Neruda, of course, but some Spanish poets, too. One quartain in particular haunted him: "It was lies / lies become sad truth, / that his footfalls were heard / in a Madrid that exists no more."

Ernesto's first biographer, Cuban writer Aldo Isidrón, made it clear that Ernesto was not a typical Argentine: "He did not have a ear for music. He couldn't even identify a tango. He had to learn dance steps by rote," and in order to be able to dance, even if it was only now and then, he had to have his friends tell him whether the tune was a fox-trot or a tango. According to his cousin, "La Negrita," "even though he was tone-deaf, he would dance, and would always ask the ugliest girls to dance, so they would not be left out."

In Córdoba, he lost Negrina, the dog who had been with him since Alta Gracia. An employee of the city dog pound found her wandering the streets and threw cyanide on her back; the dog died of poisoning almost immediately after licking herself. Ernesto got his friends together to look for the murderer, but in vain. Frustrated in his plan for vengeance, he organized a funeral with all the trappings, including the coffin.

Meanwhile he kept playing rugby with the Granado brothers. His friend Barral remembers him as the toughest of the group, and he still needed his inhaler on the sideline. It was then he earned the rude nickname he was very proud of.

They called me the Hog.
Because you were fat?
No, because I was filthy.

His fear of cold water, which sometimes brought on asthma attacks, led to a less than wholesome attitude toward personal hygiene. His aversion to bathtubs and showers would stay with him for the rest of his life.

In those days, he developed not only his bad hygiene but also his antimilitarism. After a military coup had taken place, he spoke out about it in class: **The military don't let the masses be educated, because if the people were educated, they would not accept their rule.** A small uproar broke out in the room. The teacher took fright and expelled Ernesto from class.

At the end of 1943, Granado was in jail because of a university strike against the military, and Ernesto used to go and visit him. Granado asked that his friends speak out and demonstrate at rallies. Ernesto answered that he would not take to the streets unless they gave him a pistol.

He was not overly interested in political action, neither then nor two years later, although he was caught up in activities from time to time. He did go with a friend, student leader Gustavo Roca, to a demonstration that was broken up by the police. But the myth of teenage militancy is dismissed by his own words: **I had no social concerns as a teenager and took no part in political or student activism in Argentina.**

In 1943, then, Ernesto was a fifteen-year-old whose face was losing its childlike look. His grades at the Colegio Nacional Dean Funes matched his interests: very good in literature, terrible in English; very good in philosophy, awful in music; good in history, lackluster in mathematics and natural history.

The following year, in another attempt to turn chaos into order, Ernesto began to draw up a philosophical dictionary from his reading; he kept up the effort for two years. The habit of recording his reading matter and making notes on the books he read would stay with him. As time went by, and circumstances and rereading changed his outlook, he would make notes on notes. Only a chaotic person can be so orderly.

Elections held on February 24, 1946, ratified the presidency of Juan Domingo Perón, but Ernesto was not yet old enough to vote. He volunteered for military service, but was declared unfit because of his asthma.

He graduated from the Colegio Nacional Dean Funes and decided to study engineering. Why did he not choose literature or psychology, which seemed to be the greatest interests in his youth? Was he developing a practical approach that was overriding his youthful passions?

Ernesto went to Buenos Aires, where he moved in with his aunt Beatriz and his maternal grandmother Ana, to whom he had always been close. He enrolled in the school of engineering at the university.

As the son of a middle-class family that could not afford many luxuries, he spent his vacations studying to qualify as a laboratory technician in soil mechanics, along with Tomás Granado. Both passed and were assigned jobs. Ernesto worked on highway plans and public works projects in small towns between Córdoba and Rosario. Toward the end of the year he wrote to his father:

> **the boss was telling me I was the only lab technician he had known in ten years who would not accept the [gifts of] food, and one of only two or three who didn't take bribes. You may be afraid that I was too considerate with them, but I made them stop and redo a good part of the highway.**

While struggling with builders who were used to making their jobs easier by greasing palms, he heard about the assassination of Gandhi, his childhood hero, which deeply upset him.

He decided to continue working rather than return to school, and to study engineering in his own time. He wrote to his father: If I can study an open university course [i.e., the engineering topics, for which he had requested programs] I will stay all winter, as I estimate I would save between 80 and 100 pesos a month. I earn 200 a month and have a place to stay, so I spend on food and a few books for entertainment.

But the best-laid plans . . .: Ernesto's grandmother Ana was taken ill. He quit the highway department and went straight to Buenos Aires to look after her. She had had a cerebral hemorrhage and suffered a subsequent hemiplegia—one side of her body was paralyzed. He spent the next seventeen days by her bedside, feeding and caring for her, until she died.

Without doubt, those long days he spent at the deathbed of his beloved grandmother—as well as, perhaps, his own experience as an asthma sufferer all those years—led him to a change of direction. He would drop engineering and study medicine. He started on a radically different course.

2. Remembrance of Leading Players Past

Setting off from Córdoba in 1950 on a 3,000-mile trip by motorbike across Argentina. While on the journey he studied for his medical school exams.

A LECTURE THEATER IN THE SCHOOL OF MEDICINE. A COUPLE OF DOZEN students posing in front of a naked and gutted corpse on a slab. Tradition, necrophilia, or professional challenge? Some of the students are wearing slight, timid smiles; most have assumed serious and decorous expressions, as befits future doctors. The only one grinning openly, almost offensively, almost out of sight in the back row, is twenty-year-old Ernesto Guevara. There are three women in the photograph, one of them a girl with a round face but a hard expression, maybe because her eyes are a little apart and she is staring intently. She is Bertha Gilda Infante, known as Tita to her friends.

She reminisced:

> I heard his deep warm voice several times. The irony in it gave him and all the rest of us courage when we faced something that shook even the most unflappable of those future Galens. You could tell he was provincial by his accent. He was a handsome easygoing boy. His bearing, a mixture of shyness and haughtiness, maybe recklessness, obscured a deep intelligence, an insatiable thirst for understanding, and, far down, an infinite capacity for loving.
>
> **When I began to study medicine most of the concepts I now have as a revolutionary were then absent from my store of ideas. I wanted to be successful, as everyone does. I used to dream of being a famous researcher, of working tirelessly to achieve something that could, decidedly, be placed at the service of humankind, but it was just personal triumph back then. I was, as we all are, a product of my environment.**

The smiling Guevara seemed to be taking things seriously that first year. He spent ten to twelve hours a day in the library. The department secretary, Mario Parra, remembered: "I knew him because the librarians pointed him out to me as a prime example of the right way to study. While studying, he spoke to no one." But was he studying medicine? For in that first year he enrolled in only three courses and his grades were not remarkable—"good" for descriptive anatomy in April 1948, "good" for parasitology in November, and just plain "pass" for embryology in August. He was certainly concentrating, but the object of his interest was not so obvious.

Then what was he doing in the library? He read literature, of course. He read psychology and studied medical subjects that interested him, rather than the courses he was enrolled in. Could he have been spending time away from home because there was tension in his family?

The Guevaras had already moved to Buenos Aires in 1948. His father had rented a small office on Paraguay Street. Some writers suggest that quarrels between Celia and Ernesto Senior had reached their limit and that the couple were on the edge of breaking up, They compromised on a semi-separation: Ernesto Senior would live in his office but would visit the family home. There is some problem in winnowing out the truth, and the meaning of the truth.

The same sources say the couple fought over Don Ernesto's "carousing" and his economic ventures, which usually ended in disaster. Whether this was true or not, the fact is that Ernesto Junior spent more time at the College of Medicine library than at his small and sparsely furnished room on Arroz Street.

There is a story behind Ernesto's white shirt, which appears in so many of his photographs from that time—a true story. According to his brother Jan Martín, the shirt had a name, the weekly, because washing it once a week sufficed and, being nylon it "ironed itself." Ernesto's disheveled attire was always a subject of conversation among his family and friends. His father said that Ernesto never wore a tie and his usual costume was "odd, differently styled boots," crumpled pants, and the "weekly."

Young Guevara's love of chess came back to him during his first year at medical school. He played in matches between departments, and even got to play in a simultaneous match in the Provincial Hotel in Mar del Plata with the grand master Miguel Najdorf, to whom he lost. The strange thing was the contrast between the slow, thoughtful game of chess and the violent one of rugby, which he was still playing. "For an asthmatic to run around for seventy minutes on a rugby pitch was quite a feat," his friend Roberto Ahumada says. Ernesto stood out as a hard player with a macho style. His enthusiasm for the game would lead to his becoming a writer and editor at *Tackle* magazine, where he used the Chinese-style pseudonym Chang-Cho.

Ernesto's youngest brother, Juan Martín, who was then a little boy, fondly remembers Ernesto's fatherly treatment of him. He christened him Patatín, or Fluffy, which made the child squirm with delight. The youngster looked up to his brother as a great man, a heroic character. Ernesto taught him a rhyme: "Two friends under a tree / the thunder for to flee. The lightning struck—boom! / And the one with the St. Crispin medal / met his doom!" The ladies were startled by such wanton atheism recited by a boy with an angel face.

In 1949, Ernesto took part in the university "Olympics" held in Tucumán, competing in chess and athletics. Since he liked challenges, he also entered the pole vault competition. Carlos Figueroa said, "When they asked him where his pole was, he answered that he thought the university provided them. They got him one and he jumped, but he got nowhere, since he didn't have a clue how to do it."

Ernesto's time at university was unremarkable; his grades were all simply "pass." Politically, he kept himself on the sidelines of the activities of left-wing groups. A militant from the Young Communists who used to ply Ernesto with his organization's literature commented, "Our relationship was surly, difficult"; he portrayed Ernesto as a man with ethical ideas, but not political ones. Ernesto used to have heated arguments with Tita Ferrer, who was a Young Communist, in which he accused Marxists of being inflexible sectarians. She explained what might account for his lack of interest in university life: "Both of us, for different reasons, did not quite fit in medical school. Perhaps he knew he could find only a little of what he was looking for there."

Ernesto kept playing rugby despite the doctors' warning that it could lead to a heart attack. His father tried to talk him out of it, but Ernesto refused to listen to any advice **even if I go to pieces.** The best his father could do was to persuade one of his classmates to run alongside him on the sideline with an inhaler, so he could stop to take a few puffs now and then.

As 1949 was drawing to a close, Ernesto—who liked to think of himself as a wanderer—came up with a plan for a bicycle journey. **I'm thinking of doing a tour of Santa Fe province, the north of Córdoba, and the east of Mendoza, and studying some of my subjects on the way so I can pass them.**

Having adapted a small, Italian-made Cucciolo brand engine to power his bicycle, he set off on January 1, to the admiration of his younger brothers and sisters and the dismay of his parents at "Ernesto's capers." Outside the Italian hospital in Córdoba, he was photographed hunched over his bicycle, wearing a leather jacket, a cap, and goggles. Before Ernesto became famous as "Che," this photograph was published as an advertisement in several editions of *Gráfico* magazine, to the delight of Juan Martín, who faithfully clipped them all: "Argentine medical student Ernesto Guevara dé la Serna on his Cucciolo-powered bicycle, on which he has toured the Republic."

As I was leaving Buenos Aires on the night of January 1, I was doubtful about how much power the engine that I had mounted had, and whether it would take me safe and sound to Ilar, my final destination. However, the journey went without a hitch. There were many hours of pedaling, some motoring, and breaks at midday to study medicine under a tree. As the days went by, my flesh was weak and cried out for a mattress, but my spirit was willing and the ride went on.

On the road he met a tramp who, as well as giving him maté in a flask of dubious origin, remembered he was a barber and cut Ernesto's hair. **I sported my crew cut like a trophy when I went to the Aguilar house to see my sister Ana María.**

His sister went sight-seeing with him to the beautiful waterfalls at Los Chorrillos (**It was there I learned the first law of mountain climbing: It's easier to go up than down**). Once again he risked death, as he had done so many times since childhood: To the horror of his friends, he dove into a pool that had no more than two feet of water.

On January 29, he set off once again to the leprosy hospital in the town of Chañar not too far from Córdoba, where Alberto, the eldest of the Granado brothers, was working. During Ernesto's visit, the doctor-to-be and the specialist together treated a very young and pretty patient, who had leprosy but refused to accept the fact. Granado applied heat and cold to the unfeeling parts of her back, but she could only guess where he was doing it. Suddenly, he plunged a huge hypodermic into the affected area; she did not react. Ernesto was furious, called Alberto indifferent and uncaring. He was angry with his friend for days. Granado tried to explain that that was the decisive test, the only way to confirm the diagnosis. Ernesto seems to have been reacting to a great sin against the ten personal commandments he was drawing up: the unforgivable sin of affronting dignity. While harshness is forgivable, cheating is not.

Ernesto Guevara continued with his journey some days later. A tramp he met, as he was about to go to sleep in a sewer, asked him: "Do you really spend so much energy uselessly?"

Young Guevara wrote in his travel diary, I realize that something in me that had been growing up for some time has matured in the bustle of city life, and it's a hatred of civilization, the clumsy images of people moving like crazy to the beat of that awful noise.

On the road he met a motorcyclist who had a real bike, a brand-new Harley-Davidson, and who offered to tow him along at fifty or sixty miles per hour. Ernesto, who had learned by then that anything over twenty-five miles per hour was very risky, declined. The next day, as he was entering a town, he encountered the bike rider again, but by this time he had been killed in an accident.

Ernesto was learning more than medicine on the road; he was learning to write. Metaphors slipped into the pages of his diary; his descriptions improved and carefully detailed landscapes made an increasing appearance among the reflections of a hermit.

He finally reached Mendoza, where his aunt Maruja did not recognize him under all the filth. When she finally accepted that "that" was her nephew, she gave him a huge lunch, washed his clothes, and filled his knapsack with bread rolls. He then returned via San Luis to Buenos Aires, having covered 2,800 miles and more.

In October 1950, at a wedding in the González Aguilar home in Córdoba, he met a young woman, María del Carmen Ferreyra, called Chichina. "It was young love at first sight," his friend Jose Gonzáles says. Chichina was a pleasant, pretty teenager with big eyes, hair hanging over her face, and many admirers.

The whirlwind romance was not without its problems, however. Ernesto was the son of a middle-class family down on its luck, while Chichina was from the old Córdoba oligarchy. Her parents owned Malagueño, an estate with two enormous tennis courts, polo grounds, Arab chargers, and its own church. The workers had quarters separate from the family's house.

Ernesto paid a visit to the house in shirtsleeves and with no tie, and when Chichina's parents discovered that the relationship was quite serious, they did not seem to be impressed. "They laughed at his perpetual nylon shirt, which he washed while wearing it in the bath, and they were amused by his lack of formality and his shabbiness which, at that stupid age, made me a little ashamed. But they listened to him carefully when he spoke about literature, history or philosophy, and when he told tales of his travels, González Aguilar remembered. Dolores Moyano, who was Chichina's cousin, said succinctly: "Ernesto fell in love with the princess, surprisingly and unexpectedly. She was everything he despised, as he was for her. An impossible relationship . . .The fact that Ernesto paid no attention to his clothes, but tried to appear to be above fashion, was a favorite topic of conversation among our friends. You had to know the mentality of the provincial oligarchy to appreciate the surprising figure cut by Ernesto." Obsessed as the del Carmens were with English sweaters, leather boots, and silk ties, Ernesto's nylon "weekly" could not fail to unhinge them, but the Guevara style conquered all; and when he arrived at a party, instead being embarrassed by his poverty compared to the others' riches, he was poised and likable.

The distance that separated the two lovers made it easier for them to avoid disagreements, and the relationship blossomed. At the same time Ernesto was growing closer to Tita Infante, who was becoming his intellectual companion.

At the end of 1950 Ernesto found a new type of madness. He and his friend Carlos Figueroa acquired some factory surplus shoes, all they could afford, in a sale. They matched the shoes to make pairs and sold them off at a slight profit, then went around the streets with the mismatched shoes looking for blind people. Malicious gossip had it that after reaching the remotest footwear locker in hell, Ernesto would wear the leftovers of the leftovers.

Looking for a little money to half fill his pockets, at the end of 1950 Ernesto obtained a permit to work as a nurse on Argentine merchant ships; he began to sail on cargo ships and oil tankers the following February. He had time to study at sea, between ports where he loaded and unloaded oil.

His relationship with Chichina was confined to flying visits and the mail. He proposed to her, suggesting a honeymoon touring the Americas in a mobile home. Her parents put pressure on her, and Chichina was not very enthusiastic about the idea. Political clashes ensued; Ernesto and his friend González Aguilar were accused of being Communists, although back then young Guevara was a long way from Marxism, and was strongly influenced by Gandhi. (One of his favorite books was *The Discovery of India* by Indian premier Jawaharlal Nehru.)

On leaving the merchant fleet, Ernesto began to work with Salvador Pisani, a famous allergy specialist who had previously been his own doctor. On the side, he and Carlos Figueroa came up with a formula for an insecticide, but it came to nothing. (Had he taken after his father in quick business ventures that ended in disaster?)

Visiting the Granado family in Córdoba, in October, Ernesto and Alberto Granado were fixing Alberto's motorbike, *La Poderosa II* ("The Powerful One"). Ernesto suddenly said,

Why don't we go to North America?
"How?"
On the *Poderosa*, of course.

According to Granado, the idea came from his brother Tomás, who was also the one to suggest that Guevara was crazy enough to go along with it. Granado himself said that Ernesto, who had gone to Córdoba to see Chichina, "began dancing around, yelling that we should seal an unbreakable pact to travel together."

What both versions do agree on is that Alberto was not happy in his work, while Ernesto had just finished a job and furthermore was sick and tired of medical school, of hospitals, of exams . . .

In November, Ernesto had been working in Pisano's clinic with a new machine to grind the entrails of patients who had died of infectious diseases. In his impatience, he had not wanted to wait for the protective filter, and he caught an infection. Two days after using the machine he was running a very high fever and could not get up. After trying to cover up the problem, he was forced to ask his father to call for a nurse with a stimulant. Ernesto Senior asked Pisani to come at once. Ernesto seemed on the verge of heart failure. The next day, worn out, he got up to take an examination. According to his father, he was exhausted. But the word "exhausted" was not in the Guevara lexicon.

3. The Discovery of Latin America

At the shore of the Mambo-Tambo pool in the Amazons during Guevara's first Latin American trip, with Alberto Granado

ERNESTO AND ALBERTO'S TRAVEL PLANS WERE A BIT ODD: THEY WERE TO go from Córdoba to Buenos Aires to take their leave of Ernesto's parents, then along the Atlantic coast to take their leave of Chichina, and then south to the lakes and over to Chile before taking a decisive turn northward.

The departure took place toward the end of 1951. They almost crashed into a streetcar after taking off from an endless farewell at the Granados' home, then left Buenos Aires on January 4, after hearing the same recriminations that they had heard in Córdoba. Celia asked Alberto to do what he could to get Ernesto to return and finish his studies: "A degree never goes to waste." Another member was recruited to the expedition at this stage, a police dog called Comeback, who hung on to the overloaded motorbike by his claws.

From Buenos Aires they went to Miramar, a small resort where Chichina was spending the summer with her family. **The two days we had planned stretched like elastic into eight, and with the sweet-sorrowful taste of parting mixed with my inveterate halitosis. . . . Alberto saw the danger and imagined himself alone on the highways of America, but never raised his voice. It was between me and her**

They finally separated (**after much drooling, my companion Alberto Granado dragged me off**). Chichina lent him fifteen dollars to buy a swimsuit, and Ernesto swore he would starve rather than spend the money on anything else.

The bikers arrived in Bahía Blanca on January 16. Ernesto burned his foot on the cylinder during a fall in the outskirts of the town, and the wound did not heal properly. They were held up when he fell ill in Benjamín Zorilla.

They finally crossed the border into Chile on February 14, after striking a deal with the owner of the tug *Esmeralda:* He would take the bike across on the tug, while in exchange Ernesto and Alberto worked the bilge pumps. Ernesto had an asthma attack. **We paid our fare and *Poderosa*'s with the sweat of our brows.**

They had a serious accident as they were leaving Temuco: **Without warning the bike skidded over** and hit the ground. Miraculously, they were unscathed, but the frame was broken as well as the aluminum chassis protecting the gearbox. Welding the *Poderosa*'s frame—Ernesto was by now calling it the *Weakling*—back together used up the remainder of the pair's funds.

While they were fixing the bike, they fell in with a group of Chileans in Lautaro and ended up drinking wine with them. In Ernesto's words:

> **Chilean wine is delicious and I drank like a demon. We went to the local dance. . . . A particularly friendly garage mechanic asked me to dance with his wife as the wine did not agree with him. The woman was hot and flushed with Chilean wine and I took her by the hand to take her outside. She tamely started to go along but then realized her husband was watch-**

ing and told me she would stay put. I was no longer open to reason and began a tussle, dragging her over to one of the doors with all eyes on us. She tried to kick me, and as I was still dragging her along, she tripped and fell slap onto the floor. We were chased toward town by a bunch of furious dancers, and Alberto was smarting because the husband made us pay for all the wine.

Granado later said that Mad Serna told him quite seriously: We must promise not to seduce women at local dances any more.

By Santiago, the bike had passed away—"like the body of an old girl-friend," Granado said in farewell. The loss of the bike meant a loss of status. As Ernesto put it, To a certain extent we had been knights of the road; we had belonged to the long-standing "wandering" aristocracy and had calling cards with our impeccably impressive titles. Now we were just two hitch-hikers thumbing it to Valparaíso.

On March 8, they stowed away in the bathrooms on board the *San Antonio,* bound for Antofagasta. We spent two and a half days in the bathrooms. Whenever someone tried to open the door, a throaty voice would say "Taken!" Next, a mellifluous little "excuse me." And when the coast was clear, we would go to the next bathroom along to repeat the responses. Then they gave themselves up.

From Antofagasta they moved on to mining country. Ernesto was quite shaken there by how miners were exploited by the British companies in the area (the company's grandeur is built on the ten thousand bodies lying in the graveyard). During their stay they met a Communist miner; Ernesto's opinion of him is most interesting: It's a crying shame that they repress people like this. Apart from whether collectivism is a danger to a decent life, the Communism gnawing at his entrails was no more than a natural longing for something better.

On March 23, they left Chile, having covered 2,200 miles, from south to north.

Their first impressions of Peru were to do with tiredness: Our knapsacks felt as if their burden had increased a hundredfold. They walked up to a peasant's house in the middle of the night. The doors were flung open when they introduced themselves as doctors and Argentines—"from the land of Perón and Evita, where they don't fuck the Indians, like they do here," the peasant said.

From March 24 to March 31 they slowly made their way toward Cuzco after touring Lake Titicaca, eating occasionally, hitching rides in trucks along with Indians and animals, and seeing for themselves the racism and ill-treatment meted out to the indigenous people.

Ernesto was quite taken by the Inca world of Cuzco. His choice of words went crazy, his metaphors ran wild, and he waxed lyrical in the pages of his diary. Cuzco was an evocation, the intangible dust from another era settling on its streets. There was without doubt an archaeologist crying to be left out in doctor-to-be Guevara. But if he was taken by Cuzco, he was bowled over by Machu Picchu. He gathered data that he would use in an article a couple of years later.

They left the archaeological site on April 6 to head for the leper hospital at Huambo, one of the objectives of the journey. Ernesto was struck by a terrible asthma attack on the way and, despite two shots of adrenaline, grew sicker as night fell. They were spending the night in a police station. Granado greatly feared he might be seeing a case of spasm due to tetanus, as the needles were not washed properly, and that Ernesto might die there, but another dose kept the asthma at bay. **I watched the rain while wrapped up in a blanket belonging to the policeman on duty, as I smoked one black cigarette after another, which relieved my fatigue somewhat. I fell asleep just after dawn, leaning against a pillar in the hallway.**

The pair wandered around the country until the end of April, practicing a little medicine and witnessing the brutal racism of Peruvian society. They finally arrived in Lima on May 1. **We were at the end of one of the most important stages of the journey; we didn't have a cent, or any chance of getting one soon, but we were happy.**

In Lima they went to see Dr. Hugo Pesce, a leading light in leprosy research, a Marxist, a clinician treating and researching diseases that affect the poor, especially malaria and leprosy. Pleased to see two wandering doctors who shared his interest in leprosy, Pesce gave them a warm welcome. Thanks to him and his assistant, Zoraida Boluarte, the pair were put up in the Guia Leper Hospital, which was run by strict Salesian nuns.

They left Lima ten days later. On saying their farewells, Pesce asked for their comments on his latest book, *Latitudes del Silencio* ("Latitudes of Silence").* Ernesto could not help himself and crucified it, accusing Pesce of describing landscapes badly and of being pessimistic in his analysis of Indians. That got Pesce's back up: How dared Guevaras after all Pesce'd done for them? Ernesto said that truth was like that, it hurt. Pesce humbly took the point. The two young Argentines took away with them their grateful memory of the doctor, and also a couple of suits that Pesce gave Ernesto, who was in rags by that stage.

They now made their way toward the Amazon. Ernesto wrote a letter to his parents: **If you don't hear from us in a year, look for our shrunken heads in some American museum, as we are going to cross Jivaro country.**

Going up the Peruvian Amazon on a boat called the *Cenepa*, they were friendly—"without interfering," as Granado put it—with a free and easy girl (Guevara called her a slut, which was strong language for him) who liked to hear their tales of wandering during the endless, mosquito-ridden days and nights. Ernesto remembered Chichina now as one remembers someone from an interlude that is over.

*Translator's note: This book does not appear to have been translated into English.

At San Pablo, a leprosarium in the depths of the jungle, they gave consultations and treated patients, studied with the doctors, fished in the river, and played soccer with the lepers.

Ernesto turned twenty-four on June 14, **St. Guevara's day.** "Fuser was in fashion." Three days later, he achieved something that satisfied him greatly: He swam across the Amazon diagonally, two and a half miles downstream. He was panting, but delighted, when he reached the shore. — cold H_2O?

Reaching the Colombian border, they had to cross over to Leticia by canoe. While wandering around on the Colombian side, they met the manager of the Leticia "Independiente Sporting" soccer team and convinced him of their talents; they agreed to train the team for an indefinite time and to be paid by results. It was the best job they had during the journey. The two brilliant coaches introduced man-to-man marking and achieved spectacular results in a matter of hours, after a practice game with forwards marking defenders.

They finally played in a knockout tournament, winning the first game thanks to a goal by Granado, whom the local fans dubbed Pedernerita, in honor of the crack Argentine player, for his dribbling. Ernesto was a superb goalie. They had made amazing progress with the team, but it was time to leave. Though they were urged to stay on as coaches, they drew their pay and flew to Bogotá on a military cargo plane.

They were astonished at the number of heavily armed police on the streets in Bogotá and they could feel the weight of Laureano Gómez's dictatorship. They ate in a student canteen and slept on chairs in a hospital.

One night, Ernesto was using a small penknife to draw a map in the dirt to find his way around Bogotá, some policemen arrested him, and confiscated the knife. Sick and tired of Colombia and its police, Guevara and Granado crossed the Táchira River into Venezuela on July 14.

But high prices in Venezuela forced them to drink water in Barquisimeto while the rest drank beer, and the asthma was still afflicting Ernesto. They drew up an initial plan on the way: If Ernesto managed to transport some horses to Buenos Aires on a cargo plane through a relative of his, and Granado managed to get work as a doctor, then the trip would end for now. If they failed in both respects, they would move on toward Mexico. But at the end of their first week in Venezuela, Granados found work in a leprosarium in a nearby town, some twenty miles from Cabo Blanco, and the representative of the horses' owner who was connected to Ernesto's uncle had no objections as long as Ernesto obtained a U.S. visa (the return flight to Argentina made a stop in Miami).

During a farewell drink with some friends they had made during their few days there, Ernesto could not help getting involved in an argument with a UPI journalist, and with the Venezuelan middle-class way of thinking while he was at it. He ended with an abrupt **I'd rather be an illiterate Indian than an American millionaire.**

Ernesto flew from Caracas to Miami in the cargo plane transporting the race horses. They were supposed to spend only a day in Miami, but one of the plane's engines broke down; he had to wait with just one dollar in his pocket while it was repaired. He made a deal with a boardinghouse, promising to pay them after returning to Argentina. He frequented the library, lived on a diet of milky coffee, walked ten miles a day from the boardinghouse in downtown Miami to the beaches, and got into trouble with the police for siding with a Puerto Rican who was saying bad things about U.S. president Harry Truman. Tita Infante later recalled Ernesto telling her that "the twenty days he spent in Miami would go down as the toughest and most unpleasant in his life, and not just because of the economic hardship he had to endure."

When the plane was finally repaired and Ernesto returned, the family was waiting for him at Ezeiza Airport in Buenos Aires and saw him disembark among the horses. The prodigal son was home again. He was thinner and doubtless had a more mature look about him, although he did not lose his permanently adolescent face. Was that it? Shortly after rewriting his diary he would comment: **The person who wrote these lines passed away on reaching Argentine soil again. . . . All this wandering around our "Greater America" has changed me much more than I thought** José Aguilar said as much, and pointed out one aspect of the change: "What I noticed after his first journey was that he was very interested in politics."

How much, though? What politics, and what tendency? The truncated diary he had written over those eight months ended with a decidedly vehement and hard-line credo:

> **I will be on the side of the people and I know that because I see it written in the night that I, the eclectic dissector of doctrines and dogmatic psychoanalysis, will take to the barricades and the trenches, screaming as one possessed, will stain my weapons with blood, and, mad with rage, will cut the throat of any vanquished foe I encounter.**

These seemed to be mere words, for now.

4.   In Through the Out Door

Ernesto at twenty, in Cordoba

FROM SEPTEMBER 1952 ONWARD, ERNESTO WORKED LIKE MAD TO prepare for his exams, hour after hour in the National Library on Rodríguez Peña Street in Buenos Aires. Tita Infante remembered years later: "He was capable of stopping to really ponder a problem that fired his passion: leprosy, allergy, neurophysiology, advanced psychology . . . and he was just as capable of calling up to chat the night before the exam."

In January 1953, he paid one last visit to the La Malagüeña estate to see Chichina. Had they formally split up by then? Did Ernesto propose and get turned down? Did Chichina not want to share in his madness? The separation was permanent.

The research article about allergy that Ernesto had been working on in Pisani's clinic was published that same month. His colleagues there later recalled the most trivial things, the sort of things people remember when a novel is written about a vanished person—for example, one day he came to the clinic wearing mismatched shoes from his business venture. He read strange things: an archaeological book about the Incas bought with money given him by his aunt. He told blue jokes to the lab technicians, corrected his colleagues' syntax, flirted with a co-worker, Lira Bocciolesi, to whom he half seriously, half jokingly proposed that she should accompany him on his next trip. What trip? There would be a trip, as Ernesto was obviously just passing through Argentina. He had discovered Latin America and had now gone beyond the restrictive future envisioned for him as a doctor in Buenos Aires. (Liria, who was very shy, was frightened by the proposal.)

Ernesto began to write, starting with diary entries, about his recent Latin American odyssey, a book entitled "A Travel Diary," which he would never finish.

On April 11 he took his last exam, in clinical neurology. A few hours later he called his father: **This is Dr. Guevara speaking.**

The family was happy, and it seemed Ernesto's future was clear: He would work with Pisani. But then it was **Dad, I'm off to Venezuela.** Off to catch up with Granado in Venezuela, where there was the chance of work as a resident doctor in a leprosarium in Maiquetía. The family feared the worst, because of his asthma, the cold on the highways, travel on second-class trains, and hunger. The worst thing was that his mind was made up. Granado was working in Venezuela. "Venezuela" was any old thing, anything that was far away. The wanderer in him had won.

Young people came and went at the family home for two months while Ernesto prepared for his departure, putting some money aside, getting his degree and his license to practice medicine. His old friend from Alta Gracia, Calica Ferrer, was to be his companion this time.

The farewell party was a family affair; Ernesto's sister Celia made a curry. The young people danced while Ernesto, the wallflower, watched them. For him, dancing was a waste of time. As he stood looking on from a corner as the party got into full swing around him, his mother, Celia, said to her niece, "I'm losing him forever. I'll never see my son Ernesto again." She was wrong, but the Ernesto she was to see years later would be someone else.

The second Latin American trip, 1953

O N A COLD AND GRAY DAY IN JULY 1953, ERNESTO GUEVARA, ALONG WITH Calica Ferrer, said good-bye to his family at the Retiro Railroad Station in Buenos Aires. The two travelers had less than $700 between them. The farewell party would remember the way the young man walking down the platform suddenly hoisted his green canvas bag up, shouted, **Here goes a soldier for America!** and without so much as a backward glance ran closer and closer to the slowly moving train until he grabbed a handrail and jumped onto one of the cars.

Ernesto's parents were dismayed. Now that he'd made a superhuman effort to graduate, he was throwing everything to hell. In search of what? his father wondered. Adventure? A soldier for America—all right, but in which of the many wars currently being waged in the continent?

They left with fourteen packages, mostly farewell presents, and food for the journey. Ricardo Rojo, who met up with the adventurers later, described Calica Ferrer's qualifications for being Dr. Guevara's travel companion: "he would have to be prepared for endless walks, despise any kind of dress sense, and put up without any quibbling whatsoever with the hardship of having no money at all."

They had to cross two thousand miles of monotonous and desolate pampas to reach La Paz, Bolivia, and without the satisfaction of being able to go there directly. They traveled second class with Indians who worked in the sugar mills in Jujuy, but, as Ferrer said, "We sat in second-class seats but with people who were first-rate."

In La Paz they rented a shabby room on Yanacocha Street with two nails knocked into the wall from which to hang their belongings. Ernesto wrote to his parents on July 24:

> **I had been expecting to work for a month as a doctor in a tin mine, with Calica as my assistant. We've given up on that one** [the doctor who promised them work had disappeared]. **I am a little disappointed at not being able to stay here; this is a very interesting country living through especially restive times. The agrarian reform takes effect August 2 and all sorts of uproars and riots are expected throughout the country. . . . There are people dead and wounded from the shooting we hear every day. The government has proven almost completely ineffectual at controlling the mass of peasants and miners, but the latter do respond to a certain extent and there's no doubt that the Falange** [the opposition party] **will be on the side of the MNR* if they take up arms.**

It was not easy, even for the astute young Argentine doctor, with his constant curiosity and almost professional powers of observation, to define which way the Bolivian revolution was going. At times, he saw it as a failure whose corrupt leaders would end up throwing it straight into the arms of imperial-

---

° MNR: Movimiento Nacional Revolucionario, National Revolutionary Movement.

ism. At other moments, he could not help admiring the terrific fight put up by the miners, and the clashes that had caused two thousand casualties. **They have fought fearlessly,** he wrote in a letter to his longtime confidante Tita Infante. Ernesto sympathized with the agrarian reform, but did not see anyone who could carry it through. He could discern three wings in the MNR, the winning party: first, the conciliatory sellout right wing, represented by Hernán Siles Suazo; then, a center that was slipping to the right, led by Victor Paz Estenssoro; finally, the left wing headed by Juan Lechín, the miners' leader, **who himself is an upstart, a womanizer, and a playboy.** Ernesto felt that the revolution could withstand outside attacks, but would split up on account of internal disagreement. What he did not know was that in the course of time he would run into all three of these characters again, under completely different circumstances.

Ernesto watched and thought over the social unrest from the lively cafés on 16 de Julio Avenue to the Camacho market, where he tucked into the tropical fruit before ending up installed in the bar at the Sucre Palace Hotel. He used the bar as a vantage point to watch the movement in a city crowded with workers' and miners' demonstrations. **It was a picturesque demonstration, but not a virile one. Their slow plodding and lack of enthusiasm stripped it of its strength and life. The connoisseurs said that the miners' lively faces were missing from the throng.**

Ernesto visited the Agrarian Affairs Ministry with Rojo, whom he had met in the house of a rich Argentine. Here he saw an exhibit about how peasants were sprayed with DDT along with the crops. Ñuflo Chávez from the left wing of the MNR gave him an explanation that was only a rationalization of why campesinos visiting the museum were similarly humiliated, and the pair left unhappy. The MNR was not a party of the people; it was a party without cadres, with a bureaucratic vacuum with leaders who whooped it up in cabarets while the people outside were forming armed guards.

On one occasion, Calica asked Ernesto, in his capacity as kitty treasurer, for money to get washed with and Ernesto, quite seriously, told him that was needless, that food came first and cleanliness afterward. Calica insisted, and Guevara told him he would have to skip breakfast in exchange for the bath. A few hours later, a washed and brushed Ferrer watched Ernesto drinking café con leche with cookies until the doctor relented and treated his friend.

Ernesto's way out of Bolivia took him back to his old love, archaeology. He visited the ruins at Tihuanaco and then the Isla del Sol in Lake Titicaca. He wrote to his mother: **I realized one of my most cherished dreams as an explorer when I found a statue of a woman the size of my little finger in an indigenous graveyard.**

They crossed the Peruvian border on August 17 at Yunguyo and were detained by the customs guards, who checked over their books and the information they'd collected about Bolivian agriculture.

Ernesto became an archaeologist again on August 21, when he took photographs in Cuzco. He would later used them to illustrate an article with material about his first trip to Machu Picchu, called "The Stone Enigma." **I don't** know how many more chances I'll have to admire it, but those gray mounds, those purple and colored peaks that provide a backdrop for the bright gray ruins, are one of the most marvelous spectacles I could imagine.

Ernesto's archaeological enthusiasm was too much for Rojo, who split off from the group and went on to Lima. Guevara was insatiable and visited more ruins, struck with amazement. He described the difference between Granado and Calica as travel companions: One would lie down in the grass and dream about marrying Inca princesses, while the other would complain about the dogshit he trod on in every street in Cuzco. He doesn't smell that intangible evocative stuff of which Cuzco is made, but the smell of stew and dung.

In Machu Picchu again, he wrote, full of emotion: Citizens of Latin America, may ye reconquer the past. In his article, Ernesto would pick up a message left in his hotel by an American—"I'm lucky to have found a place that has no Coca-Cola ads"—and would protest at the major museums being plundered, with major works going out of Latin America.

There were no archaeological ghosts milling around Ernesto's head in Lima, so he was able to observe the symptoms of political deterioration exhibited by the repressive and bloodthirsty military dictatorship led by Manuel Odría. In a letter he wrote later, he described the political atmosphere as "suffocating" and the government as unpopular and propped up with bayonets. His plans were unclear. He told Tita: As to my future life, I know little about bearings and less about schedules.

On September 26 the pair set off for Huyquillas in Ecuador, then to Puerto Bolívar and from there to Guayaquil, where they met up with Rojo again. Rojo recalled that Ernesto won a bet about the state of his underwear. To demonstrate, he took it off and placed it on the floor. Before the astonished stares of his friends, an object of indefinable color, encrusted with dirt from the roads they had traveled, stood up all by itself.

Rojo would later tell of how he suggested they go to Guatemala, where a revolution, principally among the agricultural workers, was under way. Ernesto's version of events is different: There was our economic plight. . . . It all came down to a joke that Gualo García, whom they'd met in Peru, made: Why don't you come with us to Guatemala, boys? The idea was there, and it needed just a little shove for me to make my mind up.

In order to pay for the journey, or at least the start of it, they sold part of what little clothing they had, and finally sailed from Guayaquil for Panama on October 24.

In Panama, Ernesto and Gualo García lived off the kindness of a student leader, Rómulo Escobar, who invited them to stay at his home since they could not afford a boardinghouse. It was not a peaceful household; the police used to arrest Escobar regularly for political reasons. Ernesto ate at a cheap restaurant, the Gato Negro ("Black Cat"), a meeting place for local student leaders and poets. It was in Panama that he made his début as a journalist: His piece on Machu Picchu was published in *Siete* magazine.

They finally found transportation to Costa Rica but Ernesto, who took no notice of anything but his own whims and was never put off by hardship or hurry, said he would not leave Panama without first seeing the Queen of England, who was due to pass through on an official visit.

They arrived in Costa Rica at the beginning of December, leaving behind the suitcase full of books that had caused them so many problems at many other borders. Escobar, entrusted with its safekeeping, would hold on to the contents for many years. Ernesto's first words from San José were addressed to his aunt Beatriz in Buenos Aires; in the head-hunting tone he adopted to frighten his more conservative relatives, he told her he had had the chance to **pass through the domains of the United Fruit Co. and was convinced again how terrible these capitalist monsters are. I have sworn by the image of the late lamented old comrade Stalin not to rest until these octopuses have been vanquished.**

In the Soda Palace café in San José, Ernesto fell in with a group of Cuban exiles who had just clashed with the Batista dictatorship by raiding the large Moncada army barracks. He seemed skeptical of what he was told by Calixto García or Severino Rosell about Fidel Castro, the young lawyer who united the flower of youth with his moral discourse and few weapons: **Pull the other one!**

He finally headed for Guatemala. The trip from the Nicaraguan border was to be the toughest part of the journey.

Just as they were waiting in Nicaragua for someone to take them to Honduras, Rojo showed up in a jalopy with the Beberaggi Allende brothers. It was a pleasant surprise. They traveled in the car to Managua, Nicaragua, where Ernesto picked up a telegram from his father offering him money, which quite disgusted him. **I think they ought to know by now that I won't ask them for cash, no matter what state I'm in.**

They set out for Guatemala, where the brothers were thinking of selling the car, but their money ran out so they sold it bit by bit, first the jack, then the lights, and whatever else came to hand. They would have to get to Guatemala with what was left.

6. Guatemala: The Moment of Truth

In La Marquesa, on the outskirts of Mexico City, 1955

N December 1953, Ernesto wrote to his mother:

> *This is the only worthwhile country in Central America, even though its capital city is no bigger than Bahía Blanca and is just sleepy. Of course, all regimes lose something when you get close to them; here, just to confirm the rule, you do get high-handedness and robberies, but there is a real atmosphere of democracy, and cooperation from the foreigners who have ended up dropping anchor here for various reasons.*

A place to drop anchor? At long last? In Guatemala, a country shaken up by the changes enacted by the liberal popular government headed by President Jacobo Arbenz, which was at daggers drawn with the U.S. monopolies?

On December 20, a few days after arriving in Guatemala City, Ernesto went to see a Peruvian called Hilda Gadea, one of the rich assortment of Latin American exiles with whom the city teemed, to see if she could find him a cheap boardinghouse. Hilda described the two young men at that first meeting:

> They were about twenty-five or twenty-six years old, thin and taller than usual in our part of the world, between 5' 9" and 5' 10". Guevara was very white and pale, with brown hair, big expressive eyes, a short nose, regular features, very good-looking on the whole . . . with a slightly hoarse, very manly voice, which you wouldn't have expected from his seemingly weak appearance. His movements were nimble and swift, but he gave the impression of always being very calm. I noticed that he had an intelligent and observant look and that his comments were very sharp. . . . He gave me the impression of being a little vain and full of himself. . . . I would later find out that asking favors bothered Guevara and that he was suffering from an asthma attack, which forced him to stick his chest out so he could breathe. . . . Like many Latin Americans, I was wary of Argentines.

Hilda's kind description omits the fact that Ernesto's shoes were all worn out and he only had one shirt to his name, which he wore with the tails half hanging out.

Following Hilda's recommendation, Ernesto, along with Gualo and Rojo, moved into a flophouse on Fifth Street.

A few days later, Ernesto received a visit from the commercial attaché at the Argentine embassy, who was to play a decisive role in his life: He would keep him supplied with maté and would later provide him with a safe refuge.

The grateful Argentines visited Hilda in her boardinghouse three days after their first meeting, when Guevara was suffering from a bad asthma attack. Hilda could not have made too big a first impression on Ernesto, either. At twenty-seven, two years older than he, she was a short, plump intellectual. She took after her Indian grandmother, with Asian-looking eyes. She had an interesting political background: She had been exiled by the dictatorship led by General Manuel Odría in Peru because of her activities with the Popular

American Revolutionary Alliance (APRA), and was working in Guatemala City at a government agency that helped to encourage cooperatives and small farmers. One of Hilda's co-workers, Myrna Torres, was more impressed than Hilda with the newcomers, and wrote in her diary on December 27: "I met a very attractive Argentine boy."

Meanwhile, the trials and tribulations of Ernesto's most recent journey were catching up with him, and his asthma attacks were unusually severe. His suffering did not, however, prevent him throwing himself into a search for work. A few days after his arrival, he wrote his mother:

> **I am currently looking into whether I can get work at the leprosarium here, for 250 quetzals and the afternoons off, but there's nothing fixed as yet. Nonetheless, I'll sort myself out somehow, as people here are easygoing and there's a lack of doctors.**

Harold White, a tall, skinny, gray-haired American philosophy professor of about fifty, joined the group of exiles. (I engage in small talk with a gringo who doesn't speak a word of Spanish; now we have a language of our own and we cover great wonders. Some say this gringo was forced into exile because the FBI were after him, and others say he is with the FBI. The fact is that he writes furiously anti-American articles and reads Hegel, and I don't know which side he's batting on.) Ñico López, another newcomer, was a tall, unkempt Cuban with curly, shaggy hair, four years younger than Ernesto. A son of Spanish immigrants, he had run away from school, founded a rebel group called the down-and-outs, and taken part in the July 26 actions, raiding the Bayamo barracks in Cuba the same day as the Moncada raid.

> **I feel quite small when I hear Cubans make grandiloquent claims with completely straight faces. I can make speeches ten times as objective, and without using commonplaces; I can read them out better and convince the audience that what I'm saying is right—but I don't convince myself, whereas the Cubans do. Ñico used to leave his heart on the microphone and that was how he roused a skeptic like me.**

Some more exiled Cubans joined the group a few days later. Because their lack of funds, they appealed to Ernesto to give them free medical treatment. The exiles also swapped reading material. It was White's doing that, after their first conversations (held with Myrna acting as interpreter, and then in a strange hybrid language), Ernesto began by defending Freud but ended up reading Pavlov. With Hilda, the topic was Sartre, whom they both admitted to admiring. Hilda loaned Ernesto books by Mao Zedong. The first arguments cropped up; Ernesto had a run-in with Rojo, who seemed too moderate to him. As Ernesto saw it, change in Latin America would not come about through lukewarm reforms; the revolution would be violent. Hilda tried to calm him down; Ernesto lashed out—I don't want any one to calm me down!—and then apologized: Fatso gets my back up.

At the beginning of January, Ernesto provided a first stocktaking in a letter to his aunt Beatriz:

> **This is a country where you can breathe deep and fill your lungs with democracy. The United Fruit Company backs every other paper, which I would close down in five minutes if I were Arbenz, as they are a disgrace but even so can say what they feel like saying and help to paint just the picture that the U.S. wants: that this is a den of Communists, thieves, traitors, etc. I won't try to say it's a country of plenty, not by half, but there are chances to work honestly and, if I can avoid some irritating red tape, I'll stay here a while.**

An exiled Venezuelan doctor got Ernesto an interview with the public health minister, who told him that if he wanted to practice medicine he would have to take a one-year refresher course at a local university.

The Cuban gang of rogues offered Ernesto a way out by suggesting a different line of business to him; selling pictures of a miracle-working Christ, printed on tin, mounted on wooden boxes and backlit through the print. **For the time being, I'm selling pretty prints of the Lord of Esquipulas on the street, a black Christ who works all sorts of miracles. . . . I already have a rich store of tales about the Christ's miracles, and am constantly building it up.** But street sales seem not to have gone very well for the small gang of atheists: Che was dreaming of food; they were "starving" him in the flophouse.

The political situation was getting tense during Ernesto's second month in Guatemala; the possibility of a coup was growing as military conspiracies, backed by United Fruit, were discovered. Ernesto meanwhile began to make contact with the Guatemalan left. On the second Saturday in February, he went to see Alfonso Bauer, chairman of the National Agrarian Bank and a member of the policy committee of the party coalition supporting Arbenz, at his bungalow. Ernesto criticized the clashes and sectarianism among the parties belonging to the front that supported Arbenz. He thought they were too trusting and believed that a true people's resistance was not being organized.

Shortly after, Ernesto took part in the First Democratic Youth Alliance Festival, an open-air fête combining sporting and political and cultural events. There he met Carlos Manuel Pellecer, congressional deputy for the Guatemalan Communist Party, who made an atrocious impression: **He's a typical representative of a domineering bureaucracy.** But Ernesto wrote to his aunt on February 15:

> **My position is in no way that of a dilettante, all talk and nothing else; I've thrown in my lot with the Guatemalan government and, along with it, the PGT [the Guatemalan Workers' Party], which is Communist. I have also been in touch with in-**

tellectuals that way inclined who publish a magazine here, and I have been working as a doctor with the unions. That has put me in conflict with the College of Surgeons, which is completely reactionary.

Best wishes stood in for good intentions at this time. Ernesto probably sympathized with the Guatemalan left, although he was no more than an observer, removed from the process. He may have had the intention of going beyond that, but no more. His work as a doctor with the unions was no more than an offer they had made him, which came to nothing. Ernesto certainly was in conflict with the no doubt reactionary and corporate-minded College of Surgeons It is doubtful, though, that this bureaucratic institution was harmed by young Dr. Guevara's hatred. . . . Despite his good intentions, Ernesto was still an outsider and Latin America—Argentina, even—was just background and scenery.

Tension was mounting in Guatemala and Ernesto decided to keep an option open, just in case. He asked his father for the address of one of his old friends in Mexico, the filmmaker Ulíses Petit de Murat. Toward the end of February, Ernesto summarized his precarious economic situation:

> **One peso a day for giving English lessons (Spanish, I mean) to a gringo, and 30 pesos a month for helping out with a geography book that an economist here is writing. Helping out means typing and transferring data. Total, 50, and if you take into account that my food and board cost 45, that I don't go to the cinema, and that I don't need medical treatment, it's bountiful.**

Despite this "bountiful" income, Ernesto fell two months behind with boardinghouse rent. He made ends meet by getting a job painting advertisements in the street. Meanwhile, it seems the sweetest opportunity will come to nothing, as the cooperative members don't feel much like paying for a doctor. Ernesto's relations with Hilda Gadea, strengthened by shared intellectual curiosity, were growing closer. They discovered a common interest in poetry; she lent him a book by César Vallejo while Ernesto gave her one by Juana de Ibarbouru. She introduced him to León Felipe and Walt Whitman. They found they were both fans of Kipling's "If." Ernesto chipped in with some prose and introduced her to "The Skin" by Curzio Malaparte and *Mamita Yunai* by Carlos Fallas.° She helped him translate White's book and lent him her typewriter. All this led to long and involved discussions of Marxism, during which Ernesto reproached Hilda wasting her time trying to be militant in a liberal, popular party like the APRA, whose head, Victor Raúl Haya de la Torre, had been to Guatemala and left a rather negative impression on Dr. Guevara.

One way or another, they were embarking on something akin to an intel-

---

°Translator's note: This book does not appear to have been translated into English.

lectual engagement, with their long conversations and long walks in the countryside. One day they went to Sacatepéquez to see a village fair. The hour grew late, and they could not find any way to get back. Hilda was very concerned that she might have had to spend the night: "What will they think at my boardinghouse?" Ernesto managed to get her back to spend the night in Guatemala City. An intellectual and quite conservative engagement, by all accounts.

It was about this time that Ernesto formally declared himself to Hilda. He told her he had had an affair with a nurse at the general hospital where he did voluntary work now and again, but that he was a free agent. He proposed marriage. Hilda was alarmed, and avoided the topic.

Ernesto's living situation got worse and worse in April, so he went to live with the Cubans in their boardinghouse, where he shared a floor to sleep on. Finally, he was told that a job application he'd made to work in the Petén area had been rejected.

In their later memoirs, both Ricardo Rojo and Hilda Gadea suggested that Ernesto did not get the job because he refused to join the Guatemalan Communist Party (PGT), which was a condition of employment. Hilda recalled that an indignant Ernesto protested to Herbert Zeissig, a young Communist: He did wish to join the PGT, but not just to get a job. Amorality and opportunism got his back up.

Ernesto's Guatemalan visa was about to expire, so he decided to leave the country in order to enter it again. He said good-bye to Hilda, who believed that he would never return, that his wandering spirit was stronger than his interest in Guatemala. Ernesto left his things with her, along with a promise to come back.

He traveled to El Salvador **half on foot, half thumbing it;** the Salvadoran police confiscated some of his books at the border. In El Salvador, they picked him up for going around talking about agrarian reform and reading poetry to casual acquaintances. Fortunately, matters went no further than a dressing-down and a recommendation to stick to love poetry and avoid politics. A week later he was in Guatemala again, telling his friends how awful the situation in El Salvador was—how the estates had armed gangs in the pay of the plantation owners—and recounting his experiences with the police.

In a letter to his mother, Ernesto spoke passionately of the Mayan ruins he had visited, but disavowed any intention to become an archaeologist: **It seems a bit of paradox to make the main aim in your life investigating something that is already dead and past caring.** He acknowledged that his practical dreams centered on **something like genetics,** but the only thing he was sure of was that **Latin America will set the stage for my adventures in a much more important way than I might have thought; I really think I have come to understand the place, and I feel distinctly a Latin American, different from everyone on earth who is not.**

Curiously, only in this letter did he mention Hilda's name to his family for the first time (Ernesto the prude, who mentioned everything in his letters, except his love affairs!): **I drink maté when available and get into endless discussions with comrade Hilda Gadea, an APRA supporter whom, with my usual delicacy, I try to convince to leave that shitty party. At least she has a heart of gold, and helps me out in every aspect of my daily life (beginning with my lodgings).**

Years later, Ernesto's father would salvage from among his old papers an article written about Guatemala that April—"Guatemala's Dilemma," a draft in which Ernesto sketched out the tension of the Guatemalan situation and whose end is worth repeating, as it clearly shows what was passing through his mind: **It is high time for the big stick to be fought with a big stick, and if it is time to die, then better to do so like Sandino than like Azaña** [Manuel Azaña y Díaz, the president of defeated Republican Spain].

The last chapter in the unconsummated Guatemalan revolution began May 15. The CIA, backed by the United Fruit Company, had been preparing a coup d'état, and when a shipment of Czechoslovakian arms arrived—the only weapons the Arbenz government could buy, because of the U.S. blockade—it became a pretext to put the plan into action. A small army of mercenaries, led by Colonel Collos Castillo Armas, was waiting on the Honduran border; it stepped into action. The mercenaries were armed and financed by the CIA and supported by aircraft flying from Nicaragua, then under the dictatorship of Anastasio Somoza.

Castillo's private army entered Guatemala amid a blaze of propaganda and pressure; the civilian population had been bombed beforehand. Two days later, Ernesto wrote to his mother: **Two days ago, a plane machine-gunned the city's poor neighborhoods, killing a two-year-old girl. The incident managed to get everyone behind the government, along with all those who came as fellow-travelers, like me.**

At first he was optimistic: **Arbenz is a guy with guts. . . . The people are in very high spirits. . . . I have already signed up to carry out emergency medical aid and have joined up with the youth brigades to receive military training, to go as far as necessary.** This is true. A few days before, Ernesto had gone to the headquarters of the Augusto César Sandino Brigade, a meeting place for leftist Central Americans, where he met with Rodolfo Romero, the Nicaraguan brigade chief, and volunteered to accompany him on guard duty.

Romero recalled:

> I handed him a Guatemalan army-issue Czech rifle and he asked me, **How do you use one of these?** I gave him quick instructions on how to assemble and take it apart in the field, and that first night, during the blackout, I took him to the highest part of the building, to do his first guard duty, from two until six in the morning.

Ernesto formally enlisted as brigade medic shortly after. The atmosphere became increasingly tense. The blacked-out city was bombed night after night.

It was a strange war, in which rumors and misinformation were more important than facts, a war of the airwaves in which Colonel Castillo's columns, though immobile, were "advancing" on Guatemala City, of pressure from the U.S. embassy, from the clergy, from officers who did not want to fight, from attacks on merchant ships. . . . Toward the end of June, the Guatemalan army had managed to stop the small group of mercenaries, but rumor had it they were still advancing. The bombings became worse and were carried out with absolute impunity.

Ernesto thought that the mercenaries could be stopped if the people were armed. **And even if the city were to fall, the fight could go on in the mountains.** He was suggesting, as did other young activists from various left-wing groups, that volunteer brigades be mobilized toward the border with Honduras.

Arbenz finally gave the order to arm the people on June 25, but his own military commanders refused to carry it out. The regular army did not want to fight. Troop casualties had been only fifteen dead and twenty-five wounded; most casualties in the Guatemalan counterrevolution had been sustained by civilians during the bombings.

On June 27, under pressure from the U.S. embassy, the military demanded Arbenz's abdication. The deposed president's sad voice was heard on the radio that day: "Someday, the dark forces that oppress the downtrodden colonial world will be beaten. . . ." And then Arbenz took refuge in the Mexican embassy.

Ernesto met up with Hilda, told her he was going to Mexico, and proposed marriage for the second time. But Hilda was very hesitant to commit herself. A few hours later, the city was in the hands of a military transition government which, in a matter of days, ended up making a deal to turn power over to the coup leaders. For safety's sake, both Hilda and Ernesto changed their address.

There is a legend among Guevara buffs that Ernesto spent the week following Arbenz's overthrow frantically helping exiles find refuge in embassies, or stashing arms in the homes of democratic youth activists. Dolores Moyano later recounted how Ernesto did spend three sleepless days fully active with urban brigades; other sources paint a picture of a crazy Argentine organizing the resistance. In those terrible every-man-for-himself days, Ernesto doubtless participated in some minor tasks with a group of militants who began to think beyond the chaos that obtained in their respective parties. And he most probably engaged in some form of resistance. But it was evident that everything, then, seemed useless, and there was not much left to do. Still, these activities did seem to be of interest to stool pigeons and the police.

Finally, knowing full well that foreigners would be closely scrutinized by the repressive official forces and the military coup leaders, Ernesto accepted the advice of his friend and maté supplier, Sánchez Toranzo, and took refuge in the Argentine embassy. It was there he met the Cuban Mario Dalmau and Humberto Pineda, Myrna Torres's boyfriend.

Hilda was detained shortly afterward while trying to pick up some clothes from her old lodgings. In her first interrogation session, she was asked about Dr. Guevara. She ended up in the women's prison. Hearing this news, Ernesto wanted to turn himself in so they would release her, but his friends stopped him.

On July 4, he wrote to his mother: **Mama, everything has happened like some amazing dream . . . treason is still the army's legacy . . . Arbenz was not up to the circumstances, and the military shat their pants.** He closed with an intimate confession, which, without meaning to, gave still another picture of the adventurer-observer that he was:

> **I'm a little ashamed to say that I actually had a whale of a time in those days. That magical feeling of invulnerability . . . made me squirm with delight when I saw people running like crazy when the planes came, or at night, during the blackout, when the city was filled with gunfire. By the way, I might tell you that light bombing is very imposing.**

And he gave his first impressions of the new regime:

> **If you want an idea of this government's orientation, I'll give you a couple of details: One of the first towns taken by the invaders belonged to a fruit company where the employees were on strike. On [the mercenaries'] arrival, the strike was immediately declared over; the workers were taken to the cemetery and killed by having grenades tossed at their chests.**

Although Ernesto knew the police were after him, he frequently left his refuge in the embassy and one night helped to take Humberto Pineda out of the embassy confines in a car trunk because Humberto wanted to stay behind and fight on in the underground.

Hilda was released on July 28 and, although she could not enter the Argentine embassy, she did begin to swap messages with Ernesto. Aircraft turned up toward the end of August to pick up Argentines sheltered in the embassy, and Ernesto's family took advantage of the opportunity to send him clothes and money. He wrote to his mother: **You seem to have sent me too many clothes and spent too much on me. It may sound a bit ungrateful, but I don't think I deserve it . . . my basic motto is "Travel light, on strong legs and with a fakir's stomach."** He gave his Cuban friend Dalmau five dollars out of the money his parents had sent him, and turned down an invitation to return to Argentina.

On the streets of Guatemala City, police were harassing supporters of the overthrown government; nevertheless, Ernesto left the embassy and turned up in the restaurant where Hilda ate breakfast. People who knew the couple watched with frightened eyes as they walked through the city. Ernesto told Hilda he had dropped his passport off at the Mexican embassy to apply for a visa, and that he was off to Lake Atitlán for three days. As ever, he showed a remarkable disregard for danger and a remarkable ability to do something as "normal" as going on a tourist jaunt amid all the turmoil. Everything went off without a hitch; Ernesto spent three days in the peace and quiet of the Guatemalan countryside, probably putting his ideas in order. Toward the end of the third week in September, nine months after arriving in Guatemala, Ernesto Guevara took a train again, resuming his wandering existence. Hilda traveled toward the Mexican border with him for a while, then disembarked and went back to Guatemala City. They both felt they were saying their farewells for good, although Ernesto said he would wait for Hilda in Mexico City.

On the train, Dr. Guevara met another young man on the run from the military dictatorship: Julio Cáceres, known as "El Patojo" ("The Boy," "Shorty," "The Kid"), who **was several years younger than I, but we struck up a lasting friendship straight away.**

Ernesto was leaving behind a chapter in his life that was to make a strong impression on him, a story of what was and what could not be: a revolution stranded at the halfway mark, and a character, Guevara himself, who was also left stranded halfway—for the moment, anyhow. Was he condemned to be an observer all his life?

7

Ports of Call

The ascent of
Popocatépetl on
October 12, 1955—
Columbus Day.
Ernesto carried an
Argentine flag in
his knapsack, which
he planned to plant
in the crater of the
Mexican volcano.

With Fidel in prison. This is the first photograph of Che that Batista's
police were able to get their hands on. He was being held in the Interior
Ministry's detention center in Mexico City, in 1955. One of the Mayo
brothers took the photo.

I T WAS SEPTEMBER 21, 1954. MEXICO WAS A NEW HORIZON, THE UNKNOWN. There was no connection between the new arrival and the country he had just come to, except for an obscure family tie. His great-grandmother, Concha Castro, had been born in Mexico during the nineteenth century and lost her fortune in the course of the U.S. invasion and the subsequent annexation of Mexican territory.

Shortly after saying good-bye to Hilda, that young Argentine doctor, aged twenty-six years and a few months, surname Guevara—yet to be known as Che—together with his recently acquired traveling companion, Julio Roberto Cáceres, El Patojo, took another train, this time to Mexico City. The city was then milling with Latin American exiles: Puerto Rican independence fighters; Peruvians, mostly APRA supporters, who opposed the Manuel Odría dictatorship; Venezuelan enemies of the despotic government of Marcos Pérez Jiménez; Cuban supporters of Moncada opposed to Colonel Fulgencio Batista; Guatemalans taking refuge after the recent coup; anti-Somoza Nicaraguans fleeing jails and torture; and Dominicans avoiding persecution by dictator Leónidas Trujillo.

It took Ernesto less than a week to put his emotions into enough order to write a first impression: **The city, the country rather, of graft, greets me with all the indifference of a big animal, which neither wags its tail nor bares its teeth at me.** "Indifference" fits the bill exactly. The specter of conservatism and apathy haunted Mexico. The country had watched the CIA-sponsored coup in Guatemala with absolute indifference, but with some very honorable and notable exceptions. Former president Lázaro Cárdenas had come under fire from the conservative press for having dared to point out publicly what was happening south of the border. President Adolfo Ruiz Cortínes, who looked like a small-town lawyer, a little bohemian but very smart, was too busy patching up the social disaster dressed as progress that he had inherited from the Miguel Alemán administration.

Guevara and El Patojo moved into downtown Mexico City. In an imposing urban landscape the outcasts' view—from a sublet maid's room on Bolívar Street—was of clothes hanging in the afternoon breeze, of endless rooftops, of washtubs and gas tanks. The Mexican capital was the Court of Miracles, the land of hardship.

Guevara set down his sense of the country, of the future, and of his survival in letters home: **Here, too, you can say what you like, but on condition you pay for it someplace—in other words, it's dollar democracy.** In his letters he spoke, as always, of new journeys, of plans for going from one place to another, as if the superhighway, the stellar freeway he had lived on for the last ten years, were endless; his goals had not **changed, and my next port of call is still Europe, followed by Asia. How, though, is another story. As for Mexico, I can tell you nothing definite other than this general impression, and the same goes for myself.**

In a letter to his father, he added the United States to his list, **if they let me in.** But for now Mexico was clearly a safe harbor, where he could lick the wounds from Guatemala and satisfy his curiosity. His priority, however, as in so many other cash-strapped moments, was still survival: **I have been around enough in Mexico to know that things here will not be easy, but I come with a bulletproof spirit.**

If poetry is an intimate space, and the poet, good or bad, uses poems to say what he would not put down in a journal, his memoir, or his correspondence; if the poem or a snatch of lyric gives us a glimpse of the inner life—then young Dr. Guevara's Mexico poems will say more about him than his essays. In one, entitled "Dark Self-Portrait," he wrote:

> *I am alone in the inexorable night,*
> *And with a certain sweetish smell of the tickets.*
> *Europe calls me with a voice like vintage wine,*
> *A whiff of pale flesh, of art treasures.*
> *On my face I feel the soft impact*
> *Of the song of Marx and Engels.*

In those early days, Ernesto fell back on one of the few contacts he had in Mexico, a friend of his father's, the Argentine filmmaker and scriptwriter Ulíses Petit de Murat, who worked for the once powerful Mexican film industry, now in relative decline. Petit de Murat fed him some enormous steaks—a gastronomic symbol of Argentine nostalgia—offered to put him up, and even talked of the possibility of obtaining a scholarship for him. Ernesto made his apologies and gave his thanks; there must have been something about the man he did not like, as he kept his distance. As always, he preferred his difficult independence.

He fell into his first job, as he had with everything in these last few years. As Rafael del Castillo Baena, a Spanish refugee and owner of the Foto Taller studio, tells it, "I had set up on the corner of Morelos Street. A friend of mine, who had a photography business on the corner of San Juan de Letrán Street, sent him. . . . I gave him a camera, no strings attached. He could pay me for it as and when he had the money."

This was a case of solidarity from one political refugee to another, from one who just *knows.*

El Patojo had no money whatsoever, and I had just a few pesos. . . . Together we did some off-the-books work, taking photos in parks, with a Mexican partner who had a small laboratory where we did the developing. We got to know every foot of Mexico City, walking from one end of it to another to deliver the photos we had taken, struggling to convince all kinds of clients that their little baby really did take a cute photo and that it was well worth paying a Mexican peso for such a treasure.

Rafael del Castillo Baena added, "He began to take pictures and came by every day so I would develop the rolls of film he had shot at parties or on the street. Every week he gave me something toward paying off the camera. . . . One day, he told me he was a doctor. What, a doctor taking photos at parties and on the street?"

That job fed us for a few months, and we were making our way, bit by bit.

Another accident let Ernesto practice medicine again, although not under the best conditions. A Central American doctor introduced him to Dr. Mario Salazar Mallén, who ran a couple of research groups at the General Hospital and the Cardiology Hospital. Salazar Mallén first offered him an internship in the allergy ward at the General Hospital, which according to Hilda Gadea was poorly paid, and according to Che was not paid at all.

There, in Mexico City, Ernesto had an encounter that planted the seed of the momentous change in his young life. On the street, he bumped into the Cuban Ñico López, whom he'd known in Guatemala and who'd come to Mexico with a compatriot seeking treatment for an allergy. Shortly afterward, taking advantage of an amnesty offered by Batista, Ñico returned to Cuba, but Ernesto stayed in touch with the small group of Cubans to which Lopez had introduced him.

Finally, with survival just about taken care of, Ernesto could afford to take stock of his situation in the wake of what he had just lived through in Guatemala:

> The middle ground can be taken to mean nothing other than the forecourt to betrayal. . . . The bad thing is that, at the same time, I have not decided to adopt the decisive attitude I should have taken so long ago, because deep down (and on the surface, too) I am an incurable drifter and have no wish to see my career interrupted by iron discipline. . . . I do not even know if I shall be an actor or an interested spectator in the action.

At the beginning of November 1954, he wrote his mother:

> I am not doing anything new. I am still making a living from photography and there are no great hopes that I can quit before long, even though I'm now doing research every morning at two hospitals here . . . in the afternoons and on Sundays I work at taking photographs, and at night I study a little. . . . I think I have told you that I am now in a decent apartment and cook and do everything myself, as well as taking a bath every day thanks to the plentiful hot water here. As you can see, I am quite changed in this respect, but am just the same otherwise, as I barely wash my clothes and then badly, as I still cannot afford to pay for a laundress.

A few days later, the quasi-homelike atmosphere that Ernesto had built up around himself was enhanced by the arrival of his friend—practically his fiancée—Hilda Gadea, who had been deported from Guatemala. She arrived in Mexico City on the plane from Tapachula and got in touch with Ernesto immediately: "I put a handkerchief over the phone to disguise my voice, and asked, 'Is Dr. Guevara there?' But he recognized me instantly." They met up just minutes later, at the Hotel Roma, where Hilda had checked in.

> Ernesto once again raised the possibility of our getting married. I told him we should wait a while yet, as I had just arrived, and wanted to settle in and look for work. I had not really made up my mind, which he realized. It bothered him a little. I got the impression that my rather vague answer had made things somewhat tense between us. He then decided we would just be good friends. I was somewhat taken aback at his reaction . . . I had only just arrived and we were already quarreling.

They kept seeing each other, though there was a bit tension in the air. Hilda lived in a boardinghouse on Reforma Street with another exile, a Venezuelan poet called Lucila Velázquez. Ernesto called her a couple of times a week, to take her out to eat, to visit one of Mexico City's marvelous museums, or to go to the movies.

Another accidental encounter improved Dr. Guevara's working life: on a streetcar, he met Alfonso Pérez Vizcaíno, the bureau chief of the official Argentine news agency Agency Latina de Noticias. Pérez Vizcaíno offered him a job as press photographer, steadier work than wandering the streets.

El Patojo's work situation also improved; from delivering photos and collecting payment, he moved up to the post of night watchman in the Fondo de Cultura bookstore. Ernesto joined him now and again, keeping watch in a sleeping bag and taking the opportunity to read. On November 29, he wrote to Tita Infante:

> **At the end of every month I have to do a balancing act and starve to make ends meet. . . . I have felt like giving up, at times—or been pessimistic, rather. . . . When this happens as a temporary thing, in one-day spells, I solve it by drinking some maté and composing a couple of verses. . . . All I ever do is run from anything that bothers me; even today, when I think I am on the way to meet the struggle head-on, especially in social matters, I calmly carry on with my wanderings wherever events may take me, without thinking of taking up the fight in Argentina. I must confess that this is my biggest headache, because I have this terrible struggle with chastity (when I'm there) and desire (to wander, especially all over Europe) and I see that I shamefacedly prostitute myself every time the occasion arises. I meant to give you advice when I began, but ended up telling you about my problems.**
>
> **I earn my keep taking pictures of brats in the park and reporting on Argentines who turn up in these parts for the Agen-**

cia Latina de Noticias, Perón's miscarriage. . . . A good scientific welcome has given me grounds for medical optimism and I have been working in a hospital—in allergies—for free, like one of the Seven Dwarfs. It has turned out well in any case, as Pisani [his university professor in Buenos Aires] **is miles ahead of any other allergy specialist in the Western world. . . . This leads me to think that my economic luck may change, too, as success in these happy, godly parts turns to dough if you are not too much of a drip, as they say around here.**

In that same letter, Dr. Guevara tried to encourage his friend Tita, who had fallen victim to one of her frequent depressions, with a piece of advice about sex:

Remember that that little itch we call sex needs to be scratched now and again; otherwise it gets out of hand, takes up every waking moment, and makes a real mess. You may think this is all stupid, but deep down I know you do not, and that there is something in what I'm saying and that not the least important is that it keeps [you] **from seeing a way through your problem.**

His economic luck did not change, but his relations with Hilda did: "In the last week of November, he took me to the cinema to see *Romeo and Juliet,* a Soviet film that featured a ballet. We really liked it and discussed the universal appeal of Shakespeare, whose plays we knew. We made up on that occasion."

At the beginning of December, Hilda and her friend Lucila moved into a small apartment in the middle-class Condesa district, which they furnished very cheaply. Ernesto was a frequent visitor. Judging by the account in Hilda Gadea's memoirs, relations between her and Ernesto were stormy; they often broke up. Curiously, in Guevara's copious correspondence with Argentina, there is no mention of his relationship with Hilda. It seems that, either because of a strange prudishness or because he did not consider the matter to be important, he simply omitted it. In the last few weeks of 1954, a year that, for Dr. Guevara, ended with ever-present economic uncertainty (he was once reduced to selling toys on the street), his curiosity drove him to the university, to be an nonmatriculating student at classes given by the legendary Jesús Silva Herzog, the economist behind the 1938 nationalization of Mexico's oil wells.

Toward the end of the year, Ernesto had resumed work on writing "The Role of the Doctor in Latin America" (**I may not know much about medicine, but I have Latin America down pat**). He was earning 700 pesos a month as a writer and photographer at the Agencia Latina and was hoping to round it up to a thousand with his street photography.° He was spending three

°Translator's note: 700 pesos was worth U.S. $56 at this time.

whole mornings a week at the hospital and was still writing of the need to visit Europe, now adding the "Cortisone"—"Iron Curtain zone"—countries to his wish list. He kept his diary meticulously, as he had been doing for so many years and which some day would be revealed; and he read, in an urge to become familiar with Mexico, the best he could find on the country's recent history, like John Reed's *Insurgent Mexico* and Martin Luis Guzmán's *Memories of Pancho Villa.*

Around this time, the young Guevara tried to make a political summing-up of Latin America: **The way the gringos treat Latin America . . . was making me more and more indignant . . . then came Guatemala and all the business that is so hard to talk about. . . . Just when I left reason to grasp something like faith, I cannot say, can't even estimate, because the road was really long and there were a lot of setbacks.**

The end-of-year holidays were part of the by now chronic ups and downs of his relationship with Hilda. Ernesto and El Patojo were invited to have supper on December 24 with her and her Venezuelan friend at their apartment. Guevara, however, was delayed visiting his Cuban friends at María Antonia González's house, a frequent meeting place for exiled supporters of the Moncada raid. Then he left early to pick up his sleeping bag, so he could keep El Patojo company on the night shift at his watchman's job. Hilda took offense at the delay and swift departure, and became depressed. Although they spent Christmas Day together, walking in Chapultepec Park, the story was repeated on New Year's Eve, when Ernesto stood Hilda up completely. Hilda thought she might breaking things off if Ernesto cared more for solidarity with his Guatemalan friend than for her. Theirs was like a relationship between teenagers: full of doubts, misinterpretations, breaking up and making up.

New Year's Day, 1955, found the couple making up again and walking around Toluca. The reconciliation was contentious throughout January. On the twentieth, Ernesto gave Hilda, as a belated New Year's present, a copy of *Martín Fierro* that Ernesto had dedicated: **To Hilda, so that when the parting comes, you will keep a substratum of my wanderlust and militant fatalism. Ernesto.**

In February, Ernesto pressed his marriage proposal again. Hilda accepted and fixed the date for March. Ernesto asked her, Why not now? She suggested marrying on the first anniversary of their meeting. The engagement did not last long, however. Between the pages of a book he had lent her, Hilda found a negative of a photo of a woman in a swimsuit. This brought on a fit of jealousy. Ernesto was annoyed at her starting a squabble about the picture. He told her it was nothing; the woman was just Petit de Murat's daughter. "He said I was just finding excuses not to get married, that he was breaking things off that time, and that we would not even be friends now," she said.

They did not see each other for a week, and the breakup seemed to be final. However, Hilda fell ill and asked for a professional visit from Dr. Guevara. Ernesto diagnosed tonsillitis that had spread to her ears; he treated her with antibiotics. They were back together again.

Their love life did not seem to be very meaningful to Ernesto, or at least not enough for it to show in the constant stream of letters to his family in Buenos Aires, where he made no mention of it. The topic of future journeys, on the other hand, kept cropping up; it might almost be described as an obsession. He told his father that France and the "Cortisone" were in his sights, and Chairman Mao as always, at the end of my roaming, or almost at the end, as the scholarship is still on the way. To enable him to make these journeys, my ammunition will be three or four scientific works which [typical modesty] are very good.

A chance to relieve his economic hardship came at the beginning of March 1955. The Agencia Latina de Noticias, for which he had been working, offered him a well-paid job: covering the fourth Pan-American Games. I had to be a beat reporter, photographic editor, and host to journalists arriving from South America.

Ernesto set up an improvised team with his friend El Patojo, the Cuban Severino Rosell, and a Venezuelan exile, who provided a darkroom for developing and printing. It was, Rosell would recall years later, "a small photographers' collective." Guevara threw himself into the job, which lasted from March 6 until March 20, and without stopping work at the hospitals where he did his research into allergies.

> My work at the Pan-American Games was exhausting in every sense of the word, as . . . I did not sleep more than four hours a night on average . . . since I was also the one who developed and copied the photographs. All this work did have a small monetary reward in the form of some 4,000 pesos due me after all that toil and trouble.

Years later, *Bohemia* magazine rescued some of Dr. Guevara's photographs: a Peruvian woman in midair during the high jump; the sprint in a bicycle race; the men's 110-meter hurdles final; the Brazilian gymnastics team, looking bored. . . .

But the story was not to have a happy ending:

> When all the toil and trouble was over and everyone who had covered the games had been conveniently congratulated, a laconic cable from the Agencia told us it was suspending transmissions and that each correspondent should do what he felt best with the personnel of whom he was in charge (no word of salaries). Hearing this news and throwing myself heart and soul into the business of biting my ass was one and the same thing.

Despite his overwhelming workload, during those days he returned to the subject of marriage. As Hilda Gadea put it:

When he came home, he asked seriously whether I had made up my mind. His tone of voice was calm, but firm, and he was almost giving me an ultimatum. And as I really had, I said yes, that we would get married in May. . . . After that I asked him if he had been sure I would say yes. He quite seriously answered me, **Yes, because you knew that you would lose me this time if you said no.**

There then followed the trying business of overcoming the bureaucratic obstacles thrown their way by the Interior Ministry, which seems to have spent years just making life impossible for penniless foreigners.

With a wedding coming up and in the midst of another working crisis, some good news broke: **Luckily, I have been given lodging and board at the General Hospital, and maybe the odd mislaid peso will find its way into my fingers (I spend it most drunkenly on melon juice).**

In a letter to his mother, he explained that the scholarship consisted of room and board and laundry, but no money. Olivia Salazar, Mallén's widow, remembered years later that her husband invited Dr. Guevara to come and live at their house, but Ernesto, arguing that he did not wish to abuse a friendship, "preferred to stay put, in a sleeping bag on an examination table in a small office and instruments room in the hospital." These were the "lodgings" he spoke of in the letter to his parents.

———

In order to earn his board and room in the hospital, Ernesto submitted a paper entitled "Cutaneous Research Using Semidigested Alimentary Antigens," which was to be presented at an allergy conference in Veracruz and published in the May 1955 edition of the *Ibero-American Allergology Review*.

He was also working on another half-dozen projects, all with their ups and downs.

Laura de Albizu Campos, a Puerto Rican living as an exile in Mexico at that time, said:

> He was doing experiments on cats' brains, studying nerve cells, cerebral cells, according to stimuli, which he determined according to the reactions. . . . I think he paid a lady a peso a cat, but the lady had a group of Mexican boys who were the ones that picked the cats up, and I always used to ask him if he hadn't used up all the cats in the neighborhood, and he would burst out laughing.

With Dr. David Mitrani, he used to go and eat tacos at the little stands outside the Medical Center after working in the laboratory. They were working on several other experiments, two of which made a stir in the medical community: "on alimentary antigens and on the action of histamines on a cat's uterus. . . . By day he did his research, while at night he worked as an assistant professor of practical human physiology in the old medical school."

With his usual biting wit, Ernesto said in a letter to his father: I spend twenty-four hours a day talking about diseases and how to cure them (although I do not cure anything, of course), and to Tita Infante he summed up his research as follows: Scientifically, I am a first-rate failure: All my great research projects have been a washout . . . and I am confined to presenting a modest paper in which I repeat in Mexico Pisani's work in Argentina on semidigested food.

By the end of April, Hilda had found work, first at the Economic Commission for Latin America and the Caribbean and then in the Pan-American Health Office. She and Ernesto spent all their spare time fighting Mexican bureaucracy at the Interior Ministry to try to obtain a marriage license.

Although the wedding was scheduled, there is little or no mention of it in Ernesto's letters to Argentina. The wish lists of possible, impossible, and hypothetical journeys were still appearing, though. To Tita Infante, he wrote: I hope, Tita, that around the corner in any old European city, we will meet soon, me with my belly full and you with a degree in your hand. For now, that is the most we can hope for, but the future is for the people.

———————

Ernesto's contact with the Cubans made him change his list of potential journeys: The next step could be the U.S. (very difficult), Venezuela (feasible), or Cuba (probable). But I have my heart set on Paris and will get there even if it means swimming all the way across the Atlantic.

Ernesto Guevara was, at this stage in his life, essentially a drifter. During the twenty-two months of his stay in Mexico there were 161 mentions of possible or hypothetical journeys in his correspondence with his family and two friends alone. This obsession with travel was reflected in a poem he wrote at that time:

> The sea beckons with a friendly hand
> My meadow—a continent—
> Unrolls itself softly and indelibly
> like a bell tolling at eventide.

Ricardo Rojo, a compatriot of Guevara's, arrived in Mexico City on April 30, 1955, from the United States, where he had spent a year in exile, and immediately looked up Ernesto. "He was thinner and, despite having been a street photographer, still had the unmistakable appearance of a university student on vacation."

The next day was May Day, and Ernesto went with Hilda and Rojo to watch the parade. A sad travesty of a labor parade passed in front of the exiles. One Mexican progovernment labor organization after another declared its allegiance and tameness. Not too big a parade, and weighed down by routine. The left-wing parties, the POCM and the Communist Party, and dissident workers' groups, like the railroad workers, were being repressed by the police and had been excluded from the official parade. Ernesto commented: **The Mexican Revolution is dead—and has been for a while, without us realizing. . . . The parade of organized workers looks like a funeral procession. . . . They are gathered together by the budget, the government payroll. Let's go, pal.**

Rojo spent just a week in Mexico City, during which he and Ernesto went to a meeting of a group of Cuban exiles, whose headquarters was in the Imperial Building. Without meaning to, they became involved in a heated debate. At that time, an amnesty bill was under consideration in Cuba for those who had assaulted the Moncada barracks in 1953, and in particular for the leader of the action, one Fidel Castro. The Cubans followed the new developments, advances, and setbacks with their ears glued to the radio. Fidel was freed two weeks later, on May 15.

There were echoes of this Cubanization of Ernesto's interests in a letter written to his parents at the end of May: **Havana in particular is grabbing my attention, filling my heart with landscapes, mixed up with views of Lenin.**

Meanwhile, overwhelmed by the legal obstacles the Mexican immigration authorities threw in the way of their getting married ("How about that, the lady is Peruvian and wants to marry an Argentine"), Hilda and Ernesto decided to live together anyway. Dr. Guevara gathered the scant possessions he had at the hospital and moved into the apartment that Hilda and her friend Lucila had on Rhín Street, a very austere place where the closet consisted of just two planks and a couple of cloth-lined strips of wood.

On May 18, they went on an "engagement trip to Cuernavaca." Hilda marked the occasion as "our real wedding day."

On June 17, Ernesto wrote to his mother: **The Agencia Latina fired me owing me 6,000 pesos. They have paid me now, but just 3,000, with which I have to pay a whole pile of debts.** He related how, expecting the whole amount, he had gone to look for a passage to Spain (as part of a planned journey to Poland), but pulled out when he was given just half the money, as he was **really hard up.** As ever, he tried to strike a balance in the letter: **This tough and inhospitable Mexico has treated me fairly well after all and, despite being ripped off, I will take something more than money with me when I go: my respectable name on a series of more-or-less worthwhile articles and, most important of all, a settled set of ideas and aspirations where there used to be just haze in my brain.**

There was no mention of his de facto marriage.

Despite his attempt to convince his mother that the scientific work was not going too badly, the conditions were very poor: **I am working here in a bacteriology . . . and a physiology lab** [what's more] **in a specific area of allergy where I have to make equipment out of thin air, where we do not have so much as a lousy Bunsen burner.**

In mid-June, Ernesto embarked on a scarcely advisable venture for an asthmatic: He set off to climb Popocatépetl, one of the volcanoes close to Mexico City. The expedition was a failure, but Ernesto wrote a memorable account of it:

We burst with heroism but failed to reach the summit. I was ready to die trying and leave my bones behind, but a Cuban friend who accompanied me on the ascent had two frozen feet, so the five of us had to come down. When we'd descended a hundred meters (which is a lot at that altitude), the storm let up a little and the mist cleared, and then we realized that we had almost reached the edge of the crater, but we could not turn back up then. We had spent six hours struggling against the snow, which found its way to our pubic hair at every step, and with our feet soaked thanks to our carelessness in not wearing the right gear.

The guide got lost in the fog, thus avoiding a crevice, which are pretty dangerous, and we were all dead tired from struggling against such soft and abundant snow. On the way down, we slid downhill, toboggan-style, just like in the swimming pools in the mountains, and with the same outcome: None of us had pants left when we got to the bottom.

My feet thawed out when we got down, but my face and neck are burned all over, as if I had spent a whole day sunbathing at Mar del Plata. Right now, my face looks like something out of Frankenstein, what with the Vaseline I put on it, and the oozing blisters. Furthermore, my tongue is in the same state, as I wiped it in the snow. Mountain climbing is lovely, but one thing bothers me: An old-timer of fifty-nine came along and climbed better than any of us.

Was life like that? Was he a street photographer, poorly paid medical researcher, permanent exile, no-great-shakes husband, letter writer, poet, and diarist, the latter two privately?

Yes, and more besides.

He finished a letter to his mother this way: The main thing is that I feel like something out of a tango, a bit Argentine, I mean, a feature I've nearly always disowned. I think this is the first sign of old age (which in the end is tiredness), or else I long for the peace of home sweet home.

But Ernesto Guevara, who had just turned twenty-seven and was scared of settling down and getting sidetracked from his Latin American wandering, was about to set off on a remarkable journey.

Late in June, on a visit to the Cuban exiles in Mexico City, Ernesto met the younger of the Castro brothers, baby-faced Raúl, who had had to leave the country after the recent amnesty because the Batista government had accused him of planting a bomb in a cinema. Raúl's Marxist background and his record of taking part in the Moncada raid must have made him much more attractive to Ernesto than the Latin American exiles he had been in touch with so far, experts in juggling dreams and mixing up illusions with reality and living on fairy tales of a triumphant return.

The two talked several times, in the new home Ernesto had set up with Hilda, as well as at the dive at number 6 Ramón Guzmán Street, where the young Cuban was staying. They spoke of Raúl's legendary brother, Fidel, and his expected arrival in Mexico. Though Fidel had planned to stay in Cuba to organize a revolutionary network opposed to the dictatorship, censorship, and sundry repression against his comrades had finally convinced him to go into exile and organize an armed return.

In the second week of July—it was **one of those cold Mexican nights,** though the season was summer—he met the eldest of the Castro brothers, the undisputed leader of what was beginning to be known as the 26th of July Movement, or M26, the resistance to Batista. Fidel arrived in Mexico on July 8 and met Ernesto at María Antonia González's flat, where the Cuban exiles landed one by one.

That first conversation between Fidel and Guevara lasted eight or ten hours, according to what witnesses later remembered, and it made a lasting impression on them both. From eight P.M. until dawn, they discussed politics, the international situation, their respective views of Latin America, and, above all, revolutions. In particular they spoke of Ernesto's version of events in Guatemala, and of the coming revolution in Cuba.

Guevara, who by this stage of his life had become aloof, a man who kept his emotions under wraps, was struck by Fidel's snake-charming magic. The following day, he wrote in his diary: **To have met Fidel Castro, the Cuban revolutionary, an intelligent, young, and very self-assured guy, is a political event. I think we hit it off.**

When he got home, he told Hilda: **Ñico was right in Guatemala when he said that Fidel is the best thing to come out of Cuba since Martí. He is going to make the revolution happen.**

A couple of years later, he told Argentine journalist Jorge Ricardo Masetti:

> **Fidel struck me as an extraordinary man. He faced up to the most impossible problems and solved them. He had an exceptional faith that once he left for Cuba, he would get there; that once he got there, he was going to fight; and that in fighting, he was going to win. I shared his optimism. Things had to be done, to be fought, to be settled. You had to stop whining and fight.**

Other meetings followed quickly after that first one. At the end of a meeting at number 43 Rhín Street, the apartment where Ernesto and Hilda lived, Hilda asked Fidel why he was in Mexico. He replied with a four-hour monologue by the end of which Hilda herself was convinced that she should throw in her lot with the July 26 group. When Fidel had gone and they were alone, Ernesto confessed to his wife that he thought Fidel's plan was madness, but feasible and realistic madness. . . .

From that meeting, we have Hilda's description of Fidel: "Very pale and tall, stocky without being fat, with very black, shiny, curly hair; he had a mustache. His movements were swift, nimble, and surefooted. . . . He could have passed for a good-looking bourgeois tourist, but then when he spoke . . .

A few days later, Ernesto asked Hilda:

What do you think of these Cubans' crazy idea of invading a completely mobilized island?

"It's crazy, all right, but you can't argue with it."

Just what I think. I wanted to know what you'd say. I've decided to join the expedition. We're holding talks, and will soon begin our preparations. I'll go along as a doctor.

The utopian adventurers' boat had acquired some new oars.

Raúl Castro, however, took it into his head to be a bullfighter, and practiced passes with his friends every chance he got. Raúl's passion was hardly sensible. When he wasn't "bullfighting," he accompanied Ernesto through the alleyways of Mexico City, hunting for cats for Dr. Guevara's experiments.

The Rhín Street apartment was broken into around that time. There was little for the thieves to take, except for the young couple's most precious possessions: Hilda's typewriter and Ernesto's camera. Guevara was indignant; he told Hilda it was the work of the FBI, and they decided not to report the matter to the police. But now the doctor could no longer work at photography, nor could the couple finish the book they were working on together, "The Doctor's Role in Latin America," which Ernesto had been writing for years, Ernesto used to dictate while Hilda typed. "The Doctor's Role" was to be a long essay in fourteen chapters, covering not only public health problems, clinical problems, and the economy of disease and its geopolitics, but also projections for the "socialist future" of medicine in the continent. The book would stress that the revolutionary doctor had to stand up to state structures in thrall to the powerful absentee landlords and foreign monopolies, and would seek to define a medicine in which profit and plunder would not prevail. The book was never finished.

The postponed wedding, meanwhile, came unstuck over umpteen bureaucratic requirements. Ernesto and Hilda began to think that maybe they should get married in an embassy. The Peruvian embassy, said she; the Argentine embassy, said he.

At the beginning of August, Hilda realized that she might be pregnant, and told Ernesto so when he returned from the hospital. At first he was doubtful—**You're joking**—then he was glad. That afternoon, he gave her a Mexican silver bracelet, using some of the money he'd been paid by the press agency.

Finally, they found a way of getting the wedding sorted out. Guevara got a hospital colleague to put him in touch with the authorities at the courthouse in Tepoztlán, a small town thirty minutes from Mexico City that was well-known for its colonial convent. In Tepoztlán, they could be married "Mexican-style," i.e., without a license. And so, on August 18, an official fortuitously named Angel married Hilda Gadea Acosta and Ernesto Guevara Serna, who had been accompanied by a small group of friends.

Jesús Montané, a director of the anti-Batista movement in exile, and the poet Lucila Velázquez were the bride's witnesses. Montané was standing in for Raúl Castro, who attended the ceremony but for reasons of security did not sign the certificate. Drs. Baltazar Rodríguez and Alberto Martínez Lozano—the latter was a native of Tepoztlán and had arranged the wedding—were the groom's witnesses. On returning home, Ernesto threw a barbecue, to which Fidel came.

Hilda's family was notified by telegram, while Ernesto told his own by letter sometime during the next few weeks. Complaining at not having been informed, Hilda's family sent $500 and clamored for a church wedding. Ernesto replied:

You're right to complain at our not having informed you of our wedding when it took place. The child is definitely on its way; biological reactions and a whole series of clinical data allow me to be absolutely certain. . . . I am very sorry to have to tell you that our shared political and religious convictions rule out anything other than a civil wedding.

The way Ernesto conveyed the news of his wedding to his parents and his aunt Beatriz is curious. In a letter to his mother dated September 24, more than a month after the wedding, he wrote: I will tell you the news officially so you can pass it on: I got married to Hilda Gadea and we are to have a child shortly. He didn't say a word about his new wife—not even who she was or where she was from—and he buried this reluctant-seeming wedding announcement in a pile of other news. On October 8, he wrote to his aunt Beatriz: You must have heard the news about my love life from my mother; I got married and I expect a Vladimiro Ernesto in a short while; obviously I expect him, but my wife will have him. He did not even mention the marriage in his letters that month to Tita Infante. What was behind his delays and his playing the matter down? Fear of middle-class rejection by his Argentine parents and relatives? Distaste for marriage? For someone whose correspondence contained detailed accounts of events and aspirations, the trivializing way he told his family and friends that he'd gotten married is a little strange, if not suspicious.

Travel was still a passionate concern. In a letter to his new in-laws, Ernesto commented on the possibility of a journey to Cuba as if it were part of a tourist itinerary, and he added his plans to visit China and France. Also, he insisted that sooner or later Hilda and he would go to Paris, like any other urban middle-class Argentines. And the list did not stop there:

Our wanderings aren't over yet; before settling for good in Peru, a country I greatly admire, or in Argentina, we would like to discover Europe and a couple of fascinating countries like India and China. I am particularly interested in the new China, since it is in tune with my political ideals.

In those days, Ernesto even asked Hilda to check into the possibility of a journey to Africa.

Had he not committed himself to the Cuban expedition? Did he have his doubts concerning the feasibility of the plan? Certainly, he was fascinated by Fidel's personality, and the proposal had taken hold of him, but Dr. Guevara must still have had a trace of skepticism left. How many times had revolution been spoken of in the little world of political exiles in which he had been moving for years? How many plans had been made and broken? How many countries had been freed in word only?

The conflict between Ernesto's leaning toward the life of a wanderer and travel writer, and the need to move on to political action and stop being a mere observer is echoed in one of his poems, "Here":

> *I am a mestizo in another respect, too.*
> *In the two forces that quarrel over my intellect . . .*
> *And both attract and repel each other.*

Of those months Hilda said:

> Ernesto was very worried about a patient in the hospital, a laundress he called old María. He was very moved when he told me she was in a bad way with acute asthma. He was so worried about her that I began to feel jealous because she was always on his mind. He used to rush every morning to see her. . . . One day, very downhearted, he told me she probably wouldn't last the night, and so he went to the hospital to be at her bedside, watching over her to do his best to save her. She died that night, suffocating from her asthma.

The death of the old laundress made a big impression on Dr. Guevara. He felt personally disturbed at the wretchedness the woman lived in with her daughter and three or four grandchildren, and saddened that she died "with neither pain nor glory," as they would have said in Mexico then.

The old woman's death inspired a work by the physician-poet. It was not a good poem, but little by little he described the woman's misery, the hospital ward, and her death from asthma. There is a promise that **your grandchildren will live to see the dawn,** and a rhetorical but sincere-sounding end: **I swear,** written in capital letters.

A military coup against Perón took place in Argentina on September 16. Ernesto devoured the newspapers in Mexico and wrote to his parents and his aunt. He had already commented on the first coup attempt a couple of months before, worried that his anti-Perón family may have been involved: I hope things are not as bad as they say and that no one is mixed up in trouble where there is nothing to be done.

Now, with the military cracking down on grassroots Peronist organizations, he told his mother that anything that the oligarchy liked could not be good, and that there was nothing healthy in the conservative elements rejoicing at Perón's fall. He also took the opportunity to remark to her that your old enemy has fallen and to predict a future for Argentina as a dependent banana republic.

Meanwhile, life went on in Mexico. Perón and Argentina were a long, long way away. Hilda recalled: "One day we went to see *Curtain Up* with Cantinflas. I don't remember a film that made him laugh so much . . . The scene where Cantinflas dances the minuet when he finds himself unexpectedly onstage was what made him laugh the hardest." Guevara went to see the movie more than once; he surely remembered Dr. Velenza, a Peruvian psychologist whom he met during his first journey in Latin America and who told him that the only way to understand pan–Latin Americanism was to see Cantinflas.

This anecdote is frequently pertinent in the history of the years to come. When he wanted to laugh at himself, Ernesto would draw on his resemblance to Cantinflas, a resemblance that did not yet exist in 1956. Ernesto in those days looked more like a young and clean-shaven version of John Garfield, but taller and a little stockier.

He lived in a condition of indecision and uncertainty back then. Fidel carried on with his organizing and his recruitment campaign from a distance, while Ernesto spent his time discussing possible names for the baby with Hilda (Hilda Victorina or Ernesto Vladimiro), learned from one of the Cuban exiles how to cut hair, and tried his knowledge out on innocent patients in the hospital. (All knowledge is useful; it may come in handy someday, don't you think?) He moved with Hilda—but without Lucila—to apartment 5 (according to the attorney general's records) at Nápoles Street. The new place was just as modest as the old, but larger.

And he fulfilled his ambition to climb to the top of Popocatépetl. On Octobe 12, 1955, Columbus Day or the Day of the Race (in Mexico), to celebrate the mixing of Europeans with the native race of Mexico, Ernesto climbed the old volcano with a crowd. A tough climb, especially for an asthmatic, eight miles long and over 17,500 feet high.

Fidel left for a fund-raising tour of the United States on October 29, accompanied by Juan Manuel Márquez. In his absence, Raúl fell ill and was treated by Dr. Guevara. There they met the Soviet diplomat Nikolai Leonov, a friend of Raúl's. Ernesto asked him for some Russian books. The Russian gave him his card, not knowing what trouble this simple act would cause him several months later. Hilda's memoirs mention Ernesto reading books that Leonov brought for him.

At the end of October, Ricardo Rojo stopped in Mexico on his way back from New York to Argentina, and immediately got in touch with Guevara. According to Rojo, Ernesto followed events in Argentina closely, but had no intention of returning. He had not left Argentina to get away from Perón; while Guevara may not particularly have liked him, he liked the man's opponents, Frondizi and others, even less. Guevara answered Rojo's repeated invitations to return:

What is there to go back to? A military government, which right now is trying to get the working class out of the country's politics. Let us suppose this government goes away, another goes away yesterday, your friend Frondizi comes and you yourself get to be a minister. What could you do? A government with good intentions but no far-reaching changes.

According to Hilda Gadea's memoirs, the arguments between Guevara and Rojo grew very bitter, as Fatso seemed to Ernesto to be quite conservative.

Rojo recalled: "At that time, I recommended Guevara for a job with Mexico's biggest publisher, the Argentine Armando Orfila, who ran the Fondo de Cultura Económica (FCE)." Apparently they didn't hit it off. Ernesto was selling books on commission for the FCE, but was not one for asking favors.

There are two accounts of the conversation that night, one by Orfila and another by a Cuban leftist named Raúl Roa, who happened to be present.

"He looked—and was—very young," Roa said. "His image was painted on my retina: bright intelligence, ascetic pallor, asthmatic breathing, bulging forehead, thick hair, dry expression, energetic chin, serious manner, inquiring look, sharp thinking, words stored up, vibrant senses, a clear laugh, and a mind clouded with magic dreams that just shone out from him." Two other anecdotes can be salvaged from Rojo's memoirs: He and Ernesto were at a meeting with Cuban exiles in a smoke-filled room in the Imperial Building in downtown Mexico City, where Rojo first heard the broad outline of the invasion plan. It drew a sarcastic laugh from Rojo: "You know where we lock people up in Buenos Aires when they've got ideas like yours? In Vieytes." No one needed to tell Ernesto that the place was a mental hospital.

Roa's second anecdote is of an interview with León Felipe, a Spanish poet exiled in Mexico, who obviously made quite an impression on the Argentine doctor. Ernesto knew his work well and would quote it repeatedly throughout his life. Rojo's sketch reveals much: when Ernesto and León crossed their legs during their conversation in a Mexico City café, you could see that both men's shoes were worn through in the sole.

Finally, in November 1955, the much-postponed honeymoon took place. Ernesto and Hilda decided to go to the south of Mexico and tour the former Mayan country. They had no particular schedule in mind.

In Mexico City, Ernesto had managed to keep his asthma in check by sticking to a strict diet of beef, fruit, and vegetables, and eliminating fish, chicken, and eggs, to all of which he was allergic. But the asthma came back when they went down to the coast. A terrible attack laid Ernesto low in Palenque. Hilda tried to give him an injection, to which he reacted aggressively. Hilda recalled:

> He rebuffed me violently. I realized this was not strictly to do with the injection, but rather because he did not like to be protected, to be helped when he was sick. I was dumbstruck by his harsh attitude.
> **Sorry. It's not your fault. It's this disease that gets me out of sorts. Don't worry, it's silly, it's not worth staying upset about.**

Mérida, Chichén Itzá, Uxmal.

Ernesto climbed the pyramids frenziedly, like a boy discovering a new adventure, like an explorer coming across the find of his life, fascinated by the imposing spectacle of the ruins, hyperactive, up and down, taking photos.

His fascination can be seen in a poem about Palenque:

> *What strength keeps you beyond the centuries*
> *Alive and kicking as in youth?*
> *Which god blows, at the end of the day*
> *The breath of life into your stelae?*

In Veracruz, Ernesto almost got into a brawl with some drunks in a bar where he and Hilda had gone to eat fresh fish: the beer drinkers insisted in "his queen" going to have a drink with them, and Dr. Guevara stood up to them in true Mexican style, ready to break their faces. **You can try what you like with me,** Ernesto said to the most aggressive of the bunch, just like something out of a home-grown Mexican film. The story had a happy ending, because the owner of the bar threatened to call the police if things got out of hand.

They went by boat up the Veracruz coast shortly after; Ernesto remembered his long voyages as a teenager and enjoyed himself while the rest were seasick. He ran from one end of the deck to the other, taking photos.

Back in Mexico City, Guevara got some good news: he'd been offered a lectureship in physiology at the National University. He wrote to his mother on December 5, skeptically: **I cannot see myself as a teacher, even in primary school.** But in his letters he kept talking of the lectureship, though it was never to materialize. He used it as a masquerade, a cover, so as not to mention what was really happening: Fidel had returned from the United States; preparations and training for the expedition had begun.

The survivors would remember the winter of 1955–56 in Mexico City as harsh, dusty, bitterly cold, damp, and gloomy with rain. This is what Cubans remembered; for them, the absence of sun and palm trees was depressing and nerve-racking. In photos from those days, they look like a bunch of poor boys, "poor but polite," with their hands always in their pockets, looking for money that isn't there. Ernesto Guevara, with his forelock hanging down, his permanent scowl, his frayed shirt, and his overgrown-boy looks, looked odd beside these very formal Cubans, with their ears sticking out under their awful fifties haircuts, with thin mustaches penciled on their upper lips. They were all so far removed from the magnificent, irreverent, bearded, and long-haired characters later to descend from the Sierra Maestra and the Escambray.

Turning up in Mexico at the end of '55 and the beginning of '56, alone or in groups of two or three, working their way over from Havana, Camagüey, Miami, Costa Rica, or San Francisco, bringing a phone number, a contact address, a name—these people did not come to be unwilling exiles moaning about their fate. They came to join an armed invasion of Cuba. A phrase from their leader was particularly captivating, a sort of awesome promise. In New York, on October 30, 1955, Fidel said: "I can tell you with absolute certainty that in 1956 we shall be free or we shall be martyrs." And Fidel, a thirty-year-old lawyer, was known not just for his rhetorical ability, but because his words were usually accompanied by deeds.

The original plan, which was being drawn up little by little, was to organize a landing in the east of the island. The invasion was conceived as something of an epic dream that linked the traditions of the nineteenth-century independence struggle with Guiteras in the thirties and the long Cuban history of exile and armed return.

María Antonia González's apartment in downtown Mexico City became the headquarters and main meeting place. Curiously enough, it was a couple of blocks from a grocery store called La Antilla. If revolutions have hearts and minds, then they have to have a home, too.

On arriving in Mexico in February, Juan Almeida described the place:

> The apartment is small, cramped, as if many people had slept there the night before. When more than three people sleep in a house, it is very hard to get them to pick things up early. The place is plain, with a living room, a dining room, a bedroom, a bathroom, a small kitchen, and a long narrow little patio. There are some folding beds spread out over the living room and dining room, and some more in the bedroom. We later found out that they set them up at night and take them down by day.

This and other safe houses in the city were to host "Gino the Italian," a former partisan with the Venetian branch of the anti-Nazi resistance during World War II, who now lived in Cuba; Miguel Sánchez, known as "the Korean" for having fought with the U.S. Army in the recent war; Guillén Zelaya, the only Mexican in the group; Calixto García, one of the first exiles, who tried to be a baseball player in Mexico and ended up as a movie extra; Dominican Ramón Mejía del Castillo, known as Pichirilo, and Ernesto's lanky friend, labor leader Ñico López Fernández, who had returned from Cuba at Fidel's request and who "was seen to sleep on park benches in midwinter and faint from hunger rather than stretch his hand out to ask for donations from the rich exiles." Also Universo Sánchez, a peasant from Matanzas and a former Communist; Ramiro Valdés, from a poor family in Artemisa, who had had the glory of capturing sentry posts at the Moncada barracks; navy man Norberto Collado, tortured by Batista's police with burning, being hung by his testicles, and slung onto a garbage dump, who used to show off his war wounds; and Juan Almeida, who had also taken part in the Moncada raid. Almeida quickly took a liking to Mexico City; his favorite outing was to take his Mexican girlfriend, who went by the name of Lupita, to eat tacos by the Tepeyac hills.

These men were joined by a group of women—many women, as the Movement had an unmistakably female cast. It was mainly women who set up the financing networks, who built up the infrastructure in Santiago, Cuba, and in Mexico. María Antonia Orquidea Pino stood out in Mexico, untiring, organizing without money, setting up safe houses, and, at times, paying the rent by pawning odds and ends. She was wonderfully tough; Ernesto told Hilda, **Don't be surprised at the foul language she often comes out with, that's part of her character; she's a respectable lady and a great comrade.** Along with María Antonia, there were Fidel's sisters; also Mexican Piedad Solís (who was married to Reinaldo Benítez), and Melba Hernández, a key activist in the Moncada operation, who together with her husband, Jesús Montané, was in Mexico and participating in the network infrastructure and its tricky financing.

These were to be the new people in Dr. Guevara's life. They were anything but innocents. They belonged to a generation—and to a subgroup of that generation—owed a blood debt by the Batista dictatorship. It gave them a tragic sense of purpose and a very peculiar relationship with history.

At the end of 1955, Ernesto, so as not to lose sight of his calling as pangalactic traveler, studied Russian at the Soviet-Mexican Cultural Relations Institute, read a lot of books on economics (including the first volume of *Das Kapital*), and began to study typing on a new typewriter, **battering away at the machine with more verve now, and almost without looking at the keyboard. When I've gotten the hang of it, I will learn embroidery.**

Fidel cooked Christmas dinner for the Guevaras, Melba, and Montané. The menu was very Cuban—"Moors and Christians": *yuca* (cassava) and *mojo*. The meal was not without its share of tension: Ernesto and Hilda's marriage was not faring very well, being held together only by the imminent arrival of their child.

Due to Fidel's penchant for roping into his plans anyone careless enough to allow it, a new personality had joined the group. He was Mexican all-in wrestler Arsacio Vanegas, the owner of a small printing press. This man was put in charge of the recruits' physical training.

The first stage was long walks. As almost all of the prospective revolutionaries lived in the south-central part of the city, they would meet outside the Lindavista Cinema, eight or nine kilometers away from their safe houses, and walk from there to Zacatenco, in the far north end. Vanegas would recall years later that they used to walk to the meeting place, as there was no money for bus fares. "We used to just have just water and a bread roll for breakfast."

The hard training began in January of 1956. Ernesto cut bread and pasta from his diet in order to lose weight. He neglected his allergy experiments at the hospital and did not take up the lectureship in physiology he had been awarded.

Vanegas not only supervised the walks and the hill-climbing, but also gave them training in self-defense at a gymnasium he had rented on Buchareli Street: "All-in wrestling, some karate, fall techniques, kicks, how to climb walls."

Hilda remembered that at first Che "came home aching all over and I had to rub him with liniment." But his muscles were not his main problem. On one of their hill-climbing exercises, Vanegas found Guevara breathless. **Look, mate, I don't want anyone to find out about what you've seen. You see I suffer from asthma.**

To us, looking back over the years, the training does seem somewhat absurd, games for adolescents with much free time and little discipline. But they were much more than that and evidently had their uses, these walks down Insurgentes Avenue, climbs up Zacatenco hill, Chiquihuite, or the Ajusco, sometimes weighed down with knapsacks.

In February, the training got serious, and risky: Fidel obtained permission to practice at "Los Gamitos," a firing range on the outskirts of the city that was normally used for practice by a rifle club. The invaders-to-be used rifles with telescopic sights to fire on a target at 600 meters, or on live turkeys at 500. Whoever got a bull's-eye rejoiced at the noise the bullet made, the more so if he hit the turkey, as the prize was that he got to eat it. The marksmanship training, combined with the walks and the wrestling, would last for three months.

It was at that time, according to Hilda Gadea's memoirs, that Ernesto learned to tell the difference between the openings of Beethoven's Fifth and Ninth symphonies. This made the doctor so happy that he dashed off a letter to his mother about it. Guevara's musical education did not have many such triumphs; with his pathetic musical ear, he could not do what any old Argentine can—i.e., sing tangos—and had to make do with reciting them.

I would give my right arm to be able to play the guitar, he told his wife.

"But you'd need it to pluck the strings," she answered.

On February 15, at about seven in the evening, the child the couple was expecting was born at the Sanatorio Inglés in Mexico City.

Her name is Hilda Beatriz and she makes me happy twice over. First, because her arrival has put the brakes on a marital disaster, and second because now I am totally certain that I will be able to go [to Cuba] despite everything, that my inability to live with her mother is greater than the affection I have when I look at [the baby]. For one moment, it seemed to

me that the mixture of the child's charm and consideration for her mother (who in many respects is a great woman and loves me almost to a fault) could turn me into a boring father figure . . . now I know it will not be like that and I will keep going with my Bohemian lifestyle until, who knows when, I'll land my sinful bones in Argentina. Then I'll have to do my duty; stop playing knight-errant and gird up for a real battle. As for the child, I cannot tell you; she's a lump of purplish flesh who suckles every four hours like clockwork and spews most of what she suckles with slightly less regularity.

Ernesto was a tremendously happy man. As he didn't usually express his emotions, his joy unsettled everyone. As Myrna Torres said, "He looked happy to be a father; he seemed more human."

There was just one dark cloud on the horizon: the doctor's worry that his daughter might have inherited his asthma. He watched her continually, on the lookout for some symptom. Fortunately, none appeared.

A couple of months later he told his mother: **She has turned out exactly like Mao Tzedong. She is more spoiled than most kids and eats the way, according to my grandmother, I used to—meaning she suckles without drawing breath until the milk comes out of her ears.**

———

A key figure in putting Fidel's plans into effect was Alberto Bayo, a remarkable character who had lost an eye in combat as a colonel in the Spanish Republican army and was now living in exile in Mexico. Fidel had been in contact with him since 1955. On hearing the Cuban revolutionary's plans, Bayo offered to give a series of lectures on guerrilla warfare. Fidel not only took him at his word, but pushed him even further, reminding Bayo that he was of Cuban origin and asking him to join the group he was to train. The colonel accepted. Years later, he wrote: "I got drunk with enthusiasm." The only reservation he had about getting involved with the planned invasion or even the fixed date, was with the curfew. That was madness.

Were they serious about this? There they were, being trained by a has-been wrestler who made them take endless walks along the avenues of Mexico City, rowing in a lake used by adolescents playing hooky, learning to shoot in a rifle club, and now dumped into the hands of a one-eyed colonel whose main claim to fame was his loyalty to a republic that had lost a war.

They were serious, absolutely serious, because they rowed and walked as if possessed, because the group's discipline was extremely rigid, because they all wanted to shoot Batista out of power, which was why they shot down the poor turkeys with so much venom, because behind closed doors Colonel Bayo taught his zealous recruits with the utmost seriousness all about sabotage, guerrilla warfare tactics, irregular-army discipline, fire patterns, the use of light artillery, shooting at aircraft, camouflage . . .

Ernesto Guevara wrote later:

My almost immediate reaction, on hearing those first classes, was [to believe in] **the possibility of victory, which I had thought was very doubtful when I joined up with the rebel commander. I had been linked with him from the start—a bond of sympathy between romantic adventurers, based on the belief that it was worth dying on a foreign beach for such a pure ideal.**

Another member of the crew, a character as remarkable as Bayo and Vanegas, was Antonio del Conde, whom the Cubans dubbed "El Cuate."* El Cuate was the owner of a small gun store in downtown Mexico City. Once Fidel had whipped up his enthusiasm, he began to supply arms to the Cubans and became an invaluable collaborator, full of the spirit of solidarity and adventure. By way of reward, Fidel offered him 10 percent of the value of the arms he transferred, but del Conde began to deliver them at cost and ended up putting money from his own pocket into the project.

As a result of El Cuate's abilities and somewhat questionable methods, twenty hunting rifles with telescopic sights began to turn up in pieces from Toluca and Puebla, bought unassembled from the arms factory and put together in the gun store's workshop, along with five Remington automatics bought in the United States and legally brought to Mexico, and a variety of arms smuggled across the northern border. The purchase included twenty Johnson automatics, some Thompson submachine guns, two .50-caliber anti-tank guns, and a Star pistol with a folding butt, as well as backpacks, canteens, and boots from Guanajuato.

Eventually, El Cuate became even more involved and offered Fidel the cellar where the first stockpile was set up, as well as a house belonging to some of his in-laws in the exclusive Lomas district, where they occasionally kept arms in the closets.

Bayo rented a ranch, the Santa Rosa, in Chalco, an hour's drive from Mexico City. A property belonging to one of Pancho Villa's old supporters; the Cubans bamboozled him by saying it was to be bought by an important Salvadoran politician and suggesting that while the place was being refurbished, it could well be rented for a token amount. The former Villa supporter, Rivera by name, charged just eight dollars a month.

In the second half of May 1956, Ernesto told Hilda that the time had come for him to train out of town. The doctor did not realize then that the separation was to last several years.

---

*Translator's note: *Cuate* means "buddy" or "pal" in Mexican slang, and is as peculiar to Mexico as "Che" is to Argentina.

He was not the only one burning his bridges. Colonel Bayo dropped everything to devote himself to training "his" Cubans full-time. He left behind not only the classes he was giving at the aviation school but also his furniture.

Activities got under way immediately in Chalco: firing practice, arduous night marches ("no smoking allowed," Universo Sánchez would recall), combat exercises, and theory classes. Bayo was in charge of training and became military head; Guevara was named personnel chief. His appointment was unpopular with some of the Cubans, who were annoyed that a position entailing such responsibility had been given to a non-Cuban. Fidel intervened personally to thank "some one who was not born in our land being willing to shed his blood for it," but Ernesto was hurt. "He was a man with no ambitions, who became inhibited when anyone contested him," Fidel would recall, years later.

The ranch was barely habitable, so the future expeditionaries slept on the floor and spent a good part of their time building latrines and swatting at a plague of flies, so many that they made the white walls look black.

At night, there were candle-lit chess matches between Dr. Guevara and Bayo, and political debates. The Cubans' political orientations were very diverse. On the one hand were Fidel, Juan Manuel Márquez, and Felix Elmuza, with a liberal, Martí-like political background; on the other were Raúl and Ñico López with a more extreme social outlook, and other militants with almost no political background at all.

> **I remember that in an intimate discussion, in a house in Mexico, I supported the idea that the Cuban people had to be offered a revolutionary program; one of the Moncada raiders—who unfortunately had left the July 26 Movement—answered me with words I would always remember, saying, "Things are very simple. What we have to do is organize a coup. Batista organized a coup and took power on that very day, so we need another to get him out. Batista has made a hundred concessions to the Americans, so we will make a hundred and one." It was all about taking power. I argued with him that we had to strike a blow based on principles, that the important thing was knowing what we would do in power. . . . Fortunately for us, he and others who thought like him left our revolutionary movement and went their separate ways.**

Ernesto attributed such simplistic proposals to a group that was preparing to make a revolution for the benefit of a bunch of bad elements, mainly those in Miami.

Bayo's memoirs confirm that Ernesto was obsessed with doing everything well, with surpassing himself, with never failing. His overwhelming competition with himself and with his own limits turned him into "a [number one candidate] for promotion, and he got top marks in all the training activities, ten out of ten."

Ernesto was not the only one to push himself to the limit. Bayo was also determined to be more than just a trainer; he wanted to go to Cuba with the expeditionaries. On the ranch,

You have no idea what he did. As he wanted to go on the expedition and was so fat, he went on a water-only diet. In just two weeks he lost ten kilos. He wanted to lose another ten, but time was running out. What a magnificent old man!

It was in those days that Dr. Ernesto Guevara, recruited as expedition doctor, definitely came to be known to everyone as Che. While some Cuban expressions found their way into his Argentine vocabulary, as did Latin American expressions picked up throughout the continent, and while he was fascinated by the Cubans and their cleanliness (two baths a day! even in the freezing cold water at Chalco!), there was a time-honored Argentine custom he could not shake off: he interspersed his conversation with *che,* used as the Mexicans used "hombre," and addressed everybody as *Che.* The Cubans found this very funny and nicknamed him Che.

It was also while on the ranch that Che wrote one of his worst poems, an epic dedicated to Fidel, the main virtue of which was that it reflects the fascination the Cuban leader had for the Argentine doctor:

> *Let's go, blazing prophet of the dawn*
> *Along the unfenced winding pathways*
> *To free the green alligator you love so much.*

The seriousness with which Ernesto had taken up his commitment to the revolutionary undertaking was also evident:

> *And if iron should cross our path,*
> *We shall ask for a shroud of Cuban tears*
> *To cover the guerrillas' bones*
> *On the road to Latin American history.*
> *Nothing more.*

It is well known that since the beginning of Fidel's stay in Mexico, Batista's police had had a plan in motion to assassinate Fidel. It's also known that the naval attaché at the Cuban embassy was implicated and that a hired gunman had been brought from Cuba to recruit local gangsters. The locals, promised a fee of $10,000, had contracted to kill Fidel. But the news reached Castro's ears and the plot faded away to nothing. At the same time, however, Cuban embassy officials had approached the Mexican authorities to find out what they knew about the Cubans and offer them money for information. These approaches had met with success.

On June 20, 1956, the Cuban embassy's pressure and their attempts to bribe the Mexican police paid off. That night, Fidel was in the safe house on the corner of Kepler and Copérnico; with him were Ramiro Valdés, Cándido González, and Universo Sánchez. They met Ciro Redondo and half a dozen other recruits who were quartered there. Suddenly, looking out the window, the Cubans noticed two strange characters checking over Ciro's car, a battered 1942 Packard. Fearing the worst, Fidel split the group and walked off with Universo and Ramiro, but they were attacked by the police several blocks away. Fidel tried to resist and drew his gun, but surrendered when the police used Universo and Ramiro as a shield.

The police drove the three men around Mexico City, threatening them and demanding identification; Fidel replied that he would identify himself to the relevant authorities. They were then taken to the DFS, the Federal Security Headquarters.

Cándido González and Julio Díaz were detained as they left the house, then taken to the fourth precinct and tortured. They were bound hand and foot and shoved under freezing water—the so-called wishing-well. The police then detained the Mexican Guillén Zelaya, who came to look for them.

Ciro Redondo, who had managed to escape the first round of arrests, was worried because there was a shipment of arms in his Packard. He was detained with Benítez while opening the car to unload them.

All this was no accident. A roundup was under way, and the Mexican police were acting under pressure from or in agreement with Batista's police.

Another raid was carried out in the late morning of June 21, this time on María Antonia's house at number 49 Emparán Street. The agents used the revolutionaries' code, three knocks on the door. María Antonia and Almeida were rounded up then; Evaristo Venereo, who had informed them, escaped through the bathroom window.

That same day, federal agents turned up at the Guevaras' home. Hilda was accused of receiving correspondence for a subversive group. She was detained the following day, along with the baby. In the DFS offices at the Plaza de la Revolución, she was shown a telegram addressed to "Alejandro" (a pseudonym for Fidel) and asked insistently about Ernesto. Hilda stuck to their previously agreed-upon story: Dr. Guevara was in Veracruz. El Patojo, who was living in the rooftop room in Che's house, was also picked up; both he and Hilda were released later.

In one of the revolutionaries' few strokes of luck at that time, a Cuban who saw Fidel being arrested managed to get word of it to the ranch, where Raúl had time to hide the arms.

During the first interrogation session in the DFS, Fidel suggested that Universo should sound things out, to see if a bribe could settle matters. As Universo later recounted,

> Captain Gutiérrez Barrios said:
> "I'm in charge."
> "Look, we're decent people. How can we settle this? We could give you some gratuity and you might let us go. . . ."

"And you, how much are you offering?"

"Twenty-five thousand dollars."

We did not have that kind of money, but I felt like saying that, and shit, he grabbed me, handcuffed me and told me afterward that we offered him so much he thought he had latched on to something big, something to do with drugs.

Gutiérrez Barrios later recalled:

We found a more or less well-drawn sketch map of Mexico City with its highways and Chalco marked on it. . . . I sent for Fidel and I said:

"Spare us a confrontation there that would be no use either to you or to us."

Fidel decided to accompany the federal agents to the training center to avoid a shoot-out. Once there, he asked the fighters to keep discipline, telling them the Mexican police would take charge of everything. Che almost got away, because he was up a tree on guard duty when the jeeps arrived. But the others insisted he come down, saying, "Fidel's calling us all out." Raúl, on the other hand, did manage to escape.

Finally, the detainees were gathered in the Miguel Schultz Prison in the San Rafael district; a small detention center, run by the Interior Ministry, it was a way station for foreigners who were to be deported.

Although Almeida would say, years later, that Gutiérrez Barrios knew he was dealing with "decent people" and treated them carefully "to avoid confrontation," the interrogations ranged from friendly to brutal. Chuchú Reyes was tortured to get him to identify El Cuate, the mysterious arms supplier. Che was accused of being a Communist; the police threatened to torture his wife and baby. From that moment on, he refused to cooperate in the interrogation, saying that if they were savage enough to do that, they should count him out—that though he had been supplying information about himself up to this point, he would keep quiet from now on.

The decision to speed up final jail sentences for the Cuban revolutionaries came from President Ruiz Cortines, who ordered that they be charged. The attorney general sent fourteen officials from the Ministry of Public Affairs to question them. The police told the press that "Dr. Guevara has, for years, had links with the Russians." Ernesto confined himself to admitting the obvious: yes, he was part of the July 26 Movement; yes, he was at the ranch; yes, there were arms (who knew who fired them?); yes, Fidel Castro did want to overthrow Batista. Apart from his statement, however, Ernesto, who was never one to duck a debate, went from noncooperation to open argument when the agent from the ministry set about discussing Marxism with him. Gutiérrez Barrios intervened to keep matters from becoming even worse: "Counselor, he already said he's a Marxist-Leninist. Just go and list the charges."

The Miguel Schultz Prison fare was soup and bread; the cold, which was so severe it peeled the paint from the walls, to the Cubans seemed even worse. The twenty-eight prisoners suffered from the fear of being murdered or deported to Cuba—where who knew what might await them in Batista's jails—and the fear that all those months of preparation had gone to hell.

There followed a strange limbo during which the detainees' destiny was in others' hands. On June 27, the conservative press, specifically the newspaper *Excélsior,* fanned the flames, accusing Che of having links with other revolutionary movements in Latin America and of relations with the Russian expatriates. These allegations, based on his membership in the Russian-Mexican Cultural Relations Institute, made serious trouble for Nikolai Leonov, the Soviet diplomat who had lent Che books by Ostrovsky and Furmanov. His card had turned up among Che's papers, and it was made public that Leonov was "the liaison with the revolutionaries." Leonov was recalled to the USSR for having involved the Soviet legation in a scandal.

Hilda, together with Ernesto's family, managed to get a distant relative working at the Argentine embassy to intervene. Ernesto's Guatemalan friend Alfonso Bauer, now exiled in Mexico, turned up at the Miguel Schultz jail to talk the matter over. Ernesto answered him: **Poncho, I came in here with a group of comrades, and I'll leave with them, thank you very much.**

On the outside, Raúl Castro and Juan Manuel Márquez set up the legal defense. They found two lawyers, Ignacio Mendoza and Alejandro Guzmán, who accepted the case and immediately requested that the prisoners no longer be held incommunicado. At the same time, a document signed by Raúl Castro and Márquez appeared in the newspapers pointing out that the Cubans held in detention were at war with the Batista dictatorship, but had not participated in Mexican politics.

Tension was high, but morale was not low. Photos taken at Miguel Schultz—which was not, strictly speaking, a jail but a temporary detention center for those about to be deported—looked festive. In one, a sort of family photograph, in which smiles abound, Che stands out in his white suit, stretched out in front of the group like a goalkeeper. Almeida is smiling brightly, and María Antonia, in dark glasses and holding a small Cuban flag, stands proudly in the center of the group.

In another, more informal photograph, the barracks or dormitories in the detention center can be seen: white metal hospital beds; a huge muddle of chairs, bedside tables, books, and clothes; and there, in the middle, Fidel in a dark suit watching a very young bare-chested Che Guevara doing his pants up. The photo, taken for *Mañana* magazine, would, curiously enough, end up in Batista's secret-police files. It was the first picture the Cuban dictatorship's secret service had of the Argentine doctor.

From abroad, Raúl Castro and Márquez had been trying to get in touch with former president Lázaro Cárdenas, so he might intervene with the Mexican government. They finally reached him through his old nanny in Jiquilpan. Cárdenas received the Cubans' defenders, who asked him to intervene with the interior minister, but the former president went further and said he would communicate directly with President Ruiz Cortines.

On July 6, when the detainees' situation was still uncertain, Ernesto offered his parents the explanation he had long owed them. In a long letter, he told the story of his relations with the July 26 Movement and of how he had been misleading his parents with the story about working as a lecturer over the previous months. He described his role as

> **physically preparing the youngsters. This is what all the events of my past have led to. The future is divided in two: medium-term and the immediate. I can tell you that the medium-term ones are linked to the liberation of Cuba. I either win with them or die there. . . . As for the immediate future, I have little to say, as I do not know what will become of me. I am at the judge's disposal and it will be easy for the Mexicans to deport me to Argentina, unless I obtain asylum in a third country, something I think would suit my political health.**

Almost in passing, he mentioned that, whatever happened, Hilda would take Hilda Beatriz back to her family in Peru, and that the couple's separation was now a fact. In the same letter, he explained that he did not like the idea of his letters being read so he would write less often in the future:

> **We are about to go on an indefinite hunger strike to protest the unjustified detentions and the torture some of my comrades have been subjected to. The whole group's morale is high.**
>
> **If for any reason, which I do not expect, I can no longer write and I have lost my mind, please consider these lines as a farewell—not a very eloquent one, but a sincere one. All through my life I have been stumbling along the road in a search for my truth, and now, with my daughter to carry on after me, I have come full circle. From now on, I would hardly consider my death more than a frustration, like Hikmet*:** "I will take to my grave / only the sorrow of an unfinished song."

The immigration authorities freed twenty of the detainees three days later, on July 9, when the hunger strike was about to begin. They used a strange bureaucratic expression: "You have been invited to leave the country." Universo Sánchez, Ciro Redondo, Colonel Bayo's son, and several others were freed, on parole, on the simple condition that they appeared to sign in once a week. Only Fidel, Ernesto Guevara, and Calixto García remained in jail. The last two of the others were accused by the media of being Communists, and were expelled from Mexico on the pretext that their immigration documentation had expired.

Cárdenas's intervention with the Mexican president was the first success. The Mexican government seems to have reconsidered matters, deciding that it did not want to do the Batista dictatorship a public favor; neither, though,

---

*Nuzim Hikmet, twentieth-century Turkish poet.

were the Mexicans attracted by the idea of freeing all the Cuban revolutionaries. Once again, it was a question of establishing the principle of power, the
answer to that obsessive "Who's in charge here?" that has been the manic and
ultimate issue in Mexican politics since the forties. Fidel was offered friendly
deportation to Uruguay; this the July 26 Movement leader refused, because
it would have disrupted the invasion plans.

The prison days went by. Ernesto played soccer; on Thursdays and Sundays he received visits. He would play a while with little Hilda, until she fell
asleep, her mother said, "and then he would watch her for ages and amuse
himself with the faces she made in her sleep."

Ernesto's mother had chastised him for his actions; on July 15, he replied,
Not only am I not a moderate but I will try never to be one, So she
would not get the wrong idea about his situation, and would know that his
sense of humor was intact, he also was forced to explain that **the stains** [on
the letter] **are not bloody tears, but tomato juice.**

Fidel was freed on July 24. What were the terms of the negotiation? Was
the former president's pressure sufficient? Fidel promised his two comrades, who remained hostages, that he would not begin the expedition without them.

Finally, fifty-seven days after entering, Che and Calixto walked out of the
Miguel Schultz Prison. There were rumors of a hefty bribe in there somewhere. Che himself told Hilda they got out **on account of a large sum of
money that Fidel had to pay to settle the immigration business.**
Fidel set forth his relationship with Mexico briefly: "The incident is over and
done with, and I don't want Cubans to retain any trace of resentment toward Mexico. Prison and mistreatment are all part and parcel of our work as
fighters."

Years later, Che would say:

> **The fact is that Fidel made some moves that, we might almost
> say, compromised his revolutionary attitude in favor of friend-
> ship. I remember outlining my case to him: a foreigner, ille-
> gally in Mexico, facing a pile of charges. I told him that he
> should not in any way hold up the revolution for my sake and
> that he could leave me; that I understood the situation and
> would try to go and fight from wherever the Mexican author-
> ities sent me to and that the only effort he should make was
> to get me sent to a nearby country rather than Argentina. I
> also remember Fidel's curt answer: I won't abandon you. And
> that is how things turned out, because precious time and
> money had to be diverted to get us out of that Mexican jail.**

Now, forced into stricter secrecy, with the safe houses shot, with no
money, obliged to find new homes and reorganize training, the core group of
exiles frantically began to step up security to protect the arms that had been
salvaged and to rebuild the movement's finances.

A camp was established in Mérida, and several arms caches were set up in Mexico City. María Antonia took charge of the housing network; she had to pawn her own goods and clothing with the Monte de Piedad brokers to meet costs.

In one of many trips made around the country to look for useful training areas, Fidel discovered that El Cuate Conde was part owner of a battered yacht kept near the port of Tuxpan.

"If you fix that boat up, I'll go in it."

"That boat's useless."

The boat was still half owned, because El Cuate had only half paid for it, by an American, a certain Robert B. Erickson. Although it carried a Mexican flag, it was called *Granma* (presumably in honor of the American's grandmother). Unfortunately, it was just sixty-three feet long and had only one deck. Fidel and the others felt it might be useful for an expedition composed of dwarfs, and not many of them. Its two 250-horsepower Gray motors, its theoretical capacity of twenty passengers and crew (tightly packed), and her keel, damaged in a hurricane the year before, bore out El Cuate's reaction. Erickson asked $15,000 for his half share of the boat, on condition that the buyers take a house on the banks of the Tuxpan River for another $2,000. Fidel appealed to former Cuban president Carlos Prío Socarrás, now exiled in the United States. He did not have a good opinion of the man, but this was not the time for turning up one's nose at possible help. With no boat there could be no expedition. "It will be the only contribution we accept," Fidel told a U.S. journalist a few months later.

The possibility of an airborne invasion had been dismissed a few days beforehand, and there was no other boat to hand. So, El Cuate and Fidel (who pretended to be his brother) Erickson bought *Granma* and immediately set about refitting her, boosting the power output of the two diesel engines, increasing the available space by dismantling needless additions and appurtenances, and adding water tanks.

After being set free, Ernesto Guevara spent three days at home, packed his bags, and said good-bye. A week later, via a go-between, he proposed that he and Hilda see each other in Cuautla, where he went by the name of Dr. Ernesto González. When Hilda saw him, she asked what he was doing for money. She was obsessed with the idea that he should not be living off the movement, even though he had not worked in the hospital since May and had no income.

At that period, in September, Che was obliged to live undercover as **the Interior Ministry committed the grave error of believing in my word as a gentleman and freed me on condition that I leave the country in ten days.** He made sporadic visits to his daughter, little Hilda, and once recited to her a poem by Antonio Machado, dedicated to General Lister: "My word goes from the hills to the sea / If my pen had the power of your pistol / I would die happy." Apparently seven-month-old Hilda liked the ring of Machado's poetry: she cried and complained, asking for more, when her father finished.

The final recruitment phase was under way. Dr. Faustino Pérez returned from Havana at the end of October, and Camilo Cienfuegos, the multitalented tailor, joined up. He had a scar on his leg from a bullet wound he had sustained in a student protest and had left his U.S. exile in response to a rumor that "something big is cooking in Mexico." Efigenio Ameijeiras joined up after, leafing through the magazine *Bohemia* one day, he discovered that his brother had been murdered in the wake of the Moncada raid. He was a taxi driver in Mexico City, who had come from Costa Rica with a false passport. It was not just militants who turned up to swell the ranks of the invasion, however; a swarm of Cuban military intelligence agents also came to Mexico and, among other things, took photographs at the airport.

———

Several key meetings in those last few months defined the relations between the invaders and the dissident social groups within Cuba. The meetings were amiable, but Fidel refused to change or postpone the plan despite pressure from several directions.

The first and perhaps most important meeting took place at the beginning of August, when Fidel had just gotten out of jail. Frank País, a young schoolteacher and a key member of the revolutionary organization in eastern Cuba, met Fidel. (He had been recruited to the July 26 Movement after Fidel left Cuba.) Frank told Fidel that he was in favor of postponing the invasion until the urban networks that had been set up were better prepared and could carry out an uprising to coincide with the landing. Fidel stuck to his political promise. Both left the interview very impressed. In Frank, Fidel had found the urban coordinator M26 needed. The general guidelines for joint action were then drawn up then. An urban action was to take place along with the landing.

In August Fidel held another meeting, with another central figure in the democratic left-wing opposition: student leader José Antonio Echeverría from the Revolutionary Directorio. They signed a letter of agreement and outlined a pact to coordinate revolutionary activities. Fidel advised the Directory of his intentions, and the latter promised to support the landing with armed actions in Havana.

Still another contact took place in those final months, this time with representatives of the Communist People's Socialist Party (PSP), particularly their student director, Flavio Bravo, a fellow alumnus of Fidel's from the University of Havana. Only minimal agreements to coordinate came out of the interview, as the PSP was opposed the invasion in principle. Flavio wanted to convince Fidel and the July 26 Movement of the benefits of opposing the dictatorship with civil action by a coalition. Fidel turned a deaf ear to him.

Frank País returned at the end of October to finalize details; he went back to Cuba with the text of a telegram notifying the movement of Fidel's plans, along with an agreement that the uprising would be timed to coincide with the landing. He bore another piece of information, too: the landing would occur in the Niquero area, in the foothills of the Sierra Maestra.

At the beginning of November, Ernesto wrote to his mother:

> **I have given up on my case being solved legally. I am writing to you from no particular place in Mexico, where I am waiting for things to be sorted out. This air of freedom is, in reality, the air of secrecy, but that doesn't matter: it gives things the tone of a very interesting mystery film.**

His hideout in those days was a rooftop room in his friend Alfonso Bauer's house in the Narvarte district of Mexico City, which he shared with Calixto García and other Cubans. We spent the days working in secrecy, hiding where we could, shunning any public appearance as much as possible, and we hardly ever went out on the street. They had a narrow escape when the house was broken into and the police went up to the roof to investigate. The cops apologized to Dr. Guevara, who turned on the charm, posing as a poor professional. "The thief must have been the boyfriend of one of the maids," the police said as they left.

As for his relationship with Hilda, he wrote Tita Infante:

> **It may interest you to know that my marriage has almost completely broken down and we will definitely split up next month, when my wife goes to Peru to see her family for the first time in eight years. There is a trace of bitterness in the separation, as she was a loyal companion and her revolutionary conduct during my forced vacations was irreproachable, but our spiritual discord was great; I live with an anarchic spirit that makes me dream of new horizons.**

Hilda's version, given in her memoirs, differs; she points out that the separation was meant to be temporary and due only to the circumstances. Hilda Guevara—little Hilda—recalls, however, that her mother used to tell her that when her parents split up in Mexico, Ernesto wanted a separation to avoid commitments, but that they would see how things went when they met again. Given the danger of the Cuban venture, Che did not wish to leave his wife uncertain about her status.

Fidel rented another ranch, this one in Abasolo, in the state of Tamaulipas, near the probable point of departure. It was in an ideal situation, being very remote. Faustino Pérez was put in command. Sixteen of the future expedition members gathered there at the end of October, then another twenty.

The final push was not without tension. The house searches continued in Mexico City; the Mexican police confiscated an arms shipment in mid-November; two safe houses fell; and Pedro Miret was one of the Cubans arrested. Fidel went to see Gutiérrez Barrios, who told him that the Mexican police were getting information from the Cuban secret service, which had doubtless infiltrated M26.

> **We found out there was a traitor in our ranks, whose name we did not know, and that he had sold an arms shipment. We also knew he had sold the yacht and a transmitter, although the legal sales contract had yet to be drawn up. This first batch of information served to show the Cuban authorities that the traitor effectively knew our innermost secrets. That also saved us, by showing us the same thing.**

Fidel was more precise: "The one who supplied the information made a run for the Mexican border. We found out that he was handing over one safe house after another, and was then going to hand the boat over. That is why we rushed things so much." The identity of this oft-mentioned traitor was to remain one of the Cuban revolution's great secrets. His name was never made public.

Meanwhile, Che was hiding out on the roof at the Bauers' house—being an ideal guest, according to the householder: "He had an equally deep-seated habit: he read like a demon, always with his maté gourd in his hand. He tried not to make any fuss; we had to beg him to come down to eat." Fidel turned up one day without warning and had a hard time getting to see Che. The Bauers denied knowing Ernesto, but Fidel insisted he knew Che was there, put his foot in the door, and would not budge until they let him in.

On November 21, two men deserted from the Abasolo ranch and thus put the whole invasion in jeopardy. Fidel made a decision: from November 22 on, the mobilization order began to circulate among the dispersed groups of future invaders. The rendezvous was set for the twenty-fourth, at a landing stage on the Tuxpan River, a few miles upstream from the small port of the same name in the state of Veracruz.

Che recalled: **The order to depart came to us suddenly; we all had to leave Mexico City with just the clothes on our backs, in groups of two or three . . . to avoid the traitor giving word to the police.** Che left his bed unmade, his maté gourd lying out, and his books open. A few days later, when his friends became worried and forced the padlock, they discovered what Che's final reading matter had been: *The State and Revolution* by Lenin, Marx's *Das Kapital,* a work by Germán Arciniegas, a field surgery manual, and an obscure work entitled *Como Opera el Capital Yanqui in Centroamérica* ("How Yankee Capital Operates in Central America").° The group based in Veracruz and Jalapa departed their hotel in Tecolutla, leaving their belongings behind (and probably not paying the bill, either). In the rush

---

°Translator's note: It has not been possible to identify the author or to learn anything else about this book.

to get away and under pressure from leaks, the expeditionaries, who had had a small arsenal, left with hardly any automatic weapons. That was not the only hardship, as Che was to recall: **I had to go just like that, without my inhaler, and I had a terrible asthma attack on the way. I thought I would never get there.**

The expeditionaries finally gathered in Tuxpán on the twenty-fourth, in the rain, after journeying for miles in cars or buses from Mexico City, Veracruz, Jalapa, and Ciudad Victoria, where the recruits who had previously been at the Abasolo ranch were holed up in flophouses. Thanks to a mix-up in the organization, a small group under the command of Héctor Aldama was left high and dry in the Aurora Hotel in Poza Rica. They never did get the order to mobilize.

Individuals who at first seemed to want to go along afterward, with one excuse or another, dropped out, so the number of expeditionaries was limited. In the end, eighty-two of us boarded the Granma. **Guevara's version is not exact; in the end many more than eighty-two finally came aboard. Fidel would later tell:**

There were eighty-two men on the *Granma*; we could not take some who were left over. Do you know how we picked them? According, of course, to who had the most experience, the most practice, etc., etc., and in the end there were about fifteen in the same category, and then we said: "How can we take the largest possible number of those [left]?" and we picked them according to their weight and their size. The smallest of all our troops were chosen in the end, and three or four fat guys were left out. They did not come, and there was no way to convince them it was only on account of their size.

Besides the "fat guys," some others were left. Pedro Miret, a key cadre, was awaiting trial in Mexico. El Patojo was rejected by Fidel because he did not want the expedition to become a "foreign legion." El Cuate was kept out; his participation at the end of the expedition was confined to running up down the Gulf of Mexico as far as Isla Mujeres in case the *Granma* should break down. Bayo was rejected because of his age, and no one could console him. Even Vanegas had to say good-bye to Che with tears in his eyes.

A small group acted as a farewell committee. Melba Hernández, Piedad Solís, and El Cuate watched the little yacht fill up with men. The volunteers scurried onto the boat, almost on top of one another, because there had been a rumor that they would not all fit and many might have to remain on land. After so many months of waiting, no one wanted to stay on the sidelines.

The supplies were placed under an awning, with Fidel supervising for the first few hours. The *Granma*'s two engines fired up at 1:30 A.M. on November 25. The boat steamed away from the improvised jetty with its lights out. Shipping had been prohibited due to bad weather, as a *norte* was wreaking havoc in the Gulf of Mexico, with constant rain and strong winds.

There were eighty-two men crammed on board, elbow to elbow, huddling against the cold of their last night in Mexico. Sánchez Amaya, one of the expeditionaries, said, "You couldn't take so much as a step on that bit of deck." They were in a state of mingled unease, fear, and hope. And they were "comely," not in the strictly correct Spanish or Mexican sense, but in the Cuban sense of being brave and daring. And they were really "comely" in proposing to topple a military dictatorship with eighty-two poorly armed men on a frail little boat. A couple of years of doubts, of building up for their mission impossible, were over. As people would have said then, it was "in God's hands now."

More than 35,000 armed men, alerted by police and stool pigeons, were waiting for them. Along with the police were an army equipped with tanks, ten warships, fifteen coast guard vessels, and seventy-eight fighter and transport planes.

For now, the *Granma* was dancing on the waves, facing the full fury of the *norte,* leaving Mexico behind. In time, the memory would be a good one for Che and his comrades. They would remember willing help and smiles, rather than kickbacks and police torture; the long walks along Insurgentes, and the tacos, rather than the cold and the loneliness. Che would remember Cárdenas's solidarity with them, the beauty of the Mayan pyramids, and even old María—not the high walls in the Miguel Schultz Prison.

8

Granma Takes On Water

In the Mexico City prison. Che is the white man in the front of the group of Cubans, some of whom would be together on the *Granma*.

THE YACHT SAILED DOWNSTREAM, CROSSING THE RIVER MOUTH IN HALF AN hour, riding well below her waterline, with her stern low and the men huddled, crouching, on the deck.

Fidel Castro, speaking years later:

> We had tested the *Granma* in still waters and what's more, with just a few crew members. Nobody knew enough to realize that if eighty-two men got onto the boat, weighing a few tons between them, plus weapons, water, fuel, food . . . then it would slow the boat down considerably. It didn't just slow down, it nearly sank. . . . It was a nutshell bouncing around in the Gulf of Mexico.

That was not the expedition's only problem. Despite all the safety measures and precautions taken, a mysterious and still unknown stool pigeon in the July 26 Movement network was able to transmit a first report which, although vague, managed to put the dictatorship's troops on alert. The message that arrived at the Cuban army high command said: "Boat sailed today with plenty staff and arms from Mexican port."

The voyage had only just begun, but Dr. Guevara already had work on his hands.

We began a frantic search for antihistamines to treat seasickness, but none were to be found. About five minutes after the Cuban national and July 26 Movement anthems were sung, the boat assumed a ridiculously tragic appearance. Men with anxious faces were grabbing their stomachs. Some stuck their heads in buckets and others flopped down in the strangest positions, immovable and with their clothes vomit-stained. Apart from two or three sailors and four or five others, all eighty-two aboard were seasick.

Near daybreak, the decision was made to leave Mexican territorial waters as soon as possible to avoid the coast guard. The helmsman set an eastward course, which was difficult to hold because of the hurricane that was blowing.

It was cloudy at dawn on November 26, and rainfall had soaked the yacht's crammed decks. The boat was making 7.2 knots instead of the expected ten. As evening fell, hunger was becoming more of a problem than seasickness, and the orange sacks on the poop deck were opened. Guevara urged the sickest to drink some liquids, at least. He himself was in a bad way, suffering from a severe asthma attack. Jesús Montané commented: "The expedition had to set off in a hurry . . . and Che wasn't able to gather the medicine he needed to ward off his asthma attacks. . . . We were all struck by the stoicism and self-sacrifice with which he bore his suffering. No one heard a single complaint from him. It was only because comrade Faustino Pérez had had the foresight to take some adrenaline ampules with him that Che could alleviate some of the violent attacks."

The expeditionaries were uncertain about where they were going. They were skirting the Yucatán Peninsula, some forty miles from the coast, so as to avoid the Mexican authorities. René Rodríguez, who was there as cameraman, "but with neither camera nor film, because we didn't have any money to buy any," thought the closest part of the Cuban coast was at Pinar del Río, and several others seemed to go along with him.

Fidel took advantage of the relatively calm weather to adjust the rifles' telescopic sights and to test the machine guns. "No one would stick their head out on the port side—a target had been placed on that side on the bow, and they were firing at it from the poop deck." In the middle of the test firing, the group leader suggested aiming at some dolphins swimming near the boat. Chaos ensued. Efigenio Ameijeiras, the former Havana taxi driver, who was trying out his Thompson machine gun, recalled: "I was one of those who argued that they shouldn't fire, because the sailors were saying it was bad luck."

On November 27, the third day of the journey, while *Granma* was north of the Yucatán, Norberto Collado, one of the helmsmen, realized that "there were just a few sacks of oranges in the hold, a few dozen hardboiled eggs that barely stretched to one meal, one half-rotten ham, and two tins of ship's biscuit." Part of the food had been left ashore in the hurry to leave. Fortunately, seasickness had wreaked such havoc with the invaders' stomachs that the lack of food was not noticed for the first few days. Fidel imposed rationing when he discovered how critical the situation was.

To make matters worse, engineer Chuchú Reyes, although very proud of the twin diesel engines, to which he had devoted much time and care, found that the clutch was slipping on one of them and that the engine speed could not be increased. Only by keeping the *Granma* at half speed could they avoid burning the engine out. On top of this, one of the hoses from the fuel injection pumps had split, the boat was mysteriously taking on water, and the bailer was not working properly.

That day, under an overcast sky with shafts of sunlight peeping through the clouds and no bursts of rain, the *Granma*, Fidel's "nutshell," overloaded and with its speed cut by 30 percent, headed on a new course, away from Cape Catoche at the end of the Yucatán Peninsula and much farther south of Cape San Antonio in Cuba. The expedition never managed the hoped-for ten knots, sailing at seven and a half knots an hour at best.

"Requested work sold out. Disclosure Publishers," the first telegram said. "Urgently need send college diploma. Love, Bertha," said the second. We will never know what the third one said, because its recipient, Aldo Santamaría, had to eat it when he was picked up by the Havana police several days later. The telegrams had been sent from Mexico to alert the July 26 Movement network in Santiago, Havana, and Santa Clara that the expedition was at sea so that, as planned, the urban uprising could coincide with the landing. But just when was the *Granma* going to reach Cuba's Oriente Province, given the delays caused by the storms, overloading, and engine failure?

Meanwhile, some expeditionaries, seasick and overcrowded, thought only of survival. Chuchú Reyes, the engineer, recalled: "Some comrades spent three days huddled in a corner without moving."

Guillén Zelaya, a young Mexican who had joined up with the expedition, remembered that the Argentine doctor continued to suffer from asthma attacks. Years later, an American journalist picked up the story that after a particularly terrible attack Guevara was given up for dead, that someone told Fidel as much, and that the latter answered: "If he's dead, throw him overboard."

On Wednesday, November 28, the boat was still taking on water, but the general outlook brightened up a little. We discovered that the water pipe on the boat was no such thing, but an open valve leading from the toilets. Two other versions were to crop up over time. According to Chuchú Reyes: "One of the toilets was blocked by the comrades being sick all the time; it overloaded, the flap through which it flushed was jammed open, and seawater began to enter the toilet, too." Fidel's version was this: "We were desperately bailing out, but the problem was quite simple, we found out later. The boards that were normally above water were less watertight [than those normally below] and at first began to leak, but as the boat sank under the weight and they got wet, they expanded and thus plugged their own gaps." Whatever had happened, the fact is that the men had spent the three previous days bailing the boat out in shifts.

On November 29, the fifth day at sea, the boat drew away from Mexico and the west of Cuba to steer a course toward the Cayman Islands, to the south of Cuba, skirting Jamaica. Some fishing boats appeared in the distance, and Fidel ordered the decks to be cleared, readied for combat, as weapons were raised from below. It turned out to be a false alarm, however.

What the expeditionaries on board the *Granma* could not have known was that the Batista dictatorship was mobilizing forces all over the island, and the air force was under orders to search for suspicious-looking boats in coastal waters; also, the U.S. Navy, without apparent reason, was gathering forces in Santiago de Cuba, where a submarine, several destroyers, a frigate, and an escort ship had anchored.

The next day, Friday, November 30, the boat's radio began to pick up alarming news. An uprising had broken out in Santiago, and there was fighting in the streets. There were sporadic shoot-outs and acts of sabotage in other Cuban cities, but it was in Santiago where the uprising seemed most extensive. There were reports of fighting in the police station and at the maritime police headquarters, and of snipers on the city's rooftops.

On board the *Granma* there was a feeling of anguish, of being out of it, stranded in the Gulf of Mexico while their comrades were fighting. The uncertainty, the delay, were like a dark pall drawing over the invaders. Then, as the hours went by, reports seemed to confirm that the affray was dying down and the rebels were being beaten.

Fidel and the pilots discussed a change of plan: instead of trying to land near the port of Niquero, which by now would be under close military surveillance, they would try to approach a beach called Las Coloradas, to the southeast of the original spot. From there they would travel by truck to attack some nearby towns and then head for the Sierra Maestra.

By December 1, Batista's army's sources had managed to confirm (doubtless thanks to their informant in Mexico) where the revolutionaries intended to land, and sent the following communiqué to the navy and air force:

> Begin search by Air Force planes, white yacht 65 ft., chain running almost whole length boat, nameless, Mexican flag, sailed Tuxpan, Veracruz state, Mexico, 25 November. Estimated heading Oriente province. Report results CEN. General Rodríguez Avila.

After circulating the same wire dozens of times, they happened to correct it: for "chain" read "cabin."

Meanwhile, on board the boat, according to Raúl Castro's diary: "a cigarette butt was priceless." In the night, we set a head-on course for Cuba, desperately looking for the Cabo Cruz lighthouse, lacking water, oil, and food. There were only ten fourteen-gallon drums of fuel left, the *Granma* was taking on "a lot of water," and, at two in the morning, with a storm blowing, the situation was worrying. Lookouts took turns peering into the darkness for a shaft of light on the horizon, which never appeared. Roque climbed the little lookout post, to the see the light from the cape, but lost his footing and fell in the water.

A frantic search began in the dark which lasted for hours. They turned in wider and wider circles, failing to locate the comrade among the high waves in the choppy sea. Fidel insisted and ordered the boat to turn back. It was a moonless night.

Leonardo Roque had spent an hour on his own in the middle of the sea, thinking of his mother and father and how nice it would have been to die some other way than by drowning, for instance in a real revolution, when the yacht appeared in front of him and he heard Fidel shouting for him. After a thousand and one mishaps, they managed to fish him out of the rough water, and the two doctors, Che Guevara and Faustino Pérez, gave him artificial respiration.

Just after we set off again, we could see the light, but the boat's erratic progress made the journey's final hours seem endless. At dawn on Sunday, December 2, after 172 hours at sea, a journey of more than seven days instead of the planned three, the expeditionaries could see the outline of something that looked like dry land.

Fidel asked one of the pilots, Onelio Pinto: "Is that the Cuban mainland? Are you absolutely sure we're not in Jamaica or some key?"

"Yes."

"Then let's have the motors full steam ahead and let's head as fast as we can to the nearest coastline."

They did not get very far, as the boat ran aground on a mud flat that they figured was some 2,000 yards from shore. Visibility was only fifty yards, and they could just make out the contours of land masses with sparse vegetation. The day was warm, seventy degrees.

A short while later, they would know they had landed in front of a mangrove swamp, at a place called Belic, a mile and a half from their intended destination at the Las Coloradas beach.

9

The Disaster

In the Sierra Maestra with Fidel, at the beginning of 1957. As far as his image goes, this is "pre-Che," as Guevara had not yet acquired his trademark beret and his beard.

Fidel said to me:

"Abandon ship!"

So I dived into the water, with my backpack and everything, but was almost immediately stuck in the mud. I then grabbed the anchor chain and told Fidel what we had there was a swamp. He said to me:

"Forward, dammit!"

T**HAT WAS HOW RENÉ RODRÍGUEZ, THE FIRST MAN TO LAND, WAS TO RE**member his initial contact with the island of Cuba on December 2, 1956.

Chest-deep in the water, the expeditionary force began to wade away from the *Granma.* The lifeboat was lowered; the high command and the advance guard disembarked. The men advanced along the seabed, which extended into a mangrove swamp. Mud, water, and mire, a difficult tangle of roots to break through, and not a sign of dry land. There was a nagging doubt that they might have disembarked on a small key cut off from the mainland. **An hour after beginning the landing, we had advanced a few hundred yards without hitting dry land. [We were] in the middle of a swamp, surrounded by clouds of gall midges and mosquitoes.**

The yacht that had run aground was observed by the occupants of two small cargo boats, the *Tres Hermanos,* carrying coal, and the *Gibarita,* carrying sand. The latter turned northeast to notify the authorities.

After a couple of hours struggling through the mangrove swamp, the first men arrived on dry land, facing a row of coconut palms. Some were so exhausted they had to be carried in their stronger comrades' arms. Luis Crespo, a Cuban country boy, went back to help Che, who was suffering from an asthma attack. As the son of an asthmatic, Crespo knew full well how terrible the affliction could be.

"Here, let me give you a hand."

No—what are you going to help me for?

"Come on, the swamp's worn you out."

No, dammit! Like hell you're going to help me. I came here to fight, not to be helped.

Crespo finally managed to take Che's backpack from him.

The rear guard was still on board, with Raúl Castro in charge of organizing the unloading of the last of the military equipment, when a navy launch appeared in the distance. Shortly afterward, Coast Guard Vessel No. 106 opened fire on the mangrove swamp; the shots seem to have been the signal for the air force to appear. A Catalina began to bomb the area. **Wading through the mangrove swamp, we were not sighted by the air force, but the dictatorship's armed forces were already hot on our heels.**

They made their first contact with some campesinos. Crespo entered a house just as the gunshots and the bombing were heard. The campesinos told them they were at the Las Coloradas beach. **We made dry land, and wandered, stumbling along, like an army of shadows, of ghosts, as if driven by some obscure psychiatric program. Our men had suffered seven days in a row of hunger and sickness during the crossing.**

Efigenio Ameijeiras came upon Che:

I saw him sitting in the mud, leaning against some mangrove bushes. I
dropped down by his side. He saw I was exhausted and asked me:
  What's up with you, then?
"Man, I'm worn out." He slowly got up and cracked an affected,
seemingly self-mocking smile, and said to me:
  Want me to help you?
"Who helps you?" I answered. "You look like you're drowning."
  You know, I'm having an asthma attack.
"Damn, sorry, man! Let's see if we can carry on." As I got up, I asked
him, "Weren't you that Argentine doctor handing out pills on the boat?"

Eight members of the expeditionary force, led by Juan Manuel Márquez,
had gotten lost. Fidel ordered the column to advance into the mountains, and
to try to head for the Sierra Maestra.

The next day, December 3, **we walked at a slow pace, with reconnaissance planes constantly overhead. We ate just once. Luis Crespo got lost at night.** Fidel harangued the group in a low voice: anyone
splitting off from the main body would have to look for the Sierra Maestra
himself.

The United Press International bureau chief in Havana wired a scoop to
his subscribers: "Fidel Castro dead." This was not the first item of disinformation broadcast by the major press agencies; nor, over the next three years,
would it be the last.

Juan Manuel Márquez, who had ended up several miles ahead of the
group before the rendezvous on dry land, rejoined it the next day. Hunger was
hanging over them. Efigenio Ameijeiras reckoned that they had gone without
full regular meals for two days traveling by bus in Mexico, with just one meal,
then seven days at sea, with no hot meals, just biscuits and the oranges of not-
so-fond memory. On top of that they now had to add a two-day hike.

**We left by night and walked until 12:30 A.M. We halted for three
hours in a sugar cane plantation. We ate a lot of cane and left a lot
of traces behind; then we walked until dawn.** They camped out at first
light in a sugar cane plantation, Alegría de Pío, that belonged to the U.S. New
Niquero company. Che could not have known how plain their trail was. The
last two campesinos to have encountered the column gave exact details of
their movements to the Rural Guards, so the dictatorship was able to gather
forces and close off access routes to the Sierra Maestra. At that very moment,
a company of guards with 140 reinforcements was lying in wait at the Alegría
de Pío sugar mill, just a couple of miles away.

**We went along, exhausted from a walk that was difficult
rather than long. There was no longer anything left of our
military equipment except rifles, cartridge belts, and a few
soaked rounds of ammunition. Our medical supplies were
gone; most of our backpacks had been left behind in the**

swamps. New boots had blistered most of the troops' feet. But the new boots and foot rot were not our only enemy. By dawn on the fifth, there were few of us who could have taken so much as another step. People were fainting, walking short distances and asking for long halts. For this reason, a halt was ordered beside a sugar cane plantation, in a thinly wooded copse relatively close to the high mountain. Most of us slept that morning.

Aircraft flying overhead should have warned them, but the rebels were so inexperienced that some of them were actually cutting cane while the planes flew low.

Che was occupied treating the blisters on his comrades' feet. René Rodríguez recalled: "Che treated me, and put Merthiolate on my mud-caked feet. He was a great revolutionary, but a lousy doctor." I seem to remember the last treatment I gave that day. The comrade's name was Humberto Lamotte and that was to be his last day. I can still recall his tired and distressed expression, carrying the boots he could no longer wear as he hobbled from the first-aid tent to his post.

It was 4:30 P.M. and Che had sat down beside Jesús Montané, the pair of us leaning against a tree trunk, talking about our respective children. We were eating our meager rations—half a sausage and two crackers—when a shot rang out and, in the space of seconds, or at least that was what it seemed like in our apprehensive mood, a swarm of bullets flew around the men. Efigenio Ameijeiras wondered later: "I don't know how any of us got out of that one."

The proximity of death is not conducive to rationality. There is no logic in it; rather, it brands the memory with the most absurd images, the most disjointed memories:

I don't know when or how things came about. My memory is hazy. I remember how, in the middle of the firing, Almeida came up to me to ask what orders there were, but there was no longer anyone to give them. As I found out later, Fidel tried in vain to gather the men together in the nearby sugar cane plantation, which could be reached by just crossing the property line. The surprise had been too much, the gunfire too heavy. Almeida took charge of his group again.

Just then a comrade dropped an ammunition case at my feet. I pointed this out to him and I remember well how he answered me, with worry written all over his face: "This is no time for ammunition cases." And he immediately headed off to the sugar cane plantation.

Maybe that was the first time I had to make a practical choice between my vocation for medicine and my duty as a revolutionary soldier. I had a backpack full of medicine and an ammunition case in front of me; together they weighed too much to be carried. I grabbed the ammunition case and left

**the backpack behind, and crossed the clearing between me
and the canebrake. I can remember Faustino Pérez perfectly,
kneeling at the boundary line, firing his machine pistol. Near
me, a comrade called Albentosa was walking toward the cane
plantation. A burst of gunfire just like the others hit us; I felt
something hit me hard in the chest, and a wound in my neck.
I gave myself up for dead.**

The bullet had hit the ammunition case and struck Che such a blow on the
rebound that he thought it was lodged in his throat. He leaned against a tree,
ready to die. Albentosa, vomiting blood through his nose and mouth
because of an enormous wound from a .45, shouted something like
"They've killed me" and began to fire like mad, every which way.
You couldn't see anyone just then.

Che managed to say to Faustino Pérez, I'm fucked, and although the latter told him it was nothing, Guevara could see

**in his eyes that I was done for. I immediately began to think
what would be the best way to die just then, when it seemed
everything was lost. I remembered an old Jack London story
where the main character leans against a tree trunk and pre-
pares to end his life with dignity when he knows he is condemned to freeze to death in the . . . wastes of Alaska. It's the
only image I can recall.**

By his side, Che could hear calls for them to surrender. The reply of one
of the fighters (later attributed to Camilo Cienfuegos) would be etched in
Che's memory: "No one surrenders here, dammit!"

**Ponce drew up, anxious and panting, with a bullet hole that
apparently went through one of his lungs. He told me he was
wounded and I showed him, quite indifferently, that I was too.
He dragged himself over to the cane plantation, some other,
unharmed, comrades with him. For a moment I was left alone,
stretched out there, waiting to die. Almeida came over to me
and encouraged me to keep going, which I did, despite the
pain, and we went into the cane plantation.**

Almeida ordered Che to carry his rifle and plug his wound, which was
bleeding profusely. He also tried to restore order, telling the men crossing over
with him to fire at one of the light aircraft

**which was flying low, shooting bursts of machine-gun fire,
wreaking more havoc amid scenes that were Dantesque at
times and grotesque at others. As if in a kaleidoscope, men
went along screaming, the wounded crying for help, fighters
hiding their bodies behind cane stalks as if they were tree**

trunks, others, terrified, asked for silence with their fingers on
their lips amid the racket of the gunfire—and suddenly there
was a terrible cry of "Fire in the canebrake!"

It was Juan Almeida's encouragement that kept Che and others going on
the way to the sugar cane plantation. The group gathered itself and broke up
again; some split off; and then along came Ramiro Valdés, Benítez, and Chao,
who crossed the edge of the field together and were then able to go uphill.

Che followed along as if lost in a fog:

I was thinking more of the bitterness of defeat and my imminent death than the events of the engagement. I walked and
walked until we reached the canopied mountain. We marched
until the darkness and the trees—which were so thick we
couldn't see the stars—stopped us, without gaining much
ground from where we had fought. We decided to sleep all together, all piled up, attacked by mosquitoes, and racked by
thirst and hunger.

10

No Place to Go

With Raul Castro in the Sierra Maestra in 1957

T HE DAY AFTER THE LANDING, JUAN ALMEIDA'S GROUP, INCLUDING THE wounded Che, wandered through the hills without knowing where the rest of the expeditionary force had headed, hearing shots in the distance but not knowing who had fired them. They had no water and had suffered another misfortune:

> Our only tin of milk had suffered an accident at the hands of Benítez, who'd been entrusted with its safekeeping. He had put it in his pocket upside down—i.e., with the holes to suck on facing downwards. So when it came to have our ration—an empty pillbox filled with condensed milk, and a swig of water—we were dismayed to see that it had all leaked into Benítez's pocket and onto his uniform.

Chao convinced them that wandering around the way they were doing would lead them head-on into an ambush, so they agreed to take cover in a cave and walk by night only. The five expedition members made a pact to the death in that cave: they would fight if they were discovered, and would not surrender. It was the heroism of despair.

It is typical of Che's stoicism that in all that he wrote about those terrible moments, he never, even in his diary, mentioned the wound in his neck. Almeida, on the other hand, recalled that the wound was bleeding profusely when they found Che, but that the next day it had clotted and did not seem so severe.

On the night of December 7, they tried to reach the Sierra Maestra, guided by Che, who was in turn following what he supposed to be the Pole Star. A good while later, I found out that it wasn't the Pole Star, which would have led us due east; it was just by coincidence that we went approximately that way until daybreak, when we reached some cliffs right by the coast. Thirsty after eating the raw flesh of some crabs they had come across, the men were forced to drink the rain water that had collected in some rocks.

> We sucked [it] out using the little pump from an asthma inhaler; we only drank a few drops each.
> We walked along listlessly, aimlessly. A plane flew over the sea now and then. Walking through the reefs was very tiring, and some suggested we should walk next to the cliff face, but there was a serious disadvantage to that—we could be seen. In the end we lay down in the shade of some bushes, waiting for the sun to go down. At nightfall we found a little beach and washed.

Che's diary entry for December 8 ends with a pathetic We ate nothing.

Searching for water, Che came up with an experiment that turned out to be a complete failure.

> I tried to repeat something I had read about in a semiscientific publication or some novel. It said that fresh water mixed with

a third part of sea water was very drinkable. . . . We did that with what was left in the canteen and the outcome was a sorry one, a salty potion that earned me criticism all around.

That night, under a tropical moon that deserved a better occasion, they came upon a fishermen's hut with uniformed men in it. Not thinking twice, they ran toward it desperately, shouting for the men inside to surrender, only to discover they were Camilo Cienfuegos, Pancho González, and Pablo Hurtado. After going over the nightmarish ambush at Alegría de Pío over and over again, the group swapped crabs for pieces of sugar cane and walked on with the nagging awareness that they might be the only survivors of the *Granma* expedition.

The fact did not escape us that the sheer cliff faces and the sea cut off any possibility of getting away if we were to run into enemy troops. I can't remember now whether it was for one or two days that we walked along the coast, just that we ate some prickly pears growing on the shore, one or two apiece, which didn't keep our hunger at bay, and that we were racked with thirst, as the few drops of water we had left had to be strictly rationed.

On Tuesday, December 11, the exhausted group, which had reached the banks of the Toro River, saw a house in the distance, and, after careful reconnaissance, what looked like the outline of a soldier:

At first I thought it was best not to approach, as presumably they were our enemies or perhaps the army was billeted there. Benítez thought the opposite, and the two of us ended up advancing toward the house. I was waiting outside while he crossed a barbed-wire fence. Suddenly I clearly saw a uniformed man in the shade, holding an M1. I thought our time had come—or at least Benítez's; I could no longer warn him, as he was closer to the man than to me. He had almost reached the soldier's side when he backtracked and told me in all innocence that he had returned because he had seen "a man with a gun" and thought it best not to ask him anything. Benítez and all of us were really born again.

Che could not have known how right he was. The house belonged to an army collaborator, Manolo Capitán, who had turned nine *Granma* expedition members over the day before; eight of them were murdered in cold blood.

By climbing a cliff, the group managed to reach a cave where they could hide during the daylight hours. From there **we could take in the whole view perfectly; it was quite peaceful, men landing, others boarding a navy ship. It seemed to be a relief operation. We could count about thirty men.**

They were forces under the command of Lieutenant Julio Laurent, a naval intelligence officer. The man had murdered Che's friend Ñico López, along with some other expeditionary members, in cold blood five days before, and had done the same with another group of captured rebels on December 7, machine-gunning them in the back.

> We ate nothing that day, strictly rationing the water, which we passed around in the eyepiece of a telescopic sight so we each had exactly the same amount, and at night we set off again so as to put some distance between us and the place where we spent one of the most agonizing days of the war, what with the hunger and the thirst, the feeling of defeat, and the overwhelming, palpable, unavoidable danger that made us feel like rats in a hole.

Luck was with them that day; they came across a brook while heading northwest.

> We hit the ground and drank avidly, like horses, until our empty stomachs could take no more water. We filled our canteens and carried on.
>
> That night, we continued our pilgrimage until we reached the vicinity of a house, where we could hear the sounds of a band. Once more, an argument broke out; Ramiro, Almeida, and I felt we should in no circumstances go to a dance, or whatever, as the campesinos would give away our presence in the zone immediately, even if only out of casual indiscretion. Camilo said we had to go and eat in any event. In the end, Ramiro and I were given the mission of going into the house, bringing news, and obtaining food. As we got close, the music stopped and a distant voice could be heard saying something like, "Let's drink to our comrades in arms who so brilliantly . . ." which was enough for us to steal back as quickly as possible and tell our comrades just who were enjoying themselves at that party.

At two A.M. on December 13, with the hungry and desperate group's morale very low, they came upon a campesino's house. Again they argued about whether to approach it. Fortunately, it happened to belong to be Alfredo González, a Seventh-Day Adventist who, along with his shepherd, belonged to one of the July 26 Movement networks run by Celia Sánchez from Santiago and Manzanillo to support the expeditionary force.

Some collapsed there and then. The news was bad. They heard that at least sixteen members of the expeditionary force were dead—murdered after being captured, not killed in combat.

> They gave us a friendly welcome, and right then an uninterrupted feast got under way in that campesino hut. We spent

> hours and hours eating until day dawned and we could not
> leave. Campesinos came in the morning. They had been told
> we were there, and wanted to meet us, give us something to
> eat or bring us some present.
>
> The small hut we were in soon became sheer hell.
> Almeida lit the hellfire with his diarrhea and then eight other
> bowels showed their ingratitude and poisoned the confined
> surroundings. Some of us even vomited.

Reports coming in fleshed out the rumor that Fidel was alive and being sheltered by Celia Sánchez's network, led by Crescencio Pérez, the father of the rebellion in the mountains.

> The campesinos' gruesome tales made us leave our guns well
> hidden. Armed with just our pistols, we tried to cross a very closely
> watched highway. They split into two groups and began to climb the Sierra. Almeida and Che had taken the precaution of keeping at least two Star machine pistols, but the rifles stayed in the campesino's house with Hurtado, who was seriously ill.

When they arrived at the house of a shepherd called Rosabal the next day, they heard that Hurtado had inadvertently talked too much; that had led to a betrayal. The army had captured both him and the weapons.

> As soon as he heard the terrible news, this comrade [Rosabal]
> got in touch with another campesino, who knew the area very
> well and said he sympathized with the rebels. That night they
> led us out of there and to a safer refuge. The campesino we
> met that day, Guillermo García, was one of the key cadres in
> Celia's network.

Che's small group spent December 15 in a cave and the next few days going from one campesino's house to another. The farmers protected, fed, and transported them. Finally, at dawn on December 20, they arrived at the farm of Mongo Pérez, Crescencio's brother. There Fidel, Raúl, Ameijeiras, Universo Sánchez, and half a dozen other survivors were waiting for them. One of Crescencio's sons, who had been briefly arrested shortly before because he was suspected of having helped the expeditionaries to break out of the army cordon, noticed that the Argentine with the group was ragged, barefoot, and shivering; he asked for a canvas sack to throw around himself as he was dying of cold.

Fidel did not conceal his delight at seeing them, but dressed them down for having left their guns behind. Fidel's rebuke was very harsh.

> You haven't paid the price for the mistake you made, because you pay with
> your life for leaving guns behind in those circumstances. Your guns were
> the only hope of survival you would have had if you had run into the army.
> Leaving them behind was criminally stupid.

Ashamed, Che omitted any account of the reprimand from his diary, confining himself to mentioning his asthma and saying that he slept badly.

Eleven days later, a small note bearing a Manzanillo postmark arrived in Argentina by express mail. Che's family, having read in the press and been told by a witness that he had fallen with a chest wound, had believed him dead. Dear Folks, I'm fine, I've spent just two and have five left [out of the proverbial Latin American cat's seven lives]. I'm still working in the same line. News is patchy and will continue to be, but take my word that God is an Argentine. It was signed "Teté," Che's childhood nickname.

11.   River Plate Resurrection

The Sierra Maestra, 1958. Already in command of the Fourth Column of the Rebel Army.

66 **I** HAD NEVER SEEN AN ARGENTINE IN MY LIFE, NOT EVEN IN FILMS, I think, and it was . . . 'Yes, Che,' 'No, Che,' 'Three bags full, Che,' " Crescencio Pérez's son Sergio said years later, explaining how Ernesto Guevara was sentenced to be known as Che among the country people in the Sierra Maestra.

And this Che went around in a sorry state until shoes and clothes, and even an atomizer from a mountain store, were found for him, although it seems the latter did not ward off a terrible asthma attack. The legendary "group of twelve" was recovering after the bitter days following the attack at Alegría de Pío. The twelve were not twelve, however; counting the first campesinos to join up, **there were about seventeen of us**, all that was left of the eighty-two expedition members on the *Granma*. **The roll call of the victims was long and painful: Juan Manuel Márquez himself, Ñico López, Juan Smith, [and] advance guard captain Cándido Gónzalez, Fidel's adjutant and a impeccable revolutionary.** The vast majority had been captured and shot in the back, tortured and thrown into a cave, or killed and their bodies dumped outside a cemetery.

Then Fidel Castro's optimism began to take hold on the men, his old magic, proven in Mexico, began to reach the survivors of **that little group who had yet to get to know each other well.** Now they were **talking about winning, about attacking.**

Fidel was a unique character. Meeting with the first group of survivors on December 18, he asked his brother Raúl:

"How many rifles have you got?"

"Five."

"Well, that plus the two I've got makes seven, so we can win this war now."

His optimism turned out to be contagious.

> **Already back then, on those long-drawn-out nights (long because our inactivity began at nightfall) under the trees of some wooded area, we began to draw up plans and more plans, plans for the moment and, a little later, for victory. Those were happy hours. I savored my first cigars (which I learned to smoke to keep the mosquitoes away). The fragrance of the Cuban leaves soaked into me as prophesies of the future crowded on top of one another.**

The training began; campesinos in Crescencio's network began to recover lost weapons. Che's rifle turned out to be faulty, and Crescencio ended up with Che's Star. Fidel ordered a surprise practice attack on December 23 and asked Faustino Pérez to give a false alarm. Faustino went to Che, who was on guard duty above a coffee plantation, and shouted that the Rural Guards were coming. Che calmly asked him for some facts and figures—how many Guards? coming from where? and so on—until Faustino had to admit the truth. In his diary, Che wrote: **Combat drill. I ran over to bring the news; people mobilized well, and were willing to fight.** Shortly afterward, Faustino went off to get back in touch with the M26 urban networks; three liaison officers from Manzanillo arrived with bullets and sticks of dynamite. We know from Che's diary that he asked one of the boys to bring him some books, and we even know what they were about: one on Cuba's history and the other on its basic geography. He received them a week later. Raúl Castro wrote in his diary: "There was even a book on algebra for Renaissance Man Che Guevara."

Two days after Christmas they were marching again, the way paved for them by Crescencio Pérez's knowledge of the region and his political influence. Where Fidel and his message were not known, Crescencio was, and people accepted whatever he told them. On December 27, under a ceiba tree, Che made his début as a chef, barbecuing a bullock Argentine style. His diary entry said: **It turned out well but took a long time. The countryfolk in the column didn't quite get the idea. They said the beef was half-cooked.**

The days went by and, little by little, people were recruited. The first campesinos would come along, sometimes unarmed, sometimes bringing weapons our comrades had left behind in friendly houses or canebrakes after running for safety. Guillermo García, a key figure in the resistance network that had been operating in the Sierra Maestra since November, joined up at the end of December, along with three *Granma* expedition members who had been lost and rescued by Celia's organization. By the end of the month, the column had twenty-four members, including a dozen campesinos.

For the last week of the month, they had been camping out at a place called La Catalina, and on December 29 they ate the remains of the barbecue which, according to Raúl, "stank, even with a lot of bitter oranges in it." Firing practice for the recruits continued. They saw the new year, 1957, in under rain. This was a group of nonpersons, the dead come back to life, since Batista had announced over the radio and in the press that the threat had disappeared, that Fidel was dead, that the expedition members who had landed had been dispersed or killed. Meanwhile they were preparing for their first engagement.

> **On January 14, 1957, a little more than a month after the surprise attack at Alegría de Pío, we halted at the Magdalena River. It is separated from La Plata by a ridge projecting from the Sierra Maestra, which runs down to the sea where it is between two small pools. We held some firing practice there, ordered by Fidel so as to train the men a little. Some were shooting for the first time in their lives. We got washed there, too, after having left hygiene behind for many days; those who could changed their clothes.**

Years later, in an interview with Mexican journalist Víctor Rico Galán, Che recalled that Fidel was fat and had not trained hard in Mexico, so he had some trouble climbing the hills. He got up them only because of his iron willpower.

"And what about you, with your asthma?"

I have a bit of willpower, too.

On January 14, toward five o'clock in the afternoon, a young campesino in Cabezos de la Plata saw a couple of armed men arrive:

> I took them for a pair of Rural Guards. They asked me questions, I gave them coffee. We talked about roads, about campesinos, they asked me to sell them a hog which, by the way, I didn't charge them for out of fear. Then a group turned up that scared me even more. They were led by a big, unusually tall guy asking thousands of questions, and somebody else with him who spoke slowly and deliberately, in a low voice, introducing himself as a doctor. He took my pulse, checked me over, and said to me, You're as strong as an ox.

The visitors were Fidel and Che. The campesino was called Dariel Alarcón, and his future would be linked to Che's. He joined the guerrillas a few days later.

Fidel had chosen the La Plata barracks for his invaders' baptism of fire, but it is not clear why, since the column had no bullets. On January 15, they sighted their target.

> The La Plata barracks. It was only half built, with galvanized tin temporary walls and half-naked inhabitants, among whom we could see some enemy uniforms. We were able to observe how at six o'clock, as the sun went down, a launch full of guards would come along; some would get off and some would get on. . . . We decided to leave the attack until the next day.

They began to draw closer on January 16 and crossed the La Plata River at nightfall. They were lucky enough to run into two campesinos who gave them two pieces of vital information: the number of soldiers in the barracks—around fifteen—and the fact that Chico Osorio, the overseer of one of the region's large plantations, was to pass through before long. He was well-known for torturing the campesinos and as an informer. Shortly afterward, he turned up drunk, on a mule, and with a bottle of brandy in his hand.

> Universo Sánchez asked him to halt in the name of the Rural Guard, and he swiftly replied "Mosquito," which was the [Guard's] password.
> Despite our gallowslike appearance, we were able to fool Chicho Osorio, perhaps because he was drunk. Fidel indignantly identified himself as an army colonel who had come to

investigate why the rebels had not been wiped out yet. He was, he said, going up into the mountains, which was why he was bearded. And what the army was doing was "garbage." Chicho very submissively told him that as a matter of fact the guards did spend their whole time in the barracks, doing nothing but eating; they made meaningless sorties, and he emphatically said the rebels had to be got rid of.

Unwittingly, the drunken foreman was making a reverse list of whom to trust and whom not to.

Some twenty-odd names were reeled off, and the stool pigeon kept on talking. He told us how he had killed two local men, "but General Batista let me go free right away." He told us he had just slapped a couple of campesinos who had been "a little ill-mannered," and that, according to him, the Guards couldn't do such things; they let the farmers speak without punishing them. Fidel asked him what he would do if he got his hands on Fidel Castro, and he answered with a gesture that he would cut off his balls,

as well as those of Crescencio Pérez. Then he showed them his boots, Mexican ones and said, "From one of those sons of bitches we killed."

A chill ran through the rebels' ranks: the boots had belonged to one of the rebels from the *Granma*. There, without knowing it, Chicho Osorio had just signed his own death warrant. On a hint from Fidel, he ended up agreeing to guide us to catch the soldiers by surprise and show them just how ill-prepared they were and how they were failing in their duty.

The rebels cautiously approached the barracks to take up battle stations. Just then, three guards on horseback passed in front of the group,

hauling a prisoner behind them who was on foot and tied up like a mule. He passed by my side and I can remember the poor campesino's words as he said, "I'm just like you," and the reply from a guard, whom we later identified as Corporal Basol, "Shut up and keep going before I help you with my whip."

The fighters took up positions. They were thirty-two strong—eighteen from the *Granma,* plus fourteen campesinos who had thrown in their lot with the harebrained revolt. They had twenty-two guns among them, and very little ammunition. If the attack ended in failure and the rebel column couldn't capture any ammunition, they would be in a very dangerous situation.

We thus drew closer and closer to the enemy positions until we were about forty meters away. It was a clear moonlit night.

[At 2:40 a.m.,] Fidel began the shooting with two bursts of machine-gun fire, followed by all the guns we had available. We immediately asked the soldiers to surrender, but to no avail. [They answered each call to surrender with a burst of fire from an M1.] **As soon as the firing broke out, Chicho Osorio, the stool pigeon and murderer, was executed.**

The guerrillas responded shot for shot. Universo Sánchez had nine bullets and gave two of them to Crespo. The group had a couple of Brazilian grenades; Che and Crespo moved up and threw them, but they did not explode. **Raúl Castro threw a stick of dynamite, but it had no nipple, and therefore no effect.**

Fidel ordered Universo to throw the grenades.

"I already threw them."

"No, no you didn't."

But he had. So Fidel told him he had to burn the houses down, and handed him some matches. It did not seem like an easy mission in the middle of the shooting. Camilo Cienfuegos had a try, too; finally, Universo managed to set fire to one of the huts.

By the firelight we could see it was just a place where they stored coconuts from a nearby grove, but we managed to intimidate the soldiers who then abandoned the fight. One of them ran off, almost bumping into Luis Crespo's gun, and was wounded in the chest. Luis took his gun from him and we kept on shooting at the house.

Battles spawn as many different accounts over time as the number of men who took part in them and, despite the detailed accuracy of his reports, Ernesto Guevara always tended to play down his own acts of bravery. According to Crespo, Che was a man who pushed things to the limit, and it was Che who threw himself into the middle of the fray, grabbed the wounded soldier, and took his gun. The latter said, "Don't kill me," and Che didn't take it in; instead he said something like **The doctor's on his way.**

Fighting was meanwhile going on elsewhere. Juan Almeida and his platoon were confronting some marines in another cabin. Twice Fidel had to repeat the order to advance. The second time the guerrillas charged.

Camilo Cienfuegos, taking cover behind a tree, fired at a sergeant who was running away, and used up the few rounds he had. The almost defenseless soldiers were mercilessly wounded by our bullets. Camilo Cienfuegos was the first, from our side, to go into the house where they were shouting that they surrendered.

Before they checked to see whether their comrades were wounded, even whether they themselves were really still alive or just keeping on out of inertia, they had one obsession: get guns and ammunition.

Eight Springfields; a Thompson machine gun and about a thousand rounds—we had used up about 500. . . . Furthermore, we also got cartridge belts, fuel, knives, clothing, and some food. . . . On their side, two dead, five wounded, and three prisoners. Some got away. On our side, not so much as a scratch.

The blow struck at Alegría de Pío had been returned. The men from the *Granma* were beginning the revolution.

Che began to practice medicine again. After seeing that the wounded soldiers were treated and leaving them in the care of their surviving comrades, Fidel ordered the column to open fire on the cabins that were still holding out. Then, even though it was night, the column went uphill toward the Sierra, **heading for Palma Mocha, where we arrived at dawn. We moved on quickly, looking for the steepest parts of the Sierra Maestra.**

They went over the events on the way. A victory, even a minor victory like this one, is harder to believe than a defeat. The rebels were not the only ones commenting on the events; as Batista had temporarily relaxed censorship, news of the La Plata engagement echoed through newspapers and international news agencies. The dead had come back to life. When the adrenaline wore off, Che commented parenthetically in his memoirs: **We did not want to fight, by any means; we did it because we had to.**

On their way up to the heights of the Sierra, the rebels met with an exodus of campesinos. The Rural Guards had spread rumors that their huts were about to be bombed. Both Che and Raúl reported on the **sad spectacle** in their diaries. The army intended not just to empty the area immediately around the guerrillas, but to prepare for a widespread eviction.

As no one knew of our presence in the [immediate] **area, it was clearly a maneuver by the foremen and the Rural Guards to evict the campesinos from their lands and possessions. But the lie had been made truth by our attack, so terror was rampant and it was impossible to stem the campesino exodus.**

Fidel made his début as a guerrilla tactician. He foresaw that the army would not be able to ignore an attack like that at La Plata and would send detachments to pursue the guerrillas, so he set up an ambush, the first of many by the rebel army. The chosen spot was a couple of huts on the banks of the **Arroyo del Infierno, a short, narrow stream that flowed into the Palma Mocha River.** The ambush was set up in a horseshoe formation, with seven small combat posts; the abandoned campesinos' huts were in the middle.

Efigenio Ameijeiras remembered that Che left the camp on a reconnaissance mission on January 19 and returned through a clearing in the woods in front of Camilo's post. On his head was one of the spoils of the clash at La Plata, a complete corporal's helmet from Batista's army, which I was wearing with pride. Thinking the army had arrived, Camilo asked no questions but opened fire on him with a rifle. Che had to wave a white handkerchief and shout "Don't shoot!" Camilo laughed and said, "You bastard, you took me prisoner once when you were careless but now you surrender!"

This incident showed just how much tension we were all under, waiting for combat to relieve it. At times like that, even those with the steeliest nerves begin to tremble at the knees, and everyone is anxious for the high point in war, which is combat.

Three days later, the ambush party heard gunshots nearby. They discovered much later that it had beem Lieutenant Angel Sánchez Mosquera's column, about which they heard a great deal in succeeding years. The shots they'd heard marked the execution of a Haitian campesino who had refused to act as a guide for them.

As we thought the soldiers were nearby, [we didn't forage for food and] there was no breakfast or lunch. Countryman Crespo had found a group of chicken nests and rationed the eggs there, leaving one behind, as usual, so that the hens would keep laying. That night, because of the shots we had heard, Crespo decided we should eat the last egg, and that's what we did.

Suddenly, at midday, one of the guerrillas turned up at the campesino's houses, and according to witnesses the following dialogue took place:
"Right, they're here," the guerrilla said to Fidel.
"Oh, fine, let them through," Fidel replied, thinking he meant the campesinos who owned the huts.
"No, I mean the soldiers!"
Fidel, whose rifle had a telescopic sight, opened fire and shot one of the soldiers.

I soon found there was a soldier trying to hide from the shooting in a hut near my position. I could see only his legs, because the roof blocked the line of sight from my elevated vantage point. My first shot in that direction missed; the second hit the man right in the chest. He dropped his gun, which stuck in the ground by its bayonet point. Crespo covered me and I got to the hut, where I saw the body and stripped it of its gun, bullets, and some other belongings.

Che did not describe how he went up to the dead man in the middle of the shooting and risked being caught in the crossfire. What did he see? This was the first man he knew he had killed; maybe his shots had hit another of Batista's soldiers in the attack at La Plata, but it would have been impossible to be certain in the heat of the battle. Now it was possible. Years later, Che avoided the question and confined himself to a medical description: **He received a gunshot wound in the middle of his chest, which must have burst his heart and caused instant death.**

Che requested permission to go and collect the rest of the rifles, but Fidel refused. The objective had already been achieved. **The battle was unusually furious, and soon each of us was running in another direction.** It appeared that casualties had been inflicted on the advance guard of troops, which might have numbered up to 300 men. Strangely enough, both forces would move in parallel to avoid each other over the coming days, during which they would often be just a few hundred yards apart without knowing it.

Five soldiers were killed, but the guerrillas did not measure their successes only in terms of enemy casualties; they had used up 900 rounds, while capturing just seventy and a rifle. **It wasn't a total victory, but neither was it a Pyrrhic one. We had measured our strength against the enemy in new situations and had passed the test.**

Over the next few days the guerrillas approached the Caracas area, where some tentative links with the campesinos had been made. A sorry sight met their eyes: the army had been through the place and terrorized everyone into leaving.

Despite the victories, **the situation was not a happy one at that point. The column had yet to cultivate a battle-hardened attitude and a clear ideological awareness. One comrade would walk out one day, another the next. Members asked for missions in the cities, which were often riskier but which meant not having to live under the tough conditions upcountry.**

Conditions were even tougher because a traitor had infiltrated the ranks. Eutimio Guerra, a campesino in whom they had placed a great deal of trust from the first, had been captured by the troops under a Major Casillas and had agreed to betray the guerrillas. He was promised 10,000 pesos and an army rank if he killed Fidel. Thanks to the information he provided, campesinos who had collaborated with the guerrillas had their houses burned down. Guerra turned up at the Caracas camp, and the next day requested permission to see his supposedly sick mother. Fidel not only granted him permission but even gave him some money. Eutimio quickly went to the military and gave away the location of the campsite.

On the morning of the thirtieth, after a cold night and just as we were getting up, we heard the hum of airplanes, which we could not place as we were in the brush. The kitchen fire was

a couple of hundred yards downhill at a small water hole, where the head of the advance guard was.

We suddenly heard the clatter of a fighter plane, the rattle of machine guns, and, soon after, the bombs. Our experience was very limited back then and we could hear shots everywhere; .50-caliber bullets explode when they hit the ground, and when the attackers came close they gave us the impression they had come out of the brush itself. At the same time we could also hear machine-gun fire from the air. . . .

Eutimio himself, on board a Beaver light plane, had pointed out the guerrillas and marked the spot. Fortunately, the bombing was concentrated on the original campsite, from which they happened to have moved the night before.

Che stayed in the rear with Chao, a Spanish Civil War veteran, to pick up those left behind when the column dispersed. The pair joined up with Guillermo García and two others, and spent the day looking for the rendezvous Fidel had fixed—at the Humo Cave, **which we knew by name, but did not exactly know how to find. So we spent the night in uncertainty, hoping to see our comrades, but fearing to meet the enemy.** The campesinos they ran across were very frightened. Ciro Frías, a muleteer who had collaborated with the guerrillas, had his merchandise requisitioned and his tent burned; worse, his brother was killed and his wife arrested. Tension ran high and one of the recruits, a campesino called Sergio Acuña, deserted. He

just quietly dropped his rifle and cartridge belt and abandoned the guard detail entrusted to him. We wrote in our campaign diary that he had taken with him a country-style straw hat, a can of condensed milk, and three sausage links. What really hurt us back then was [losing] the condensed milk and the sausages.

That day, February 1, the uncertainty ended with Crescencio Pérez appearing uphill **with a long column comprising almost all of our men and some new people who had joined up from Manzanillo, led by** Roberto Pesant. The Manzanillo people brought with them items that were priceless just then, such as surgical equipment and underwear. **I got some underpants and undershirts, with initials embroidered on them by the girls in Manzanillo.**

The group moved through the Sierra, over known territory. The guerrillas' survival now depended on their mobility. Campesinos who supported them were being harassed. Hunger bit now and then.

I can still remember, as if it were one of the greatest days in my life, the time when countryman Crespo turned up with a can of four pork sausages—he had saved them from before— saying they were for friends; Crespo, Fidel, someone else, and

I tucked into those meager rations as though they were a sumptuous banquet.

Che was going through a bad time, with swamp fever on top of his usual asthma attacks. To cap it all, he also fell victim to severe diarrhea and dehydration. Nor was he the only one suffering from the harsh Sierra conditions: Ramiro Valdés was plagued by an old leg wound; Ignacio Pérez was also wounded; and several new recruits could not take the pace and were granted leave.

Afterwards, the ones who stayed and stood up under the initial trials and tribulations got used to the dirt, the lack of food, water, shelter, and safety and to living constantly with a rifle at hand. Our only shield was the cohesion and stamina of the guerrilla hard core.

Eutimio had returned, arguing that his mother was well again and pushed his deception to the limit by predicting air raids.

Eutimio would say, with a soothsayer's face on him, "I tell you, they'll strafe Donkey Hill today." Then the planes would strafe Donkey Hill and he'd jump for joy at having got it right.

On one of the last nights before his betrayal was discovered, Eutimio said he had no blanket, and could Fidel lend him one. It was cold back then, in February, on the hilltops. Fidel answered that that way they would both be cold, that instead they should sleep together under the same blanket so that their two overcoats could cover the pair of them.

Fidel recalled years later, still in amazement that, "he had two grenades and a pistol and he slept right next to me!" But the grenades were not enough, he needed to have some support to carry out the final assignment. After slyly sounding out Universo Sánchez and Che, Eutimio decided it would have been very difficult to escape after killing Fidel and scrapped the idea.

Over the following days, the guerrillas seemed to be caught in a situation where they were being manipulated by the Army, who had the initiative. These were relatively quiet days. On January 28, Che wrote to Hilda in Peru, asking her for photos of little Hilda Beatriz, whom he had last seen in Alfonso Bauer's house in Mexico, and gave her a synopsis of the first engagements . . . Raúl's diary entry for February 8 said: "I began to study French with Che today, who has a great accent and is very intelligent," and later on, "Fidel, Che and I made a hut, where the rain was worse inside than out. I picked a right pair of slobs for this job."

The impasse with the Army was broken on December 9 when a campesino reported the presence of a 140-man column in the vicinity.

> From our position on a bald mountain top, we could indeed
> see them in the distance. Furthermore, the campesino said he
> had spoken with Eutimio, who told him the area would be
> bombed the next day. Fidel began to suspect something was
> up; the oddness of Eutimio's behavior had at last dawned on
> us, and the speculation began.

Shooting started at 1:30 P.M. A section of Casillas's column, led by Eutimio, had pitched camp at the top of the hill, where they unwittingly stumbled on the army. A shot rang out just then, followed by a volley. Then the air was full of volleys and explosions triggered by a concerted attack on the place where we had previously camped out. The campsite emptied very quickly.

Two soldiers had died, and so had one of the rebels: a campesino named Julio Zenón Acosta. Che was very fond of him and had been teaching him how to read. He was my first pupil in the Sierra. . . . Wherever we stopped I would teach him his first letters. We were at the stage of distinguishing between A and O, between E and I.

Che confessed that his only contribution to the combat was to run away: I effected no more than a "strategic retreat" at full speed in that engagement. He lost his backpack full of books, medicines, and food in the process.

> There was an unwritten law among the guerrillas that who-
> ever lost his personal possessions . . . had to sort things out
> himself. Among the things I had lost was something very pre-
> cious to a guerrilla: the two or three tins of food we each had
> back then. When night fell, everyone naturally got ready to
> eat his tiny ration. Camilo, seeing I didn't have anything, as
> blankets aren't good to eat, shared his only can of milk with
> me, and I think that was when our friendship began, or be-
> came closer.
> While sipping the milk, each of us carefully making sure
> it was shared out evenly, we talked about a whole host of
> things. The conversation generally revolved around food, as
> people tend to center their conversation on problems affect-
> ing them, and we were obsessed with food in those days.

On February 12, the small column reached El Lomón, where they rendezvoused with Fidel. Their ranks thinned by desertions and disorderly retreats, they numbered only eighteen. Meanwhile Eutimio's treachery had been discovered. Four days later, at Epifanio Díaz's farm, Fidel met with the key urban cadres: Frank País, Haydée Santamaría, Armando Hart, Vilma Espín, Faustino Pérez—back from his mission in the cities—and Celia Sánchez. It was a gathering crucial to the revolution.

Frank País made a big impression on Che:

All I really knew then was that he had the look of a man totally dedicated and faithful to a cause—and furthermore, that that man was a superior being. He gave us a quiet talk on order and discipline while we cleaned our dirty rifles, counting the bullets and arranging them so as not to lose them.

At that time Haydée and Frank's idea was that Fidel should leave the Sierra Maestra and go to another Latin American country, from where he could reorganize the movement. This notion did not last ten seconds—Haydée and Frank didn't even dare suggest it. What Fidel asked for was ammunition and coordination.

The outcome of the meeting was a new coordination between the Sierra and the cities; it was decided that recruitment and concentration of weapons should be organized in the Sierra Maestra. Minutes of the meeting show Fidel saying that his "exterminated" column was giving the army a lot of trouble; he called for a war in the cities (this was already brewing), as well as for the execution of torturers, the burning of canebrakes, and the sabotage of public services and communications routes. To round things off, he wanted an economic campaign and a general strike.

Che was sidelined at those first meetings held by the July 26 Movement national leadership. He was just another fighter, and his status was ambiguous at that, since he was a medic. He was also from another major event that took place at that time. The urban movement had been preparing a journalistic coup, an interview with Fidel in the Sierra. Experience with *Bohemia* magazine and the newspaper *Prensa Libre* had convinced them that censorship could gag any of the media in Cuba, and distributing the underground paper *Revolución* was more and more difficult. So they decided to offer the interview to the international media instead. Faustino Pérez contacted Ruby Phillips, the Havana correspondent of the *New York Times,* and offered her an exclusive. She relayed the offer to New York and quickly got the go-ahead. New York assigned the interview to Herbert Matthews, a fifty-seven-year-old journalist and head of the editorial desk, who was well known for his international work and particularly for his magnificent coverage of the Spanish Civil War twenty years earlier.

A complex operation organized from Havana brought Matthews from New York to the Sierra via Havana and Santiago. Fidel tried to make the guerrillas adopt a somewhat martial bearing during the meeting and asked one of the men, Fajardo, to appear military. Years later Fajardo laughingly recalled: "I looked at myself, I looked at the others with their broken shoes held together with wire, caked in filth."

That was not the only absurdity in the interview. Fidel, avoiding the question of how many men he had under arms, pointed to those around him and said, "This is my high command." What he did not say was that there was no army for them to be the high command of. Perhaps this did not impress

Matthews, who had seen other revolutionary armies in his time, but the fact that Fidel was alive and well was a world scoop in itself.

Matthews's report appeared in the *New York Times* on March 24–26. He described the climate of resistance that prevailed, especially in the island's two main cities, and elucidated Fidel's status as a leader. Following on the heels of reports that Fidel was dead and his forces disintegrated, the *Times* story dealt a strong blow to the régime—a blow whose force was renewed some months later. When censorship was temporarily lifted in Cuba on December 26, the interview was reprinted in several newspapers and broadcast on the radio. The Cuban Defense Ministry angrily replied that the interview could "be considered a chapter out of a science fiction novel," and the Oriente Province military chief was even more ridiculous, claiming that nothing could get past the blockade enforced by his troops. The uproar aroused world interest, and two days later Matthews topped off his story by publishing Fidel's autograph and several photos, taken with a box camera, showing the two of them together in the Sierra.

Che noted the following, as if the involvement of an American bothered him: **Matthews's visit, naturally, was very brief.**

Execution

This mule's name is "Ernesto."

AFTER THE MEETING AND INTERVIEW, THE GUERRILLAS HAD TO GET ON the move again. As they were preparing to leave, the news that Eutimio Guerra was in the area made them mobilize a search. Ciro Frías captured Guerra and took him to the camp; when the guerrillas searched him, they found a sidearm and grenades, along with a safe-conduct signed by Casillas. Guerra was shouting, "Shoot me, for God's sake, but don't read it!"

> He fell on his knees in front of Fidel and simply begged to be killed. He said he knew that he deserved to die. He seemed to have aged in a short time, and a good number of gray hairs could be seen in his temples, something we hadn't noticed before. It was an extremely tense moment. Fidel rebuked him harshly for his betrayal; Eutimio admitted his faults and just wanted to be killed. For every one of us who saw it, the moment when Ciro Frías, a family friend of his, spoke to him was unforgettable. Ciro reminded Eutimio of all he had done for him—of the little favors that he and his brother had done for Eutimio's family—and of how Eutimio had betrayed them, first by giving Frías's brother away and getting him killed by the Guards a few days later, and then by trying to wipe out the whole group of us. It was a long and pathetic tirade that Eutimio listened to in silence, with his head hung low. He was asked if he wanted anything, and he said, yes, that he wanted the revolution—us, in other words—to take care of his children.

Universo, who was ordered by Fidel Castro to shoot Guerra, later said, "I would have shot him ten times over. Che came along and, between the two of us, we carried him out of the place so as not to kill him in full view of everybody. I gave him a bottle of rum, which he drained in one gulp on the way. He kept saying, 'Kill me.'" Just then, a heavy storm broke and blacked everything out. The sky was criss-crossed by lightning in an uncommonly heavy rainfall, and the air filled with thunder. In Universo Sánchez's words: "I was carrying a rifle, and then Che grabbed a .22 PAC pistol and shot him right there. 'Dammit, Che, you killed him!' He fell face up, gagging. And, what with the thunder, it was hellish, horrible."

Che, who was not much given to beating about the bush or half-truths, never publicly admitted to executing Eutimio, the traitor. In a future account, he would only say,

> There was a flash of lightning, and then a roll of thunder, so that none of the comrades nearby were able to hear the gunshot when Eutimio Guerra met his death.
>
> We buried him right there the next day. . . . Manuel Fajardo wanted to plant a cross on the grave, and I refused as it would be very dangerous for the farmers there to have such evidence of the execution in plain view. He then carved a little cross on a nearby tree.

Eutimio's denunciations to the soldiers hit the campesino communities in the Sierra very hard, even after his death. On April 25, the army fired on Dariel Alarcón's house and murdered his wife. The guerrillas moved on again. At that time, we were moving slowly, in no fixed direction, hiding out among the hillocks.

Che was struck with another asthma attack on February 22 and, as if to pay for Eutimio's execution, he had no medicines on him. The attack was so severe that in his memoirs he would speak of this as the toughest stage of the war. He dragged himself across the hills with great difficulty for a week. On February 28 the army was seen marching toward the campesino house where the guerrillas were resting. It was a well-equipped group of soldiers, who were coming specifically to occupy the high ground. We had to run quickly to reach the edge of the hill and cross over before the troops could cut us off. It wasn't too hard to do, since we had sighted them in time.

But the soldiers had sighted the guerrillas as well, and began to fire on the hut with machine guns and mortars.

> We made it to the top easily, most of us, and kept on; I had a hard job of it. I made it, but I was having such an asthma attack that every step was difficult for me. I can remember the hard time Crespo had helping me to walk. When I couldn't keep up, I asked them to leave me behind. The campesino, in that way our troops talked to their comrades, kept saying to me: "You Argentine piece of shit, you walk or I'll beat you all the way."

Manuel Fajardo recalled with admiration years later how "Crespo just threw Che over his shoulder, backpack and all!" Efigenio Ameijeiras's version was less flattering, however:

> When the mortar and machine gunfire first sounded, it was like a life-giving elixir for the struggling Che. I might say that of all of us running there, he did his fellow countryman Fangio proud. He later confided that the best cure for illness was the presence of enemy soldiers.

In their escape, the guerrillas came upon a hut at a spot called Purgatorio. Fidel decided to leave Che behind there in the company of a dubious recruit, Luis Barrera, known as El Maestro. According to Efigenio Ameijeiras: "By dawn we had to leave him to take his chances while he waited for medicines in an area infested with the Rural Guards. . . . We said goodbye to him, some with a hug, others with a handshake, leaving a man at the mercy of betrayal." Fidel, in a moment of generosity, gave us a Johnson repeating rifle, one of the treasures of our guerrilla group, with which to defend ourselves.

> The campesino ran an errand for me and brought me enough adrenaline. We then went through ten of the toughest days

during the fighting in the Sierra. I walked along from tree to tree, with a rifle butt for support, in the company of a frightened fighter who trembled every time firing broke out, and had a nervous attack every time my asthma made me cough in some dangerous spot. We took ten days to reach Epifanio's house again, though it was really just over a day's march away.

Che reached the rendezvous on March 11. Army patrols abounded, and Fidel and the rest of the guerrillas had yet to arrive. Instead, news of substantial reinforcements from the cities came a couple of days later, and bad news with it. Frank País had been arrested in Santiago, and Armando Hart in Havana.

On March 13, as we were waiting for the new guerrillas, news of an assassination attempt on Batista was broadcast by radio, and some of the dead were named. First, there was student leader José Antonio Echeverría, and then others, like Menelao Mora.

Unsuccessful attacks had taken place on the National Palace and on a radio station. Both actions were organized by the M26 command, as the first salvo in the movement's strategy of urban guerrilla warfare. This initial engagement had resulted in substantial casualties among the students, but did not prevent M26 from fighting on against the dictatorship.

Meanwhile, Che clashed with the captain in charge of the reinforcements that had arrived:

Who are you? Che asked.

"Jorge Sotús. Why?"

I have orders from Fidel to take charge of you as soon as you arrive and to take you to the rendezvous.

"No way. I don't trust anybody. I'm the one in charge of these troops."

What did you say?

"I have orders from the Plains leadership to take these reinforcements to Fidel."

Tomorrow is another day, Che said, swallowing his pride.

The students from Santiago sang around the campfire that night.

The reinforcements consisted of fifty men, only thirty of whom were armed. They had two machine guns with them, a Madsen and a Johnson. We had become veterans in the months we had spent in the Sierra, and saw in these new recruits all the faults the men from the Granma had. . . . The difference between the two groups was enormous: ours was disciplined, compact, and battle-hardened; the greenhorns were still suffering from the illnesses that newcomers to the Sierra get, they were not used to having just one meal a day,

**and they wouldn't eat anything they couldn't identify. Their
backpacks were full of useless things and, to lighten the load,
they would get rid of a can of condensed milk rather than a
towel (a heinous crime among guerrillas). We took the opportunity to pick up all the food left on the way.**

The troops marched off up toward the Sierra but made very slow progress,
as they were poorly trained. Sotús was one of the worst, but Che did not dare
to confront him, even though he had orders from Fidel to take command.

**At that time, I still had a complex about being a foreigner, and
did not want to push things too far, although the troops looked
very uneasy. After short hikes that were made long by lack of
preparation, we came to a place in La Derecha where we were
to wait for Fidel Castro.**

Fidel's arrival on March 24 brought all the guerrilla forces together.

**There, Fidel criticized me for not asserting the authority in-
vested in me and leaving it in the hands of the newcomer
Sotús. . . . New platoons were formed also, with all the men
brought together to form three groups headed by Captains
Raúl Castro, Juan Almeida, and Jorge Sotús. Camilo Cienfuegos would command the advance guard and Efigenio Almeijeiras the rear guard. I was named medic to the high
command, where Universo Sánchez was squad leader. . . . We
discussed what we could do there and then. I felt we should attack the first post we could, so as to break in the new comrades. But Fidel and the rest of the council thought it would be
better to make them march for a while so that they could get
used to the rigors of life in the jungle and the mountains, and
to climbing up steep mountainsides. It was thus decided to
head due east after elementary practical guerrilla warfare
classes, and to march as far as possible while seeking the
chance to surprise a group of Guards.**

The eighty-man column spent the end of March and all of April marching and training. Che joined up with Crespo and Fajardo, who had formed a
food collective. He protested that they both favored carrying reserves in their
backpacks, while he preferred to gorge now and go hungry later, rather than
carry anything. It doesn't suit me to join in with you two because I eat
a lot, even if I don't eat every day. Then he would say, always arguing: It's
better to die on a full belly than an empty one. But Crespo remembered
that in spite of his words, he shared everything; if he had so much as a piece
of "candy, he would break it into three with a stone."

Experience was having its effect on the marchers. Veterans were
showing the new recruits how to cook and get the most out of their

food, how to pack a backpack and how to travel on foot in the Sierra.

It was at that time the rebels began to let their beards and hair grow, maybe as a way of telling veterans apart from novices. Country boy Crespo was the first to stop cutting his hair. Fidel cut his hair, but let his beard grow; Che did the same, didn't quite sprout a beard. The rebels with their bushy beards began to become a legend in the Sierra; while General Batista's government denied their existence, they were forging closer relations with the campesinos. At just that time, the government even flew some journalists several thousand feet up in an air force plane, to show them there was no one in the Sierra Maestra. It was a pointless exercise, which did not convince anyone.

As a means of breaking through the smoke screen of disinformation, the July 26 Movement organized another interview with a U.S. journalist. So Haydée Santamaría and Celia Sánchez climbed up the Sierra on April 23 with CBS's Robert Taber and a cameraman. The high point of the interview took place at the peak called Pico Turquino (whose ascent was an almost mystical operation), the loftiest and most inaccessible spot in the Sierra Maestra. The photograph of the guerrillas shouting "Long live Cuba!" with their rifles held aloft, which would symbolize the Cuban revolution for years, was taken just then.

Che was in a good mood at that time: he had finally obtained a canvas hammock.

> The hammock is a cherished possession, one I hadn't succeeded in getting sooner because of the guerrilla law that canvas ones be given only to those who have already made hammocks from sacks. This was to combat laziness. Everyone could make a sackcloth hammock, and once you had you were eligible to get the next canvas one that came along. Because of my allergies I couldn't use a burlap hammock—the fluff was a real problem—and I had to sleep on the ground. As I didn't have a burlap hammock, I wasn't due to get a canvas one. These little day-to-day details were all part of the discomforts of guerrilla life, and to which each gets used to. But Fidel noticed and revoked the order so I could have a hammock.

When they descended Pico Turquino, Che's asthma attacks became worse; he was in a bad way and therefore marching at the tail of the column, so his Thompson submachine gun was taken from him. It took them about three days to give it back to me and they were among the bitterest days I spent in the Sierra, disarmed as I was, when we could have run into the Guards at any time.

They were still developing their relations with the campesinos.

> I had to fulfill my duties as a medic in those days at every place we came to. It was pretty monotonous, since we had lit-

tle medicine to offer and there was not much variety in the cases arising in the Sierra; the tell-tale signs of poverty were women prematurely aged and toothless, children with bloated bellies, infested with parasites, suffering from rickets and general vitamin deficiency.

I remember a little girl watching the consultations I was giving to the women of the area, who came in an almost religious frame of mind to discover the cause of their suffering. When it was her mother's turn, this little girl, having watched all the other consultations in the hut I was using, whispered in her mother's ear: "Mama, this doctor has the same story for everybody."

The guerrillas and the campesinos were blending into a whole, without anyone knowing at what stage of the long march it happened, or when what was proclaimed became true, when we became as one with the campesinos. I only know, as far as I am concerned, that those consultations with the country folk in the Sierra turned the decisions we just jumped to into something more solidly based and thoughtful. Those long-suffering and loyal inhabitants of the Sierra Maestra never suspected the role they were playing as forgers of our revolutionary ideology.

Coming and going along the highways and byways of the Sierra Maestra, Dr. Guevara got lost. He spent three days wandering around in the brush until a campesino showed him the way to the campsite. I was greatly moved by the warm reception I got when I met up with the column again.

Now that May had begun, there were marches up and down the eastern part of the Sierra Maestra: the guerrillas were looking for an arms shipment that was due to arrive at Santiago. Reports on the shipment were contradictory, and it was very important because the column's ranks had been swollen by young campesinos. One of the advance guard went off in search of a contact in one of the expeditions; he was captured by soldiers from the Pino del Agua garrison and murdered.

The arms existed, but the rebels' sources of information were faulty; rumors took the place of news. Had the weapons fallen into the army's hands? During the wait, another American journalist, Andrew St. George, turned up. Che dealt with him, as nobody in the group spoke English and the two could at least communicate in French. While St. George was there, the Taber interview was broadcast on U.S. television. The news cheered up everyone except Andrew St. George, whose poor little journalist's heart was broken. The day after hearing the news he sailed off in his yacht from the Babún area to Santiago de Cuba.

Word of the Taber broadcast wasn't the only important piece of news to reach the rebels. At the trial of captured *Granma* expedition members, one judge voiced his disagreement with the government by voting against the sentence imposed on them. The man in question, Judge Manuel Urrutia, was risking his life in doing so.

While waiting for news about the arms, the rebels spent their time fighting mosquitoes, learning how to survive in the appalling, unhygienic conditions of the Sierra, and slowly spreading their influence and enlarging their network of collaborators. Those were times when

> **our sense of smell was perfectly in tune with that lifestyle. We could tell the guerrillas' hammocks apart by their smell. Our worst enemy was the "macaguera," a type of horsefly that . . . would sting you in uncovered places. If we scratched the stings, they easily became infected because we were so dirty.**

The arrival of the arms was confirmed on May 18. When they were picked up,

> **it was the most amazing sight. There, on display before the fighters' beady eyes, were the instruments of death. Three mounted machine guns, three Madsen machine guns, nine M1 rifles, ten Johnson automatic rifles, and six thousand rounds of ammunition. Although the M1 rifles only had 45 rounds each, they and the other arms were handed out along with the rest, according to each fighter's merits and his time in the Sierra.** [Che was given one of the Madsens.] **I still remember taking delivery of that machine gun, crappy as it was.**

The guerrillas now numbered over 150, and they included some rather extraordinary characters. One was a likable young campesino, the "Cowboy Kid," the kind of youth of whom legends are made. His path would cross Che's again. There was a fifteen-year-old farm boy called Joel Iglesias. Joel's first impression on encountering the column was not heartening: "We saw a bunch of skinny people, pale and bearded, in very poor shape, who stank to high heaven." Fidel rejected him on the grounds that he was just a boy. But Joel, like so many other campesinos, had come to stay, and whereas other rejects went home, he hung around until Che intervened on his behalf by asking him:

Can you carry this sack?

The sack was full of heavy machine-gun ammunition. Joel lifted it and thereby assumed his role as adjutant.

On May 23, Fidel granted leave to those who had turned out to be least reliable, and the guerrillas' ranks were **reduced to 127 men, mostly armed, of whom about eighty were well armed.** The rest had the almost useless weapons.

On May 25, the group heard that revolutionaries commanded by Calixto Sánchez had landed from the yacht *Corinthia* in the Mayarí area. On the basis of this vague news, and unaware of what had really happened—nearly all of the group was captured—Fidel decided to begin the action they had delayed for two months. The *Granma* survivors were moved by the thought of a group of recently landed men fighting for their lives while being pursued by the army. They believed that action on their part could **draw some of the enemy's forces so those people could reach a place where they could regroup and begin to fight.**

The decision led to an argument between Che, who proposed an immediate ambush of an army truck entering the Sierra, and Fidel, who felt they had to launch a full-blown attack on a barracks. That, Fidel argued, would be incontrovertible proof of the guerrillas' presence:

> **it would come as a huge psychological blow and be known across the country. That would not happen after an attack on a truck. In that case the army could just say that some men were killed and wounded in a road accident and, although people would suspect the truth, they would never know of our effective presence as a combat force in the Sierra.** [Fidel made his decision,] **but I was not convinced.**

Years later, though, Che acknowledged that Fidel was right and would say, to excuse himself, that **at that time, everyone was itching so much for a fight that we were ready to adopt the most drastic attitudes without being patient or, probably, being able to take the long view.**

13.   Scratching the Dirt

Che Guevara and Camilo Cienfuegos in the Sierra Maestra

A CAMPESINO WOMAN WHOM CHE CALLED AUNT CHANA TELLS IT AS SHE saw it: "Fidel and Che would set to drawing plans, scratching the dirt with a stick. They seemed to be thinking about building hospitals, building schools, building highways, because they would leave a whole load of lines in the dirt." This postrevolutionary version of events is a pretty one, but probably does not quite coincide with reality. The lines scratched in the dirt were a schematic layout of how Batista's troops were deployed in the barracks at El Uvero.

Fidel ordered the eighty well-armed members of the column to move off on May 27; it took them eight hours of marching by night to cover the ten miles between their temporary campsite and the approaches to the barracks, because they were taking very strict **precautions.**

The lines traced by Che and Fidel's twigs showed the sentry posts and the main quarters at the sawmill. The latter were not to be fired on, **as there were women and children there, including the manager's wife. She knew about the attack but did not want to leave as that might arouse suspicion. The civilian population was our main concern as we went to take up our battle stations.**

Fidel was at the top of a hill overlooking the barracks, with Raúl Castro's platoon opposite him. Che had been asked to cover a gap beside Camilo's platoon with his machine gun. He was accompanied by two new recruits who had been appointed orderlies. One, Oñate, had been honored with the nickname "Cantinflas." Joel Iglesias, the other, later said that "Neither Cantinflas nor I had the faintest idea of what combat was, and neither of us had so much as seen a war movie."

The various platoons had trouble getting to their stations—which was crucial, as Fidel's plan called for small details of guerrillas to be strategically deployed around the barracks. But daylight was running out, so Fidel fired the first shot at 5:15 P.M. **When Fidel opened fire with his telescopic sights, we could tell where the barracks was by the gunfire that responded within seconds.** The squads began to advance.

> **Almeida went from his sector toward the post charged with defending the entrance to the barracks; on my left I could see Camilo's cap with a cloth hanging down from it over his neck, like a Foreign Legion képi, but with the Movement's insignia. We advanced in the midst of widespread gunfire.**

Even Celia Sánchez was taking part, with an M1. Che's squad was joined by a compañero named Manuel Acuña. **The defenders put up a hard fight, and we had reached the flat open stretch, where we had to advance with infinite care, as the enemy fire was constant and on target.**

But Che did not slow down. Acuña commented: "We continued to advance on the barracks, firing all the while . . . but they did, too. You could feel the bullets, *ping, ping, ping,* as they whistled around your head and when they hit something, a stick or a rock, the sound was *tac, tac* . . . and there we were, advancing with Che."

Almeida saw Che shoot his way forward, "defying the gunfire, in a rush of bravery . . . and after him came munitions carriers Joel and Oñate and then Manuel Acuña, who seemed to be spurring Che on with his rifle: 'Come on, Che, you can do it!' "

> From my position, just fifty or sixty meters from the enemy outposts, I saw two soldiers running out from the trenches in front. I fired at both of them, but they took cover in the main quarters, which were out of bounds to us. We kept advancing although there was only a small stretch left, without so much as a blade of grass for cover, and the bullets were whistling dangerously close to us. Just then I heard a moan nearby and some shouts in the fray and thought it was some enemy soldier wounded and crawling. I asked him to surrender. It turned out to be a comrade, Mario Leal, Manuel Acuña's nephew. He had a head wound. I briefly inspected the wound, with entry and exit in the parietal bone. Leal was passing out as paralysis crept up his limbs on one side, I cannot remember which. The only bandage I had to hand was a scrap of paper. I placed it over his wounds.
>
> The comrades told afterward of how Eligio Mendoza, a scout, grabbed his gun and threw himself into combat. A superstitious man, he had a "saint" that protected him, and when they told him to take care, he answered disparagingly that his saint defended him from everything. He fell a few minutes later, when a bullet hit him in the chest and smashed his trunk. The well-entrenched enemy troops pushed us back, with several resulting casualties; it was difficult to advance through the central sector. In the sector by the Peladero road, Jorge Sotús tried to go around behind the enemy's position with an orderly called the Policeman, but the latter was instantly killed. Sotús had to dive into the sea to avoid certain death, and in any practical sense was out of action from that moment on. Other members of his platoon tried to advance, but were likewise beaten back. A campesino comrade, Vega by name, I think, was killed. Manals was wounded in one lung. Trying to advance, Quike Escalona ended up with three wounds—in his arm, buttocks, and hand. The post was entrenched behind a strong wall of tree trunks and was making mincemeat of our men with machine-gun and semi-automatic fire.

Fidel then ordered Juan Almeida and his squad to make an all-out attack; he knew that, as Sergio Pérez said, "apart from the blow to our morale, if we didn't take the barracks we would have no ammunition left for our guns." Almeida got up with a shout and advanced; shortly, four of his squad were wounded and Almeida himself had been hit by two bullets. He had been told so many times over the previous days that he would get himself killed if he kept fighting so recklessly, the rebels gave him up for dead. Then he reacted. Before entering his shoulder, one of the bullets had ricocheted off a pocket in which he was carrying a tin of milk and a spoon. Guillermo García: "Almeida took hold of the tin and began to drink bloodstained milk."

On hearing shouts that Almeida was wounded, Che stood up and moved forward, firing constantly and shouting, over and over: We've got to win! Little Joel followed him with the ammunition. Acuña was wounded.

> This push overpowered the post and opened the way to the barracks. On the other flank, well-aimed fire from Guillermo García's machine gun had liquidated three of the defenders. The fourth ran out, and was killed as he did so. Raúl, with his platoon split into two, made a swift advance on the barracks. It was the action by Captains Guillermo García and Almeida that decided matters. Each liquidated his assigned sentry and prepared the way for the final assault. [As usual, Che played down his own part in the combat.]

Headquarters received news that Che was wounded. Acuña, the old man, said that he would go after Che, even though he himself had taken two bullets, but the information was false.

> On my left, some comrades in the advance guard . . . were taking prisoner several soldiers who had made a last stand. From the stockade in front of us, a soldier came out signaling that he would surrender his weapon. Shouts of surrender began to ring out all around us. We quickly advanced on the barracks, when we heard a final burst of machine-gun fire which, I later heard, took the life of Lieutenant Nano Díaz.

There were fourteen dead soldiers in the barracks, and also

> several parrots that the guards kept in the barracks were killed. You just have to think of the size of these tiny little creatures to have an idea of all the bullets that had hit the wooden building.
>
> I have told the whole story in a few minutes, but the battle lasted approximately two hours and forty-five minutes, from the first shot to when we took the barracks.

On entering the barracks, the rebels began to take charge of the wounded. The medic in Batista's ranks, an aged, gray-haired man, was so nervous he did not know what to do.

> My knowledge of medicine was never too great, the number of wounded coming in was enormous, and I had no urge to de-

vote myself to healing at that time. But when I went to hand over the wounded to the medical officer, he asked me how old I was and, just like that, when I had qualified. I told him, "Some years ago," and he answered, very frankly: "Look, kid, you take charge of this, because I've only just qualified and have very little experience." What with his lack of experience and his natural fear of the situation, the man had forgotten every last thing he knew about medicine. So I had to swap my gun for a medic's uniform—an act that, as it happened, consisted of just washing my hands.

Fidel remarked years later: "While we were treating their wounded and releasing sixteen prisoners, they were murdering the *Corinthia* expeditionaries in cold blood."

The rebels had sustained fifteen wounded.

In Batista's ranks, [there were] nineteen wounded, fourteen dead, another fourteen prisoners, and six escaped. If you consider that there were eighty fighters on our side and fifty-three on theirs, that made approximately 133 in all; of those, thirty-eight, or more than a quarter, were put out of action in just over two and a half hours of fighting. It was an assault by men who advanced bare-chested against others who were defending themselves in an almost unprotected place. It should be acknowledged that there were displays of courage on both sides.

Che found a second to congratulate his young assistant: You've done well; you've earned your olive green uniform. Joel Iglesias was about to walk out—they were just going to give him a *uniform* when what he wanted was a gun! And, naturally, Che also spared a moment to say good-bye to a guerrilla named Cilleros, who was gravely wounded and had to be left behind.

I was only able to give him some tranquilizers and bind his chest up tight so that he could breathe more easily. We tried to save him in the only way possible back then, by taking fourteen prisoners with us while leaving our two wounded, Leal and Cilleros, in enemy hands and with the word of honor of the medic there. When I told Cilleros this, with the regulation words of comfort, he greeted me with a wry smile that said more than mere words could at a time like that; it very well expressed his conviction that he was done for. We knew that, too, and I was tempted to kiss him on the forehead; but my doing that, more than anyone else's would have been a sign that our comrade's condition was hopeless. Duty told me I was bound not to ruin his final moments by confirming something about which he was almost absolutely certain.

That day, the column climbed up the Sierra once again to bury their dead. In the brief ceremony, Fidel pointed out that difficult days were looming. The army would certainly send its forces after the guerrillas. While the main corps, under Fidel's command, would try to go as far from the area as possible, Che would stay behind in charge of a small column with the wounded. In the morning, we saw the conquering troops off; they took their leave of us sadly. My assistants, Joel Iglesias and Oñate, stayed behind with me, along with a scout called Sinecio Torres, and [Juan Vitalio] Vilo Acuña, who stayed to accompany his wounded uncle [Manuel. Also remaining were seven others who had been wounded, four of them seriously].

Strangely enough, the July 26 Movement's urban networks had planned an uprising in Camagüey for the very same day as the guerrilla attack on the sawmill. May 28. They hit the naval base to get arms and then headed for the Escambray massif, in the center of the island. There was also an uprising in Havana. The first operation was a failure—the M26 was betrayed and thirty-five men were captured and tortured—but the Havana action was a success. At two A.M. a powerful bomb blast blacked out a broad swath of Havana.

Meanwhile, aircraft flew over the part of the Sierra where the two guerrilla columns were separating. With the help of two workers from the sawmill, Che and his group managed to reach an abandoned hut four kilometers away. After resting for a day, **eating plenty and disposing of a good number of chickens,** they were forced to leave in a rush because there were rumors the army was near. Almeida, who had two serious wounds, complained bitterly that Che's soup must have been very tasty but that what with the hurry he could not swear to it.

> **With the few men at our disposal, we began a short but very difficult march, which consisted in going down to the so-called Del Indio Brook and climbing up a narrow trail to where a campesino called Israel lived with his wife and brother-in-law. We had real trouble moving the comrades in such steep country** [with three of them in hammocks], **but we did it.**

In order to transport the wounded, they were forced to set down their faulty weapons and their baggage. Che, having by now learned from experience, went over the trail backward, wiping out tracks and picking up weapons, even if they did not work. He had no wish to be crucified again by Fidel.

The most prudent course of action was to mobilize as soon as possible. The small group left the hut and headed for the bush—just in time, as the army captured the family that had given them shelter and started combing the area. The arrival of three new volunteers would at least make future movements easier. The wandering group saw the signs of a major army mobilization; there were frequent overflights, and there was news of troop landings and rumors that military columns were heading for the Sierra.

The marches were tiring and incredibly short. The wounded had to be moved one by one, as they had to be carried in hammocks hung from thick tree boughs, which literally destroyed the porters' shoulders; they have to change over every ten or fifteen minutes, so you need six to eight men to carry one wounded man in these conditions.

One very rainy morning, some very exhausted men turned up at the home of young Ramón "Guile" Pardo. This was the safe house Che had been expecting to reach; several guerrillas would take shelter in it over the months to come.

Che made a very valuable contact in that zone on June 3. He met David, the foreman at a nearby plantation. As so often, the meeting was symbolic. Che was eating a lemon, peel and all, and David offered him food—cheese, butter, and crackers. Che replied that he would take it to share with the wounded. The relationship flourished, and David moved from acting as quartermaster for the new guerrilla cell to liaison officer with Santiago, where he would later be arrested and tortured barbarously. His main concern after reappearing was to assure us that he had not talked.

The group kept a cautious vigil in the Pardo house for almost a month, with hardly any contact with the outside world, while the wounded gathered strength. Sometimes rumors found their way to them—for example, they heard that Celia Sánchez had been arrested or killed, which would have been a tragedy for the guerrillas, cutting them off from the urban network. The army, meanwhile, tried to empty that isolated area with evictions and bombings, while Che was setting up a campesino network of liaisons and friendship.

Despite his usual habits of hygiene, Che used to go down to the banks of the Peladero River close to the house to bathe in a pool of clear water. His asthma had returned and become worse, since there was no medicine. It forced him to be as immobile as the wounded; I managed to stave off the effects of the illness by smoking the leaves of an herb, which is the folk remedy in the Sierra.

Aunt Chana described Che during an asthma attack:

> He stayed calm when his asthma came on, taking shallow breaths so as not to intensify it. There are people who get hysterical with an attack, who cough and open their eyes, their mouths, but Che tried to contain it, to tame it. He would flop down in a corner, sit on a stool or a stone, and let it be. . . . Oh Lord, it was a shame to see such a strong, handsome man that way . . . but he didn't like pity. If you said, "Poor thing," he would dart you a quick glance that said nothing and meant very much.

The group's ranks kept on growing with young campesinos joining up, despite Che's intention to keep the number to a minimum as long as they had no more weapons. No fewer than forty people passed through the column, but desertions were continuous too; some left with our blessing, others against our will. The column never numbered more than twenty-five to thirty men. There were twenty-six when they decided to move on, when the wounded had recovered, the partly useless weapons had been repaired, and medicine for asthma had been obtained through the network.

While they were on the march,

> on June 16, I made my début as a dentist, although I was conferred the more modest title of "Tooth-Puller" in the Sierra. My first victim was Israel Pardo, who stood up to it well. Nothing short of dynamite would have pulled the tooth of my second patient, Joel Iglesias. He still had it at the end of the war; my efforts had been to no avail. My lack of expertise was compounded by a lack of pills, so we had to spare the drugs and use a lot of "psychological anesthetic."

Joel: "He would shout insults at me by way of treatment. I knew it was the first time he had pulled teeth, and I have been terrified of dentists ever since."

While his patients—among them a Haitian campesino who was one of his first victims—may not have appreciated his efforts, Che would come to like the tooth-pulling business. For years, while he shunned medical commitments, he took to dentistry with such gusto that a legend grew up around him, about his glee whenever he learned that someone in his vicinity had a toothache.

There were new recruits and more desertions on the march.

> The radio spoke of violence all over the island. On July 1 we got news of the death of Josué País, Frank's brother, along with other comrades, during a running battle under way in Santiago. Although our hikes were short ones, our troops were feeling worn out; some of the new recruits requested leave to "accomplish more useful missions in town."

It was while moving in search of the main column, in the La Mesa area, that Che met a campesino who would become crucial to the guerrillas' future relations with the locals. Polo Torres, whom Che nicknamed "Captain Barefoot," was a man of medium height, wearing a hat that almost covered his very green eyes; he always went without boots or shoes.

Polo greeted the guerrillas with a pork stew that was too much for the hungry rebels: Polo, this is sabotage. We'll all either puke or have the galloping shits.

While skirting El Turquino and avoiding the troops in the area, Che lost an important ally: the guide Sinecio, whose morale had been weakening.

> It was very difficult to keep up the troops' morale, with no weapons, no direct contact with the leader of the revolution, practically groping our way along, with no experience and surrounded by enemies who loomed large in the minds and

**stories of the country folk. The lack of enthusiasm among the
new recruits, who came from the plains and were not used to
the thousand and one difficulties of the Sierra trails, made for
a continuing crisis in the guerrillas' spirits.**

On June 16, contact was made, first with patrols from Fidel's column, and
then with the leader of the revolution himself. Che introduced his column as
follows:

They're my troops.

In Crespo's words: "What he had with him was a ragtag bunch, some with
shotguns, some with machetes, buckets or tins."

As well as meeting up with old comrades, Che was truly delighted to receive a new recruit, a Dr. Julio Martínez Páez, whom he immediately gave a
"little gift," his box of medical instruments. **As of today, I have left medicine behind to be a guerrilla fighter.**

In Che's absence, Fidel had been working in the Sierra in collaboration
with two liberal opposition figures, Felipe Pazos and Raúl Chibás. The three
drew up a political program that propounded a civilian revolutionary front, rel-
egating the army to the sidelines of public life and rejecting any mediation by
the United States; also called for were, of course, the immediate release of political prisoners, freedom of information, the restoration of suppressed con-
stitutional rights, municipal elections, a fight against corruption,
democratization of the unions, and a literacy campaign. There was also a timid
proposal for agrarian reform based on unused land and compensation for
plantation owners. The writers of the document insisted on naming a provisional president. Fidel had offered the post to Chibás, but he refused. The
document, dated July 12, was made public and opened the door to broader-
based negotiations abroad.

Che was very critical of the document's limited scope; later papers show
him to have been deeply suspicious of it. He even accused Pazos and Chibás
of using the agreement as the first step toward betraying the armed struggle.
Indeed, the document did mean a step back from the the July 26 Movement's
most radical proposals.

> *We weren't satisfied with the agreement, but it was necessary; it
> was progressive at that time [and] we also knew that it was im-
> possible to impose our will from the Sierra and that we had to rely
> for a long while on all sorts of "friends."*

Just what were the political aims, the plans for the country, being discussed in the Sierra back then? What were Fidel's goals? What were Che's?
Probably they had only vague ideas about the need for radical agrarian reform,
the desire for extensive social change—socialist strands of thought half worked
out in Che's head. Maybe the only thing the men in the Sierra clearly understood was that they had to end Batista's dictatorship in the only possible way,
militarily.

The flag of the July 26 Movement in the Hombrito Heights, where Che had his encampment at the end of 1957. The rebels flew the flag to provoke Batista's air force.

O N July 5, Fidel Castro wrote to Celia Sánchez: "Our troops are becoming more select and effective by the day. By recruiting, by disciplining, and by throwing out what is of no use, we are building a real army." This was doubtless the reasoning behind the decision to form a new column. Who would lead it? Fidel must have taken Juan Almeida's military prowess into account, or Raúl Castro's seriousness, but ended up plumping for Che. Why? Che had not been notable as a military man in the guerrillas' first months. Although a daring fighter, he was not Cuban; he had been a medic until very recently; and his rank was that of an ordinary soldier. What did Fidel see in Che? Was it that his rigor, his drive, his determination to do the impossible and his egalitarian stance made him an example, or had he demonstrated his leadership ability in a difficult situation when left alone with the wounded? Whatever the reason, Fidel, whose intuition was usually on target in military matters, was on target again.

The column, in a childish attempt at disguise, was to have the number 4. Che's squad was to be assigned three captains with their platoons: Ramiro Valdés, Ciro Redondo, and Lalo Sardiñas.

> This column, which they called the "campesino eviction column," was made up of seventy-five men dressed and armed any old how, but I felt proud of them nonetheless. I was to feel much more proud, much more linked to the revolution, if that were possible, and more willing to show I deserved the stripes I had been given, several nights later.

On the night in question, he and Fidel were signing a joint letter to Frank País; Fidel told Che to "just put 'Commander' " as his rank.

> **That was how, almost in passing, I was named commander of the guerrilla army's No. 2 Column. . . . The share of vanity we all have in us made me the proudest man on earth that day. The mark of my rank, a little star, was given to me by Celia, along with one of the wristwatches that had been handed over in Manzanillo.**

The column's weaponry seemed to consist of museum pieces, mostly shotguns, but there were also Colts, Remington rifles meant for target practice, bolt-action Winchesters of the kind used by cowboys in the North American Wild West, blunderbusses, .22-caliber rifles, Savages, and Springfields and Garands that had been captured from the enemy.

Che's area of operations was set up to the east of El Turquino, near the El Hombrito zone; he was to have some independence of command, but to communicate with Fidel's column by messenger. One of his first steps was to name Arístides Guerra as the column's quartermaster. Guerra's cover had been blown on the Plains and he wanted to fight, but Che persuaded him that setting up a supply network was a tougher and more difficult task.

While the column was heading east, toward the most inaccessible hills in the Sierra Maestra, one of the men deserted. The one sent after him tried to run off, too; *his* comrade shot and killed him after vainly ordering him to halt.

> I gathered all the men together on the hill at the scene of these macabre events, telling them what they were about to see and what it meant, the reason why desertion was punishable by death and the reason for carrying out a death sentence against all who betrayed the Revolution. We went by, Indian file, in strict silence, with many comrades still stunned at their first sight of death and of the body of the man who had tried to abandon his post. Maybe they were moved more by personal feelings toward the deserter, and by a political weakness natural at that stage, than by lack of loyalty to the revolution.

Frank País was murdered in Santiago on July 30, at the end of a week in which the tightening police cordon had forced him to move from house to house three times. Frank had been captured by Colonel José Salas Cañizares, the notoriously brutal police chief, in a roundup; recognized by a policeman who had been at school with him, he was taken into an alley and killed. Che did not hear the news until some days after the event, when a spontaneous strike was under way in Santiago. In Frank País, we lost one of our bravest fighters, but the reaction to his murder showed that new forces were joining in the struggle and that the people's fighting mood was on the rise. It also showed how much influence the July 26 Movement had earned in the cities, particularly in Santiago.

At exactly that time, Che's column saw its first combat, during a raid on the barracks at Bueycito. The column was backed up by an M26 cell in El Dorado; a rolling attack was planned. But things did not turn out as intended. A car braked in front of the barracks and lit it up, giving the agreed-upon attack signal, but then Ramiro lost part of his platoon in the dark, the car could not get away, and the dogs barked like crazy. Che advanced toward the town center.

> [On] the main street, I came across a man and gave him the "Halt! Who goes there?" Thinking I was a comrade, the man identified himself: "Rural Guards." When I made to aim at him, he leaped into the house and slammed the door; inside I could hear tables and chairs being turned over and glass broken, while someone jumped out the back silently. There was almost a tacit agreement between the Guard and me, since it was not worth my firing. Neither did he shout any warning to his comrades. The main thing was to take the barracks.
>
> We kept advancing . . . the barracks sentry moved forward, alarmed by the number of dogs barking and probably by the noise of my encounter with the soldier. We bumped into each other, just yards apart. I had the Thompson ready, he a Garand. I had Israel Pardo with me. I yelled "Halt!" and the man with the upraised Garand made a move. That was enough

for me, and I squeezed the trigger with every intention of filling him with a clip-load of bullets. But the first shot misfired and I was defenseless. Israel Pardo tried to fire, but his faulty little .22 rifle didn't work, either. I don't really know how Israel escaped with his life; I can only remember for myself that, in a rain of bullets from the soldier's Garand, I ran with never-to-be-repeated speed, vaulted around the corner, and dived into a side street, where I fixed the machine gun. The soldier, however, had unwittingly given the signal for our attack. He huddled behind a pillar when he heard shots all around him, and that is where we found him when the combat, which only lasted a few minutes, was over.

When the first shots were fired, Ramiro Valdés and his platoon swooped on the rear side of the barracks and cleared it. Of the twelve guards, six were wounded, while the rebels had one dead. The column left the town after burning the barracks down, and were given cold drinks and beer by the townspeople as they went.

Up above California, the arms were handed out. Even though my participation was minimal and not at all heroic, since I'd faced the few shots there were with my backside, I bagged a Browning machine gun, the barracks' prize possession, and dumped the old Thompson and its dangerous bullets that never fired when called for.

The Argentine journalist Rodolfo Walsh remarked of Che's account years later: "As far as I recall, no [other] army chief, general, or hero has admitted to running on two occasions." (The first had been when the rebels were surprised at Altos de la Espinosa.)

The Bueycito attack took place shortly after a guerrilla action by Fidel at the Estrada Palma road, during the Santiago strike, and in the midst of widespread challenges to the dictatorship. Three revolutions were taking place in Cuba at that time: one in Santiago, which affected the vast majority of the middle classes and even members of the economic aristocracy; a young and very radical one in Havana; and the beginnings of a campesino war against the dictatorship in the Sierra Maestra. This last was acting as a flashpoint and stimulus for the other two. The masterstroke performed by Fidel and Frank País had been to make the three coincide and be self-sufficient.

Che was a key player in the campesino war, but what was his image? According to Ricardo Martínez, a young radio commentator who went up to the Sierra Maestra at that time with a group of colleagues, "Broadcasts by government radio and the right-wing press accused Che of being an international Communist, a professional hit man, who cruelly killed the prisoners he took from the Batista forces. They repeated over and over again."

The reporter's first impression of the rebel leader shows that the newsman was somewhat naive:

It was nighttime; he was leaning on a hut, by the light of a candle or lamp, with his hair tousled and sweaty, his face greasy, with his very special stare, his features accentuated by the contrast of light and shadow. I didn't doubt for one moment that he was everything the propaganda said he was. He gave us roast tidbits to eat, but even that could not wipe the image away.

Martínez's group was not the only one to join the newborn column. On August 3, thirty-four men climbed up to El Hombrito, including two teenagers whose future would be linked with Che's: the Acevedo brothers, then fourteen and sixteen years old. As the group had no arms, only twelve of the volunteers were accepted; the Acevedo brothers were left out. They made "such a fuss" that Che approached them and asked if they were students. He gave Rogelio an algebra test, the results of which were not impressive. The fourteen-year-old Enrique told him that history and geography were okay, but otherwise . . . Che laughed, but did not accept them. They stubbornly tagged along as the column marched, and would have died rather than be rejected. They finally managed to join up, thanks to Ciro Redondo's intervention. Che was becoming surrounded by teenagers. Leonardo Tamayo, a fifteen-year-old campesino whose father had previously joined elsewhere, had the following exchange with him:

What have you come here for?

"To do the same as you."

It seemed as good an argument as any to Che. He used Leonardo as a messenger several days later and discovered that the little Tamayo could fly over the hills, accomplishing in one day what others did in two. From that moment on he was part of Che's entourage.

There were others, like Oniria Gutiérrez, the first woman to be accepted into the column. She was a seventeen-year-old campesina, whom Che treated like a daughter, giving her his blanket. Sixteen-year-old Harry Villegas came with a group of men armed with shotguns. Che: You think you can fight a war with those guns?

Then there was Guile, the youngest of the Pardo brothers, who had joined up at the beginning of 1957 and in whose house Che holed up at the time of the war of the wandering wounded. And René Pacheco, a young seminarian from an orthodox religious background, who had been brutally tortured at the Bayamo barracks. And Alberto Castellanos, a streetwise young man from the shantytown at Victoria de las Tunas who'd worked as a shoeshine boy, drugstore assistant, and newspaper seller. Alberto was sent back because he was unarmed, but would return some months later to join up.

What did Che see in all those teenagers? Where others just saw illiteracy, lack of military experience, and immaturity, what did he see? Doubtless he saw tenacity, a reflection of his own stubbornness, and a fireproof will. And he was to treat them accordingly, with the same rigor with which he treated himself.

Over the following months, the deeds of these youths and others would become the stuff of legend.

And what did these young people see in Che? Castellanos's description is precise:

> I had imagined him to be a huge, tall, stocky man. I was used to hearing Argentines spoken of as tango singers wearing scarves, with that Buenos Aires way of talking, and I thought that was the way he had to be. I imagined him as an actor in Argentine films. But he made no special impression on me when I did see him; in fact, I was rather disappointed. He was a skinny, ordinary guy like any of us, and I exclaimed: "So this is Che?"

After the first military engagement, Che headed for a zone through which he had passed before, the **valley called El Hombrito** —Little Man—**with the two enormous boulders that gave it its name.** He would spend time there training the recruits, and also fighting illiteracy, as only four or five out of the whole column could read. To Joel, his assistant, he said: **I spoke to Fidel about you, and he asked me why I didn't make you a lieutenant, but I answered that as you couldn't read or write, I couldn't appoint you.** To encourage Joel, he appointed the boy chief of his noncommissioned squad and ordered him to look for a notebook and pencil, and he began tutoring him at night by lamplight.

With Pacheco, instead of playing the role of teacher, Che became a student and spent his time learning Cuban history. Little by little, books by José Martí found their way up to the Sierra Maestra, as did volumes of poetry by José María de Heredia, Gertrudis de Avellanada, Gabriel de la Concepción, and Rubén Darío; these made a change from Emil Ludwig's biography of Goethe, which, according to a photograph, Che was reading at the time. The photo shows him lying under a blanket in his hut, holding the book, with an enormous cigar in his mouth.

He was also getting the group into shape. Some ran off during the bombings; when he caught them, he would really dress them down: **Those hotshots from the cities who are the first to shit themselves and take off when they hear the bombs are the ones who'll have to work hard.**

On August 29, Che got word that the army was climbing up to the El Hombrito area. He deployed two platoons along the possible routes, one to enter into combat, and the other—which had the worst weapons—to **open "acoustic" hostilities.**

> **As dawn broke, we began to see men moving, coming and going and milling around as they woke up. Shortly after, some put their helmets on. . . . We saw the head of the column come up, making their way with difficulty. The waiting seemed eternal during those moments, and my finger was itching to squeeze the trigger of my new weapon, the Browning machine gun, ready to enter action against the enemy for the first time.**

But the rebels' plan turned out not to be very realistic, as the soldiers appeared to be well spread out. When the sixth one went by I heard a shout up ahead and one of the soldiers raised his head in surprise. I opened fire immediately and that man fell. The firing spread right away and the six men vanished from the trail with the second burst of automatic fire.

The column they were facing, led by one Merob Sosa, had 205 men in its ranks and Che had just seventy-two, poorly armed ones at that. Even so, the army column scattered as soon as the shooting started. Castro Mercader's squad attacked, but the enemy column regrouped and began to fire on the rebel positions with bazookas. The fallen soldier was searched, but had only a revolver on him. The rebels' Maxim machine gun would not work, so this "acoustic section's" hostilities spread panic rather than causing casualties. In that state of affairs, Che was forced to give the order to retreat squad by squad and set up a second line of defense in the high mountain.

He was the last to withdraw, as he would be in all combats from then on. The arrival of a platoon of reinforcements sent by Fidel strengthened the guerrillas' position; in any case, the Guards did not advance but confined themselves to burning the body of a rebel killed in the skirmish and to exchanging shots from a distance.

> This engagement showed just how little combat readiness our troops had, with their inability to fire accurately on enemy soldiers moving such a short distance away. . . . Nonetheless, it was a great victory for us. We had stopped Merob Sosa's column in its tracks, and it withdrew at nightfall. . . . We had achieved all this with a handful of half-way effective weapons against a whole company of 140 men, at least, fully equipped for modern warfare, who had fired a good number of bazookas—and maybe mortars—on our positions. But they'd fired so randomly, every which way, just like the way our men fired on their advance guard.

The combat would have a sorry aftermath: Merob Sosa's troops murdered several campesinos and used their bodies as "proof" that rebels had been killed in combat.

On August 31, Che reported to Fidel on the success at Bueycito and the growth of his column to one hundred men. He also discussed who should replace Frank País in Santiago. He suggested someone who could combine the role of a good organizer with experience in the Sierra, so that he would not have an outsider's view of the guerrillas' problems. He proposed Raúl Castro, Almeida, Ramiro Valdés, or himself for the task: I do so without false modesty, but without the least desire to be picked. And, he added: I stress this point because I know the moral and intellectual stature of these puny leaders who will try to replace Frank.

Che's hostility toward city people was curious; although it is true that his experiences with them had been negative at times, his assessment arose from profound ignorance of the July 26 urban movement. In the end, René Ramos Latour, a radical nationalist and labor organizer who had done a stint in the guerrillas' ranks, was chosen to replace Frank País. The polemic between Che and "the Plains" was about to begin.

At that time, Che's and Fidel's columns were marching in parallel. They met and then split up again to take action against Pino del Agua. They knew there was a small garrison there, and Fidel meant to attack it, with Che lying in ambush as backup to deal with the defenders' reaction.

As they approached the garrison, there were some desertions; one man killed himself on being disarmed for insubordination. Che also tried to disencumber the guerrilla column of its least capable fighters; he held a meeting at which he announced that anyone who wanted to could leave. His manner was friendly when he told the teenaged Acevedo brothers to go: they could not stand the pace and were a danger to the column. On their last legs, still the brothers refused: "Over our dead bodies." Che became furious and was about to expel them, but Ciro Redondo intervened and they were granted another week.

On September 5, there was an uprising of sailors in the city of Cienfuegos. These men were involved in a conspiracy within the armed forces; they belonged to a group that later became known as "the true military" and were linked to the July 26 urban networks. The conspirators scored a first success by taking the city. Instead of withdrawing to the Escambray mountains along with the townspeople who had joined in, however, they stayed in the city, expecting their rebellion to spread. Instead they were hit by the full weight of the régime's forces. The waste of lives, fighters, and weapons was tragic, as was the lack of coordination and the sailors' inadequate grasp of guerrilla tactics. It was also evident, however, that the régime's defeat of the popular uprising had isolated it even more.

Che meanwhile entered San Pablo de Yao on September 8, **amid widespread jubilation in the town, which we took control of peacefully in a few hours (there were no enemy troops). And we began to make contacts.** Perhaps the most important of these was Lidia Doce, a forty-five-year-old woman of campesino origin who had gone to work as a servant in Havana after her divorce and then returned to the Sierra. She would be a key part of Che's networks.

On September 10, as planned, Fidel's column entered Pino del Agua and took the sawmill. Fidel suggested the route to be taken next. They began their march the day after, while Che's column lay in ambush for the army.

A tropical rainstorm began.

The enemy soldiers were far more concerned about the rain than the possibility of an attack, which gave us the advantage of surprise. The man in charge of opening fire had a Thompson machine gun, and he did begin to shoot, but he could hit

nobody under those conditions. General shooting broke out. The soldiers from the first truck, who were more shocked and surprised than wounded, jumped down to the road and ran behind an outcrop for cover.

The guerrillas' plan worked and the first three trucks fell into their trap. None got through, and the rest of the troops were routed. Resistance by those in the first few trucks was thwarted by Lalo Sardiñas and Efigenio Ameijeiras's platoons.

On taking the first truck we found two men dead and one wounded and still ready to fight although in his death throes; he was finished off without being given a chance to surrender, which he could not do as he was half-conscious. This act was committed by a fighter whose family had been wiped out by Batista's army. I severely reprimanded him, not realizing that there was a wounded soldier listening to me. He had covered himself with some blankets and was lying still at the back of the truck. When he heard all this and our comrade's apologies, the enemy soldier told us of his presence and asked us not to kill him. He had a gunshot wound in his leg, a fracture. He stayed by the roadside while the fight proceeded in the other trucks. Each time one of our fighters went past him, the man would shout, "Don't kill me! Che says don't shoot prisoners!"

The tally of enemy casualties was not substantial, but the guerrillas picked up crucial weaponry: **a Browning automatic rifle, five Garands, a machine gun and ammunition, and another Garand rifle were snatched up by Efigenio Ameijeiras's men.** The guerrillas celebrated by having hot chocolate for breakfast, while light aircraft, followed by B-26s, flew menacingly overhead.

Che regrouped in El Hombrito toward the end of September and from there sent occasional messages as a liaison with René Ramos Latour, who had taken charge of the underground network in Santiago and Manzanillo and the backup for the Sierra. Ramos Latour complained that Che was not cooperating and had tried to set up a competing network, without relying on theirs, and that he had written to everyone except the group he was supposed to be working with. On October 3, Ramos Latour wrote a detailed letter asking Che not to use contacts he just picked up without knowing whether they could be trusted or would abide by discipline as they weakened the organization and the movement's centralization efforts. The people Che had linked up with were not the best, he stressed: "Don't be trusting, don't give them any authority." It was better to link up with Santiago which, after all, was only twenty minutes from La Palma. Ramos Latour finished by saying, "We hope to get everything you need to you in short order. We are also working on setting up supply centers in the two zones you mention." He also explained the structure he was building up:

The contributions owing to you to meet expenses in the Sierra are coming in to us, in cash, from every town and province in the country. Until now, only Manzanillo and Bayamo had been ordered to set aside collections for meeting the needs of troops in nearby areas. All the rest send most of what they obtain to the Revolutionary Directory, which takes charge of meeting these needs.

Ramos Latour had good reason to try to better organize links between the Plains and the Sierra, but Che was not wrong, either, in organizing his own supply routes which reported directly to the guerrillas. Tension mounted as Che pressed forward with his effort to obtain autonomy for the guerrillas and began to set up another support network.

Around that time, Che met Rafael Mompié, a trusted guide from Fidel's column. They went hill-climbing together; on one of those climbs, Che took some books out of his backpack. On seeing the countryman's reaction, Che offered him a book; at this, Mompié admitted he could not read. Mompié recalled: "He stopped reading, marked the page with his forefinger, and stared at me for a while. He said nothing, and began to read again. I took that look as meaning that I had to learn. . . . That look stayed with me and marked me for life."

The following days were taken up with training and marches, interrupted when a deserter named Cuervo was captured. He had been plundering campesinos in the zone and had taken part in a gang rape. When the man arrived at the camp, he tried to shake Che's hand, but the latter curtly answered that he had summoned him to have him shot, not to greet him.

The distance between their two columns forced Fidel and Che to communicate in writing during those months, and they covered topics ranging from the loftiest strategic-political analysis and military proposals to the most surprising details, taking in every variety of the absurd on the way. An example is this note from Che to Fidel:

> Camilo says you gave him a pistol, but he didn't accept it, thinking that I had one (but you took it from me). He ended up with no pistol, but, at the same time, he had asked Chicho for one—Soto's—and when he changed columns, he did not give it back. Chicho ended up worse off. You work it all out.

Several days later, on the way to the Peladero River to link up with Fidel's column, the guerrillas collected revolutionary taxes in the form of a mule. He was immediately named after his former owner, Balanza. While the guerrillas were wondering whether to eat him or take him along, the mule won his spurs by

> making headway downhill in places where you had to slide down holding on to lianas or grabbing on to ledges as best as you could. . . . He gave a demonstration of extraordinary gymnastic gifts, followed by a repeat performance when we

crossed the Peladero River. In an area full of large stones, he made a series of breathtaking leaps between the rocks, and that saved his life.

Balanza became Che's mule.

But there was more going on than acrobatic mules. Tension had been in the air over the preceding months. Enrique Acevedo, who was forever condemned to the rear guard among the *descamisados,* the "shirtless ones" (Che's Argentine-sounding joke, reviving the name given to the Peronist masses in his youth), described things that were far from idyllic: "The column was a monastery compared to the Chinese whorehouse that was our platoon."

While Che was away from the column consulting with Fidel, Lalo Sardiñas punished a disorderly comrade on impulse and, while trying to hit him on the head with a pistol, accidentally fired it and killed him in the act. Enrique Acevedo recalled:

> All hell broke loose. Many who had been looking for an honorable way out of the guerrilla campaign took advantage of the situation; some were friends of the dead man and others were just onlookers. . . . Crazy Robert grabbed a rifle and flew at the captain—now under arrest—with the aim of killing him. Lieutenant Cañizares raised his voice and said he would leave the troops if justice was not done quickly.

We were on the verge of a mutiny. I immediately placed Lalo in custody. The comrades were very hostile toward me and were demanding summary justice and execution.

Physical punishment was forbidden among the guerrillas, and furthermore, many thought the killing had not been an accident. On the other hand, Sardiñas was a highly esteemed fighter. Finally, the dispute had all but destroyed discipline in the column. Fidel personally intervened, staging an open trial to hear people's opinions. Both he and Che were in favor of punishing Sardiñas, but certainly not of condemning him for murder, which would imply a death sentence and the firing squad. After a heated debate,

it was my turn to speak to ask people to think the matter over. I tried to explain that the comrade's death should be imputed to the conditions of the struggle, to the situation of the war itself, and that, most definitely, the dictator Batista was the guilty party. But my words did not sound very convincing before that hostile audience.

By the light of torches and in the dead of night, Fidel made his summing up. His enormous powers of persuasion were put to the test that night. The final vote was split: seventy-six favored some other form of punishment, and seventy wanted the death penalty. Lalo was saved. The decision, however, led one group to desert the guerrillas, and one Conte Aguero, relying on the confessions of Crazy Robert, made use of the story in the pages of *Bohemia* magazine to portray the guerrillas as a band of wicked delinquents. Lalo Sardiñas was demoted and sentenced to winning his stars back by fighting alone with a small patrol against the enemy. . . . To replace Captain Sardiñas, Fidel gave me one of his best fighters, Camilo Cienfuegos, who was promoted to captain of our advance guard.

Dariel Alarcón also came along with Che's friend Camilo.

Che's reduced ranks marched the next day to put down outbreaks of banditry that had occurred in other parts of the Sierra Maestra.

While on the march, Enrique Acevedo noted:

> There's something about Che that intrigues me. He has had a pet for several days now, a white mouse, which travels in his backpack. When we rest, he takes it out and puts it on his shoulder. It . . . climbs up to his beret and plays around. I'm struck dumb when I look at him. I take him for such a tough guy, and then he amazes me with such human touches. This makes me think I just see the inflexible chief in him. I'd like to get to know him a bit better one day.

Camilo, moving fast, had captured "Chinaman Chang" and his band, which had been laying waste to the Caracas region, murdering and torturing as they went. Along with Chang, a campesino who had raped a teenage girl was summarily tried and executed. Some of the band were acquitted and three others subjected to a dummy firing squad. When the three found they were still alive after the shots were fired over their heads, one of them gave me the strangest spontaneous demonstration of glee and acknowledgment—a loud kiss, as if I were his father.

The events were witnessed by the journalist Andrew St. George, who had returned to the Sierra and

> whose reports in Look magazine won him a prize in the United States for being the most sensational of the year. The deception we tried out for the first time in the Sierra may now seem barbaric, but no other punishment was possible for those men—we could spare their lives, but they had a range of serious crimes behind them. The three joined up in the rebel army and I had news of brilliant behavior from two of them during the whole insurrection. One belonged to my column for a long time and, in discussions among the soldiers that arose over war stories and doubting some of those that were being recounted, he would always say with marked emphasis, "Now I'm not scared to look death in the face, and Che is witness to that."

Two or three days later, Che's column detained another group, this one made up of former guerrilla fighters who had been stealing food arriving from the Plains

GUEVARA, ALSO KNOWN AS CHE

and, going down that road, had sunk so low as to commit murder. In those days in the Sierra, a man's economic status was basically measured in terms of how many women he had. Dionisio, in following that tradition and considering himself a potentate on account of the powers the revolution had conferred upon him, had set up three houses, in each of which he had a wife and abundant supplies. During his trial, Fidel indignantly accused him of betraying the revolution and denounced the immorality of supporting three wives with the people's money, he replied with campesino naiveté that there weren't three, but two, as one was his own (which was true). Two other spies sent by [the pro-Batista gangster and paramilitary leader Rolando] Masferrer were shot, after confessing and being sentenced.

A new case of banditry gave rise to a serious dilemma for Che. It involved a fighter called Echevarría, who had formed a small group that had been committing holdups in the area.

The Echevarría case was pathetic because, while he admitted his crimes, he did not want to dishonor his family by being shot by a firing squad. He implored us to let him die in the next combat; he swore that he would look for death that way instead. Echevarría, whom we called "Cross-eyes," wrote a long and moving letter to his mother after the tribunal condemned him to death: he explained the justice being done in the sentence about to be carried out on him, and exhorted her to be loyal to the revolution.

Also shot was Barrera, "El Maestro"—the same odd character who had accompanied Che in the difficult early days. He had later deserted the guerrillas and passed himself off as Che, Dr. Guevara, raping several campesino girls.

Che himself was not present when these men were captured and executed. He was in the heart of the Sierra, in the El Hombrito area, striving to create a stable base there. He encouraged the peasants to plant crops, organized the messengers to keep a closer watch on any army operations, set up new supply networks, and even built a bread oven, as well as setting up a field hospital.

Lidia Doce was active in this enterprise, as was a young campesino woman, Delsa Puebla, known as Teté. There was also María Mercedes Sánchez, an urban fighter who had taken part in an assassination attempt on a high-ranking military officer in Holguín and was known as Carmencita in the Sierra. She shared Che's liking for Neruda's poetry; he placed her in charge of literacy projects.

Argentine journalist Jorge Ricardo Masetti reported some months later:

The first schools in the Sierra were set up shortly after the arrival of the rebel army. The countryfolk had never been to a church: there weren't any in the mountains. They were illiterate, but very intelligent. They had never eaten bread, nor beef. They ate cookies occasionally, but never even suspected what bread was until Guevara's troops installed the first campesino bakeries. They saw the cows and knew their meat was delicious, but it was only after the rebels arrived and began to distribute the cattle and slaughter them that they tasted steak. And yet 90 percent of them had been born in the richest part of the very rich island of Cuba.

And while he was setting up the base, the arrival of two students, Geonel Rodríguez and Ricardo Medina, and a 1903 mimeograph machine, allowed Che to begin one of his most cherished projects: to publish a Sierra newspaper, *El Cubano Libre* ("The Free Cuban").

Che wrote to his contacts in the Plains:

> **The newspaper is entirely edited and copied onto stencils, but there's not enough ink to run it, and the lack of paper will limit us to 700 copies. It also suffers from a basic omission: there is no article signed by Fidel. Luis Orlando had agreed to take charge of making it look more like a newspaper. It is worth sending all the material along those lines that you can, as the newspaper could be very useful.**

A few days later the little newspaper appeared with a section written by Che and signed "The Sniper." He wrote to Fidel:

> **I hope that its poor quality will shock you into contributing something with your byline. The second issue's editorial will be about cane-burning. Noda wrote about agrarian reform in the current issue, Quiala about the reaction to crime, the doctor about real life for Cuban campesinos, Ramiro about the latest news; I explained the name, wrote the editorial and "off target." I assigned the stories. We urgently need news of all actions, crimes, promotions, etc., and regular communication so that we can set up a special press corps.**

But Che's happiness was overshadowed by news that an agreement had been signed in Miami, whereby the already feeble joint program against the dictatorship was to be watered down even more. Worse, the agreement would take leadership away from the July 26 Movement, instead giving prominence to traditional Cuban organizations that, although they may not have been allied with Batista's dictatorship, represented the old traditions of corruption and politicking.

The Miami Pact had been approved by the July 26 Movement's overseas delegation, headed by Felipe Pazos, and was signed on July 1. It led to bitter recriminations among the left wing of M26 on the Plains (Ramos Latour called the signatories "political hacks standing on our dead bodies") and in exile (Carlos Franqui in Costa Rica denounced the pact as risking a "mediating" U.S. intervention). But Che felt betrayed and totally isolated in his doubts, since he was unaware of the reaction of the Movement as a whole and of Fidel himself, who disowned the pact in the Sierra on November 10.

The misunderstanding was cleared up several days later; Che wrote to Fidel:

> **The messenger has just arrived with your note of November 13, and I confess that, along with Celia's note, it filled me with calm and joy. This is not for personal reasons, but for what it means for the revolution. You know full well that I don't trust the national leadership people in the least, neither as chiefs nor as revolutionaries.**

He went on to propose getting rid of the entire national leadership entirely, as if they had all been implicated in the pact.

On November 8, meanwhile, in Havana, the July 26 Movement organized a spectacular show of force, setting off a hundred bombs, loud fireworks, and explosives in the capital. The concert of noise and fire began at nine at night.

The régime, now on the defensive, was counterattacking on several fronts. Several days later Che was warned by Fidel that Sánchez Mosquera's column was making inroads once again on what the guerrillas considered their territory. After some fruitless ambushes and a failed attempt by the guerrillas to set off a mine in their path, the Guards advanced by truck and on foot, shielding themselves by mingling with the local people. Che tried to close the cordon around them, but they found their way out along an unguarded trail, burning huts as they went.

In trying to close in on the army, Che arrived at a farmhouse where there was a guitar player and a trio of other musicians; the campesinos threw a party, with dancing and singing. It was the first Cuban campesino party Che had seen. The presence of a dog reminded him of a puppy they had been forced to kill on the march, so it would not give away their position by barking. This experience gave rise to his best short story, "The Murdered Puppy," which he wrote some years later.

The pursuit, though, came to nothing; for the troops it was to be just another terible hike across the Sierra.

> **The army passed through six of our ambushes, and we didn't fire at them. Some** [of our fighters] **say they didn't shoot out of consideration for the children all around the soldiers. I didn't shoot because I was 500 meters away, there were many enemy soldiers, and I had lost contact with the other ambushes; I was behind a banana tree—not a very large kind of tree in the Sierra Maestra—and two awesome P-47s were flying overhead all the time. Well, as the intellectuals say, we had to eat shit.**

On November 24, after fruitlessly chasing Sánchez Mosquera's column, Che wrote to Fidel:

> We already have the armory working full-tilt, although we haven't been able to make light mortars because Bayamo isn't much help—he doesn't send us materials. I oversaw the manufacture of two prototype grenade launchers, which I think may bring good results. We have already made a few very powerful mines, but we haven't exploded any yet, and the army took possession of one of them. The shoemaking machinery has been installed and set up to make all kinds of footwear and leathergoods, but we have not received any material. We have the beginnings of two farms for raising pigs and free-range poultry. We have built an oven that will probably bake its first loaf the day after I write this, the anniversary of the landing you set up for us. We have begun to build a little dam to supply the area with hydroelectric energy. We have set up a permanent hospital and will build another with good hygienic conditions. We already have the materials. The area is being covered with air-raid shelters. We intend to stand fast and not give this place up for anything.

And in a postscript:

> News keeps coming along, as if in the movies. The Guards are now in Mar Verde. We'll make our way there at full speed. You'll read the next installment of this fascinating story later. [And he finished off:] I forgot to tell you that the July 26 Movement flag flies at the peak of El Hombrito, and we'll try to keep it there. We raised another one in Corcabá to try to ambush a light plane and the P-47 came and shot our asses full of shrapnel (literally, but only little bits of it).

The flag atop the mountain was twenty feet wide and was not there just to challenge Sánchez Mosquera to climb up and remove it, but also to provoke light aircraft. The flag bore a New Year's greeting from the July 26 Movement, and the column posed for a photograph in front of it: Che in the middle, unarmed, with a long branch he was using as a walking stick. It was like a family photograph with the patriarchal grandfather, a bunch of teenagers, and their moral mentor Che in the middle, with his bus driver's cap.

The flag's presence triggered dozens of bombing raids. (Years later the movie director Sergio Giral would gather campesinos who remembered those raids and have them looking at a sky from which the bombers had long gone and say, "Air raid.") Che himself finally had to order the flag taken down to prevent a group of children from doing it under threat from Sánchez Mosquera's troops.

The Mar Verde battle took place on November 29.

A messenger reported to Che that some 500 yards away soldiers were stealing chickens; these men were part of the advance guard sent by Sánchez Mosquera, who was only a few miles away. Camilo's troops were elsewhere, and Che had to set up two ambushes to close off two of the army's possible routes. After separating his squadrons, Che set up an ambush with his small squad on the trail that went down to the sea, the way he thought the army was most likely to go.

In the early hours of the morning, with the ambush set up, the alarm was given. We could hear the soldiers' steps almost on top of us. . . . At that time, I was armed only with a Luger pistol and felt anxious about what would become of two or three comrades who were nearer to the enemy than I, so I rushed the first shot and missed. As happens in such cases, widespread firing immediately broke out and the house where most of Sánchez Mosquera's troops were was attacked.

Joel Iglesias and two other rebels from Che's squad went in search of the men from the troops' advance guard and took the same trail as the soldiers, through the tunnel in the brush. I could hear them calling for surrender and promising to let the prisoners live. Then suddenly I heard a quick volley of shots, and the comrades told me Joel was seriously wounded.

Joel himself tells it:

Che ran out to me, defying the bullets, threw me over his shoulder, and got me out of there. The Guards didn't dare fire at him, as they heard somebody call him Che. Later I questioned them, and they told me he made such a great impression on them when they saw him run out with his pistol stuck in his belt, ignoring the danger, that they didn't dare shoot.

Joel, all in all, was extraordinarily lucky. Three Garands let fly at him, almost at point-blank range. His own Garand was hit twice—the butt was broken—his hand was grazed by another bullet; the next grazed his cheek; two more hit his arm and two his leg, and he was grazed by some others. He was covered in blood, but his wounds were really relatively light.

The three soldiers surrendered soon after. Vilo Acuña wanted to shoot "those dogs" in his anger at seeing Joel lying there bloodied, but Che told him: Look, those guys could have killed me but didn't want to. We won't solve anything by killing *those* dogs; the ones we have to kill are the top dogs, the ones provoking these dogs here. These are just working stiffs, with no ideology whatsoever.

Sergio del Valle and Che gave Joel a field dressing while the fighting continued. Then they sent him to the rear with the prisoners, where Dr. Martínez Páez operated on him using rum as an anesthetic.

On interrogating the soldiers, they discovered that Sánchez Mosquera was entrenched with a company of one hundred men, with machine guns and plenty of ammunition.

> **We felt that it was best not to push for a face-to-face encounter, which would have doubtful results: our forces had approximately the same number of men but far fewer weapons, and Sánchez Mosquera was on the defensive and well entrenched. We decided to harass him to make it impossible for him to move until nightfall, the best time for us to attack.**

But the opportunity was lost because another column of Guards came up from the coast and new ambushes were needed to hold them back. That same November 29, while the rebels were confined to besieging and beleaguering Sánchez Mosquera's column, army reinforcements broke through the blockade and forced a rebel withdrawal. Just before, Ciro Redondo had died trying to force his way through the enemy lines. **We were grief-stricken, and the death of our great comrade Ciro Redondo came on top of our not being able to take advantage of the chance to beat Sánchez Mosquera.** Some days later Che wrote to Fidel: **He was a good comrade and, above all, an unwavering supporter of yours in his obsession with the struggle. I think in all fairness he should be given the rank of Commander, even if only for the sake of history, which is all that most of us can aspire to.**

Che brought up the rear once again during the retreat and, despite his comrades' shouting at him to duck or take cover, he persisted in standing up to fire. Just then

> **a bullet hit a tree trunk just inches from my head and Geonel Rodríguez upbraided me for not ducking. The comrade later argued—perhaps because mathematical speculation had been drummed into him while he was studying to be an engineer— that he had more chance of ending the revolution alive than I, because he never risked his life unless absolutely necessary.**

Aware of how weak his column was, of its inability to organize prolonged battles or sieges, Che had now decided to defend the El Hombrito base at all costs, He took the precaution of transporting the wounded to La Mesa, a more inaccessible area.

In less than a week they entered into battle once more, while Sánchez Mosquera's column began the climb up to El Hombrito through the Santa Ana area. The guerrillas' homemade mines did not explode and the ambushes were overrun. Although it pained him deeply, Che gave the order to abandon El Hombrito before his other patrols were cut off by the advancing soldiers. He set up another ambush on a hillock (called Altos de Conrado) sticking out from the Sierra range. There we were, waiting patiently for three days, mounting twenty-four-hour watches. The nights were very cold and damp at that altitude and time of year. We weren't really prepared for or in the habit of spending the night in combat readiness while braving the elements.

Despite Fidel's recommendations, Che placed himself in the forefront of the ambush: The men's morale had been quite undermined by all the useless agitation they were subjected to, and I felt my presence was required on the firing line. The army finally advanced toward them on December 8, under the onslaught of the guerrillas' psychological war.

We could clearly hear the soldiers in a very heated discussion; I could hear especially well, as I was looking out from the parapet. Someone in charge, apparently an officer, shouted "You'll go in front, damn you," while the soldier, or whoever it was, testily replied no. The argument ended and the troops moved on.

The ambush was set up so that Camilo could fire at point-blank range, while the rest of the guerrillas had orders to wait under cover until they heard the first shots.

While looking out (violating my own orders), I could appreciate that tense moment before battle. The first soldier appeared, looking warily this way and that as he slowly went along. To be sure, there was every sign of an ambush there; it looked strange compared to the rest of the Peladero landscape, with a little spring bubbling constantly in the midst of the verdant wood surrounding us. The trees, some of which had fallen and others that were dead but still standing, added to the gloomy scene. I hid my head, waiting for the combat to begin. A shot rang out and widespread firing followed. I later learned that it was not Camilo who fired, but Ibrahim who, made trigger-happy by nervous tension, fired before it was time. The shooting spread within a few moments.

I suddenly felt that unpleasant sensation—a bit like a burn or numbness—of a bullet wound in my left foot, which was not covered by the tree trunk. I had just fired my rifle and as I was hit I heard the racket made by people advancing toward me, hacking branches, as if charging. . . . Turning around as best as I could, and too swiftly, I drew my pistol just as one of our fighters, young Oñate, called Cantinflas, arrived. On top of the tension and the pain from the wound, here was poor Cantinflas telling me he was withdrawing because his rifle had jammed. I tore it from his hands and examined it as

he crouched by my side. His clip was just slightly bent, and that had jammed his rifle. I fixed it with a diagnosis that cut like a knife: "What you are is an asshole." Cantinflas grabbed the gun, stood up, and left the cover of the tree trunk to empty his clip in a show of bravery. He did not quite manage it: a bullet hit his left arm and went out through his shoulder blade. There were now two of us there who were hurt, and it was difficult to withdraw under fire, so we had to crawl over the tree trunks and then walk under them, wounded as we were and without sight nor sound of the rest of the men. We made way, little by little, but Cantinflas kept fainting. I, despite the pain, could move better and made it to the main group to ask for help.

The soldiers had withdrawn, certainly with some casualties, but the situation was not clear. Che ordered his men to regroup by squadrons and told Oñate to stay behind. He then obtained a horse, as the pain in his foot had returned and he could not walk. Thinking that the troops had taken the Conrado heights, Che set up new ambushes and ordered Ramiro Valdés to take command of most of the column and head off in search of Fidel, **as there was a certain feeling of defeat and fear in our ranks and I wanted to have only the minimum number of fighters necessary to mount an agile defense.**

Che's wounded foot had a great effect on the campesinos in the area. At first they could not believe it. A rumor that Che was wounded went nowhere. One woman even came to see him in the hut where he lay; she asked, "Are you wounded, Che? No, you can't be." Che had to show her the wound in his foot and tell her it was nothing serious. Years later, when this scene appeared in a documentary about the campaign, the countryfolk in El Hombrito and La Mesa would cry when they remembered it.

A day after the battle, a scouting party found that the army had retreated. But, they had burned campesinos' houses and destroyed the fledgling infrastructure at El Hombrito as they went. **Our baker's oven had been deliberately smashed, and among smoking ruins we found only a few cats and a pig that had escaped the invading army's marauding.** The destruction of the base must have hurt Che to the quick, as could be discerned in a letter he sent Ramos Latour on December 14: **El Hombrito was razed, with forty houses burned and all our dreams shattered.**

Some time in the next few days, Dr. Machado Ventura operated on Che with a razor blade so as to remove the M1 bullet from his foot; by December 12, Ramiro reported to Fidel: "He's probably taking his first steps right now."

Four and a half months had gone by since Che was first named commander, and he felt like a failure. He had led some successful skirmishes, but had not been able to seize the advantage and had had to retreat several times. He had had to surrender his cherished base at El Hombrito. He was continually clashing with the July 26 Movement leadership in the Plains and had ignored Fidel's advice and taken too many risks, as a result of which he was now wounded. In a sure sign of his discouragement, he turned command of the bulk of his column over to Fidel, with Ramiro Valdés; he himself remained in charge of only a small outpost.

It may have been too soon as yet to evaluate the two big successes he had had over those months: he had set up a very extensive network among the campesinos, who truly admired and respected him; and he had built up a magical aura around himself. Che was the fair-minded one, the one who would not ask anyone to do what he wouldn't do himself.

These two successes were to be worth much more than it then seemed and Fidel, instead of relieving Che of his command of the No. 4 Column, would realize their importance.

15.   Controversy

1958

At the end of the year, the enemy troops were withdrawing from the Sierra once more, and we were masters of the stretch of territory between the Caracas peak and Pino del Agua from west to east, from the sea to the south and as far south as the villages in the foothills of the Sierra, which were occupied by the army. An armed truce was in effect, a respite. The guerrillas were unable to operate against the army's heavily defended positions, and the army did not feel inclined to climb up the Sierra.

Meanwhile, there was a need for a new and more extensive infrastructure. There were difficulties getting food, medicines, weapons, and ammunition for the guerrillas, and in carrying on a propaganda campaign.

> **As a first step, we ordered some campesino to plant particular crops, and we guaranteed to buy their beans, corn, and rice, etc. At the same time, we organized supply routes with storekeepers in the outlying villages to bring food and some military equipment up to the Sierra. We organized trains of mules belonging to the guerrillas that not only transported food, but medicine as well.**
>
> **It was difficult enough to obtain weapons from the Plains; on top of the natural difficulties entailed by our geographical isolation, there were the needs of the forces in the cities themselves and their reluctance to hand weapons over to the guerrillas. Fidel had to fight hard to get some military equipment to us.**

The main aim of combat now was to provide weapons for the guerrillas by disarming enemy soldiers. There were even greater problems with ammunition.

Although these were urgent needs, Che did not abandon the idea of setting up a base camp and infrastructure, and soon after the loss of El Hombrito he mobilized toward La Mesa, "The Table." This was an apt name. Che named the valley surrounded by four mountains the Upside-Down Table, and one of the mountains the Table Leg. There he began to shape his ideas of a permanent base. On December 3, work began on a camouflaged camp, which was to be spread out across the valley, on a hospital, a leather works for making the boots indispensable in guerrilla fighting, and even berets (this was the origin of the bus driver's cap that Che wore now and again). There was also an armory equipped with a small lathe. They would later add a worship for making cigars. According to Che the results weren't bad, but according to Homer Bigart of the *New York Herald Tribune* and the Uruguayan journalist Carlos María Gutiérrez, they were as good as the Partagás brand sold in Havana.

A school was also up and running in La Mesa, where campesino children and even captured soldiers were taught to read. Che had Carmencita teaching the adults; other rebels taught reading as well. The Spanish journalist Meneses recalled a letter that one of the teachers sent Che, complaining pompously that they lacked the most rudimentary material for teaching campesino children, and Che's irate reply:

> **I am in joyful receipt of your missive in which you regret not having suitable implements with which to undertake your pedagogical endeavors in the sinecure assigned to you by the revolution. The puerile subjects of your academic attentions will have to make do with your genius, as I do not have the cultural arms available to which you lay claim. While on this point, I might tell you that the next time you make a man walk ten hours to give me such a pile of nitwit remarks, I'll send someone out to cut your balls off. Got that? Your pissed-off commander, Che.**

Che kept clashing with the July 26 Movement urban hierarchy over his renewed organizational work. He had already written to Fidel Castro on December 9:

> **If we see each other, or if I have a chance to write you a longer letter, I'll have to complain to you about the leadership, as I have the sneaking suspicion that they are directly sabotaging this column, or more specifically me personally. I feel that, in this state of affairs, there are only two solutions: to take strong action to prevent such measures, or to resign on grounds of physical disability—or whatever seems best to you. This feeling is not born of any grudges arising from having to abandon El Hombrito. . . . The facts are a little too tenuous to give you conclusive proof, but you will have the chance to read letters . . . in which they answer my overwhelming and urgent requests, taking issue in three pages with one paragraph of mine in which I was just doing as I was instructed with respect to unattached visitors.**

A perusal of the correspondence between the Sierra and the Plains today makes it seem that Che was excessively harsh in his judgment of his comrades in the urban networks, who were subject to the terror of Batista's police force, were often arrested and tortured, and suffered from betrayals, the difficulties arising from working underground, and constant breakdowns in communication with the Sierra.

On December 12, René Ramos Latour reported to Fidel that he had sent Che, via Bayamo, 17,000 rounds of ammunition, mostly .22 caliber, but also .44 and 30.06, as well as 2,000 pesos via Yao. Two days later he wrote to Che, saying:

> Che, I suppose most of the ammunition sent will now be in your hands. . . . I assure you that I have been driven to despair by receiving one request after another from you and finding myself practically helpless when it comes to solving things. . . . Everything I sent you was acquired

here in lots of 50, 100, 200, and we paid through the nose for it. . . . You know I'm a stalwart defender of the organization in the strict sense of the word. Nonetheless, now that I have tried to get the ammunition you requested speedily into your hands, and have stumbled over people's irresponsibility, delays, indecision, etc., I realize why you stick with Ferrer and others who brought you what the Bayamo leadership didn't know how to get to you. My despair was such that I was about to go to Bayamo and take you the military equipment myself, and abandon all the other tasks weighing us down right now. . . . Within a few days you will receive 200 jackets, 75 pairs of woolen underwear, 150 pairs of socks, the new mimeograph and some other odds and ends we're sending you.

The network seems to have improved, as Che received a little electricity generator, and would even manage to obtain a copy of volume one of *Das Kapital,* which he had begun to read in Mexico but hadn't finished. The new mimeograph allowed production of *El Cubano Libre* to resume; the newspaper would begin to reach the outskirts of the Sierra and nearby towns as January went by.

A Cuban campesino said you had to read *El Cubano Libre* by sunlight or by the light of a very big street lamp, because the stencil printing was awful. Still, it raised morale. It was one of Che's obsessions. He had spent many hours setting up the infrastructure, and had not a few fights over it—for instance, when he found out someone had used a copy as toilet paper. He almost put all the high command personnel on a bread-and-water diet.

Despite his sudden attacks of rage, Che was adored by his men and the campesinos in the area. Carmencita described him thus:

> Nobody had a bad word for Che in the Sierra; the people loved him, nobody felt hard done by, nobody blamed him for the things that happened, nobody dared lie to him, and they trusted him, trusted in his intelligence. He was a smart guerrilla fighter; they admired him, respected him, and spoke formally to him.

Che, sir . . . And it was this Che, respected by the campesinos, who took his controversy with the Plains people further than just his doubts about communications and supply networks. On November 23, Armando Hart had written to Che pointing out that they needed to keep the command structure on the Plains, that there were many opportunists trying to make contact with the Sierra and that accepting them meant weakening the July 26 Movement urban network, which had been so much trouble to set up and which was so hard to keep going, underground, in the face of repression. Hart made it clear that, regarding political differences, "I assure you that if you so much as talked to us you would understand" that the Plains people were not conservatives, nor did they want links with more liberal sectors of the oligarchy. The letter was extremely friendly and even affectionate toward Che.

On December 14, Che replied to Ramos Latour, Frank País's successor (in what he himself later described as a really idiotic letter), defending his rights and responsibilities as a guerrilla fighter against the constant objections I face over my centralizing activity. And without offering any solution, he launched straight into a confrontation with the Plains and set out political differences:

> Out of ideological conviction, I belong to those who believe the solution to the world's problems lies behind the so-called iron curtain and consider this movement one of many provoked by the bourgeoisie's urge to rid itself of the economic shackles of imperialism. I have always considered Fidel to be the authentic leader of the bourgeois left, although he himself has personal qualities of extraordinary brilliance that place him well above his class. This was the spirit in which I entered this struggle: honorably in the hope of going beyond liberating the country, prepared to go away when the conditions of the following struggle shift to the right (toward what you people represent). [And he acknowledged that at the time of the Miami pact,] I thought what I am ashamed to have thought. Fortunately, Fidel's letter arrived.

And then he closed, despite the letter's harshness, I hope there's an explanation.

Ramos Latour replied on December 18: "I have just received the letter which you yourself describe as harsh and whose content just surprises me. . . . Opinions about me by people like yourself do not actually hurt me, as you do not know me well enough to judge me. I must make it clear to you that I am giving you an answer, out of the respect and admiration that I have always held for you and which has not wavered in the least despite your words." After this elegant preamble, Ramos Latour made it clear that he wrote in the name of all the members of the national leadership on the Plains. He explained the sacrifice made when the urban networks gave up a bullet for the Sierra that they could have used to defend themselves, and cited the example of the Mayarí cell, which had delivered to the Sierra the guns it had gathered, and was fighting on, unarmed.

He moved on to define the political horizons and his view of Communism, summarizing by saying, "The solution to our ills isn't freeing ourselves from harmful 'Yankee' domination by accepting some no-less-harmful Soviet domination." He also made it very clear that the urban networks, too, were of the left: "You, like us, feel the need to rid our country of corrupt administration, unemployment, militarism, poverty, illiteracy, ill health, the lack of civil rights . . ." And he defined himself as a worker ("Not one of those who is concerned about what goes on in Egypt but will not get involved in Cuba," an allusion to the PSP Communists)—a worker who'd dropped out of his studies in sociology and law to go to war. He finished off by saying that controversy was irrelevant "as long as we keep on working for the triumph of the revolution."

But things were not to stay where they were.

Armando Hart went up to the Sierra in January 1958 bearing a letter addressed to Che and replying to his expressed mistrust of the Plains leadership. Fidel, concerned over the tone that the debate occasionally assumed, ordered Hart not to deliver the letter. However, when Hart° climbed back down the Sierra, he was captured and the letter ended up in army hands. While Hart's life was hanging by a thread, the government propaganda machine aired the debate, publicizing the dissent within the July 26 Movement, and Raúl Castro was forced to make it clear to Fidel that he had never mentioned Stalin in any letter to Che, and that a rumor that he had done so was based on the letter Hart carried that contained a discussion of Marx. The controversy appeared to have been worked out.

> **The Sierra was certain by then that it could continue to develop the guerrilla war, move it elsewhere, and thus lay siege from the country to the cities [that were] in the hands of the dictatorship, and make the regime's machinery fall apart by choking it and wearing it out. The Plains proposed a seemingly more revolutionary approach, such as armed struggle in every city, culminating in a general strike to overthrow Batista and allow power to be taken in the short run. . . . A general strike called by surprise, in secret, with no prior political training and with no mass action.**

Although he was not wrong, Che's view tended to underestimate the role that the struggle in the cities had played and continued to play in the revolutionary political process that had closed in on the dictatorship. By denying that role (maybe because he lacked perspective on the movement's history, starting with the raid on the Moncada barracks in 1953), he saw the guerrilla war as an autonomous process, rather than the vanguard of the widespread dissent that it fed, and fed on. Apart from his great intelligence and the worldview afforded him by his Latin Americanism à la Simon Bolívar, at times, as far as Cuba was concerned, Che was no more than a country intellectual who had never set foot in a city.

These debates were not Che's only concern. Apart from military matters, he also had plans in his head to launch a radio station from the Sierra. The matter had been discussed earlier at Frank País's behest, but by this stage it was more a matter of linkage between Fidel's command and the leadership in Santiago.

On December 23, 1957, one of Che's officers told him he knew a technician in Bayamo who thought he could set up a transmitter in the Sierra. Che gave him the go-ahead and ten pesos to make the connection. The radio technician, Eduardo Fernández, had a small repair shop in Bayamo and was a member of the July 26 Movement network. Within a few days, he met Che in the El Hombrito camp: "I found him completely absorbed and enthused by the matter."

°Hart's life was spared, although he was imprisoned on Pinos Island.

On January 8, 1958, Che wrote:

Tell Daniel [René Ramos Latour's nom de guerre], **Deborah, or whomever, in the leadership that I have a technician who promises to set up a broadcasting unit in two weeks, at a cost of approximately 500 pesos. The equipment may come via Havana. The technician lives in Bayamo, Zenea #54, his name is Eduardo Fernández.**

Two weeks later, Ramos Latour had agreed to the project: "I am waiting for the technician to tell us what equipment he needs, so we can get it to him."

In Santiago, "Daniel" Ramos Latour met Fernández at a secret rendezvous. A little later, the necessary equipment began to appear in Havana. A small transmitter was assembled and then transported (in pieces again) to Bayamo. That was just the beginning. It turned out to be extremely difficult to transport the transmitter to the heart of the Sierra Maestra and build it. It first had to be taken to the quartermaster's stores in the Sierra foothills, avoiding the army cordon on the way. Then it entered the Sierra in a jeep with two women sitting on it, covering it with their wide skirts. The next stop was Ciro Redondo's grandmother's house; then porters carried the equipment on their backs across several ranches until one of Che's patrols finally took delivery. In the second week of February, the rumor that they had their own radio station working began to go the rounds of the rebels.

Che was meanwhile working on another of his pet projects in La Mesa: the armory. With the support of Oris Delfín Zaldivar, with whom he had been working since the days of the El Hombrito camp, he was developing

our latest weapon, to which we ascribe exceptional importance: the M-26, also called Sputnik, a small tin bomb. It is first launched using a complicated piece of apparatus, a sort of catapult made of the elastic bands used in an underwater harpoon. It was later improved so that we could fire it from a rifle, using a blank cartridge, which gave the device a greater range. These little bombs made a lot of noise and were really frightening, but, as they were armored only with tin plate, their lethality was limited; they caused only light wounds when they exploded near some enemy soldier.

On February 16, Fidel gathered his forces to make a strike, again on Pino del Agua. It was more of a harassment and ambush operation than an attempt to take the barracks, which was now being guarded by a whole company.

Fidel personally commanded the attack, with Camilo leading the advance guard. Guillermo García's platoon lay in wait to ambush possible reinforcements to the besieged barracks. At five in the morning, Camilo began the advance, but discovered that the army's guards had withdrawn into the barracks.

The guards had installed a rudimentary alarm system consisting of wires running along the ground with cans tied to them. They rattled when anyone stepped on or touched them. However, the soldiers had meanwhile left some horses grazing, so when the advance guard tripped the alarm, the guards thought it was the horses moving around. Camilo was thus able to advance practically right up to where the soldiers were.

The rebels launched an ineffective bombardment, and then Camilo's advance guard engaged the army's forward positions. In a few minutes, Camilo's forces had wiped out resistance, seized eleven weapons, among them two machine guns, and taken three guards prisoner, while killing seven or eight. But the defenders immediately regrouped and our attacks were halted.

The rebels sustained several casualties in attempting to continue the attack. Among the wounded was Camilo himself, hit in the leg.

Despite his wound, Camilo dived back to try to recover a weapon, in the first light of dawn and the midst of hellish gunfire. He was wounded again, but was lucky enough, for the bullet went through his abdomen and out of his side without hitting any vital organs. While Camilo was saved, the machine gun was lost. Some isolated comrades, from positions close to the barracks, bombarded the building with Sputniks or M-26s, spreading confusion among the soldiers.

At midmorning, calm reigned, broken only by the odd burst of machine-gun fire. A little later, Fidel's plan to ambush reinforcements proved prescient. An enemy company made its way from Oro de Guisa and fell into the ambush headed by Paco Cabrera. Fidel had set the ambush up for just this contingency. The advance guard from Batista's army was wiped out, with eleven dead and five prisoners, a lieutenant named Lafarté among them. And the rebels captured plenty of weapons.

A second ambush failed because the soldiers managed to discover the rebels' positions and, although Raúl Castro had to withdraw, the siege at Pinar del Agua held up.

During the night, I insisted that it was possible to undertake an attack of the sort that Camilo had carried out and overwhelm the guards stationed at Pino del Agua. Fidel was not in favor, but agreed to try the idea out; he sent forces commanded by Escalona, made up from Ignacio Pérez's and Raúl Castro Mercader's platoons. The comrades approached and did all they could to reach the barracks, but were repulsed by the soldiers' rapid fire; they quickly withdrew without trying to attack again. I asked to be given command of the strike force, which Fidel allowed reluctantly. My idea was to get as close as

possible and, using Molotov cocktails made from the gasoline at the sawmill itself, set the wooden houses on fire to force either a surrender or a disorderly withdrawal, firing after the soldiers as they went.

Fidel, however, was not convinced and sent Che a note:

> If everything depends on the attack from this flank, with no support from Camilo and Guillermo, I don't think any suicide action should be undertaken because we would end up with a lot of casualties without attaining our objective. I recommend, sincerely, that you take care. My final order is that you should not take part as a fighter. Make sure you lead our men well, which is essential right now.

Che considered the situation and reluctantly decided not to enter combat, telling a messenger: **Tell Fidel to go. I'll stay a while longer. I have discovered that cordite is the only cure for asthma.** The column withdrew under a raid from B-26s that was more nuisance than harm.

When Che got back to the La Mesa campsite, preceded by Camilo on a stretcher, he discovered that the newspapers were reporting that he'd been wounded. He met the Uruguayan journalist Carlos María Gutiérrez, who described him thus: "The pockets of his olive-drab tunic were overflowing with papers, notebooks, and pencils . . . [and] the side pockets of his pants were as full as saddle bags and sagging under the weight of bullets, socks, and a few books." Che welcomed him with a gruff: **You're the Uruguayan? Have a maté.**

Che had introduced the habit of drinking maté to the Sierra. Where did he get the maté? His aunt Beatriz sent it to him. But what was the amazing network that connected his aunt Beatriz in Argentina with the end of the world in the Sierra Maestra?

Carlos María Gutiérrez was to get just one exclusive from the elusive Che, who was more interested in talking about photography than in answering questions. He preferred to be reserved. "His defensive weapons are sarcastic wit and a wry smile. He looked me over as though weighing up my impertinence or my naiveté. Che knew how to build his redoubts and raise his drawbridges. But he also had an intuitive friendliness and his bluntness left no scars." One day, Gutiérrez recalled, he was informed that Che had invited him to move his hammock to the very hut of the high command. "I went to thank him for the favor, but Guevara cut me off sharply. **It's not for you, I just don't like drinking maté alone.** "

Che affectionately tormented Camilo in the hospital, doing things like taking his cap away and laughing at him.

Fidel's participation in the second combat at Pinar del Agua

provoked a group of officers to send him a document . . . asking him, in the name of the revolution, not to risk his life for no good reason. I don't think that somewhat childish document, which we drafted out of the highest motives, deserved

so much as to be read by him and, needless to say, he took not the slightest notice of it.

It was somewhat amazing that commanders and captains, platoon chiefs who, following the law of the Mau Mau, personally led in combat by example, should have asked Fidel to do the opposite. Efigenio Ameijeiras said:

> It was quite a gas to see one of those greenhorns, some of whom were not much more than teenagers, stand up in the heat of battle and shout, when everybody was nose down to the ground and the bullets were whistling in our ears: "You there, look at me! The Mau Mau law." He would then stand straight up in the midst of the bullets and fire on the enemy. The one he was shouting at would imitate him. . . . That, all in all, was the Mau Mau law, to fight on foot and to advance into the bullets or fire right on the planes. Man's play, which seems like fool's play.

And the fools' ranks grew. Two new columns broke off from the main one on March 1: Almeida, in command of No. 3 Column, headed off toward Santiago; Raúl Castro, at the head of No. 6 Column, advanced to form a second front, also closing in on Santiago. Their departure coincided with the birth of Radio Rebelde.

For in the meantime, Fernández, who had moved to La Mesa, got the transmitter up and working, using ham frequencies for the first tests. When he found it was working he broadcast the "Invaders' Anthem." He learned that the broadcasts were getting through, but that he had picked the wrong spot, as the transmitter was in a depression between the mountains. Che decided to move the transmitter to Altos de Conrado. Two men who knew something about radio announcing, Orestes Valera and Ricardo Martínez, joined the rebels' ranks at that time; and Olga Guevara, a teacher in Che's column, would be roped in, too.

On February 24, Cubans heard for the first time the words, "This is Radio Rebelde, the voice of the Sierra Maestra, broadcasting throughout Cuba on the twenty-meter band daily at five P.M. and nine P.M. . . ." But Che was sarcastic: **Our only listeners were Pelecho, a campesino whose hut was on the hill opposite the transmitter, and Fidel, who was visiting the campsite . . . and heard the broadcast.**

Fernández explained that "the twenty-meter band isn't appropriate for broadcasting within Cuba; it's rather for long-range communication. So it could be heard in Pinar del Río, but not in Santiago . . . although it could be heard perfectly well abroad."

One day in Venezuela, Abel Tamayo, from the July 26 Movement committee in exile, ran into a meeting screaming, "We've made contact! I've caught it!" Radio Rebelde was coming in. Strangely enough, the network of relays set up by the Venezuelans, supported by Radio Rumbos and Radio Continente, and later Radio Caraco in Colombia, could be heard in Cuba, so Venezuela acted as another relay for Radio Rebelde, and the possibility of setting up a radio network was discussed.

Radio Rebelde existed; the armory was working.

It was also at that time that the People's Socialist Party—the Cuban Communists—sent Che a pair of cadres in response to a request for teachers. Pablo Rivalta and Armando Acosta were given the mission of drafting campesino members of the PSP into the struggle and of joining up personally. Che told them firmly that the idea above all was to set sectarianism aside and not to behave like Party members: **You people are capable of creating cadres that fall to bits in the darkness of a prison cell, but not of forming cadres that can take a machine-gun post.**

This was not to be the case with Acosta and Rivalta.

There were other recruits, too, like Batista army lieutenant Lafarté, who had such a crisis of conscience that he decided to join the guerrillas, and Mark Herman, an American who had picked up military know-how in Korea. The new recruits made it possible for Che to set up a new camp in a part of the Sierra called Minas del Frío, to serve as a guerrilla training school for young campesinos and where, in addition to military instruction, there was educational and political training, too. The school grew under almost continual air raids, with the pupils building fortifications and digging trenches. Joel recalled: "The main test in that school was the hunger you had to live with . . . what with that and the bombing, 50 percent of those who entered dropped out."

It was at that time that Che broke his own rule about keeping a distance from campesinas and the urban fighters who often had to take refuge in the Sierra. He fell in love with a young campesina he met in Las Vegas de Jibacoa. Zoila Rodríguez was an eighteen-year-old of mixed race—very pretty, according to Joel—the daughter of an unmarried blacksmith in the Sierra who supported the movement.

Zoila described the meeting years later, breaking the silence that until then had covered that part of Che's life:

> It was about four in the afternoon. I was shutting a cow away [in the shed] when he arrived. He was riding a mule and came with another comrade on horseback. He was dressed in an odd green color, with a black beret. After saying hello, he asked if El Cabo (my father's nickname) lived there, because Che wanted him to shoe his mule. I told him there was no problem, that I could do it as my father had taught me how.
>
> While I was shoeing the mule, I gave him a sideways glance and realized he was staring at me, but in the way that young men look at girls, and I got really nervous. When I went to pick a rasp out of the box of horseshoes, he asked me what I was doing and I told him I had already cut the hooves and had to even them out so as to put the shoes on. Guevara asked if it was necessary to make them look so pretty. . . . He kept staring at me that way. . . . It was a slightly roguish stare—seemed as if he wanted to scold me for something I had not done. When I had finished, I offered him coffee. He told me he liked it without sugar, which was how I made it for him.
>
> He was interested in me—what I did, where I had learned to shoe

mules, whether I was married. I told him I was unmarried, but had a daughter. When he took his leave, he said:

Tell El Cabo that Guevara was here.

Zoila found him "a funny and very handsome young man. He made a big impression on me; the truth is, I can't deny I liked him very much as a woman, especially his look. His eyes were so pretty, and he had a calm smile that was enough to melt any heart."

That night El Cabo told his daughter that Che was an "extraordinary man." When she asked why, the old man said: "He's here to get rid of our misfortunes, the hunger, the dirt, and the poverty."

Days later, they entered a relationship that was to last several months.

Building at Minas del Frío was meanwhile making progress. Che was thinking of building a proper hospital with several wards; the work was all done amid air raids, because the air force discovered the campsite two weeks after the first building was put up. **From then on, for three months, we suffered from air raids, day and night.**

"The best defense against bombs was a stick between clenched teeth. Another one was the caves. But the very best defense was to lose your fear of them," the campesinos in the area used to say, following Che's instructions to the letter. Che behaved erratically during the air raids; at times he'd stay put, not running for cover, just watching the planes, as if he wanted to prove something, to show something.

In Minas del Frío, Che chose a new member for his entourage, sixteen-year-old Jesús Parra, whom he had found suffering from malaria in Fidel's headquarters. Parra had been a shoeshine boy and a kitchen assistant, and had also taken a three-month typing course. He could type twenty-five words per minute, which was more than enough for what Che had in mind and for the guerrillas to call him the intellectual. It was to Parra that Che explained why he had so many teenagers around him: "He said that teenagers were crazier, they took more risks and didn't think very much." Was he describing himself?

These young men were training with sticks in place of guns, studying Cuban history, and going hungry; they even organized a hunger strike, which Che put to a stop with seven words, ten insults, and a threat to have them all shot. To punish them he made them go for five days without eating, "on hunger strike." Castellanos, who was sitting this one out, summed up: "Che realized the situation was serious, that the punishment was severe, but there was nothing else to do, as there was no food."

That same Che, according to Lafarté, "had a little jar of water beside his hammock in case he had to take pills at night. In the morning, he would wet his fingertips and wipe his bleary eyes, saying: **I'm getting much too wet, Che, I'm getting myself too wet.** "

Zoila Rodríguez came to stay at the camp, and Che moved his hammock to a little grass hut where they would both live. Zoila helped out in the kitchen and the hospital, and also carried messages to and from Manzanillo. "I fell deeply and sweetly in love. I was committed to him not only as a fighter, but as a woman." She was to be a fount of mountain wisdom for Che.

> He used to ask me many things about the Sierra Maestra—what the plants were called, what they were used for, especially the medicinal ones. He was very interested in two, one of which we call pito, with very green, razor-sharp leaves that can be used to stem the flow of blood, and the ya-magua, which is also useful for bleeding. He wanted to know about the animals and birds in the mountains.

16.   The Sierra and the Plains

THE JULY 26 MOVEMENT NATIONAL LEADERSHIP HELD A MEETING TO FIX immediate strategy aims in the Sierra Maestra on March 10–11, 1957. Because of the régime's political isolation and the growing urban resistance movement, the leadership decided it was time to take advantage of political tension by calling for a general strike.

Years later, Che would say the strike was **decreed by the Plains with the Sierra's consent, as the guerrillas did not feel capable of preventing it.** This is a false reflection of what happened. Fidel Castro, of course, did not oppose the strike, and while doubts did exist among other cadres in the Sierra, they did not prevail.

Che, who did not take part in the meeting and had never set foot in a city in Cuba, did not have a clear idea of what was happening in the cities and could scarcely have made a political appraisal of the situation.

Fidel had prepared a call for a general strike that would be primed by the M26 and immediately spread. A workers' front had been set up, apparently united but actually very sectarian. Three important arms shipments were expected. The guerrillas were to try to support the strike by mobilizing several squads to descend to the Plains and wait for events to unfold. Even apart from the mistaken idea that events would take place as planned, this may have been the least inspired part of the plan: enlisting the full rebel army in the effort to overthrow the régime by striking.

The relationship between Che and Camilo Cienfuegos, who was to lead a patrol in the plains near the Sierra in the El Canto region, was an odd mixture of bullets and friendship. When Radio Bemba, which never hesitated to broadcast rumors, said that Che was capable of eating anything, Camilo, a bloodthirsty trickster, caught two cats in the La Otilia campsite and cooked them, betting that when Che found out what the meat was, he would not eat it. He extended a formal dinner invitation to Che, who replied, **I think the cat's out of the bag, Captain.** Che had his own sources of information in the camp.

"Commander . . ." Camilo replied, and stood to one side as Che tucked into the cats.

The letters between the two commanders were also tinged with black humor. On April 21, Guevara wrote:

> **You poor devil. I got your news when I was about to set off for your area to give [illegible] a piece of my mind. I have authority from the giant to do so . . . you may do what you like in the area, but don't take too many risks; you want to see the end of the party, which seems to be coming soon. Finally, here's a reminder of a night in La Otilia:**

> *There was an old man from Timbuktu*
> *Who read some old books in a zoo*
> *He felt so cerebral*
> *But was et by a zebra*
> *And I might do the same to you, too!*

Camilo, whose previous letter had commented on Che's handwriting, wrote on April 24: "I didn't know you people spoke Chinese so well." But then his tone changed:

> Che, my soul-brother. I received your note and see that Fidel has put you in charge of the military school; I'm glad we'll have first-rate soldiers available. When I was told you were to do us the favor of coming here, I was not too pleased. You've played a key role in the struggle and while we need you during the fighting stage, Cuba will need you more when the war's over, so the giant's right to take care of you. I would like to be at your side all the time; you were my chief for a long time and you always will be. Thanks to you, I now have a chance to be more useful. I'd do anything not to let you down. Your friend, as always.

Che was running the military school and at the same time engaging in one skirmish after another with Sánchez Mosquera's forces, which were occupying Minas de Bueycito.

Che led what was perhaps the most important such engagement by accident, but strangely enough made no mention of it in his memoirs. It happened in a place called Bernabé, on land belonging to a plantation owner who had refused to sell cows to the rebels, arguing that he would get into trouble. But then he had reported their presence to the army. Sánchez Mosquera sent a company to take the cattle and clashed with a group of rebel gunmen guarding them from the army. Che was in the vicinity, was attracted by the noise of gunfire, and, without realizing it, found himself in the middle of the fray. He began to shoot at the soldiers surrounding the ranch. A rebel who saw the action recalled, "He would fire two, three, or four shots, duck down and run back and forth, and hit the ground. The soldiers were shouting at him: 'Don't run, you coward!' A hundred to one, and they called him a coward, but they didn't go after him."

As Che's luck had it, a rebel patrol that had gone in search of him gave him covering fire while he and the gunmen withdrew with the cattle toward La Mesa.

That was the last combat action before the general strike. Years later, Efigenio Ameijeiras listed the milestones along the road to revolution:

> The Moncada raid, November 30; the *Granma*; Alegría de Pío; La Plata; the Herbert Matthews interview, March 13; *Corinthia*; the El Uvero barracks; the death of Frank País and the strike he made almost nationwide; the two battles at Pino del Agua; San Lorenzo, Mota, and El Hombrito; Front II and the "Frank Muñoz" Front; No. III; the Revolutionary Command's guerrillas in the Escambray mountains; the night of the 100 bombs; the kidnapping of Fangio; Camilo in the Plains. All this, and the uprisings in the East, Camagüey and Las Villas, had made it clear just how serious the revolutionary movement was.

Action got under way following the capture of a radio station in Havana and the broadcast of Fidel's strike call. Santiago, still smarting from the failure of the strike the previous November, did not carry out the action with the same intensity, and the mistakes piled up. The weapons did show up as promised and the strike did break out, but in isolated spots, which allowed the government to focus its backlash.

The problem was not lack of social ferment, but lack of planning. People were being asked to confront the dictatorship without any weapons. The movement thus depended on the militias, which were few and poorly armed, and on coordination with the Sierra, which had a limited range of action. Furthermore, the strike call had been limited. The July 26 Movement had hoped to pull other organized workers' groups along with them, but they were poorly organized even within its own ranks.

At the beginning of the action, there was rejoicing in the Sierra. The Argentine journalist Jorge Ricardo Masetti was at headquarters at the time, he described how Fidel received the news, shouting and dancing for joy, saying that now they would all go down to Havana. Even Che had not given up the strike up as lost on the third day; it was fizzling out in Havana, but it was still holding forth in other cities. Nonetheless, the movement bled itself dry in heroic but inchoate confrontations. The failure of the strike set Batista's army on the offensive.

In the days following the April strike, Che was on his way to visit Fidel's headquarters with a guide when they found a hut where the army had just destroyed a convoy taking supplies to the rebels. The desolation of the area, the bodies of men and animals frightened the guide, who

> **refused to follow me, alleging he did not know the area. He just got on his mount and we separated on friendly terms. I had a Beretta. I entered the first of the coffee plantations. . . . When I arrived at an abandoned house, a fearsome noise made me jump and I almost fired, but it was just a pig, also frightened. Slowly and with great caution I covered the few hundred meters between myself and our post, which I found was totally abandoned. . . . That whole scene holds no meaning for me except for the satisfaction I felt at conquering my fear during a run that seemed endless until I arrived, at last, on my own, at the command post. I felt brave that night.**

Che was cut off several days later during a clash with Sánchez Mosquera's troops:

> **The enemy had fired a few mortar salvos, but without getting any sort of range. For a moment the firing became intense to my right and I set off to visit the other positions, but when I was halfway there the firing began on the left. I sent my adjutant I don't know where and was cut off between the firing on both sides. On my left, Sánchez Mosquera's troops, after firing a few mortar shells, were climbing up the hill, making a terrible din. Our men, lacking experience, did not manage to fire more than the odd shot, and ran off downhill.**

On my own, in a bare paddock, I caught sight of several soldiers' helmets. One of this group ran downhill, chasing our men who were making their way into the coffee plantations. I shot at him with the Beretta but missed, and immediately drew some rifle fire. I ran in a zigzag, carrying a thousand rounds of ammunition in a huge leather cartridge belt on my shoulders, cheered on by enemy soldiers shouting derogatory comments at me. I dropped my pistol as I came close to the shelter of the trees. My only proud moment that sad morning was to stop, retrace my steps, pick up the pistol and run off, accompanied this time by clouds of dust thrown up by the rifle bullets hot on my heels.

When I felt I was safe, with no idea where my comrades were or how the offensive had ended, I rested awhile, sheltering behind a large rock, in the middle of the hill. My asthma had held off long enough to let me run a few meters, but now it hit me with a vengeance, and my heart was beating wildly in my chest. I felt branches being broken by someone approaching, but I could no longer keep on running (which is what I really wanted to do). This time the noise turned out to be one of our comrades, a recent recruit to our ranks who had lost his way. He soothingly said, "Don't worry, Commander, I'll die with you." I didn't want to die, but rather to say something to him about his mother, although I don't think I did. I felt like a coward that day.

A little later Che, who had left the command of No. 4 Column in Ramiro Valdés's hands, headed off to take charge of the recruits' military-training school. While waiting for the army's inevitable offensive in the wake of the strike's failure, Fidel had ordered that food supplies be built up in the Sierra, that cattle be requisitioned, and that the watches be stepped up. Also in anticipation, Radio Rebelde was transferred to the La Plata area, the safest part of the Sierra Maestra, where it resumed broadcasts on May 1.

Masetti, the Argentine journalist, was back in the Sierra at that time, as his first transmissions had not gone through and he had to rerecord his interviews with Che and Fidel. An impassioned book, *Those Who Fight and Those Who Cry,* grew out of the two meetings; so did a close friendship with Che who, it was well known, did not make friends easily.

The interview with Che was recorded in the middle of an air raid, and Masetti happened to say that the sound of the bombs would make good background, so Che took him outside the shelter to get the noise on tape. In a second interview, in Fidel's presence, "Guevara took it upon himself to offer a contrast to Fidel: every time Fidel got mad, Che cracked jokes."

The national leadership held another meeting on May 3, in Altos de Mompié. Che was invited to attend by Ramos Latour and Faustine Pérez, with whom he had sustained debates.

The meeting was tense; the outcome of the strike was obviously unfavorable, and Fidel took the opportunity to put the blame on the Plains. It is probable (this is a matter for speculation as, if minutes were taken of the meeting, they have not been published) that Fidel leveled three charges at the city leaders: that they had overestimated the cities' role in the overall struggle; that sectarianism in the labor movement had led to its refusal to cooperate with other groups, especially the People's Socialist Party (PSP); that the militias on the Plains had been organized as if they were **parallel troops, but had no training, and were untried by battle and the rigorous selection process of combat.**

All in all, the fault lay in thinking that the revolution could stem from the cities, with the July 26 Movement assuming a paramount role and the rural guerrillas serving as a mere resistance and propaganda device, rather than an essential military force.

The opposing viewpoint, which Che shared, was that the guerrillas in the Sierra were central and that all other forces had to be placed in their support. After **heated arguments** they finally reached agreement that the rural guerrilla movement would be buttressed as the central force in the struggle. Meanwhile the Plains would keep up the pressure in the cities, which was cutting off the régime politically and creating a breeding ground for militants. The actual events and the momentum of the Cuban revolutionary process would achieve this result naturally over the coming months, if the guerrillas in the Sierra could only hold out against the offensive being prepared by the government in order to capitalize on its recent success.

After an exhausting and often heated discussion, those present decided to replace Faustino Pérez and David Salvador and bring René Ramos Latour up to the Sierra. Fidel would remain in overall command of the troops and would coordinate the militias on the Plains. These groups would now be subordinated to the needs of the guerrilla columns. The structure of the organization in exile was to be changed; Carlos Franqui was called up to the Sierra to take charge of Radio Rebelde, and Manuel Urrutia was confirmed as candidate for provisional president.

Faustino Pérez who, in spite of the angry debates, was held in great esteem by Che for his bravery and honesty, would make a quick trip to Havana to arrange for his own replacement. Ramos Latour, whom Che had underestimated and whom he would come to appreciate enormously in the future, was appointed commander of a column in the Sierra Maestra.

(Despite all these agreements, when Franqui arrived from Miami on May 29, he found that communications between the Sierra and the Plains had broken down completely. "They accepted me not just because I came by plane, but because I came from Miami, not from Havana or Santiago.")

At the end of the meeting, Che was commissioned to inspect lines of defense in the Sierra where, according to Fidel, the army would first try to make inroads during the expected offensive. **This little patch of territory had to be defended by not much more than two hundred serviceable rifles when Batista's army launched its search-and-destroy mission several days later.**

THIS MAY WELL BE THE LEAST DOCUMENTED PART OF ERNESTO "CHE" Guevara's military history during the Cuban revolution. Che did not devote any of his *Reminiscences from the Revolutionary War* to it; his diaries have not been published; and in his *A Revolution Is Born*, he gave barely two paragraphs to the offensive.° This may be because Commander Guevara could not have liked his own part in it very much. Fidel Castro was keeping him on the sidelines because he had future plans for him and had stripped him, temporarily, of his command. Che, a man who systematically sought the front line, was to act primarily as a consultant and liaison during one of the bloodiest chapters of the Cuban revolution.

On May 8, Fidel, complaining that his pens did not work and that he had only a dirty old pencil stub to write with, sent a note to Captain Ramón Paz, telling him that news of army landings had reached him. This was the first of many alarms indicating that the expected government offensive had begun. Rebel territory had been the scene of feverish activity over recent days: unexploded bombs dropped by the air force had been made into land mines; plans had been drawn up to block off access routes to the Sierra; there was an intensive search for weapons; and the revolutionaries were trying to rebuild the July 26 Movement network in exile. They even tried to set up a primitive telephone line in the Sierra.

Che was constantly on the move, running around the eastern part of the zone (where Fidel was in command and Radio Rebelde had its transmission center) and Minas del Frío (where he tried to speed up training in the recruits' boot camp, as that was to be the mainstay of a new column).

Dr. Julio Martínez Páez remembered one of the rare moments of calm before the offensive began. The men were tired—exhausted—from digging trenches in the Sierra. Che had just returned to La Mesa after a meeting with Fidel. He strung up his hammock between two trees in the woods, ready to sleep. But he was called on to take up medical practice again, to treat a suppurating leg wound. And so behold the fearsome Commander Guevara, painstakingly using a twig and some cotton thread to make a splint for a bird.

———

Fidel and Che were constantly in touch during the second week of May. Fidel sent Che several notes, commenting on various ways of mining the trails and path leading to the wildest parts of the Sierra. Fidel's language was remarkably precise, and had a curious way of switching suddenly from overall strategy to minute detail: "Che: You need to pick up the two hundred-pound bombs. I'll send a couple of the others to take the place of the big ones. As each hundred-pound bomb has two fuses, instead of two explosions we can now have four, simply by using the round mines . . ." (Fidel, May 12). Or "Che: We have just found the solution to the problem we've been having with factory-made electric fuses. Use the current from five cells; connect them directly without using

°Translator's note: The latter book appears neither in the bibliography nor in the Library of Congress online copyright catalogue. Its Spanish title is *Una revolucion que comienza.*

a coil. We just blew three grenades up at once, 15 meters apart . . ." (Fidel, May 19). Among the practical military details ("Yesterday, I hung a patent metal grenade from a branch two meters high and detonated it. It sent deadly shrapnel flying everywhere") there was a more personal note: "Furthermore, we haven't spoken for days now, and that is almost a requirement. Here, I miss the old comrades" (Fidel, May 19).

On May 19, this quiet, relatively nostalgic interlude came to an abrupt end with a first clash in Las Mercedes, a small coffee-growing town that had been abandoned by the dictatorship's forces. This turned out to be the prologue to an all-out attack by government troops on May 25. The army had fourteen battalions prepared for the offensive, one with field artillery and another with tanks; six of these would go into action at one time. Rebel-occupied territory at that time was eighty miles across, but only a little more than three miles would separate the army columns intending to converge on La Plata.

In order to prepare for the attack, Fidel had regrouped the guerrilla forces, and ordered Che to form a new No. 8 Column with recruits from the training camp.

> **Fidel articulated the principle that it was not the number of enemy soldiers that mattered, but rather the number of men we would need to make our position invulnerable. And we were to stick to that tactic. So all our forces were grouped together around the headquarters in order to set up a compact front. On May 25, in the middle of a meeting between Fidel and some campesinos—they were discussing how they might harvest the coffee crop—the expected offensive began. The rebels there had not many more than 200 useful rifles among them.**

The confrontation began when the army's advance guard fell into an ambush at a place called La Herradura, near Las Mercedes. The rebels resisted mortar fire and air raids for thirty hours. The army finally entered Las Mercedes, but the rebels did not sustain a single casualty. Of this first round, Efigenio Ameijeiras said there were "neither winners nor losers; each side [was] stalking the other very closely."

Fidel had assumed direct command of the defense; his concerns and Che's movements at that time can be traced from the communications between them. It is obvious from their notes that the rebel forces suffered from grave shortages. In some notes Fidel is concerned about a rifle he repaired and another he made from odd parts; in others he speaks of the telephone line that was being installed inside rebel territory and would never be finished. On May 28, he sent a note complaining that coded messages were arriving, which he could not decipher because Che had taken the codes with him. A day later, Che was in the training camp at Minas del Frío and received an order from Fidel to send recruits to build up fortifications at the trenches. The last note was apprehensive: "There'll be weapons if we can hold out for ten days." They did not have to wait ten days; that same afternoon Carlos Franqui came in from Miami on a light aircraft with 20,000 rounds of ammunition, electric fuses for mines, and thirty Italian carbines.

Che spoke to the recruits at the training school on May 30 and began to form a structure for the column. Most of the men chosen were unarmed. Meanwhile, the fighting was becoming widespread. The army managed to advance four miles, but was held in check by Juan Almeida and Ramiro Valdés's columns. The battle lasted six days. Ameijeiras described the first engagements vividly:

> You had to move along pathways so narrow the men could walk only in Indian file, or along flattened trails made for horses and teams of mules. In that sort of terrain, an enemy can't use either tanks or heavy artillery, and air support in that group of mountains can be very relative. It wasn't so easy there to shoot straight with field guns, machine guns, and rockets, and cluster bombs have only a limited effect.

At the beginning of June, the army advanced northward and consolidated its position at Las Mercedes after three days of heavy fighting. Rebel territory was being squeezed. Fidel wrote to Che telling him that he was to act as operations coordinator; if the army managed to break through the Habanita line, which Che was covering just then, Crescencio Pérez should be on the other side so as not to abandon a whole swathe of territory.

On June 4, however, Ramiro announced that Che had arrived with a shipment of arms for his column, but two days later reported that the army was still gaining ground: "Their intent is quite clear to me: as they advance on one flank, they force us to cut off all the access routes to the Sierra. The situation is urgent."

On June 10, when there were air raids on the coast and it seemed the troops on the ships would come ashore, Che kept moving along the broad front, doubtless in agonies of frustration at not being able to lead a column into action. He took charge of communications and supplies, employing Lidia Doce again: she went up and down the Sierra, fetched and carried vitally important documents, and kept us in touch with the outside world. Fidel commented years later that "there was no point in stationing Che or Camilo at the head of a squadron; we had to keep them to lead columns afterward."

The situation was very dangerous. The government troops that had entered via Santo Domingo were now four miles from the rebel headquarters, while the ones that had landed to the south were in a position to advance along the Palma Mocha and La Plata rivers and meet up. With another two columns advancing from the west toward Minas del Frío, the government troops might have been able to surround the rebels. As Almeijeiras pointed out, "It was a critical moment for the guerrilla command." Fidel then sent for Camilo Cienfuegos, who was on the Plains, and asked him to join forces with the inner circle of defense and break through the blockade. Camilo was called up so as to better cover our patch of territory, which held priceless treasures, like a transmitter, hospitals, and arms dumps—and furthermore, an airstrip, located among the hills in La Plata, where a light plane could land.

Around June 16, Fidel ordered the La Mesa zone to be abandoned, pulling Almeida's, Ramiro's, and Guillermo García's columns together for a strategic withdrawal. The rebels' aim now, he said, must be to protect and defend their core territory for three months before moving on to a counter-attack.

Fidel wrote Che on June 17 that troops were advancing on Santo Domingo, which could not be allowed to happen. He requested two men with Garands and five with M1s: "This order to be carried out forthwith." Che replied:

> You will by now have news from Las Vegas. I don't think I should send you men who in any case have yet to arrive, because then the El Purgatorio road would be left undefended. I haven't intervened directly, but have followed your orders and left you in charge of Las Vegas. Understand, though, that I should be in closer contact. You must tell me at once how the men are to be deployed after, as I expect, Las Vegas falls tomorrow. And tell me whether I may take the initiative in a rearguard action with men from elsewhere. [Crescencio had some men available in Habanita.] I must have an answer before dawn.

On June 19, two rebel squads struck a heavy blow against an army battalion that had landed and was moving uphill. Fidel wrote to tell Che and ask him for "the seven men you have left who have automatic weapons." A little later he sent him a second note which shows that the pressure had not abated despite this first successful engagement: his forces had detected the presence "of enemy troops [somewhere] on the shore, which have not been located. All I have here is my rifle." Fidel also underlined the need to send the squad he had requested that morning:

> We run the risk of losing not only the territory, but also the hospital, the radio station, the ammunition, the mines, the food, etc. . . . We do not have the men to defend such a large area. . . . We will have to attempt a defense by regrouping before throwing ourselves back into irregular action.

On June 20, the rebels were defeated at the other end of the front, at Las Vegas. Che, entering the town on muleback, was almost captured in the middle of the road. Enrique Acevedo, who was relocating the mines (the continual changing of ambushes forced the rebels to keep digging up mines and burying them again) as he went uphill toward Loma del Mango in the rain, saw Las Vegas fall under the combined forces of the Guards and napalm from the air force. While passing a hut, he was stopped: the commander wanted to talk to him.

> I saw the Argentine in front of me, looking me up and down. I didn't know what to do. I felt like hugging him, but I was caked in filth. I looked at him and smiled.
>
> **May we know the reason for your not protecting the detonator from the rain?**
>
> Damn, I thought, he doesn't recognize me. Didn't he have anything nicer to say, considering we hadn't seen each other for five months? A bit pissed off, I mumbled that it all happened very fast and ended up saying, "Besides, all of us are wet."
>
> He looked up. I knew it was a bad day. He chewed me out in one sentence:
>
> **What a pity; you never change. Get out!**
>
> We flew off toward our rendezvous. A few minutes later, one of his escorts caught up with us and handed us a couple of pieces of nylon [to use as ponchos]. I mouthed a few words of thanks.

On June 20, Fidel ordered the rebel troops to regroup again; if they did not manage to stop the Guards, they would have to disband the columns and organize irregular guerrilla groups to infiltrate the lost territory. Fidel ordered Che: "Take charge of the Maestra line from El Purgatorio to the Altos de Mompié. Move the line back this way and transfer the squads to that zone, which will be reinforced by twenty men from Las Vegas. Mobilize everyone, even Crescencio's men."

An ambush led by Ramón Paz inflicted twenty-one casualties on the army as it advanced on the La Plata River on June 23. That was a needed first respite. Four days later, in the midst of continual clashes, Camilo's column arrived in the Sierra Maestra. Fidel was enormously happy. "At the best possible moment," he said.

But the rebels' situation was still precarious. They were holding out under constant bombing. The army had occupied Las Mercedes and Las Vegas, was close to Las Minas, controlled the coast and Santo Domingo, and could force its way through to the rebel command at La Plata in two hours. Fidel made plans for Radio Rebelde to be blown up if the front fell, and for the various columns to become wandering guerrilla groups that would try to make their way to the enemy's rear. The terrain now favored the rebels, however: the army was moving through the steepest part of the Sierra, a landscape ideally suited to ambushes. Furthermore, the regrouping ordered by Fidel allowed Che to march small groups astonishing distances in a few hours to plug gaps or set up more ambushes.

Che continued to work as a coordinator and organizer, but couldn't resist approaching the front line.

Vicente de la O, a doctor:

We were in Mompié . . . and Che, along with a guerrilla group of five or six men, was watching movements by the guards who had taken Minas del Frío. I was making a phone call, and at one point he said to me:

Listen, don't ring so much, just once and then hang up, or the guards will hear us.

He was lying in ambush in a bush no more than thirty meters from the soldiers.

The first engagement with Sánchez Mosquera's troops took place on June 28 in the vicinity of Santo Domingo. Lalo Sardiñas killed twenty soldiers in one company, and took twenty men prisoner with their weapons. Fidel blocked off the army's retreat by moving Camilo's, Almeida's, and Duque's troops.

Two days later, fighting was still under way in that zone, with one army battalion practically destroyed; meanwhile, in the Las Mercedes zone, Che was keeping in check the troops advancing toward Las Minas. Harry Villegas recalled: "We were commanded to halt in front of a house. Before we realized what was happening, the army was there and had opened fire. We began to run, they fired at us, and we ran faster, until we managed to get out. I think Che never ran so hard in his life—it was like a track and field meet."

The battle of El Jigüe began on July 11, when an army battalion was ambushed and held up, then closed in on as part of an operation led by Fidel personally. Che was keeping up the pressure on Las Minas, and fighting continued in Santo Domingo. That day a mortar bomb made a direct hit on a house where the writers of *El Cubano Libre* were eating; it killed Carlitos Más and Geonel Rodríguez, one of Che's best-loved cadres.

While Fidel successfully kept up the siege of El Jigüe, the army made a decisive thrust in the Minas del Frío zone and dislodged a group of poorly armed defenders to take the schoolhouse. Che, who was on his way back from La Plata, ran into the recruits as they were retreating. His first reaction was **You assholes, they took Minas del Frío off you. Well, now you'll have to take it back again.** Later, after he had cooled down, he would see it was an impossible mission.

The continual arrival of wounded made Che turn doctor once again; he had to perform an emergency operation right there in the woods.

A little later, he organized a successful ambush at the river, while the soldiers were trying to replenish their water supply. The rebels could not retake the school, but did manage to stop the army's advance with small ambush parties and prevent it from coming to the aid of the soldiers who were surrounded at El Jigüe. **Minas del Frío was the last point taken by the army.** Fidel wrote to Che: "I congratulate you on having managed to overcome the crisis there; our spirits have been raised by the knowledge that we face no danger from that quarter."

The siege was maintained. Fidel used loudspeakers to bombard the besieged soldiers with words, and used the radio to make false reports that induced the air force to bomb its own troops. On July 18 the rebels routed reinforcements that were on their way up from the sea. Over the next few days, attempts to relieve the besieged troops failed and Fidel, in a masterstroke, offered to free the besieged men in exchange for a surrender mediated by the Red Cross. Negotiations began on July 20, and Fidel ordered Che to mobilize toward Las Vegas, where he took delivery of 253 demoralized prisoners on July 23.

Just as the commission formed by Carlos Franqui, Faustino Pérez, and Horacio Rodríguez was taking delivery of the prisoners, they beheld "the spectacular appearance of Commander Guevara riding on a donkey." Che made an offer to the captain in charge of the troops in Las Vegas, to which he had been laying siege in the previous hours: he and his men could leave if they surrendered their weapons. Che warned him they would not be able to fight their way out.

While siege was laid to another group of soldiers, a clash took place on July 25 in Santo Domingo; there Ramón Paz and René Ramos Latour tracked down members of an army battalion who were taking food and supplies to Santo Domingo, and routed them. In the following days, however, Sánchez Mosquera's men managed to break through the siege, though they sustained casualties as they went. Sánchez Mosquera himself, whom Che considered a personal enemy, sustained a head wound in the withdrawal. The rebels meanwhile lost one of their bravest captains: Ramón Paz.

Fidel began to mobilize men to reinforce the siege on Las Vegas. (Camilo said Fidel was "begging some unknown god to bring some troops our way.") He tightened his grip on the battalions that were attempting to relieve the besieged troops. Che resumed talks with their commanding officer, Captain Durán. In Rafael Mompié's words, "It was a quick conversation, lasting maybe some fifteen minutes. . . . Che looked at his watch and said: **It's ten o'clock; at half-past ten we'll be fighting one another again.** They shook hands and took their leave of each other."

A little later, shots were heard and the Guards began to leave, apparently unarmed. But they had not only burned just part of their supplies, they were carrying hidden weapons. They tried to break out with the help of a light tank and under an air raid that was meant to cover their retreat. The rebels fell upon them, mainly for their weapons and ammunition. The light tank got stuck and was abandoned, to be bombed shortly after by the air force so the rebels could not capture it. Mark Herman destroyed an armored truck with the rebels' bazooka. Che was right there, at the head of his gang of teenagers, pushing forward.

While some stopped to engage stragglers from the Guards, Che went ahead with a small group, captured dozens of soldiers, and ran on among the trees to take the ones who were fleeing. One group, including a Captain Durán, surrendered to Ramón Silva. A hundred soldiers were taken prisoner, but René Ramos Latour, already wounded, was hit while leading his squad's withdrawal. Frank País's successor was dead by the time Che arrived. His loss was a terrible blow to the guerrillas, particularly to Che, who had argued long and hard with him but respected him enormously. There was an account to settle.

A new siege operation began almost immediately, focused now on Las Mercedes. Fidel wrote to Che on July 31: "I think the men are contributing much less than before: everyone is exhausted and so many officers have been killed." Verdecia and Paz had fallen, along with Ramos Latour and Cuevas. And there was to be no respite. That same day, Camilo informed Che that government reinforcements, headed by tanks, were drawing near on the Sao Grande road.

The front was in a state of tension. Fidel was obsessed with the captured tank and tried to repair it; Che had lost the use of his mule Armando, which had been wounded during an air raid that threw Che from the saddle. On August 5, a battle against the reinforcements began and the rebels were able to halt their advance. Two days later the army withdrew. Annoyed at not having been able to capture the besieged soldiers, and hearing that two tanks had gotten stuck in a mudhole during the retreat, Che said: **Let's grab those tanks off them.**

In Andrés Menes's words:

> When he said, that my flesh crawled, because we knew full well what tanks did. When Che said again, *Follow me, we're going to take the tanks,* we counted to ten. We followed him because he marched on ahead, and for no other reason. When we got to the stream and saw that the tanks had pulled themselves free [and were gone] . . . my body and soul came together again. It's not that I was scared of the army, but that I had a lot of respect just then for those iron hulks.

On August 10, as the offensive was in its final phase, the latest surrender of prisoners was being discussed in Las Mercedes. Fidel again had the wit to see that a returned prisoner who deeply hurt the enemy's morale was more useful than a prisoner who had to be tended and guarded.

Che had sent Delsa Puebla, Teté, on ahead with orders to propose that negotiations be opened, with the Red Cross as mediators; to fraternize with the soldiers; and to observe trenches and emplacements: **Well, Teté, wash your uniform and iron it, you need to be all smart when you go, with your July 26 bracelet, and don't let them take it from you.**

Later, Fidel entered the camp with Celia and Che to negotiate with Colonel Neugart. The colonel sounded out the rebels: how would they react if Batista were deposed by a military coup?

With the release of the prisoners, the counteroffensive was over. The rebels were the masters of the Sierra Maestra again.

After two and a half months of hard fighting, over 2,000 enemy troops were dead or wounded, had been taken prisoner, or had deserted. [The army detained almost 600 men for insubordination or desertion at the end of the offensive.] **They left 600 weapons in our hands, including a tank, twelve mortars, twelve machine guns, twenty-odd automatic rifles, and countless other automatic weapons, as well as a huge quantity of supplies and all sorts of equipment, to say nothing of 450 prisoners, who were handed over to the Red Cross when the campaign was over.**

The rebel army had sustained fifty casualties—a fifth of all the forces that had fought against the army in that zone—but 600 volunteers had joined up by the end of the campaign.

We had broken the back of Batista's army after that final offensive on the Sierra Maestra, but it had yet to be beaten.

The Invasion

THE REVOLUTION WAS SCARCELY GETTING ITS BREATH BACK AFTER defeating Batista's offensive when Fidel Castro, in one of the most brilliant of his military decisions, decided to take advantage of the government's general weakness and disarray and immediately launch a counterattack. In a plan that was very bold: The final strategy was then drawn up. There would be a three-pronged attack, entailing a flexible siege of Santiago; of Las Villas, where I was to march; and of Pinar del Río at the other end of the island, where Camilo Cienfuegos had to march.

Che originally thought that a large column of 120 to 150 men could be moved to the center of the island, to the other mountain range, the Sierra del Escambray, in vehicles because I have ordered a study of a quarter or half of the route and I believe it can all be done by motor. He was to trying to obtain the trucks in which I am exceedingly interested.

Fidel made an appointment on August 17 to meet Che two days later at the Altos de Mompié to finalize details. Guevara attended in the company of Zoila Rodríguez. He and Fidel held a long conversation on their own in La Plata, and the entire matter must have been settled then: the next day, on Radio Rebelde, Fidel announced the end of the government offensive and cryptically told of the departure of "invading columns" from the Sierra Maestra to other parts of the island. Once more, military prudence took a backseat to psychological effect. Just as in 1956, when the *Granma* expedition had been announced in advance, Fidel opted for the huge political advantage that would accompany news of a counterattack. This enhanced the rebels' image in the eyes of the population, which had become used to the "Mau Mau" keeping their word.

On August 21, Fidel issued written orders:

> Commander Guevara has been assigned the mission of leading No. 8, the "Ciro Redondo" Column, into the province of Las Villas. . . . No. 8 Column will set out from Las Mercedes between August 24 and August 30. The column's strategic objective will be to strike unceasingly in the central region of Cuba until enemy forces are totally immobilized.

Two days earlier, a similar order had been given to Camilo Cienfuegos, who was to head the No. 2 ("Antonio Maceo") Column, also in the west of the island.

At about this time, Fidel introduced Che to a campesino with a charming name, Edilberto Enamorado—Enamored Edilberto—who would serve as a guide in the operation's initial phase. Is it good luck to have people with names like that around? Pepín Magadán and Enamorado led a small group that had been taking supplies up to the Sierra Maestra, and Fidel entrusted them with Che's safety during the first phase of the invasion.

Well, looks like I'm going out.

"Out?"

Yes, I'm going off to the Plains. . . .

But this conversation had to be repeated over and over before it actually happened. At that time, they were saying in the Sierra Maestra that if the Guards did not come up, then they would go down after them. But getting people to volunteer was no easy task. The counteroffensive had worn a lot of cadres out with its three months of nonstop marching and fighting, on top of which a lot of campesinos from the mountains did not want to fight in unfamiliar terrain, and the Plains made them especially nervous. It was one thing to face soldiers on one's home ground, and another to descend into territory unknown to one. Most of those fighters had never visited any of the country's provincial capitals.

Enrique Acevedo, a fighter who had just turned sixteen and swapped his M1 rifle for a Garand, recalled:

> There was a split in the platoon, and not many were ready to leave the mountains. Six stepped forward to volunteer, including Lieutenant Alfonso Zayas, who had been my chief for a few months. I tried to bring the others around, and some joker said, "You must be a born masochist, the way Che's hammered you recently and you come back for more."

Che was meanwhile making lists of fighters obtaining guns and ammunition, and trying to make life a little easier for his ragged troops. There are several handwritten notes in which he scribbled down possible formations of the column, signed "Commander Ernesto Guevara" and then, underneath, " 'Che' Guevara." In agreement with Fidel, he named Ramiro Valdés second-in-command of the column. Fidel, meanwhile, was to act as quartermaster:

> This morning I sent you the men who have the Garand rifles from Crespo's formation. Do as you see fit with both. Send back anyone who is no use to you, with another weapon, and tell me how many Garands you have gathered and how many you think you will need.

A rumor was going around the mountains to the effect that Che was to go down to the Plains in a "firefighting" operation. Young Acevedo:

> Despite the silence surrounding the column's movements, the jungle telegraph is working full tilt. Well-informed sources say that we'll be leaving on September; others, making their début as strategists, say that the objective is the Cristal mountain range, but a minority say it's Camagüey.

The list of soldiers was being drawn up bit by bit; it consisted mostly of young campesinos who'd proven themselves in the last offensive. Some volunteers came along, like Joel Iglesias, Dr. Vicente de la O, and Dr. Oscar Fernández Mell, who had been working miracles from one end of the Sierra Maestra to the other since he'd joined up after the failed strike in April. About a third of those who were to march with Che had risen up in arms during 1957, most had fought in the battle at Las Mercedes, but only three had been part of the original *Granma* expedition: Che himself, Ramiro Valdés, and René Rodríguez. The average age of the men was twenty-four and **90 percent of our column was illiterate.**

Camilo's column set off on August 22; Che's departure was delayed while he waited for a light aircraft to come from Florida with sorely needed ammunition. **More than a hundred rifles were now useless because the fighters had no ammunition.**

Batista's air force was constantly bombing Las Mercedes, seriously hurting the local civilians although it had little effect on the fighters, who were spread out into platoons. On August 23 alone, there were twelve raids that used 250-pound bombs and rockets. Harry Villegas recalled that when he was in Guevara's platoon, Che once said to him: **Let's get out of here, because this is where the next one is going to fall.** Which was just what happened. Che seemed to have a sixth sense when it came to "knowing" where the bombs would fall.

Enrique Acevedo again:

[The air force attacking Las Mercedes]
After they finished with the bombs and rockets, they made several passes with machine-gun fire and then finally withdrew. I slowly got up, covered in dirt and stones. The house was in ruins, and as I approached I saw the shelter was empty; a rocket had struck some seven or eight yards away and knocked it over, with the beams sticking up in midair. . . . I kept sniffing around till I finally came up with what I'd been wanting to examine for a whole year—the Argentine's rucksack. It was unmistakable, with his bedtime reading in it. No one knew what he read—the members of his squad kept that sort of thing a closely guarded secret. . . . I rifled through his rucksack at once, finding nothing, thinking the books were at the bottom and were bound to be political, Stalin, Mao, and maybe Lenin . . . I managed to find a book in the middle of a really worn-out change of clothes, and was terrifically disappointed to see that it was *A Connecticut Yankee in King Arthur's Court,* and nothing more. I carefully repacked the rucksack and put some bits of rubble on top.

On August 24, Che called a meeting of the column; he gathered 300 fighters together and spoke of the mission. He painted a grim picture of the outlook; it's reported that he said: **We'll have soldiers for breakfast, aircraft for lunch, and tanks for dinner.** He underscored the fact that there would be ten to fifteen soldiers for each rebel fighter. For security reasons, he did not mention the objective, but Joel recalled:

He went over the fact that we would be off to unknown and unaccustomed terrain, where the population had no prior preparation and we would be under a lot of strain. What with enemy action, hunger, thirst, cold, all sorts of shortages, and possible estrangement from the population, it was possible that only 50 percent of our column—and maybe even less—would survive.

Che knew what he was doing; his idea was to make a selection from among that group of extremely young campesinos, who'd been shaken up by the revolution but were still not totally committed. After this dramatic and very Argentine speech, he went on to ask for volunteers—but not for hands to be raised. Rather, he told the rebels to think things over and give him the word through their platoon commanders in three days. He also gave three-day passes to those with family in the mountains.

The volunteers for the brand-new column gathered at the end of August in El Jíbaro, a country house in the foothills of the Sierra Maestra. About half of the 300 fighters Che had spoken to had volunteered. While they waited for the light aircraft, a hurricane with the friendly-sounding name of Daisy was battering southern Florida and said to be heading for the coast of Cuba.

Zoila Rodríguez demanded to join the column. She wanted to be considered just another fighter; she had taken part in risky actions in the past. Guevara gave her a flat no, instead asking her to look after his mule, Armando, who was recovering. Years later Zoila recalled that, out of love for Che, "I looked after that animal as if he were human." We know little about this separation (Che's diary for those few months has yet to be made public); still, we might suppose that both seem to have been aware that wartime liaisons are made and broken all the time, and that this separation was to be for good. It was not the first time Che had taken his leave of a woman that way.

The aircraft from Florida was to land on the twenty-eighth, five and a half miles from where the column had gathered. Che went out into open country with a small patrol to pick up the cargo, but the aircraft had been spotted and an enemy plane was machine-gunning it where it had landed. The army was nearby and the rebels unloaded the plane under fire. Under fire, Faustino undertook to do what was necessary to keep the plane from falling into enemy hands: dousing it with gasoline and setting it on fire. Che left out the fact that he was there, too, also under fire.

A pickup truck carrying a load of uniforms was lost, but the rebels managed to salvage guns and a radio. Unfortunately, the aircraft did not bring anything amazing, as you can imagine. For one thing, its cargo included no ammunition, which was nothing short of a tragedy in the circumstances: here were 144 hand-picked fighters armed with Garand, Springfield, San Cristóbal, and M1 rifles, but with an average of just 120 rounds each. Twenty-nine fighters had no arms at all.

Transportation was still a key problem. We were going to begin the march in trucks, thinking it would take us four days. Fidel wrote to Che: "Pepito has told me about the business with the trucks. Tell him to arrange it in line with your plans. Tell him to get the ones he needs, wherever and from whomever, but whenever possible they should come with food."

Che also had Blas Oreste trying to obtain transportation: **Tell me about the trucks, which I am especially interested in.** However, Blas managed to obtain only one truck, a green '52 Ford, from a rice farm; the farm's other truck was broken down. In the end, Che could not even use the Ford: **the enemy troops advanced on the airport and intercepted it with the gasoline in it, so we had to continue on foot.**

On August 30, Che sent a note to Fidel: **This time it seems I'm saying good-bye for good.** The army had concentrated five battalions and two tank companies in the vicinity, so the fighters were anxious as they waited to depart.

The column was in battle formation and ready to leave by seven P.M. Che met with the platoon chiefs and gave the orders: to march in silence, leaving no tracks, following all orders. And no smoking. Only Leonardo Tamayo was authorized to pass Che's orders on to the platoons; he would communicate with Captain Mark Herman, who was in the advance guard with Lieutenant Manuel Hernández at the head.

Sixteen-year-old Joel Iglesias led the forward platoon with the command group, in which Che, Ramiro Valdés, Miguel Álvarez, and a group of medics were to move. Captains Ángel Frías and José Ramón Silva led the third and rear platoons, respectively.

Javier Fonseca, a campesino from the mountains, described our leading player as he was then: "Che was looking a lot more weatherbeaten by now, and I don't know if it was just because his beard had grown and his hair was almost down to his shoulders, but he had less of a little boy's face and more of a chief's."

The column began to march shortly before eight P.M. on August 30, in the middle of a terrible downpour caused by Hurricane Daisy. Joel, who was convalescing from his wounds, went on horseback, as did Che, Ramiro, and Dr. de la O. The rest of the men went on foot, Many of them were shoeless, their uniforms in rags. They halted after marching four miles, sliding in the mud all the way. In his first communiqué to Fidel, Che would mistakenly date the departure **nightfall on the 31st**. It wasn't the first such mix-up about dates; the rebel leaders hardly slept, and the days seemed to run into one another. **All was quiet as we passed a point the guards had abandoned, but we couldn't continue more than a little under six miles, stopping to sleep on a hillock on the other side of the road.**

The marchers set off again at eleven P.M., arriving at an abandoned estate at 5 P.M. The men were worn out, having walked seventeen miles with fully loaded rucksacks. Fernández Mell would remember that march years later: he was carrying a full backpack *and* a knapsack with forty pounds of medicine.

The next day and into the night, in total silence, the marchers crossed a nearby highway which several supporters of the July 26 Movement were guarding, In the afternoon, aircraft had flown over the marching rebels, who were under cover, and an army patrol had gone by two hours before they crossed the highway.

We crossed the road and took three trucks, which broke down with terrifying regularity, and came to an estate called Cayo Redondo, where we spent the day with the hurricane approaching. The Guards came close, about forty of them, but they went off without fighting. We followed with the trucks, being helped along by four tractors, but it was just impossible and we had to leave them behind the next day.

Part of the column had to travel behind on foot, as they could not all fit into the trucks. Progress was slowed by thick mire and hurricane-force winds. The rigors of the march were taking their toll of the troops' clothes and their footwear. The rebels laid down planks to cross streams. The trucks bogged down in the country roads. **We had indeed found trucks but, also on September 1, we met up with a severe hurricane, which devastated all roads except for the central highway, the only paved one in that part of Cuba.**

Now it was Hurricane Ella's turn. Joel thought that at least they could be thankful that the wind and rain were keeping the air force away.

Speculation about their destination continued, but Che kept it secret. The army was closing in on the column, but it was obvious they were not too eager for a confrontation in that hellish weather.

Despite Che's desperate attempts to keep going with the trucks, using tractors to pull them out of the mud, it was just not possible. Enrique Acevedo said:

> At midnight it was our turn. It was the third time we had to shove the thing out with our shoulders. Everything was wet; it hadn't stopped raining. Che, who was walking past just then, gave orders for us to get off the truck and pull it out of the mud. There was no answer from inside. One or two got down, but the rest didn't budge. The Argentine lost his temper and cursed and raised his gun. To be on the safe side, we all dived out headfirst and pushed, or at least pretended to.

Dr. Fernández Mell said, "In the column they used to say you had to love Che for nothing."

Finally, despite Che's insistence, the trucks had to be abandoned or the guerrillas would still have been trying to drag them along in the mud when day broke. The next day, September 2, Che gave the order to scatter the trucks and hide them. **We continued on foot with a few horses and came to the banks of the Cauto River, which we could not cross at night, as it was very high.**

"The Cauto was quite a sight, risen to the banks," Fernández Mell said. "Trees and drowned animals were being washed away by the current." One of the guerrillas, Alfonso Zayas, added, "What a sight! It looked like the sea! The catch was that we had to get to the other side, and most of us couldn't swim."

Che wrote to Fidel:

> **We spent eight hours today** [crossing it] **and tonight we leave the peasant's house to follow the route as planned. We have no horses but can get more on the way; I plan to reach the assigned operations zone with everyone on horseback. Accurate estimates of my time of arrival cannot be made due to the many obstacles we encounter on these godawful roads. I will try to keep you informed along the way to create efficient messenger routes and tell you what we learn about the people there.**

During the night, the rebels were able to get horses, mules, and donkeys—eighty-nine mounts in all—and Che wrote his first report to Fidel at the El Jardín estate, but changed the date to throw the army off the scent in case the note was captured. The message ended: **For now, just greetings from here to the far-off world which barely appears on the horizon.**

After crossing the Salado River on September 4, the column was warmly welcomed by some local campesinos and received forty-eight pairs of boots sent by a supporter of the July 26 Movement.

That day Che formed a punishment squadron within the column, dubbing it the *descamisados,* or shirtless ones. The contrived metaphor was typical of him: he explained that shirtless people are untrammeled by possessions and are outside norms. Che put Armando Acosta in command and ordered him to be very strict with the men. The *descamisados* were stripped of their weapons and had to earn them back in combat. The first member of the squadron was a fighter who had argued with his platoon leader. (The day before, Che had made a man go without food for two days because he had fired a stray shot.)

At dawn on September 5, the column crossed Tamarindo Brook; Che, who had dismounted to ford the brook, got his foot stuck in the mud and lost a boot when he tried to pull free. He limped along with one foot bare for the rest of the day's march. The guerrillas, exhausted after the six-mile march along hellish trails, rested on Saturday, September 6, in a sugar plantation called La Concepción.

Camilo Cienfuegos had meanwhile been marching in parallel, and Che had had frequent contact with him. He turned up at the plantation and made quite an entrance, charging into Che's hammock on horseback and toppling him out. This terrified the guerrillas who didn't already know them—*Will the Argentine stand for this?*—but Camilo and Che were used to sharing private practical jokes of the kind that few people would put up with. The two commanders had their photograph taken together, Che barefoot.

Che spent the day nursing his feet, washing clothes, and talking to groups of campesinos who approached the column. The support for the rebels in the Sierra Maestra was strong in the region; Che had to turn away would-be volunteers, as this was not the ideal moment for recruiting campesinos. He ordered two more fighters to join the descamisados, one for having dismantled a rifle without permission, the other for having lost bullets. He himself was worn out, so much so that he collapsed in the middle of a conversation with the Doctors de la O and Fernández Mell. At first the medics thought something serious was wrong, but then they realized that Che had keeled over because he'd fallen asleep standing up. It was not just the aftereffect of the tension and the marathon marches in stormy weather (where, as Joel said, "a six-click march turned out to be thirteen after you zigzagged across the poor terrain"); he had also used up his rest periods meeting and talking with the countryfolk.

September 7 was a holiday and the fighters ate beef. Che wrote to Camilo:

> **This afternoon I'm off to the rice farm, which must have been taken by now. . . . There are [said to be] 400 regulars at Jobabo. Probably crap, but action must be avoided. Send me your whereabouts and keep people on the alert so as not to get attacked in case we meet, as they say we will.**

Actually, there were twenty-three soldiers in Jobabo, but although they knew of the column's presence, they preferred to play possum.

> Everything indicates that the regulars don't want to fight—and we don't, either; to tell the truth, I'd be scared of a retreat with 150 rookies in unknown territory like this. But a guerrilla war fought with thirty men could do wonders in the area and revolutionize it.

The column set off again at four P.M. for the Bartés rice farm. They crossed the Jacobo River on the border between Oriente and Camagüey provinces. "Che was a very good swimmer," Joel said. "So when we had to cross a river and had nothing to cross over on, he'd ford it time and again, carrying rucksacks and weapons, swimming with one hand and holding things aloft in the other to keep them dry."

The column reached the rice farm at night; the advance guard secured the zone and, as usual, were joined by a few campesinos where they halted. Che ordered a crop-dusting plane to be put out of action. They entered the farm store, where Ramiro Valdés took note of everything that was taken and scrupulously paid for all of it.

With Pablo Rivalta's help, Che had been meeting with campesinos in this zone, helping to set up a union. He also met with the estate owners, trying to make them raise the miserable wages they offered and pay revolutionary taxes to the rebel army.

> **In passing, I laid the foundations for a rice-workers' union in Leonero; I also talked about taxes, but they knocked me down. It's not that I backed down in front of the owners, but I do**

> think the rate is excessive. I said this could be negotiated and
> left it for the next one who turns up.

(Che never did find out about it, but the operation worked. Two weeks
later the rice farmers raised wages and paid taxes to the July 26 Movement.)
    That same day, Che began a second report to Fidel:

> After exhausting days of marching, at last I can write to you
> from Camagüey. There are no immediate prospects of the pace
> picking up from an average of three or four leagues a day,
> since the troop is only half-mounted and have no saddles.
> Camilo is around someplace, I waited for him at the Bartés
> rice farm, but he didn't show up. The Plains are fearful: there
> aren't so many mosquitoes, we haven't seen so much as a sin-
> gle helmet, and the aircraft look like harmless doves. We have
> trouble listening to Radio Rebelde via Venezuela. . . . Someone
> with a social conscience could work wonders in this region,
> and there are a lot of hills to hide in.
>   As for my future plans, I can tell you nothing as far as the
> route is concerned, because I don't know myself, it rather de-
> pends on particular and random circumstances. Right now,
> for instance, we're waiting for some trucks to see if we can get
> rid of the horses, which were perfect in Maceo's aircraftless
> times but are very visible from the air. If it weren't for the
> horses, we could calmly walk by day. It's mud and water sea-
> son, and the Fidel-like moves [shouts of Dammit!" and "Hell!"]
> that I've had to make to get the howitzers through in a fit
> state, they're amazing. It's taken colossal efforts to swim
> across several brooks, but the troops have behaved well, al-
> though the punishment squadron is working full tilt and
> seems likely to become the largest in the column. The next re-
> port will leave by a mechanized route, if possible, from Cam-
> agüey city. Fraternal greetings to those up in the Sierra, which
> we can't see anymore.

Che had a tense meeting with the owner of the rice farm. When he arrived
with his escorts, he found that a small banquet had been prepared for him in
the dining room. It was a great temptation to men who had been eating badly,
but Che brought his ubiquitous pride and spartan nature to bear and would
not accept anything from the American owner. After much pressing, he did
allow his escorts to have a brandy. There is no record of the conversation, although there is of Che's comment as he left: I would die smiling, behind
a rock on the brow of a hill, fighting against people like that. Whether
the phrase has been embellished over the years or whether Che forgot his
usual reserve, it was another example of the anti-U.S. sentiment he had developed in previous years.
    Again the column set off at night, with a motorized group using a jeep, a
light truck, and a water truck. Che and his escort, Leonardo Tamayo, lost their

way for a while when they fell asleep on horseback. The advance guard, five men in a light truck driven by Ramiro, arrived at the sugar mill belonging to the La Federal estate. It consisted of five isolated houses in the middle of a plantation of about 40,000 acres—1,200 *caballerías*—whose owners paid miserable wages to their workers but had hired seven soldiers and a Rural Guard corporal to man a permanent security detachment.° The Guards, alerted by rumors that there were rebels in the vicinity, tried to set up an ambush. The flashed signals in the rebels' direction at signals dawn. Ramiro Valdés responded by switching his truck's headlights on and off three times, probably thinking he had come across men from Camilo's column. The rebels approached, there were shouted exchanges of identification—"July 26 Movement!" "Rural Guards here!"—and then the shooting began.

One of the rebels—Marcos Borrero—tried to take cover behind some empty gasoline drums and was killed. Mark Herman was wounded in the ankle, and the guerrillas' fire killed one soldier. Fortunately for Che's column, a supporter of the July 26 Movement had cut the telephone lines so the soldiers could not get in touch with the Elia sugar mill. Ramiro withdrew and found Che 500 yards from the entrance to the sugar mill. Guevara immediately ordered two ambushes to be set up and personally took command, keeping the column in reserve. The soldiers had meanwhile barricaded themselves inside their cottage and adopted firing positions on the second floor. Their corporal was wounded. One soldier threw down his rifle and cartridge belt and ran out. (Afterward, when the rebels questioned him, the soldier recounted how he and two campesinos from the estate had tried in vain to make contact with the rebels to warn them about the ambush.)

Angel Frías, who was in charge of fighting the army cavalry, had stepped up the pace as he heard the shots. Che tried to take in the situation, to determine what he was up against. The rebels who had been moving by truck were taking positions and firing on the house. Roberto Rodríguez—the Cowboy Kid—and Enrique, the younger Acevedo brother, volunteered to make a frontal assault on the house. Che said it was very dicey and they would be killed, but he accepted.

They made the attempt at seven A.M. while their comrades fired on the windows. They found the ground floor empty and carefully climbed the stairs, covered by Angel Frías. The two volunteers entered one of the rooms and fired on what they thought were the yellowish uniforms of the Rural Guards. Immediately, there was chaos in the hallway. Acevedo was wounded in both arms during the almost face-to-face firing, the Cowboy Kid found himself confronting five soldiers, and Frías broke his ankle throwing himself down the stairs to get out of the line of fire. From the floor, Frías shouted that he would throw grenades at the soldiers. The Cowboy Kid continued to fire. And the soldiers surrendered.

The ambush at the mill cost the column one dead and three wounded. The rebels entering the cottage began to shout angrily that the Guards should

°In Cuba a *caballería* is about thirty-three acres of land.

be killed, but Che pulled rank and said that the prisoners were not to be touched.

Marcos Borrero was buried and the column's medical corps attended to the wounded in an M26 supporter's house some three miles away, where they operated on Enrique, made a cast for Frías's foot, and nursed Herman.

The army was now alerted to the rebels' presence, and responded by requesting air support. The first reinforcements came from the Francisco and Elia sugar mills. Che dispersed the column on a nearby hill, set up ambushes on the approaches to the estate, and prepared a withdrawal. The regulars ended up falling into the ambush set up by Ramón Silva, most of whose men were sleeping off their exhaustion. Shots were exchanged and one of the guerrilla fighters wounded, probably in the crossfire from his own men. He later died. Silva regained the position and the army withdrew with two wounded. Lieutenant Colonel Suárez Suquet, who had been in charge of the fruitless hunt for the elusive rebel column, flew in from Nuevitas to take command of the operation, but the rebels fired on his Piper as it flew overhead. They wounded the pilot, punctured the fuel tank, and forced a landing. The column meanwhile pulled out gradually and moved back toward the hill.

The army lost contact and took the sugar mill in reprisal, then forced the workers to kneel at machine-gun-point. Later, some were accused of having collaborated with the column and were jailed. Borrero's body was dug up and abused. What the army could not do in combat, it could invent on a desktop: subsequent dispatches mentioned fifteen rebel casualties.

On September 8, Che's and Camilo's columns were marching practically alongside each other. No. 8 Column had three wounded and some Guards held prisoner. Some fell asleep, exhausted, after crossing a river and others lagged behind and constantly had to be picked up, all of which made for slow progress. Che quickened the pace, a fortunate decision: Lieutenant Colonel Suárez Suquet arrived at the La Federal estate with reinforcements and two B-26s began to bomb the hill where the rebels had been taking cover.

The column camped at Laguna Baja, where they made contact with M26 supporters. Che asked them to take Enrique Acevedo with them—he had lost a lot of blood—and took his leave of his youngest fighter: **Don't go shooting your mouth off out there and telling people you're a captain, because you're really just a lieutenant**—a sidelong way of telling him he had been promoted. Enrique was taken away by a member of the Cienfuegos underground in a taxi, with a new haircut and a long-sleeved shirt to cover up his wounds.

Some food and a little rest were to be had at a farm belonging to an M26 member, who returned the money Che and Camilo paid for the food. The exhausted troops collapsed and fell asleep on the spot. The doctors nursed the fighters' feet—there was no rest for medics. Everyone was suffering from a plague of mosquitoes, gall midges, and other insects, and had to wrap them-selves up in blankets and sheets. The sentries had the worst of it, so the watches were reduced to a half-hour instead of two hours. The two columns took their leave of each other in the early evening. Camilo took motorized transportation provided by the movement and handed over his horses, which Che's column would use later.

Che set off at 9:30 P.M. on September 10; speed and mobility were the watchwords of guerrilla warfare. They reached the sugar mill at the Faldigueras del Diablo estate toward 4 A.M., where people linked to the M26 gave them food and boots. Che had a severe asthma attack then, and asked for medicine to help him stay awake. He mustered some strength from some-where or other and met local workers who were members of the M26 or the People's Socialist Party; they had had frequent struggles against eviction by the landowners, the King Ranch Company.

The march got under way again at six P.M. on September 11. There were problems—guides got lost; the column breaking formation, troops lagged behind—all of which put Che in a stormy and aggressive mood. The 150-man guerrilla column was marching in platoons, by night, so as not to be an easy tar-get, but this ensured that the troops would sometimes lose their way, and each other. The men were exhausted; they fell asleep on horseback, dropped to the ground, and kept sleeping. As Alfonso Zayas put it: "Back then . . . a bed of nails would have done." The next day, though, the column had new guides and could march by day with its one hundred horses in open country, sheltered from the enemy air force. They reached the San Miguel del Junco sugar mill by nightfall. Having received word of an army ambush in the vicinity, Che dropped the idea of marching farther that night. M26 supporters had seen a column of trucks and armed soldiers—about five hundred, they said. Che smiled and asked if there were not three hundred. Still, it was a dangerous zone; they would have to cross the highway between Camagüey and Santa Cruz del Sur.

———

The rebels had more and more contact with the M26 network, and got the im-pression that it was widespread but not very coordinated. There were more prospective recruits; Che temporarily accepted three boys from Victoria de Las Tunas, since Alberto Castellanos had recommended them. Che had re-jected some fifty unarmed men who had wanted to join up over the previous week.

The column marched off again toward 11 P.M. on Saturday, September 13; they now had four trucks, two jeeps, and a Pinilla Rum delivery truck provided by the townspeople of Victoria de las Tunas. For security reasons, the trucks kept fifty yards apart on the bad, muddy trails that ran alongside the railroad tracks. They stopped off at small ranches, where three impromptu volunteers joined up without Che even finding out about it. The trucks broke down and Che again had to raise Cain, gun in hand, to make his troops pull them out of the mud. It transpired that Camilo had had a confrontation with the army the day before. Tamayo commented: "Camilo was moving a distance ahead of us, but that made the road as dangerous as if it were mined, because the army would come in to fill the gap." It was therefore almost inevitable that, what with exhaustion and lack of reconnaissance, the column walked into one of the many ambushes that the army had set up, at the Cuatro Compañeros country house. The advance guard found a tractor oddly parked in the middle of the road and, by the time they realized why it was there, it was too late, the soldiers opened fire. It was 4:45 in the morning; the rebels were still half-asleep, and in a nightmare at that.

Che ordered the rebels not to open widespread fire; rather, those in the advance guard were to contain the enemy. He arranged a rendezvous at a hill to the south, a mile and a half away. Zayas recalled: "We couldn't tell whether south was north or west. You can just imagine what happened." Che ran up and down amid the gunfire trying to reorganize the column. Pablo Rivalta left his backpack in one of the trucks in his concern to bring back those who had set off on the wrong side of the road—a loss that would have serious consequences. Meanwhile:

> It was chaos. As we did not know the zone at all, we were ordered to march to a hill we could see in the dawn's light, but to get there we had to cross a line along which the guards were marching both ways. We had to fight to clear the way for those comrades who had fallen the farthest behind.

The arrival of a train in the middle of the engagement disconcerted the fighters even more. Che ordered bazooka fire to prepare to take the train out, but withdrew the order on discovering that there were no troops in it. The rear guard kept the army in check, and during the action José Ramón Silva was wounded. He continued to show exemplary stoicism despite having suffered a fractured right shoulder.

Che ordered Silva relieved; Fernández Mell attended to him on the nearby hill while the rebels covered them with machine-gun fire, wasting bullets—which is unusual in a guerrilla war. Silva had lost a lot of blood, so they tried to give him plasma, but the transfusion apparatus did not work—fortunately, as it turned out that the plasma was no good.

The rebels kept the army from taking the railroad track and splitting the column in two. We had to keep fighting on the railroad track, over a distance of no more than two hundred meters, to contain the enemy's advance, as we were short of men.

The army air force arrived at 7:30 A.M.—two B-26s, two C-47s, and a light aircraft. Joel:

> While the air force began to strafe us with bombs and machine-gun fire, the dictatorship's soldiers tried to advance again. Most of the column had crossed the tracks. The fighting started up again, most intensely where

Che was. The soldiers were also advancing over the savanna, taking cover behind the few trees, shouting for us to surrender . . . [but] the attack was repulsed, and the dictatorship's soldiers had to crawl away.

Armando Acosta was now in charge of the rear guard. **The skirmish lasted two and a half hours, until 9:30 A.M., when I gave the order to withdraw, having lost comrade Juan, whose leg had been smashed by a bomb.** The main body of the column had made it to the hill under very ineffective strafing, but some had gotten lost. Joel remembered:

> Around 9:30 a.m., Che ordered some comrades to stay and offer resistance at the railroad track while the rest went farther uphill. A whole lot happened as we made the traverse in small groups. Even Che fell asleep during a ten-minute break he gave, along with the rest of the group who accompanied him, and was most upset when he woke up well after the allotted time.

A group of campesinos offered to set out and look for the stragglers. They set up several ambushes up as the men gathered together. Three platoon chiefs were wounded at that time, and three lieutenants were lost.

At a camp between the San Antonio and Cayo Cedro estates, Che took the opportunity to treat the column to a critique. He began with a breakdown of the errors that had led them into the tractor ambush: the lack of reconnaissance; letting tiredness and listlessness get the better of them. Those who had lost their backpacks were severely upbraided, as were those who had abandoned weapons or ammunition. And, once he'd gotten started, Che turned all his anger on himself for having lost control when the truck was bogged down just before they reached Cuatro Compañeros.

The column marched off at six P.M. that same day. Army forces had been mobilized from the east toward the zone. That was the "invasion's" first success: forcing troops to move away from the Sierra Maestra.

On September 17, they ate just once, at three P.M.; the last to eat were Herman and Che. Beef, rice, half a can of condensed milk, and off again at five A.M. They arrived at the La República estate at dawn. **The men began to regroup in the days following; ten stragglers showed up in Camilo's column.**

They set out again at 11:30 P.M., Che riding a mule and suffering from an asthma attack. The mule got stuck in the mud; Che tried to pull it out. Alfonso Zayas, who was by his side, tried to help and could only hear Che wheezing.

> I felt simultaneous annoyance and admiration at the great effort he was making. He always carried this device to help him breathe, but it wasn't much use just then. If I stayed to help him, then the other comrades would not be able to get through.

Che, gasping, told Zayas: **Go on, go on, I'll catch up with you.**

He did catch up, a little later. But he was not the only one on the edge of exhaustion; the whole column was worn out. Joel recalled that "the pace was slow and heavy. The column had been ravaged by the long marches which, given our physical state, tended to get shorter. We were thirsty and hungry, and the mosquitoes, the deadly mud, and the rain took a great toll on us."

As they were camping out on September 18, someone found some of the rodents known as *jutías* and, hungry as the troops were, the hunt began, and they caught some. Che, who was reading, saw the hunters go and forbade them to use rifles.

The column marched off in the afternoon and arrived at Laguna Guano at eleven that night. Some campesinos there told Che that the army had 250 men gathered about nine miles away, so the guerrillas marched on. They had been marching six to ten miles inland, in grassy terrain alongside the coastal swamp, about ten or twelve miles a day.

Relations with the campesinos were very good; wherever the column went there was support and food, although not very much of the latter.

> **Despite the difficulties, encouragement from the campesinos was never lacking. We always found one willing to act as a guide or a scout, or to provide just enough food to keep us going. There wasn't, of course, the unanimous support we had in the Oriente province, but there was always someone to help us out. At times we were given away as soon as we had passed an estate; that was not due to any direct action by the campesinos against us, but to the conditions these people lived in. They'd been turned into the estate owner's slaves and, afraid of losing their daily bread, they told the boss of our passage through the region. The boss, in turn, would graciously inform the military authorities.**

The social conscience of the Camagüey campesinos in the cattle-rearing zones is minimal and we had to face the consequences of a lot of squealing. Che made this point again elsewhere, but he was wide of the mark. His impression was based on constant ambushes and the ever-present threat of the army, and did not do the country people justice. A review done years later of army dispatches showed that denunciations were very few and far between.

On September 20:

> On the radio we heard a report from [General Francisco] Tabernilla about how Che Guevara's column had been routed. It turned out that, in a rucksack, the army had found a notebook listing the names, addresses, arms, ammunition, and supplies of the whole column. Furthermore, one of the men in the column, a member of the PSP, had left behind his rucksack containing party documents.

There is no record of Che's reaction, but it could not have been gentle. The capture of Acosta's and Rivalta's rucksacks, which contained not only PSP material but also details of the column's members, would allow Tabernilla to began a worldwide propaganda campaign, with a news conference in which he spoke of "Fidelism-Communism." In that same conference, the former sergeant from Batista's clique hotly denied the rebel invasion of Camagüey and gave assurances that "the groups that made inroads from the East were struck down by the army." He cited sixteen guerrilla casualties and said the "outlaws [had been] put to flight."

The phony news of our death made the troops very happy. Nonetheless, pessimism was gaining ground little by little. Hunger, thirst, weariness, the feeling of helplessness toward the enemy forces that were coming closer and closer, and, above all, the terrible foot rot which the campesinos call "mush" made every step our soldiers took sheer hell and had turned us into an army of shadows.

They were an army it took some trouble to keep active. Zayas recalled:

One day when we were sleeping in a grove beside a brook and the hour was growing a bit late, I heard a noise like palm leaves falling from the trees: it was Che cutting the ropes holding up the hammocks, as the comrades had overslept. To tell the truth, everybody was dead beat. He didn't cut my rope, because I threw myself out quick, but I was struck by the fact that the fall hurt me more than if my hammock rope had been cut.

There was a droll event in the midst of the suffering. Che, with his usual strictness, thought a guerrilla named José Pérez Mejía had deserted. Nothing of the sort: the man rejoined the column, explaining that he had fallen asleep and gotten lost while answering a call of nature.

September 23–25: **We had no scouts and were following the broken trail left by comrade Camilo.** A campesino apologized for not being able to offer them more to eat and drink in his house: Camilo had been through a few days before. . . . **We have been walking almost nonstop between swamps since the twentieth. More than once we had to abandon the few horses we had. Foot rot is beginning to take its toll on the troops.** Che also suffered a persistent, exhausting, three-day asthma attack.

Leonardo Tamayo: "We wanted to head for the central region of the province, but he said we should go south. The south was the most inhospitable part, and that's where we went." Che surmised that the army would look for the easiest ways out of the Sierra del Escambray and block them. "The army could not think of three things at once."

Che sent a squad led by Ramón Pardo and Dr. de la O to the store at the

Aguila rice farm, where they got some food and also some tractors with rakes and carts.

Nonetheless, the trap closed in on September 29.

> **We had left the Aguila rice farm storeroom behind and entered the grounds of the Baraguá barracks when we found that the army had completely blocked off the line we had to cross. The Guards discovered us as we marched, and our rear guard fought them off with a couple of shots. Assuming that the shots had come from government troops waiting in ambush, according to their persistent habits, I ordered that we wait for nightfall, thinking we could get through then. When I found out that there had been a skirmish and the enemy knew exactly where we were, it was too late to try to get through: it was a dark and rainy night, and we had no reconnaissance of the enemy's well-entrenched position at all.**

Che told Acosta that he had been responsible for the clash with the army: Those shots will cost us very dear.

We had to retreat using a compass, sticking to the swamps and sparse hills to throw the aircraft off track as they were really focusing their attack on a wooded hill nearby.

They were almost surrounded by the army on September 30. Although the soldiers did not know the exact position, they knew the guerrillas were inside their cordon. Five companies had been deployed; it was a wet and rainy night. Che sent reconnaissance missions out to try to find a gap in the cordon, ordering them: Don't shoot, even if you're shot at. Guile Pardo and Acosta drew impossibly close without being detected. The soldiers fired at random, but the rebels stayed down in the mud and did not return fire. The army had reserves every fifty meters, and a small train brought them food and supplies.

Che was not the only one to be exasperated by fighting blindfolded. Lieutenant Colonel Suárez Suquet, who had taken command of the chase, remarked to another officer: "You see, this hasn't finished, and it never will."

At five A.M. on October 1, Che ordered the guerrillas to march through a flooded swamp, splitting up into small groups to camouflage themselves. He met with the column commanders at four P.M. to order another reconnaissance. Joel Iglesias remembered:

> The comrades' exhaustion was such that at times they stayed put when army aircraft passed overhead and strafed us. We were knee-deep, waist-deep, in water and to keep ourselves more or less out of it we had to sit beside some big trees that had little islets around them. We were in the swamp for about three days, surrounded. We used to bed down on one of those islets and throw leaves on it. The ground was soft, like quicksand, and gradually we sank into it until we were half underwater, but we were so exhausted we would just sleep on, with just our chests and head out of

the water. We'd see [Che] get up every now and again and go over to the comrades, especially those having the hardest time of it, to raise their spirits, talk to them, and tell them we had to be strong, we had to hack it, we had to get through.

I had to really chew the invaders out in the middle of the brush. They were barefoot, starving, and undisciplined. They had gallows-like, deathly expressions. They took no notice. At times it even took physical punishment to goad them on. I told them they were writing an important chapter in the history of Cuba, even if they didn't know it.

Under those conditions, Che called a meeting of the officers in the column and for the first time gave them details of the mission in Escambray. He told them the objective to set up a guerrilla war there, to cut the island in half and take pressure off the Sierra Maestra. He talked about the political work to be done in combining the groups fighting in the Escambray, about the idea of building foundations like those in the Sierra. In that same meeting, he was pressed by the younger officers, who wanted to make advance by fighting their way through the cordon. Che insisted that they would be at a disadvantage in combat and had to avoid it unless there is no other way out. Fernández Mell recalled: "He kept on answering that the time was not ripe yet, that for now it was nature we had to fight to get to the Escambray."

Another patrol, led by Rogelio Acevedo, tested the cordons limits again. In the dead of night they provoked some soldiers into firing on them to see if there was a gap in the cordon. Finally, they found one at the end of the Baraguá pier and reconnoitered. When they reported back to Che, he saw light at the end of the tunnel and immediately ordered them to go through. Again under cover of night; no lights; no noise. The advance guard crossed over and set up ambushes on either side of the railroad track while the rest of the column went through, wading chest-deep in the water with their rifles held aloft.

We went through that muddy lagoon, doing our best to dampen the noise of 140 men paddling through the mire, and walked almost two kilometers until we crossed the tracks almost a hundred meters from the last army post. We could hear talking. The paddling, impossible to avoid, and the moonlit night made it almost certain the enemy would realize we were there, but the lack of combat-readiness we have always seen in the soldiers of the dictatorship made them deaf as posts.

It was eleven P.M. on October 2.

For the next three days, the column advanced by night,

in saltwater swamps. A quarter of the troops had either worn-out shoes or none at all. In pestilent swamps, without a drop

of drinking water, with the air force constantly strafing us, without a single horse to take the weakest through the unforgiving marshes, with our shoes destroyed by muddy sea water, and plants cutting our bare feet, we were in really dire straits as we struggled through the Baraguá cordon and into the famous stretch from Júcaro to Morón.

The army kept the pressure up, and the air force often flew over.

Our psychological situation was like that of the early days in the Sierra Maestra: we saw a possible squealer in every campesino. We could not set up contacts with the July 26 Movement, because a couple of supposed members refused my request for help; only from the PSP did I receive money, nylon ponchos, some shoes, medicine, food, and guides. They said they had requested help for us from the organizations in the M26, but got the following reply, which should be noted for the record, as I have no evidence: "If Che sends us word in writing, we'll help him; if not, he can fuck himself."

Meanwhile, the Revolutionary Directorio forces in the Escambray were following the march's progress in broadcasts by Radio Rebelde. They were to send one of their guides to try to make contact, and later a patrol of armed men. Men from a group called the Escambray Front II and from the M26 were doing the same.

On October 7, the column made its first contact with guerrillas from the Escambray. Che got his first impression of tension between the M26 and Front II, which had splintered from the Directorio and was led by Eloy Gutiérrez.

They had a whole string of complaints about Gutiérrez's actions, and told me that Bordón had been taken prisoner and things had reached the point where the groups had been close to pitched battle. I felt a lot of dirty linen needed to be washed in public here, and sent one of the M26 people to summon Bordón.

Che reported the same day to Fidel, pointing out that

in order to try and clean up the dross from the column I have ordered that leave be given to whomever requests it. Seven took the opportunity and I will give their names for the Revolution's black books. . . . The day before, Pardillo went missing and was suspected of having deserted from Joel's platoon.

Again, Che was excessively harsh and unfair in judging his men. Of the seven who requested leave, it developed that one was a scout, who went home and took up arms with another rebel group there; another was detained in Camagüey and murdered by the army; a third was detained by the army and kept in jail until the revolution was over; and a fourth returned to Escambray and joined up with Che again. As for Pardillo, he had not deserted; he ended up joining the guerrillas with a group of rebels he had mustered in the area.

The night marches continued. Che cut a comical figure in those days, with a boot on one foot and a shoe on the other. Some relief from the tension came from following the World Series, in which the New York Yankees were playing the Brooklyn Dodgers. Most of the guerrillas were rooting for the Yankees, but Che, just to be different, rooted for the Dodgers, although he admitted he did not know the least thing about it.

Their main problem now was the air force, while the army was trying to set up another cordon to prevent them from reaching Las Villas and cut them off at the Jatibonico River.

> The air force caught up with us on October 10 and strafed the hill where we were. They used light aircraft and no one was hurt, but we had no time to recover, none at all. Another downpour, an enemy attack, or news of the latter's presence would force us on our way again. The troops were more and more tired and disheartened. Nonetheless, when the situation was most tense, when only by dint of insults, pleas, and all sorts of outlandish measures could I get the exhausted men to walk, a single distant sight brightened their faces and gave our guerrillas new life. That sight was a blue blot to the west, the blue blot that was the mountainous massif of Las Villas, which our men were seeing for the first time.

On October 11, the column's advance guard occupied the main quarters at a rice farm. We surmised that the army knew our situation from the phone calls we intercepted: "The rats have been precisely located."

Che then decided to close himself up in the house, to stay put all day. The rebels found huge amounts of cheese in the house, which they immediately gorged themselves on and which after several days without eating gave the whole column tremendous constipation.

> According to reports picked up from the army phone conversations, the army didn't think we were capable of walking the two leagues between here and the Jatibonico. Of course, we did them that night and swam across the river, even though we soaked almost all the weaponry and had to walk another league before reaching the safe refuge of a hill. Crossing the Jatibonico was almost symbolic of coming out of darkness and into the light. Ramiro said it was like an electric switch turning the light on, and it was just like that. But the mountains had been turning blue since the day before and even the most reluctant hill dweller was dying to arrive.

On October 12, Colonel Pérez Coujil wrote an amazing missive to Lieutenant Colonel Suárez Suquet:

> Our clear and specific mission is to capture Che Guevara, dead or alive, and all the outlaws with him. By no means can he get through any part of the cordon. You have sufficient forces under your command to accomplish this mission; moreover, the air force will assist you. If the whole troop section has to go, you can count on its being there. Strictly obey, and make sure your orders are obeyed. Each soldier [shall conduct himself] as a soldier and a man. This is just the time when we must give due obedience to General Batista and show the bears and the rats for what they are.

The lieutenant colonel's high-flown rhetoric had little to do with reality, however.

———

The rebel column moved on in strenuous nighttime marches over those two days. The army, which had been following them, wanted nothing to do with them—they were now the job of the troops at Las Villas. Those troops were nearby when the rebels reached the vicinity of the Vitico rice plantation; Che sent Silva's platoon to monitor and contain them, if necessary. But the government soldiers received a message—in a bottle thrown from a aircraft—with orders to withdraw.

On October 13, the Directory column in the Escambray launched an operation on the small towns of Placetas and Fomento to distract the government forces trying to cut off the "invaders'" columns. The combat lasted for four hours; the garrisons in both towns were unsettled by rumors that Che's column had arrived.

On October 15, **after an exhausting day's march, we crossed the Zaza River.** It was running high and Tamayo lost one of Che's shoes, which he was carrying, but was spared some trouble because another comrade found it farther downstream. They say Che sighed when he crossed the Zaza River and said: **The end is in sight.**

Acosta, who had traveled ahead of the column and had been a political organizer years before in that same area, had made contact with the PSP network in order to obtain food, clothing, and footwear. Che was astonished when, in a campesino's hut on the other side of the Zaza River, he was given coffee without sugar, the way he liked it, rather than the usual sugar-laced coffee much loved by Cubans. Then came the explanation: Acosta had been there.

On the night of October 15, at 3:30 A.M., the advance guard came across four men. The exchange was to stay forever in the memories of those who heard it:

"Halt! Who goes there?"

"Good people and campesinos."

"Campesinos? No, you're armed, you're Guards."

"No, not Guards. We're from Escambray, from the 'May 13' Directorio."

"Come here. We're Che's men."

That was when the legend was born. All over Cuba, people knew that Commander Guevara had arrived in Las Villas province and had broken the cordon. Radio Rebelde took charge of broadcasting it. Fernández Mell described it best: "We had marched 554 kilometers as the crow flies, but it was more in actuality. . . . During that time, forty-seven days, we had eaten just fifteen or twenty times, and had passed through two hurricanes as well."

The legend of the invasion, whose chroniclers have been inaccurate, is not based on trivial military engagements like the two Che fought at La Federal and Cuatro Compañeros. The stuff of the real legend is that awesome forty-seven-day march in inhuman conditions. It is Che's tenacity, his caution—so out of keeping with his fighting spirit—in avoiding traps and ambushes, and his brilliant ability to evade combat. The journey was to take on its real meaning in the course of time. For now, the revolution was able to cut the island in two.

19.   More Hills, More Problems

THE PATROL FROM THE DIRECTORIO WARNED CHE'S COLUMN THAT ARMY ambushes had been set up along the way. That very night, October 15–16, 1958, the rebels crossed the last cordon of guards on the highway between Trinidad and Sancti-Spiritus. The soldiers made threatening gestures, but did not act. Che had already told the armed men from the Directorio: You'll see, we'll get through now without their firing so much as a shot at us, and that's how it was.

On October 16, the Invasion forces, with their feet wounded, bloody, and ulcerated from the ravages of foot rot, and only their faith unharmed, entered Escambray. The rebels in Che's column felt safe now that they were in mountainous country again. Joel Iglesias later reported: "Despite their being tired, all the troops were happy and some even sang the national anthem."

The first camp was set up at ten A.M., October 16, in the ruins of a hydroelectric plant in the coffee plantation on the Cantú estate. The Directorio group went on to Dos Arroyos to report the column's arrival.

In those two days, Che made contact for the first time with practically all the forces operating in the region: with Manuel Quiñones from the provincial PSP leadership, who brought money had a confidential report for Che; and with a group from the July 26 Movement that included the Las Villas financial officer, Leonor Arestuch, and the workers' section leader, Joaquín Torres, among others.

The M26 cadres gave Che information about the army reinforcements. Che, in turn, asked for medicines to cure trenchfoot, and for medical equipment, clothing, and footwear. He made an appointment to see them the next day in Lomas del Obispo. Che spoke in private with Torres, who struck him as not much of a worker considering he was a labor leader.

Che not only got in touch with the urban section of the July 26 Movement but also spoke with the leaders of a small guerrilla group led by Pompilio Viciedo and Sindo Naranjo, whom he asked for information about Front II in Escambray.

The first signs of tension with Front II, the breakaway group from the Directory, were appearing; there, in the Escambray foothills, Che received

a strange letter, signed by Commander Carrera, who warned the revolutionary army column under my command that it was not to go up into the Escambray without first making clear what it was going for and I was to stop and explain before taking any action.

The letter was a circular dated October 10, which said: "Any organization with an armed group intending to fight in this area without prior agreement or authorization from the Front II high command, will first be warned and then expelled or exterminated by the Front II army."

For Che this was more than a test of strength or even a provocation; it was downright offensive. There was obviously a storm brewing; nonetheless, we kept calm and talked with some captain—who, we later found out, had murdered four fighters from the town who had wanted to leave Front II and join the revolutionary ranks of the M26. The captain's name was Sorí Hernández.

Che gave the column two days' rest in the Cantú camp, where the men could wash themselves. According to a campesino, "Che stripped off his ragged clothes, gave them a 'shakedown' as we say here, and put them back on again."

For Che, the rest was not welcome; he was dying to go out with some troops and the awful bazooka to smash up some barracks. There mustn't be even one little barracks left in the mountains. Entering into combat with the enemy again after forty-five days of avoiding confrontation was the priority, but the political situation in the area, the strained relations between different rebel forces, and the absence of a camp all forced him to devote time and patience, especially his scant patience, to other work.

> **The task at hand when we first arrived in Escambray was well defined: to harass the dictatorship's military structure, above all its communications. The immediate aim was to prevent the elections** [called by Batista in an attempt to recover some legitimacy for the régime] **from taking place, but the work was hampered by the lack of time remaining and by discord between the revolutionary factions.**

The rebels moved off again, farther into the mountains. That the fighters were exhausted was obvious: they lagged behind and fell asleep on the way.

> **We camped out near the top of a mountain called Del Obispo, which can be seen from the city of Sancti-Spiritus and has a cross at its peak. There we managed to set up our base camp again and immediately inquired after a house where one of the items guerrillas appreciate most was supposed to be waiting for us: shoes. There were no shoes; the Escambray Front II forces had taken them, even though they had been obtained by the M26.**

Now there was a second interview with people from Front II, among them Commander Carrera, the one who had signed the famous circular. It was an unfriendly meeting, but not a stormy one. He had already swallowed half a bottle of liquor, which was also about half his daily quota. In person, he wasn't as aggressive or objectionable as in his recent missive, but was obviously unfriendly. Carrera had a reputation for being wild; men from the Directory had censured him for his bloodlust, and for firing his pistol at anyone he thought was a stool pigeon.

Having smoothed over relations with Front II, Che's made it his first priority to recuperate from the rigors of the march and bring under his command the most important M26 guerrilla group operating in the zone. The column had more men under arms than Che did—202 fighters, led by Víctor Bordón. Che sent a note to their camp at San Blas, asking that Bordón come and see him; so, in the third week of October, Che met Bordón's troops at a place called Las Piñas. The meeting was strained at first, as Che seemed to have contradictory information about Bordón's group and his conflicts with Front II. The troops couldn't have struck him as sufficiently battle-hardened, and he probably didn't like the flamboyant cowboy hat worn by the former sugar worker, either.

Che's troops could hardly have made a good impression on Bordón, for that matter; years later Bordón said: "When we got there, we saw a group of physical wrecks, exhausted, barefoot, ragged. . . . Che was suffering from a heavy asthma attack."

Che started off with a provocative question: **How many of your guerrillas have you got there?** Bordón answered: "They're not mine, they're from the M26." Che then launched into an awe-inspiring speech to the new troops: one-man command, iron discipline, stepping up the fight; anyone who didn't like it could leave his arms and go. Bordón would comment very succinctly years later: "A meeting very much after Che's style, very curt." There were only 110 or 115 left of the 202 men Bordón had brought along. Che made Bordón, then commander, a captain under him. Relations between the two were excellent from that moment on.

On October 21, after having shored up the home front, the long-awaited meeting with people from the Directorio was held at Dos Arroyos and El Algarrabo. It was an emotional meeting and the troops got along well. The Directorio had some infrastructure set up in the zone, which must have pleased Che and reminded him of his painstaking efforts in El Hombrito to set up a campesino school, an armory, barracks, a radio station, and an electrical plant.

The meeting was attended by Commanders Rolando Cubela, Tony Santiago, Faure Chomón, and Mongo González. Che wrote a greeting: **On arriving at the Sierra del Escambray . . . from the Directorio's general headquarters we, the men of the July 26 Movement, give testimony of our thanks for this fraternal welcome. . . .**

They soon got down to business: unity in the movement. The Directory stated that it was ready to act jointly—but not with Front II, which they accused of "talking and behaving like bandits"—and that they understood how Che, a new arrival in Escambray, must have had trouble understanding the strained relations between the forces.

The split between the Directorio and Front II was very recent—it dated from that August—which heightened the tension. Faure, whom Che had met briefly in Mexico when Echeverría met with Fidel Castro, asserted that Eloy Gutiérrez, the Front II leader, had sold out to the old-line politicians and that the U.S. might well be behind him. Che stuck to his brief and insisted on unity at all costs among forces willing to take arms against the dictatorship. Faure recalled the following exchange:

" 'We would not unite with someone who has sunk to being a bandit,' I said. Che gave me a penetrating glance. I knew what he was thinking, and I explained:

" 'I'm not speaking as a sectarian. You've come to unite, but I have to warn you.' "

Che then proposed, **Let's make a plan between us; then I'll make a separate one with Gutiérrez.**

There is a photograph of Che and Ramiro Valdés meeting with the Directorio chiefs (Cubela, Faure, Castelló, René Rodríguez). Che and Ramiro have their shirts open to their navels. Che wears a small peaked cap rather than his usual beret, into which he could barely stuff his long hair, and he smokes a huge cigar. Their faces, in keeping with the importance of the meeting, are very grave.

At that meeting, Che met a man who would be linked to his future, a captain from the Directorio. Víctor Dreke was a wiry twenty-seven-year-old black man with a piercing look. He was almost killed by a gunshot wound during the diversionary action the Directorio undertook when Che's column arrived. Dreke recalled:

> Che was a legend when he came to Escambray in '58. I was wounded and they took me to the meeting place. Faure introduced all of us and told Commander Guevara how I had been wounded during the attack on Placetas. Che treated me in his role as doctor. Castelló, our doctor, explained to him where the wounds were. We talked about the shot that almost killed me. We had a small office and a typewriter and Che, very humbly, asked us to lend it to him. He was the commander of the Revolution in Las Villas, but he went around asking permission. . . .

The fact was that, whereas Che may not have clearly seen a way through to unity, he did seem to feel extremely comfortable with this group of fighters, who had graduated from the student movement and who seemed to have no duplicity about them. He decided to set up a camp in the Directorio's zone rather than to the east, which was Front II territory. The column moved to a place called Gavilanes.

Some mementos of the invasion were still with the troops—notably their unhealed wounds and the sores on their feet.

A campesino saw Che go by on horseback with ammunition belts crossed over his chest and a floppy-eared dog in front of him. When did he get that dog? Its name was Miguelito and it turned up in another photograph, in which it lies in a hammock in front of a campesino's house.

That same week, Che held a crucial meeting with Enrique Oltuski, the M26 coordinator in Las Villas. The meeting was not friendly in the least. Che said straight off: **I don't think you've handled things very well in Escambray.** Oltuski replied that, in seeking an alliance with what seemed the most important force, Front II had drifted away from the Directorio. When Front II was formed there was an agreement whereby it's members would recognize Fidel's nationwide leadership and the M26 would place itself under Front II's command in Las Villas. But the Front II people ended up trying to boss Bordón around. They stole supplies from the M26, and in the end left the Directorio and M26 with depleted pockets.

Che told Oltuski that Gutiérrez Menoyo had been avoiding him. (Che had sent Tamayo to him to arrange a meeting and warned him: **Tamayo, we may have to fight not only the army but Front II as well. Go in firing from the hip; don't let them catch you out.** Gutierrez refused, and replied that Che wouldn't have gotten any different reception if he had come himself.

The conversation with Oltuski turned to agrarian reform and the desirability of not entering into direct confrontation with U.S. interests at first. "And although I thought I was a hard-liner on both issues, he was tougher than I, and went further," Oltuski said. Oltuski was one of the authors of the M26 agrarian program, which seemed moderate to Che; and it provided for land distribution based on taxing big landholdings heavily, and for selling lots and granting loans to smallholders. Che became angry, and his argument followed Zapata's line, "Land for those who work it."

"But Che, we have to tread carefully on these matters, we can't show our hand early on, because the Yankees will flatten us."

You really are a hayseed! You think we can make a revolution behind the Americans' backs? Revolutions have to be real from the start, so every one can know what they are about, so we can win the people over. You can't disguise a real revolution.

The conversation lasted all night. Oltuski, who mistrusted Communists, had seen Armando Acosta in Che's camp and knew he was a PSP member. Che, widely known as an independent Marxist, thought the Cuban Communists were moderates and opportunists who had been skirting the real problem—the Bastista dictatorship—and that the way to face up to it was with gunfire. The conversation went on; the fighters in the camp went to sleep, and it was cold. Oltuski left with the impression that Che was attaching more importance to political than to military problems. Beyond their differences, however, each had found an opponent worth arguing with.

In Gavilanes, on October 23, 1958, Che wrote his last report to Fidel on the invasion. A couple of days later, he decided to begin operations against the barracks in the mountains, and held a stormy meeting with a Front II commander named Peña, who was

> **famous in the region for running after the campesinos' cows. He emphatically forbade us to attack Günía de Miranda because the town was on his patch; when we argued that the patch was everyone's, that it had come to a fight and we had more and better weapons, he just said that our bazooka was canceled out by 200 rifles, that 200 rifles can make as much of a hole as a bazooka. Period. Front II had earmarked Güinía de**

Miranda for taking and we could not attack. Naturally, we paid no attention, but we knew we had some dangerous "allies" there.

Other witnesses portrayed the meeting as being more hostile than Che's account would indicate. At one point, Peña told Che: "I can do more with the four hundred rifles I have than you with your bazooka, all your invaders and your balls put together." He seems to have rattled Che's cage there. They sat talking on the floor of a guano shack until finally Che stood up and laid his M-1 on the floor: **Look, Peña, the day I have to take arms against my comrades will be the day I stop fighting.** He finished: **If you haven't taken Güinía de Miranda within five days, we'll take it.**

Che did not wait five days.

On October 25, as the army bombarded the mountains, Che asked Faure for a couple of guides and the next day split his column into two groups. Acosta and a few recruits moved up to a place in the most inaccessible part of the Sierra del Escambray called Caballete de Casa, a 1,200-foot hill from which the cities of Placetas and Sancti-Spiritus could be seen in the distance. Che had picked it for a campsite and a training school.

He himself moved with the rest of the column to the Las Piñas estate, where he interviewed members of a small M26 cell who had collaborated very actively with Bordón's troops. These campesinos then guided him to the Güinía barracks, a brick building with a tin roof and a garrison of twenty-six men.

The four platoons of No. 8 Division took up positions while Bordón's troops set up ambushes on the approaches to the town. The signal for the assault was to be a bazooka shot, but the first two shots were too high, and widespread gunfire broke out. Che got mad and cursed the bazooka man. He then ordered them to find some gasoline for Molotov cocktails. At first they couldn't find any—the Chinese-owned grocery store was closed—and, then, when they succeeded and the bombs were ready, Amengual and Cabrales, approaching the barracks to throw them, were spotted and killed by machine-gun fire.

And another guerrilla, Eliseo Reyes, "San Luis," was almost killed when a Brazilian grenade he threw bounced back at him; fortunately, it did not explode.

The bazooka failed again, twice; they had to repair it with flashlight batteries. Joel remembered:

> We couldn't see for the dirt thrown up by the bullets, but the hillock shielded us. In that situation and with that much fire . . . Che saw that the bazooka man kept missing; he got angry, got up, went over and took the bazooka from him, and stood right there, with bullets flying everywhere. I don't know how he lived through so many bullets. He grabbed the bazooka to fire it. . . . I stood in front and tried to push him back behind the hillock. . . . Then he shoved me really hard and we practically had an argument.

But Guevara prevailed. All he needed was for the bazooka, much maligned by Peña, not to work. At about the fifth attempt, it fired and scored a direct hit on the barracks, killing one guard and wounding two others. Six soldiers ran out in the back and the rest surrendered.

Bordón would later justifiably comment that "disregard for safety was Che's Achilles' heel."

The fighting ended at about five A.M. The whole town cheered the guerrillas, according to the corporal who commanded the guards. As a matter of fact, Corporal Maximiliano Juvier was near retirement age and had been left with just fourteen well-armed men. Che disarmed him, dressed him down, and sent him home, after letting his wife know that he was all right. It was not the last time that Che and the corporal would meet.

The victory was not profitable by any means —thousands of rounds had been used up, and only 600 or 700 bullets and four Springfield rifles were captured—**but was a political coup that showed our willingness to get things done.**

On the way back to Gavilanes, a couple of fighters, the Cowboy Kid and Figaredo, approached Che and floated the idea of forming a assault group to be armed with automatic weapons and used in attacking barracks like those at Güinía. Che accepted and asked them to go and draw up a list of volunteers for what was to be dubbed the "suicide squad."

On October 27, Che had finished designing the setup for the guerrilla camps. El Pedrero in Gavilanes would be in a large estate surrounded by mountains; at Caballete de Casa in the high mountains, the most inaccessible camp, recruits were to be trained. Work went on at full speed; wooden huts were put up in a matter of days. Set in the dense forest, they were invisible from the air. In El Pedrero, Che billeted himself at the house of Lina González, a woman who later remembered him very well: "He had a nice, somewhat mischievous smile."

Che had his work cut out for him: the charade of "elections," with which Batista intended to give his government a veneer of legitimacy, had to be dealt with. The watchwords in the mountains were "abstention" and "sabotage."

> **The run-up to November 3—election day—was a time of extraordinary activity: our columns were mobilized all over the place, almost completely blocking off the influx of voters to the polls in those regions. . . . Almost everything from transportation for Batista's soldiers to the flow of goods was halted.**

The key military action, however—an attack on the Banao barracks east of the mountains, in the opposite direction from Güinía—was not a success. Little time was spent in preparation, the guides did not direct the troops well, the bazooka misfired again, and there were several casualties among the guerrillas. The fight lasted all night, and Che gave the order to retreat at dawn to avoid being caught in the open by the air force. Bordón recalled:

The retreat was sheer hell. Che was suffering from an asthma attack and had no medicine to treat it with. All the men were tired and he made a superhuman effort to stay on foot.

We picked up some horses on the way and Che mounted one of them. A young fighter [named Soto] saw this and complained. Che heard him, dismounted, and walked along with the column. The sun was up by the time we got to an estate they called a coffee plantation.

We began to organize the camp so we could rest and then Che sent for me. The asthma attack wouldn't go away. *Tell Soto to come here.* Che asked the comrade to take a seat. The grass was wet. He talked for a long while with Soto, explained why he had accepted the horse and why Soto shouldn't see this as pulling rank. *All right, kid?* he asked paternally, patting the fighter on the right shoulder. Soto began to cry.

The elections turned out to be a failure for the government. The *New York Times* correspondent figured that only 30 percent of those eligible had voted—in some places less than 10 percent—despite the pressure and fraud. As expected, Batista's candidate, Rivero Agüero, was elected. The failure of the elections in *Las Villas* came about spontaneously, as there was no longer time to organize passive resistance by the masses and guerrilla activity at the same time.

Che was wrong here. Antielectoral action and mobilizations were probably not coordinated, but Che saw spontaneity where actually there was well-prepared organization, action, and propaganda. When Che arrived in Camagüey there was already an M26 network there with widespread social influence centered in Santa Clara, Camagüey, and Sancti-Spiritus, and spreading up the Sierra del Escambray through the towns to villages and farms in the massif. Actions carried out by the network, reorganized by Oltuski after the failed strike in April, were staged in various places and at different times, from Güinía, where a group led by the town doctor and connected with Santa Clara by a taxi driver obtained arms and engaged in sabotage. Women at the University of Las Villas devoted themselves to buying ammunition for the fighters and to propaganda. Not a day went by in the region without some action: recruitment of students, campesinos, and small-business employees; collections of revolutionary taxes for the M26; thefts of arms or food; or collections to buy the guerrillas clothing or footwear; and there was almost nonstop armed action. Workers at the Flor de Lis tobacco factory in Las Lomas were paid a production bonus in kind and donated 95 percent of it to the guerrillas.

Maybe the network's weak link was the attitude of the M26 action chief in Las Villas, "Diego" (Víctor Paneque), who thought that the movement should be led from the cities. This was clearly opposed to Che's forthright view, in the wake of the April strike, that the network should revolve around the guerrillas in the mountains. Che would soon take action: We completely changed the combat network in the cities when we arrived. We swiftly transferred the best militiamen from the cities to the training camp to train them in sabotage which turned out to be effective in rural actions.

A photo of Che taken in the days following Batista's electoral failure shows him leaving the Caballete de Casa camp mounted on a horse, rather than his usual donkey. Che is very upright and proud, with his back straight, his pockets bulging with a thousand and one bits and pieces of crap, and a grenade hanging from his belt.

He had good reason to be happy. Caballete de Casa had been converted at top speed into—finally!—the rear base he had always wanted. It was fortified and it served to assemble men and give them military training while arms were being obtained for them.

The base also had a headquarters, a radio station, small tobacco, leather, and metal workshops, and an armory. Serious work was done at Caballete with campesinos from the area; Larrosa's platoon of riflemen was formed there, young Front II fighters were won over, and student activists came from Santa Clara and even Havana, drawn by the mystique of Che and his invasion. Sources indicate that between 600 and 1,000 recruits passed through the camp in the following month and a half.

Che put Pablo Rivalta in charge of the base and commissioned Vicente de la O to begin implementing the agrarian reform program in the liberated zone. Land distribution was under way by November. The La Diana estate near Banao, which belonged to the governor of Las Villas province, was shared out among campesinos. And on November 8 Military Order No. 1 was issued, which, among other things, included a draft of Che's agrarian reform, providing for immediate confiscation of land belonging to those who served the dictatorship and investigation into any estate of more than thirty *caballerías*. Anyone who had worked as a farmhand or had paid rent for two years or more was to become the owner of the land worked on.

Once again it was a political problem that made Che lose his temper over the agrarian reform and land distribution program:

> **After many arguments . . . which tried our patience endlessly and during which we put up with more than we ought to, according to Comrade Fidel's fair judgment, we came to a compromise: we were allowed to implement the agrarian reform throughout the Front II zone as long as Front II was allowed to collect dues.**

Meanwhile, the Invasion's main aim was being fulfilled as the month went by. Ramón Silva's platoon blocked the Trinidad–Sancti-Spiritus highway, and the central highway from one end of the island to the other was obstructed when sabotage damaged a bridge over the Tuinicú River. Further attacks hampered the central railroad. The most agitated zone, the east, received government help only by sea or air, and that more and more precariously. The enemy defense was showing increasing signs of deterioration.

A small cloud darkened the horizon. Among the actions Che had proposed to sabotage the elections was a bank robbery, a joint action between the urban militias and the guerrillas. The idea was to use money from the raid to finance urgent needs. Enrique Oltuski was in "total disagreement"; he and Víctor Paneque opposed the idea strongly. Otulski though that bank raids would not improve the movement's public image, and he pointed out that money was pouring in to the organization from conservative groups that foresaw the imminent collapse of the régime and wanted to be in the winners' good books. Oltuski offered 50,000 pesos from the treasury instead.

In early October this reply prompted an angry letter from Che. Reproaching Oltuski because the bank action had already been agreed upon and because people from the Plains did not keep their word, Guevara said he didn't give a damn if the people's leaders threatened to resign, as Oltuski had hinted:

> **I must regretfully remind you that I have been named commander-in-chief. . . . Whether I resign or not I will use the authority invested in me to rid the villages bordering the mountains of all fainthearts. . . . Why haven't any campesinos found fault with our idea that land should be for those who work it, while the big landholders have? And has this got nothing to do with the main body of fighters supporting the idea of bank raids because not one has so much as a cent to his name?**

Things did not stop there. In all good faith, Oltuski asked Che for a receipt for the 50,000 pesos, to which Che replied that between comrades that was an insult. I wouldn't have asked for yours for any amount of money, although I'd ask Gutiérrez Menoyo for a receipt for a hundred pesos.

Strangely enough, this money trouble brought about a journey that was to change Commander Guevara's future. The M26 financial officer, Dr. Serafín Ruiz de Zarate, led a commission of M26 members up to the Sierra del Escambray to hand the 50,000 pesos over to Che. He was accompanied by Martha Lugioyo, Graciela Piñeira, the doctor Adolfo Rodríguez de la Vega, and Aleida March, an activist in Santa Clara who had played an important part in carrying messages and transporting workers during the April strike and the Cienfuegos uprising. The commission stayed in El Pedrero for three days and nights; as they were preparing to leave, a messenger reported that March and Rodríguez de la Vega were wanted by the police. So they stayed on in the Escambray mountains, Rodríguez with the column and Aleida in Placetas.

Ernesto Guevara's relationships with women have been treated by his chroniclers and biographers with a caution verging on Victorian puritanism. But compared to the treatment of his relationship with the woman who was to be his last partner, they seem puritan dementia. This may be due not just to the timid hagiographic desire to separate public from private life, but also to Aleida's incredible modesty in refusing to grant interviews. (Among thousands of press articles on Che and his comrades, the author, despairing, was able to find just one, no more than ten lines long.) They also understate her at times very important role in the revolutionary process, as will be seen when the battle of Santa Clara is described. Consequently it is difficult to learn more about Aleida than her second surname (Torres) and some of her activities in the Las Villas resistance. There is not one biographical sketch of her in all the hundreds of books on the Cuban revolution.

Those three days in Placetas, and how Ernesto and Aleida fell in love, have thus remained in shadow. Alberto Castellanos, one of Che's bodyguards, tells us:

> I wasn't there, but when I got back I saw such a good-looking girl that I immediately asked who she was. They told me she was a great revolutionary fighter, very brave, who had been active in the underground in the province of Las Villas. She had learned that the police had raided her house and were looking for her, so the M26 leadership had told her to stay in Escambray. Aleida and Che fell in love, and I say that because when I saw her and made a flirtatious comment, Che gave me such a look that I said to myself "Get out of there, Alberto, you'll only be in the way."

Curiously, another man from the commander's platoon, Harry Villegas, denied that it was love at first sight: "That love affair didn't come about superficially like some people think; they didn't just see each other and love followed. It didn't start platonically or as love at first sight, but was one that arose as the struggle progressed."

Faced with a man as reticent as Che in showing signs of affection or revealing his emotions, and a woman as self-effacing in acknowledging her own position as Aleida, it is very difficult to disentangle fact from fiction. Did Che send Aleida wildflowers by a guerrilla messenger? Did he write in his diary, **Tonight I am going to woo Aleida,** and then do just that? Did they spend a moonlit night in a coffee-drying room? Or not? In any case, Ernesto Guevara and Aleida March were partners by the beginning of December.

The influx of volunteers grew during the first week in November. Among the newcomers two would be especially significant in Che's future: Alberto Fernández Montes de Oca, known as Pacho, a twenty-five-year-old from the east, and twenty-two-year-old Jesús Suárez Gayol "El Rubio" ("Blondie"), from Pinar del Río.

Pacho Montes de Oca liked to mix it up. He returned from exile in Mexico, where he got lost in the jungle on a bungled attempt to reach Cuba in which his brother Orlando was killed; he went underground in Santa

Clara and was going under orders to Escambray when his cover was blown.

Suárez Gayol, an M26 student leader, had to leave Pinar del Río when his cover, too, was blown. He had burned his feet before coming to Escambray, in an action during which a radio station had been set on fire. Ventura, one of the most notorious torturers among Batista's police, mistook another boy for Suárez and had just ordered his execution. But Che did not want to accept Suárez when he saw the condition he was in: "Don't forget I'm a doctor and I know you can't walk in that state." But the student's stubbornness got him sent to Caballete de Casa along with Montes de Oca, who was put in charge of a platoon of recruits.

Finally, on November 7, Che wrote a note to the Directorio:

> **Difficulties that had arisen between ourselves and the organization called Escambray Front II became worse . . . until they came to a head with an act of outright aggression committed against one of my captains located in the San Blas zone. This delicate situation makes it impossible to reach agreement with the aforementioned organization.**

Che also told the Directorio that he was in a position to negotiate an understanding with Front I, the PSP had placed the guerrillas from Yaguajuay and from Plains organizations at his disposal. The letter finished with a request for a meeting with the Directorio. They replied on the thirteenth: "You have only been in our insurgent zone for a month and have already become a target of the worst kind of defamation and affronts. All of this will make the doubts about Front II we expressed at our first talks seem quite convincing."

The meeting, which took place a few days later in the town of La Gloria, was attended by the Directorio's high command and the cadres from No. 8 Column. Some time was inevitably taken up in discussing what to do about Front II. This time Che was the most radical one present; he cursed Eloy Gutiérrez no end. Apparently someone from Front II had been posting bills on campesinos' houses saying that fighters not subordinating themselves to Front II discipline would be expelled or shot. **I had no idea of what was going on in Escambray, and I ask you to forgive my being predisposed against you people. Shit, we're really badly informed.**

Faure Chomón recalled: "He considered the possibility of our prosecuting them jointly for betrayal and misappropriation of supplies, and taking forceful action against them, before beginning an offensive." But the rebel offensive could not be postponed for too long, and so they decided to set aside the Front II issue, close a deal between the the Directorio and the guerrillas, and immediately begin joint operations under joint command. It would appear that Che sounded out the Directorio cadres as to whether they had any objections to the PSP joining the deal; they had none.

The immediate result of the talks in La Gloria was two small actions toward the middle and the end of November. Directorio troops headed by Commander Rolando Cubela attacked the town of Caracusey and troops from Che's column made a surprise attack on the town of Cabaiguán, where they remained for several hours appropriating equipment from the Cubacán radio station and the phone company installations, as well as fuel from the RECA refinery. (These materials would supply No. 8 Column's future radio station.)

And either tensions between Che and Front II were not as high as the Directorio cadres maintained, or Che was making an effort to keep a united front in the province of Las Villas; the Front II leader, Eloy Gutiérrez, traveled in the jeep from which Che directed the operation, along with Che's second-in-command, Ramiro Valdés, and Dr. Oscar Fernández Mell.

At about that time, Oltuski and Marcelo Fernández—one of the national M26 leaders—met Che again in the mountains, doubtless to smooth over tensions between the urban underground and the guerrilla leadership. Oltuski:

> Che arrived toward midnight. We were dozing on the school floor. There were greetings and then Che said:
> **Now we've had the first clashes, it's high time we tried to make some inroads into this zone.**
> As he was talking, he grabbed some pieces of meat with his dirty fingers, and he ate them with immense relish—they must have tasted wonderful. He finished eating and we went outside. We sat down at the side of the trail, Marcelo, Che, and I. Che gave us cigars. They were really coarse; they must have been rolled in the zone by some campesino. I breathed in the strong, bitter smoke, and felt warm inside and slightly dizzy. Beside me, Che was smoking and coughing, with a damp cough as if he was all wet inside. He smelled bad. He smelled of rotten sweat. It was a clinging smell and I fended it off with the tobacco smoke.
> Our conversation was gruff, but we did not fight much that night. Maybe Che was tired; maybe the bad tobacco made us a bit dopey. Che and Marcello had some verbal sparring. Among other things, they discussed the M26 program. Che promised a written contribution.

They discussed not only the program but also the urban underground's refusal to enter a broad front with the PSP Communists. Despite their disagreements, however, Oltuski told Marcelo Fernández as they went down the Escambray mountains: "I'll fight alongside Che when I come back to the mountains."

The opportunity was not to arise, however; events accelerated too fast. Among the campesinos and fighters at the end of November, "word had it that the army was going to launch an offensive in the hills, that Sánchez Mosquera was coming, along with a certain Colonel La Rubia. . . ." Rumor followed the army's trail: "They're in Fomento"; "They're in Cabaiguán"; "They've got tanks and jeeps and everything." "Crap, boy, crap. Those guards aren't coming up here."

They did go up, but did not bring everything with them. There were about a thousand soldiers from antiguerrilla Battalions Nos. 11 and 22 and, what was more dangerous, they had six Stewart armored cars with them.

Che located his command post in Manacas, near El Pedrero. He had 150 invaders at his disposal, plus Bordón's troops, support from the Directorio column, and a growing force of recruits who were already gathered at Caballete de Casa.

On November 29, the army troops set off and by daybreak had arrived at the foothills of the guerrilla-occupied territory:

> **They advanced from Cabaiguán and took the town of Santa Lucía, and took Punta Gorda after setting off from Fomento. Our forces countered with flexible resistance, gradually surrendering ground that was taken at great sacrifice by the enemy, which had continuous tank support.**

A campesino who admired Che's ability said years later: "Lucky for us Che was a damned good strategist and had deployed men on all of those hills, so wherever the guards popped up, we gave them hell and they stayed boxed in on the trail without making much progress."

> **On November 30, the enemy's left flank advanced to a place called Conuco with tank and air support, but Captain Joel Iglesias's fighters stopped them there and forced them to withdraw to Santa Lucía. The central flank made a traverse to the town of Mota, with tank support, and the right flank reached the town of Sitiados, and that was the extent to which the tanks were able to dodge our defenses and advance.**

Bordón's troops checked the advance in a street called Culo del Perro ("Dog's Behind"), which led to the El Pedrero cemetery. **On December 1, enemy efforts to advance were hampered all along the front and cost them many casualties. Commander Camilo Cienfuegos personally intervened in the defense of the left flank at the head of a select group of veterans from his column.**

(Camilo's men were temporarily at Che's campsite; Fidel had written to Camilo on October 14 ordering him to postpone the second part of the invasion of Pinar del Río and deploy his column in the northern part of Las Villas.)

Camilo meanwhile blocked the tank route by felling a palm tree, and his cohort of fighters halted the column's advance. The campesinos' version of the story has Che and Camilo fighting side by side for the last time.

It is both surprising and indicative of the importance Che attached to the matter of unity that on December 1, while under attack, he was able to formally meet with Cubela and Castelló from the Directorio and sign (in the middle of bombing raids) what was to became known as the El Pedrero Pact. It was a simple declaration of joint aims, underlining the groups, common ground and total coordination, and stating the intent to launch new operations. The pact ended with an invitation to unite in order to overthrow the dictatorship; the PSP agreed eight days later.

The offensive by Batista's forces soon spent itself in the face of rebel ambushes. Che had learned his lessons from the Sierra Maestra very well:

> **The entire right flank of the enemy was defeated and put to flight on December 2, whereby we acquired plentiful supplies from the enemy, as well as a tank with caterpillar tracks and a 37-mm cannon, and pursued the army to the vicinity of Fomento, where they took refuge. They were meanwhile forced to abandon the town of Mota.**

On December 2, Che, in spite of the bombing, held a supper at El Pedrero to celebrate the *Granma* landing. There were still bullet holes in the walls of Lina González's kitchen from the machine-gun fire. Lina said, "Che used to sleep in this house sometimes. He never rested for more than two hours at a time, poor thing. You had to be brave to stay here, because they bombed us every day."

> **The enemy set twenty-one campesinos' houses on fire with their tank cannons before withdrawing from the town of Sitiales. On December 4, the enemy tried to recapture Mota and their advance guard fell into one of our ambushes** [organized by the Cowboy Kid and Alfonso Zayas] **with the following results: eight dead and thirteen seriously wounded on the enemy side.**

This clash was the last action by Batista's forces in the offensive against liberated territory in the Escambray. As if to celebrate, No. 8 Column's radio station went on the air with Hiriam Prats as its operator. The first transmission was a link-up with Radio Rebelde.

Camilo's column got its station on the air a few days later; the following radio conversation between the two rebel leaders took place:

> Tell us what enemy movements are like over there and tell us if there's anything new. Tell us, by the way, what kind of tank you picked up, because the messenger who went over there told me he had seen it, but couldn't tell what type it was.
>
> **Camilo, I can see this is eating you, eh? It's a tank with caterpillar tracks, whose markings are a little scorched, but it's very nice, of American make and I think it will come in handy for us. . . . The technicians there are working on it, fix-**

ing a few little faults. . . . **There are no problems in our lines now, but I think they will have some in theirs any minute. I heard you tell Fidel you were going to take Santa Clara—well, hands off, because that one's mine. You just have to stay put.**

As far as the Santa Clara business goes, okay, fine, we'll draw up plans later, to take it jointly. I want to share the glory with you, I'm not greedy like that. I'll give you a little break in the cordon there: I'll throw 7,000 riflemen into the attack. These guys are dying to see some action and have been disarming every soldier in the barracks here these last few days . . . it's amazing what these boys will do to get rifles.

Che was interviewed again on December 12, this time by the column's radio station, which would transmit in the Escambray and be relayed from the Sierra Maestra via Radio Rebelde. It was a very formal interview and a little dry. Che still had not lost his fear of journalists, even his own.

"What kind of reception did you and your men get in the small towns in Las Villas?"

Well, the reception was fantastic. We couldn't have asked for a better one. We did have some problems with revolutionary sectors operating in the zone, but our subsequent action cleared those differences up in the end.

"What do you think, Commander, about the condition of the dictatorship?"

I think it's on its last legs. If external factors intervene, it may keep going a little longer. In any case, popular forces are so strong that collapse is inevitable. I think the interventionist factor ought not to arise because of the widespread revolutionary spirit among the Cuban people.

"Well, Commander, compared with previous struggles in the Sierra Maestra, how do you see the struggle in this area?"

In the Sierra Maestra, we had to begin our struggle as a group of almost unarmed men, with no ammunition and almost without campesino support. Our action got better and better, but the Sierra Maestra is a forbidding place, with few communication routes. In Las Villas, on the other hand, we are a little way from the big cities and the central highway, and we receive a great amount of support from our supply lines in the Plains. The conditions are better.

"Do you like it more, then?"

It's not that I like it more. Being more comfortable doesn't mean that I like it more; I feel a great affection for the Sierra Maestra, where we began the struggle and where we built ourselves up as a revolutionary force.

"What can you tell us about the government's recent major offensive, which you and your men bravely repulsed?"

Well, it wasn't just repulsed by the men under my com-

mand; it was also humiliatingly lost by the dictatorship's army, which would not fight, but retreated and left arms and other supplies in our hands.

"And what do you think about the offensives in this province?"

I think it is necessary and vital to break communications between the east and west, and I think that Santa Clara is virtually in our hands, and will be when a real offensive is launched with all the revolutionary forces grouped together.

"And one last question, Dr. Guevara. Do you figure we can all have supper together on Christmas Eve?"

Well, we can all have supper together; the question is where. In any case, I hope we all have supper together in harmony . . . those of us who are still here.

20. The Lightning Campaign

The capture of the Fomento quarter in Che's offensive in Las Villas,
December 1958

O N December 15, without any prior warning or special preparation, Che unleashed his own very special brand of blitzkrieg. In the
early evening, squads from the combined forces of the No. 8 and Directorio columns began to block off the approaches to Fomento, a town of
some 10,000 inhabitants with an army garrison 140 strong. Captain Ramón
Silva's forces cut the Fomento–Placetas rail tracks at a place called El
Nazareno and set up an ambush. Che wrote a note to Cubela: **Rolando,
we've already destroyed the Falcón River bridge and laid siege to
Fomento. We need your cooperation for the Báez road.**

A squad from the Directory column led by Captain Juan Abrantes, a Mexican, advanced on Báez at the left flank of the Fomento front and took it without a fight. Captain Alonso Zayas's squad entered Santa Isabel at nine P.M. Che
was using a variation of his guerrilla experience from his time in the Sierra
Maestra and the little tricks picked up during the combat against barracks in
December: seal the area off; set up ambushes; take advantage of the enemy
being barricaded; demoralize the army with propaganda. Contemporary accounts confirm, however, that behind the attack was the pressing need to acquire arms and ammunition. Most rifles were down to twenty rounds each
after the Batista offensive, and there were hundreds of unarmed volunteers
waiting in Caballete de Casa.

At 6:30 A.M. on December 16, three of the column's squads, led by Zayas,
Joel Iglesias, and Manuel Hernández, began to make their way into the city.

Half an hour later, Aida Fernández, the Fomento telephone operator, received a surprising call from the Santa Isabel base. A man with an odd South
American accent asked to be put through to the army garrison commander,
Lieutenant Pérez Valencia, a thirty-two-year-old career officer. Bald, with an
imposing mustache, he was the son of poor campesinos. Years later he said,

> When I picked up the phone, I knew it was Che asking for me. He told
> me he had the garrison surrounded and stressed that any resistance was
> useless. He urged me to avoid bloodshed by surrendering to his forces. He
> said my men would be freed on condition that they left the rebel-
> controlled zone as soon as the surrender was agreed to. I answered that I
> would not accept his offer.

Pérez Valencia had 150 men under his command, better armed than the rebels
and with ample ammunition. He had set up defenses using the garrison, the
telephone exchange, the Baroja Theater, and the Florida Hotel, in which he
planned to trap the rebels, and he expected to take the offensive after the
fighting started and he received reinforcements from Santa Clara.

Che at first acted with just three platoons, keeping the rest waiting in ambush along the approaches to Fomento.

In the course of the morning, as they were advancing toward the garrison
to set up positions twenty-five meters away, the rebels led by Manuel Hernández attacked and forced an army squad to surrender in the vicinity of the station; they suffered just two casualties.

The siege began. Local people came out onto the streets to join the rebels. They made Molotov cocktails, raised barricades, and transported the wounded. At nightfall, anonymous citizens set fire to the curtains in the cinema, burning the building down and forcing the troops defending it to surrender. All the army squads had now given up, except for the most important, the one at the base, where Pérez Valencia was stationed with 121 men. Che was forced to make a crucial decision: should he maintain the siege or withdraw to the mountains? The ambushes were still in place; the enemy had not sent reinforcements from Santa Clara and had not even mobilized soldiers from the nearby bases at Cabaiguán or Placetas. But the rebels' lack of ammunition was a serious problem. The column began the attack on Fomento with an average of forty rounds per gun. It was therefore not only essential to make the enemy surrender, but also to grab his ammunition.

If Che was in a difficult situation, then Pérez Valencia was in a rather odd one inside the base. Although he could not possibly have known it, his 121 soldiers were besieged by fewer than a hundred rebels, and they were not as well armed as his men. However, the rebel fire did not just consist of bullets from Garand and San Cristóbal rifles; the guerrillas also threw myths into the fray. The lieutenant stuck to the most basic military discipline, ordering his men to "resist and wait for reinforcements." Che followed his instinct and kept the siege up.

Batista's air force went into action at dawn, strafing the squad lying in ambush on the Fomento–Placetas highway. They also bombed nearby farmhouses, the Spanish Community building, and the Red Cross headquarters, producing eighteen civilian casualties. However, **despite the air force strafing our rebel army, the dictatorship's demoralized troops did not come across country to support their comrades.**

Four platoons were now raiding the base. The one led by the Cowboy Kid was making its début as a suicide squad in the common meaning of the term. Because the rebel cordon was so tightly drawn—twenty-five to thirty meters from the base at some points—the action to increase pressure was very dangerous.

Amado Morales was a member of the suicide squad.

> Tamayo climbed up onto the roof of a clinic . . . and began to fire at the soldiers opposite him. I jumped over a reed fence to take a position in a nearby home, and chose a small terrace where there was nothing to take cover behind but a wall too low to give us enough cover. Comrade Sergio Lemus also took a position there. I only fired a few shots and was wounded by enemy fire. A few minutes later, a gunshot hit Lemus in the head, and he died instantly beside me. Comrade Hugo de Río dragged me out of danger.

Del Río added: "The Cowboy Kid and I saved our skins by jumping backward like lightning."

The suicide squad was not the only one to sustain casualties in that encounter. Joel Iglesias, the young captain, received a gunshot wound after dangerously exposing himself to enemy fire. The bullet entered his neck and broke his lower jaw. He was rescued under fire by men from his own squad. Thinking he would die, he asked them to notify Che and then was taken unconscious to a clinic right in Fomento. Che came running. Joel was one of the campesino boys with whom he had lived through some of the toughest times in the Sierra Maestra and during the invasion. He told the doctors, as if his orders could stop the flow of blood, that the boy was not to die.

Captain Manuel Hernández was also seriously wounded.

Despair began to take hold among the rebels. The siege had entered its second day and although their casualties were relatively few, those wounded or killed were of the utmost importance to the rebels. Two platoon captains were among them. The air force strafing was terrible.

Leonardo Tamayo:

> The Cowboy Kid planned to set fire [to the Fomento barracks], but it was surrounded by walls with high brick ramparts and difficult to enter. The army was posted in crenellations all along those ramparts. The Kid then came up with a bright idea (for me back then, that is; now I think it was the stupidest idea going): We would look for gas tanks and pipes. We'd join the pipes together until they could be connected to a spray pump, and we'd blow gasoline at the barracks. We thought of disconnecting the pump from the tank and setting the gasoline on fire inside the tube. It was hare-brained. We would have been the ones to get burned. The plan was not carried out as we did not find the equipment.

Electricity and water to the barracks were cut off, and many of the soldiers were wounded, but the resistance continued. Night was falling on December 17 when Che, despite the growing risks, made one of the most daring decisions in his time as a guerrilla fighter: to keep up the siege.

The revolutionaries drew closer and closer to the barracks' ramparts throughout the morning of December 18. Another invader, Mariano Pérez, was wounded. Che withdrew the ambush parties and concentrated the rest of his squads on the barracks. He was betting everything on one card. The strafing continued.

Che's strategy proved correct. The soldiers in the barracks could not hold out much longer, and the land reinforcements were not on their way, maybe because they thought the attack on the barracks was the bait for an ambush. Commanding officer Pérez Valencia:

> I came to the conclusion that I had nothing more to defend. The advance guards in the hotel and cinema had fallen under rebel fire, and the rest of my men were exhausted and with no spirit left. We had sustained sev-

eral casualties and had no way of treating the wounded or burying the dead. . . . After informing the officers of the decision, I ordered the white flag to be shown.

It was just after four in the afternoon.

Che entered the barracks and sat down facing the defeated officer. A photo of the meeting shows Che talking and smoking a cigar in front of Pérez Valencia, looking as if he were there by chance and this was not his sort of thing.

Che first ordered his medics to treat the army's wounded and then commanded the soldiers to hand over their weapons. The men from No. 8 Column were meanwhile flying the M26 ensign outside the barracks to celebrate their victory. Che made a detailed list of the military equipment captured: two jeeps, three trucks, one mortar, a .30-caliber machine gun, 138 rifles and light machine guns, and 9,000 rounds of ammunition. The long list also included eighteen pairs of shoes, four typewriters, and an alarm clock. **Over a hundred rifles were taken by the freedom fighters.** The No. 8 Column was well aware of how much each and every item taken from the enemy was worth. The guerrillas took 141 prisoners.

At the end of the battle, the air force raided the area again, and Che denounced this to the Red Cross:

> **. . . savage machine-gunning, of which the victims are civilians in the city of Fomento and the surrounding areas, which have no military significance whatsoever and have caused the deaths of two children in Fomento and in which two civilians were wounded in the town of Las Arenas.**

At the end of the battle, Che announced promotions—to captain, Robert Rodríguez (the Cowboy Kid) and Orlando "Olo" Pantoja; to medical captain, and Oscar Fernández Mell. The distribution of weapons also began. Part of the booty was sent to the Caballete de Casa camp to start arming the reserves.

The townsfolk were on the streets. A sunny and newly promoted Captain Roberto Rodríguez was photographed sitting in a recently captured jeep, surrounded by admiring girls and rebels with beards in various stages of growth. The twenty-three-year-old Cowboy Kid was quite a character with his bushy beard (but no mustache) and flowing hair covered with a cap that seemed to float precariously above his head. He was short of stature. He looked like a naughty little boy, covered in ammunition belts and grenades, with a rifle that seemed bigger than he was slung over his shoulder. This is a man who, according to Che, **diced with death.**

Zobeida Rodríguez approached Che. She should not have been there; she had no rifle and had stayed behind in Punta Gorda because you cannot go and take a barracks with a Winchester, but she "went along freelance" and fought with another seven comrades from the reserve. Che found about it and censured her. Zobeida apologized and repeated the words from the horse's mouth: "Arms must be won in combat." Che answered, **Okay, half an orange,** and gave her a Garand.

One photo in particular sums up the victory at Fomento: An enormous Cuban wall flag is draped over the back of a jeep; another flag hangs the front; Che stands on the seat, addressing the crowd. The people of Fomento, unarmed, cluster around the Voice of the Revolution, speaking to them in an odd-sounding Argentinean accent. They are hanging on his every word. The relationship was a new experience for Che, who hitherto had only known the mountains and swampy plains of the invasion in Cuba. He had argued with and harangued campesinos many times, but was now talking for the first time to townspeople, to workers, craftsmen, small traders, students, housewives, secretaries, and clerks: the urban base of the revolution.

With help from the Directorio, the M26, and the recently reorganized unions, new civilian authorities were named in Fomento.

In contrast to their actions after attacks on other barracks, the column did not seem to be in any hurry to withdraw to the safety of the Sierra del Escambray. Was the battle for Santa Clara about to begin? What lessons had Che learned from Fomento?

To begin with, he lost no time in sending the squads under Captain Olo Pantoja and Lieutenant "San Luis" Reyes to the east of their occupied positions, toward Santa Lucía, to confront troops from the army's No. 38 Squadron, which was only now sending the belated reinforcements. The squads also aimed to paralyze rail traffic to Oriente Province, and they blew up a railroad bridge on December 19, thereby cutting off Cabaiguán from Sancti-Spiritus. The derailed train had been carrying food to Santa Clara; the cargo was distributed among campesinos in the zone and taken to the soldiers held prisoner in the Manacas camp. From there, the squad advanced to La Trinchera to cut a second bridge with oxyacetylene torches.

While Che was preparing the column's next central action, the air force continued to bomb the region's highways and the outskirts of towns, thinking to prevent Che's squads from approaching other towns. But Colonel Ríos Chaviano's troops were still holed up in various barracks in the area, rooted to their spots, waiting for their time to come, harassed by the waves of hatred buzzing around them, and hit by the legendary invincibility of the rebel army, the "Mau Mau." They were strafed over the airwaves by transmissions from Radio Rebelde and from No. 8 Column's transmitter and its twin sister in the north of Las Villas.

On November 19, Camilo Cienfuegos's column laid siege to the Yaguajay barracks in the northeast of the province. That same day, Military Order No. 67 from Che was broadcast.

Given the successful outcome of the struggle for liberation in Las Villas province, the zone covering the Natividad, Amazonas, Santa Isabel, and Agabama sugar mills is declared

> Cuban Free Territory. All Batista's union bosses are hereby ordered to stand down forthwith, and workers' general assemblies are called to elect new leaders.
>
> —Commander Che Guevara

Now Che had to choose between consolidating liberated territory and taking advantage of the enemy's defensive stance to continue on the attack. This decision would imply a sea change from the mentality of the early days of guerrilla warfare, and an invitation to turn the guerrilla squads into besieging forces, though without abandoning their mobility. A similar military project was under way in Oriente, under the direction of Fidel Castro, whose columns were beginning to complete a cordon around Santiago de Cuba, wiping out barracks and broadening their bases of support throughout the province. Che's original mission, that of cutting the island in two, was accomplished. Would he go further?

On November 21, at eight A.M., sixty-one hours after the surrender at Fomento, No. 8 Column simultaneously attacked army barracks at Cabaiguán, forty-three miles east of Santa Clara by the Central Highway and eight from Sancti-Spiritus, and the barracks at Guayos, four miles east of Cabaiguán by the same route.

Che had opted for a blitzkrieg, **to give the enemy no quarter,** and began to draw up a battle plan that would take him to the outskirts of Santa Clara in a few days, if his troops' performance and the army's response remained as it had been.

At five A.M., four columns directed by Che—one of which was the suicide squad led by the Cowboy Kid—as well as forces from the Directory exited their vehicles in the outskirts of Cabaiguán, a town of 16,000, and began to make their way in.

Batista's forces, under the command of Captain Pelayo Gómez, consisted of ninety soldiers and policemen; they were deployed in the barracks, in the upper floors of the Escogida de Breña tobacco works, and at a microwave transmitter half a mile from town. There were, in addition, several snipers posted in Cabaiguán's tallest buildings.

The rebels took the tobacco works first. Two of them managed to reach the roof, then broke a window and opened fire inside. The six soldiers surrendered almost immediately. Che then ordered an advance on the microwave station, which had a garrison of ten men, while the barracks was besieged.

Che had set up a blockade on the Central Highway, toward Placetas, to prevent reinforcements from turning up, and a second one outside Guayos, at the bridge on the River Tuinicú on the way to Sancti Spiritus. These containing forces would allow the attackers at the barracks to fight without danger from crossfire for some time. If the army was as slow as usual to react, the rebels could expect over forty hours of calm for the rear guard. The air force was the chief trouble. It made its usual appearance: five B-26s bombed the approaches to the besieged towns for five hours.

The Cowboy Kid's squad met resistance while reconnoitering enemy positions. Later, however, during one of their usual fits of madness, they were preparing a commando attack on the hill where the microwave station sat; fortunately, the Guards in the station surrendered at the urgings of one of the soldiers inside, who later joined up with the rebel forces.

Next came the barracks occupied by Captain González's forces. The squads advanced over the houses, jumping from rooftop to rooftop, crossing backyards and knocking down walls. Che tripped on a TV antenna while jumping off a roof, and fell on top of some flowers planted in tin cans in a yard. He had an inch-long cut above his right eye and a sprained wrist. An X ray taken after he was transferred to Fernández Mell's clinic revealed that he also had a fractured elbow and a painful wound in his arm. Che refused a tetanus shot, as he thought it might react with his asthma and leave him paralyzed and out of combat. From then on he **was eating aspirins like cookies** for the pain.

The barracks was still under siege at eight P.M.

The fighting in Guayos took a lot less time. Shooting began in the town at seven A.M., after a clash at the bridge over the River Tuinicú, where the squad commanded by Olo Pantoja and San Luis held up reinforcements coming from Sancti-Spiritus. The squad then blew up the bridge after putting its guards to flight. They withdrew after the military counterattacked, although they did maintain the blockade on the Central Highway.

Víctor Bordón's troops fought on two fronts: against the soldiers guarding the barracks and against the police who, under the command of José Rojas, son of a well-known Santa Clara police colonel, were stationed as snipers on top of the Alcázar Cinema.

Pantoja's and San Luis's squads entered the town. Marcelo Martínez, a member of the squad, recalled:

> When we got to the railroad embankment at Guayos, things were looking ugly and besides, we didn't even know the place. The snipers posted in the town hotel had a clean shot at us when we entered, forcing us to bail out of the jeep at the right-hand end of the embankment. We took shelter in the doorway of the old Lycée and began to return the fire. It was a knock-down drag-out fight.

San Luis, over eager, ran out firing wildly. The others warned him of the danger, but his mood and the gunfire deafened him and on he went. Olo ran out after him. They fell in a burst of machine-gun fire from the hotel. Olo had two gunshot wounds, one in his chest, the other in his arm. San Luis was hit on the left side of his back. One of the fighters ran up to drag them off, but they answered that the wounds were "nothing," and kept firing as blood stained their clothes. They left the field reluctantly.

At ten in the morning on December 22, the barracks fell to Bordón. His troops captured a dozen firearms and plentiful supplies. Only the snipers in the cinema were holding out, but they waved the white flag at two P.M. At about that time Olo Pantoja and San Luis returned to the town, having absconded from the Manacas camp, where they had received first aid.

Combat was renewed at dawn in Cabaiguán. Che's men were reinforced by Bordón's and Pantoja's troops. The rebels sustained another casualty when José Ramón Silva was seriously wounded for the third time since the invasion began. The wound was to cost him his arm.

At two in the morning on December 23, Che, recently treated and unarmed, entered the barracks in the company of the Cabaiguán curate to parley. The officer in charge greeted them high-handedly. Commander Guevara told him: **I'm Che and, as the winner, I'm the one to dictate terms.** A short while later, the soldiers surrendered. There had been forty-five hours' fighting. **The barracks' surrender was agreed to based on the rebel's political principle of freeing the garrison on the condition that the soldiers went out of the liberated territory. We thereby gave them the chance to hand over their weapons and save themselves.**

The rebels captured ninety prisoners, eighty-five rifles and submachine guns, and plentiful supplies. It was a resounding—but again, excessively costly—victory. Three rebel officers were wounded, one seriously. To fill in the gaps, Che promoted Ramón Pardo (Guile) and Rogelio Acevedo to captain on the spot, and made Leonardo Tamayo a lieutenant.

The regulars were disarmed, released, and sent to Placetas, where they were detained by their own comrades without food, under orders from above. The Guayos and Cabaiguán garrisons had caught the highly contagious bug of defeat.

News had arrived, meanwhile, that Armando Acosta's squad had pulled off a miracle. The city of Sancti-Spiritus had been taken, its surrender speeded by a popular uprising that Acosta himself had brought about. The rebel captain's smart move was given a helping hand by a rumor among the townsfolk to the effect that Che and Camilo were coming to take the town in the company of someone called Joan of Arc who wanted to avenge the murder of her family at the hands of the dictatorship.

Che's guerrillas were now operating on a thirty-mile-long front along the Central Highway, between Sancti-Spiritus and Placetas. His offensive was running like clockwork. The last shots in Cabaiguán were still echoing when the squads of what had now been formally designated the Rebel Army were ordered to mobilize rather than sleep. They marched toward Placetas less than two hours after the soldiers surrendered.

Rogelio Acevedo's squad occupied the town of Falcón between Placetas and Santa Clara on December 23, and set up an ambush to contain the mythical reinforcements; simultaneously, a Directorio column entered into action. Faure Chomón:

> We are putting pressure on Placetas. César Paz entered with a unit yesterday and held a gun battle. He spoke through a loudspeaker and met with popular acclaim. He then withdrew and the air force bombed and strafed the approaches to the town. But we came out unscathed. We are maintaining the siege. . . . Some soldiers came over to us today, among them a lieutenant with his arms.

At 4:30 A.M. on December 23, here was the situation in the south of the Las Villas province: The Rebel Army held all the barracks to the north and east of the Escambray, with the exception of Manicaragua, which was under attack by a Directory column. Rebel bases in the mountains were being converted into training camps for the reserves; the influx of captured weapons had made this possible. Sancti-Spiritus had been taken by Captains Acosta and Castillo and, after the Cabaiguán victory, Che sent along the squadrons of Olo Pantoja and San Luis, who were convalescing. These fighters were to reinforce the advance on Jatibonico. Attacking barracks farther and farther east was the best way to prevent the dictatorship from sending reinforcements from its relatively fresh reserves at Ciego de Avila.

The guerrillas began to make their way into Placetas at dawn, with the gunshots from Cabaiguán still ringing in their ears. The garrison, totally demoralized, had asked for the town to be evacuated. Over a hundred soldiers were stationed there, "lacking in morale and totally discouraged by fighting rebel forces that completely outnumber them, doubtless by fifty to one," said an army report—grossly exaggerated: Che did not have as many as 200 men at his disposal for the attack on Placetas. The evacuation to Santa Clara had been ordered in response to the report, but it came too late: Placetas was already surrounded.

The firing began at 4:30 in the morning. Víctor Bordón's troops entered at one end of the town, and Directorio troops led by Rolando Cubela entered at the other. The suicide squad attacked the enemy position at the cinema, Abrantes attacked the town hall, and Alfonso Zayas's column attacked the police headquarters. Hugo del Río said, "You should have seen how the population helped us in those far-off places where we were fighting. Often so many people ran out into the street that it became dangerous. They could have been hit by enemy fire."

Che arrived at Placetas toward 6:30 in a jeep driven by his escort Alberto Castellanos. Just then, Captain Julio Martínez Páez was taking the cinema and the Cowboy Kid, having captured the microwave station without firing a shot, was fighting on the railroad embankments.

Che spoke to Faure Chomón by telephone from a store on Placetas. Chomón was waiting in ambush at Báez, southeast of the city, to prevent the army from using the second-class road.

What's the situation?

"There's an ambush set up with a .30-caliber machine gun at Falcón, in case any reinforcements come."

Any sign that they've sent reinforcements from Santa Clara?

"No, none; they haven't got to Falcón."

Che laughed. **These people are done for.**

Zayas's forces in Placetas were meanwhile keeping up the pressure on police headquarters with .30-caliber machine guns, mortars, and grenades. The police asked to parley at five P.M. and surrendered half an hour later.

Now the rebel fire focused on the barracks, where 104 soldiers were stationed. The Cowboy Kid's squad attacked from behind and Bordón's from the front. Che was on the firing line. Calixto Morales remembered: "I can see him in Placetas as if he were here right now, with the snipers firing and Che acting as if it were nothing."

The revolutionaries gained a surprising recruit in Placetas: Lieutenant Pérez Valencia from the Fomento post, who had been at the Manacas campsite for several days, had been won over to the M26 cause. He said: "I asked Che to put an M26 bracelet on me. As he complied, he whispered to me, **I'm promising you nothing.** I answered that I only asked them to let me fight."

Then, using a loudspeaker, Pérez Valencia urged the barracks defenders to surrender: "Stop the bloodshed; this is Valencia speaking, and I'm here under Che's orders, with my gun and all. The rebel army is not what you think it is." The captain gave way. Che entered to negotiate with the officers, speaking very politely and quietly according to a witness. However, Lieutenant Hernández Rivero, the chief of the defenders, stated arrogantly that he was an academy officer and would defend Batista to the death. Che could not help laughing. The soldiers then went over their chief's head and began to surrender.

The townspeople thronged the streets as soon as they heard of the rebel victory. People were shouting and the church bells were ringing. Over 150 men surrendered and 159 rifles were captured, along with seven submachine guns, one .30-caliber machine gun, a mortar, grenades, and ammunition.

On December 22, a few days before the fall of Placetas, Fidel had sent Che a message saying it was a mistake just then to hand prisoners back to the enemy; even if the rebels couldn't use them in combat, they could at least give them garrison duties. Che had held on to the prisoners from Fomento, although he later freed them. He had also freed those from Cabaiguán and Guayos, practicing a tactic used by Fidel himself time and again in the Sierra Maestra: using the defeated men to demoralize the enemy. There is no record of Che's reply to Fidel, but he doubtless found tactical arguments to justify the line he was taking. In Placetas, however, instead of freeing the prisoners directly, he handed them over to the Red Cross, which would delay their return to the army by several days.

A few hours after the fall of Placetas, Che entered Yaguajay, where Camilo and his column were laying siege to the army barracks. They met in the Narcisa sugar mill with a crowd of interested campesinos who had come to see the two commanders together. Camilo told Che, "I know what I'm going to do after we win: I'm going to put you in a cage and tour the country charging people a nickel to come in and see you. I'll make a fortune!"

At the meeting the two commanders discussed future action. Should Camilo raise the siege at Yaguajay and join Che in the Santa Clara offensive? Had the time come to attack the provincial capital? Che detailed his plans and they agreed that Camilo would keep up the pressure on Yaguajay, but would send some of his troops to participate in Che's future operations.

While the two commanders were drawing up battle plans for the immediate future in Las Villas, an armored train, the dictatorship's best weapon, had just left the Ciénaga workshops in Havana and was headed for Santa Clara. Its departure had been held up by continual sabotage, and it was understaffed when it did leave. More and more men had deserted and would continue to do so on the way; even the commander eventually ran off to the United States with a million pesos from the soldiers' payroll. But the armored train and its machine guns entered Santa Clara on Christmas Day, and lay in wait for Che's troops.

Directorio forces attacked the barracks at Manicaragua; that same day, Armando Acosta and Orlando Pantoja's combined forces entered Jatibonico. Che then ordered Víctor Bordón's column to operate along the highway in the south, which ran between the Sierra and Cienfuegos. Bordón was to move up and cut off communications between Santa Clara and Havana. With his forces putting pressure on the army and simultaneously operating to contain any potential reinforcements, Che prepared another surprise for the dictatorship. He celebrated Christmas by advancing on Remedios and Caibarién towns five miles apart on the north coast of Las Villas province, northeast of Santa Clara.

The operation began at midday on December 25. The two army barracks, together with police and sailors, had twice as many troops (some 250) as the Fomento barracks where the Las Villas offensive began, and this time Che was going to deploy only a fraction of his column, without even the support of the Directorio fighters. On the other hand, morale was sky-high among the four platoons (the Cowboy Kid's suicide squad, plus those led by Zayas, Álvarez, and Acevedo) and their 120 men. They had been hardened in urban combat, and their enemies were demoralized and on the defensive.

The rebels entered Remedios in broad daylight and opened fire on the town hall and the barracks. The first to fall was the electoral tribunal building, where the suicide squad attacked a group of officers who surrendered without much resistance. Fighting broke out at the police headquarters and the barracks, where a total of 200 soldiers were posted. Once the fighting was under way, a new squad joined in, led by Captain Alberto "Pachungo" Fernández Montes de Oca and composed of forty-five recruits from Caballete de Casa, who were armed with weapons recently captured from the army.

Before operations at Remedios had finished, No. 8 Column troops began the attack on Caibarién. The townspeople came out on to the streets and surrounded the rebels, telling them that Batista's men had taken refuge in the Rural Guard and naval headquarters. Navy captain Luis Aragón surrendered the navy post without a fight. For the rebels, former Army Lieutenant Pérez Valencia acted as a mediator. Che also scored a point in the psychological war by broadcasting the invitation to surrender to the commander of a nearby navy frigate. The commander rejected the offer, but agreed to stay on the sidelines during the combat. It was a partial victory—one that disappointed Che; he had told his men they could dismount the frigate's guns to use afterward in Santa Clara.

Meanwhile, a fierce battle was heating up at the Remedios police station. As the rebels approached the building, the Cowboy Kid, in command, ordered them to stop, and to stay where they were until he gave the word. Then he ran around the corner of the building, in order to get at the water supply.

Two fighters, not having heard his order, followed him, and the Kid, thinking they had disobeyed his command, slowed down in the middle of the bullets flying from everywhere to dress them down.

A little later, after the water to the besieged station had been cut off, the rebels attacked with Molotov cocktails, and soon the building was in flames. Shouts of surrender could be heard. The attack was caught in a memorable photograph that shows a glassy-eyed and staring Cowboy Kid, surrounded by his men, overwhelmed by fatigue and tension, and the old country house with flames coming out of its windows in the background.

The siege closed in on the army barracks that night. The suicide squad was going to finish off the job, which the other squads had begun. Lieutenant Hugo del Río commented:

> We had already taken so many positions that we were right next to the barracks stables. Miguel [whose column was to relieve them toward the end of the attack, by Che's orders] arrived, so we thought we were getting a rest, as we had not slept for days, but it was not to be. The Mexican, the Cowboy Kid, called us together and told us we were to head for Caibarién. Miguel asked him, "Where's this barracks we have to take?" The Mexican, putting his hand on a wall, said, "This is the barracks, right here."

The suicide squad entered Caibarién at dawn on December 26. Droves of townsfolk had already joined in the siege and aided in Guile's platoon's fight against superior forces. The two squads kept the pressure up throughout the morning of December 26. The gunfire was constant; the barracks water supply had been cut off, and the soldiers could not so much as stick their heads out. The resistance continued, however, to the despair of the besieging troops. They tried to set the barracks on fire by burning automobile tires, but without success. Then the Cowboy Kid commandeered a fire engine, ordered its water tank to be filled with gasoline, and brought it up to the barracks in order to spray the building, at the risk of blowing everyone up. He warned the soldiers in the barracks over a loudspeaker, and a white flag soon appeared in one of the windows. The lieutenant in charge of the post did not want to surrender; apparently he had committed some crimes against the population and was afraid of reprisals. The Cowboy Kid was indignant and challenged him to shoot it out face to face rather than continue to endanger his soldiers, who no longer wanted to fight. Some rebels were meanwhile disarming the soldiers a few yards from where the conversation was taking place. The lieutenant insulted the Cowboy Kid, who answered that he was very tired and was going to catch some sleep while his soldiers thought the matter over. Without further ado, he dropped into a camp bed and fell fast asleep. This was the last straw for the guards' morale; they surrendered at once.

It was the morning of December 26. The Remedios barracks had fallen into rebel hands a few hours before. More than 200 guns and 250 prisoners were taken in Remedios and Caibarién. The army's official dispatches would later turn the 120 rebels into 1,200.

While Che's troops were fighting in Remedios and Caibarién, an important change was under way on Batista's side: Joaquín Casillas Lumpuy was taking command of the campaign in Lasillas, replacing the indecisive Ríos Chaviano. Casillas's record included abuses committed in the Oriente zone during the war, as well as the murder of Jesús Menéndez, the leader of the Communist sugar workers, in Manzanillo in 1948, early in Casillas's career. Batista made the change because he suspected Ríos Chavano of conspiring with General Tabernilla to find an easy way for the dictatorship to get out from under the dictatorship's part in the rebellion.

A December 27 Cuban military intelligence report on the state of Batista's troops in Santa Clara showed very objectively what Colonel Casillas was up against: "The troops in the province seem, in general, very pessimistic and complain that at no time in fighting against superior numbers have reinforcements and supplies been sent when asked for." The report was erroneous on one account: Batista's troops had faced, throughout the fighting, either equal or inferior numbers but never superior ones. In addition, the rebels were less well armed. But they took the offensive and made up for their shortages with tremendous morale and excellent teamwork.

In ten days Che's troops had snatched from the dictatorship 3,000 square miles of territory with almost a quarter of a million inhabitants. They had taken twelve barracks from the army, the Rural Guard, the police, and the navy in eight towns; they had forced garrisons to withdraw from another half dozen towns; they had taken almost 800 prisoners and captured almost 600 guns and plentiful ammunition. They had operated very flexibly and stepped up the pace of the offensive as and when they discovered the enemy's weaknesses, and all at a very low cost in dead and wounded (just eleven dead throughout the campaign). But perhaps the most brilliant feature of Che's guerrilla warfare campaign was how swiftly he reacted in taking the offensive, and its startling pace. Sixty-one hours went by between the fighthing in Fomento and in Guayos, but just two hours between the fall of these cities and the taking of Placetas, and just twelve hours between the taking of Placetas and the beginning of the attack on Remedios and Caibarién. Che had taken advantage of all the enemy's weaknesses, and of the amazing strength of his Invasion forces, those young and apparently tireless campesinos, brave to the point of madness, jokey, smiling, highly motivated, with a strong sense of solidarity, buoyed by popular admiration, and led by captains and lieutenants who did them more than justice and who had paid for the offensive in blood. By then none of the captains had come through the Invasion unscathed; several rebel lieutenants had also been wounded before their promotions to captain.

It was almost time for Santa Clara. On December 27, in Placetas, the situation of the joint forces of the Directory and the M26 could have been summed up as follows: to the east, the squads of Orlando Pantoja and San Luis had had to withdraw from Jatibonico due to the arrival of army reinforcements—including tanks and armored cars—and strafing by the air force. Even so, the platoon, which by then was a small column of almost a hundred, was holding out.

The situation was also difficult for Víctor Bordón's forces, who were northwest and southwest of Santa Clara and closing in to cut off the provincial capital. The small column of seventy-five men had been moving in a circle from south to north, had taken a number of small forts, and were seeking to securely blockade the central Havana–Santa Clara Highway, fighting all the while. They were attacked from the rear by a column of armored cars coming from Santa Clara and led by Casillas Lumpuy himself, who knew that he would be totally surrounded by the rebels if the route to Havana was closed off. Bordón fought a rearguard action, then blockaded the highway the following day using railroad cars welded together. To the northeast, Camilo's No. 2 Column was keeping up the siege on the Yaguajay post and controlling a vast swath of land. To the south, part of the Directorio's forces had closed in on the city of Trinidad.

The revolution's decision-making center in Las Villas was briefly billeted in Placetas, in a lower-class hotel built in 1912 and bearing an impressive name, the Grand Hotel Tulleriás. Its owner had ordered a cleanup so the rebels would have a room in good condition. Guevara met with his second-in-command, Ramiro Valdés, and Directory commander Cubela by the light of a paraffin lamp, the electricity having been cut off. He was faced with the riskiest military puzzle of fighting experience: the attack on Santa Clara. Che found himself having to choose between giving Camilo and Faure time to take Yaguajay and Trinidad, or annexing their troops to his own so that he wouldn't have to advance on Santa Clara with only the depleted No. 8 Column and Directorio forces.

The underground (and even UPI; on the wire was news that Batista was planning to send 2,000 reinforcements to Santa Clara) had provided plenty of information about the troops Che's men would be facing: 380 soldiers on the armored train, with mortars, cannons, and bazookas; 1,300 garrisoned in the Leoncio Vidal barracks, the province's main base; a garrison in the airport; 250 to 300 men at the Rural Guards' No. 31 Squadron barracks, with tanks and armored personnel carriers; 400 policemen, informers, and soldiers at the police station, armed with two Comet tanks and two personnel carriers; and another 200 soldiers at various other posts.

Batista's ground forces totaled almost 3,200 men; to them, constant air support would have to be added. Che was particularly concerned because **we had a bazooka without shells and had to face a dozen tanks, while we also knew that to fight the tanks effectively we had to get to the residential areas of the city, where tanks lose a lot of their usefulness.**

For the attack, Che had seven platoons totaling 214 men: a hundred from the Directorio column; about fifty recruits from the Caballete de Casa camp who had just been armed and were led by Pablo Rivalta (some of them were former Front II fighters who had switched sides); and his own forces. Military manuals would probably agree that what Commander Che Guevara was preparing was madness. He was going to take the initiative against a garrison whose forces outnumbered his nine to one *and* had far superior firepower; he was excluding a substantial part of his guerrilla force—Camilo's and Faure's men—from the operation; he was advancing with fighters who had barely slept or even rested in ten days (some men from the suicide squad had not slept at all for three days, and neither had Alfonso Zayas's men) and had little ammunition. A people's war, however, does not go by the book. Che knew that a swift response would prevent the dictatorship from reinforcing Santa Clara, that he was facing demoralized forces, and that he had popular support on his side. Above all, however, he had at his disposal the amazing fighting power of his men—battle-hardened over the previous eleven days, convinced of the justice of their cause, and sure that victory was at hand. They were counting on the army being cut off in the city it intended to defend and on being able to pick off the military posts one by one. Che thought it would be a long battle.

Che was mistaken only on the last point.

The single matter left to resolve in the Placetas hotel room was the central command for the offensive. Che had to be sure his column would not face enemy tanks or be exposed to aerial attack in open spaces as they entered the town.

Antonio Núñez Jiménez, a geographer who had just joined the column and to whom Che gave the fancy title "head of topographic services for No. 8 Column," was the one who had to solve the problem:

> He asked me to find a way into Santa Clara for his troops without their being discovered by the enemy. We couldn't set off from Placetas and use the Central Highway, nor could we take the Santa Clara–Camajuaní highway or the trunk roads where we were. . . . But there was another way. A country road, not used very much, went from La Vallita to the outskirts of Santa Clara, passing through the university campus.

No. 8 Column's platoons began to assemble in the main street at Placetas between eleven A.M. and noon. Simultaneously, the Directorio forces began to gather in Manicaragua, twenty miles south of Santa Clara, to wait for the order to advance.

21.   The Mau Mau in Santa Clara

Inside Santa Clara, in the battle to take the city, with Aleida March, who several months later would become Che's wife. During the battle she acted as a guide for the column, thanks to her familiarity with the city, where she had worked underground for several months earlier. Last days of December 1958

As the rebels headed for Santa Clara, their reputation preceded them. That they were called the Mau Mau meant that they were men of honor, who magnanimously released their prisoners after explaining to them the reason for the revolution. They treated both their own wounded and the enemy's, they never abandoned comrades in battle, they gave warning of their attacks, they avoided useless bloodshed, they avenged offenses against the people, and they were never defeated.

Captain Rogelio Acevedo followed in the celebrities' wake, with an enormous responsibility weighing on his seventeen-year-old shoulders. He had been sent ahead with his squad on reconnaissance missions. The suicide squad followed him, and then came the rest of the column, headed by its commander, Ernesto Guevara, known as Che, of whom it was said that he could be in all places at once while also fighting where he stood. Next to him, in a red Toyota jeep, rode a woman called Aleida March, who knew the city like the back of her hand and would open the doors to popular support for Che. She would also clear a path for him along the roads, on the rooftops, and in the alleyways.

The city was calm; police sirens had not been heard for twenty-four hours. The soldiers were holed up in their barracks or in the defensive positions detailed by their commanding officers. Acevedo's advance guard approached Santa Clara in two jeeps at two in the morning. He arrived at the university and first encountered a couple of streetwalkers from the neighborhood; he asked them for information, but obtained no useful intelligence about the army. Batista's forces did not appear; the rebels found only milk trucks on their way into the city.

The second contingent of rebels arrived at the university at daybreak. Che Guevara came two hours later, at around six A.M., while Acevedo, who had gone ahead with his column, was taking the CMQ radio station, two kilometers down the highway.

Lolita Russell, an M26 sympathizer living on the road into Santa Clara, saw Acevedo's skinny, dirty men arriving. Her mother greeted them from the door with shouts of "¡Viva Cuba libre! Long live free Cuba!" Her father asked, "Are *these* Che's men, the ones who are coming to take the Leoncio Vidal barracks?" She harangued him: it was morale that counted. . . . Her father told his wife, "Lola, start packing, because when they come back this way, we'll have to go up with them to the hills."

A very young rebel asked Lolita, "How many soldiers has Batista got in the city?" She told him five thousand, and seeing the look on his face, asked, "Is that a lot?"

"I don't know if it's a lot—but with the chief we've got, it won't be. That much I do know."

Acevedo sent Pacho Fernández's platoon ahead, and they managed to further penetrate the outskirts of the city and set up an ambush in a side street. Fernández saw a milk delivery truck and let it go by, thinking, Who knows when the townspeople will be able to get milk again in the next few days? A truck carrying army forces drew up some minutes later and gunfire broke out, killing a soldier. The first enemy column appeared shortly afterward. After a brief clash, Fernández's squad withdrew to regroup with the column.

The greater part of No. 8 Column began to advance from the university toward eight in the morning. They went in two long lines, Indian file, along the ditches. Che was in the middle with a small escort. Harry Villegas: "When we entered Santa Clara, people were saying that Che was coming with three women: one blond, who was Aleida, one dark, who was me, and a frail one, who was Parrita. They were confused by Parrita and me, because we had haystacks of hair and no beards."

When the advance guard got to the CMQ radio station, they found two students holding a soldier, whom they wanted to hand over to the rebels. While they were interrogating him, a Jeep turned up on the highway; they shot at it and it backed away, tires screeching. Acevedo gave the order to advance, because the men in the jeep were bound to give their presence away. Guile Pardo said,

> We had advanced about 300 meters when all of a sudden a light tank appeared at a bend in the highway, and opened fire while on the move. We immediately stood and returned fire. I remember going over a wire fence with my rucksack and rifle, and my hat didn't even fall off.

The guerrillas took up positions in doorways and fired back. The light tank withdrew, but not before killing five rebels and leaving several wounded and bleeding on the highway. Just then, shots began to be fired on the advancing column's left flank. They came from soldiers from the armored train, who had taken up positions on the Capiro hill.

An improvised blood transfusion center was set up in the university's Faculty of Pedagogy. Dr. Adolfo Rodríguez de la Vega recalled:

> Fernández Mell and I bedded down in a corner of one of the university lecture halls. We stayed asleep even though the planes were strafing. At times broken glass fell on us from above, but we didn't feel a thing. The wounded began to arrive at about one o'clock. . . . We had arranged for only the most serious cases to be treated there. The rest could be taken to Camajuaní, which was close by.

The rebels reached the railroad tracks and set up a first line of defense there, to cut off the soldiers on the hill and hold up any reinforcements appearing on the highway. Meanwhile, the air force had been bombing since 8:35 A.M. Ten B-26s and F-47s flew over the city and strafed the outlying neighborhoods. A bomb that fell opposite the maternity hospital destroyed eight houses. The rebels approaching the Capiro hill and the Directory forces approaching the Los Caballitos barracks were strafed with particular intensity. Unlike the people of the Escambray, the population of Santa Clara had not previously been under bombardment, and they were terrified. The city was left shaken by the bomb blasts.

The Directorio troops had entered Santa Clara along the Manicaragua highway toward ten A.M. There were about a hundred men in a convoy of trucks preceded by two cars. Their progress had been slow because of obstacles placed along the way by the rebels themselves, but there had been no clashes with the army. Their objectives were the Los Caballitos highway patrol barracks and the Rural Guards' No. 31 Squadron headquarters, where 400 soldiers were waiting, backed up by four tanks. After the first clashes with army squads, the column split into two and advanced under the bombing.

By eleven A.M., the Directorio's troops were 600 yards away from the barracks. Nieves and Dreke's groups took up positions in the Coca-Cola building and the Cabrera maternity clinic. Abrantes began the attack on Los Caballitos and was repulsed, but Lieutenant López's forces managed to scurry over to the enemy's rear. Dreke reported:

> At about eleven in the morning or noon, the situation became very critical, as some soldiers had left the squadron headquarters in light tanks and were firing on our positions and on the comrades posted around the houses. The guards were firing and then retreating to the barracks, while others were advancing in the light tanks.

In the Leoncio Vidal barracks, Colonel Casillas was in despair; he had no clear idea of what was happening to him, except that he had the Mau Mau on the streets, harassing the military posts, and that he was on the defensive. He called the high command at the Columbia base in Havana to ask for reinforcements to be airlifted from Cienfuegos and for more bombing raids. The Columbia base responded by ordering a new wave of bombing; the B-26s and Sea Furies attacked Santa Clara neighborhoods again. The actions lasted from 10:42 A.M. until 4:54 P.M.

A harsh voice with an Argentine accent, somewhat blurred by exhaustion, was heard from CMQ: Che, calling the population to collaborate with the rebels. **The régime's military situation is getting worse by the day, as its soldiers do not wish to fight.** The message was rebroadcast at two A.M. from Sancti-Spiritus and relayed from there by Radio Tiempo, Unión Radio, and Radio Nacional. A mysterious network passed on a message: Che asked that streets be blocked off to prevent armored cars from moving, and ordered the city's water and electricity supplies cut in order to increase pressure on the garrisoned forces. Another (and even more powerful) network in Santa Clara began to carry out Che's orders, blocking streets with cars that had flat tires, and with mattresses and furniture thrown out of windows.

A girl asked Che to pose for a photograph as he was leaving Station CMQ, and he agreed.

Che was perplexed; the situation was far from clear. True, his forces were making their way into the city, but they were far outnumbered and the light tanks made a great difference. A counterattack could have been fatal. Che told Fernández Mell that at least a month's fighting would be needed to take Santa Clara. The pressure had to be stepped up.

Che ordered the actual infiltration into the center of the city to begin. While Ramón Pardo's platoon, supported by the suicide squad, engaged the soldiers from the armored train who had been firing from the Capiro hill, the rest of the rebels advanced on the center of Santa Clara. They found, to their surprise, that people opened their doors to offer them glasses of water or cups of coffee.

On the southern front, the Directorio troops took advantage of the waning light after the bombing to launch a counterattack, which forced the Los Caballitos troops back into their barracks. On the Santo Domingo front, west of Santa Clara, Víctor Bordón's troops had engaged, and managed to hold up, an enemy convoy with reinforcements for the city. In the approaches to Jatibonico, Olo Pantoja, and San Luis Reyes's platoons tried to ambush and check the advance of reinforcements headed for the garrison.

At nightfall, the rebels had come out ahead, despite their casualties and their very slow progress. They had managed to block reinforcements coming from the east and west of Santa Clara, and they had practically taken Trinidad. With great difficulty, they were beginning to put pressure on the central districts of the city. The army, despite its enormous superiority in matériel and numbers, had not been able to launch a counterattack or even to mobilize its huge reserves in the Leoncio Vidal barracks. Civilians were barricading the streets to prevent tanks from coming into action.

That morning, as Captain Acevedo was setting up a machine gun in a house near the university, the owner, Professor Luis García, had asked if he would be allowed to retreat with the rebels if there was a withdrawal. Acevedo answered: "There'll be no retreat here, Doctor." It seemed he was about to be proven right.

On the night of December 28, Che regrouped his forces and tried to learn some sad lessons, to identify the most important things that the day had to teach them. He sent a message to Cubela: **We could barely advance. We lost four dead and several wounded. We will try our luck tonight. Give me your exact position so I can act more precisely. Che.**

Che did not sleep that night, but ran up and down the railroad tracks with an escort looking for a weak point in the armored train, and for the best place to pull up the rails. Shortly before dawn, using a yellow D-6 Caterpillar from the Santa Clara Agronomy Department, the rebels did destroy the rails, at a spot two and a half miles from the train. Now the army would not be able to pull the train back to the Leoncio Vidal barracks. Captain Acevedo recalled that Che "would at times do or order things whose immediate purpose escaped us, but which were the product of his great intuition as a fighter."

Once the train and the Capiro hill were cut off, Che ordered the advance into Santa Clara to proceed. The suicide squad was sent to attack the police station, Acevedo's men to fight in the area of the courthouse and prison, and Alberto Fernández's small platoon to the Grand Hotel. Captain Zayas's squad was ordered to fight the troops on the Capiro hill and Captain Alvarez to reinforce the Directory troops, who were contending with forces from the No. 31 Squadron headquarters and the Los Caballitos barracks. The reserve squad, led by Lieutenant Pablo Rivalta, was ordered to enter the Del Condado district and attack the Raúl Sánchez Building and the Martí Building and to undertake a holding operation against the forces from the Leoncio Vidal barracks. Cut the central forces off and attack the weaker positions—those had been Che's principles over the previous month.

Che's forces entered Santa Clara. Rivalta had been born in the neighborhood, so his men may have known where they were headed. But that was not the case with Acevedo's forces, who were advancing along the opposite sidewalk—or with the suicide squad, which was totally lost in Santa Clara. Che himself, who knew no more of Cuba than the Sierra Maestra, the Sierra Escambray, and the route he covered between them during the Invasion, had had to use the underground leadership to find his way in the blacked-out city, and particularly needed Aleida March's help. Santa Clara was now cut in half.

By dawn on December 29, the rebels were dispersed throughout Santa Clara. Years later Che was to comment, maybe in recalling that night, that **the guerrilla fighter is a nighttime fighter; to say that is also to say that he has all the features of a nocturnal animal.**

December 29 was to mark a turning point in the fighting in Santa Clara. Batista's army had managed to recover from the initial surprise, to mobilize and deploy its troops, and to counterattack against the guerrillas, whom they vastly outnumbered and outgunned. But Che's front was invisible—a nonexistent firing line that kept moving forward, cutting off enemy strongholds, immobilizing soldiers, and obtaining support from the population. Several years later, Che wrote a line in his book *Guerrade Guerrillas, Guerrilla Warfare,* that was to drive military theorists mad, being imbued with Che's particular humor: **There are no definite firing lines. A firing line is more or less theoretical.** Back then, on December 29, no mapmaker could have drawn the dividing line between soldiers and rebels; it did not exist. The rebels had infiltrated and blended into the urban landscape, broken through Colonel Casillas's defensive cordon, and hit straight home.

The Directorio's troops, which were attacking the Los Caballitos barracks, began a new approach at dawn. Rolando Cubela was injured in a burst of machine-gun fire, so Gustavo Machín Hoed, who had come to Che's forces from the Directorio, took charge of the attack.

Santa Clara, meanwhile, again lay helpless beneath an air raid: two B-26s were strafing the city. The journalist José Lorenzo Fuentes reported:

> Those living in the most fought-over zones fled their houses, horrified. Old people, women, and children were wandering the streets with small bundles of clothes under their arms, looking for the safest place to shelter and save their lives. Hunger, suffering, and terror were written on their faces. The air force was strafing the rooftops, and groups of civilians were wounded or killed. Many bodies had to buried in backyards without so much as a coffin. A twelve-year-old boy was hit in the chest by machine-gun fire, and his parents could not even come close to him.

Acevedo's platoon attacked the barracks and the courthouse. Rivalta's entered the Del Condado district—where he was well known—amid popular acclamation. People came out into the street and gave the rebels food and coffee. Molotov cocktails began to be made, and citizens' militias were set up in the neighborhood. Pressure was brought to bear on the vicinity of the Leoncio Vidal barracks. The military made a couple of attempts to break through using tanks, but were driven back by gunfire and did not persist. Che brought the combat zone command headquarters closer, from the university to the Public Works Department offices and buildings on the Central Highway, less than a mile away, at the point where the railroad tracks had been pulled up.

Despite the initial successes, the fighting was not easy. **Our men were fighting against soldiers supported by armored units; we put them to flight, but many paid with their lives, and the improvised hospitals and cemeteries began to fill up with the dead and wounded.**

The Cowboy Kid's squad had taken over the railroad station. First Lieutenant Hugo del Río took a remarkable phone call there:

> The phone rang and I picked it up. It was a military chief asking me what the situation in the zone was like. I replied that the rebel army was on the city streets. He then told me not to worry, as the police would soon restore order. I answered that that would be difficult, since the rebel army dominated the situation. He asked who was talking. I answered First Lieutenant Hugo del Río. He asked whether I was with the Guards or the police. I answered neither, but the rebel army instead. . . . He became somewhat nastily annoyed and said it would take courage to come and see him at the Esperanza barracks. I informed Che, and he told me to go.

Toward one A.M., Che spoke with two of his captains, Guile Pardo and the Cowboy Kid, in a house belonging to Dr. Pablo Díaz. He had been directing military operations on the run, turning up suddenly at one point or another wherever in the city fighting was under way. He had a chaotic—but at least broad—view thanks to his contact with all the combat zones and his constant control of the action. A little later, the fighting for the police headquarters began, as did the attack on the Capiro hill, led by Guile's and Alfonso Zayas's platoons.

The rebels split into three groups and climbed the hill, lobbing grenades to flush out the soldiers. They were fired on with mortars. The rebels used the hill itself as cover from the train and managed to dislodge the soldiers in a frontal attack, with hand-to-hand fighting. The troops went down the other side of the hill and took refuge in the train cars. Toward three P.M., the train retreated to escape fire from the rebels, who were now taking advantage of being able to shoot downhill. The two locomotives pushed the train swiftly backward, but after about four kilometers the engineers suddenly realized that some twenty meters of track had been pulled up a short way ahead. The train buckled and ran off the rails. The locomotive crashed into a garage and destroyed some cars there. The noise was incredible—not just the crash, but the screech of metal from the derailed cars. The novelist Edmundo Desnoes observed:

> The train was lying immobile, all askew. Green Coca-Cola bottles, dark Hatuey beer bottles and colorless ones of Cawy; cans of Libby's tomato juice, of Bartlett pears, Campbell's soup, of asparagus and peas, were thrown all over the cars, overturned and twisted from end to end in the smoke and dust that enveloped the convoy.

Lieutenant Roberto Espinosa, with part of Guile's squad (Guile was with Che in the city center just then) advanced on the railroad cars at the junction of Independencia Street and the Camajuaní highway and captured forty-one soldiers without giving them a chance to react. Espinosa recalled: "The guards didn't dare to leave the train, so they didn't know how many of us there really were. We never stopped firing at them, and if anybody stuck his head out, that was that. Besides, they were confused by the crash and the derailing."

Eighteen rebels now controlled the 350 soldiers left on the train. A .30-caliber machine gun was set up on a rooftop thirty-five or forty yards away and riddled the cars' unarmored roofs. The first Molotov cocktails began to rain down on the train. Having taken three of the twenty-two cars, Espinosa kept up the pressure on the rest.

Che and Captain Pardo were in the town center engaging a tank when they were told of these events. Che got to the scene as fast as he could, then could not resist the temptation to throw himself into the middle of the fighting. He climbed onto the roof of one of the derailed cars, where there was a 20-millimeter cannon.

A very interesting fight then got under way, in which men were driven out of the armored train with Molotov cocktails. They were incredibly well armed, but willing to fight only at a distance, from comfortable positions and against a practically defenseless enemy, like the colonizers with the Indians in the American West. They were harassed by men who threw bottles of lighted gasoline at them from nearby points and adjacent cars. Thanks to its armor plating, the train became a real oven for the soldiers.

While he was fighting, a messenger came running to report that reinforcements for Batista's men were coming along the Camajuaní highway. Che left Pardo in command of the assault forces and headed off to organize the defense.

The shooting and Molotov-throwing continued. An hour later, Pardo proposed a truce. After talking to a sergeant, who threatened him with a Thompson submachine gun and refused to surrender, and then with the train's chief medic, he managed to speak to Commander Gómez Calderón, who agreed to parley with Che, but only on board the train. Pardo sent a messenger to find him. Che reappeared shortly; the news of the army's advance from Camajuaní had proved false, and he had not gone far. With him was Leovaldo Carranza from the Red Cross, who climbed up a lamppost and waved the white flag with the red cross in the middle of it to clear Che's way to the train. He heard a voice behind him saying, "Are you scared?" Aleida was there, smiling.

Leaving his gun behind, Che went halfway to meet Commander Gómez, who was carrying his. When Che pointed this out, he handed his pistol over to Carranza.

"I want to speak out of earshot of the troops," Gómez said, and Che agreed. They walked over to a railroad car together.

"Commander, I give you my word of honor that if you let us return to Havana, we won't fire another shot," Gómez said.

Che smiled. **I believe in your word of honor, but I cannot allow those bullets to kill more Cubans, either here or there.**

Che gave the troops a quarter of an hour to surrender and made the commander personally responsible for any subsequent bloodshed. But Gómez did not last the fifteen minutes. Seconds later the soldiers began to get down, unarmed.

The rebels gazed in amazement at the booty they had captured, like Ali Baba in the cave, like Pizarro finding the Incas' treasure: six bazookas, five 60-millimeter mortars, four .30-caliber machine guns, a 20-millimeter cannon, thirty-eight Browning light machine guns, grenades, 600 automatic rifles, a .50-caliber machine gun and almost a million rounds of ammunition: **their anti-aircraft guns and machine guns; their fabulous quantities of ammunition** . . . It was more weaponry than all the rebel forces put together had in Santa Clara.

The arms were taken to different parts of the city. By Che's order a bazooka quickly found its way to Camilo Cienfuegos in Yaguajay. As agreed, Che ordered three of his men—Dr. Adolfo Rodríquez de la Vega, Antonio Núñez Jiménez, and Serafín Ruiz de Zárate—to take the disarmed prisoners (almost 400 of them) to Caibarién, to be handed over to the commander of a navy frigate tied up there and be transported to Havana. Guevara had to get prisoners off his hands: he could not spare the men to guard them while the battle was in full swing. Besides, he was thinking about how demoralizing it would be when the defeated soldiers from the train turned up in Havana. Meanwhile the situation remained rather absurd: three revolutionaries transporting 400 men.

The air force began to bomb the wreckage of the train shortly afterward. Che asked an M26 activist to take a message to be broadcast from the radio station asking that reinforcements be sent down from Caballete de Casas, now that there were weapons to arm them with.

In Santa Clara, meanwhile, the rebel advance continued. Alberto Fernández's platoon was advancing on the Vidal barracks, after some heavy fighting on the way. The Cowboy Kid's squad, guided by a teenager, was approaching the police station. The Directorio forces were closing in on the No. 31 Squadron barracks. Hugo del Río's platoon joined forces with the Cowboy Kid's after a dramatic confrontation in which they collided with a light tank and an armored car and exchanged fire.

Although there was no electricity, a large number of townspeople continued to follow the fighting into the night; they found out about the armored train by listening to CMQ, which had been made operational by a group of underground M26 members under Che's orders. The station was using an auxiliary power plant and could be heard on battery-powered radios. The airwaves carried the following message:

> Attention; this is the Ciro Redondo Column, No. 8 Column of the July 26 Movement Rebel Army speaking. In a few moments we shall broadcast a message to the people of Cuba and especially Las Villas, about the advance of the rebel forces storming Santa Clara. Over three hundred officers and men belong to the Army Engineering Corps have just surrendered.

The next morning, December 30, Radio Rebelde denied in international news agency wire reports that Che was dead:

> For the peace of mind of relatives in South America and of the Cuban people, we wish to assure you that not only is Ernesto "Che" Guevara alive and in the line of fire, but he has occupied the armored train that we referred to some moments ago and will soon take the city of Santa Clara, which has been under attack for some days now.

The weaponry on the train had been used to mobilize the rest of the reserves in the camps at Caballete de Casas, El Pedrero, Gavilanes, and Manacas to reinforce the troops in the combat zone. Thanks to these new forces, the momentum from the day before, and the full support of the population, the various rebel squads were able to chalk up more victories.

The air force launched thirty sorties against the city that day. Shortly after the bombing, the Los Caballitos barracks fell into rebel hands. Some soldiers desperately tried to break out and make it to No. 31 Squadron headquarters, but were caught in the crossfire between the rebels and the Guards. Several were killed or wounded, and the Directory took the rest prisoner.

The fiercest fighting that day was at the police station, defended by almost 400 policemen supported by light tanks and commanded by Colonel Cornelio Rojas. Rojas had good reason not to want to surrender: he was known for his recent torture and murder of civilians. The Cowboy Kid's squad had engaged the station, but the rebels were having great difficulty in approaching it. Even with five other squads and some of Che's platoon helping them out, they had no more then seventy men among them. They could not move freely in the narrow streets around the station, and several had already been wounded. To make matters worse, the police station, facing the Del Carmen park, was just 500 yards away from the Leoncio Vidal barracks: a counterattack might be launched at any time. Emérido Meriño had been drawing his squad closer to the police station, fighting house by house, picking off the guards one by one; by now his hat looked like a sieve. The Cowboy Kid ordered him to use a new tactic to find a better position from which to launch an attack: now they would advance *through* the houses. They began to knock down walls, with cooperation from the neighbors, and thus advance toward the church opposite the police station. A series of invisible avenues began to crisscross the neighborhood.

They advanced over the rooftops, too. The Cowboy Kid was taking too many risks, and his comrades chided him for it. As usual, he answered: "You never hear the bullet that's going to get you." He took up a position on a rooftop in Garofalo Street, some fifty meters from the police station, along with Orlando Beltrán and Leonardo Tamayo, who had recovered from his wounds at the Cabaiguán hospital. Orlando had this to report: "We had barely taken cover, and then we saw a group of six guards running across the park. We attacked them, but two tanks that were nearby began to fire at us with their thirty-caliber guns."

Tamayo provided the rest:

> I shouted, "Kid, hit the deck, or they'll kill you!" but he didn't. Just after that, I shouted, "Hey, what's up, why aren't you firing?" He didn't answer. I looked and saw he was covered in blood. We picked him up immediately and took him to the medic. But the wound was fatal, a shot in the head from an M1.

Che was advancing through the houses toward the positions from which the police station was being attacked when he saw the men carrying the Cowboy Kid's body. His grief-stricken words when he found that his most aggressive, flamboyant, and fearless captain had died were these: **They've killed a hundred of my men.**

After ordering that the Kid's body be taken to the hospital, Che went to the cordon surrounding the police station and named Tamayo and Hugo del Río joint commanders of the platoon. Some soldiers wept while they fought. The pressure on the station was stepped up:

> **We had managed to take the power station and the entire northwest of the city, broadcasting the news that Santa Clara was almost in rebel hands. In that announcement, which I made as commander-in-chief of the armed forces in Las Villas, I remember I had the sad duty of informing the people of Cuba that Roberto Rodríguez, the Cowboy Kid, was dead. He was short in stature and in years, the chief of the suicide squad, who took his life in his hands a thousand and one times in the fight for freedom.**

Shortly afterward, Orestes Colina encountered Che, who had an enemy prisoner, a lieutenant, with him. In a fit of anger, Colima said, "What we have to do is kill this one." Che calmly replied: **Do you think we're like them?**

Zayas's squad was fighting to take the provincial government headquarters, which was protected by snipers on the roof of the Grand Hotel. There was fighting in the prison, in the courthouse. The soldiers fighting in the Carmelite church surrendered.

Night fell.

The day had also favored the rebels fighting on the other fronts in the city. In spite of air raids, Bordón's column liberated Santo Domingo for a second time and took the bridge over the Sagua River. To the east, in Jatibonico, San Luis and Olo Pantoja's platoons had been meeting with fierce resistance from enemy columns supported by armored cars, and had had a great day ambushing them. In Trinidad, the Directorio forces commanded by Faure Chomón had taken the last Batista stronghold there, the jail.

Ramiro Valdés, No. 8 Column deputy commander, had been in command of troops fighting on the eastern front since December 29. Now he took charge of getting the new "subcolumn" into shape, using Olo's and Acosta's platoons. This move allowed Che not only to bolster the holding operation and widen his range of options, but also to create a strategic reserve in case things did not turn out as planned in Santa Clara. Although he was placing all his bets on one single action, Che did retain the option of saving an important force from a possible defeat and thereby keeping the ability to rebuild the front should that prove necessary.

On December 31, a young journalist met Commander Guevara in the Public Works Building, where the Rebel Army's operations room was located. The bomb blasts from Batista's B-26s, still raiding the city, could be heard in the distance.

> Someone by my side pointed out Che to me, and indeed there he was, skinny, with his hair all matted, his arm in a sling, his uniform in shreds. Anyone would have taken him for the most ordinary soldier, were it not for the penetrating and unusually bright stare emanating from that tired face.

Che, on the verge of exhaustion, still had to handle the police station, which had cost him one of his best captains, and the Leoncio Vidal barracks, which, with its 1,300 men, still had firepower superior to all the revolutionary forces in the city. He also had to dislodge the snipers posted in the Grand Hotel and the courthouse, and take the Rural Guards barracks confronting the Directory column.

Che planned one last blow, which he based on an accurate assessment of the attitude prevailing among Batista's soldiers: their tendency not to take the offensive. He had the responsibility of throwing into combat, for the fourth day in a row, troops who had barely slept and were worn down by several weeks of continuous fighting, who had sustained major casualties among their commanding officers, and who had often fought against superior enemy forces that enjoyed tank support.

> I remember an episode that summed up the spirit of our forces in those final days. I had admonished a soldier for falling asleep during combat and he told me he had been disarmed for having missed a shot. With my usual terseness, I answered him, "Win yourself another rifle by going unarmed to the front line . . . if you're capable." Later, in Santa Clara, when I was encouraging the wounded at the blood transfusion center, a dying man touched my hand and said, "Remember, Commander? You asked me to go after a rifle in Remedios . . . well, I won it here." It was the fighter who'd missed the shot. He died a few minutes later, and he looked happy to have demonstrated his bravery to me.

The dead teenager was called Miguel Arguín.

There was fighting everywhere in Santa Clara that morning. Opposite the police station, the suicide squad, supported by reinforcements and wishing to avenge the death of the Cowboy Kid, was preparing the final attack. Inside the station, Colonel Rojas had murdered one of his men, a Captain Olivera, because he wanted to surrender. From the Carmelite church, which had been taken the day before by a group of rebels who had made a hole at the back, fighters were harassing the headquarters. A tank driver trying to leave the headquarters was hit in the head by a rebel bullet and his body stayed where it was. The dead inside the station were beginning to decompose, and the wounded could not be treated. The police were hungry, demoralized, and constantly under fire. Towards four P.M., Colonel Rojas asked for a truce to remove the wounded. Tamayo granted two hours and hinted that Rojas might consider surrender. They negotiated in the middle of the street, but did not reach an agreement. When the firing was about to get under way again, the colonel spoke once more to Tamayo, who walked off toward the station followed by some rebels, whom he had to stop. Once inside, he spoke directly to the policemen, telling them that if they no longer wished to fight, they should just throw down their guns and line up outside. The policemen began to leave the station as if Colonel Rojas himself had given the order. There were 396 of them, and just 130 rebels surrounding them. Rojas escaped in the confusion. The townspeople who entered the station found instruments of torture in the cellars.

The police station was not the only place to fall. The provincial government building, with its hundred soldiers, was attacked by Alfonso Zayas's forces in the front, and in the rear by Alberto Fernández's platoon, which managed to enter the building by knocking some walls down. There, Captain Pachungo Fernández, grenade in hand, took some soldiers by surprise and forced them to surrender.

Captain Acevedo's forces took the courthouse despite the tanks defending it. Five aircraft raided the city with 500-pound bombs, which destroyed houses as if they had been made of paper. The bombers struck particularly hard at the recently taken courthouse, but the anti-aircraft guns captured from the armored train were brought into action and the planes vanished from the skies over Santa Clara. The jail then fell to the rebels; the political prisoners were released, while the common criminals took advantage of the turmoil to escape through a hole in a wall. Rebel platoons coming from the city center began to put the Leoncio Vidal barracks under pressure, as did Rivalta's forces from the Del Condado district, who managed to dig themselves in a hundred yards from the base.

Fighting was under way at the Grand Hotel, where there were a dozen snipers on the tenth floor, as well as policemen and torturers—members of the hated SIM, the Military Intelligence Service. They were fired on from the park and the buildings opposite. Alberto Fernández led a group assigned to set fire to the second floor using Molotov cocktails. The soldiers were trapped in the hotel; their water had been cut off and they had no food. But they had wounded many civilians and militiamen crossing the park by sniping at them from the roof, and they still had ammunition. The squad led by the youngster Acevedo took part in a "window-breaking contest" with Batista's snipers. They were getting closer and closer.

In midafternoon, Che heard on the radio that the Yaguajay garrison had surrendered to Camilo's forces, which were now free for the final attack on the Leoncio Vidal barracks.

Colonel Casillas Lumpuy spoke to Batista at ten P.M., telling him that the city was about to fall to the rebels and that he urgently needed reinforcements. He did not get so much as a false promise from the dictator. After haranguing his officers and men and demanding heroic resistance from them, Casillas Lumpuy disguised himself in a straw hat and mufti and, claiming he had to make a tour of inspection in the province, escaped from the barracks together with his operations chief, Fernández Suero.

Batista's forces had just three armed enclaves left: the Grand Hotel, No. 31 Squadron headquarters, and the Leoncio Vidal barracks. Che knew that the final offensive on Santiago de Cuba was about to begin and that he urgently needed to mop up those three pockets of resistance. The year 1958 was about to end.

Day One of the Revolution

In Havana, before Fidel's arrival. The situation was not yet completely clear, although militarily, the 26 July Movement and the Revolutionary Directorio controlled the country. Ramiro Valdés, Camilo Cienfuegos, Che, Carlos Franqui. First days of 1959

I N THE EARLY HOURS OF JANUARY 1, 1958—AT 3:15 a.m., TO BE PRECISE— four Aerovías Q civilian aircraft took off from the Columbia military base on the outskirts of Havana. Before climbing into the first one, Fulgencio Batista told General Eulogio Cantillo he was putting him in charge of the country, the business, the whole kit and caboodle. Then he vanished into the skies. Batista was off to exile in Miami, although his entourage changed its flight plan on the wing and instead landed in Santo Domingo, home to that other bloodthirsty dictator Leónidas Trujillo. The Havana newspapers carried an Associated Press wire report that "government troops, with tank and air support, have routed rebel troops in the outskirts of Santa Clara and thrown them back toward the east of Las Villas Province."

Day had yet to break in Santa Clara; the guards in No. 31 Squadron headquarters had stopped shooting. Víctor Dreke cautiously drew near. A white flag was waving from a window. Rolando Cubela, back with the troops after a lightning visit to the hospital, had just received a brief note from Che: **Rolando. Demand unconditional surrender. I will support you with the necessary forces. Greetings. Che.** No. 31 Squadron now surrendered. A rumor that Batista had fled made the rounds of the soldiers who had given themselves up. The rebels looked at each other in amazement. Was it all over? Captain Millán, in charge of the troops who had surrendered, was granted permission by the Directorio to use a microwave relay to contact the Leoncio Vidal barracks; the officer in charge there answered him with insults. The civilians came out onto the streets and, overjoyed, looked at the defeated soldiers in front of the barracks, which was pockmarked by hundreds of bullet holes. The prisoners were taken to Che at the rebel command headquarters.

The Grand Hotel was also about to fall. The snipers cut off on the tenth floor had had to drink coffee from ashtrays and had looted the bar. Captain Alfonso Zayas posted a tank in front of the hotel and shot the windows to pieces. Lieutenant Alberto Fernández's troops attacked and the snipers surrendered. The dozen policemen, stool pigeons, and torturers came out with their hands up and were showered with insults.

Only the Leoncio Vidal barracks was left. Colonel Cándido Hernández had taken charge there, replacing the runaways Casillas Lumpuy and Fernández Suero. Lieutenant Hugo del Río contacted the regiment from a radio in a patrol car captured from the police headquarters, and the officer who answered requested a truce. Del Río answered that only Che could grant the request but agreed to look for him to inform him of it. He found Che in the command headquarters in a meeting with the geographer, Antonio Núñez Jiménez, and Dr. Adolfo Rodríguez de la Vega. He and Che went to the patrol car and contacted the regiment by radio again. Che agreed to send Núñez Jiménez and Rodríquez de la Vega to talk with Colonel Hernández. Shortly afterward the latter requested an indefinite truce, to which the emissaries replied that the only available option was unconditional surrender. Colonel Hernández, arguing that his brother and his son had already lost their lives in the fighting, that he had done more than enough to serve his country, handed over the command and the decision to his next in line, a Commander Fernández and his superior officers. Fernández then insisted on speaking with Che.

Just as the negotiations were about to begin, a broadcast by General Cantillo, speaking from the high command headquarters in Havana, was received at the Leoncio Vidal barracks.

> **The news was very contradictory and extraordinary. Batista had fled the country that day, and the armed forces command came tumbling down. Our two delegates established radio contact with Cantillo, advising him of the offer to surrender, but he reckoned it was not possible to accept as it constituted an ultimatum and that he had occupied the army command under the strict orders of its leader Fidel Castro.**

Hernández asked Núñez and Rodríguez to talk to Cantillo, who offered them a truce. They repeated that there could be only unconditional surrender. Cantillo tried to trick them, saying he had nominated a provisional government under Fidel Castro's orders and that under such conditions he could not hand over the barracks. The conversation ended amid insults.

A few hours earlier, at 7:30 A.M. at the main quarters in the América sugar mill, Fidel Castro went to the door to drink a cup of coffee, cursing the irresponsible rebels for wasting ammunition by shooting into the air to celebrate the new year. The surprising news of Batista's flight, picked up by Radio Rebelde, made Fidel angry: the dictator had escaped and the event smelled like a coup d'état. He began to gather his captains together to march on Santiago.

The news was confirmed. Supreme Court judge Carlos Piedra was now president. Cantillo, who had been conspiring with the aid of the U.S. embassy to find an easy way out of the revolution, was army chief.

Fidel set a piece of paper on a wardrobe and wrote: "Revolution, yes, military coup, no." Then he wrote a call for a general strike. He took a jeep to the Radio Rebelde station to record the message. It was on the air by ten A.M. and was later relayed by dozens of radio stations across the country and in Latin America.

Che heard Fidel's message at about the same time as he received the latest information from the besieged barracks.

> **We got in touch with Fidel immediately, giving him the news but telling him our opinion of Cantillo's attitude, which was just what he thought, too. To create a military junta would just waste the revolution by forcing it to negotiate with the remains of the dictatorship.**

Commander Hernández insisted on speaking to Che. Núñez and Rodríguez went with him. Che was very sharp with the regiment's new commander. He reportedly said:

Look, Commander, my men have already discussed this matter with the high command. It's either unconditional surrender or fire, but real fire, and with no quarter. The city is already in our hands. At 12:30 I will give the order to resume the attack using all our forces. We will take the barracks at all costs. You will be responsible for the bloodshed. Furthermore, you must be aware of the possibility that the U.S. government will intervene militarily in Cuba; if that happens, it will be even more of a crime as you will be supporting a foreign invader. In that event, the only option will be to give you a pistol to commit suicide, as you'll be guilty of treason to Cuba.

Commander Hernández went back to talk matters over with his officers. Soldiers were already deserting their posts and fraternizing with the rebels. The military hesitated. With a few minutes left before the appointed time and with the rebel rifles primed and ready to fire, they agreed to a negotiated surrender: they could leave the barracks unarmed and be sent to Havana via Caibarién. Those who had committed violence against the population would be excluded from the agreement.

As the negotiations proceeded outside the barracks, and with ten minutes left before firing would resume, the soldiers began to throw their weapons down of their own accord and walk unarmed over to the rebel lines. It was 12:20 P.M. on January 1, 1959. With the fall of the Leoncio Vidal barracks, the battle for Santa Clara was over. The rebel forces took the airfield without firing a shot.

Photographs show the townspeople of Santa Clara looking in amazement at the smashed-up boxcars and the mass of twisted iron that are the wreckage of the armored train; the victorious rebels in front of immobile tanks; the bearded young rebels, the *barbudos,* in front of the pockmarked barracks, now in silence; groups of Batista's disarmed soldiers around a young rebel who is lecturing them; Che giving instructions beside a tank, holding his injured left arm up with his right. Below the beret with the metal crossed-swords badge on it, his eyes are glassy with fatigue; a cigar hangs loosely from his lips, and he's cracking a smile.

Fidel urged the final attack in a quick succession of communiqués over Radio Rebelde that demanded the surrender of the Santiago garrison and ordered Che and Camilo Cienfuegos to advance on Havana. Che was to take the La Cabaña fortress and Camilo Batista's stronghold at Columbia. Víctor Mora's column was ordered to take the cities of Guantánamo, Holguín, and Victoria de las Tunas. The general strike in Santiago was called for three P.M.

Enrique Oltuski, the July 26 Movement regional coordinator, who had been frantically traveling, with one mishap after another, as to bring a message to Che from Fidel, arrived at Santa Clara in the midst of street parties. He found Che in the operations room at the Public Works Building:

> Che was standing behind a large bureau, opposite me. He had one arm in a a cast and a sling made from a black rag. We briefly exchanged greetings. He waved at me to wait while he gave instructions to a rebel who, too young for a beard, had let his hair grow.
>
> The room was small and completely closed in. I began to feel hot. Then I could smell the clinging odor of Che's body. The time went by very slowly. I took Fidel's message out of the lining of my pants; it was the order to advance on Havana. Finally, the rebel left and I handed the paper over to Che.
>
> When he'd finished reading it, he turned to the window and looked outside:
>
> **Yes, I already knew. We'll set off in a few hours.**
>
> "But how?"
>
> **We managed to establish radio contact with Fidel.**
>
> I felt enormously frustrated. . . .
>
> **He has already designated a civil governor of the province.**
>
> He was referring to a man from his column (Captain Calixto Morales), but at the heart of the matter was the political mistrust in which Che held us, the representatives from the Plains.

In Havana, meanwhile, as soon as the news broke that Batista had fled the country, students began to gather at the university, and M26 banners were unfurled on the university hill. The population crowded the streets. There was looting in the Biltmore and the Sevilla Plaza hotels and the casinos. M26 militias took over newspapers sympathetic to Batista. The police machine-gunned the boroughs; political prisoners in the Príncipe prison were freed. The Resistencia Cívica group took over the CMQ radio station. In the midst of the turmoil, urban M26 and Front II cadres began to fill a very precarious power vacuum, as there were still thousands of Batista's soldiers in the barracks who might rush in to set up a military dictatorship. The police abandoned various stations, and only a few precincts fired in response to the growing crowds on the streets.

At two P.M. U.S. ambassador Earl T. Smith, accompanied by the rest of the diplomatic corps, met with Cantillo (not with President Piedra; they were under no illusions about where power really lay). The United States was looking for a way, with the departure of the dictatorship, that would avoid backing Fidel and the M26 but would also exclude forces loyal to Batista and keep up the appearance of neutrality. The takeover sector was the "good military" group, headed by Colonel Ramón Barquín and Borbonet, who had conspired to overthrow Batista. They were in jail, but Cantillo gave way to U.S. pressure and at seven P.M., released the officers from Pinos Island, along with M26 leader Armando Hart.

The people were out on the streets. Street parties were engulfing Santa Clara with cheering and shouts, and the rebels were the crowds' booty. Singing and dancing were the order of the day in the liberated city, but there were also demands that captured torturers be sent to the firing squad.

Oltuski also recalled:

> The news that the dictatorship's army had surrendered spread throughout the city and thousands closed in upon the building where we were. They knew that Che was there and no one wanted to miss the opportunity to meet him. We had to put guards at the entrance to keep from being overwhelmed by the mass of humanity.
>
> On the floor above was an improvised prison for war criminals from the forces of repression who, one by one, were being uncovered and caught by the people.

The sources contradict each other concerning names and numbers, but there is no doubt that in the hours following the liberation of Santa Clara, Che signed death warrants for several of Batista's policemen whom the people accused of being torturers and rapists, beginning with detainees who had acted as snipers in the Grand Hotel, including Casillas Lumpuy, who was captured by Víctor Bordón's men while attempting to leave town. **I did no more and no less than the situation demanded—i.e., the death sentence for those twelve murderers, because they had committed crimes against the people, not against us.** As it happened, Casillas was not executed but died in a struggle with one of the guards taking him to the firing squad. The photo of Casillas in a short-sleeved checked shirt, trying to take a rifle from the soldier guarding him, was to go around the world. Police chief Cornelio Rojas, who had been arrested in Caibarién while attempting to escape, was shot a couple of days later.

Whereas Che's and the Directory's fighters kept a tight grip on weapons and the situation on the street in Santa Clara, the crowds in Havana were exacting a long-delayed justice. A sort of reasoned and selective vandalism took hold of the crowds, who attacked the gas stations belonging to Shell, which was said to have collaborated with Batista by giving him tanks. They also destroyed the casinos belonging to the American Mafia and the Batista underworld, trashed parking meters—one of the régime's scams—and attacked houses belonging to leading figures in the dictatorship. (They threw Mujal's air-conditioning unit out the window.) There was no control by the repressive apparatus of the dictatorship, which was falling apart by the second with the massive exodus of Batista's cadres; neither Cantillo nor Barquín could fill the resulting power vacuum, because the revolutionary forces refused to enter into negotiations. Television studios were taken over and witnesses gave spontanous testimony to the horrors of the now-ended Batista régime.

The surrender of Santiago was agreed to at nine P.M. Fidel entered the capital of Oriente Province; Judge Manuel Urrutia swore him in as president; and he announced his march on Havana and reiterated his call for a revolutionary strike. Radio Rebelde declared a liquor ban in the occupied cities.

Che began to regroup the separate platoons in his column in Santa Clara. Víctor Bordón's and Ramiro Valdés's forces were called up. Cars with loudspeakers cruised the streets, calling the rebels to rejoin the column. Che found out that some fighters were taking cars abandoned in the streets by escaped Batista supporters; he angrily ordered the keys to be handed over. **They were not going to ruin in one second what the Rebel Army had maintained as a standard: respect for others. They were going to Havana—by truck, bus, on foot, but it was the same for everyone.** He really chewed out Rogelio Acevedo, who was still a teenager and had requisitioned a '58 Chrysler.

During this time, Che received a communiqué from Eloy Gutiérrez Menoyo, placing the Front II forces at his disposal. **There was no problem. We then gave them instructions to wait as we had to settle civilian affairs in the first major city to be conquered.** A fighter named Mustelier asked Che to grant him leave to go and see his family in Oriente Province; the commander tersely told him no.

"But, Che, we've already won the revolution."

No, we've won the war. The revolution begins now.

Camilo arrived at the head of his column that night, and the two friends met up in the Public Works Building while Camilo's column prepared 600 sandwiches and twenty-four crates of Hatuey malt beer. They were to be the first to set off for Havana. By order of Fidel Castro, Che marched without the Directorio forces that had accompanied him during the previous days of fighting in Santa Clara. Why? Was Fidel's decision due to a burst of sectarianism, or to political mistrust, in those moments of uncertainty, of a force composed in large part of the radical student wing? Was it due to a desire that the July 26 Movement alone capitalize on victory? The reason behind this unfortunate decision will never be clear. A little earlier, Che had met with Faure Chomón from the Directorio, who had just arrived from Trinidad. He had to explain to Faure that his orders were to march alone to the capital. After a month of complete cooperation between the two revolutionary forces, it was no easy task to explain why Fidel had excluded Chomón's troops (or at least kept them on the sidelines) from the final offensive.

Oltuski remembered:

> There were few of us left in the Public Works Building. The fatigue accumulated over many days had taken its toll, and some went home; others lay down on the ground or on the sandbags in the ramparts.
>
> Everybody was asleep in the hall, except for Camilo—who had just arrived—Che, and I. Camilo was pouring out his endless witticisms relating the funny aspects of his latest adventures. We were stretched out on the floor, leaning on some sacks, in the faint lamplight coming in through the windows.
>
> Somebody came and brought a basket full of apples and then we realized it was the new year—and, despite the differences that had arisen

between us, I felt good among those men. The noise was building up outside, and then some rebels came in and said they were ready. We stood up and went out. The night was cool. The air was filled with the sound of engines and light from motor headlamps. There were few bystanders around at that time. Relatives of some of the murderers were lying against the walls, asleep.

Camilo's column set off toward Havana at 5:50 A.M. on January 2.

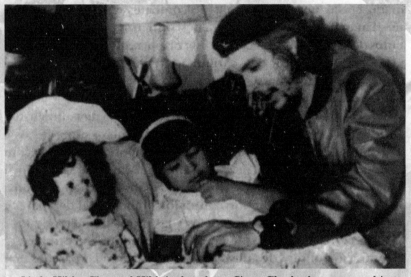

Little Hilda, Che and Hilda's daughter. Since Che had no money, his friends took up a collection to buy a doll to give the little girl when she arrived in Havana.

THROUGHOUT THE MORNING OF JANUARY 2, CARS WITH LOUDSPEAKERS drove around the streets relaying a message that was also broadcast on Radio Rebelde and repeated over and over: "Members of Number 8 Column are hereby advised that by order of Commander Ernesto Che Guevara, they are to regroup immediately at the camp, to get organized and march on."

Toward three P.M., some 400 men lined up outside the Leoncio Vidal barracks and left Las Villas in jeeps, trucks, and tank transports. Che traveled in a decommissioned olive-colored Chevrolet, with Aleida March and his entourage: Harry Villegas, Hermes Peña, Mendoza Argudín, and, at the wheel, Alberto Castellanos. It was not very comfortable with six in the car. Che, who was not too confident of the countryfolk's driving abilities, threatened with a smile that: **I'll shoot anyone who hits a pedestrian or crashes.**

A second contingent from No. 8 Column, headed by Ramiro Valdés, who had to gather some soldiers, would follow later.

Meanwhile in Havana, with the remains of Bastista's dictatorship either fleeing or collapsing, sporadic gunfights were breaking out between urban militias and the police or paramilitary forces such as Senator Mansferrer's "Tigers." The Príncipe prison was raided and the inmates freed. Cars cruised the streets with their hoods up. In the early afternoon, workers gathered in the Central Park in support of the revolution. The July 26 Movement flag was flown from surrounding buildings, and posters supporting Fidel appeared.

The 150-strong Angel Amejeiras column—militiamen who had been operating in the city's outskirts and were led by Che's old friend Víctor Paneque—was the first to enter the city. They billeted themselves in the Sports Palace. Eloy Gutiérrez Menoyo arrived at the head of the Escambray Front II column, which was quartered in the Vedado Institute. **He had "heroically" entered Havana. We thought it might be a maneuver to try to build their strength up, to take power or stir something up. We already knew them, but were getting to know them better by the day.**

The advance guard from Camilo Cienfuegos's column entered the Columbia base at 5:15 P.M. with no opposition from the "good" military officers who had replaced Batista's men in command at the country's most important military base. Camilo received a call there from Che, who was halfway to Havana with a column whose ranks had been swelled by militiamen.

Che beheld Havana, the country's capital city, for the first time in the middle of the night. He had heard a thousand tales of Havana, but had never seen it. He went up the Boyeros road to the La Cabaña camp in a three-car convoy. Che did not hesitate; he walked straight in, just as Camilo had done some hours before. He was received by Varela, a "true military" officer, who immediately handed over command to him. Varela had spent the previous hours refusing to eat or drink, terrified that the garrison, loyal to Batista, might have poisoned him.

Is that what victory was like? A lackluster entry into a barracks in the dead of night whose commanding officer surrendered before being asked?

Che assigned guard duty and ordered that accounts be drawn up and weapons be strictly accounted for. He then deployed the 600 men who were now in his column. At dawn he went to CMQ, the most important radio and TV station in Havana, where he was held up at the door by militiamen in the July 26 Movement urban network who did not recognize him. But he was allowed through without having to make too many explanations, and managed to establish radio contact with Fidel, who was in Bayamo with Camilo, who had flown east to report on the bloodless occupation of the garrisons in Havana.

Che was worn out, but as Antonio Sánchez Díaz—"Pinares"—one of Camilo's officers, put it: "You couldn't rest in Havana, either on your laurels or in bed; the place was buzzing."

The eighteenth-century fortress of La Cabaña dominates Havana, looking out over a deep bay, a complex of barracks, moats and forts, casemates, and office buildings. The ramparts are covered in ivy and colonial-era cannons can still be seen on the old patios. In the early hours of January 3, Che assembled the 3,000 soldiers from Batista's army who were in the fortress and made a conciliatory speech; The rebels still did not know what to expect from them. **The guerrillas will have to learn about discipline from you, and you will have to learn from the guerrillas how to win a war.** He had not slept.

In one of the barracks offices, Che found a sergeant behind a typewriter. He stared at him.

Did you take part in the fighting?

"No, I'm an office worker."

Have you tortured anyone?

The man shook his head. Che asked him if he could type. He nodded.

Go, take off your uniform and come back here.

He thus struck up a friendship with José Manuel Manresa that was to last for the next five years.

There were celebrations in the streets, and the general strike began. In those first three days, 800 exiles flew back from all over the Americas. Fidel slowly and surely buttressed his political conquest rather than consolidating the military victory as he advanced toward Havana. He later said: "I had some trouble getting the column on the move and calling it to order with machines here, there, and everywhere, and I'll say it was just as well we didn't have to fight. The way things were, an order for mortar fire would have led to a journalist shooting pictures."

The news of a new government, first broadcast by Radio Rebelde, had now made the newspapers: Manuel Urrutia was president, Dr. José Miró Cardona prime minister; the cabinet was dominated by the moderate bourgeois opposition, with a sprinkling of July 26 Movement members, but minus the other two allied forces in the rebellion, the Communist People's Socialist Party and the Directory. The rebels were in almost complete control of the army (they had taken over the post of commander-in-chief and named regional commanders, although they did relinquish command in Santiago for several days to Rego Rubido, a Batista supporter who had been minister of war) and the police (whose new head was Efigenio Ameijeiras). They were also in charge of the recently created Ministry of Embezzled Goods (Faustino Pérez) which would investigate corruption in Batista's administration; the Ministry of Education (Armando Hart); the Health Ministry (Julio Martínez Páez, a medic from the Sierra); the Interior Ministry (Luis Orlando Rodríguez); the Labor Ministry (Marcelo Fernández); and the Communications Ministry (Enrique Oltuski). The liberal opposition was a bland group. All in all, an odd government.

Some of those excluded showed little readiness to accept the fact. To show that they occupied some space in the revolutionary process, the Directorio column entered Havana at four P.M. and occupied the National Palace.

After Carlos Franqui arrived in Havana, the July 26 Movement's *Revolución* became a widely circulated newspaper. The movement took over the plant and offices of a pro-Batista paper. An advertisement ran on an inside page showing, in plain fifties style, a bearded rebel (grenade in belt) and a painter finishing a slogan declaring "All our trust" between the two figures. The ad also praised the DuPont Interamerican Chemical Company; that love affair was to be short-lived.

On the night of January 4, the Directorio announced that it would expect to set forth three conditions at meetings with President Urrutia in the National Palace. On January 5, while Fidel was still marching toward Havana, Che met Camilo in the Columbia base. Carlos Franqui was present:

> Then Che turned up in his Bohemian suit, calmly smoking a pipe and looking like a revolutionary prophet. There was trouble in the Presidential Palace. The Revolutionary Directorio had moved in there. Che hadn't been to see Faure Chomón, and Rolando Cubela hadn't wanted to receive him. . . . The Directorio never took to Urrutia. . . . There was no lack of mistrust, intrigues, and so on, on one side or the other. . . . Camilo half-jokingly said we should fire a couple of cannonades to warn Cubelas that he'd better hand over the Palace. As I had no liking for the Palace, I said it sounded like a good idea to me, but Che, with his responsible attitude, said it wasn't the time for cannonades of that sort; he patiently went back to the Palace, met Faure Chomón, and worked things out.

A confrontation had been avoided, but dissension had not. The Directorio agreed to leave the palace, and its troops then occupied the University of Havana, but Faure Chomón issued a statement to the press saying: "We understand that what is happening in Santiago de Cuba is not correct; we believe that if our sacrifices are not to have been in vain, the entire revolutionary movement should be organized in one single revolutionary party." Naming Santiago the provisional capital was a tactical measure by Fidel to prevent the emergence of a conciliatory government in Havana. The designation would not last a week, and that annoyed the unfairly sidelined members of the Directorio.

That night Che took a light plane to the Camagüey airport in the middle of the island to report to Fidel on the situation in Havana. Fidel was slowly approaching Havana in a triumphal convoy. The two commanders had not seen each other for almost six months, since Che left the Sierra Maestra at the head of No. 8 Column. They were later to be joined by President Urrutia, who flew in from Santiago. The World Wide Press photo taken of them shows Fidel and Che sharing knowing smiles.

U.S. Ambassador Earl Smith was far from all smiles when he left the Columbia base after meeting with Camilo to ask the rebels not to execute General Cantillo. Smith, frankly hostile to the winners, would later say that the bearded revolutionaries reminded him of characters from a movie he had just seen about John Dillinger.

On January 5, after constant delays and several false starts, President Urrutia landed at Boyeros airport on the outskirts of Havana. Camilo had decreed martial law and deployed men from his column. The Directorio handed the palace over to Urrutia at seven P.M. Strife among the revolutionaries had been held in check. Martial law was lifted during a first cabinet session. Earl Smith turned up toward the end of the meeting; accused of having been Batista's most important prop, he was not popular, and his presence and pretensions of dictating conditions angered the armed revolutionaries. *Bohemia* magazine reported: "The fighters' anger was checked only out of respect for our northern neighbor."

Che gave his first interviews in his office in La Cabaña, in a narrow room with a desk at one end, whose best attribute was four small windows looking out over Havana Bay. The Capitol dome could be seen in the distance. He spoke first to the Argentina newspaper *La Tarde,* then to *Revolución* and *El Mundo,* and over the following days to *Prensa Libre, Bohemia,* and a host of international correspondents. For a whole week he was waylaid by the press. First he offered a counterattack: **To label "Communists" all those who refuse to bow down is an old dictator's trick; the July 26 Movement is a democratic movement.**

The interviewee answered phone calls, each of which hurt his injured wrist. He was not quite comfortable with the press, not used to the flood of journalists: **what we are doing for the freedom of the people is not for publication, and even less so are aspects of our personal lives.** In one of those interviews from the first week of the revolution, someone told him the anecdote about how Batista's army's broadcasts used to call him the "rebel on a donkey." **Praise indeed,** Che replied.

He did not quite feel as if he fitted in, maybe because he did not understand what his place and position were at that stage of the revolutionary process. Even his opinions on agrarian reform were cautious: **One of the basic measures will be to give campesinos the treatment they deserve,** he said, as if a radical agrarian reform were not essential for him, as if he did not know what rights the countryfolk had after contributing to the victory. He offered commonplaces, such as **Unity is an essential factor** or truisms, such as **The lie has been given to the assertion that you cannot rebel against the army in Cuba.** He seemed unsettled ideologically, lacking in clarity, inclined to self-censor his comments to the press. He obviously had not found a place for himself in the victory.

The journalists found Aleida March among the rebel army officers in Che's entourage. They were not in Las Villas, and Aleida was an unknown quantity. She also granted an interview, one of the few she ever gave:

> I can't say I'm Che's secretary, because I'm a fighter. I fought beside him in the Las Villas campaign and took part in all the engagements there. That makes me his orderly. . . . When it became practically impossible for me to continue living in Santa Clara, due to my revolutionary activities, I decided to join the ranks of those fighting the dictatorship by taking up arms. . . . I confess that I found life there difficult at first, but then got used to it, especially after our first clashes with the enemy were over.

They could get no more out of her.

On January 8, Che heard the popular acclaim that greeted the arrival of Fidel's column from the La Cabaña fortress. Through binoculars, he watched the jeep at the head of the column, in which Fidel stood beside Camilo. The crowd made it physically impossible for vehicles to move.

Fidel consolidated his unarguable status as a popular leader in just one day. His speeches at the Columbia base, with pigeons landing on his shoulder and Camilo by his side—"Am I doing okay, Camilo?"—his calls to order as a way of promoting change; his clear wish, shared with the people, to dismantle the apparatus of Batista's dictatorship; and his magic aura allowed him to bridge the gap with the Directorio and bring popular pressure to bear on them. For a couple of days the Directorio was on the defensive, forced to explain why they had taken possession of arms stores. In consequence, they made a political retreat.

The next day, Fidel rid himself of the "true military" officers and moderate Batista supporters; Barquín was sent to the Military Academy, Borbonet was named chief of a tank battalion, and Rego Rubido was named ambassador to Brazil. Ameijeiras declared that the police would be under the command of the rebel army rather than the Interior Ministry, and Che and Camilo ordered the militias to be disarmed.

A little later, on instructions from Fidel himself, a State Security apparatus was set up at meetings attended by Raúl, Che, Ramiro Valdés, and a PSP cadre, Osvaldo Sánchez, who had extensive conspiratorial experience in the Cuban Communist underground.

It was also in those January days that Che confronted Gutiérrez Menoyo and the Front II men. U.S. journalist Richard Harris described a meeting among Camilo, Che, Raúl and four Front II commanders: Gutiérrez Menoyo, Fleitas, Carrera, and William Morgan. The atmosphere was extremely strained, so much so that at one point the commanders drew their guns. But this time Camilo was conciliatory. The Front II leaders were demanding that they be allowed to keep their ranks after joining the rebel army, and Che brutally cut them short.

Carrera asked: "Why make distinctions between Front II officers and yours?"

Who gave you your stars?

Carrera shouted, "They were won in combat!"

In what combat?

The meeting ended with no agreement reached. Raúl Castro ruled that each case should be decided on its own merits.

Months later, Che would record:

> **After a few days the first bill from the Capri Hotel came in, signed "Freitas": 15,000 pesos in food and drink for a few freeloaders. When the time came to assign ranks, almost a hundred captains and a fair number of commanders were aspiring to the fat of the land, as was a large and select hard core of men represented by the inseparable Menoyo and Fleitas, who were aiming at all sorts of official state positions. These weren't well-paid jobs, but they all had one feature in common: they were the civil service posts where all the stealing went on before the revolution. Finance Ministry inspectorates, tax collection jobs, all the places the money used to end up and pass through their greedy fingers—they had their hearts set on those posts. . . . From the very first there were serious differences which led to sharp words being exchanged, but our apparent [was this a Freudian slip?] revolutionary good sense won through and we gave way for the sake of unity. We stuck to our guns [,however]. We would allow no stealing, nor would we give posts to those we knew aspired to being traitors, but we did not get rid of them. We temporized, all for the sake of a unity that was not entirely understood. That was one of the sins of the revolution.**

Beyond the "sins" of compromise, however—which doubtless could not be laid at Che's door—Fidel had succeeded in making the small and reliable rebel army into the guarantor that the revolution would not be interrupted or aborted over the following days. But what type of revolution? Headed where?

Che had been relegated to the second rank, but he did not want to be in the front rank. He had no vocation for power and did not hanker after it. Neither did he have any idea how far the revolution would go and what his role in that process would be. Nothing is known about his talks with Fidel in those days; there are only a few photographs and press articles showing a look of concentration on Che's face as he listened to Fidel at night in the Columbia base, or two days later as they both sat on a camp bed. What is clear from the photographs is that Fidel did the talking and Che the listening.

In any case, the breathing space achieved coincided with the arrival of

Che's family in Havana. He went to meet his parents at the airport on January 9. As she hugged her son, Celia Guevara told the press: "We haven't seen each other for six years, since that day we saw him off at Retiro station in Buenos Aires, when he left to work in a leprosarium in Venezuela."

Che's father looked warily at the dozens of bearded and armed men, the ragged rebel soldiers wearing necklaces strung with dogs' teeth, seeds, medals of the Virgin, crucifixes, amulets.

A series of photographs of this visit reveals both the need Che had for a breathing space, for peace and quiet (a need that had built up in him over the previous months), and the affection he felt for his mother. Celia and he are sitting on a sofa. His mother, a cup of coffee in her hand, seems to be talking to him. Che has a cap, rather than his usual beret, in his lap and is leaning against the backrest. His eyes are closed, his mouth half open. His brother Juan Martín, beside him, stares at the camera. A second photograph shows Che leaning his head on his mother's shoulder. His eyes are shut again; he is physically exhausted.

Che's father asked him what he intended to do with his medical career now. **Look, old man, take my medical diploma; since you're called Ernesto Guevara like me, you can put a plaque with your name and "M.D." on it in your construction office and start killing off people, no problem.**

When his father pressed him, Che answered seriously: **I know I left medicine behind some time ago** [although several days later he was given an honorary Cuban medical diploma by the National Medical School and did not turn it down]. **Now I'm a fighter working to prop up a government. What will become of me? I don't even know where I'll lay my bones to rest.**

Communication was not easy. So many years of separation had divided them, even if they had not become complete strangers. Che was now a tough and very self-assured man. When his father asked him for a jeep to tour the Sierra Maestra, he answered: **I'll put a jeep at your disposal, with a soldier who has been over that route already. But I tell you what, you'll have to fork out for the gas and the food.**

Along with Che's parents came two journalists with whom he had bonds of great friendship, Carlos María Gutiérrez and Jorge Ricardo Masetti, who were to cover the triumph of the revolution. They had attended the first meeting of what was jokingly called the "Free Press Club," founded in a hut in the Sierra Maestra. Che was soon to involve them in a large-scale journalistic operation.

He had meanwhile also undertaken a policing action, maybe because his contacts in the PSP had warned him about how important it was to do so. He confiscated the files of the Bureau of Repressing Communist Activities (BRAC), one of the plethora of secret police organizations from Batista's era, founded probably with the aim of investigating agents and stool pigeons who had infiltrated the police. The outcome of this operation was the arrest of BRAC's deputy chief, Castaño, and a press conference during which the media was shown proof of an assassination attempt on Fidel organized by the BRAC.

On January 13, picking up his role as educator, which the war had curtailed, Che opened a Military Cultural Academy in the La Cabaña base so that he could continue teaching the campesinos in his column to read and write. He also wanted to offer other possibilities in life to his radicalized countryfolk in arms. The poet Nicolás Guillén and the pianist Enriqueta Alamanza would pass through the academy in quick succession. Havana students would give literacy and basic education courses.

In Havana, Che kept up the Spartan life and strict discipline he had had in the Sierra. He shared four rooms in one of the base houses with Aleida, Oscar Fernández Mell, and his escorts. He ran the camp from a small office until Dr. Adolfo Rodríguez de la Vega complained to him: "Look, we're eating shit, you can't run the regiment from here, it has to be run over there." He kept the teenagers in his entourage—Villegas, Argudín, Castellanos, and Hermes Peña—under strict parental control, forbidding them to use garrison cars and punishing them when they played hooky to sightsee in a Havana dazzling to young campesinos. His friend Julio Cáceres, El Patojo, was shortly to travel from Mexico to join the group.

Che set up several small workshops to make in-house supplies and placed a lieutenant and the hard-headed accountancy student Orlando Borrego, who had joined the column in the Escambray mountains, in charge of them. They were euphemistically called the Free La Cabaña Workshops.

In the meantime, the summary trials and subsequent executions of Batista-era torturers were producing the first signs of tension between the fledgling revolution and the U.S. government. On the one hand, extradition requests were not granted for Senator Mansferrer, who docked his yacht in Miami with $17 million that he had embezzled, or for Ventura, one of the worst uniformed murderers in Batista's police forces. On the other hand, Senator Wayne Morse accused the revolution of indiscriminately shooting its opponents, and this was repeated in *Newsweek* magazine—the first sally in a major anti-Castro campaign by the U.S. press.

According to the British historian Hugh Thomas, 200 pro-Batista soldiers and policemen had been shot by January 20, in an atmosphere charged by daily media reports of the former regime's secret burial sites and its torture, rape, and murder of unarmed youths. The secret burial sites were shown; files were reopened concerning the massacres of defenseless campesinos during the offensives in the Sierra Maestra. The *Chicago Tribune* reporter Jules Dubois reviewed one case for the U.S. press; the condemned, a policeman, had confessed to torturing and murdering at least seventeen young people during the urban uprisings.

Fidel launched a counterattack to the U.S. campaign in a speech he gave January 21 at the National Palace, comparing the crimes committed during the dictatorship with those judged at Nuremberg and asserting the people's right to see justice done and to carry out the executions. He asked for a show of hands: was justice being meted out to the torturers? According to Carlos Franqui, who was editor of *Revolución* at the time: "Fidel's question was answered by an overwhelming 'Yes!' A private nationwide survey showed 93 percent in favor of the trials and shootings." Che was present at the gathering, but took no part in the demonstration. At the same time, his journalist friends and other Latin American professionals began "Operation Truth" to counteract U.S. statements.

U.S. pressure was a burning question; feeling ran high among the supporters of the revolution, and Fidel felt that to give in at an early stage to U.S. pressures would be to abrogate Cuba's sovereignty. *Revolución* reported that the shootings were the reply to "barbarians who had gouged out eyes, castrated, burned flesh or ripped off testicles and fingernails, shoved iron into women's vaginas, burned feet, cut off fingers—whose actions, in short, made for a frightening picture." And the paper summed up: "Just yesterday we heard Che replying to a group of militiamen who wanted to teach a lesson to some informants who were still on the loose: **Neither you nor anyone else can take matters into his own hands. There are revolutionary tribunals. If anyone acts on his own behalf, I'll order him to be locked up and tried by a revolutionary tribunal, too.** "

Without a doubt Che was in favor of the summary trials, but the tales woven by Cuban exiles, in which he was the "Butcher of La Cabaña," presiding over most of the shootings in Havana, are flights of fantasy. Revolutionary Tribunals No. 1 and No. 2 did sit at La Cabaña, the first trying policemen and soldiers, the second (which did not pass death sentences) trying civilians. RT1, presided over by Miguel Ángel Duque de Estrada, did pass the death sentence in some cases, at least two dozen of which were in January. Che did not sit on either tribunal, but did review appeals in his capacity as commander. He could have had no doubts as he ratified the sentences; he believed in the justice of what he was doing and over the previous years had become very tough-minded about such situations.

Hilda Gadea arrived in Havana on January 21 with their daughter Hilda Guevara, now almost three years old. Oscar Fernández Mell picked them up at the airport at Che's request. A little later, the meeting postponed since their days in Mexico took place. According to Hilda, "Ernesto, with his usual frankness, spoke to me of another woman he had met in the battle for Santa Clara. . . . At first he rejected the idea of divorce, but to my way of thinking there was no other solution."

Their conversation may have been confined to ratifying their earlier agreements to separate and to making some decisions about the child. She was to be brought up in Cuba, where Hilda Gadea too would remain for the time being. A photograph of Che's meeting with his daughter has survived: in a room in a house I cannot place, a longhaired Che in an oilskin jacket talks to little Hilda; beside him is a doll as big as his daughter, white and motionless, quite a contrast to the girl, who listens attentively with her chin in her hand, not looking at her father's face. The doll was bought by a group of Che's comrades to give his daughter, as he had no money in his pockets.

Finally Che reacted to what seemed to him the governments' misdirection. Everything he had been bottling up inside him, in his head, poured and poured out in one of the best speeches he ever made. It was January 27, and he was giving a talk at the Sociedad Nuestro Tiempo—"Society for Our Times"—which seems to have been a cultural front for the PSP. The talk was entitled "The future of society under the the the Rebel Army."

(While the fact he was speaking at that meeting may have been in the nature of an invitation from the PSP to the left wing of the July 26 Movement, that same day Blas Roca, who had been the party's leader forever, was speaking elsewhere. Were he and Che in competition?)

Che began by talking about the rebels' time in Mexico and about some M26 members, veterans of the Moncada raid, who then left the revolution because they thought that the entire problem consisted of simply getting rid of Batista and taking power themselves.

He analyzed the guerrillas as a far-flung group, physically broken up but fighting on; since they were **lodged in the Sierra Maestra, but not transplanted into it,** the incorporation of the campesinos was a key factor. It was they (**the straw hats joining up**) who had been brutalized by Batista's army and drawn by the sound of those two magic words: agrarian reform.

And here he found his anchor, the meaning of his presence, his place in the scheme of things: to remember the social content of the revolution and in particular the agrarian element.

He had already touched on this in those unsettled weeks in January, when he began to react politically by publishing an article, "Campesino War and Population," about the forced exile of campesinos under pressure from the army. It was as if he wished to recall the agrarian features underlying the revolution that now dominated the cities.

Once the point had been made, he reviewed the April 1958 strike in just one aspect: **The July 26 Movement was strengthened by the outcome, and the experience taught its leaders a great truth . . . *that the revolution did not belong to one group or another, but had to be the work of the entire Cuban people.***

He then mentioned again the agrarian spirit that the guerrillas had built up: **Neither in the Sierra Maestra nor anywhere else did the men and women of the rebel army ever forget their basic mission, which was to improve the campesinos' lot, to incorporate them into the struggle for land.**

The principal strand of his talk was the story of the rebel army, but its main thrust came back to the same point again and again. When he told the story of the counteroffensive and then the offensive by the rebel columns, Che said:

The campesinos were invisible collaborators who did all that the rebels could not do; they supplied us with information,

watched over the enemy, discovered his weak points, swiftly brought urgent messages, and spied among the ranks of Batista's army itself.

Che then recalled the ascent of the ten thousand cows that the rebels had forced the landholders to turn over to the campesinos: **The campesino children drank milk and ate beef for the first time.** And he pointed out: **The dictatorship meanwhile gave them systematic house-burning, eviction and death. . . . A napalm bomb dropped on a coffee plantation meant the destruction of livelihoods over an area of 2,100 square meters; what it ruined in a minute would take five or six years to replace.** Recounting the Las Villas campaign, he stressed that **we advanced with the agrarian reform as the rebel army's spearhead.**

He finally came to January 1959: **The agrarian revolution has not been completed with Law No. 3.**° He underlined the need to attack the large landholdings and timidly confronted the idea that expropriated property should be paid for in advance and in cash, according to the constitution. When it came to designing a program, the emphasis was clear: imperialism would be the enemy and **the large landholdings were the root of all economic evil.** Che stated that the reformers had to **expect countervailing measures from those who controlled 75 percent of the Cuban market.** He thus foresaw a U.S. invasion when the confrontation between social reform and the empire came to a head (an issue he had set forth in *Revolución* on January 20). The memory of Guatemala was speaking.

As we have an armed democracy, we have an instrument for change. **We have the Rebel Army, which must be in the front line of any struggle, [but] our army is not yet trained for newly acquired responsibilities.** It had to be trained, and taught to read and write. It is important to note that at the forefront of Che's thinking at that time were the rebel army, the revolutionary front parties, the men from the Sierra. The July 26 Movement, which he saw as a hodgepodge of tendencies, with the urban middle class preponderant, was not uppermost in his mind.

He finished by saying: **Our revolution has meant . . . that all armchair theories are just that—theories. . . . Agrarian revolutions have to be made;** *you have to fight in the mountains, then take the revolution to the cities.* He was talking not just about Cuba, but about the rest of Latin America.

His speech was the voice of the left wing of the July 26 Movement writ large, an appeal to Fidel and even to the PSP. It was a question phrased as a demand: Where is the Cuban revolution going?

Che was visited in Havana by Russian journalist Vasili Chichkov on Janu-

---

°Law No. 3 was a revolutionary law of the July 26 Movement and the rebel army and concerned land reform.

ary 30. He was suffering from an asthma attack, was being given injections and was flat out in bed, in his undershirt and stockinged feet. The room struck the Russian as being very Spartan, with an M1 and a pistol holster hanging from a nail, two beds, a chest of drawers, and an old mirror.° Chichkov asked for permission to take a photograph. Che agreed to put a shirt on, but not shoes.

The Russian asked Che what the key to the Cuban revolution was; Che replied: **The campesinos are the basis of the revolution.**

Fidel suddenly came into the room, followed a little later by Raúl Castro and Vilma Espín. Leaving the Russian high and dry, Fidel and Che sat down and began to hatch plots on the bed.

Were they talking about the future of a revolution that had just begun?

°The Chilean senator Salvador Allende paid Che a visit around that time and had a similar impression:

> In a large room furnished as a bedroom, piled high with books, flat out in a camp bed, bare-chested and wearing just a pair of olive drab pants, was a man with a piercing stare and an inhaler in his hand. He motioned me to wait while he tried to ease the severe asthma attack he was having. For ten to fifteen minutes I was able to watch him and see the worry in his piercing glance. . . . Then we spoke, very openly, to the point.

24. The Battle for Agrarian Reform

Marriage to Aleida, June 1959. The passenger is his friend Óscar
Fernández Mell.

O N FEBRUARY 5, 1959, COMMANDER GUEVARA SEEMS FINALLY TO HAVE found enough free time to catch up on his correspondence, to answer the letters that must have been arriving at La Cabaña since the first days of the revolution. Seven of his replies have survived, three of which were replies to people who had volunteered to fight to liberate Santo Domingo. To these he pointed out that they were needed in Cuba just then, where there are enormous difficulties to be overcome. In another, to William Morris of Florida, he spoke of racism: You may be absolutely sure that in a few years the difference between black and white will be just a matter of skin color, as it should be. He thanked the poet Pedro Revuelta for verses and songs, closing with a greeting from a revolutionary who never turned out to be a poet. In the last, to a fellow countryman in Buenos Aires, he spoke of the burning issue of that time in Cuba: The shootings are not just necessary for the people of Cuba, but are also ordered by the people.

On February 7, *El Oficial* published an obscure decree whereby Cuban nationality "as by birthright" was acquired by rebel commanders born abroad who had held their rank for at least a year in the revolutionary process. This was clearly framed for just one person, Commander Ernesto Guevara, in homage and recognition.

Che made his début as a Cuban national the next day, with a very radical speech in favor of agrarian reform, wherein he identified himself with the campesinos again. I'm quite a countryman by now; city air wasn't made for me. In El Pedrero, where he had pitched one of his camps during the Las Villas campaign, he launched a call for a radical agrarian revolt:

> Today, we are set on going to the big landholdings, even on attacking and destroying them. . . . The rebel army is ready to carry the agrarian reform through to its final consequences. . . . The agrarian reform must be brought about in an orderly fashion, so no abuses occur. . . . But on land that the people have [occupied, taken] as part of the revolution, not one commander from our forces, not one soldier will fire on the campesinos, who have always been our friends. . . . If anyone should try to evict them, they are quite within their rights to grab a weapon and keep that from happening.

Che also mentioned the formation of campesino associations, where the voting would come up from the grass roots.

He was particularly disheveled and under particular strain. He wore a cap instead of his black beret with the five-pointed star on it, with his shaggy loose hair sticking out in every direction. He was also suffering from a severe asthma attack. A woman asked him if the campesinos' houses burned by the dictatorship would be written into the history books.

No, we won't write them into history . . . we'll rebuild them right away.

Sure enough, the rebel army began construction of housing in El Pedrero shortly afterward.

A reading of history with hindsight has turned 1959, year number one of the Cuban revolution in power, into a debate over the confrontation between pro-Communists and anti-Communists about what direction the revolutionary process would take. A view from within would instead place the emphasis on the furious debate over the need for, and the extent of, the agrarian reform. This was a source of friction and strain among the wide range of groups who could claim to be victors in the revolution. If we take the pulse of events as they appeared in the daily newspapers, radio scripts, speeches by cadres, the formation of social action groups, and the memories of witnesses that have filtered through to us, and if we factor out their bias, we can be certain that agrarian reform was the burning question of year one of the revolution. The reform would have to take place in a country dominated by big landholdings, **where 1.5 percent of landowners owned 46 percent of the country,** where two-thirds of farmworkers were landless day laborers, sugar mill workers, farmhands in big landholdings, or sharecroppers.

It is within this framework that Che's definition of the revolution is found, and with it his definition of the left wing. Land was occupied by the campesinos in Las Villas Province in the days leading up to and following the El Pedrero speech. In response to these takeovers, President Manuel Urrutia summoned Camilo Cienfuegos, who was in charge of the armed forces in Havana, and Ramiro Valdés, maybe in his capacity as second in command of No. 8 Column, the main force in the Las Villas region, and asked them to keep the spontaneous agrarian revolt in check, to rein in the invasions, and make the campesinos wait for a law to be drawn up. Camilo and Ramiro answered that their men would not fire on the countryfolk.

In a February 11 television program, "Economic Commentary," Che insisted on his Zapata-style view of agrarian reform: expropriation without compensation to the big landholders, and land distribution.[*]

The first face-to-face meeting between the two wings of the revolution took place on February 13. Prime Minister Miró Cardona, a representative of the most conservative sectors in the government, had already tendered his resignation on January 17, arguing that there existed a parallel power to the government, in the form of Fidel Castro and the rebel army, and that Fidel should take Miró Cardona's place in order to end a situation that was paralyzing the process of institutionalization. Now he resigned again. Fidel stepped into the post, an action of which he would later say: "I would rather have held myself back."

Meanwhile, Che was working at a feverish pace, educating the Rebel Army

[*]The battle cries of the legendary Mexican revolutionary Emiliano Zapata (1879–1919) were "Land and freedom" and "Land for those who work it."

and organizing recreational activities at the La Cabaña base, among them a children's club where the members could spend time with the soldiers. He took part in several meetings with the children, whom he called *barbuditos*— "little bearded ones"—and told them stories about the Sierra, made them piñatas, and taught them how to assemble and dismantle rifles.

At about the same time he became angry with a fellow countryman of his, an Argentinian who owned the Shanghai Theater, where the sex shows included bestiality and sadomasochism. Che wanted to throw the owner in jail and even said it would not be a bad idea to have him shot.

His exhaustion was making him ill. Dr. Fernández Mell criticized him for not taking care of himself; he was going without sleep, smoking like a chimney, and grabbing a bite to eat whenever he remembered. He was diagnosed as having a dangerous case of pneumonia. Later, Dr. Conradino Polanco checked an X ray and discovered double pulmonary emphysema that was spreading in his right lung.

The doctors ordered rest and Fidel, over Che's objection, ordered him to take a vacation at a house on Tarará Beach, near Havana, that had belonged to a well-known Batista supporter. Despite his protests that the place was too luxurious, Che moved in with Aleida and his escorts.

The three guerrilla doctors urged him to stop smoking entirely; after some argument, he ended up agreeing to smoke just one cigar per day. Núñez Jiménez, at that time Che's secretary, recalled:

> The following morning, I went to pick up the order of the day from Che and found him smoking a cigar about half a meter long, made by some admirers among the Havana tobacco workers. With a roguish smile he told me: *Don't worry about the doctors. I'm obeying their orders— just one cigar a day, no more, no less.*

He was supposed to have withdrawn from all activity, but received visits from his daughter twice a week. And at the end of February and the beginning of March, a secret committee met at the beach house to draft an agrarian reform bill. This was the revolution's crucial issue for Che, as he again made abundantly clear in an article published in *Revolución*, "What Is a Guerrilla Fighter?" In it he praised informal discipline, and stressed the importance of reconnoitering terrain and moving swiftly. But the agrarian issue was the main thrust: **A guerrilla is, basically and above all, an agrarian revolutionary,** so the rebel army was the standard bearer for agrarian reform, and that, he believed, was to provide **the July 26 Movement's historical definition.** He mentioned that 80 percent of the rebel army, as well as half its officer corps, was made up of campesinos, and concluded: **the Movement did not invent agrarian reform, but will implement it.**

While Che rested in Tarará, the government launched a series of breathtaking social reforms: it took over the telephone company on March 3, and the metropolitan buses three days later; rents were cut by 50 percent on March 10, and the price of medicines was lowered by law some days later. Along with these measures, Law 112 was enacted, whereby property embezzled by officials in Batista's government was confiscated.

Toward the middle of March, Che wrote to his friend Alberto Granado (I'll give you the biggest hug one little macho can reasonably receive from another) telling him he had planned to go to Venezuela with Fidel, but an illness kept me confined to bed. He was up and about a week later, however, and attended an *en bloc* government meeting called by Fidel on April 9. Ministers of the government, guerrilla commanders, and July 26 Movement cadres took part. Despite its importance, there are scarcely any records of the meeting, which seems to have been heated. Tension was appearing among three groups just then: a left wing, led by Che and Raúl, which was frankly socialist and sympathized with the PSP; a right wing, backed by moderate sectors of the government and connected in some cases with members of the agrarian oligarchy; and a second left wing within the July 26 Movement, represented mainly by cadres from the Plains, such as Carlos Franqui, Faustino Pérez, Marcelo Fernández, and Enrique Oltuski. This last group combined its anti-imperialism with strong criticism of the Communists, whom they considered hidebound and sectarian, and who were relatively independent of Fidel. Fidel, characteristically unconfrontational, held himself above the conflicts. He was the indisputable leader of the revolution, and the rebel army and most of the population lined up behind him. His dealings with the people, whose welfare is his first consideration, and his strict adherence to principle, [are] the key to the fanatic welcome he draws wherever he goes.

Among other things to be discussed was whether to suspend trials against war criminals. The slow progress of some trials was being criticized; it was an issue that kept tension high in Cuba and increased tension in international relations. The lack of legal guarantees was another sore point. According to Franqui, there was a clash between the Castro brothers—one of the few of which we know—because of Fidel's decision to stop the shootings. Raúl was opposed to this move.

There is scant information about whether or how the central issue—the content and extent of the future agrarian reform—was discussed. But it can hardly be believed that the tensions arising in year one of the revolution were not in fact much greater than Cuban history recalls later. Reflections such as this by Che regarding Camilo's role seems to confirm it:

> All of us, the majority at least, have a lot of peccadilloes to confess to from those days, a lot of suspicion, mistrust, and even occasional dirty tricks; we considered our ends very just, but our methods were at times—many times—incorrect. But it could never be said that Camilo had recourse to any of them.

Apart from the tensions, Che devoted himself to two media projects for which he would have great affection, the independent news agency Prensa Latina—"Latin Press"—and the magazine *Verde Olivo*—"Olive Drab." Prensa Latina was the product of Latin American correspondents who had been in the Sierra Maestra and was backed by a Mexican industrialist, Castro Ulloa. Masetti figured importantly in the agency's leadership, as did Che and Oltuski, who at that time was communications minister. Che was a prime mover not only in an ideological sense, but also in dealing with problems of organization and providing strategic information. He took an active part in meetings and paid frequent, unannounced nighttime visits to the staff. The Argentine writer Rodolfo Walsh, who became part of the project, recalled years later:

> At Prensa Latina, we never knew when Che was going to appear. He would just show up. . . . The only sign of his presence in the building would be two campesinos wearing the magnificent Sierra uniform. One would place himself next to the elevator, the other in front of Masetti's offices, submachine gun in hand.

The news agency began to take form in April, but did not start operations for another three months.

Verde Olivo, the rebel army's official magazine, was born on April 10, when several minor publications were merged by Che and Camilo. The magazine, which Che planned as a voice of the left wing of the M26, was published under very difficult circumstances. It was financed by collections from the fighters and printed during downtime in print shops, using paper and ink contributed by one or another newspaper. *Verde Olivo* almost immediately caused tensions with some more conservative army cadres, such as Huber Matos, the military governor of Camagüey, who called the magazine *Olive Red* and sabotaged its distribution.

At the end of April and the beginning of May, Che took part in a demonstration by tobacco workers, who were strongly influenced by the PSP, and was given a contribution toward the work of agrarian reform. He also appeared on television, saying that Cuba should keep diplomatic ties with the whole world (aside from the Cold War); visited Santiago de Cuba, where he spoke at the university; took part in the May Day parade at Matanzas to honor thirties revolutionary Antonio Guiteras; and welcomed Fidel when he returned from a tour of Latin America.

There is no record of the meetings held between the two at that time, but doubtless agrarian reform was the main topic. There was much speculation about the probable content of the reform. Fidel considered it not only an initial response to the needs of the campesinos, but also a means of arbitrating the concerns of the various forces making up the revolutionary front at that time. Franqui said that Fidel delayed announcement of his the decision in order to make a greater impact. Núñez Jiménez, on the other hand, felt that Fidel delayed so as to rally public opinion first.

The bill said that the landowners were offering to turn over **ten thousand heifers** to the campesinos. The *Diario de la Marina* ("Navy Daily," a mouthpiece for the most conservative sectors in the country) which had been pro-Batista until very recently, **warmly supported** that, calling it **a very** "responsible" agrarian reform.

In an article he wrote at the time, (it was published a month later), Che heralded the agrarian reform as **the government's first great battle** and described its aims as

> **forthright, all-inclusive, but flexible. It will put paid to big landholding in Cuba, but not to Cuban means of production. This battle will absorb much of the people's and government's strength over the years to come. Land will be freely given to campesinos. And whoever can demonstrate that he is really its owner will be paid with long-term compensation bonds.**

Ofn May 17, Fidel summoned the government and several rebel commanders to the old headquarters at La Plata, in the heart of the Sierra Maestra, where the bill was to be signed into law. It provided for the confiscation of plantations of over 1,000 acres (10 percent of the farms in the country). The expropriation would be paid for with bonds maturing after twenty-nine years and paying annual interest of 4.5 percent, based on the value of land declared in tax returns. Nationalized lands would then either be split up or turned into farm cooperatives to be administered by the state. Tenant farmers, partners in cattle ranches, and day laborers would be given preference in land distribution. Land that remained inactive would return to state ownership. Plots could not be divided and could be sold only to the state. In future, only Cubans could buy land. As far as specialists were concerned, the act was very moderate in taking on only large sugar plantation owners, and in not extending land distribution to all farm laborers and partners.

Agriculture Minister Humberto Sorí Marín, who had been working on a more moderate bill, opposed the act and as a protest did not accompany Fidel to the signing ceremony. But the act must have seemed too bland to Che; though one of its prime movers, he gave a talk at the University of Havana instead of being present at the signing. He described the act later as **our first timid law, which did not dare take on so basic a task as suppressing the plantation owners.**

Fidel's attempt at mediation failed to mollify the right wing of the government, and agreed even less with U.S. interests in Cuban sugar plantations, but it did not go far enough for the left. Tensions now spread to groups allied with the various factions. Blas Roca, speaking for the PSP, accused Fidel of unleashing an anti-Communist campaign. Meanwhile the Communists and the July 26 Movement were vying for control of the unions, which were ridding themselves of their old pro-Batista framework. It was not to be the last time that the PSP was reminded of its inconsistencies and timidity in the fight against the dictatorship.

This rift in the revolutionary front was incidentally echoed by Che, who expressed his disdain of ideological prison cells in a letter to a woman who had asked him for the July 26 Movement's official doctrine: **I don't think it's possible to write according to a strict doctrinaire line—and besides, there is no official July 26 Movement.**

On May 25, Aviation Minister Pedro Luis Díaz Lanz's light plane went down in the Ciénaga de Zapata swamp. All the commanders, Che included, joined in the search for him. The old Sierra hands' esprit de corps reappeared; Fidel directed operations with map in hand. The plane was located; everyone aboard was unhurt. But meanwhile another light plane, this one with Raúl on board, was trapped in a storm, ran out of fuel, and had to make a forced landing in a swamp. Off went the old comrades on a new and riskier search, which also ended in success. The planes were old and unsafe, and the rebel commanders were flying from one end of the country to another in technically appalling conditions. They flew as they had fought, testing and pushing themselves to the limit.

Rumor had it that at the Columbia camp Camilo had performed a crazy stunt, swinging from the skids of a helicopter, and that he once offered to take Che from his camp to La Cabaña in a copter without knowing how to fly the thing. Not only did Che not dissuade him; he accepted willingly, while those watching swore they would never make it. Che was himself learning how to fly at the time and was frequently flown from one end of the island to another by his own personal pilot, Eliseo de la Campa, whom he met in La Cabaña while bringing in the wounded from Escambray.

Che's personal armed forces file has survived. A form filled in by hand reads as follows:

NAME AND SURNAME:	Ernesto Guevara Serna
	Married, age 30
STUDIES:	Medicine
PLACE AND DATE OF ARMED ACTION;	Mexico
FRONT AND COLUMN SERVED IN:	1-4-8
RANKS AWARDED:	Lt. Medic, Capt., Commander
AWARDED BY:	Fidel
BATTLES TAKEN PART IN:	[left blank]
WOUNDS RECEIVED:	2

Signed: Che

He drew a line through the box marked "Race," as he considered it irrelevant. In short, he was as gruff and laconic as usual. This gruff character, who at times seemed to be surprised to find himself where he was and reacted by smashing decorations and ignoring hierarchies, received the decree divorcing him from Hilda Gadea on May 22 and formalized his relationship with Aleida by marrying her on June 2.

Che had his wedding picture taken with a very beautiful and serious-looking Aleida March. He looked a lot like Cantinflas, as if he was not quite sure what was going on, contemplating with raised eyebrows a table that bore flowers and a cake. His uniform was clean but not too neat: the upper pockets were crammed full of stuff. The photograph also shows Raúl Castro, looking like the eternal teenager, with a very pretty Vilma Espín, the pilot Eliseo de la Campa, Alberto Fernández Montes de Oca, and Alberto Castellanos, in whose house the wedding was held. Camilo, his old buddy, wasn't in the photograph, but had played his usual practical joke beforehand, telling the guests they would have to bring their own food. Knowing Che's Spartan and frugal nature, many people fell for this and turned up with entrées and desserts. Another photograph shows a smiling Che at the wheel of a dilapidated car with an enormous cigar in his mouth; Aleida is next to him, and Fernández Mell, who was living with them, is in the back seat.

Tension was rising again in the country as the large sugar mill owners and ranchers in Camagüey reacted to the Agrarian Reform Act. They felt betrayed after delivering 5,000 heifers no one asked them for in the hope they'd be spared more drastic measures. The ever-witty Camilo said in response: "Even though they handed over the heifers we'll wring their necks." The government replied by taking over the landowners' fiefdoms, including several large American ranches, whose absentee foreign owners were "the soul of counterrevolution," as historian Hugh Thomas put it.

Fidel's action against the ranchers was protested by the right wing of the government, which complained that the expropriation was the result of Communist influence. The first official U.S. reaction to the agrarian reform was a timid diplomatic note asking for swift and effective indemnity.

Díaz Lanz's defection to the United States added fuel to the flames of the anti-Communist campaign against Fidel under way there. Fidel reacted by shuffling his cabinet on June 11. Out went ministers linked to old pre-Batista politics, along with relatively right-wing members of the July 26 Movement such as Mederos, Roberto Agramonte, Humberto Sorí Marín, and Angel Fernández. In came nonsocialist left-wing members of the M26—men from the Sierra, and one member of the Revolutionary Directorio: Raúl Roa, Serafín Ruiz de Zárate, Pedro Miret, and Pepín Naranjo.

For months, Che had been working on an article entitled "A Revolution Begins," to be published in June in the Brazilian magazine *O Cruzeiro*. It gave a brief history of the revolution, followed by his evaluation of the possible impact of events in Cuba on the rest of Latin America.

> **We are now placed in a position in which we are much more than just factors of one nation; we are now the hope of unredeemed Latin America. All eyes, those of the great oppressors**

and of the hopeful oppressed, are now turned our way. The development of popular movements in Latin America will depend to a great extent on the future attitude we display, on our ability to solve manifold problems, and each step we take will be watched over by the ever-present eyes of the great creditor and of our optimistic Latin American brothers.

25. "You Cannot Dream in the Shade of a Pyramid"

O N JUNE 12, 1959, CHE BECAME ONE OF THE FLEDGING REVOLUTION'S roving ambassadors. Was the trip really necessary? Che seemed to think, at the time, that he was getting a vacation he hadn't ask for, that Fidel looked on him as someone he had affection for but wished to keep at a distance. Nevertheless, the disciplined Commander Guevara packed his bags and set off just days after his wedding. Fidel said good-bye to him at the Havana airport. Che, due to his scruples that official trips should not be vacations in disguise, would not take Aleida with him. He felt he was punishing himself, and in letter to his family confessed that he missed her terribly throughout the journey.

The delegation was something of a motley crew. Fidel had included Captain Omar Fernández and the well-known radio commentator José Pardo Llada, arguing that he wanted the latter to join in "the government's duties." He had also brought out of relative political retirement an activist from the previous generation, the economist Dr. Salvador Vilaseca, a man in his fifties, because the right-wing economists from the July 26 Movement did not want to accompany that radical Guevara. Pardo spitefully described the rest of the group:

> Lieutenant Argudín (a mere boy of sixteen) and Pancho García, a dumb-looking character who never had anything to with the revolution, but who for some reason appeared as Che's secretary and right-hand man. . . . A Guatemalan dwarf they called El Patojo was also part of the group, and looked as if to him an olive-drab uniform was fancy dress.

Che, recently turned thirty-one, took his role as roving ambassador very seriously, as he took everything seriously. With the same tenacity and care with which he undertook to learn a job, but without making too many concessions to the formality demanded by this particular job, Che threw himself into his ambiguous mission as an ambassador. Was he to open doors, set up trade links, or gain good will for the revolution?

After arriving in the United Arab Republic on June 16, he moved into the deposed King Farouk's summer palace. His first meeting with President Gamal Abdel Nasser was quite cool. Both sparred a little, sounding one another out. Che went so far as to question the extent of the Egyptian agrarian reform and thus provoked an argument. He strongly maintained that the fact that the plantation owners had not left the country indicated that the reform was not really serious.

Relations with the countries of the Middle East were still cautious and would remain so over the next few years, but there would be some improvement. Che met President Nasser, visited Damascus, the Suez Canal, and Alexandria. He performed the obligatory anti-imperialist obeisances, paying homage to those who died during the Anglo-French invasion of 1956, and he even took part in naval maneuvers in the Mediterranean.

Salvador Vilaseca, who had been named to the delegation after the others, arrived in Cairo a day late. Delighted to learn that he had taken part in Cuban revolutionary movements in the thirties, Che fired off one question after another. Were they terrorists in the struggle against the Machado dictorship? What separated them from the People's Socialist Party? "He even made me draw sketches of the bombs we used to make, and discuss the devices."

On July 1, the delegation, now also including Pardo, arrived in India. Che met with Prime Minister Jawaharlal Nehru and laid a wreath on the tomb of Gandhi, his childhood hero. He later also visited the Jama Masjid temple, where the creator of nonviolent resistance as a political philosophy had been cremated. But Che mused aloud to the others in his delegation: **Nonviolent resistance is no use in Latin America; ours has to be active.**

Che committed his first diplomatic gaffe at a dinner with Nehru and Indira Gandhi. While laying into a dish of shrimp with Rabelaisian relish, he repeatedly asked Nehru what he thought about Mao Zedong and Red China. The only reply was a prudent silence. It was a dialogue of the deaf.

The Cuban delegates made a whirlwind tour of India, visiting Calcutta, Lucknow, a nuclear research institute, a sugar research institute, textile factories, and a sewing-machine factory; meeting with ministers—in short, doing anything Che thought might be useful to the Cuban revolution. But despite his apparently boundless energy, he was having a bad time. He revealed what was on his mind in a very frank and not at all gruff letter to his mother, his constant confidante. Dated "approximately July 2," it said, in part,

> **My dreams of visiting all these countries has come true in such a way as to thwart all my happiness. Instead, I talk of economic and political problems; throw parties where the only thing lacking is for me to put on a penguin suit, and I forsake untainted pleasures like dreaming in the shade of a pyramid or over the tomb of Tutankhamun . . .**

Regarding India: **New and complex protocols which make me panic just like a child . . . One of my lieutenants has come up with a standard reply for everything. It's something like "joinch-joinch" and it works beautifully.** And finally a heartfelt reflection:

> **A sense of mass considerations, as opposed to individual ones, has become rooted within me; I am the same old loner trying to find his way with no personal help, but I now have a sense of my historical duty. I have neither home, nor wife, nor children, nor parents, nor brothers. My friends are friends as long as they think politically as I do—and nonetheless I am happy. I feel not just a powerful inner strength, which I've always felt, but as though I'm doing something in life; I feel that I have a capacity to give something to others and an entirely fatalistic sense of my mission, which makes me quite fearless.**
>
> **I don't know why I'm writing all this; maybe I just miss Aleida. Take it for what it is: a letter written on a stormy night, above the skies of India, far from my homelands and my loved ones.**

The uncommon seriousness of his reflections was also mirrored in the fact that instead of the usual jokes he signed the letter tersely with his name: Ernesto.

To outward appearances, Che was still Che. At a Chilean diplomat's house, he demonstrated his yoga abilities by standing on his head in the middle of the floor. Agra fascinated him, and he couldn't stop taking photographs. In Delhi he had a severe asthma attack while climbing down from a large fortified tower and had to lie flat on the ground to get his breath back.

Che left India with two presents—a silver model of the Taj Mahal and a sari that Nehru gave him for Aleida—and the feeling that diplomacy was not for him.

He went to Burma on July 12, and to Thailand three days afterward. On July 15 he arrived in Tokyo. Once more the diplomatic routine dictated numerous, not always profitable, visits. He was taken aback by Japan's industrialization, but also by its loss of national pride, its **indisputable kowtowing to American power.** when his asthma improved, he made three personal requests to his hosts: to see Mount Fuji, to take in a sumo wrestling match, and to visit Hiroshima to pay belated homage to the victims of the atomic bomb he had deplored as a teenager.

Events were proceeding at a breathless pace in Cuba while Che was in Japan. The clash between the right and left wings of the revolution, staved off until then, finally broke out. Fidel confronted President Manuel Urrutia, whom he accused on television of playing into the hands of the country's most conservative sectors. Fidel's complaints also included the president's lack of tact in awarding himself a large salary and his frivolous anti-Communism, grist for the mill of the defector Díaz Lanz, whose counterrevolutionary campaign in the U.S. was in full swing. In hopes of easing U.S. pressure, Fidel resigned as prime minister. The people reacted strongly, calling a general strike and holding a peasant march on Havana. The one who ended up resigning was Urrutia. Osvaldo Dorticós, named as the new president, did not accept Fidel's resignation.

On July 26, Che tried to telephone Fidel from Tokyo, but couldn't reach him. The Cuban revolution was taking a new turn to the left, and here he was in Japan. What was going on?

Che arrived in Jakarta, Indonesia, on July 30. The fact that no one but a minor embassy official was there to receive them at the airport speaks volumes about how the tour was organized: the Indonesians had forgotten their visitors were coming. The hotel they were booked into had no water. **Never mind, those of you who wash. I learned to be a stinker in the Sierra Maestra.**

President Sukarno received Che the day after. At that time the Indonesian president appeared to be the leader of an independent anti-imperialist movement in Asia. But Che described him as "a libidinous old man." He met the left-wing cadres in the government and other ministers and made the by-now repetitive visits to sugar mills and tobacco factories. A break came in Bali, **an earthly paradise,** with echoes of Gauguin.

After Indonesia came Singapore, where Che was stranded for two days by mechanical trouble with the airplane. Then Hong Kong, where he looked over all the cameras in the airport shop before picking a Leica and a small Minox.

During his free time he wrote something that seemed to his colleagues like notes for a guerrilla warfare manual, and the excellent story "The Murdered Puppy." The weather wreaked havoc with his asthma and kept him from sleeping. In Pardo's words, "he would stumble like a sleepwalker to the bathroom, where he would shut himself away to undergo his long and laborious inhaling. He would then go back to bed and sit still for a while, until he could lie down and sleep again." The journalist in him noted his nighttime thoughts: **I love my inhaler more than my pistol. . . . I tend to think deep thoughts when the asthma hits me hard.**

On a lightning visit to Ceylon, he met the president and signed an agreement to sell 20,000 tons of sugar. He was fascinated by the local archaeological ruins. By August 8 Che was in Pakistan, where he met the head of state, Mohammed Ayub Khan. He arrived in Yugoslavia for a six-day visit on August 12, after quick stops in Cairo and Athens (where he was upset at not having time to visit the Acropolis, which he had dreamed of doing since his days in Mexico). Yugoslavia was the first socialist country he had been to on the tour, but he doesn't seem to have been impressed. Maybe his thoughts were taken up with what was happening in Cuba. He confined himself to noting that **we were impressed by Tito's massive popularity, comparable to that of Nasser in Egypt and our own Fidel.**

Just what was Fidel doing? He was disarming a conspiracy between the most conservative of the Cuban ranchers and the Dominican dictator Leónidas Trujillo. Using cadres from Front II, he captured an airplane bringing arms from Santo Domingo, an operation in which the CIA was probably involved. Meanwhile, the government also cut textbook prices 25 percent and electricity charges 30 percent.

And what was Che doing? He was making a hasty trip to the Sudan to visit its president. The end of the journey was drawing near. On August 27, on his way to Madrid, he stopped off in Rome just long enough to visit the Sistine Chapel. He had looked forward too much to Europe to spend only a few hours there. He moved on to Morocco after a brief transit stop in Madrid. There, it was more protocol, and the pro-Franco Moroccan monarchy looking askance at the Cuban revolution. There was just one happy moment: the prime minister invited Che to eat a sheep Arabian-style, squatting and with his fingers. Che felt right at home with this return to a guerrilla lifestyle.

After a stop in Madrid to deal with the plane's technical problems and make a rapid circuit of used-book stores with Vilaseca, they ended their journey on September 9. Che had been away from Cuba for almost three months.

With Colonel Bayo, the man who had trained him for warfare in Mexico.
Cuba, 1960

ERNESTO GUEVARA RETURNED TO CUBA ON SEPTEMBER 19, 1959. AT THE airport, he reported on the sympathy the Cuban revolution had evoked in other parts of the world. He would later say that, in the view of the Asians,

> the other Latin America is fading away now—the one where
> nameless men toil miserably mining the tin that keeps down
> the pay of Indonesian tin workers, who are being martyred;
> the Latin America of the rubber barons in the Amazon, where
> malaria-ridden men produce the rubber that depresses rub-
> ber workers' wages to even more of a pittance in Indonesia,
> Ceylon, or Malaysia; the Latin America of the fabulous oil
> fields, that mean oil workers in Saudi Arabia, Iraq, or Iran
> cannot be paid more; the Latin America whose cheap sugar
> means that a worker in India cannot be better paid for the
> same brutal work under the same inclement tropical sun.

Che briefed Raúl Roa at the Foreign Office about the journey on September 11. On a kind note, *The New York Times* would report that Che had surprised observers in Havana with his negotiating ability.

Humanismo magazine published his article about the journey, entitled "Latin America from an Afro-Asian Standpoint." He also wrote several articles for *Verde Olivo*—basically reportage, but always with a particular emphasis, such as postatomic industrialization in Japan, the contrasts in India, the need to learn from state planning in Yugoslavia, and the virtues of small trade links with Ceylon and Pakistan. He discussed the issues in a week-long television program and in a press conference.

Che made one of his finest speeches at the Police Academy on September 30. He emphasized the theme that young police officers, as the branch of the revolutionary army that had most day-to-day contact with the people, had the obligation to become spokespeople for public opinion. That and the need to keep public order, he said, appear to be contradictory, and as a result many members of the armed forces—not just the police, but all the branches—have been high-handed with the public. The instances are minimal, but they do exist and may contaminate the rest.

He insisted that public servants owed their positions to popular will, and thus defined the essential task of the new police officers, a revolutionary radical version of what a police officer should be. Besides avoiding the temptation to be authoritarian, he or she should

> be constantly informing us—not on conspiracies against the
> state, as we have a watchful people who will help us out there.
> But [the police must] . . . observe the popular reaction to mea-
> sures adopted by a minister or the government in general,
> and know what is thought of them. . . . This is not to be able to
> put people on file or punish them for expressing an opinion.
> Quite the contrary, it is to analyze opinion, to see how truly

**we act according to those opinions and what people really
think about those actions. The people are never in the wrong;
we make the mistakes and need to be corrected by them.**

On October 7, Fidel Castro gave Che a new job in addition to his other
duties. He was already director of the Armed Forces Training Department (responsible for organizing the rebel army's education); in charge of *Verde Olivo,*
the military band, and the departments of cinema and plastic art, and military
commander of the La Cabaña base. This new job was a complex one. Fidel
wanted Che to lead the industrialization project of the recently created National Agrarian Reform Institute (INRA).

Che had been assigned a seemingly impossible task: to coordinate activities among a group of industries and workshops that had been nationalized and
become a department of the INRA. Some of these were embezzled facilities that had been recovered, others facilities taken over under
the provisos of Labor Act 647; others had simply been handed over
by their owners; still others, the government had bought; and some
were newly built. Nearly all were small businesses.

He was assisted by a group of economists sent by the Chilean Communist
Party and headed by Jaime Barrios, Raúl Maldonado, and Carlos Romeo. The
Chileans were commissioned by the INRA but saw Che as a representative of
the left wing of the revolution and offered their services as free independent
advisers. Rounding out the group were José Manuel Manresa, whom Che had
discovered at La Cabaña; Julio "El Patojo" Cáceres, who was living in Che's
house; and Orlando Borrego, the rebel officer who had organized the workshops in the Sierra Maestra.

Raúl Maldonado was witness to the surreal quality of the small ministerial department:

> The eighth-floor offices were bare. There was a desk at the back, with
> Che's feet on it, a group of armed young men behind him, seven or eight
> empty desks in front of them, and a bit of light as we got out of the ele-
> vator. It made for an absurd picture: Aleida was filing Che's fingernails.

The primary aim was to run the businesses and keep them going no matter what, so as to keep workers employed. The first and most obvious idea was
to organize them according to types of product and to coordinate workshops
and factories with companies. They had to improvise. They appointed managers whom they believed to be honest, but no one on the team had any experience in industrial management at all, let alone at a factory or company
level. An appeal was launched among guerrilla cadres and militants from the
labor movement (some from the People's Socialist Party); with the money
raised, a small management school was founded and a central fund was set up
in order to pay wages.

The industrial picture when the revolution began, as Che was to sum it up
a year and a half later, was awful:

An army of unemployed workers numbering 600,000 . . . a whole host of manufacturing plants making goods using raw materials from abroad, foreign machines, and foreign spare parts; undeveloped agriculture, choked by competition in the capitalist market; and large plantations, whose land [was used] to plant cane for large-scale sugar production and [whose owners] thus preferred to import food from the United States.

Che appealed around that time to his travel companion Vilaseca the economist to start giving him advanced math classes. A relationship began at the chalkboard, where they went from elementary mathematics to advanced algebra, mathematical analysis, geometric analysis, and differential and integral calculus. Vilaseca recalled that classes were held "twice a week, on Tuesdays and Saturdays at eight A.M. On rare occasions he canceled, saying he was going to sleep, that he couldn't take any more. On Saturdays we had one, two, three, even five hours."

Despite his new workload, Che spoke in Cabaiguán to commemorate the arrival of No. 8 Column. The occasion was captured on film along with shots of many of his former comrades-in-arms; these may be the only photographs in which Che's usual malicious half-smile was replaced by a free, boisterous laugh.

The next day, Che began a series of speeches-cum-debates at the country's three main universities, beginning with the University of Oriente Province, in order to discuss the widening gulf between the revolution and institutes of higher education. The students, noted for their support of the March 13 Directorio, were now on the sidelines, and, in keeping with their professors' liberal opposition to the government, were resisting pressure to join the revolutionary process. They defended their autonomy, on the one hand, and their political stance on the other. Che met the debate head-on with a question: **Is it an inevitable fact that universities should become conservative, or even flashpoints for reaction?**

Che's speech in Santiago was very critical. He tried to convince students of the need for universities to join the government's plans, even at the risk of losing their autonomy. He also asked for controversies and confrontation to end, because students had to take part in setting standards for society and making it a priority to have the kind of studies that were needed for the revolution to progress. However, he did not open with threats or political pressure, but **called for a natural discussion, as bitter or as heated as you like, but always healthy.**

Some months later, the University of Las Villas awarded Che an honorary teacher's degree, which he felt he did not deserve (**all the teaching I've done has been in guerrilla camps, and has consisted of cursing and setting a tough example**). Accepting the degree as an honor for the Rebel Army, dressed in olive drab rather than an academic gown, Che asked the university to **paint itself black, to paint itself with the people, with work-**

ers, with campesinos, to open its doors to social outcasts, those segregated by racism or economic factors, and he complained about the fact that the government has no voice in Cuban universities.

Three months after the Santiago speech, it was the University of Havana's turn to take Che's scolding when he complained that in the name of autonomy its students were frivolous: the school had low standards and conferred an abundance of liberal arts degrees, which were useless in the labor market; there was no economics faculty, a huge omission. He complained that there was no coordination of academic schedules at the country's three major universities, and no provision for students to work toward their degrees and still be able for both their studies and their obligations to society. Why can't the university march alongside the other universities, on the same road as the revolutionary government and in step with it?

Then after apologizing for causing a controversy in front of television cameras, Che defended the word "coordination" against the diehard advocates of autonomy. He provided a rousing finish to his speech by demythifying the idea of vocation, using his own personal experience as an example and joking: I began university as a student of engineering, ended it as a doctor, and have since been a military commander; now you see me as a public speaker. It seems somewhat surprising that Ernesto Guevara should rail against the idea of vocation, freedom of choice, and volition, when his own personal history had been a continual demonstration that volition cannot be imprisoned within the confines of reason. But the pressures arising from the revolution's technical shortfall must have been overwhelming at that time.

On October 10, Ernesto Guevara took part in a ceremony in Santiago de Cuba honoring the memory of Alberto "Pacho" Montes de Oca's brother, Orlando, who "disappeared" during the dictatorship. For the first time in many years, Che set foot in a church, as the dead fighter's mother wanted a religious service.

Raúl Castro was appointed armed forces minister the same day, which aroused an angry reaction from Huber Matos, the army commander in Camagüey. This skirmish came on top of an air raid by Díaz Lanz from Miami, which caused many civilian casualties. (First reports blamed the casualties on the bombing but Che, who made no compromises with truth, said years later that two were killed and fifty wounded by the bombs dropped and by fire from our anti-aircraft guns.) Huber Matos resigned that very day, along with fourteen other officers, accusing Fidel of having fallen into the hands of Communism. Fidel reacted by ordering Camilo to Camagüey to disarm and detain Matos and his men.

Five days later, at a rally outside the National Palace to protest the air raids, Che asked the crowd: Will this revolutionary government and this people here give way to foreign pressure? Will it back down? This met with shouts of "No! No!" He slipped a revealing phrase into the speech: We won't be another Guatemala!

A new rift appeared in the government. The National Bank president,

Felipe Pazos, said he would resign when Fidel threatened to court-martial Huber Matos for treason; the government's left wing disagreed with Fidel.

The division widened during the ensuing debate, which included several ministers and Che. Faustino Pérez, Enrique Oltuski, and Ray said that although Matos might have split with the revolution, no treason was involved in his resignation. According to Franqui, Raúl Castro said that Matos's stance was counterrevolutionary in the face of foreign aggression, and he had to be shot. With Oltuski and Ray repeating their arguments in favor of Matos, Che jokingly said: **We'll have to shoot the lot.**

Fidel stopped the discussion in its tracks: Matos had to go to trial, he insisted, and he asked the dissenters to resign. Che then intervened in favor of Oltuski, Faustino, and Ray, saying that if they were brave enough to stick to their position at risk to their lives, they should stay on as ministers. But Fidel said they no longer had the trust of the revolution. A reshuffle then began to take place. Oltuski stayed on temporarily; the others left the government in November, to make way for Martínez Sánchez and Osmany Cienfuegos (Camilo's brother), whose political positions were closer to Raúl and Che's.

Huber Matos was to be tried on December 11. The charges of treason were not proven in spite of his evident differences with the revolutionary line, his disagreement with the agrarian reform, and his flirting with the idea of large plantations.

On October 29, meanwhile, an Argentinian newspaper published an interview with Che, in which he proposed a radical review of relations with the United States: **Without doubt, Latin America needs a few *barbudos*.**

That same afternoon, Camilo Cienfuegos vanished while flying a Cessna 310 from Camagüey to Santa Clara on a tour of inspection. A huge rescue operation began at dawn on October 30. Che flew off in a Cessna to search; the navy was mobilized and campesinos combed the area. The whole country was on edge: Camilo was doubtless one of the most popular and best-loved figures in the revolution. The aircraft had vanished without a trace. A reconstruction of the events revealed that he probably changed course to avoid a storm and perhaps headed out to sea. The search continued for a week, encouraged at times by false leads; and then, nothing. There was some anger in Che's words, as he had lost one of his very few friends:

> **The enemy killed him, and they killed him because they wanted him dead. They killed him because we have no safe planes, because our pilots cannot acquire the experience they need, because, overloaded with work, he wanted to be in Havana in a few hours. . . . And his character killed him, too. Camilo had no respect for danger; he had fun with it, played with it. It attracted him and he handled it. To his guerrillalike mind, a cloud could not stop or twist a charted course.**

The revolution had lost one of its rarest leading cadres, as it had previously lost Juan Manuel Márquez, José Antonio Echeverría, Frank País, and René Ramos Latour.

A month later, Che called for a mass rally of workers in Manzanillo to do a day's voluntary labor, the first such large-scale work mobilization in Cuba. An educational complex was being built in Caney de las Mercedes and was to be named after Camilo Cienfuegos.

It was a Sunday. Usually, building construction was done by soldiers from the Rebel Army, many of them from the early days of No. 8 Column, like the eighteen-year-old officer Rogelio Acevedo. Now, however, they were joined by the Manzanillo shoemakers, who came from the city on buses; they had stood out in their fight against the dictatorship, and Che affectionately called them the "stone-throwers." They were joined by campesinos from the Sierra, bringing coffee and food. Che arrived at eight A.M. on a light plane at the Estrada Palma sugar mill airstrip. His appearance with Aleida met with rousing applause and repeated shouts of "Che! Che! Che!" After a very brief speech, he went to the Estrada Palma quarry to break rocks. For several Sundays he came from Havana to spend eight hours on construction of the school complex.

27. "Every Time a Guevara Starts a Business, It Goes Bust"

O N November 26, 1959, Ernesto "Che" Guevara received his certificate of Cuban nationality. That same day the government announced that he had been named chairman of the Cuban National Bank. Many years later a joke was still going the rounds (Fidel Castro himself would echo it): At a meeting of the Cuban revolutionary leadership, the prime minister asked whether there was an economist in the group who would volunteer to run the bank. Che, who had been dozing, thought the question was "Any Communists?" and raised his hand.

It is said that Che's father reacted to the news by saying: "My son Ernesto handling funds for the Republic of Cuba? Fidel's crazy. Every time a Guevara starts a business, it goes bust." Reactions varied. The U.S. ambassador lodged a protest with the president over the appointment and offered three alternative suggestions, without receiving a reply. Pardo Llada, Che's former travel companion, appeared on the radio show *The Spoken Newspaper,* and welcomed Che's appointment. He echoed popular opinion when he said: "Only a fool could be unaware of the enormous danger entailed in trying to halt revolutionary momentum on the economic front. To defend our economy at times like these we need capable, brave, and honest hands."

Che himself explained years later:

> When the revolutionary government came to power, the chairmanship and vice chairmanship of the bank went back to those who were there before [the coup], Dr. Felipe Pazos and Dr. Justo Carrillo. As the revolution got under way, a bottleneck could be seen: economic programs and the drive toward rapid advancement of the revolution were being strangled, and [the cause] was precisely located in the credit institutions. Nonetheless, the respect many of us had for Dr. Paxos's intellectual ability led to quite a delay before he was replaced with some one obviously much less exalted as an intellectual figure [Che's eternal sarcasm], who knew nothing about banking but operated according to the revolutionary government's guidelines.

On taking charge of the bank, Che had to hand over the running of the INRA's Industrialization Department. The Industrialization Department was my handiwork, and I only half let go of it [Orlando Borrego, who reported to Che, was left in charge] like a prematurely aged father, to get bogged down in the kindred science of, for heaven's sake, finance. At that time, the Industrialization Department was running forty-one small and medium-sized businesses, employing 2,253 workers. Che later told the U.S. economists Leo Huberman and Paul Sweezy that he preferred industrial management to banking:

> When I took on the chairmanship of the bank, however . . . we
> saw there was more to it than wanting or not wanting to get
> rid of the roadblocks to our programs in the banks and lend-
> ing institutions; the problem was the system itself. Even
> though, in current conditions, the procedures used by foreign
> banks were not any different from those our own civil ser-
> vants used, the foreign banks were still closely enough in-
> volved in our affairs that they were able to run the whole
> outfit. They also had a share in several of our credit associa-
> tions, and all our guidelines, the fundamentals of our new pol-
> icy—sometimes concerning really delicate matters—were
> available to them. Furthermore, credit was granted haphaz-
> ardly, and the banks that had the ability to make money did so
> in the most profitable way they could find, setting the nation's
> interests completely aside.

Taking office on November 27, Che implemented a series of controls regarding import licenses, financial transactions payable in foreign currency,
the import and export of currencies, and the selling of dollars to tourists and
other people from abroad. These measures were designed to control foreign
currency reserves.

Che's presence and management style at the bank worried the old-school
functionaries, one of whom complained that "the chairman's waiting room is
full of longhaired people with guns." Those longhaired people were Che's
teenage followers from the Sierra, countrymen now formally members of his
escort and with first-lieutenant rank: Hermes Peña, José Argudín, Alberto
Castellanos, Harry Villegas, and Leonardo Tamayo.

This remarkable group was joined by Salvador Vilaseca, who was offered
the post of manager. Vilaseca remembered the following conversation years
later:

"Look, Commander, I don't know anything about banks."

Neither do I, and I'm chairman—but when the revolution asks
you to do something . . .

"Okay, when do I start?"

Guevara's appointment to the bank chairmanship came at the end of the
Huber Matos crisis in the July 26 Movement. When Che arrived, many of the
financial officers who had worked with Pazos departed, leaving a skills vacuum.
It was partly filled by two of Che's "Chilean" group of advisers from the Industrialization Department, Raúl Maldonado and Jaime Barrios.

Che then entered into a frenzy of activity. He spoke at public meetings,
continued to work on the manuscript that became his guerrilla warfare
manual, and wrote up episodes from the war in the Sierra. He also studied
math, ran the bank and the Industrialization Department, oversaw the
army's education, and regularly took part in days of volunteer work to build
schools.

To his parents, he wrote:

Cuba is living through a crucial moment for Latin America. Once I wanted to have been one of Pizarro's soldiers—however, all this is enough to satisfy my thirst for adventure and my desire to experience the heights of history. Well, I haven't missed that. Today, it's all here; an ideal for which to fight coupled with the responsibility of setting an example that doesn't depart from it. We're not men, but work machines, fighting against time in difficult and brilliant circumstances.

His few free moments became even fewer. According to his escorts, Che used to send for his daughter Hilda on a Sunday from time to time, and spend the day at home with her. He never slept more than six hours a night, and most nights it was less. His personal finances were also very rickety. He refused to draw the various salaries that came with his several positions, taking only his commander's pay of 440 pesos a month. Of this, he gave 100 pesos to Hilda Gadea for their daughter, paid fifty in rent for his house and 50 to pay off a used car he had bought, and spent the rest on household expenses. Tamayo said, "He had a good library only because people gave him books as gifts."

Che slowly began to learn about banking, as he tried to control capital flight and to liquidate the Batista-era banks and undo the shady deals that had been conducted in the past. There were companies that had been able to incorporate using 16-million-peso bank loans, while having just 400,000 pesos in capital from the management. And even that sum hadn't come out of the "owner's" pocket; it represented the 10 percent discount he obtained from his suppliers when he bought the machinery.

Che meanwhile continued to spur agrarian reform; when the first land deeds were awarded to campesinos on December 9, he said: **The death certificate of the big landholding system has been signed today. I never thought I would write my name with such pride and joy on a death certificate for a patient I helped to treat.**

At the beginning of 1960, Che entered into a dispute with Las Villas labor leader Conrado Rodríguez, whom he threatened to take to court for defamation of character. Rodríguez had accused Che of sheltering Batista supporters—in particular National Bank secretary José Santiesteban—by giving them jobs. Che would explain that he had been particularly unbending with his coworkers. Rodríguez, he said, **has an appalling reputation, so he has no business making accusations** [and it is] *astonishing that someone like that would have the effrontery (as far as I am aware he was not brave, he only went up to the Sierra to organize, and didn't fire a shot),* to slander Santiesteban. Though the latter had not been a revolutionary and had worked with the Batista government, he had sympathized with the revolution during the Batista era, and he was honest.

The accusation was a bit less than disinterested. As a union leader, Rodríguez had been paid a bonus by the state lottery in the Batista era; he had asked Santiesteban for work in the INRA after the revolution, but had not been given it. Santiesteban offered Che his resignation when the accusation was made, but Che did not accept; he took the offensive instead. The debate became an attempt on Che's part to prevent a witch-hunt.

Che's position as central bank chairman in a society still ruled by capitalist market tenets and which only had a small nationalized sector did not stop him from making high-flown statements: **It may strike you as very odd that [the National Bank chairman] should cross swords with private property. . . . But I'm still more of a guerrilla than a bank chairman.**

Much was being said about this guerrilla who had accidentally wound up as bank chairman. A small leaflet was making the rounds of Havana at that time, with a slogan ascribed to Che saying: (literally) "You can put your foot in here, but you cannot lend a hand," or "you can butt in, but don't try to do anything." Che was most indignant when he found out, swearing the words were not his, saying that **you couldn't put your foot in it here or lend a hand.**

On February 4, Che tangled on television with the most conservative circles in the country, represented by the Navy's newspaper *El Diario de la Marina.* The paper objected to the state industrialization policy Che was promoting at the bank. He attacked Cuban-style free enterprise, in which companies like Cubanitro, with 400,000 pesos in market capital held 20 million pesos' worth of outstanding state loans—this in a country with 700,000 unemployed; such free enterprise created a permanent trade deficit totaling $127 million in 1959. Che told his viewers that U.S. pressure was building up and U.S. banks had suspended import credits.

Several days earlier, Che had told *Bohemia* magazine that his policies were based on a revolution that **could be characterized by the phrase "left-wing nationalism."** But he doubtless wished to go beyond that. With economic pressure from the United States mounting, it seemed that if a national social security plan was to be developed, there was no alternative to more radical action. The *Wall Street Journal,* quoted by Hugh Thomas, said knowingly that sources of credit in Europe and the United States were being closed to Cuba, which would thus have no recourse other than to go to Russia.*

Private meetings among Fidel, Che, Raúl Castro, Emilio Aragonés, and leading Cuban Communists were taking place at the end of 1959. Without doubt, one of the subjects frequently discussed at these meetings was the possibility of Soviet aid if U.S. economic pressure increased. But Fidel did not want the Cuban Communists to be his only go-between with the Soviet Union. He therefore appointed Antonio Núñez Jiménez to head a mission to the socialist countries to explore trade possibilities, although Núñez had not been able to obtain any major concrete agreements elsewhere. The contact was to be engineered by the Communist Party of the Soviet Union's representative

*Translator's note: I am paraphrasing here: Taibo quotes from a Spanish translation.

in Cuba, one Alexeiev, who was posing as a journalist, as Cuba didn't want the appearance of ties with the Soviet Communist *Party*. Alexeiev was a strange and atypical Russian, who wore tropical clothing, spoke Spanish, paid dawn visits to Che at the bank, smoked cigars, and even cracked jokes.

The Cuban revolutionary leadership took the opportunity of a visit by top-ranking Soviet Politburo member Anastas Mikoyan to Mexico to send Héctor Rodríguez with an invitation to visit Cuba, and that was how the first representatives of the Soviet government itself came to land on the island. Mikoyan arrived in February 1960.

Che was present when Fidel and the rest of the cabinet welcomed Mikoyan and heard his initial declaration: "We are ready to help Cuba." He was present throughout the tour in private conversations and public engagements. Che was doubtless one of the strongest Cuban government advocates of close links with the Soviet Union.

But what was the U.S.S.R. to Che?

It was four novels about the October Revolution and the war against fascism. The heir to socialist mythology. Lenin's homeland. The birthplace of Marxist humanism. The cradle of egalitarianism. The alternative, in a polarized world, to U.S. imperialism.

It was not the Moscow show trials. The gulag. The persecution of dissidents. The bureaucratic anti-egalitarianism. The badly planned economy. The Marxist façade and cardboard underpinnings of the Soviet Union. None of these formed part of Che's political culture in 1960.

Mikoyan played the part. He laid flowers at José Martí's statue, was booed by Catholic students, signed a minor agreement concerning the sugar trade.° Above all, his presence was a warning to the United States, more and more bent on isolating Cuba, that the Soviets were evaluating the country's possibilities for Russia in the great Cold War geopolitical game.

Che reflected the opinion of at least some of the Cuban revolutionary leadership on a television program one month later. Commenting on Soviet aid and the possibility that it had been given only to annoy the United States, he said: **We may admit that that is true**, and finished with a provocative **and what do we care?**

Che's escort was forced to work overtime during the visit. Alberto Castellanos recalled:

> We had spent a whole week with Mikoyan, with almost no time to eat, and then his party went to visit Celia Sánchez's house. It was about ten P.M. and we were ravenously hungry. One of the comrades told us that Osvaldo Dorticós's secretary lived nearby, and that she would surely have food. So off we went. We began to fry eggs and eat her out of house and home. Then someone came to look for us and said: "Who's with Che? He's stand-

°Translator's note: José Martí, a nineteenth-century Cuban patriot, independence fighter, poet, and martyr, is revered by Cubans everywhere to this day. (He was the author of the lyrics to "Guantanamera.")

ing on the corner." I ran out and saw he was very stern and angry. *Where were you?* he asked. I told him I was hungry and he told me: *Me too. You always eat when I do, it has to be the same way for all of us.* He kept me confined to a room in the house for three days.

In 1960, Che was the subject of four pieces of photojournalism. One piece includes a shot of the old Mexico City street photographer, now a leading player, visiting his former comrade-in-arms, Dr. Vicente de la O, whose wife had just had a baby son (naturally named Angel Ernesto). An unusually affectionate Che holds the newborn baby, who is looking warily at his beard. It is a tender image; was Commander Guevara ready to be a father again?

A couple of weeks later, while giving a speech, Che was photographed by Fernando López, a photographer whom Che had unkindly dubbed "Chino-lope" (there aren't many Cuban Chinese photographers, or many called López). It was as evocative as the one taken by Alberto "Korda" Diez three days later, but less well known; it was criticized the year after Che died by an out-of-date social realist, who called it "mystical." In it, a longhaired Che gazes slightly upward; the background is blurred. His right hand rests on a chair, his left hand props up his chin, and his index finger holds up the edge of his nose. El Greco believed that catching someone in that kind of pose told the character's story.

Three days later, on March 4, as Che was on his way to the bank, the French ship *La Coubre* blew up in Havana harbor with seventy tons of Belgian weapons on board. The casualties were terrible, with seventy-five dead and over 200 wounded. On hearing the explosion, Che made his way to the arsenal pier and helped out in the rescue operation. Everyone had the same question: accident or sabotage?

Gilberto Ante, a photographer with *Verde Olivo,* found Che rescuing the wounded, but the latter angrily forbade him to take any photographs. He felt it was improper to be the object of curiosity at an accident.

The next day, Korda, from the newspaper *Revolución,* snapped two shots of Che at the public funeral for the victims of the explosion. An unidentified man was on the right side of the negative, and the leaves of a palm tree on the right. Korda skillfully left out the peripheral elements and homed in on Che's frowning face, which has a very particular look to it, with his left eyebrow slightly raised, his beret with the star on it, a jacket zipped up to his neck, and his hair waving in the breeze. Years later, the Italian publisher Giacomo Feltrinelli found the photograph in Korda's house and made a poster from it. Tens of thousands and then millions of copies went around the world. It is the best-known picture of Che, Che as icon that has since flooded walls, book and magazine covers, banners, placards, and T-shirts, and it would provide a contrast to that other photograph, circulated by the Bolivian military, of Che dead on a slab in the Malta hospital—a comparison symbolic but no less powerful for that. Strangely enough, the picture editor from *Revolución* did not choose to run Korda's picture that day.

On March 20, Che spoke on television. In a harsh and more confident tone, with an attitude different from the one he had in 1959, he proposed a new path: We have the privilege of being the most-attacked country and government, not just at the moment, but probably throughout the history of Latin America, much more so than Guatemala and maybe even more than Mexico . . . when Cárdenas ordered the expropriation.° He also made it clear that a fairer society had to redistribute wealth: To conquer something, we have to take it from someone, and it is just as well to speak clearly instead of hiding behind concepts that can be misinterpreted.

Between his three jobs, Che found time in April to start writing regularly on international politics for *Verde Olivo,* under his old byline from the Sierra days, "The Sniper," and using his old column title, "Off Target." The first article was dedicated to Harry S. Truman, whom Che called a "macabre clown" for ordering the bombing of Hiroshima and Nagasaki, and for now advocating intervention in Cuba. With this column, he set the tone for the rest of the series, from the titles that always contained a joke, to the very combative and informative style of the writing. Over the following five months Che published eighteen articles, covering elections in Argentina; U.S. bases in Latin America; Korea; the politics of the blockade; the Organization of American States; U.S. Vice President Richard Nixon, Guatemalan dictator Miguel Ydígoras; and Nicaraguan dictator Anastasio Somoza.

In a fit of workaholism, Che began another series of articles a month later, which would force him to write something every week. This series, on military matters, was called "Advice to Fighters." It ran for seven months and covered topics such as "Using Machine Guns in Defensive Combat," "Disciplined Fire in Combat," "Defense Against Tanks," and "Pocket Artillery."

It seems as if Che wished to make up for all the journalism he had not practiced in his lifetime. The most sacred thing in the world [is] the title of writer, Che said in a letter to Argentine writer Ernesto Sábato.

Guerrilla Warfare the book Che had been working on since the middle of 1959, was published in the spring of 1960. It was naturally dedicated to Camilo:

It was hoped that this book would have the support of Camilo Cienfuegos, who was to have read it and checked it over, but fate prevented him from doing so. These words and those that follow may be considered a homage . . . to an impeccable revolutionary and a brotherly friend.

The book was a manual and a compendium of the lessons that Che had learned as a guerrilla fighter in the Cuban revolution. He lost no time

°Translator's note: President Cárdenas expropriated U.S.- and British-owned oil wells in 1938.

in expressing the three key ideas; they are on the first page of the first chapter:

> **popular forces can win a war against an army. . . .** [There is no need to wait for] **a revolution; a flashpoint of insurrection may bring it about. . . . In Latin America, the battleground for the armed struggle must be fundamentally in the countryside.**

The book was intended to prod the traditional left out of its quiescence, and its main thrust was contained in these three points. Che did place them in context, however, noting that a guerrilla outbreak could not come about in a country where the government had come to power by popular consensus and that, on the other hand, labor's struggles were not to be scorned. Starting from the understanding that a guerrilla fighter was a **social reformer,** the book slowly peeled away the layers of down-to-earth anecdotes to reveal their significance and to develop them into maxims. It painted a picture of a guerrilla fighter who at times seemed to be excessively in the image of Che himself, or at least in the image he wished to paint of himself (**smoking of cigars, cigarettes, or pipe tobacco is a complementary and very important habit in a guerrilla fighter's life, as the smoke puffed in rest periods is a great companion for a lone soldier**), including his defects (**sweating on continuous marches, his sweat drying on him to add to more sweat, with no chance of washing regularly, although this does depend on a personal disposition, as with everything**). The book provided a wealth of advice on campfires, the best way to form a squad, commitment to campesinos, teaching by example, how to convert a rifle to a Molotov-cocktail launcher, the area over which gunshot is dispersed, and the virtues of withdrawal, before reaching very well thought out conclusions on cruelty at the time of fighting and on war as the only training for war.

There was a surprising lack of Marxism's usual stilted language and clichés, no trace of the scholarly prose usual in manuals. Anecdotes proved once again to be Che's best tool as a writer and even as a theorist. The U.S. political analyst James Higgins later recounted how a friend told him that the *Monthly Review* edition of the book looked like a Boy Scout manual, and that this is what he found fascinating about the text—its simplicity and compactness. He was not wrong.

Che was shy about requests for autographs and, while he did not give copies of the book to his friends and workmates—they had to pay their 50 cents—he did give them to board members at the National Bank, as a provocation, so his vocation as a guerrilla fighter who had accidentally wound up as a banker would be clear. He offered a copy to an American named Finley, who was Chase Manhattan's representative in Cuba. When Finley said he had already read it, Che quizzed him and was surprised to hear the banker summarizing chapters. Che then offered him more copies to take to the United States.

This was scarcely Che's first outing as an author, and it was not his best book, but it was not to be his last, if he could help it. He told Ernesto Sábato that some day he would write another book on *the revolution,* **a real work of inspiration.**

The situation in Cuba was meanwhile heating up. The government faced a hidebound Catholic hierarchy and clergy, who were waging a very virulent anti-Communist campaign. There was also a spiraling conflict with the pro-Batista and liberal newspapers *El Diario de la Marina* and *Prensa Libre.* Both had been subsidized by the Batista government.

Information began to filter into Cuba about CIA action in Miami, where the U.S. intelligence service was organizing two groups of Cuban exiles. The first, which was not pro-Batista, counted Manuel Artime, Varona, and Aureliano Sánchez Arango among its ranks; the other was made up of pro-Batista military figures, who were starting to train in Guatemala with the blessing of the Ydígoras dictatorship.

Che accompanied his mother, who was in Cuba, to the Hemingway fishing tournament on May 16. According to photographs, Che must have cut a striking figure, bare-chested but wearing his beret. As always, there was a book in his hands or hidden away under his seat as he pretended to fish.

I have really only one project . . . to industrialize the country, said Che in a speech in May. It was an obsession born of the realization that Cuba's economic structure could make no progress as long as the country depended on producing cheap raw materials and had to import manufactured goods. Che had been playing a more active role in the work of the Industrialization Department, the three other members of which had been joined by Jaime Valdés Gravalosa, a twenty-eight-year-old lawyer who was a friend of Faustino Pérez. The main issue at their meetings was to make the INRA immediately hand over businesses received by the Ministry of Embezzled Goods or nationalized, and consolidate them according to product. The Industrialization Department would clear up the bookkeeping and, by offsetting losses in some with profits in others, try to make the firms pay their way without laying off workers.

U.S. economist Edward Boornstein, who was working in the consultant's office next to Che's at the bank, reported that apart from his day-to-day tasks, the commander was concerned about industrial planning. All of this was during a frenzy of other activity—receiving guests, making visits; taking math and economics classes at night from Jaime Barrios at an octagonal table in an adjoining office. The evenings were drawn out by visits from guerrilla commanders with their war stories. Aleida March and José Manuel Manresa were disturbed by Che's workload and tried to stave off some of the work that came Che's way: a torrent of reports to study, of writing, of speeches to prepare, and of visits to bank branches. During one such visit he found a poster above a teller saying: "I'm serving the people." On leaving the bank, Che suggested that Vilaseca tell the man to turn the poster around, so that *he* would be the one to get the reminder.

Che also took on more days of voluntary work. He gave an interview to Jean-Paul Sartre and Simone de Beauvoir, who reported: "You might say that sleep has left these people and also emigrated to Miami." Che owed many ideas and hours of reading to Sartre. On another day, the U.S. journalist I. F. Stone visited him. Stone's book *The Hidden History of the Korean War* had been one of the things that first opened Che's eyes when he read it in Mexico.

> Guevara greeted me with a warmth I found puzzling until I learned that, a few years earlier, the U.S. embassy in Mexico . . . had bought up every copy it could find of *The Hidden History of the Korean War* when it came out in Spanish translation. The remaining copies were all the more widely read. . . . Che welcomed me as a fellow rebel against "Yanqui imperialism."

Stone recalled that Che

> was the first man I had ever met whom I thought not just handsome but beautiful. With his curly, reddish beard, he looked like a cross between a faun and a Sunday School print of Jesus Christ. . . . What struck me most of all was that he seemed in no way corrupted or intoxicated by the power that had suddenly fallen into his hands.

Indeed, Che was a person who had no regard for money, and whose friends had to buy him coffee when he was out, as he carried no coins in his pocket. When he was best man at Fernández Mell's wedding, he wore torn battle fatigues full of holes.

"How can you wear that uniform?" someone complained.

It's my summer uniform.

On June 14, he began discussions with workers to prevent a wave of pressure for raises among the most organized sectors in the labor movement: Industrialization calls for sacrifices; forcing its pace is no picnic, and we'll see about that [raises] in the future. Che also explained that we oppose raises because they do no more than produce inflation and do not allow jobs to be created. He put the number of unemployed at 300,000 which, although half what it was when the revolution ended, was still unusually high.

At the Industrial Technical School two weeks later, Che repeated that explanation. If no more goods were produced, raising wages was just printing more money, but money that is worth less as the country's production has not yet increased to the extent needed for that money to be issued.

Liborio Noval, a photographer with *Revolución*, bumped into Che in the Martí district, where a housing project was being built.

Did you guys come to work?

"Yes, Commander, we came to cover the event."

No, no, I mean really work, with a pick and shovel, and pushing wheelbarrows.

"Well, we will if we have to."

Good. Hang your cameras up over there and come with us.

And so Noval spent the morning pushing the wheelbarrow that Che had filled with sand, cement, and stones. From then on he began to follow Che in his voluntary work on Sundays—heavy manual labor that Che did not do just for form's sake—until Che asked him to stop; his colleagues from the Monday ministerial meetings were giving him a really hard time because of Noval's many photographs. Cubans are hard to stop when it comes to jokes.

At the beginning of July, the United States suspended its quota of sugar imports, which had provided for buying a substantial part of Cuba's national output at a fixed price above market levels. The Cuban government warned that it could proceed to nationalize the sugar industry. Graffiti appeared on walls in Havana: "No quota but no landlord."

On July 17, Che's weekly column in *Verde Olivo* mocked U.S. paranoia. The United States had accused Cuba of setting up bases for Soviet submarines on the island. The article recalled Camilo's reply when he was asked about Soviet submarines: there was only one, Camilo said—the one that used to take weapons to El Turquino, which had legs on it. **Camilo looked quite seriously at the man, who did not dare to doubt Camilo with his fearsome beard. Now, once again, we are in an era of many-legged submarines.**

There were no submarines, but Belgian and Italian weapons purchased in the first two years of the revolution were being quickly replaced by Soviet weapons bought at better prices.

The U.S. press stepped up its campaign against the Cuban revolution, in which Che was variously described as the "shadowy power behind Castro" (in a headline over a piece by Tad Szulc in *The New York Times*), the "sinister man behind Fidel Castro" (F. Sondern in *Reader's Digest*), "Castro's brain" (*Time* magazine) and the "Red dictator in back of Castro" (*U.S. News & World Report*).

On July 20, the U.S.S.R. purchased the 700,000 tons of sugar left over from the harvest. As the Polish intellectual K. S. Karol said, "The socialization measures began to gather like a tropical storm."

The escalating confrontation between the United States and Cuba dated back to the first months of the revolution and entailed steadily more hostile measures and countermeasures on both sides. When the sugar plantations were expropriated, the United States made an impossible demand: that payment be made in cash, but on the basis of the land's actual value rather than its declared taxable value, which was lower.

With threats to lower the sugar quota and President Eisenhower's authorization by Congress to do so, the clash moved on to encompass the subject of oil. The Soviet Union had offered Cuba 300,000 tons of crude oil at preferential rates, as well as credits for industrial equipment. U.S. companies Standard Oil and Texaco refused to refine the Soviet oil and then refused to supply any crude. On May 29, the Cubans took tankers containing Soviet oil to Shell. The oil companies abandoned the refineries, which were nationalized on June 10. After the oil companies were nationalized, the electricity utility refused to accept 30 percent price cuts or to work with Soviet oil; **the blockade tightened, they eliminated the sugar quota, we nationalized the power stations, we nationalized the electric utility.** On July 9, after the sugar quota had been reduced, U.S. companies were ordered to undertake notarized inventories. **There were very spectacular and quick exchanges of blows.** A month later, on August 6, Fidel nationalized thirty-six sugar refineries and their plantations, to which were added the oil refineries, the telephone company, and the electric utility.

While this quick succession of events was taking place, Che was at the bank trying to prevent capital flight; in the same four months, he had shored up the Industrialization Department, which he foresaw as a probable mainstay of nationalized industrial economy; sent José Manuel Irisarri to personally withdraw Cuban gold deposited in U.S. banks; prepared to liquidate state-owned banks from the Batista era while trying to avoid firing their employees; and worked publicly to promote the move toward nationalization.

By July 10, Enrique Oltuski and Marcelo Fernández, from the anti-Soviet left wing of the July 26 Movement, had left the government, as they foresaw closer links with the Soviet Union. Allowing their departure was a grave error; it would deprive the government of a revolutionary element to balance its future relations. Che, despite being a diehard advocate of close Soviet ties, had no doubts of Oltuski's revolutionary stance and recruited him to the Industrialization Department to make use of his abilities as a business organizer.

Che meanwhile gathered together Alberto Mora, Raúl Maldonado, and Jacinto Torres from the PSP, and told them loud and clear: **We have to monopolize foreign trade.** He told them to appropriate Bansec and turn it into the Foreign Trade Bank. Without a trustworthy staff, they had to improvise, using "economists" who had been journalists and even a twenty-three-year-old who had worked for an export company.

Three months later, during a reception at the Habana Libre hotel,* Che received the Foreign Trade Bank report, compiled by Mora and Maldonado. The young commander and his economic adviser turned up dirty, worn out, and proud to hand over the two-volume report to Che: "We felt like heroes." Che took the report without even giving his thanks. Maldonado would later say: "He expected everybody to work like he did. He was a seductive character who would make you work terrible hours and be pleased to death to do it."

*Translator's note: The "Free Havana," formerly the Hilton.

A bank official from the old school, who was amazed at the speed with which the clashes were taking place, asked Che: "Where is all this going to end?"

It's clearly going to end in gunfire.

Amid the escalating tensions, Che took part in the July 26 anniversary ceremony in the Sierra Maestra, and two days later in the first Latin American Youth Congress. At the first gathering, he reacted like a doctor when he saw **children whose physiques would make you think they were eight or nine years old and who nonetheless were nearly all twelve or thirteen. They are truly the children of hunger and poverty, the offspring of malnutrition.** At the congress he met for the first time a man who had made a marked impression on him in the past, former Guatemalan president Jacobo Arbenz. Che promised him that what had happened in Guatemala would not be repeated in Cuba, where the people would fight to defend the revolution.

Che met in August with French economist René Dumont, an expert in agrarian issues, who had been acting as an adviser to the revolution. He wanted Che to act as a go-between to "make Fidel understand" certain economic realities. **You can't make everything get done that you want to get done.** Dumont pointed out the need to increase farm production without raising wages, of which Che was well aware, as may be seen from his statements to urban workers. "I also explained to Che that the fall in prices at the campesinos' stores risked increasing consumption by campesinos too much, and I proposed that this should be offset by retail taxes." **We'll receive Soviet watches costing nine pesos each and sell them for forty,** said Che by way of refusal. "He was not aware of the dangers of overconsumption in the countryside [causing shortages and inflation] because stocks were limited and imports were falling."

Dumont suggested to Che that cooperative members work without pay on building houses, especially after the sugar harvest, as they would then appreciate their homes much more. He also suggested that work be done during the relative idleness of the rainy season. Participants could be paid partly in stock certificates or in a share in the cooperatives. The members had no money, but they had time, as there was still unemployment. "I gave him my overall impression that they did not seem to feel part of a business that really belonged to them," but rather like government employees. To many, it seemed morally acceptable to steal from the cooperative, since idlers earned the same as hard workers. Dumont had hit the nail on the head: nationalization and state takeovers did not necessarily add up to socialism.

According to Dumont, Che reacted violently: **You have placed too much emphasis on the need to give cooperative members a sense of ownership. In 1959, there was a marked tendency here toward workers' councils and doing things as in Yugoslavia. It's not a question of giving them a sense of property, but a sense of responsibility.** Che pointed out that it was a mistake to have set up cooperatives—they were acceptable in the Soviet Union or Hungary, but not in Cuba, where the peasants were really proletarian.* As Dumont saw it,

> Che then developed a stance that was very interesting in principle: a sort of idealistic vision of the socialist man. He would become a stranger to commerce; he would work for society, not for gain. Che was very critical of Soviet industrial success, where he said everyone worked to earn more money. He did not think there was a new Soviet man, and did not see a great difference between him and an American. He consciously refused to be part of creating *another American society, even if it does belong to the state.*

Che replied on August 9 to a letter from a citizen concerning Cuba's new paper currency, which was being printed by American Banknote and was signed merely "Che." Guevara's critics would then make a cross ("cruz" in Spanish) in front of the signature, making it "Cruché"—read "Khrushchev."

> **Criticism has arisen over my signing banknotes with my guerrilla name. Although I could not care less to what use counterrevolutionaries will put this fact . . . I am pleased to tell you that while my way of signing is not customary for bank chairmen, [these are] usually men whose ideologies are very different from mine and who have arrived at their posts, again, by very different routes from the way I arrived at mine in this National Bank. By no means does this imply that I am making the documents any less important, just that the revolutionary process is not over yet and that, furthermore, scales of values must change.**

Che did not care less about the antics of his detractors. He was the Che who made informal everything he touched, and naturally aroused heated controversy.

On August 19, Che spoke at the Health Ministry. To constant applause, he recounted his life story as a doctor and Latin American traveler. Six months earlier, he had acknowledged that he did not wish to leave medicine behind altogether and that he felt linked with the medical profession by the Health Ministry because **the ministry is related to social struggles.** He set forth the key ideas of a new brand of medicine: to **organize public health so as to provide treatment for the greatest possible number of people** and to work to foresee the foreseeable. He told how some months previously a group of recently graduated students refused to go to the countryside if they were not given special compensation, **which is logical from the point of view of the past.** But now a new vocation of public service was coming into being. He spoke of the need to change from, at best, practicing charity to

---

*Che saw cooperatives as a modified form of capitalism in that they involved a sense of ownership rather than work for the general good.

practicing solidarity. And he finished with his favorite remark by Martí: "The best way to say is to do." One of the greatest revolutions within the Cuban revolution was under way.

A day later, Che was visited at home by Nikolay Kudin, who was to be the Soviet embassy's economic attaché. Kudin was surprised at how Spartan Che's home was:

> We went down a small corridor that led to a little room with a wardrobe, a table, and three plain chairs, all of which were made from worn-out pine. The table wasn't covered by a tablecloth or oilcloth, and there were no curtains over the windows. There was no decoration in the room, and not so much as a straw mat on the cracked marble floor. An unshaded bulb hung from the ceiling and lit the room with a very weak light.

On October 10, Che published "Notes for a Study of the Cuban Revolution's Ideology" in *Verde Olivo*. This was his first public statement as a Marxist—not a Communist, but an unorthodox Marxist; its aim, in Che's words, was to provide an **explanation of this curious phenomenon that intrigues the whole world: the Cuban revolution.** Though unsuccessful, the essay was a first attempt to reconcile orthodox sixties Marxism with the unique nature of the Cuban revolution; it was an attempt to put reality into the rigid frame of theory, to file it down and make it fit. In *Che's Revolutionary Humanism*, Roberto Massari says: "With a beginner's enthusiasm, he took up his studies of Marxism again . . . under the direct influence of the manuals . . . with inferiority complexes when faced with the theoretical cadres from the old Stalinist People's Socialist Party and, above all, the mirage of the U.S.S.R. as the home of socialism."*

The curious thing about Che's article is that in it he did not explain what he had set out to do, but confined himself to tracing different periods in the Cuban revolution and the process whereby it turned from a struggle against a dictatorship into an agrarian revolution, which was gradually radicalized upon clashing with U.S. imperialism. Perhaps the best part of the essay was its timid Latin American unorthodoxy; Che criticized Marx's analyses Bolívar and of the 1846–47 U.S. war against Mexico.

Che was not at his best, either, in the interview he granted Laura Bergquist of *Look* magazine. He had previously denied interviews to U.S. journalists while granting them to Irish and Indian ones, so there was some tension underlying the meeting, a "meeting of antagonists." Che's replies make him look deliberately terse, as if he wished to get the matter over with. Bergquist got the impression that Che was an austere revolutionary monk, who kindled more enthusiasm among young Latin Americans than Castro himself. And she was decidedly fed up with having had to wait from the appointed eleven P.M. until 2:30 A.M., when she saw Castro himself leaving Che's office.

*Translator's note: Massari's book does not appear to have been translated into English. The Spanish title is *El Humanismo revolucionario del Che*.

She asked Che whether Cuba was not just exchanging U.S. domination for Soviet.

It is naive to think that men who fought a revolution for freedom such as ours would bow down to any master. If the Soviet Union had demanded political clientage as a condition for aid, we would not have accepted.

The interview went ahead amid verbal sparring. Che laughed when he was called the brains behind the revolution and pointed out with a smile that the tactic of trying to set him against Fidel would not work; he became angry when he recalled that the U.S. press had published an article libeling his wife and ex-wife. He did, however, welcome the articles' use of the phrase "a pragmatic revolutionary" . . . I am not much given to speculation and am not known for being a theorist.

He finished cautiously. When Bergquist asked him what came next, he replied: That depends on the United States. With the exception of the agrarian reform, all our measures were taken in direct response to aggression.

At that time a report was being compiled (which Che, despite being National Bank chairman, was not to see), that revealed that Cuba's expenditures of foreign currency totaled three times its income, so that reserves would dry up in four months' time.

On October 13, the U.S. government declared an embargo on all goods to Cuba and an economic blockade. The response was forthright. Between October 13 and 14, 400 banks, sugar mills, and factories were nationalized; immediately afterward, an urban reform act was passed, handing over housing to residents or freezing rents. The Industrialization Department thereby received another 227 businesses to add to the 390 it already ran, as well as 160 sugar mills and all the mines on the island.

Commander Ernesto Guevara's televised speech on October 10 focused on economic problems; he outlined the restrictions that the boycott and the embargo would cause. With his usual passion for truth and refusal to hide information from the public, he predicted: These temporary shortages will not be overcome for the time being. First there were temporary shortages of razor blades, and eggs became scarce just as the speech was being made. Consumption has soared and the increase in production has been great, and naturally we cannot import. The same goes for many products. He predicted again that some industries will be paralyzed. In reviewing the situation of nationalized industry, however, he was optimistic, because in that first stage factories did raise production. Only eight or ten businesses of those nationalized were losing money, and just three of them seriously. The managers have performed miracles at times.

Finally, in response to concern that the embargo was a prelude to a U.S. invasion, and to the news that counterrevolutionaries were setting up a base in Guatemala, he said: Well, like everyone, I think they will come. And I also believe that . . . they will not be able to get away again.

What will be the overall result? That our revolution will be buttressed.

He confessed to the cameras that he was no longer, as he spoke, chairman of the National Bank. I quit that job a few days ago. What then, was his role in the revolutionary government? What were his new responsibilities? Why had he left the bank? Che was to travel the next day, on what now really was a crucial tour for the fledgling revolution.

28.   Factories and Deodorants

Moscow, 1960

O N OCTOBER 22, 1960, COMMANDER ERNESTO GUEVARA TRAVELED VIA Madrid and Prague to Eastern Europe at the head of a delegation that included Héctor Rodríguez Llompart, Alberto Mora, and Raúl Maldonado. They were on a key mission to obtain credit, aid, and an outlet for blockaded Cuban goods so that the island nation's economy might survive.

After meeting with Czechoslovak premier Antonín Novotný in Prague, the delegation obtained its first credit—$20 million for the transportation industry—but the really crucial negotiations were to take place at the heart of the Soviet empire's overcentralized bureaucratic apparatus, in Moscow. The delegation traveled there on October 29; two days later, following the ritual visit to the Lenin Museum, the negotiations began.

Soviet premier Nikita Khrushchev opened the talks by saying: "Anything Cuba wants will be granted." Anastas Mikoyan was present as guarantor of the negotiations. For the Soviets this was a geopolitical operation; for a fascinated Che, a question of his country's survival when faced with an ever-tightening blockade. In the first round, Commander Guevara began by apologizing and asking for the Soviets' patience. He acknowledged a lack of clarity in the requests he brought, as well as his lack of awareness about whom to ask for what in the various socialist countries. Maldonado recalled:

> The working sessions were pandemonium. We had to organize the Cuban delegation, first of all. We took almost a whole floor in the Sovietskaya Hotel, and assigned a different room to each country's delegation. We had to work out with each delegation what they wanted and what we wanted, what one and the other had to offer. The Soviets simplified the plan. Everything would be at market prices.

Che was invited to take part in the parade commemorating the anniversary of the October Revolution, and his presence drew an enormous ovation, **Something I personally will never forget.** He was ushered up to the podium—a great distinction, as only heads of state and top-level Soviet bureaucrats were there. **And when I was there, the people cheered me with thunderous cries of support for Cuba.** He had encountered the myth of the October Revolution. His political naiveté and lack of malice let him meet, as well, the phantasmagoria of an egalitarian revolution, and a socialism that did not exist. Years would have to pass before he could discover the sad reality behind the authoritarian, bureaucratic and anti-egalitarian socialism of the U.S.S.R.

He may have felt a kinship with the ghosts, but the bureaucrats' gray suits and ties, their dull and formal attire, did not change Che's style. Alberto Mora upbraided him because they were on their way to a protocol ceremony and Che was very sloppily dressed. He apologized (!) and pulled his trouser legs out of his boots. **Alberto, you're right.**

In Leningrad,* they visited the legendary battleship *Aurora,* the mother

---

*Translator's note: Now once again known as St. Petersburg.

of the revolution. A photograph shows Che with a camera around his neck and a military overcoat obtained who knows where. On November 14, in Stalingrad,† Che saw a documentary on the World War II battle that had left such a marked impression on him as a boy.

The first rounds of negotiations took place between October 31 and November 14. The Cubans urgently sought an outlet for their sugar, in exchange for oil and spare parts to keep their industry running. They needed small industrial plants in which to manufacture substitutes for imported goods. They had difficulty with differences between equipment and machinery—the electricity ran at 50 cycles on one side of the Atlantic, 60 cycles on the other—as well as with conversions of specifications: the U.S.S.R. used metric measurements, while Cuba, colonially assimilated into the U.S. market, used pounds and inches, unlike the rest of Latin America.

In addition to their successes, they made several very costly mistakes:

> **We took the Foreign Trade Ministry digest and said to ourselves: we import so many spades from such and such a place [so]. . . . let's make a spade factory. We import so many machetes; let's build a machete factory. We import so many brushes . . . let's build a brush factory . . . bicycles, copper wire . . . We did not take one basic fact into account: that a country, small as it may be, still needs to develop its own raw material bases. . . . We built up a policy of import substitution. . . . And in the long run the policy was clumsy. . . . We merrily made calculations about the factories we would build in the allotted time.**

Furthermore, as the Cubans would discover years later, they were unwittingly buying obsolete low-yield and high-cost technology.

Che was in China by November 17, and five days later attended a reception at the Sino-American Friendship Association in Beijing, where he was welcomed with a standing ovation lasting several minutes. Did the Chinese people see a possible future ally in Guevara and the radicalized Cuban revolution?

The pictures show Che eating rice voraciously and with great gusto alongside Chinese functionaries. He was nonetheless a sui generis diplomat, who always seemed to be out of place, to be interested in what others saw only as background, and to be uncomfortable at receptions. Che looks very awkward in a documentary that shows a Chinese girl giving him flowers with a kiss.

Che met Mao Zedong in Beijing. The Argentine lawyer Ricardo Rojo remembered that Che had such a severe asthma attack during the meeting that he it affected his heart attack and he fainted.

To judge by the television report Che gave to the Cuban people a couple

†Translator's note: Known since 1961 as Volgograd.

of months afterward, Che was very taken by China: **Truly, China is one of those countries where you realize that the Cuban revolution is not a unique event.**

The agreements reached in China were very beneficial to the Cubans: $60 million in interest-free credits to mature at 15 years, plus an outlet for part of Cuba's sugar. Che, however, was most interested by the attitude of the Chinese, especially when he spoke with Zhou Enlai, who wanted to change the agreement's last paragraph and eliminate the phrase "disinterested aid." Zhou said the Chinese were not disinterested but that their bias was political rather than economic: Cuba was in the forefront of the anti-imperialist struggle. The final version used the word "aid" by itself. In the same conversation, the Chinese delegation added that the word "loan" applied to the $60 million was a formality, that if Cuba could not pay **it was not at all important.** Later on, Che discovered that China had just finished paying the U.S.S.R. for weapons used in the Korean War. Commander Guevara blanched. One socialist country charging another for weapons used to defend a third one?

On November 24, while Che was traveling, a daughter was born, the first of the Guevara-March children, named Aleida after her mother. Che thus began the bad habit of being outside Cuba when his children were born.

The delegation split up at the end of the China tour. One part went to Vietnam while Che, following an interest kindled by his reading over the years, went to North Korea, where he met Kim Il Sung on December 3. He signed an agreement with the Koreans three days later, then returned to Moscow. North Korea was perhaps the country **that made the greatest impression on me.** He noted how the war had devastated the country—destroyed it: **nothing was left of the cities,** industry had been ruined and livestock killed, and not one house was left standing. **North Korea became a country of dead people,** but was rising from the ashes.

Back in Moscow, Che made a speech that was, according to the brief descriptions of it that exist, a simplistic tribute to the glories of an old revolution that Che did not see as being on ice. "He said that from the moment he set foot in the Soviet Union he felt it was the home of socialism on earth. He added that the revolutionary spirit born in 1917 lived on in the Soviet people." He thanked the Russians for the demonstrations of popular affection they offered him throughout his journey.

The delegation next went to the German Democratic Republic to sign another agreement. The Cubans were granted a credit in the GDR out of sheer solidarity, as the country was at a low point in its economy and produced its own sugar.

The members of the delegation still remember with horror how their deal was copied on such poor quality paper that when Che started to sign it, a small inkblot he made just grew and grew. Che became furious at the German television crew, who kept on filming: **What the hell is going on! What kind of animals have we got here?** The delegation had to go back to their hotel to draft the final page again. It was almost as much of a headache as the loss of the final page of an agreement with Romania several days earlier.

In Moscow on December 18, they reached a final agreement. The main plank was a sugar deal. Che had found an outlet for 4 million tons of sugar at 4 cents a pound, which was above the world market price. Most was to be purchased by the U.S.S.R. and China (2.7 million and 1 million tons, respectively). China was an essential market for future prospects, **because of the small per-capita sugar consumption in that country and because it could absorb our entire harvest of 7 million tons.**

The first 100-million-peso credit from Mikoyan was used to build a steel mill. An agreement was also signed whereby Soviet geologists would study the Cuban subsoil and come up with a mining investment plan for copper, nickel, and manganese. **There is an even more important issue underlying manganese. Everyone knows the Nícaro mining complex has only been partly working and the Moa is completely mined out.**

The agreement turned out to be a failure in this respect, however, as the Soviet technicians did not know how to operate the modern equipment installed by the U.S. companies that had owned the mines.

The Cubans also bought a spare-parts factory and a file factory. No one knows why, but at the time Che thought they were strategic.

On December 22, the delegation returned home via Prague, where the Czechoslovak government doubled credit to Cuba, from $20 million to $40 million, basically for building vehicles, tractors, motorcycles and truck engines. Che admitted to being impressed by the industrial planning that the Czechoslovak officials said they had mapped out until 1980.

Che made it clear that he understood the agreement had a political background—solidarity in the face of the isolation the United States intended to impose—rather than being due to the delegates' virtues or their tough negotiating. The situation was such that even countries like Korea, Vietnam, and Mongolia, which did not need sugar, agreed to buy 20,000, 5,000, and 1,000 tons respectively if the United States violated its purchase agreement in future, **which seems very likely.**

Che later reported the outcome of his tour on Cuban television. The revolutionary press hailed it as a success because **we were caught in a net that would have been impossible to cut in a regime that was not revolutionary.** The net result was that an outlet had been found for a substantial part of future Cuban sugar production; in exchange, the negotiators had obtained oil supplies and technical assistance for mining and nickel production, as well as purchasing twenty-one industrial plants with soft loans, with a hundred more contracted for.

There was a little warning note in the Che's television speech:

> **Of course, for a Cuban living in the twentieth century, with all the comforts that imperialism has accustomed us to in the cities,** [the socialist countries abroad] **may seem even to be lacking in civilization. They are countries where every last cent has to be used in production for development.**
>
> **We had to table some problems that made us rather ashamed . . .**

. . . such as raw materials for manufacturing deodorants and razor blades. The Nicaraguan poet Ernest Cardenal recalled: "When he said in Russia that Cuba lacked some raw material or other used in manufacturing deodorants, the Russians said to him: 'Deodorants? You're used to too many luxuries.' " The story is quite significant. The quality of goods consumed in the socialist countries was well below what the Cuban middle classes were used to finding in their stores.

Che went on: **At the end of the day, you cannot eat soap and stuff; we must first ensure food supplies for people, because we are at war. We are in an economic war—one almost not just economic anymore—against a great power.**

On his return to Cuba, Che met his new baby daughter, Aleida. He also found tensions between Cuba and the United States greatly heightened. The United States broke diplomatic relations with Cuba on January 3, 1961, and almost all the Latin American countries quickly followed suit. It was at that time of threats and anxiety that Che met one of the people who had been most important in his past: the Chilean poet Pablo Neruda, whose verses he had recited so many times from memory along the highways of Latin America. Cuban poet Roberto Fernández Retamar accompanied Neruda to a nighttime meeting with Che at the National Bank offices. The conversation centered on Che's conviction that an invasion was inevitable, that they were on the verge of armed aggression to be supported or directly launched by the United States.

Little by little, the conversation turned to Neruda's poetry, which Ernesto knew so well. Before meeting the commander, the two poets had gone to the movies to see *Stories from the Revolution*. Che stayed away; he was embarrassed to go because the movie dealt with some of his exploits in the battle for Santa Clara. Strangely enough, Tomás Gutiérrez Alea had received a great deal of assistance from Che in making the movie; Che had also advised him on the second story, "Rebels," and even took part in the filming, persuading many of his comrades from No. 8 Column to act in the movie. Che's coyness was unwarranted. The movie was very dry and, being greatly influenced by Italian neorealism, was right up Che's alley.

On January 15, Che began another stint of voluntary work, as if he wished to make it clear that political pressure could not stand in the way of progress. This time he worked on housing construction in a slum neighborhood called Yaguas, for whose inhabitants the government was building new homes in the Martí district. One week later, Che went to Pinar del Río to take command of the military zone when the Rebel Army was placed on red alert following the inauguration of the new U.S. president, Democrat John F. Kennedy. Che's speech to the militias that day focused on the prospect of an invasion—**It is well known that the Soviet Union and all the socialist countries are prepared to go to war to defend our sovereignty** (had he been given some sort of assurance during the tour?)—and sent a message to Kennedy: **We all hope the successor to our well-hated enemy Eisenhower is a little more intelligent and does not allow himself to so influenced by the monopolies.**

On February 12, Che published an article entitled "A Revolutionary Sin," in which he recalled the old rifts within the revolutionary front in 1958 and how they came about. He began:

> **Revolutions are swift and radical social transformations that are born of circumstance. Their details are never, or almost never, matured or scientifically foreseen. They are the creatures of passions or improvisations by men in their struggle for social justice, and are never perfect. Ours was not, either. It made mistakes, and some of those mistakes are being paid for dearly.**

Che then described the relations with Front II in the Escambray mountains, how Fidel's adherents had to compromise with them at the time and how most of its members had now gone over to the counterrevolutionary side. He went on to speak of the liberals who were linked with Front II, taking each case in turn: The same sin . . . led to juicy salaries being paid to the Barquíns, Felipe Pazoses, and Téte Casusos of the world, along with other freeloaders inside and outside, whom the revolution maintained in their positions so as to avoid conflict.

Che finished by thanking sarcastically those who had gone to Miami, celebrating the fact that they had joined the ranks of Batista supporters. The agitated tone was unusual for Che. As one of his messages had been explicitly addressed to President Kennedy, this one was clearly addressed to the exiles.

29. Girón Beach*

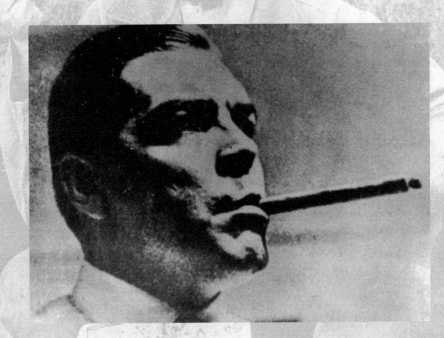

O N FEBRUARY 23, 1961, THE CUBAN GOVERNMENT CREATED THE MIN-
ISTRY of Industry. Its responsibility was the nationalized industries
that had been under the control of the Industrialization Department,
and the hundreds of new ones that had recently been added. Ernesto Guevara
was appointed minister.

In the words of Che's secretary, José Manuel Manresa:

> When we got to the office at the Industrialization Department, which Ol-
> tuski had set up for us, Che leaned on a filing cabinet and said to me:
> **We'll stick this out for five years and then we'll be off. We
> can still fight a guerrilla war when we're five years older.**
> He did tell me that he had reached a deal with Fidel. He would par-
> ticipate in the Cuban revolution for a while but later he would be free to
> carry on the revolution elsewhere.

Che did not waste time. The day after his appointment, he drew up and
drafted a board of directors for the ministry: Orlando Borrego, Enrique Oltuski (as administrator), Gustavo Machín Hoed, Alberto Mora, and, as secretary, Juan Valdés Gravalosa. The board was also joined by his "Chileans," Julio
Cáceres (aka El Patojo), and Manresa as office secretary.

The organizational structure was modeled along the lines of the Industrialization Department, with a board of directors meeting weekly, four deputy
ministers of basic industry (for heavy industry), light industry, economics
(planning), and construction. Under the aegis of each division, factories were
to be organized into "consolidated businesses," according to their production
classification. Within each organizational structure was a department to handle relations with private industry, which by this time was very small. Farm industries were outside the new ministry's brief, and were still to be run by the
National Agrarian Reform Institute (INRA) and **the Public Works Ministry, which was in charge of industries related to construction.**

The new ministry opted for a centralized structure as an initial response
to the lack of middle management and it was given centralized financial management, with no autonomy for businesses **as is the case in some socialist countries.** Che was starting up a "socialist heresy." Years later, he would
acknowledge that **this whole arrangement was built up in ignorance of
the tasks entailed, and conflicts were always arising within the
state apparatus.**

Among the problems they inherited was a large number of small workshops called *chinchales* in Cuba, which the Industry Ministry was supposed to
keep running just so as not to increase unemployment. **We were given the
unwelcome gift of a shed with seven workers and not even a toilet
in it, or the tiniest piece of machinery, or the slightest sense of organization, but seven men who needed work.**

---

*Translator's note: The events covered here are often referred to as having taken place at the Bay
of Pigs, but Giron Beach, which is on the bay, is the name used by Cubans in Havana and Miami
alike for the episode.

The ministry also received cottage industries that were impossible to bring up-to-date. Shoemaking, for example, a trade at which 15,000 people worked, could not be mechanized as that would have meant firing thousands of craftsmen. The same was true of the tobacco industry. There was a labor surplus in the factories and a lack of workers to cut sugar cane or pick coffee beans. In principle, the ministry had to keep unprofitable and blockaded industries running to supply a country demanding more and more goods.

Che moved into an office on the ninth floor in a building on Revolution Square which, according to the journalist Luis Pavón, "looked like a military camp." While trying to find trustworthy managers and facing up to the lack of technicians, he found himself in the middle of the port crisis. Edward Boornstein, in *The Economic Transformation of Cuba,* explained:

> The entire port system in Havana was designed to accommodate the Palm Beach ferry and the Sea Train from New Orleans which used to bring spare parts here in five days after a phone call. Many products used to arrive in box cars from U.S. companies and roll on from the port to Cuban factories.

The port never used to receive ships of over 5,000 tons, but everything had to change now. Among many other problems, there was not enough storage space to hold goods destined for export, and the Soviet Union had to devise a special detergent to clean out the oil tankers in Havana, so as to be able to send them out with oil and bring them back with sugar.

Things were worse on the technical front. For example, Che had two Cuban geologists. He would have 200 geologists a year later, counting Latin American, Russian, and Polish volunteers, but he really needed 2,000. **We were complete babes in the woods when it came to technical matters.**

Che set forth some criteria during his first working days at the ministry: collective discussion, individual responsibility. In addition, there were weekly review meetings by the board of directors, which could last four to five hours. Jokes were permitted, but the meetings began very punctually. Gravalosa recalled that those who arrived five minutes late were left outside. Borrego said the deadline was ten minutes. Furthermore, to make clear that he felt volunteer labor was a crucial issue, Che immediately organized a volunteer group at the ministry.

At that time, Che asked Gravalosa whether he knew an elementary school teacher who could give his bodyguards a crash course in science and letters. Gravalosa recommended his old schoolteacher, a socialist called Raúl Arteche. The bodyguards—Carlos Coello, Hermes Peña, Leonardo Tamayo, Alberto Castellanos, and Harry Villegas (who would later be sent to the industrial management school)—studied in a classroom close to the ministry. Tamayo recalled that Che paid for the classes out of his own pocket and that they caused problems, because Che would go off on his own in his jeep while the guards studied. Tamayo was forced to have words with his boss: "Che, if you don't want bodyguards, then say so right now and I'll take the matter up with Ramiro." Che must have feared the wrath of his old friend and former subordinate, now in charge of state security, because he apologized.

Villegas and Castellanos played hooky to learn how to fly, so they flunked. Che took drastic measures. He punished them by making them plow and sow a piece of nearby wasteland, shouting: You're plowboys and want to stay plowboys; you don't want to better yourselves! They obtained a tractor, but Che told them no way. Then they obtained a yoke of oxen, but that would not do, either; they had to pull the plow by hand. They ended up with a bumper crop of chilies, tomatoes, and cabbages from the wasteland plot.

Che published a feature article entitled "Compassionate Joy" in *Verde Olivo* on February 26, three days after he was named minister; doubtless the piece had been drafted during his recent tour. Two weeks later, "The Battle for La Plata" was published, and then his memoirs of the revolution appeared in quick succession under the title "Reminiscences from the Revolutionary War." This last issue vanished from the newsstands; it was a thought-provoking subject for Cuban readers. Over the following three years, Che filed other articles on a more irregular basis, since he had little time to write. His articles were detailed reconstructions of his view of the Cuban revolution, backed up by his diaries and put into perspective by the viewpoints of other fighters. Che's work style was always the same. He would tape-record a first draft, based on notes; Manresa would type it out, and Che would edit the copy several times, seeking a more fluent style and greater accuracy. He would then meet up with his old comrades-in-arms, always in the small hours before dawn, in a room at the Industry Ministry, and go over the text with them, leaning on the table and taking more notes and making sketch maps between the jokes and the reminiscences of the veterans—Fernández Mell, Zayas, Villegas, Castellanos, Pardo, Iglesias, and Acevedo.

Oltuski was one of the readers of the final drafts, and controversy arose more than once: according to "the Polack," Che was playing down the role of the urban struggle. He saw that role as comprising only recruitment, propaganda, and fund-raising. The argument would flare up again as Che criticized his friend for not accepting his version of events.

Apart from the fact that Oltuski was probably right, Che's articles had the enormous virtues of accuracy, simplicity, and sincerity. He was not afraid to broach prickly topics. Above all, he was able to recreate and evoke an atmosphere, and to sketch believable characters. Once again Che's skills as an analyst were most apparent when he used them as a tool in writing. He was beginning to publish advance sections of what was to be his second book; *Guerrilla Warfare* appeared in translation in the U.S.S.R.

Che found a way to combine the suffocating duties at the ministry with new types of voluntary work. On February 29, he was cutting cane at the Orlando Nodarse plantation with a group of women volunteers who normally did office work.

The threat of an invasion was in the air and the country felt besieged, just waiting for the inevitable.

On March 13, tighter rationing was decreed for meat, milk, shoes, and toothpaste. Oltuski recalled that:

> Once, somebody complained about the lack of food and [Che] said that that was not so, that they ate well in his house. 'Maybe you get an extra quota,' I said, half-jokingly. Che frowned, went to a telephone he had on a little table about ten feet from his office desk, and called home. The next day he called us to say: *You were right, we did get an extra quota yesterday.* And he told his secretary, Manresa: *From now on, in my house we eat out of our ration books.*

Che took things further. People would eat out of their ration books not just at his home, but throughout the ministry. Manresa recalled:

> He got me to speak to Manuel Luzardo, the domestic trade minister, to find out what [the majority of people ate] and that that was exactly what he was to be given at the ministry. It was a hell of a problem for me. This man worked twenty hours a day, had asthma and could not eat eggs or fish due to his allergies. At times I tricked him so as to improve his diet. He liked fruit and chicken broth a lot, and beef, like a good Argentine. I would cook up a barbecue for him, and tell some stories to disguise the fact, like that I had to meet with some Latin American comrades who wanted to do something or other, and I would set up a grill on the ministry roof.

Che spoke to the sugar workers in Santa Clara; he chose them because **at such dangerous times for the republic,** they served as prime symbols of workers who had systematically been ill-treated and repressed, but had still kept up the struggle. The sugar crop that had been sold to the socialist countries had nearly all been harvested. The aim was to achieve a higher degree of efficiency in milling sugar cane so as to free land for other crops. Competitions and contests were being planned. **Small material incentives and big moral ones:** banners for the winning provinces and sixty tourist trips, one for a worker from each sugar mill.

Che rose above petty inconveniences. **Unadorned reality, fearless and shameless. Truth is never bad.** In offering an initial explanation for the shortages, he said: **It should be said in all honesty that there have been shortages and there will be more in the months to come.** Che explained that 75 percent of Cuba's foreign trade was cut off by the blockade. Although the government had tried to obtain the means of refining gasoline to replace the facilities Cuba used to use in the United States, the effort had failed, not only in France but also in Belgium and Canada. U.S. businesses were putting pressure on their subsidiaries and on other companies that traded with the United States.

Che described the old character of Cuban industry as a subsidiary, used to handling few products. The managers would order what they needed from New Jersey, from a catalogue, and they could always get it, due to the usual

food shortages

overproduction in the United States. Now they were not only farther from their suppliers—a month by ship from the U.S.S.R. or China—but warehousing posed enormous problems.

Shortages, however, could be dealt with only one way, and Che got an enormous round of applause when he repeated his egalitarian message: **Everything there is will have to be shared by all of us. . . . In the new stages of the revolutionary struggle, there will be no privileged officials or plantation owners. The only privileged people in Cuba will be the children.** And he warned of harsh punishment for speculators who tried to raise prices or profit from shortages.

He made another speech in Santa Clara five days later, from which all Cuba would pick up a Mexican-sounding phrase: "You have to get right up in imperialism's face," and declared what amounted to a one-man war against bureaucratization and in favor of a new management style. He published an article in *Cuba Socialista* entitled "Against Red Tape," in which he urged that people **rein in their impulses to water down** [government measures] in **the slow bureaucratic grind.**

Che thought idealistically that he was faced with a temporary distortion caused by centralism, in a social project that concentrated the management of most of agriculture, industry, and services in state hands. **Red tape did not come about through socialism, and is not an obligatory component of it, either.** He attributed it to three causes: lack of awareness, lack of organization, and lack of technical know-how.

Che did not hold his tongue when he criticized the economic management of the revolution, in which he had always been implicated. He was particularly hard on the Central Planning Bureau (Juceplan) for having centralized industry without being able to manage it. He believed that the great antidote to red tape arising from centralization and stratification was social reaction and awareness:

> **When the country was bracing itself to resist the enemy onslaught, production did not fall, absenteeism disappeared, problems were solved remarkably quickly . . . The driving force behind this was ideological; foreign aggression made a powerful incentive.**

He proposed harsh sanctions against bureaucratic officials, and the setting up of control mechanisms. He had previously criticized factory managers, whom the government had put in place but whom the workers saw as the old bosses. Che wanted to create workers' councils to keep grassroots pressure on factory management.

To a certain extent, Che was not mistaken in thinking that the revolution had created social pressure and a strong incentive for thousands of workers to break down the barricades of red tape and push the revolution's projects along, more for reasons of principle than for material gain. A Czechoslovak study team was taken aback to find that workers in Cuban factories would speed up work when it was said that production standards were about to be set; workers elsewhere tended to slow down.

Problems began to overwhelm Che in the ministry, however, not just because of multiplying red tape: he was going mad over the lack of spare and replacement parts, which was bringing machinery to a standstill. The country had been eating into the reserves and stocks of raw materials it had had at the beginning of the revolution, and was even reducing the huge resources from the socialist countries. And because the government had reduced unemployment, awarded scholarships to the children of workers and campesinos, and cut back on imports of luxury goods, large sums of money were going into the consumer market; the result was shortages.

Several days after "Against Red Tape" appeared, Che published "Cuba: Historic Exception or Vanguard of the Anticolonial Struggle?" in *Verde Olivo*. It was a first call for the Latin American revolution, arguing against the idea that exceptional conditions in Cuba meant that a revolution elsewhere could not take place.

Is that necessary?

At six A.M. on April 15, 1961, U.S. B-26 aircraft flown by Cuban pilots and trained by the CIA bombed air bases in Santiago, San Antonio de los Baños, and Ciudad Libertad. It was the prologue to the long-expected invasion.

Following a contingency plan, Che went, as he had during other red alerts, to Pinar del Río, in the west of the island, to take charge of that region's forces. Raúl Castro took over the eastern army and Almeida the central army. Some hours later Commander Guevara spoke to a rally of militiamen returning after fighting bands of counterrevolutionaries in what was known as "the Escambray cleanup." The photographs show thousands of rifles raised in the air while Che said:

> **It is comforting to know that at least one enemy plane was definitely shot down yesterday and crashed in flames. . . . While it was still morning, we saw Universo Sánchez wounded by shrapnel, yet taking action in case the attack was repeated. . . .** [He called the counterrevolutionaries] **latter-day Nazis, cowards, criminals, and liars . . .**
>
> **We don't know if this fresh attack will be the prelude to the heralded invasion by five thousand gusanos* . . .** [but] **it will be over the dead bodies of our fallen comrades, over the rubble of our factories, with more and more determination:** [our cry will be] **homeland or death.**

*Translator's note: *gusanos:* literally "worms" or "maggots"; a term used in Cuba for many years to describe exiles.

Che was in Havana the next day for the burial of those who had died in the air raid. The funeral procession made its way down Twenty-third Street, surrounded by thousands of armed militiamen and protected by anti-aircraft batteries on the rooftops. In his funeral address, Fidel denied that the aircraft had been Cuban, as CIA propaganda claimed; he clearly saw that the aim of the operation was to destroy the Cuban air force on the ground and thus prepare for a seaborne attack. It was within the logic of this final, all-or-nothing, homeland-or-death showdown that Fidel decreed the socialist nature of the Cuban revolution.

What was crossing Che's mind? In the end, it was the still the same idea. He believed there was no other way than socialism, and events seemed to confirm it. Was there space to draw up plans for the future when Cuba was faced with war again? Over the past year, he had often thought that the Cuban revolution might have dissolved its social radicalism in the solvents of compromise and politicking. For a man who liked to leave scorched earth behind him in his personal history, a man well suited to metaphors of burning boats and bridges behind him, it could have been no less than a moment of glory when a country opened a door to heaven or hell and closed the rest.

Hours later, Che was in Pinar del Río again. Fidel thought that the invasion would come from the west, on the coastline facing the continent, so Che was in the zone where Cuban intelligence expected the first battles to be fought. That afternoon a strange accident occurred that gave birth to a whole host of rumors. Che made a sudden movement and dropped a belt with a cocked pistol attached to it. The pistol went off, and a bullet grazed his cheek. Sources differ as to whether he was wounded in his cheek or his neck, but all agree that the bullet came within an inch of penetrating his skull. Che was immediately taken to the hospital and given first aid. He was given no anesthetic for fear that an it might trigger an allergic reaction, which in turn could lead to an asthma attack, one they believed could paralyze him. Aleida came from Havana to be with him.

That same night, toward 11:45 P.M., a group of militiamen clashed with the advance guard of the invasion force, a group of frogmen who were marking out a landing zone close to Girón Beach, near to the Zapata Swamp on the southern coast of the island. The news was received less than an hour and a half later by the revolutionary command. During the same night, a fake landing organized by the CIA as a diversionary tactic took place in the Pinar del Río zone, which was under Che's command. Electronic equipment mounted on rubber dinghies was used to simulate the approach of landing craft to the coast. Commander Guevara discharged himself from the hospital.

During the night, Fidel personally organized the mobilization of militias into battalions, appealing to the resources he had to hand, including the Militia Leaders' School in Matanzas, in order to keep the invasion forces from setting up a beachhead. The revolutionary leaders became guerrilla fighters again. Labor Minister Augusto Martínez moved to the zone of operations, as did Emilio Aragonés, police chief Efigenio Ameijeiras, and Oscar Fernández Mell.

Che spoke to Fidel at eight that morning. The invaders had taken three small towns in the vicinity of the Zapata Swamp, and the first clashes had taken place. Fidel and Che still thought the landing was a diversionary tactic and the real invasion would take place elsewhere. Che requested transportation and troops who knew how to fire 120mm mortars. Fidel obtained them.

The operation, apart from the CIA's underestimation of the political tenor of the country, was not badly planned. The invaders set up a bridgehead of "liberated territory" with its own airfield, transporting the "government in exile" there and immediately obtaining its recognition by the United States and governments in Latin America. Not only was the U.S. government involved in the invasion, but the governments of Luís Somoza in Nicaragua and Miguel Ydígoras in Guatemala had provided training camps. The political alliance between Kennedy's liberal government and two of the most sinister dictatorships on the continent may only be understood within the demented logic of the Cold War.

A swift reaction by the Cuban revolution's scant air force, which had to work technical wonders to keep half a dozen craft in the air, struck the first blow against the invasion. Resistance by the poorly armed Cuban militias prevented the landing party from setting up a beachhead. Above all, Fidel the magician ran every detail of the battle by telephone and set up a trap for the invaders.

Anecdotes and thousands of witnesses attest to how three or four thousand people raced to Girón Beach. It would seem that the rush to shoot at the invaders became a particularly virulent epidemic. Stragglers, tanks that could not be moved, and latecomers were left behind as the battalions mobilized by Fidel began to approach and clash with the immobilized invaders. The first day of the counterattack was marked by a race between Fernández "the Spaniard" Duque, Aragonés, Dreke, Ameijeiras, and René Rodríguez to see who could reach the front line first, and then the beaches. This was by no means unusual; the militias fought fiercely, halting tanks and advancing under artillery fire. By April 17, the invaders had not only been held up, but were on the defensive and completely surrounded.

Propaganda in the United States put things differently: I had shot myself; I was a failure as a Communist; everything was washed up. Fidel, I think, had been wounded in an air raid or given asylum. Raúl was meanwhile lost. To sum up, the troops had already advanced and taken the port of Bayamo.

On the night of April 17–18, Fidel returned to Havana from the combat zone to receive a report from Pinar del Río, as a seaborne landing seemed to be imminent. Many warships could be seen off the coast of Mariel and Cabañas, and Che had taken defensive measures. Once it was clear that there was not going to be a second landing, Fidel mobilized anti-aircraft guns and tanks toward Girón. For an impatient man like Che, the waiting must have been unbearable.

The invaders, who had no fighting spirit and faced popular resistance on every side, withdrew from Playa Larga and regrouped at Girón, where they suffered the most devastating blows on April 18. The rebel army took Girón

Beach at 5:30 P.M. on April 19—and the invasion had failed. Shortly before-hand, U.S. boats picked up a small part of the invasion force, but left behind more than 1,500 troops and almost 200 dead. Fidel himself came to the seafront in an armored military vehicle.

Afterward, Che looked back and said: **You can't expect that a man who was given a thousand acres by his father and just shows up here to get his thousand acres back won't be killed by a countryman who used to have nothing and now has a terrible urge to kill the guy because he wants to take his land away.**

Fidel offered a statistical summary based on the captured invaders' prop-erty. The figures confirmed Che's version of events and showed what was at stake in Girón: "It was all about taking back 371,930 hectares of land, 9,666 pieces of real estate, seventy factories, ten sugar mills, three banks, five mines, and twelve cabarets."

No Time to Get Tired

A tough chess player, Che took part in several tournaments while he was Minister of Industry in Cuba, and played in simultaneous games with a number of Grand Masters.

THE VICTORY AT GIRÓN GAVE THE REVOLUTION THE BREATHING SPACE IT needed to move on to its economic development plans, amid widespread popular participation.
A few days after the invasion

> the comrades from the Sugar Federation drew up the slogan: "May 1: six million tons of sugar." I was startled when I heard the news, because I know something about how the sugar crop is progressing. I called the general manager of the sugar mills ... Comrade Menéndez, and he told me the workers had done it on their own initiative, without consulting him. . . . Well, now, it is impossible to achieve that.

Che was angry. He did not like rhetoric, demagogy, or promises impossible to keep.

On April 24, 1961, Che was back from Pinar del Río, chairing a board meeting at the Ministry of Industry. Earlier the board had reached an agreement, proposed by Che, that all the directors should visit factories and workshops twice a month to get a close-up view of their problems and that anyone who failed to do so would be docked a day's pay. The board members had been complaining that they were overloaded with work, and to have since Che had been quartered at Pinar del Río, no one expected him to make his scheduled visit, to a pencil factory in Batanabó.

At the meeting, however, Che took a folded scrap of paper from one of his uniform pockets and apologized for not having brought a typewritten report. More than one board member lost a bet that day.

Che not only produced his report, he also took a green notebook out of his shirt pocket—it was forever full of trash—and began to read his notes, observations, and criticisms: what the cadres (and he himself) used to call his outbursts. Everyone began to tremble when the notebook appeared. Then Che provided another little mystery, a multicolored pen with different nibs, which he could change according to what notes he was taking. No one dared to ask his purpose, until one day Valdés Gravalosa could not resist any longer. It's a code I use. When I write in red, it's something I have to take up with Fidel; when I write in green, with the cabinet, and so on.

The problem the board had to face that day and every day was the lack of raw materials and spare parts. That same day, however, Che confirmed that production had increased, despite the recent irregularities. In Boornstein's words: "Industrial output in 1960 had increased. The problems in the future would have to do with carry-overs and the embargo rather than management."

On April 30, Che took part in a television program during which, with his usual frankness, he broached the topic of national economic problems: We are learning as we go and naturally we learn from our mistakes. He spoke of how planning had been based on illusions—that every necessary school must be built in five years, that a merchant fleet could be created in five years, that in five years it would not be necessary to buy aircraft—and how he had soon realized that these things were not possible. Nonetheless, he did look forward (and so also succumbed to the vice of planning on illusions) to cars being made in Cuba by 1965. He spoke of how the Ministry of Industry's early actions had been laboratory experiments; the officials had not spoken to workers in factories and were not aware of thousands of possible problems. They had started from the premise that there would be no shortage of raw materials or spare parts. **We can see clearly now that the people had nothing to do with drawing up the plan, and a plan with no worker participation runs a serious risk of failure.** Although overall the plan had a 75 percent failure rate, it did produce astonishing results in some sectors; for instance, there was 75 percent growth in the iron and steel industry.

With his usual ease, Commander Guevara went on to announce that there were now 140 technicians from socialist countries in Cuba under the aegis of the Ministry of Industry, and joked about the showpiece machinery provided by the Chinese government and the ten technicians sent to assemble it: **We're trying to marry them off here so they'll stay.**

Che meanwhile took issue with the magazine *Voz Obrera,* official organ of the Cuban Trotskyist group Vox Proletaria, which **was criticizing the Technical Advisers Councils . . . saying they had been set up by the faint-hearted petite bourgeoisie in the government as a sop, to avoid really handing anything over to the masses, who were demanding to run the factories.**

And speaking theoretically, Che countered, that is absurd. From a practical point of view it is either a disgrace or a grave mistake. The main sin of the Technical Advisers' Councils was precisely that they were not set up by the masses: they were a top-down bureaucratic invention to give the masses a vehicle they had not asked for, and not asking was the sin of the masses.

The revolutionary leadership was not to be so open and generous with the Trotskyist group. What to Che called for debate, to other sectors of the revolutionary leadership called for repression. Several months later the police smashed the presses as they were printing Trotsky's classic *The Permanent Revolution.* Che criticized the action in an interview with Zetlin: **It was a mistake made by a second-rate bureaucrat. They broke the plates. It shouldn't have happened.** But it did.

Che was worried that the debate among sectors of the revolution was turning into persecution under the pressure that followed the Girón invasion. It was about this time that he issued a Ministry of Industry circular expressly forbidding workplace interrogations concerning workers' ideologies.

Socialism became the watchword in the wake of Fidel Castro's first definition of the Cuban revolution as socialist in nature. On the April 30 television program just described, Che defined the objective of the revolution as an attempt to create **an absolutely democratic socialist society.** A day later, in his May 1 speech, Fidel was already talking about "our socialist revolution."

On May 8, Che divided his time between a speech in honor of Antonio

Guiteras, the historic Cuban revolutionary of the thirties, with whom he so clearly identified, and a day's voluntary work stacking raw materials at the Machina pier.

Although the economy was having grave problems, "still, everything seemed to work, although very few people could explain why," as K. S. Karol lucidly put it. The phenomenon could doubtless be accounted for by revolutionary momentum, the use of stocks accumulated during the final years of the Batista era, the mood of change, contagious willpower, and a sense of sacrifice. A mixture of all this was working, but producing unseen economic wear and tear. The agronomist René Dumont recalled that cattle consumption had quadrupled, from 250,000 head to 1 million head, between 1960 and 1961, and that demand by campesinos was outstripping supply and thus leading to inflation. Demand for milk was growing at the same rate, and although national poultry production was rising, it could not replace the 1.5 million chickens that used to be imported from the United States annually before the blockade. Production of bananas was increasing, but increased consumption in the growing areas kept them from getting to Havana.

Che was aware of the effect of pressure placed on inadequate production by the thousands of formerly disadvantaged Cubans who had now become consumers for the first time:

> We had made the bulk of cattle available for public consumption; cows were slaughtered indiscriminately and it became fashionable to eat beef—a wonderful habit (which I have to recognize, perhaps more than anyone) but not one we could afford to the extent that the Cuban people deserve.

This was not the only problem that stemmed from agricultural management. Dumont bitterly criticized Antonio Núñez Jiménez's irrational running of the National Agrarian Reform Institute and his serious misjudgments. The Cuban revolution's justified concern for full employment was meanwhile swelling the ranks of factory workers, and Che would later confess that he had had a hundred unnecessary workers at the National Bank. If the solution was a breathtaking rate of industrialization, then Che was trying to move along a road full of obstacles. Machinery arriving from East Europe was being stockpiled in the open, where it was subject to salt damage, because the factories in which to install it had not yet been built.

Karol asserted that the Russian experts did not rein in the Cubans' wastage and impractical haste—didn't stop them from requesting factories for which they had no raw materials. But the Soviet advisers were not independent. They had few decision-making powers and were mostly accustomed to rigid Soviet hierarchies. The Cubans complained about the quality of the machinery sold to them at world prices, while the Soviets complained about the ingratitude of those buying machinery with soft loans.

Difficulties were compounded by the lack of technical managers to start up the plants. Edward Boornstein recalled that Guevara handed over the running of one factory to a twenty-three-year-old *barbudo;* the Procter & Gamble plant was run by a doctor who knew a little chemistry, and the Matahambre copper mine was run by a U.S. geologist who, although knowledgeable about mining itself, had no idea how to ventilate a mine.

A year and a half later, in 1963, Che would admit to Uruguayan journalist Eduardo Galeano: **Rushing headlong into industrialization was a blunder. We wanted to eliminate all of our imports in one fell swoop by making finished products. . . . We didn't see the enormous complexity entailed in importing intermediate goods.**

In 1965, a CIA study reported that the industrialization project had turned out to be overambitious and premature, with many Cuban investment resources tied up in projects that were unfinished and/or that produced goods of little value on either the domestic or the international market.° The causes were apparent: scarce human and material resources, lack of experience in heavy construction (the construction industry under Batista was U.S.-based and operated with U.S. technicians and machinery), and poor organization and planning. To this must be added the flight of engineers and the fact that industrial designs from the Communist bloc were unsuited for a tropical climate and in any case were of poor quality and had a short working life.)

That same month, May 1961, K. S. Karol interviewed Che, who expressed his severely critical view of the Soviet model. They spoke in French: "Che spoke the language with ease, worrying only occasionally and teasingly whether his vocabulary was not excessively castilianized." The first topic was socialism:

> **Here people learn on the job and are still beginners. . . . I myself have spoken at times to comrades who have said they didn't like this socialism business much, so I asked them: Don't you agree with the agrarian reform, or the urban reform, or expropriating the Americans, or nationalization, social justice, and everyone's right to enjoy the fruit of their labor? And they swore to me that that wasn't it, that they liked all that so much they were prepared to sacrifice their lives for it. So I said to them, If you're in favor of that then you're precisely in favor of socialism, and they went away in a calmer frame of mind.**

Karol asked whether it was not dangerous to toss doctrinaire Soviet ideological garbage, the vacuous and dogmatic Communist doctrinaire manuals, into such a political vacuum. Che said that he did not know these manuals, that he would have to ask others to tell him about them. Karol felt he couldn't explain his question further. Their experiences were worlds apart: one was a left-winger whose views were shaped by the contradictions between the rhetoric of Stalinism and its authoritarian practice, the other a Latin American radical

---

°Translator's note: Having no access to the original I am offering a paraphrase based on the Spanish translation.

whose firsthand revolutionary experience, with a Marxist ideological gloss and a very limited view of the real history of socialism, gave him an entirely different perspective. Che told Karol that Marxist formulas from manuals seemed to be a side-issue, that political education in Cuba did not depend on them in the slightest. He tried to explain that Stalinism would not prosper in Cuba, that collective farming was in line with the campesinos' wishes, not against them, that industrialization would not be achieved by sacrifice, and that a capitalist blockade of the type that had been imposed on the U.S.S.R. was no longer possible. He said it was essential to make use of the experience of Eastern Europe in building socialism, especially in training young technicians.

> I would be a liar [Karol explains] if I said now that Che's arguments persuaded me in 1961. His forceful personality and intellectual charm immediately made their mark, but I had the impression he was closing his eyes to reality in the socialist bloc because it was convenient for him to do so. A man of his intelligence and gifted with his sensitivity could not have failed to be tormented by the number of shortages and imbalances he must have noticed in the socialist societies he had just discovered. Unlike true believers, he did not chant simplistic Soviet propaganda slogans.

Meanwhile, the blockade of Cuba was tightening up and the Soviet presence, which both gave the Cubans a respite and offered them an economic model, was growing. The U.S.S.R. extended another $100 million in credit— an insignificant but significant figure.

———

Che was combining the difficulties of running industry, in which he was trying to improve on the Soviet model, with continuing to set an example by doing voluntary work. Notably, he was helping to build a school in Havana, and he was studying. He sponsored a seminar on Karl Marx's *Das Kapital*, organized by a Hispano-Soviet political economist named Anastasio Mancilla. It met every Wednesday evening. Mancilla would start talking and after half an hour Che would cast doubt upon everything he had said. The maelstrom of questions and discussion would churn until midnight or later.

Karol was not mistaken when he said that the revolution's lack of political content had apparently been satisfied with declarations of socialism, and was tending to take second place bureaucracy and Marxist manuals, and that in the process the most dogmatic cadres in the People's Socialist Party had the upper hand. Debates on art and literature were held at the National Library in June, and showed the tension among the PSP cadres running the cultural bureaucracy.

It was not only the most eclectic revolutionary projects that old orthodoxy and new converts had their eyes on. According to Karol, Che's hypercritical style bothered some cadres from the old PSP bureaucracy, like Aníbal Escalante and Blas Roca, as he was uncontrollable. Karol also recalled that there was a subdued campaign against Che on the grounds that he was a "left-winger." Ironically, it had been Che and Raúl Castro who first opened the door to the textbook Marxists in the ranks of the revolution. A year later Che was to confess that **we blindly trusted in the PSP's organizational authority and . . . swept our own criticism** [of the PSP] **aside . . . a bleak time was beginning.**

Che was meanwhile basically concerned with keeping the country's rickety industry going. There was one important achievement. The Moa nickel plant was beginning to work successfully. A Cuban engineer, Demetrio Presilla, had figured out how to start up the plant and use its brand-new technology, which the Soviet technicians could not understand. When nationalized, Moa **did not have a single Cuban mining department manager; they were all** [North] **American.**

Presilla had promised that he would find a way to up start the plant if Che came up with a commercial outlet for the nickel. Having obtained the necessary contracts during his tour of the U.S.S.R., Che visited Moa every week to see the progress of the project and to deal with workers' complaints about the lack of sufficient water, electricity, and housing.

Moa began to produce nickel sulfate in June 1961 and Che went there to congratulate the workers. He found a photograph of himself in the union local and said, **That guy looks like Cantinflas.**

At the beginning of August Che set out for Uruguay to take part in a conference of the Inter-American Economic and Social Council (CIES), an arm of the Organization of American States that dealt with economic relations between member states. When their plane was forced to land at Rio de Janeiro because of fog, the delegation went to the Cuban embassy; people on the street recognized Che and cheered him. **They seemed to have seen a ghost,** he said to the ambassador. He arrived in Montevideo on August 5, getting a memorable popular welcome. The crowd greeted him at the airport chanting: "Guevara's here, the masquerade's over." Ten thousand banner-waving people chanted "Cuba yes, Yankees no!" all the way from Carrasco Airport to the city center.

At Punta del Este, a luxurious beach resort frequented by members of the Uruguayan, Argentine, and Chilean oligarchies, the Cuban delegation rented a floor in the Hotel Playa. There, according to Ricardo Rojo, "they reproduced the atmosphere of Che's offices in Havana at that time, a combination of bivouac and government department, the typists mixed in with the guards armed with submachine guns. Some people cooked, others spoke on the phone, and everybody moved with amazing rapidity."

Che attended a luncheon at Uruguayan president Eduardo Haedo's residence on August 7, where the two goaded each other about the quality of Cuban cigars. A day later Che spoke at the plenary session of the CIES. **A long chain of events brings us here,** he said, and went on to enumerate: pirate aircraft flying from U.S. airports; cane plantations bombed; the *La Coubre* explosion; the refusal of oil companies to refine Soviet crude in 1960;

the final cutoff of the U.S. sugar quota in December 1960; Girón Beach; and the assassination attempt on Raúl Castro launched from the U.S. base at Guantánamo. **For all the reasons I have just given, I do not feel the Cuban revolution can talk technical matters at this assembly of illustrious technicians.**

He defined the Cuban revolution as an agrarian, antifeudal, and antiimperialist revolution that became socialist due to the way it evolved. He spoke of its successes—the agrarian reform; equality for women; no discrimination against blacks; the literacy campaign. He then turned his guns on the Alliance for Progress, President Kennedy's grand developmental plan for Latin America, which he rated as a contrivance against Cuba and the tide of revolution: **Do you not get the feeling your legs are being pulled just a bit? Dollars are given to build highways, dollars are given to build roads, to build sewers. . . . Why are no dollars given so our underdeveloped countries can just become industrial-agricultural countries? It is really quite sad.** He jokingly went to the heart of the Alliance for Progress: **Cuba is the goose laying the golden eggs; as long as Cuba's there, they give to us.**

In one of the speech's better parts, Che said:

> **The experts suggest substituting large and small holdings for well-equipped farms. We say, Do you want an agrarian reform? Take the land from one who has a lot of it, and give it to one who has none. . . . We are not opposed to their leaving us out when it comes to granting credits, but we are when it comes to leaving us out of the cultural and spiritual life of our Latin American peoples. . . . What we will never allow is for our freedom to trade and maintain relations with all the world's peoples to be curtailed.**

The message packed a huge punch. It may not have moved the technical people from the dictatorships, the cardboard democracies, and the Creole oligarchies, but Che was not speaking for those present. He wanted the ear of those absent: the new Latin American left, who felt that the Cuban revolution had ushered in an era of sweeping change in a continent rife with inequality.

Guevara held a news conference on August 9 in Montevideo. He told the journalists to **ask what you please** and spent two hours facing a barrage of questions; with jokes and smiles and to occasional applause, he addressed a range of topics with varying success:

On the Girón prisoners: **We offer to swap them for Albizu Campos or for tractors.**

On the incidents of skyjacking US planes to Cuba: **The U.S. is keeping aircraft turned away from Cuba.**

His voluntary work cutting cane and stacking bananas on the piers: **Don't look at me doubtfully like that, I'm telling you the truth.**

On elections: **Whenever the people want them, in a popular assembly.**

On rationing—a Peruvian journalist said it had lately been commented that the weekly 700-gram (25-ounce) food ration was one of the most underhanded tricks ever played against the Cuban people. Che answered:

> **I have no knowledge of that ration. We did have to take some action on the meat allowance, which is infinitely higher than in Peru, to fairly share what we have. In countries like Peru, rationing is different: people with money buy and poor Indians starve. Don't you think so?**

The Peruvian journalist replied, "I guess so, but it's just that—" Che: **Don't listen to him!**

On the nationalization of Catholic schools: **Now they're just schools.**

On the Trotskyists: **We decided it was not prudent for Trotskyists to keep making subversive statements.**

On the church: **[Cuba is] a nonreligious government which allows religious freedom.**

On the book *Listen, Yankee,* by C. Wright Mills: **There are some errors from our point of view, but it's a wholly sincere book.**

On the possibility of more socialist revolutions in Latin America: **They will happen, simply because they are the product of contradictions between a social regime whose time has come to an end and the people, whose patience has come to an end.**

On what he ate and drank and whether he smoked and liked women:

> **I wouldn't be a man if I didn't like women, and I wouldn't be a revolutionary if I failed to live up to my marital responsibilities if I liked women. . . . I work sixteen, maybe eighteen hours a day and sleep six hours, when I can. . . . I don't drink, but I do smoke. I don't go to shows of any kind, I'm convinced I have a mission in this world and for that mission I have to sacrifice my home . . . and all the pleasures of daily life.**

On his being Argentine: **I am of Argentine cultural extraction, and I feel as Cuban as the next man.**

Che lost his temper only once, when the Argentine journalist Luis Pedro Bonavista spoke of his "former homeland." He testily replied: **Sir, I have a bigger—much bigger—and much more worthy homeland than yours, because it's all of Latin America, sir, a homeland you don't know.**

Che addressed the CIES plenary session again on August 16; on this occasion he justified the Cuban delegation's abstention on the grounds that under the proposed Alliance for Progress **underdeveloped countries will take five hundred years to reach the same income per capita as in the developed countries.** Furthermore, he had received no reply to questions about how Cuba might apply for Alliance for Progress resources and whether it had no right to them: **We can hardly support an alliance in which one ally takes no part.** His speeches predicting the failure of the Alliance for Progress would become known as "Che's prophecy."

Che had a private meeting with President Kennedy's envoy, Richard Goodwin, that was set up by Brazilian representatives. **A meeting between two guests of a third person.** Neither was authorized to hold a public meeting, Che did not speak English, Goodwin did not speak Spanish, a Brazilian had to translate. Although Goodwin would later overestimate the meeting, it did not seem to hold much importance for Guevara.

Two days later, Che spoke at the University of Montevideo on Cuba's economic development based on its radical agrarian reform. He had spent the previous hours with his mother and other relatives who had come from Argentina to see him. The university had been attacked with stink bombs by ultra-right-wing groups, and the hall, packed with students, reeked of bleach.

Starting with a basic truth in Latin America—**Everyone has the right to eat**—Che explained the rationing necessitated by the blockade of all types of fats,[°] meat, and footwear. He insisted that the way to economic independence was to industrialize, starting up the 205 planned factories.

> **And this struggle will allow the country to grow rapidly and naturally, to come along at a fast pace, but will also have a series of results difficult to overcome. That is neither good nor pretty, but we had to do it and we don't regret it.**

The police fired on the audience as they left, killing a professor from the university; the next day, Che was accused of having taken part in a "political rally."

On August 18, Guevara traveled in secret to Buenos Aires at the invitation of President Arturo Frondizi. A plane chartered by the Argentine government flew him to Don Torcuato Airport near the capital, where presidential bodyguards were waiting to take him to the official residence, Los Olivos.

Three issues were covered at the meeting, beginning with the paths to development; Che insisted that U.S. investment could play no part, as it took more than it gave. They discussed Frondizi's concern that Cuba might enter the Warsaw Pact; Che replied: **We are not recommending that.** Frondizi then explored the possibility of elections taking place in Cuba. Che said that door was temporarily shut. At the end of the meeting, Frondizi's wife invited Che to eat a steak. **On horseback,** he said, remembering the Argentine custom of serving grilled steak with a fried egg on top.

News of the secret meeting had meanwhile leaked to news agencies and the government administration. Foreign minister Adolfo Múgica was made to look ridiculous when he denied that the meeting had taken place, and he resigned the next day.

[°]Translator's note: Lard is a staple in Cuba.

Che visited his Aunt Luisa and left that afternoon for Montevideo. A friendly meeting, he later told journalists of his conversation with Frondizi. They could not get another word out of him.

Che then met Brazilian President Jânio Quadros on August 19, in Brasília. The brief meeting ended with Quadros's public declaration of support for Cuba and for the right of peoples to self-determination.

In the months following the conference, Brazil and Bolivia, the two countries that had taken nominally independent stands toward the United States with respect to the Alliance for Progress, and the two presidents who held private meetings with Che, Quadros and Frondizi, were to fall victim to military coups. Che was dangerous in Latin America then; his very touch polarized opinions. Despite the projected image of the Alliance for Progress as democratic and progressive, Latin America seemed to face a choice between between the relatively small and radicalized group of Cuban revolutionaries or the military jackboots supported by the United States.

On his return from the tour, which had confirmed him as a leader of the new Latin American revolution, Che found that rationing had been stepped up in Cuba; there were persistent shortages of chicken, other meat, green and root vegetables, and lard. This was the first sign of serious economic difficulties. In the spring there had just been sporadic shortages, of toothpaste and soft drinks. Fidel ascribed the problem to the huge rise in the capacity for consumption and to mistaken planning, but it was evident that there was more to it than that.

Harsh reality forced the government to call the first National Production Meeting in Havana, on August 27. It was attended by 3,500 government officials, producers' organizations, and the new political party, the Integrated Revolutionary Organizations (ORI), created by a merger between the July 26 Movement, the Directory, and the PSP.

Che was entrusted with one of the keynote speeches, which showed his usual frankness and tough criticism. We have to focus on our mistakes, he said, speaking of his Ministry of Industry. The important thing is not to justify those mistakes, but to avoid repeating them. He went on to reveal that despite Cuba's deep dependence on exporting its products, there had been few stoppages in industry, and these were becoming less common. Out of forty consolidated businesses, only two had failed to meet production targets, and output had increased in all. There are two critical points, he said: First, the businesses were operating without reserves, so the slightest accident could paralyze the factories. Second, there was the abiding problem with spare parts. Che proudly stressed the great success that works committees had had in manufacturing spare parts and improvising repairs with paper clips and pins.

Che also foresaw shortages of soap (which was being hoarded), raw materials, and footwear. The latter was due to huge increases in production for the militias, people working on literacy projects, and people with scholarships, among others. There had almost been a serious crisis in tires, but that had been averted. He announced that there was a shortage of toothpaste, because reserves had run out while raw materials had not arrived. A good substitute had been made, but it hardened after a month (he laughed: the hoarders would be in trouble then). There would also be shortages of beer and soft drinks, because of the shortage of bottles, inefficient management, and lack of raw materials, which was absurd, we don't even use Cuban ones. One of the greatest failures has been in soft drinks. Coca-Cola, which we used to drink the most of, now tastes like cough medicine. This statement raised the hackles of cola-factory workers.

> There are businesses that equate quality with counterrevolution, thinking it is a capitalist vice and that in these socialist times there is no need to worry about it. . . . Quality is constantly sacrificed to cut expenses and ensure production. . . . We have argued—though not strongly enough—we have insisted that . . . socialist development and social development in a justly run country should be done for people, not for some intellectual construct. . . . There is no conflict between beauty and revolution. It really is a mistake to make an ugly article for daily use, when it could be pretty (and here comes the dynamite), because the comrades sometimes think the people can be given any old thing, that if they're given something bad . . . and supplies aren't well managed . . . and the people protest, then the people are counterrevolutionary. This is a falsehood among falsehoods. The people don't like some things that are, unfortunately, happening—that is why we are here. . . . It is no good for there to be soap in Havana if there's none in the countryside; if there's none in the countryside, then neither should there be any in Havana.

Everyone knew that Che was not speaking just to hear himself talk; he spoke the truth, did not believe that problems could be solved by covering them up, and while he announced shortages, he also insisted on equitable distribution of the goods there were. Che gave further news of problems. He criticized the Ministry of Foreign Trade, but acknowledged that in many cases the directors of businesses had not given him clear specifications. He criticized business directors who used the Havana piers as warehouses and let fly at the Ministry of Domestic Trade: There's less justification there for some of the things that have happened. He laid into the army, too: Every last lieutenant or captain thinks he has every right to grab what he can lay his hands on.

Industrial production had increased by an average of 120 to 130 percent, with a fall in textile output and a slight increase in cement. Footwear production had doubled over six months in 1961. Che continued to weave praise in with criticism—some of it severe, as in the case of matches: Matches are one of the biggest sources of shame in the Ministry of Industry; there is no one who doesn't think of the Ministry of Industry several times a day when he tries to strike a match.

In Boornstein's words: "Che's voice was filled with emotion when he listed successes in medicine production, where despite the difficulties and the need to rationalize production and not to duplicate efforts, there were no shortages in 1961."

Che finished by saying the people had to know these things, that the government had to discuss problems (and he was clearly inviting an open public debate); he advocated women's equality in the workplace and said that women would shortly be drafted into production.

Despite the conference's virtues in frankly discussing the great economic problems of the day in front of the people, something was not right with the optimism with which it closed. The 10 to 15 percent economic growth targets would not be met, and shortages were to persist, although living standards in 1961 were 60 percent higher than in 1959. Furthermore, as Commander Alberto Mora had pointed out, few countries had depended as much on the overseas market as Cuba, all of whose domestic products, especially sugar, were exported to some degree.

Che's speeches were published almost immediately in the "Obra revolucionaria" booklets, and Che said that doing so was useful to encourage people to control the government, although he later said:

> We held an assembly for criticism and self-criticism at the end of 1961, and I think it has taken a year and a half to assemble its conclusions, which have never been analyzed. It was a bureaucratic failure really . . . there was a series of problems that were indicative of the existing malaise and difficulties, but they were not addressed constructively.

Apart from the immediate effects of these debates, Che continued his campaign for openness and gave a talk on October 6 that kicked off with a self-critical description of how his guerrilla lifestyle had been transferred to his work at the ministry.

> Immediate action, unquestioning obligations. Then there was overwhelming work to do . . . there's another load of commitments that take up practically the whole day and even put pressure on time spent asleep. There's nothing to do but think of work. All this gradually leads to the abstraction of the real world and of man as an individual; people are no longer seen as people, as a human problem, but as soldiers, as ciphers in a war that has to be won, and which is stubborn and continuous. The state of tension is continuous, too. It is the great issues that occupy our minds, and compared to those everyday reality is gradually forgotten. This unknowingly happened to me, as it happened to many of us. . . . I can honestly say I do

not know a single cabaret, a movie theater, a beach or a house in Havana, I don't know how the people live in Cuba. . . . We have to do something to enable this organism to be a little more alive, not to be so dehumanized.

The self-criticism stopped there and he went on the offensive: **The other day, for the first time in ages, I made a tour** [of the offices], **starting with the eighth floor.** People panicked—they were gathered around listening to the radio.

It turns out that there's all sorts of absenteeism here— straightforward absenteeism by people who don't feel like working and don't come in; absenteeism by people who arrive late and leave on time; absenteeism by people who stay late and use that as an excuse to come in late the next day but do not really pull their weight; and absenteeism by those who go out for snacks in the morning and to see their friends outside in the afternoon. . . . On one floor I found a comrade reading the paper. Don't worry, I can't remember his face.

But Che did take time to become involved in a contest with the chess grand master Jose Luis Berreras. Che wrote to the newspaper *Revolución* to complain that the chess problems Barreras had posed in the paper's chess puzzles were very easy. Barreras took offense and published a difficult problem in the next edition, calling for checkmate in three moves. Three days later he received a note from a certain "Anon." with the problem solved in all its possible variations; shortly afterward came a phone call from Che. Chess was the only vice he allowed himself in those days. He had taken part in a tournament several months earlier, and Barreras himself had said: "Che goes actively and audaciously for instant advantage, rather than carefully planning ahead." Che once beat Rogelio Ortega by using a gambit known as the Fianchetto queen, which he had modified a little; he told his friends he called it the "Guevarovski."

But chess-player Guevara devoted the end of 1961 to his work at the Ministry of Industry and also to giving one last push to the literacy campaign, one of the revolutionary government's great efforts. On December 16, he flew the red and white "Illiteracy-Free" flag at the San Juan military base in Guane and took part in the December 23 closing ceremony for the campaign. The results were spectacular: 707,000 people had been taught to read and write, and only 3.9 percent of the population was illiterate after just two years of revolution and just one mass campaign.

The revolution celebrated its anniversary in Revolución Square in Havana on January 1, 1962. The day after, with no publicity, he flew in the lead plane in a "V for Victory" pass, and was allowed to take the controls when the formation broke up. Che's personal pilot, Homero de la Campa, had been giving him flying lessons since the end of 1959; he had now won his pilot's wings, which he valued so much they were the only insignia he wore next to his commander's star.

On January 3, it was back to ministerial duties. He opened a cookie factory, built from discarded machinery and odds and ends obtained here and there, **from scraps and hard work.** He was particularly delighted that this was **a consumer goods factory,** since there could be no socialism without producing more products for people.

Che was not known to have much of a social life, apart from going very occasionally to the movies with Aleida and his bodyguards. He always had a little problem: the theater did not want to charge him admission.

It's not yours, kid, it's the people's, so why won't you charge me? he'd tell them.

On January 6, Che made a speech to the port workers in which he explained imports, import substitution, the need for technical training, the country's dependence on imports, **not to develop but just to subsist.** He also called for increased productivity, not out of national considerations, but out of solidarity with other workers, the unemployed and the campesinos, **to create a surplus [for] the others. The others.** It seemed that he had abandoned his paternal discourse from the early days and was now speaking face-to-face with people who had obligations. The port workers had to be told that the merchandise they unloaded had an objective, a destination, and a meaning, that they had to make a tiny effort every day to make things perfect. Doubtless, the message hit home. He finished with an obvious appeal to the collective spirit: **The task is very big, so big that no one can work it out by themselves; we either work it out together, or it doesn't get done.**

Che wrote an article at that time, "The Revolution's Industrial Tasks over the Coming Years," to put in order his own ideas, which had been changing over the previous months. After describing the problems the planners had discovered, he spoke of planning as if it were a new toy, to be rationalized and coordinated, to be adapted to **the possibility of producing raw materials** [and] **our true import capacity.** The article abandoned the principle of the ministry's first attempt—swift industrialization, based on using factories supplied by Eastern Europe to produce substitutes for imports—and instead foresaw that industrial development would be slowed by the need to recognize the priorities of a social revolution: transportation, public health, education, agriculture (consumption had soared), and naturally, although Che did not mention it, military equipment. He listed the necessities for industrial development: shipping, metals, electronics and sugar chemicals.

He also set forth a major problem that had to be addressed in the future: disastrous wage discrepancies. Equally qualified jobs were paid at different rates, as a result of the old practice of each sector having separate wage scales. To level wages downward would be to deny the just achievements of one sector, but to level upward would flood the market with money that would be eaten away by inflation.

Che returned to the wage-differentials problem in a ministry meeting shortly afterward. There he stressed that there was enormous pressure from workers to level wages up, because as industries had been unified, huge differences had been found between, on the one hand, workers whose unions had been able to make successful wage claims in the past, and those in workshops or backward sectors who were poorly paid.

However, Che resisted leveling wages upward. He insisted that absenteeism was due to the fact that it did not matter whether you had money, as there was nothing to buy with it; therefore, wages had to be lowered—and who would dare to do that? I won't take that responsibility. Wages were not at real levels and led to the black market, to speculators, the rottenness of it all. . . . We cannot inject a mass of money into circulation if we have no products on which to spend that money.

———

Tensions between the new allies mounted at the beginning of 1962. Fidel did not much like the Soviet ambassador, who was close to Franqui; Soviet technicians clashed with Cuban methods and, to make matters worse, the editors of the major Soviet newspapers, *Pravda* and *Izvestia*, interviewed Fidel and then censored the published version of the interview because, instead of talking of peaceful coexistence—the Soviet bureaucracy's usual term—Fidel said there was no coexistence possible with the "Yankees."

And while relations with the Soviet Union were becoming tense, the Kennedy administration was determined to end the revolution. In February, General Edward Lansdale was put in charge of "Operation Mongoose," which fixed a timetable of operations that included guerrilla actions in Cuba beginning in August or September 1962, with the aim of producing, in the first two weeks of October, open revolt that would culminate in a new government by the end of the month. The leaders of the "Cuba project" wondered if direct military intervention had been ruled out, and were told that that key decision had yet to be made. The fact is that 716 acts of sabotage were committed by the CIA between February and October, costing Cuba both human lives and millions of pesos.

Amid the tension, Che continued to wage his own personal war to set up a new style and culture of solidarity in the workplace. He set forth his positions on workers' incentives at a Ministry of Industry board meeting; on the question whether material incentives, like prizes or money, should take precedence over moral incentives, he said:

> In general, it so happens that moral incentives are stronger than material ones in countries that are in the early stages of revolution and revolutionary ferment.
> The two are closely linked. . . . We are not planning to abandon material incentives, just to establish that moral incentives should determine workers' actions for as long as possible . . . to make moral incentives qualitative.

He offered the example of workers who had surpassed production targets and, instead of being paid extra wages, had been sent to technical schools.

Having become better qualified, they received more skilled jobs, and thus higher wages, when they returned to work.

In the same meeting he announced that all industry would be run by the state—it's already been announced—and stressed, **Oh, yes: we have to be as human as possible.** They were entering the territory of small business owners, with fifteen or thirty workers. **They're not a social danger.** He suggested they be drafted as consultants, to make use of their know-how and all the love and care they gave to their little firms.

As for his own style of work, he said: **My way of doing things is to always speak the truth. I personally think it's the best there is.** He meanwhile complained that working seventeen hours a day and being caught up in problems at the ministry left him with little time for national leadership, for the ORI or the ORI economic commission, or for the Central Planning Committee, to which he belonged. This may be why, in discussing the political situation, he cited the unity of the Cuban revolutionary command as one of the great advantages of the time: **There isn't the slightest power dispute.** This viewpoint was a little naive; perhaps it was adapted to his own distaste for power for its own sake. Bogged down as he was in the ministry, he doubtless failed to see what was happening around him. At that time the PSP bureaucracy, led by Aníbal Escalante, was taking over the ORI, and often sectarianism and authoritarianism took the place of debate and dialogue. Campesino cadres from the July 26 Movement were being displaced by Marxist bureaucrats; arrests were being made without trial, homosexuals were being rounded up, and illegal repression and arbitrary abuses of authority had developed. The Italian journalist Saverio Tutino made the following list:

> with the authoritarianism and sectarianism they showed in recent months—officials have occupied houses, used personal cars, and turned churches into stores—the PSP bureaucrats [had] more of the mentality of functionaries than revolutionaries. . . . Cadres from the Sierra [were] displaced from positions with the argument that they were not sufficiently politicized.

Despite his remarks about unity, Che must have realized something was amiss in the party. He reported that he had undertaken a survey of prize-winning workers: How many had been militia fighters? Almost all. How many were members of the party? Almost none.

At that time Oltuski had joined Che on the Central Planning Committee. He would later recall the uneasy political climate:

> In a full-blown bout of sectarianism, and in his [Che's] presence, an extremist attacked the July 26 Movement. Without thinking twice I dared to say:
> "It's true we knew little about Marxism and did not belong to the party, but maybe it was thanks to that that we overthrew Batista." He con-

ceded that I was right. . . . [But] whenever I behaved like a reverse sectarian and criticized some old Communist, Che put me in my place.

In January 1962 the Argentine poet Juan Gelman took part in a group interview of Che and other Argentines—journalists and union members; he wrote:

> At four A.M. in the Ministry of Industry. There was great enthusiasm for the revolution among some present. Che put things in perspective; he did not want it to be idealized. There were never more than 2,000 of us; some were very good revolutionaries and halfway through the fighting left the guerrillas because they missed their mothers or didn't like the water. . . .
> Someone spoke of the heroism of the guerrillas who fought on foot. I told my Argentine colleague in a low voice: "It's safest to be on foot when they're machine-gunning you from the air." Che heard me and said: *True, but you have to be there first.*
> At that time Che was facing the huge problem of the lack of cadres everywhere. He said he envied the Chinese for having waged a much longer war, thanks to which they had recruited tens of thousands of cadres. He insistently asked for our criticisms. A boy, a grassroots delegate from a big Argentine company, said he had noticed how few machines a textile worker operated. The point was not to overwork someone, . . . [the boy said,] but he thought that production would increase if workers operated more machines. Che replied that when the revolutionaries entered Havana in 1959, in their inexperience they acceded without question to all sorts of major claims by union leaders, so as to strengthen the movement by reaching agreement with them. He told the following anecdote: several days earlier, as he was supervising repair work on his office building, he met the foreman, who said: "Well, Commander, people are now working almost as they do in capitalism."

Despite the problems arising from work practices and plentiful mistakes, there was no doubt that revolutionary fervor did improve production. Industrial output—excluding sugar—grew 23 percent, **which was very impressive**, over the first three years of the revolution. And this in a difficult situation.

On January 23, Che spoke some very harsh words on prime-time television. He predicted that the sugar harvest would be a failure. Volunteers, he said, were trying to make up for the lack of manpower, and he added that the workers' brigades going to cut cane for two weeks would be covered by qualified fellow workers so that factory production would not fall off. He made an appeal for people to learn to organize work, recalling the 1961 chaos in transportation, caused by lack of planning, and remarking on how some volunteers cut cane stalks very high up, so they did not grow back vigorously.

Che calculated that, thanks to drought and lack of manpower (and the diversion of land to other crops, which he did not mention), with luck the sugar harvest would total 5.2 million tons. His estimate was not far wrong, and he was correct in foreseeing a sharp drop. The 1962 harvest totaled 4.8 million tons, down 2 million from the previous harvest.

René Dumont, echoing other critics of voluntary work, said that although that work was unpaid, transportation costs outweighed production gains. Furthermore, inexperienced cutters destroyed the cane stalks and made them useless for future growth, and those volunteers who stayed longer were paid industry wages, which were much higher than those of a regular cutter. Students from Oriente Province, for instance, brought in only 7.8 percent of the coffee crop and picked only 1.2 boxes each per day, while each farmworker picked 7 boxes per day. Dumont said that apart from the effect on students' academic work, losses were incurred because of pickers, loafing. This was doubtless a very widespread image of voluntary work, and one heavily influenced by its critics, especially those in the INRA and the ORI who were promoting the Soviet idea of rationalizing production by offering workers material incentives.

———

In a speech on February 4, Fidel made public the Second Havana Declaration. His talk strongly stated many of Che's views about the crying need for a Latin American revolution. Shortly afterward, on February 25, the Economic Commission of the ORI's national leadership was established, headed by a triumvirate: President Osvaldo Dorticós, Carlos Rafael Rodríguez from INRA, and Che himself. One of its first tasks was to take part in the debate over future income policy. Rodríguez, in those days Che's adversary, said:

> The three comrades took up the subject of wages, with Labor Minister Augusto Martínez Sánchez taking an active part. One thing that concerned Che in fixing prizes and bonuses . . . was that no worker who surpassed a quota should earn more than those who were one level higher on the pay scale. This was so the worker would be motivated to equip himself to go up to the next level if he wished to earn more. Che defended his position very fiercely.

Rodríguez then proposed that if what was needed was to raise productivity, and workers earned more thanks to economic incentives, then let them earn more. Otherwise the country would lose work "that people were not willing to do unless we paid them more." Che defended the idea of moral incentives and training as alternatives. "We adopted Che's position."

The political crisis that had been brewing finally came to a boil on March 8, when a list was published of those who would make up the national leadership of the Integrated Revolutionary Organizations (ORI). This was the culmination of a process that had begun in December 1961. The PSP was overrepresented compared with its participation in the revolution. Was Soviet aid being paid for in some way?

Che was part of the leadership lineup of twenty-five, along with Fidel and Raúl Castro. Among the rest were Ramiro Valdés, Osmany Cienfuegos,

Carlos Rafael Rodríguez, Haydée Santamaría, Emilio Aragonés, Armando Hart, and President Osvaldo Dorticós. The Directory had just one representative, Fauré Chomón. At a local level, the PSP's presence was even greater. Fidel later said: "The only ones to have organized themselves here are the PSP men, and the same thing is happening in the provinces. Who's been named provincial ORI secretary? Why, the old PSP secretary!" But the PSP's preeminence in the new line-up would be short-lived.

At an Ministry of Industry board meeting held on March 10, Che said he had spent the three previous days at a leadership meeting of the ORI without finding out the meeting's purpose. He went on to give his cadres a list of problems with the party structure: its lack of self-criticism and its intent to control everything, on the Soviet party model. He called the Ministry of Industry **a controlling body that becomes an executive body. There is no criticism.**

At the same Ministry of Industry meeting, Che reported that Fidel had ordered the leadership to fully implement rationing. **We don't eat meat at home anymore.** Che had long since imposed rationing at home, although he did not say so. **Now that our bellies are feeling the problem, the going will get tough and we can hold up our heads with more authority.**

Che was really fed up with the shortcomings in agriculture:

> **Here we are, the first socialist country in Latin America, the vanguard of Latin America, the beacon for Latin America, and there's no malanga root, no yuca, no nothing—and while the rations are more or less okay here, go to Santiago where there's just four ounces of meat a week and nothing to buy but bananas, and half-rations of lard.**

He went on to criticize the ORI: **The ORI is confused, gentlemen. The ORI has no need to deliver cement; the ORI has no need to be an employment agency or to deliver meat. The ORI is the driving force behind the revolution, not its administrative arm.**

Then he finished with an enigmatic **Well, that will soon change.**

Che's comrades on the Ministry of Industry board could not know what was behind his comments. The explanation may have been in an article by the journalist Carlos María Gutiérrez, one of Che's old friends from the Sierra. He wrote that Che was part of a secret investigating committee looking into the effects of power being monopolized by Aníbal Escalante and a group of PSP cadres, especially in the Foreign Ministry, the State Security Ministry, the Education Ministry, the INRA, and the rebel army.

Like the remark about change, Che's exhortations could not have been clear: **The revolution has to proceed at a furious pace. Whoever gets tired has the right to get tired, but not to be in the vanguard.**

Three days after Che spoke at the Ministry of Industry, Fidel addressed a university rally. His angry speech used the word "sectarianism" for the first time, a word that would come to characterize the tendency he was criticizing.

He thundered against sectarianism again three days later, in a speech to literacy workers.

On March 22, a new ORI leadership line-up was announced, with only one PSP member, Blas Roca. The rest, including Che, were members of the July 26 movement. Fidel and Raúl Castro took posts as first and second secretaries. It was a first step beginning. Appearing on television on March 26, Fidel inveighed against sectarianism in the ORI and announced the departure of Aníbal Escalante, whom he accused of building up a party of political appointees, whom you had to ask permission for everything. Along with Escalante, a group of Communists was sidelined.

The German poet and essayist Hans Magnus Enzensberger later said that this was the only way to halt the PSP bureaucracy's development of an autonomous power base. But the process of militarization; the need to be on guard against daily aggression; and the hierarchical Cuban leadership structure were setting up a political command structure with no checks or balances, whose defects could not all be blamed on the authoritarian style of the old Stalinists.

———

Che received some bad news that same spring: his old friend El Patojo had died in combat in Guatemala. Shortly afterward Che was sent a suitcase from Mexico, containing clothes and a notebook of poems. He later wrote:

> A few days ago, a wire referring to events in Guatemala brought news of the death of some patriots, among them Julio Roberto Cáceres Valle.
>
> In this laborious job of being a revolutionary, amid the class struggle that is shaking the continent, death is a common accident. But the death of a friend, a companion in good times and bad, is always painful to hear of, and Julio Roberto was a great friend.
>
> When we came to Cuba we lived in the same house, as old friends do. But that intimacy couldn't last in our new life, and I suspected what El Patojo wanted only when I saw him burning the midnight oil to study some works in the indigenous language of his country. One day he told me he was going: the time had come and he had to do his duty.
>
> El Patojo had no military training; he simply felt that duty was calling, and he went to try to fight in his own country, to repeat our guerrilla war in some way. We had a long conversation—rare in these revolutionary times in Cuba. I confined myself to wholeheartedly recommending three points to him: constant mobility, constant distrust, constant watchfulness. . . . These were the essence of our guerrilla experience, the only things, apart from a handshake, I could give my

friend. Could I recommend that he not go? What right had I, when we had tried to do something that we thought was impossible, and which he now knew was possible?

Again, we're left with the bitter taste of defeat.

This bitter taste was to stay with Che. He felt that the situation in all of Latin America cried out for action, but except for the struggle against Escalante—he had to devote every day to the Cuban economy, pressed by the need to supply a population whose demands had grown enormously.

Shortages spread to the industrial sector in March 1962, affecting items like women's underwear, men's shirts, and footwear. The rains had been light; consumer pressure on new goods increased, and overconsumption of some led to shortages of others. Children were entitled to a glass of milk per day, but adults got only a fifth of a quart per week. On the other hand, dozens of students in state schools were receiving extra food rations. Boornstein reported: "While it is true that most of the Cuban population was eating much better than in 1959 despite rationing, urban workers and the middle classes were worse off, although they could offset shortages by eating out."

Che angrily told an industry meeting that

We have been making a bunch of people rich who still don't produce yet because of the mammoth bureaucracy . . . because of badly conceived and badly executed investments, because of huge expenses we have incurred. People have money but everything has been eaten; we ate the cows; now there's no malanga root and there are umpteen other problems . . . We're responsible and we must be frank about it. . . . Does the working class want to condemn us . . . ? Well, let them condemn us, replace us, shoot us or do anything. But the problem is here.

Perhaps Che was being too hard on himself. The ministry's mistakes had been the natural consequence of inexperience; bad investments had been made in the rush to replace imports, and the factories arriving from Eastern Europe were designed for raw materials that in most cases did not exist in Cuba. Existing industry had been kept running, however—something that might have seemed impossible given the blockade and the shortages. Finally, social priorities had been fulfilled in public health and education. Priorities for 1962 were now being fixed properly, and the chaotic wage differentials were on their way to being corrected. Fidel's camp had prevented a burgeoning Stalinist party from taking hold of the ORI and dictating to society as a whole. It was all difficult, all very complicated, but Che, with his idea of "communism without a party," as the Italian left-wing leader Rossana Rosanda would put it years later, had found a substantial echo among the grassroots of Cuban society.

On April 13, the plenary session for sugar closed. Without fearing what the enemy might say, we have to admit this was a poor harvest. The main problem had been a terrible drought; besides, **we are working very inefficiently**—and more, there was the **feud between agriculture and industry. . . . I feel that agriculture is more to blame for this quarrel we have had.** He struck a positive note only in discussing Matanzas, where there had been a spectacular popular reaction to attacks by counterrevolutionaries and crops being set on fire.

Two days later, at the closing ceremony of the Cuban Workers' Council congress, Che wondered why the initiative for criticism had come from the top down, from the ministry. **Where did this apathy come from? Why did major tasks, enormous tasks involving the working class have to come about as bureaucratic initiatives?** He explained that it was a carryover from the sectarian era, of the divorce between leadership and grass roots, when the functionaries spoke for the people. The Argentine journalist Adolfo Gilly homed in on the problem two years later when he characterized Cuban labor unions as bureaucratic and vertical, incapable of expressing workers' needs, at one with the state as its rear guard rather than its advance patrol.

On April 30, Che took part in a meeting with workers at the García Lorca Theater, during which forty-five houses were handed over to the most outstanding workers in each branch of industry. One of the workers refused the gift, saying he already had a house and this one should be given to somebody else. Che congratulated him publicly. It is ironic that in a meeting to celebrate material incentives he should congratulate the only person who rejected them. Ironic, but typical for a man who never used to carry money in his pocket.

31.   The Urge to Shoot Down Planes

The cave at Portales, where the command headquarters were during the crisis of October 1962, called "the Bay of Pigs" by the U.S. and "Girón Beach" by the Cubans.

O N MAY 4, 1962, CHE MET UNION DELEGATIONS FROM ABROAD WHO had come for the May Day celebrations. Once again, informality prevailed: Che sat on a table with his green beret stuck under a shoulder strap and told the visitors about the bleak outlook for Cuba. Industry depended on imports, which in turn depended on exports. The increase in farm output had been swallowed up by the huge increase in Cubans' capacity to consume.

And despite a year of rationing, consumption was higher than ever. What was very serious was that production of sugar cane had fallen; fields had been abandoned by campesinos going to the cities, while those who were now landowners planted crops other than cane. Money was worth less because the imbalance between money in circulation and production had led to inflation. Irrational wage differentials, a throwback to the past, still existed.

It was a frank and open conversation between friends critical of the Cuban economy, and it had no overtones of propaganda.

A week later, Che achieved one of his dreams as a chess player: he played in a simultaneous game with Soviet champion Boris Spassky in the Capablanca tournament. He also took part in other simultaneous games and tournaments at the Ministry of Industry and even played a simultaneous game against the Argentine grand master Miguel Najdorf. Che was smoking a cigar; when he won some rounds, people at the match said the cigar "tasted better the smaller it got." He was unaware that at that very time the CIA was working on a plan to poison him and Fidel Castro. Like so many other such plans, it came to nothing.

———

In a speech to State Security Ministry employees, Che railed against the peaceful road to revolution in Latin America (the ass end, with weak bourgeoisies who did not stand up to imperialism). **Latin America today is a volcano. It is not in eruption, but is moved by the immense subterranean rumbling that heralds** [the revolution's] **approach.** He characterized the Alliance for Progress as **an imperialist attempt to halt revolutionary impulses among peoples by distributing a small part of the profits among the Creole exploiting classes.**

He stated two conclusions: guerrilla warfare was the way to overcome conventional armies, and

> **the nature of the struggle was continental. Can this new stage in the emancipation of Latin America be conceived of as a comparison of two local forces struggling for power over a given territory? Obviously not . . . The Yankees will intervene because the struggle in Latin America is a decisive one.**

These two ideas were to have a strong influence on his future actions.

In the same speech, he broached another thorny issue of state security. He heavily criticized excesses by the party leadership in Matanzas and the degradation of the Committees for the Defense of the Revolution (CDR), which he accused of being dens of opportunism, of treating the people badly. Although the Committees were born when the people were actively defending the revolution, it was isolated from that revolution. He told the Security Ministry employees that they should not follow the same road to isolation from the people, and not to forget that **it is much more important for us to have malanga root than to have you.** Moreover, they should not forget that while **a counterrevolutionary is someone who fights against the revolution,** [a counterrevolutionary] **is also a gentleman who uses influence to obtain a house, then to obtain two cars, then to contravene rationing and have everything that the people do not have.**

Whom was he fighting? Aníbal Escalante and the old People's Socialist Party bureaucracy had been dismantled, so who were the new anti-egalitarian bureaucrats?

———

Che's first baby boy, Camilo, was born on May 20, but Che had little time to celebrate. A huge storm was on the horizon. Tensions between Cuba and the United States were on the verge of blowing up into a global nuclear war in the months to come. A couple of days before his son was born, Che gave a speech in which he said: *"The imperialists either know or do not know what the Soviet Union is capable of doing to defend us. . . . if they are mistaken then imperialism will be destroyed to the root but there'll be little left of us, either. That's why we have to be determined fighters for peace."*

What was the Soviet Union capable of doing?

On May 20 Che was summoned by Fidel to a very private meeting attended only by himself, President Osvaldo Dorticós, Fidel, and Raúl Castro. Fidel told them that the day before he had spoken with Soviet marshal Biryuzov, who brought a proposal from Premier Nikita Khrushchev to strengthen Cuban defenses, with nuclear missiles if need be. Fidel told them he had postponed his decision.

There is no record of what the four people present discussed, of agreements or disagreements. Many years later, in 1992, Fidel said: "We didn't like the missiles; they harmed the image of the revolution in Latin America. They were turning us into a Soviet military base. We thought the missiles would strengthen socialist Cuba, instead." In any case, those present at that meeting decided in favor of the Soviet offer. Cuba was going nuclear.

———

Anecdotes about Che continued to circulate. He was driving a Chevrolet one night on the Fomento highway and accidentally ran into a bicycle being ridden by an old man. Che stopped the car and approached the bicyclist, who was in the gutter looking over the damage.

Are you all right?

The old man looked up and recognized Che. "Are you the one who hit me?"

Yes.

"What a stroke of luck. Now I can tell the old lady Che Guevara knocked me over."

Another Che story starts with Fidel arriving at a Central Planning Committee meeting and tossing a Swiss Army knife with dozens of devices and blades at Che.

"Look what they gave me, Che."

As he listened to the discussion, Che fiddled with the various parts of the knife. At one point he put it on the table between Fidel and himself, perhaps an inch closer to himself.

Now it was Fidel's turn to fiddle with the knife. After a while, he put it between himself and Che, who took it up again. All through the meeting the knife went back and forth. The meeting lasted four or five hours. Fidel finally called it a day and got up, leaving the penknife in the middle of the table. He headed for the door, then suddenly remembered and went back. Che was still sitting with his arms folded, watching the prime minister leave. Fidel looked at him, grabbed the knife, thought better of it, and said without much enthusiasm:

"Take it, dammit, it's yours."

Che took it. The narrator of the story, who had it secondhand, does not know whether he smiled.

———

Toward the middle of July, a problem arose in the pharmaceutical industry. The ORI economic commission had found that there was a surplus of some raw materials, but that the industry was requesting imports of those same raw materials. The commission had conducted an investigation whose style had been unfortunate; those investigated, including Che himself, had been insulted.

Che argued at a board meeting that he could not take action against managers for not being aware of their stock levels; it was a widespread problem. He would punish them, however, for refusing to accept the truth, even if it came from a host of thugs. Action was finally taken against the industry manager. **We have the worst of state administration, not the best.**

At the same meeting he attacked the unions: **Most union leaders are people who have no mass support.** So they worked as buck passers, transmitting pressures from above and below: "The workers say," "The minister says." Self-critical to a fault, Che said: **These are hard times. We cannot afford to penalize mistakes; maybe in a year's time we will. Who's going to fire the minister of industry** [himself] **who last November signed a plan that said ten million shoes would made, and who knows what else besides?**

He also reviewed the investments the ministry had made—for example, a yeast factory bought in Poland that required 200-odd workers to produce what it took twenty-seven to do in a German factory that cost the same. **The comrades said [it] could do better and we did not believe them because we thought it was a symptom of anticommunism, but they were right.**

Che was surprised by how backward in technology the socialist bloc was, as he was discovering day by day. The U.S. Caterpillar was **better than any Soviet tractor. Why? Because in capitalist competition, one mile per hour more in speed counts, as does a slightly better hydraulic system or four more horsepower.**

Che then appealed to his fellow ministry officials to go out on the street to listen, to observe, and to learn. **We're not going to diagnose what's going on from up here on the ninth floor.**

The minister of economics, Regino Boti, told K. S. Karol that in those days "no sooner had we plugged one gap than we had to dash off to plug another, wider one."

In July 1962, the ORI leadership sent Che to Juceplan to move it along and above all to gain some industry respect for planning. Enrique Oltuski, who had been appointed industry undersecretary, became a vice president of Juceplan, too.

The new job did not stop Che from doing voluntary work. The José Antonio Echeverría flour mill was on the verge of breaking a production record, and the workers invited Che to help. He soon learned to fill the sacks and sew them up. The dust brought on an asthma attack, but he pulled out his inhaler, kept on working, and had the honor of stitching up sack number 100,000. He thanked the workers for having allowed him to take part in the record and for enabling a minister to return to physical work.

It was about that time that Che first played golf in Cuba, in a friendly match against Fidel and Antonio Núñez Jiménez at the Colinas de Villareal club on the outskirts of Havana. He beat them; remembering his days as a caddie in Altagracia, he later said: **I knew about golf.** The scores were atrocious: on a par-70 course, Che went around in 127 and Fidel in 150.

On August 13, Soviet Ambassador Alexandr Alexeiev handed Fidel the agreement on missile bases. Fidel checked it over and gave it to Che to take to the U.S.S.R. Plans for their installation were evolving rapidly. Commander Guevara arrived in Moscow on August 27 with Integrated Revolutionary Organizations president Emilio Aragonés; the pretext was a meeting to discuss "economic matters." They met Khrushchev at his dacha in the Crimea on August 30. Although Che urged that the agreement be made public, Khrushchev declined. He did not even sign it, probably to prevent the Cubans from leaking the information. So the agreement was made without the signature of one of the parties.

On August 31, it was announced that Che had signed a cooperation agreement covering technical, agricultural, steelmaking, and military matters; no further details of the contents were given. The industrial components were made public three days later.

Che traveled from Moscow to Czechoslovakia on September 2, visiting an industrial fair in Brno. He was back in Cuba on September 5. Only three weeks had gone by, but preparatory work on the future bases had begun, which did not go unnoticed by the U.S. intelligence services. Flights by U-2 spy planes in the last week of August seemed to confirm that launching pads were being built.

The U.S. secretary of defense, Robert McNamara, informed President Kennedy, who saw the launching pads as defensive. These conversations in U.S. government circles coincided with a negative assessment of Operation Mongoose, which by this time was supposed to have arrived at the final phase in overthrowing the Cuban government. The counterrevolutionary bands backed by the CIA had been mopped up one by one, and although constant sabotage had done some damage, it had hardly made the economy collapse.

Now the U.S. government began a campaign to denounce the presence of Soviet nuclear weapons in Cuba. The Soviet Union reacted on September 11 with a statement by its official news agency, Tass, saying the action was defensive. Four days earlier, the Pentagon had given the green light to prepare a combined air and sea attack on Cuba, which was to be ready by the end of the month. The Soviet cargo ship *Poltova*, carrying the first missile, docked in the port of Mariel on September 15. The missile was taken in secret to the base at San Cristóbal. At the United Nations, Soviet foreign minister Andrei Gromyko accused the United States of warmongering.

In spite of the growing tension, Che was still very concerned over ministry matters like the quality of Cuban products. "We have to be exacting with all those items for popular consumption. . . . Somebody strikes a match to light a cigarette and then the match head falls off and the cigarette goes out." As to waste, he said:

> Over a year ago, I went through Nuevitas and saw machinery out in the open, standing unused, a kilometer from the sea. The manager . . . hadn't installed it because he didn't have a crane. . . . It could have been brought in on rollers. The Egyptians built the pyramids that way, and they moved huge stones who knows how many kilometers. But nowadays, Cuba, which is building socialism, isn't capable of moving a stone that weighs less than a ton.

On October 6, the Pentagon activated Operational Plans 312, 314, and 316, for the invasion of Cuba. They included a massive air strike. Che meanwhile moved his home again for security reasons.

On October 13, Chester Bowles met Ambassador Anatoly Dobrynin and told him there was evidence of nuclear missiles in Cuba. The ambassador, who was unaware of the facts, denied it. More U-2 overflights revealed the construction of a base at San Cristóbal to house medium-range surface-to-surface ballistic missiles with a range of 1,500 miles. There was no reason to believe there were nuclear warheads in the area, and CIA analysts did not think the missiles were ready to fly. The U.S. ambassador to the United Nations, Adlai Stevenson, evaluated the situation and told President Kennedy that the Soviet missiles were comparable to U.S. missiles in Turkey. So what was the moral basis for questioning Cuba's right to set its missiles up?

That same day, Che received the Algerian revolutionary Ahmed Ben Bella. The meeting was a gesture of solidarity between the young revolutions in Cuba and Algeria; in addition, Che and Ben Bella signed agreements, as we shall see later, to support other revolutionary projects.

President Kennedy that week rejected the most risky options that his advisers offered, such as an air strike against Cuba, and decided to impose a naval blockade. Kennedy also asked an adviser to provide the legal grounds to set it up. The tense discussions between the superpowers went back and forth. Soviet foreign minister Andrei Gromyko, visiting the United States, insisted that the missiles given to the Cubans were defensive. According to Soviet sources, there were nuclear warheads on the island at that time, but they were not mounted on the missiles.

What became known as the Cuban missile crisis erupted two days later. President Kennedy gave a nationwide live TV broadcast at seven P.M. on October 22, in which he announced that he had indisputable evidence of the bases in Cuba and spoke of setting up a naval blockade. In reply, Soviet ships were immediately ordered to ignore the blockade.

"Battle stations" were declared in Cuba the day after. According to Argentine journalist Adolfo Gilly, "It was as if tension that had long been held back was suddenly released, as if the country as one person said: at last." Che was appointed armed forces chief in the west; he went to Pinar del Río. According to his adjutant, Leonardo Tamayo, he believed that war would break out at any moment and that this time the invasion would come in his sector. He set up his headquarters at the Los Portales Cave, at the base of the hills surrounding the valley at San Andrés de Caiguanabo, on the banks of the San Diego River. It was a natural cave that had been adapted slightly in pre-revolutionary times by a landholder called Cortina, who had built some stairs and extended the "ceiling." The cave was majestic. Some terribly austere compartments had been built inside it, with communications facilities, a few camp beds, a couple of stoves, and a table made of a slab set on two stone pillars. Swallows flew among the stalactites by day, and bats by night.

Thinking that war was around the corner, Che set out at full speed to organize ammunition stores in caves and mountainous country, to review trenches and billets, to talk to people and boost morale. The idea, in the light of experience from the Bay of Pigs, was to set up a first line of defense and then, in case the invaders managed to establish a beachhead, they would withdraw to the Sierra de los Organos to fight a guerrilla campaign. Che spent his time during the red alert traveling around the zone under his command by day and reading and playing chess by night.

On October 24, Khrushchev delivered an urgent message to Kennedy: the U.S.S.R. saw the blockade as an act of aggression and he would not instruct Soviet ships to turn back. In the early hours of the morning, however, Soviet ships did slow down, return to port, or change their routes. Just one tanker, the *Bucharest,* continued to advance toward the blockade. Was the *Bucharest* to be the one to test U.S. threats?

Fidel sent an urgent note to Khrushchev two days later: "Aggression is imminent, will take place in the next 24–72 hours, most probably an air strike confined to targets they wish to destroy, next an invasion. We shall resist any attack." In the second case, he suggested that a nuclear attack be met with a nuclear response. That same day, Kennedy ordered reconnaissance flights to be stepped up.

Two days later, Fidel ordered that unauthorized planes be shot at; toward noon a U2 was shot down by a surface-to-air missile fired on the initiative of a Soviet commander at one of the bases. Tension escalated. Then, without telling the Cubans or taking them into account, Khrushchev proposed to Kennedy that the bases be dismantled in return for a U.S. commitment not to invade Cuba and to negotiate over the withdrawal of U.S. missiles stationed in Turkey and aimed at the Soviet Union. Kennedy accepted the proposal in principle. The Cubans had again been caught up in the game of Cold War politics.

On October 28, Carlos Franqui, the editor of *Revolución,* learned from an Associated Press wire that the Soviet Union would withdraw the missiles. He got in touch with Fidel. This was the first the Cuban leader knew of the agreement, and he launched into a tirade of insults: "Asshole, son of a bitch, bastard!" *Revolución's* headline the next day was "Soviets Withdraw Missiles," and crowds in the street chanted: "Nikita, *mariquita, lo que seda, no se quita*" ("Nikita, little sissy, what you give you don't take back.")

Fidel received partial information from Khrushchev the day after that. The Soviet premier said he had negotiated on the basis of Kennedy's promise of nonintervention in Cuba. Fidel stated publicly that he was opposed to an on-site inspection in Cuba, argued that the shooting down of the U2 had been justified, and told Khrushchev: "We're not impressed with danger, because it has been hanging over us for a long time now and to an extent we have become used to it."

Over the following days, the tension eased. Hilda Gadea saw Che at home on her way back from work: "I found Ernesto all dirty, his boots caked in mud, playing with his little girl on the floor . . . and with the dog, too." It was a turn to life when death was near.

In his speech to the State Security Ministry staff, mentioned at the beginning of this chapter, Che expressed anger over the missile crisis. The speech was published posthumously, probably because it denounced the role played by the Soviet Union:

It's a hair-raising example of a people prepared to be atomically incinerated so that their ashes may be used as the foun-

dations of new societies. And when, without consulting them, a pact is made to withdraw the missiles, they do not breathe a sigh of relief or give thanks for the truce. Instead they arise to give voice to their willingness to fight, theirs, and their determination to fight alone if they must.

Saverio Tutino, then correspondent for the Italian Communist newspaper *L'Unità*, tried to interview Che and met with a triple negative: **No, because he's a Communist, an Italian, and what's worse, a journalist.** Tutino later reported: "He had an aura of mystery about him that arose from his silence and his left-wing stance, his rejection of privileges, his working by night. . . . There was a rumor that Che during the crisis had wanted to shoot at U.S. planes."

32. "Even Che Couldn't Always Be like Che"

Taking a break from volunteer work on the Machina wharves in Havana.

I N ORDER TO SOOTHE ITS ANGRY CUBAN ALLIES, THE SOVIET UNION PLAYED its only card: it sent Politburo member Anastas Mikoyan to Cuba. On November 5, 1961, he met with Fidel and Raúl Castro, President Osvaldo Dorticós, Integrated Revolutionary Organizations president Emilio Aragonés, INRA head Carlos Rafael Rodríguez, and Soviet ambassador Alexeiev, the only Soviet official whom the Cubans seemed to respect, and of whom it was said that he wept in despair when the missiles were unilaterally withdrawn. It is obvious why Che was not invited. In any event, a cool atmosphere prevailed at the meeting and no communiqué was issued.

The next day, the Kremlin envoy saw Cuban officials again at his embassy's celebrations of the October Revolution. The ice had yet to be broken. To improve the atmosphere, Mikoyan made left-wing, anti-American speeches at the University of Havana, but the students criticized him and he got no official support from the Cuban government.

November went by with the feeling that when push came to shove, the island would have to stick up for itself in its deadly confrontation with the United States. As the days went by, Cuban dignity led to a refusal to accept Soviet *or* U.S. control. President Kennedy called off the naval blockade, while the Soviet Union dismantled the missile bases.

———

On December 4, Che gave an interview to the British Communist newspaper *The Daily Worker.* It seems to have been toned down before publication, because Che had railed against Khrushchev's liberalism. Commander Guevara was not in a good mood, and a week later he was sniping again, this time at *Revolución.* The paper had published Che's diary of the invasion of Santa Clara, which had been edited by **a very sharp gentleman from Santa Clara who wanted to add to events by using adjectives. The scant value of such notes ends when they lack authenticity.** Answering this and other complaints from Che, Franqui said: "We hope that one day, when the years have gone by and you have been successful in every task assigned to you by the revolution, you will be appointed a newspaper editor."

Throwing himself into industrialization again, Che found that production had increased during the crisis, despite the alerts, the need to mobilize militias, and military priorities in transportation. There was only one way to explain the fact: the people worked more conscientiously in times of crisis, despite the added problems. Political tension made a difference that no quota, requirement, or prize could achieve. It was a lesson from Che's own life: how potent social conscience and willpower could be.

Che worked in his small, austere ninth-floor office, which was decorated with a photograph of Camilo, a certificate in recognition of his voluntary labor, a drawing of a miner at work, an industrial map of Cuba, two awful gilt armchairs, a small television set, and two ashtrays. It was there he received one of his new collaborators, the Cuban economist Miguel Alejandro Figueras, whom he had drafted as manager of long-term planning, and to whom he confided that the future would be electronics, heavy industry, and computers, topics no one spoke of in Cuba in those days.

Every Monday there was a board meeting, held back-to-back with a review of one particular business in the afternoon. The discussion was often heated, but Che liked the others to argue with him. He did not like subordination, did not quash his opponents or let deputy ministers quash them.

At about that time Che presented the cabinet with a document entitled "General Tasks for 1963," in which he made several proposals: First, that the Ministry of Industry consolidate its progress to date rather than make any new investments (i.e., Cuba should not buy any new Soviet factories while still installing those already bought in Eastern Europe). Second, the discrepancies in pay scales should be sorted out and war waged on red tape; third, that the ministry insist on technical and professional training and begin the battle for quality.

The campaign for training was under way. Of the 189,514 industrial workers under the Ministry's auspices, 34.4 percent were studying. Scientific research related to industry was beginning, too. Figueras recalled that between 1963 and 1964, "ten Ministry of Industry research centers were set up, even though at that time there was the least staff."

Che Guevara was still that difficult, devoted character who brutally pressured his colleagues and was always a little reserved. Enrique Oltuski:

> We drew closer after various meetings, but without becoming friends, and even crossed swords several times in January. One day I put my hand on his shoulder as a sign of friendship and he said to me: **Why so friendly?** So I let my hand drop.
> After a few days he said to me: **You know, you're not as much of a son of a bitch as I thought!**
> Then we laughed and did become friends.

Anecdotes concerning Che's peculiar personal style blossomed. On January 21, for example, during a board meeting, Che had an unopened flask of coffee by his side. Jaime Valdés Gravalosa asked him to open and pour it, but it stayed closed. When Gravalosa protested afterward, Che told him: **There wasn't enough coffee for everyone, so there won't be any for anyone.**

Che later told his coworker Miguel Alejandro Figueras: **You know I'm not much in favor of material incentives, but I will use material disincentives. As your staff's work entails visiting two factories a month and you haven't complied, as of today no one will be paid until they get up-to-date.**

Che inspired amazing loyalty *and* hatred, both in spite of and because of his combination of austerity with brutal demands and harsh moods. He also had an impact on women staffers. Verónica Fernández, a ministry employee, later said: "Che's personality and appearance made quite an impression among the girls at the ministry, and some were even in love with him. He was a man whom nature had given handsome features. He was very masculine, with beautiful eyes. He spoke with those eyes."

Six or seven years after these events, the Nicaraguan poet Ernesto Cardenal visited Cuba and throughout his trip collected anecdotes about Che. Everyone was anxious to contribute. The result was a compilation of stories about the minister who ate in the cafeteria like any other worker, waiting in line with his aluminum tray, who would lean against an armchair, standing up, so as not to fall asleep, and who read reports at home on Sundays after a day's voluntary work. They were stories of which the following exchange is typical:

Cardenal: "Not everyone can be like Che. . . ."

Haydée Santamaría: "Even Che couldn't always be like Che. Sometimes he got tired, too, and got home worn out and just wanted to be with his kids."

In February, Che was driving himself to the limit again. Rumor in Havana had it that he had gone crazy, that he wasn't just doing voluntary work anymore, he wanted to cut all the cane by himself. On February 3, he turned up in Camagüey to try out a cane-cutting machine at the sugar mill named, like his column in the Sierra, after Ciro Redondo.

For a year, Che had been pushing projects to mechanize cane cutting and a team had been going around in circles trying to come up with an appropriate machine. There were none to be had either in Cuba or the socialist countries. The team tried everything, from copying a Hawaiian cutter they saw in a movie to adapting a South African machine, to revamping an old U.S.-made Thornton they found lying around. When they finally came up with a prototype, Che ordered a thousand cutters to be built that could be mounted on an ordinary fifty-horsepower tractor and used in regular field work. The prototype had to be tested, so Che went to Camagüey and met the local commission.

"We were scared fartless," said one of the campesinos in charge of setting up the equipment.

The test began at a farmhouse in the La Norma camp at four A.M. on Sunday, February 3, 1963. A dozen moppers-up, "Che's hatchetmen," followed behind the machine to cut high stalks and other cane that it had missed. An engineer responsible for making the machine, Angel Guerra, was there, along with Miguel Iparraguirre, who monitored the test and whom Che continually pressured not to falsify the results.

After a backbreaking day's work of nine and a half hours, they cut almost 6,000 *arrobas*.* The machine had broken down and it took three and a half hours to get it going again. Che jumped down from the tractor several times to see **what the hell is going on.**

He had tried to keep the press away, but gave way to pressure from *Revolución,* which sent the reporter José Vázquez and the photographer Korda. The journalists spent all day trying to approach Che. **This isn't propaganda,**

*An *arroba* is about 25 pounds.

he said. **There aren't any photo opportunities here.** But he finally allowed Korda and a young photographer from the Camagüey paper *Adelante* to take some photos—as long, of course, as they too grabbed a machete to cut cane. This was serious; no one was just posing for a photograph to persuade doubters that cutting cane could be partially mechanized. The photos show Che on the tractor or laboring, along with the mechanics, over the gears.

They cut 5,900 and 8,800 arrobas on February 5 and 6, respectively. The *Revolución* reporter asked Che how much they had cut on February 8, and he answered, dry as ever, **Ten thousand arrobas** *and a foot* (one of his bodyguards had suffered a cut foot). The reporter telephoned back to the paper. Che read *Revolución* the next day and said, damnit, how dumb could they get, what did they mean? **"What's a foot?"**

"Isn't that how you say 'and a little more' in Argentina?"

Oh, go away.

He began another grueling day on February 9, taking a light plane in the early morning to Camagüey for the first check-in on progress in the sugar harvest. He appeared for the meeting, at the Alcázar Theater, in overalls dusty from cutting cane. At that time, 60,500 pecks were in.

Che announced that a thousand cutters would be used; five hundred were ready, and the main idea was for the operators to improve them as they acquired practice. (The Polish journalist Karol later said: "There isn't a country in the world with a thousand cutters, and none would have produced a thousand machines without a prototype.") Che told the cane workers and the bureaucrats:

> **I'm going to blow my own horn here. I began cutting with the machine on Monday. At first it was business as usual—the universal joints broke, this, that, and the other broke, some comrades weren't careful and got hit, we even had an accident. . . . The machine is cutting four thousand pecks there where they're testing it. . . . I've cut forty-five thousand this week. . . . The machines can cut eight hundred pecks an hour in a medium-sized field. . . . I'd say that's a job for two, not one operator. . . . You can't ask people to spend twelve hours a day on a tractor.** [But he'd spent thirteen hours there one day.]

He finished by defending the machine even though it was complicated and had a high failure rate: **cutting cane is tough, exhausting work, and what's more, the canebrake never ends.** That drew a standing ovation from those present, who knew full well that the canebrake never ends.

He returned to his work at the Ministry of Industry after a day's rest and opened a barbed-wire factory. Back at the canebrake on February 11, he beat his own record, cutting 18,700 in nine and a half hours. A Canadian television team turned up, but Che did not take them too seriously and gave routine replies to their questions. They seemed not to realize how serious the matter was.

Che's backup team worked themselves to death for him. In his usual style, there were no discrepancies in rest periods, and if there wasn't enough coffee for everyone, there was no coffee for anyone. On February 12, a day without too many accidents, he cut a notable 21,400 pecks. Full of emotion, he asked Iparraguirre, **How many now?** The only way to stop him was to stand in front of the tractor and say that those working with him were exhausted. After washing in cold water he received the Bank of Moscow auditor on the spot. The Russian looked as if he did not understand why he had to go and talk business with a minister in the middle of a canebrake, much less have to listen to a tribute to the importance of mechanized cutting. Che did not seem to care too much about credits from the bank.

On February 14, Che heard that a nearby canebrake was on fire and rushed off with his team. If the cane were not cut, the sugar would be lost. His comrades tried to stop him: maybe the fire was an act of sabotage; counterrevolutionaries might be lying in ambush. There was no stopping Che, however. **Let's go!** Cutting cane in a burning field is sheer purgatory, with dust and ash floating in the air, and he had an asthma attack. He directed the group while gasping for breath, covered from head to toe in ash and drenched in sweat.

As if he had not done more than enough, on February 15, Che took part in a showpiece competition against a star operator from the Brasil mill, Ibrahim Ventura, and beat him, wearing out his machine's brakes in the process. The day after, he lost in another competition, to Roberto González at the Blanquiazul mill, on difficult, stony, and uneven ground. There were counterrevolutionary guerrillas in the zone and he drove his escort mad by refusing to take security measures. He cut 20,000 arrobas on February 17 at the Venezuela mill.

Che left Camagüey with much more than the 100,000 arrobas he had promised. The machine certainly worked, but a third of the testing time had been taken up with breakages and mechanical difficulties, so a mechanic had to be on permanent stand-by to keep the work rate up. In this case, however, claims that voluntary work ended up costing more than normal paid work were refuted. The expenses incurred by Che's team were more than outweighed by their output.

Despite the efforts at mechanization, Che had to accept a couple of months later that the sugar harvest is not going quite as well as it should. There were many reasons. One, for the sake of diversification, canebrakes had been replanted with other crops in 1962, so Che clashed with the National Agrarian Reform Institute, despite his friendship with its head, Carlos Rafael Rodríguez.

Two, there was much less manpower and much less cutting, as many campesinos shun the sugar harvest now that there is land and work. The third cause was the disparate effectiveness of voluntary work. In Camagüey, where there was traditionally a shortage of labor for the harvest, the people who went were a failure and really became more of a hindrance than a help. But voluntary work was a success in Havana

Province, where those of us who go on Sundays to do our bit can see that efficiency . . . has greatly increased. A whole host of distinguished bureaucrats are now becoming distinguished cane cutters.

Che insisted that voluntary work was the raison d'être of a society finding its solutions in collective organization. Jorge Risquet recalled that he once proposed at a meeting in Oriente Province that the best volunteer-brigade workers be given little houses to stay in while working, as a material incentive. Che asked him: Don't you think that's overdoing material incentives? Risquet replied: "Dammit Che, you've got to give people somewhere to live. The little houses aren't a big deal, and what's more they group the cutters together, ten at a time. No, I don't think that's overdoing it."

After his successful venture in cane cutting amid the larger failure, Che went back to industry. As usual, he preached that dragging the Cuban economy out of the doldrums depended on its development.

On March 24, he spoke to the workers' assembly at the Ariguanabo textile mill about the formation of the United Party of the Socialist Revolution (PURS). He also objected to the fact that in a factory where many women worked, only five of the 197 workers chosen to become party members were women. He said that either women have yet to be unleashed from bonds with a past that is not dead, or men think that women have not developed enough yet to make their numbers count. He recalled an anecdote from the ministry, about a woman who had to be transferred because her husband, an army officer, would not let her travel around the country. This is a bullheaded example of discrimination against women. . . . The past is still weighing us down.

 what about Che?

Che also visited the Marcelo Salado soft-drink factory (formerly the Coca-Cola factory) and harangued the technicians, as he had done already on television: Why doesn't the cola taste the way it did before? Pancho Hernández, the technician in charge, complained about the public criticism and said that they had made an enormous effort.

Look, I said what I said because the drink really does taste like cough medicine. Can't we make a cola as good as or better than the Americans'?

It would seem not.

Che always entered factories through the shop floor, never through the office section. A documentary made at the time shows him taking part in workers' meetings (pausing in the middle to smile). It gives the impression that he felt at home. He had harsh words for factory workers now and again, however. After visiting a motorcycle plant in Santiago de Cuba, he wrote to the workers upbraiding them because ORI members took the bikes for personal use and pointing out to them that workers have no rights over the articles they produce. Bakers have no right to extra bread, and cement workers have no right to extra sacks of cement, and neither do you have a right to motorcycles.

In that second quarter of 1963, Che's mother, Celia de la Serna, was arrested on her return from Uruguay to Argentina and accused of transporting

Communist literature. She spent two months in the women's jail in Buenos Aires, where her health suffered. It was Argentina's move in what would become their vendetta against Che. Meanwhile, a photo of Aleida March taken at home in May showed she was in the advanced stages of pregnancy, expecting Che's fourth. A daughter, also to be called Celia, was born June 14.

Che made a very bad speech on May 20, the anniversary of the PSP newspaper *Hoy*. It was full of textbook Marxism and praise for the old PSP cadres. The same viewpoint was reflected in a prologue he wrote at that time for *The Marxist-Leninist Party,* an anthology of texts on party theory and Fidel Castro's speeches. One of Che's biographers, the Italian writer Roberto Massari, bemoaned "Guevara's praise for a book with such a poverty of theory. It is odd that Che, who had been so critical of the path taken by the Soviet economy, had not the least idea of the social disaster, political authoritarianism, and repressive police state that was the U.S.S.R. Furthermore, of course, he did not have the theoretical bearings to keep himself at a distance from it. He was a prisoner of Neanderthal Marxism. As Karol correctly noted and Franqui realized, Che's ignorance prevented him from taking an overall view of the problem.

At the same time, oddly, Che opened a debate with Soviet Marxism, this time addressing its inconsistent economic management. A new magazine for debate and announcements, *Our Industry,* appeared on June 1, printed on paper made from cane bagasse by the ministry. The first issue ran an article by Che, in which he pointed out in the introduction, with no polemic, that Soviet "financial self-management" of businesses differed from the Cuban approach of centralization, which suited a small country with good communications.

The contentious reply did not come from Che's enemies, the old PSP cadres, but from one of his political offspring, the flamboyant foreign trade minister, Commander Alberto Mora. In the magazine *Foreign Trade,* without mentioning any names, Mora wrote: "Some comrades suggest that Marx's surplus value theory does not work at the moment in the state sector of the Cuban economy." Che lost no time in throwing himself into the argument, publishing Mora's article and his own reply, "On the Conception of Value, and a Reply to Some Statements on the Issue," in the third issue of *Our Industry.*

Che made it clear from the start that there was no "some comrades" about it. He placed himself, as industry minister, and Finance Minister Luís Álvarez Rom on one side of the fence, in defense of what had become known as the "budgetary financing" line, because it **is as well to set forth not only principles but also the people who sustain them.**

After a convoluted series of quotes and counterquotes, Che got to the point. The surplus value law **regulates commercial relations within capitalism and, therefore, in the event that markets are distorted for any reason** [such as heavy state intervention], **it also will be distorted.**

Mora had argued that state property was not social property yet, which was evident from the contradictions among the state-owned businesses themselves. Che replied that these contradictions at every level in Cuban industry, from the smallest workshop up, were contradictions inherent in a process. And he concluded by welcoming Mora's entry into the debate and congratulating him on the quality of *Foreign Trade*. All this was still relatively friendly and fraternal, although Mora was hurt by the unduly harsh tone of Che's article. Mora and Che had been friends, but when Che began to debate, his ironic and ill-natured tone overwhelmed Mora.

It was essentially an internal government clash between two stances on economic management, one of which was represented by Alberto Mora, Rolando Díaz, and Marcelo Fernández, the central bank chairman. The three, recent converts to Marxism, had never been PSP members, but had Soviet economic advisers. Their line was supported by old PSP hacks in the INRA. The other stance was represented by Che, described by Miguel Alejandro Figueras as "a rebel with a cause," Luís Álvarez Rom from the Finance Ministry, and Enrique Oltuski from the Joint Planning Committee, none of whom wished to carbon-copy what went on in the Soviet Union, and who said that in Cuba conditions were such that they could do things differently.

The pro-Soviet side advocated "financial self-management" for firms, using extensive bank loans, some autonomy, and material incentives as the main tool for increasing production, with wage differentials to reward productivity. Che defended industrial centralization, saying that Cuba had the best accountancy and communications in Latin America and had management experience from the U.S. monopolies that should not be wasted, especially in industry. Furthermore, the small number of factories (there were fewer in all of Cuba than in the city of Moscow) and the lack of managers made centralization necessary. For Che, self-management of factories to encourage competition between them meant a return to primitive capitalism or a move to a socialism that had lost its way and was based on competition rather than cooperation. Che sought above all to confront the idea that firms should become little monsters guided by the profit motive rather social interests.

Rodríguez, from the INRA, had spoken in terms of agriculture's "bureaucratic centralism" and the disasters it had caused at first. He and Che seemed to have reached a tacit agreement that what might be good for industry was not necessarily good for agriculture—or at least, they'd agreed to avoid confrontation. This, in any case, was only the first round.

At the end of June, Che made a flying visit to Algeria to establish closer links between Ahmed Ben Bella and the Cuban revolution. Carlos Franqui, who saw him there, later recalled that Che was becoming very critical of the Soviet Union. "He accepted some Chinese principles: to depend on your own strengths, without expecting anything from capitalism or the Soviet Union and its hegemony."

Che also met the journalist Jorge Ricardo Masetti, his man in Algiers. Masetti had run Prensa Latina, the Cuban news agency, during the revolution's early years; he resigned in March 1961 in reaction to encroaching sectarianism, but went back to work during the Girón Beach invasion. There he served on the front line—sending his dispatches throughout the three days' fighting—and interrogated prisoners. Masetti went to Tunisia with a message from Fidel

Castro, offering help to the FLN, the Algerian National Liberation Front. In January 1962, the Cuban ship *La Bahía de Nipe* landed in Tunisia with mortars and rifles for the Algerian guerrillas; Masetti supervised the distribution. The weapons were taken to a camp close to the Algerian border, and the boat, carrying orphans and wounded Algerian fighters, returned to Cuba. Masetti left Havana again at the end of 1962, having been there just long enough to meet his new baby daughter, and vanished from sight.

It was said in the corridors of power that Masetti was in Algeria on an operation that Che was running from a distance, and that doubtless had something to do with the presence of Cuban volunteers and medics in North Africa who were advising the Algerians in their fight against the Moroccan monarchy. This was true. Masetti did meet Che, and their conversations in 1963 were to affect both their futures.

Che returned to Havana in mid-July and met a delegation from Vietnam for the first time. Li Van Sau remembered: "It was early one morning in July 1963, in his office at the Ministry of Industry. We had spoken until dawn. Che explained his points of view to us regarding our struggle against the Yankees, and insisted on his idea of creating 'many Vietnams.' " For the first time, Che voiced a concept that was to stay with him until the end of his life: the struggle against imperialism was worldwide, and could only be won by multiplying the number of "flashpoints" in several parts of the Third World.°

The FLN banner on Che's desk, and a dog that fouled the ministry corridors were two new aspects of Che's life. Just when did Che obtain his monstrous tailless dog, which walked along around as if it owned the place? The dog (called Muralla—"Great Wall") attended ministry board meetings like any other member. It sat at Che's feet to be petted and have its head scratched from time to time. Muralla had learned to enter the elevator, get out at the ninth floor, go to Che's office, and scratch the door until Che opened it. He was the ministry mascot, but Che had excellent relations with all the stray dogs nearby; he commanded and fed them, and they accompanied him on guard duty. He warned the dog-catchers to leave them alone.

———

The previous year, Che had given factory managers a very short time to reach at least a sixth-grade educational level. What was a tough job to begin with became impossible as the managers worked like slaves against the lack of spare parts and raw materials, on top of their political and military duties. Even Che, who was very strict, had to bow to reality and grant them a one-year extension. Exams were given at the end of the year, and 132 out of 986 candidates failed, while a large number failed even to turn up.

On August 10, Che angrily took this up at a meeting of the Administrative Council of the Ministry. He was tough. He reinforced his warning that those who failed would be out on the street, those who rated between a "D" and a

°Translator's note: The Spanish word I have translated as "flashpoint" is *foco*. It was in common use among radical Latin Americans and political scientists, but has no fixed translation.

"C" would have a second chance, and the 260 who did not turn up would have their pay stopped until they did so.

It was a particularly acrimonious meeting. After recognizing that he had explosive working relationships, Che let fly at Edison Velázquez, a director general who had a terrible way of putting things and had said, "There are no revolutionaries in Cuba, there are no men here," and had accused those at the meeting of being loath to accept criticism. Che got up from his chair:

> **It's a lie to say that we're loath to accept criticism here. . . . I don't know why you have to put things so aggressively— there's no point, buddy, even with all the difficulties we have; this isn't a choir practice. . . . No, no, opinions have never been curtailed. A gentleman once said here that I was a revisionist, and should be taken off a factory assignment. I got really mad, because it seemed completely the wrong way to go about things, saying the minister should be taken off a job because of his personal attitude. I have always defended people's freedom to say what they like about me . . . as long as they do their job. But I do not have to put up with criticism with which I don't agree, and I have the same right as any of you to say so. . . .**

The meeting continued to heat up when Gravalosa said that the heads of the inefficient had to roll, and Che said that a fair system needed to be set up for such firings. He also said that the worst things that had been done in Cuba have not been done in this ministry. As for the Juceplan, it was so out of touch with reality, you would not believe it, except for Oltuski, who has just been to the countryside and come back much the wiser. He then criticized himself, as I have committed several infractions—playing chess, which takes up valuable time—but in general I do devote all my time to the country's problems.

Chess was the only vice he took seriously. When I left the ministry, I called my wife and told her I was going to see the other love in my life and she said, I know, you're going to play chess. It was a vice for which he was prepared to make sacrifices. Otherwise he worked tirelessly, touring factories at unheard-of hours and without warning, to talk to people and to work. Although no one was surprised when he materialized like a ghost, he sometimes got spectacular and spontaneous receptions. At the Gibara shipyard people began to shout "Che's here!" and no one could stop them.

Towards the end of the year, the Cuban Writers' Union published Che's second book, *Reminiscences of the Revolutionary War.* The edition was incomplete, and more reminiscences would be added in later editions. I didn't want it to be published in bits and pieces, but they took no notice of me and I don't see how anyone can understand it without a detailed knowledge of the revolution. The book was a great hit; there were long lines of people outside every bookstore in Cuba, and it sold out abroad as well.

Reminiscences was Che's way of dealing with nostalgia for the Sierra, a way, as he had told students at Minas del Frío in April, of returning: **Every time we come close to the Sierra, I can't resist the temptation to go back.** It was also a way not to forget: **the years go by and the memory of the insurrection fades without the events being clearly recorded, events which have indeed already gone down in Latin American history.**

In the foreword, he invited all the others who had taken part to offer their stories.

We only ask that the narrator stick to the truth, but never make a personal statement or magnify it, never pretend to have been somewhere he wasn't, or to say something incorrect. We ask that after each has written some pages to the best of his education and disposition, that he edit himself as thoroughly as possible and remove any word that does not refer to a strictly correct fact, or of which the author is not entirely sure.

Che was invited to join the Writers' Union after the book was published, but refused, arguing that he was not a writer, as much as he would like to be. He also waived his royalties from editions published in the socialist countries.

At the beginning of October a hurricane hit the Oriente and Camagüey provinces; Che toured the area. Human casualties were minor, but 500 houses were destroyed, and cows had been killed. Industry had suffered only small losses. As ever, Che was fascinated by the grassroots reaction and the people's level of organization, especially that of the brigades from the Ministry of Public Works. He received another pleasant surprise several days later, at an international meeting of students and teachers of architecture: **I had forgotten how (in my opinion) important is the social class that an individual belongs to, what youth is, the freshness of ideals and their cultural awareness just when people step out of their teens and into the service of purer concerns.**

It was about then that Che announced his departure from the Joint Planning Committee and Fidel took direct control of planning. **There's no authority in Juceplan. There'll be authority with Fidel there now, but there wasn't when I was there. Moreover, I had only one portfolio . . . a phantom economic commission that didn't decide anything.**

Che also reflected on the excessive ambition of the revolution's early days: **We wanted to build schools, and we did; to build hospitals, and we did. We built roads and tourist resorts, clubs and workers' centers. Wages went up. And we talked about development at the same time. It was impossible; the figures just did not add up.**

The industrial conflict didn't let up. At a board meeting, Che said that in addition, Cuba wasn't getting promised deliveries from abroad: **We didn't fulfill contracts with the socialist countries and so the socialist coun-**

tries aren't fulfilling theirs in return, but calmly withholding supplies.

Che was showing signs of tiring of the relationship with the U.S.S.R.; he made a very acrimonious observation regarding the agricultural disaster there. He could not understand why such failures still occurred forty-five years after the revolution. Something was very wrong. He called it an **agricultural catastrophe**. He said that the Soviet Union should not just have a fairer society than the United States, but a more productive one, too.

Furthermore, the shipments arriving from the socialist bloc were of poor quality. Raúl Maldonado: "Despair over the poor quality of the products and machinery we received from East Europe began to make itself felt. It was an indication of what might happen in Cuba."

The "indication" was already becoming fact. Che was interviewed by Severo Cazalis ("Siquitrilla") on November 11 for the newspaper *La Tarde*.

"Why has the quality of footwear deteriorated?"

Some initial lack of raw materials and the expropriation of private property led to a terrible loss of the sense of quality. We also fell victim to that. . . . But a solution is on its way, and footwear may be an immediate example. . . . You, for instance, did not tell the truth the other day, saying the prototype shoes were pretty, when many were awful.

That same day, Che reviewed a report from the Cuban Mineral Resources Institute and provided an optimistic note about Jesús Suárez Gayol, a former comrade in arms, who **is one of the few who expresses faith and enthusiasm and has a basic desire to express them out loud and to other people.**

The ability attained by the cadres in the ministry was what pleased him most. Che congratulated himself on the team he had set up. His deputy, Orlando Borrego, was a man with an **acrimonious personality,** but an enormous capacity for work. There was also Tirso Saiz, a chemical engineer, and Commander Castiñeiras, who had been an anti-Batista conspirator in the navy during the war and now bore enormous responsibilities as deputy minister for light industry. Che considered Mario Zorrilla his staffer with the most future potential; Captain Angel Gómez Trueba, though he had a **tendency to issue military-style orders,** and was **somewhat gruff,** was also **an enthusiastic and tireless worker.** Also at the ministry were Santiago Rivera and Oltuski, who had just been transferred to Juceplan.

Che was perhaps most critical of himself: **Among the personal failings each man has, mine are so clear and express themselves so suddenly in sharp contrasts, so often repeated that there's no need to describe them.** The failing that he thought most serious in his ministerial work was that he had always pushed for action (his belligerence was born of practice) and skipped discussion. Due to inefficiencies in the state administration, Che would always push first, ask questions later, and then see what happened. He recognized that it was on his initiative and without discussion at government level that the budgetary centralization method had been adopted at the ministry, that competition by example and voluntary work had begun (the latter had been criticized by Fidel for the way it was set up). If discussion had not been skipped, we might have had more clashes at one stage, but working relations would have been clarified.

> Needless to say, the poor relationship between the Ministry of Industry and the INRA, the two strongest bodies in the revolution, did nothing to help the country's economic development and did bring about many bad habits, which we are still trying to correct.

It would seem that those clashes with the INRA were not the only ones, as in the same report Che also mentioned clases with the ORI and the Cuban Workers' Council (CTC). Che did not give way on stances of his that led to conflict, as he thought the opportunity to clear the air would be lost by shunning debate and looking for ways out, as would the opportunity to sort out economic-policy disputes at the heart of the revolution. For this reason, the job of industry minister took up so much of my enthusiasm and working capacity that I was not able to rise above it and be a real national leader.

While Che's roundup of industry was glowing—he saw a huge leap forward in the quality of management in the Ministry of Industry, widespread enthusiasm, record growth in output—he also saw encroaching bureaucratization in Cuban society as a whole. The issue cropped up time and again throughout the year in speeches and ministry board meetings, even in his private correspondence. Your book on Laos was ground up by the wheels of our dangerous bureaucratic machinery, he told U.S. journalist Anna Louise Strong about her book on Chinese communes, which he praised, and he invited her to Cuba.

Allow me to admit to you that bureaucracy in our country is rock solid and well entrenched and, in its huge bosom, it absorbs paper, incubates it and sends it to whoever is concerned in its own good time, he told Peter Marucci, editor of the Canadian newspaper *The Telegraph.*

We carbon-copied the experience of brother countries and that was a mistake, not a terribly serious one, but one that slowed down the free development of our strengths and made a dangerous contribution to one of the phenomena that must be fought most in a socialist revolution, that of bureaucracy,

he wrote in the *Algiers Weekly.* And to José Matar, the director of the Committees for the Defense of the Revolution, he wrote: From what I have seen so far, the basic characteristic is the board's lack of organization, as shown by a letter dated July 12 and date-stamped here July 22 asking for my opinions by July 31, which I received at the ministry September 17.

Che knew only one way to fight bureaucracy: personal contact and personal relations between the grassroots and their leaders. The author has the account of Lázaro Buría, who was in charge of a storeroom at a metalworks when he was seventeen. She turned up one Sunday with a ministry official and asked him:

Are you the boss around here? What needs to be done?

"You've come to work?"

"That's right, voluntary work. . . . Are you the boss? Tell me, then: what needs to be done?

Buría hesitated, then recovered. He told Che to measure iron bars and count them.

Che decided to go to the deepest mineshaft when he did voluntary work at the Matambre mines. He was with the manager, his former comrade in the revolutionary war, Alberto Fernández Montes de Oca. Montes de Oca knew that the damp would bring on Che's asthma, so, when he saw him panting in the elevator, suggested they go back up. Down, Che insisted, and they went to Level 42 where he spent several hours working and talking with the miners.

A miner called Pablo was drilling 6,500 feet belowground when someone tapped his shoulder. It was Che, who held out his hand.

"No, Commander, mine's really dirty."

Che hugged him. He had no shirt, trousers, or rubber boots on, because of the heat. He picked up the electric drill, asked Pablo how to use it, drilled for some minutes, and said:

That wears me out. I don't know how you can handle that thing, with you being so small.

Che then vanished into the darkness. Pablo did not know whether what had happened was real.

Che still suffered from asthma. Dr. Fernández Mell, his old friend and comrade-in-arms, supervised the experiments he conducted to fight it. But Che was still unable to learn precisely what triggered the attacks, although he had several clues, such as weather conditions, food, and various clothing material.

He had been using a horse-doctor's remedy:

> Che would inhale adrenaline with a sprayer, which dilated his bronchial tubes. The adrenaline intoxicated him and gave him stomach pains and terrible headaches. He also used cortisone in solution; it's an anti-inflammatory agent, and plenty of liquid to dilute the adrenaline in his body. His disease was awful and odd at the same time. Che was like a barometer: he could tell when cold fronts were coming. The disease had left its mark on him, as his sinuses were inflamed due to his difficulty in breathing.

It was this character who troubled U.S. intelligence more and more. An intelligence memorandum, "Implications of Cuba's Renewed Campaign of

Incitement to Violent Revolution in Latin America," circulated among high-level officials in the Johnson administration on December 30, 1963. It warned of the increased incidence of incitements to Latin American revolution in Fidel's speeches and Radio Havana broadcasts, and in the words of Che Guevara.

33. 1964: In the Revolution's Basement

During an appearance on Cuban television, playing up his resemblance to the Mexican comic actor Cantinflas for an irreverent look at the hierarchy.

A T THE BEGINNING OF 1964, CHE UNVEILED AN INDUSTRIAL INVESTMENT plan totaling 180 million pesos, 18 percent less than the year before. More emphasis was given to agriculture and particularly to agricultural infrastructure: roads to canebrakes; storage facilities.

Miguel Angel Figueras, one of Che's cadres at the Ministry of Industry, says: "The government realized that a huge trade deficit with the socialist countries had been building up, and we felt it was time to put an end to it. The only way to do so was to restore sugar-production capacity." While the pace of industrialization had slowed despite its successes, new capabilities were set up and many small and medium-sized workshops were retooled, which was one of the main reasons our factories kept running when the U.S. blockade on spare parts took its greatest toll. They were slowing the pace down, but were still monitoring the process carefully so as to be able to correct mistakes.

These days, Che was permanently at daggers drawn with Regino Boti, the minister of economy and secretary of Juceplan, which he accused of being very formal and a den of bureaucrats. Che's correspondence with Boti, with whom he constantly argued but whom he respected, was full of jibes. He had written Boti in October 1963:

> I regret that my absence from the [Juceplan] meeting may have prevented any consultations from taking place over problems with production. For your information, neither the ships in Camagüey nor those in Oriente have suffered from hurricane damage. I am humbly at your service to provide information by phone or in writing regarding any doubts about production or any other area in which I am well versed (such as the surplus value theory).

Several months later, in February 1964, Che finished off a discussion with Boti on a technical problem by writing: I greet you, Comrade Minister, with the Juceplan war cry: Long live the letter-writing war! Down with productive work! Che wrote again on June 12, replying to a request to increase the print run for the magazine *Médica Panamericana* ("Pan-American Medicine"); he told Boti that the magazine was "crap," judging by my short and hardly edifying experience as a doctor, [and] crap serves no political purpose. Another letter, dated June 17, replied to a personal request for a lathe: Basic tools cannot be merchandise. If you have friends, go and look for the means of exploitation yourself.

At the end of 1964, Che characterized the Joint Planning Committee as a disaster. Whenever I sign a paper [I don't know] whether I am doing something intelligent or signing some monstrosity, because communication is so bad. He did hold Boti in regard, however, as one of those likable people who also looks into things, is concerned, and gets people moving. He congratulated Boti when he left the Ministry of Economy on its absorption by the Juceplan, headed by President Osvaldo Dorticós, and went to work in a factory.

Che's barbed letters were not confined to the Joint Planning Committee. He also returned a letter to Minister of Foreign Affairs Raúl Roa with a note saying: I'm sending back this shitty letter you sent so you can learn not to sign anything without reading it first.

On January 11, Che awarded voluntary-work certificates and received one himself, testifying to the hours he had put in. In a speech at a Cuban Workers' Council meeting, Che told the story of a seventy-year-old who fulfilled his quota, a woman who put in 340 hours, and another worker who put in 980 hours.

> But the important thing is not to make our factories profitable by sacrificing a few workers . . . rather, the accomplishment should be matched by the awareness acquired through work. . . . This Easter, some gifts found their way into my hands, and not small ones, either. I personally feel they could be given to the most outstanding comrades. I won't show them here as they are really pretty and might be mistaken for material incentives, which I don't mean them to be.

Then he gave them to the three exemplary workers.

He mentioned that social compulsion was good, but that people could not be forced to work, or "voluntary work" would lose its meaning.

During an interview early that year, the journalist Severo Cazalis—"Siquitrilla"—brought up the subject of the labor camp at Guanahacabibes. Che said: I know you don't approve of Guanahacabibes. Getting no reply, he asked: Would you like to go there?

The whole issue of Guanahacabibes was public knowledge, and had brought about terrible rumors and acrimonious echoes. The idea of labor camps was historically associated with the Nazi or Soviet euphemism for concentration camp. Che had frequently broached the topic at the Ministry of Industry—for example in 1962, when the manager of the leather products division said he had not been able to penalize anyone by sending him to Guanahacabibes without discussing it with the party's grassroots committees. Che replied:

> Guanahacabibes is not a feudal penalty. People are not sent to Guanahacabibes who should be in jail. People are sent to Guanahacabibes who have committed a more or less serious breach of revolutionary ethics and have been dismissed from their jobs. They work hard there, but it's not brutal.

Someone who committed larceny went to jail; the manager who covered up for him went to Guanahacabibes. The people I have seen don't leave resentful or scornful. What was more, he said, **Anyone who wants to can visit Guanahacabibes; anyone who doesn't can leave the ministry.**

Guanahacabibes, a name that made more than one Cuban official nervous, was in a small town, Uvero Quemado, in the middle of a forest on the Corrientes Peninsula. The place was originally adapted as a work camp by the armed forces and also used by the Ministry of Industry. There was a coal-mining town nearby.

Che visited the camp in 1964 with Siquitrilla, Che flying them there in a Cessna. Their first attempt failed because of a storm, and they made another.

"I think we're the only ones bent on going to Guanahacabibes no matter what," Siquitrilla said.

No, there're others who seem bent on it, said Che.

When he arrived, Siquitrilla saw about a hundred people in the rehabilitation center. They were armed, as almost everyone was in Cuba, where service in the militias had brought guns into everyday life. But there were no guards; this was not a prison.

Che asked: **Does anyone here disagree with his sentence?**

No one answered. They were there for the most varied of reasons; there were students, factory managers, and a revolutionary commander. Recent arrivals worked as lumberjacks, then went on to more complex tasks, making baseball bats or working in a chicken packaging plant. They were at constant war with rodents, who ate the crops. The camp had a bakery, a school, and and beehives. It was self-sufficient; everything was built by the people who worked there.

Under the Ministry of Industry, people were sent to work for several weeks or months at Guanahacabibes, for lack of discipline, immorality, or unsatisfactory work. Whoever was penalized could appeal for a review of the ruling, accept the penalty, or refuse to accept it. The penalty was usually accompanied by a temporary suspension from work, and people could go back to their usual jobs after they returned from the camp. Che's deputy minister Orlando Borrego added: "Che insisted that once the penalty was paid, the failing the cadre had had could not be brought up constantly; the matter was settled."

Commander Guevara liked the idea of the camp and often joked or half-joked about sending his team "on vacation" to Guanacahabibes. Che's secretary, José Manuel Manresa, later confessed that he was often threatened with being sent to Uvero Quemado. **It was, however, a unique work camp.** Though Che often went there on Sundays to work alongside the inmates, the place had a sinister reputation among middle and top management at the ministry. A historian as unsympathetic to the Cuban revolution as the American Theodore Draper maintained that Guanahacabibes was a concentration camp and that workers held it in terror. In March 1964, when Che asked outstanding workers in a meeting whether any of them wanted to be managers, one answered that nobody wanted to go and plant eucalyptus trees in Guanahacabibes. Che joked along, saying that first of all, there were no eucalyptus trees there, but **mosquitoes and other things, and if we sent everyone there who made a mistake, the place would be full of skyscrapers.**

There is the interesting testimony of Young Communist leader Francisco Martínez Pérez, who was sent to Guanahacabibes for six months after he had a personal problem while studying on a scholarship in the Soviet Union. He told Che he thought the penalty unfair, and Che asked whether he thought the experience would nonetheless help to make him a revolutionary. Martínez replied that it surely would. He worked as a coal miner in Guanahacabibes.

In February 1964, Che again took up the debate begun a year earlier over the differences between the Soviet and Cuban industrial models. In an article entitled "On the Budgetary Financing System," he wished to set forth in a simple way the differences, which were often described as **obscure and subtle.**

According to Che, the virtue of centralization was that it made rational use of resources and administration, saved labor, allowed for joint effort that enabled adjustments to be made without wage conflicts, and made investments simpler to control. On the other hand, he believed that **it is still hard to tell which shortcomings** [shortages, problems with raw materials, lack of managers and technicians] **are caused by the system's inherent weaknesses and which are mainly due to our current style of organization.**

Marcelo Fernández defended the Soviet "financial autonomy" system for two reasons: for its financial discipline and economic control, and also because it improved relations between producers and consumers, improved quality, and boosted production. Cuban factories had no incentive to charge for their merchandise, but if their wages depended on it . . . Fernández argued that he had bank statements proving that the Ministry of Industry's corporations could not care less about economic transfers, although he had to admit that in the chaos then prevailing in Cuba, the INRA's corporations were worse. He further showed that, although in theory bank credits were not used in the "budgetary financing system," the corporations managed by Che's men had run up a deficit between 1961 and 1963 and covered it with bank credits.

Che lost no time in replying. In an article published by the magazine *Cuba Socialista*, he accused Marcelo Fernández of lacking theoretical depth.

Changes in the Cuban cabinet lineup in recent months seemed to show that Che's position was gaining ground. However, this was still only the second round in the debate.

Che continued to wage his own personal wars in the Ministry of Industry. At a board meeting held on February 22, he harped on the need for members to study until **we have a team of which we can say everyone gathered here is a specialist in their field with university degrees and everything behind them, instead of being the keen amateurs that we all are now.**

The issue that seemed most important, however, was that

workers' participation in running factories today is nil, although we have sent a series of instructions. Each time I go to a factory, I ask how the production meetings are going . . . and the manager tells me, "Well, yes, the meetings are held every month, but they're dull, poorly attended, people don't take part. . . ."

Where does the responsibility for workers' lack of participation and their apathy lie? Simply in that they see the meetings as an obligation to some one, not as place to sort things out.

Che saw managers' insensibility as an aggravating factor. In a shoe factory in Matanzas that he had visited, one worker complained that he had to work in a dusty area and suffered from asthma. Che, being particularly sympathetic to such a problem, spoke to the manager, who said nothing could be done, that he could not install an extractor fan. Che insisted. The manager replied, "He hasn't got asthma, he's got tuberculosis."

There is no record of the string of profanities Che threw at him.

On February 23, Commander Guevara was cutting cane at the Orlando Nodarse plantation with a brigade from the ministry. The driver who brought the workers to the canebrake stayed inside his bus, in the shade. Che's anger boiled over as he approached him.

Hey, comrade, where's your machete?

"No, I'm not here to cut, I'm a driver."

Look, anyone can be a driver here. Either you get a machete and start work like everyone else, or you leave right now. And don't worry about the bus—if it comes down to it, I'll drive it back myself.

As with all hagiography, the story has been toned down over the years. It will line up a lot more with reality, according to what one of Che's close collaborators told the author, if the reader adds the odd "dammit" and "shit."

At that time, Che was promoting "emulations," fraternal competitions in voluntary work. Rosario Cueto, from the Young Communist leadership at the ministry, agreed to compete with Che in an emulation, and they each formed a brigade. In Cueto's words:

> I cut more cane than I'd ever cut in my life . . . because we just could not allow anybody to beat us. Everybody in my group agreed. . . . The emulation was a close-run thing. We found out that Che sent one of his guards to spy on us . . . and we began to do the same. The rivalry was so great that, I confess, I was happy when I heard he'd had an asthma attack, because that would allow us to get ahead a little in the cutting. According to the supervisor's calculations, my team won. Che said he was biased, because I was a woman so they wanted to give me an edge. Nobody accepted that argument and a terrible fight blew up. He seemed really angry and blamed the supervisor for our victory. . . .
>
> There was a meeting a few days later. They wanted to set up an em-

ulation between the Ministry of Industry and the INRA, and Che sent for me.

Che said: **I sent for you, Rosario, so you can tell us what you thought of the competition between us.**

Although I was nervous, I told them all about it and admitted I was happy when he got an asthma attack. He about died laughing when he heard me say that.

On February 20, Che answered a letter from one María Rosario Guevara de Casablanca, saying he had no idea which part of Spain his family originally came from.

Naturally, it's a long time since my forebears left Spain, with no more than they could carry, and if I'm not like that now it's because the position is so uncomfortable, but I keep living in as much poverty as they. I don't believe we are closely related, but if your hackles are raised every time an injustice is committed in the world, then we're comrades, which is more important.

Six days later, Che returned to the virtues of moral incentives in a letter to one José Medero:

To set capitalist efficiency against socialist efficiency is to confuse reality with best wishes. Socialism achieves its undoubted advantages in distribution and central planning. . . . [Referring to material incentives:] **Beating capitalism with its own fetishes, once their most efficient magical quality, profit, has been removed, seems a very difficult task to me. . . . If I make myself really obscure (it's past midnight by my watch) maybe I can be clearer with another simile. Material incentives as a driving force in socialism are like a cheap lottery, they don't bring a shine to the eyes of the greediest and nor do they shake the rest out of their indifference. I don't claim to have worked the issue out, much less to have said the final word on these contradictions and others.**

A new political crisis shook the Cuban revolutionary leadership in March 1964. It grew out of a minor matter, the trial of Marcos Rodríguez, a PSP member who had been infiltrated into the ranks of the Directory during the revolution and had betrayed to Batista's police force several activists who took part in the raid on the National Palace. Rodríguez was arrested on returning from a scholarship in Prague that some former PSP members had arranged for him, and his trial led to heated dispute.

The dispute took place vicariously between the newspaper *Revolución* and the former PSP paper, *Hoy,* which did not report the first week of the trial. Fidel Castro solomonically repressed both wings of the party. Fauré Chomón made good use of the trial to point out that Marquitos was a child of sectarianism and to launch a strong attack on the old members of the PSP, suggesting in summing up that several well-known people whom he had denounced had been covering up for him. Castro asked Blas Roca to publish Faure Chomón's speech in full in *Hoy* and turned the heavy artillery on Siquitrilla, whom he accused of yellow journalism. The journalist then left *Revolución*.

Che seemed to remain above the dispute. On March 10, he took an unusual break to go with Aleida to see a baseball game between Industriales and Occidentales at the Latinoamericano Ballpark.

On March 17, he went to Geneva to take part in the United Nations Trade and Development Conference, where he made a very forthright speech: **We clearly understand and frankly say that the only solution to humanity's problems at the moment is to completely suppress the exploitation of developing countries by developed capitalist countries.** He also denounced the extent of the blockade against Cuba, whereby products using Cuban components would now be forbidden in the United States, even if manufactured outside Cuba. Ships that had transported merchandise to Cuba would not be allowed to transport U.S. products. Dollar remittances to Cuba were to be forbidden. There was a long list of pressures on other countries, such as the threat of a suspension of aid to France and Britain. All this was happening while Cuba's relations with China and the U.S.S.R. were easing. The island nation seemed to be the butt of the Empire's hatred.

Che fascinated friends and enemies alike. In Geneva, Carlos Lleras Restrepo, the future president of Colombia, invited him to dinner, although the Colombian delegation had orders not to attend functions held by countries with which they did not have diplomatic relations.

Che took advantage of the U.N. Trade and Development Conference to study quality control in plastics and watch factories, and to stop off in Algeria on his way back.

In April, the Joint Planning Committee's 1963 balance sheets for Cuban industry were published. Che had reason to feel pleased, as although industry had attained only 84 percent of its planned output, costs had fallen by 4 percent. There still remained a problem that had been nagging at him, however, and that was poor quality, which he saw as a result of factory managers' lack of respect for the people. In a ministry board meeting Che differentiated between products whose low quality resulted from shortages of raw material, and those whose low quality was a result of bureaucracy, the cult of quantity, and lack of discipline at work.

He was clearly angry. He began to pull out items and put them on the table—deformed dolls **that look like old women,** a tricycle that was **crap,** a shoe that had two nails instead of the ten needed to keep the heel on, a defective fly zipper (**and there's 20,000 more**) which people jokingly called a Camilo (on account of Camilo Cienfuegos's reputation as a Don Juan), a bed whose legs were falling off, a shampoo that did not wash hair, colorless face powder, and ammonia that had to be filtered before use.

The conclusion was tragic: that the quality of factory products was going from bad to worse. It was not the first time that Che broached the topic; the month before, he had said that the most important thing he saw in Switzerland was the quality control there.

On May 9, Che spoke to a gathering of young people at his ministry. It was not a good speech. He suddenly seemed to see himself in a light he did not like: **This ministry, which is really cold, really bureaucratic, a den of meticulous bureaucrats and hatchetmen, from the minister downward, who are constantly struggling with stubborn jobs.**

However, he lost none of his sharp wit or humor. On May 26 he wrote to the manager of the Havana psychiatric hospital, and in passing said:

> **Another thing I'd like to know: how can you print 6,300 copies of a specialist magazine, when there aren't even that many doctors in all of Cuba? I have a nagging anxiety that has brought me to the verge of a neuro-economic breakdown. Are the rats using the magazine to enhance their knowledge of psychiatry or to fill their bellies? Or maybe each patient has a copy by his or her bedside? In any event, there's 3,000 too many in the print run. I ask you to think about that. Seriously, though—the magazine is good, but the print run unbearable. Believe me, because out of the mouths of madmen, truth always comes forth.**

There was always more than a method to Che's madness; there was a plan. In June he stepped into the arena of the dispute over surplus value theory, taking part in a theoretical debate between U.S. economists Charles Bettelheim and Ernest Mandel. He moved along twists and turns of Marxist classics, confronting quotes with other quotes. He characterized Marxism as biblical and open to interpretation, and complained that the point of reference was less and less reality and more and more the dogma of the "classics." Che stressed one idea above all: that awareness and volition could alter market pressures and the laws of economics.

In the same frame of mind, Che confronted the CTC union headquarters in June: **the unions will also have to understand that their function is not to go around making speeches or to fight with the management here and there, but precisely to work with the masses and develop new concepts of work in them.**

The problem of wage differentials was a tough nut to crack. At the end of 1963, Che had already confronted workers who were training as statistical aides and draftsmen, saying at once: **Don't think I'm too scared to face up to the working class.** But there were 90,000 wage rates and twenty-five pay scales, a crazy situation impossible for those at the top to sort out because money in circulation was increasing although production was not, and wages could not be cut when they had been fought for over long years of union activity.

Che assumed that what went for workers went for officials, too. On August 31 he wrote to the president of the Home University commission expressing his disgust at being offered payment for giving a lecture. **I find it inconceivable that monetary reward be offered a government and party leader for a job, any job at all. . . . Don't take this as anything other than a complaint at a gratuitous offense, which is no less painful for being unintended.**

During this period, Che opened a dozen factories that had been ordered from Eastern Europe, and built over the previous two years. They manufactured pencils, barbed wire, sparkplugs, bicycles, domestic utensils, refrigerators, and kitchen stoves. He was not happy with some of them. He expected to manufacture bicycles at a factory at Caibarién, but found it was merely an assembly plant for parts manufactured elsewhere. An assembly plant with a defect, to boot: **We ordered it without realizing the vast number of imported parts it needed.** But at the new domestic utensils factory in Santa Clara, he could at last **open a factory without feeling the need for self-criticism.**

He announced that his deputy minister Orlando Borrego was leaving to head the Ministry of Sugar, which was to be split off from Industry, and there were other changes. Among the advisers backing up the ministry was Alberto Mora, whom Che brought back despite the political differences that had arisen between them: **He can show us we were mistaken, and there's nothing wrong in that, or show himself that he was mistaken, and there's nothing wrong in that, either. We'll be very much the wiser in either case.** The advisers also included Harold Anders and Carlos Franco.

Che racked up 240 hours of voluntary work in the first half of 1964. He had worked practically every Sunday, and a little more besides—this on top of his regular grueling working hours. Che acknowledged the strain now and again: **It's the early hours on Sundays when you have to be pretty dedicated to flip through papers—or do anything—when you're dying to go to bed, and then it's papers and lots more papers. . . .** A month later, he handed out voluntary-work certificates for those who'd put in a total of 1,683,000 hours at the Ministry of Industry. Not just Che, but also a broad swath of the revolutionary leadership, technicians, and workers had joined in the project.

On August 9, Che played second base for Fidel's team in a game at Santa María del Mar. It was the first time he had ever played baseball.

Che's daughter Hilda came to work with him now and again. He would pile books on her and ask her to read to him. Sometimes he stretched out on the floor so she could give him a back massage.

Enrique Oltuski said that at that time, although they were no longer working together, "I still wanted to see him and went to his office every now and then and we talked forever. Manresa would ask for coffee. Che would lie down on the floor, on the carpet, and smoke cigars. He would open the windows and take his shirt off when the air-conditioning broke down. [In our conversations,] we used to set the world to rights."

Che was worried about theft by workers on the one hand, and about news of fraud by corporation managers and economic chiefs on the other. He asked the government to put anyone up against the wall who used his job as an opportunity to steal. He returned to the issue shortly afterward; this time he focused on the pilfering from storerooms that resulted from the lack of oversight in factories.

Midway through 1964, Che visited the Nícaro mining complex again to get an overview of work being done there. Figueras:

> The manager, Edison Velázquez, was a tireless worker who had ruined his health getting the business off the ground, but he had a terrible management style and he got people's backs up. The cadres needed to be renewed, encouraged and inspired, changes had to be made. There was a very harsh argument in that two-day meeting and in the end Che decided that Edison would have to go back to Havana. He had done his job and was making potentially serious mistakes. In the end, everybody met in the workers' canteen. Che and Edison sat face-to-face on huge cement benches and tables, and the rest of us kept quiet and began to slip away. They spent about two hours talking there. Che didn't want to lose him or crush him, even though they often clashed at ministry meetings.

Che's attempts to support and understand his cadres did not, however, make the management style he used with the Ministry of Industry directors one iota more sympathetic. On September 12, he initiated a "demotion" plan, as opposed to a promotion plan. It took shape in October, in a document entitled the "Special Plan for Integration in the Workplace," which laid out its provisions. Each ministry director had to work for a month in a factory he or she had previously run. **The idea is that you go to a factory to see what it is you're signing every day.** The program was compulsory for everyone from minister to deputy minister, director general to factory manager. Those who completed the "demotion" were barred from making reports: the workers were not to see them as making an inspection, because otherwise **people will immediately regard the comrades as ravenous lions.**

Some conditions were set up so as not to weaken the management structure: no more than 25 percent of the cadres at a given level would be demoted at any one time, and no deputy would go at the same time as his boss. And the program was limited to the Ministry of Industry because **not all the comrades, not even the government as a whole, support the idea; it has not been discussed.**

On October 28, Che took part in a tribute to Camilo Cienfuegos, at which he complained that rituals were getting in the way of remembering the dead and that remembrance was becoming a **sort of disciplinary task.** And he warned:

The history of revolutions has a huge basement, which is not seen in public. Revolutions are not absolutely pure movements; they are made by men and unfold amid internecine struggles, ambitions, and mutual abandonment. And once all this is overcome, the revolution becomes a part of history that, for good or ill, right or wrong, quiets down and fades away.

On November 4, Che went to the U.S.S.R. again to take part in the forty-seventh anniversary celebrations of the October Revolution. This was Che's first official contact with the Soviet *nomenklatura* after the tensions that had arisen during the missile crisis. Was the visit a move toward reconciliation? That was doubtless Fidel's aim, but Che could not leave out his critical edge, which was becoming sharper. He visited what was presented to him as a model Soviet factory and said, according to a comrade in the delegation, **This is a capitalist factory like those in Cuba before the nationalization.** He saw aberrations in planning and tricks in their "competition" because they planned to overproduce. He told the other members of the delegation that the Soviet Union was going down a blind alley economically and was dominated by bureaucracy.

In the U.S.S.R., Che was interviewed by a correspondent from the Uruguayan newspaper *El Popular* about the recent U.S. elections.

"What do you think about Goldwater's defeat?"

The answer to that is a truism. Goldwater's defeat is a triumph for Johnson and . . . did you write that down?

"Yes."

And . . . Goldwater seems worse than Johnson. But for all I know Johnson is not too good. You need great powers of self-consolation to be happy because the best of a bad lot won.

After he returned from the journey, Che told his comrades on the ministry board about an argument he had with some Cuban students at the embassy in Moscow:

Things began to get a bit out of hand when we argued. In those days, their manual wasn't the bible, Das Kapital, but the simple Marxist handbook, and they were evaluated from several angles, including some that were dangerously capitalist, from which a revisionist tendency can stem.

Che had spoken with the Cuban students about his views on moral incentives and the disaster that was Soviet "self-management"; he said he had never had such a receptive audience, because they lived and breathed the issue. In the Soviet system there was **no bond between the masses and the leaders.**

Che came to a dire conclusion: **Despite what is said, the Western European bloc has advanced at a faster pace than the bloc of people's democracies. Why?** He argued that it was because instead of depending on the people's cooperation, they went back to material incentives, to competition and wage differentials (**managers earn more and more**).

I had several brushes over in Moscow: it seems he picked up the rumor that the Soviets went around saying Che was a Trotskyist.[*] Commander Guevara told his comrades: I expressed opinions that may be closer to the Chinese side . . . with some Trotskyism mixed in. They say the Chinese divide the revolutionary movement and are Trotskyists and I'm also tarred with the same brush. He stressed that on a diplomatic trip I **am disciplined and strictly represent the government.** And although the Cuban government's official position in Sino-Soviet affairs was one of **strict neutrality, not to get mixed up at all in the Sino-Soviet dispute,** there was a strong pro-Soviet tendency. Indeed, Franqui had reported in January that Raúl Castro got angry at him and Che, calling them pro-Chinese.

As a result of the journey, Che began slowly to change his opinion of Trotsky and Trotskyism: **An opinion someone wants to smash to bits is an opinion that is good for us. You can't smash opinions to bits and that is just what stunts the growth of intelligence. . . . Clearly, you can derive many things from Trotsky's thinking.** What sort of things? He did not say.

He had the insight to know that he had to return to supposed so-called Marxist heresies and review them without prejudice. But Che had had little contact with Trotsky's thinking, or anarcho-syndicalism, or any other strand of the revolutionary European leftist movements of the first half of the twentieth century that hadn't been rephrased in the triumphalist tones of the Stalinist Soviet bureaucracy.

Back home, Che headed to the east of Cuba on November 30, to open an industrial combine. It privately annoyed him: **The "wonderful" combine is just another little stall, with backward features and generally pretty bad.** The families of those murdered during the civilian resistance were present at the ceremony, which gave it an emotional aspect. Che made a brilliant speech, reviewing the history of the uprising in Santiago as Fidel's tones sailed on the *Granma* and describing the city's importance to the revolution and the debt the revolution owed it. He concluded by celebrating the fact that the combine was to produce goods useful to the population, like nuts, bolts, washers, and cutlery.

Che also took the opportunity to review the situation in Latin America and the Congo. His words were recorded for posterity, thanks to a documentary made by Santiago Alvarez. We see a Che with more prominent eyebrows than

---

[*]Trotsky clashed with Stalin because of his belief that the spread of revolution and Communism throughout the world took precedence over everything else, even the internal development of the Soviet Union. He was forced into exile, and subsequently everyone on the left with whom the Stalinists disagreed was labeled "Trotskyist," whatever his or her actual views.

usual, who has lost his Argentine accent and speaks Cuban Spanish with good diction, into which he throws the occasional bit of Argentine syntax or Mexican idiom. Che did not speak well—he never did; his charisma lay not in words or in speechifying, but elsewhere. He used too many commonplaces, was surprisingly slow, and did not gesticulate. He was not a speaker to pick his words; he seemed to be thinking ahead of them, ahead of the next idea and the next. There was a sudden spark when he spoke of the murder of former Congolese (Zaire) premier Patrice Lumumba: **You can't trust imperialism.** He hesitated for a split second, then amplified the remark with a smile: **Not even a tiny bit.** He measured with his fingertips and let the gesture fade away as if ashamed.

At the same meeting he spoke of the forthcoming cane-cutting season: **Naturally, in the cutting in general, women cannot do much work.** He was loudly booed by the women present, and rightly so. **In general, I said, in general. Neither do bureaucrats do much work in general, but we bureaucrats must go and cut cane and do our little bit. And . . . we bureaucrats . . . did pay our way—we paid for our food with our work. I believe women can do that, too, and if not, they can help in many ways.**

Looking to the future at a board meeting early in December, he said:

> **All new investments [must] be made in such a way that productivity reaches world standards . . . just the opposite of the way things have been done so far, where every factory and chemical plant we open is technologically outdated and contributes little to the average productivity in the country.**

Above all, Cubans had to **sacrifice what must be sacrificed** to attain workplace safety and hygiene, something that had been neglected in the battle for productivity. In a document he wrote around then, "Basic Tasks for 1965," this issue was paramount along with quality control, training, and maintenance, and the manufacture of spare parts.

At the same meeting, he again warned of the dangers of bureaucracy and a new variant of it he jokingly called "flying" bureaucracy: **things no longer sleep in filing cabinets; they sleep on the move in a special sleep system, in which they go from place to place. . . . They come and go, and whenever you look for them, they're in another department, but they're never sorted out.**

He later defined the leading cadres in the revolution in terms far too much like a self-portrait, although he denied it: **It's not the case with me.** But:

> **The life of a revolutionary leader at national level is . . . a life that if it did not have the compensation of seeing a job in progress . . . would really be very disappointing. It is the price**

> to be paid in the present circumstances, I believe. . . . My chil-
> dren call the soldiers whom they see every day "Daddy." . . .
> A life like the one we lead is all-consuming. . . . We may use
> the machinery in such a way that it gives maximum perfor-
> mance for five years and breaks down in the sixth. . . . Al-
> though the cadres may look tired, I at least, have never told
> anyone, "Take a break." Too often, out of a mistaken idea of
> our future importance, we have let the spirit of self-
> preservation take root.

He declared that it was necessary to abandon a false concept of our responsibility, one that leads us to save ourselves for the future. Was
that a warning? Che announced that he did not mean to save himself.

———

On December 9 he left to address the United Nations General Assembly in
New York.

Latin America Again

With Jorge Ricardo Masetti, a great friend and founder of the news agency *Prensa Latina*. Che drew up a plan with Masetti for a guerrilla campaign in Argentina, a venture that ended in the journalist's death.

THROUGHOUT THE PREVIOUS YEARS, ALONG WITH HIS ACTIVITIES AS INDUStry minister and the various policy debates on economic and political issues, Ernesto Guevara had been quietly working on a project that was perhaps a little closer to his heart, to his vocation as a revolutionary, as he wrote to the Argentine writer Ernesto Sabato in 1960: domestic and international circumstances don't make me grab my gun again, a task I disdain as a governor but long for as an adventurous spirit.

The project included organizing an infrastructure and groups of volunteers and preparing conditions for an armed movement in the Andes. In October of 1962, he had predicted that the region was destined to be the Sierra Maestra of Latin America. The center of operations was to be mainly in Peru and Argentina (the latter was going from one military coup to another following the fall of Frondizi).

Do the speeches, the notes, the newspaper articles exist in which Ernesto Guevara put his practical plans for the future Latin American revolution, rather than simply his ideas? If this written material survives, it is part of the huge collection of papers that Aleida March and the Cuban government have not made public. What traces remain from the early sixties speak of his absolute conviction that the Cuban revolution was just the first step in the future revolution of all Latin America.

On April 9, 1961, just before the Giron Beach invasion, Che published "Cuba: Historical Exception or Vanguard in the Anti-Colonial Struggle?", an article that pointed out Cuban variants on the orthodox Marxist theory of revolution as the task of the working class, and that set out for the first time his ideas of what the second Latin American wave would be. Armed struggle was the essential means, a peasant campesino uprising advancing to the cities in armed response to poverty, abuse, dictatorships, and all the injustices of the continent.

Che foresaw an almost immediate, definite, and bloody U.S. invasion. Without underestimating the potential of an electoral contest, he saw elections as an extraordinarily remote and totally closed route to change. He later returned to the same issue in an article written during the missile crisis in 1962, "Tactics and Strategy in the Latin American Revolution." An electoral advance here, a couple of congressional deputies, a senator, and four city halls there, a big popular demonstration broken up by gunfire, one strike won to every ten lost, one step forward, ten backward. . . . Why all this waste of the people's energy?"

In those same articles, Che held urban uprisings and urban guerrilla warfare in low regard, because they were so vulnerable to betrayal. He did not exclude them altogether: I would not go so far as to say that success is impossible.

What seemed clear was that Che felt there was a way forward that had been shaped by the Cuban experience, and that the time for it was drawing near. Social tensions on the continent could find a revolutionary solution if somebody were to offer one. In a second article, he said, A new awareness is spreading across Latin America . . . the certainty that change is possible. And many machetes are being whetted.

From the last months of 1962 onward, if not earlier, Che began to devote a substantial part of his time to the Latin American revolutionary project, even while working at the Ministry of Industry. He helped set up an organization in the Cuban Interior Ministry that some called "Liberación." It was coordinated by Deputy Interior Minister Manuel Piñeiro, who received guidance from Che and Fidel but "mainly from Che," according to an interview with one of the cadres involved. Intelligence work was not its responsibility; rather, it was to undertake "operative missions" of support and solidarity with Latin American revolutionary groups.

Apart from collaborating with groups such as the Nicaraguans, who were beginning an armed struggle against the Somoza dictatorship and would later become the Sandinista National Liberation Front, Che focused his interest on the Andes.

Che held talks at the end of 1962 in Havana with Peruvian revolutionaries, including Héctor Béjar and the poet Javier Heraud, about the possibility of opening a guerrilla front in support of the remarkable work being done by Hugo Blanco in Valles de la Convencion in Peru. Blanco, who had led a powerful campesino and native struggle in one of the most poverty-stricken areas of Peru, was on the run after being accused of raiding a police station. Manuel Piñiero was in charge of setting up the practical end of a support operation.

It was decided that the best way into the guerrillas' operational zone would be by the shortest geographical route, across the border with Bolivia. Che appealed to the Communist Party of Bolivia (PCB) for help in collaborating with the Peruvian guerrillas, and the PCB then set up a support network. Luis Telleria, a member of the PCB central committee who was part of that network, had the support of Young Communists such as Julio Cesar "El Ñato" Méndez, Orlando Jimenez, and Loyola Guzmán. The group of Peruvian guerrillas entered Bolivia on January 9, 1963.

There were tangled political complications. The National Revolutionary Movement (MNR) in Bolivia, led by Víctor Paz Estenssoro, for example, was in conflict with the military dictatorship of Peru, and turned a blind eye to this group preparing an armed struggle against its neighbor. The Communist parties were loath to support someone like Hugo Blanco who, in their eternal sectarian logic, they saw as Trotskyist.

Finally, after several delays and changes of plan, the group crossed the Peruvian border near Puerto Maldonado. The Peruvian police, who had been tipped off, resisted the crossing, and firing broke out. Javier Heraud died in the confrontation. The operation was canceled and the Peruvians withdrew into Bolivia. Julio Méndez, "El Ñato," guided part of the group across the Beni jungle in that country.

It appears that while Che was collaborating with the Peruvian National Liberation Army's attempts to set up a guerrilla flashpoint, he was also helping out in an operation coordinated by one of his few close friends, the Argentine journalist Jorge Ricardo Masetti, with whom he began to speak of the project at the end of 1961. With Piniero and Che, Masetti prepared the "Segundo Sombra" operation to set up a guerrilla flashpoint in Argentina. Masetti returned to Algeria, with whose revolution he had been collaborating for the previous two years. After meeting Che there, he took training in urban-guerrilla tactics. "We have been waiting with bated breath for four and a half months," Masetti wrote to his wife at the beginning of 1963. "That's eating into the time we have to come up with the goods." That spring, Masetti and his comrades traveled to Brazil as members of a trade delegation, using Algerian diplomatic passports. They crossed the border into Bolivia, supported by Bolivian Young Communist activity again, and entered Argentina in September.

The group was known as the People's Guerrilla Army (EG). Masetti took as his nom de guerre "Commander Segundo," in homage to the gaucho Segundo Sombra, protagonist of the Argentine popular epic *Don Segundo Sombra*. As an "honorary member" of the EG Che chose "Martin Fierro" as his nom de guerre. In a speech years later Fidel confirmed that Che's presence was far more than honorary, that the EG was "his" operation, which he was directing from Cuba. According to several of his comrades, Che had planned to join at a later stage. Two Cubans were in the original group with Masetti, Captain Hermes Peña, Che's personal escort for years, and Alberto Castellanos, who had been his adjutant and driver. Even Commander Fernández Mell, another of Che's close friends, had been mooted as a possible member, but was later ruled out.

It is no coincidence that the two guerrilla campaigns, in Peru and Argentina, began in 1963. They were doubtless part of the "Andean" project Che had been working on.

On June 21, 1963, the EG moved into a farm called Emoraza and began to train in Salta and Jujuy provinces, the area that Che had toured on his moped as a teenager. One survivor of the EG said of Masetti: "He never spoke about his personal life. We knew he had a wife and kids, because he mentioned them once. One time, he even spoke of Masetti in the third person. But I didn't know it was him, and the photographs they later showed looked little like him. When I knew him he had a big black—almost blue—beard. I had trouble speaking informally to him. He was an imposing figure."

The EG first saw action at a bad political time: Argentina was having a taste of civilian government with the election of President Arturo Illia, although the supporters of former president Juan Perón boycotted the elections.

A man arrived in Bolivia in July 1963 who was to be closely linked to Commander Guevara's Latin American projects. His mission was to set up a border support network for the EG. He was José María Martínez Tamayo, also known as Papi or Ricardo, the Cuban interior minister. His support troop also included outstanding Bolivian Young Communist militants like the Peredo brothers, Roberto (Coco) and Guido (Inti); Rodolfo Saldaña; and Jorge Vázquez Viaña.

In August 1963, Luis de la Puente Uceda, a leader of the left wing of the

Peruvian American People's Revolutionary Alliance (APRA) arrived in Havana after leaving jail and founding the Revolutionary Left Movement (MIR) under the influence of the Cuban revolution. Strangely enough, Uceda had not met Che before, although he was a friend of Hilda Gadea, and had also been exiled in Mexico in the fifties. There is no doubt that he spoke with Che in mid-1963 about his plans to resume the guerrilla campaign against the Peruvian dictatorship, basing his work on a reassessment of Hugo Blanco's experience. A couple of years later, Uceda outlined his key concepts, which paralleled Che's: a continent-wide battle with the most developed Latin American countries as a support system—Mexico, Chile, Uruguay, and Argentina—there was a strong ideological similarity connecting the two projects.

Martínez returned to Havana in September after having set up the support network in Bolivia for the Argentine guerrillas. He brought back an excellent impression of the small group of young collaborators, but not of the party structure.

Meanwhile, Masetti's guerrillas were training and doing political work among the campesinos, preliminary to an armed uprising. Masetti wrote to his wife:

> We have now covered a hundred kilometers on the map, but much more in reality. Our contact with the people is positive from any point of view. We have learned a lot from the campesinos, and we help them as much as we can. But the most important thing is that they want to fight. . . . This is a region in which poverty and disease are rampant. A feudal economy holds sway. . . . Anyone who comes here and doesn't even get angry, who comes here and doesn't rise up, who can help in some way but doesn't, is a bastard.

At the beginning of 1964, the Argentine poet Juan Gelman received a message for Che from Masetti, delivered to him in Buenos Aires by Ciro Roberto Bustos (known as Lieutenant Laureano or El Pelado), a member of the EGP urban network. Che received it one morning at his office in the Ministry of Industry.

"I have a message from 'Lieutenant Laureano,' which seems to be from Commander Segundo of the EGP," Gelman said.

Che reacted very coldly, unlike his usual greeting to the poet.

I don't know any Lieutenant Laureano or Commander Segundo or EGP, or anything you're talking about.

"Let us suppose there's a guerrilla army in Salta. Let us suppose it's led by a Commander Segundo, and let us suppose again that there is a Lieutenant Laureano from the EGP, who gave me this message . . ."

Gelman later recalled:

> Che produced a cunning smile. He didn't say a thing about the matter after that, but he did talk freely of the difficulties of urban fighting,

how hard it was to bear up to the pressure of living underground, to torture. . . . And then, surprisingly, he switched to the Argentine and Bolivian Communist Parties, saying they sent arms to the EGP and then charged for them. Che thought that was funny.

There was a new twist to this story in March, 1964, when Che asked Tamara Bunke or "Tania," to his ministry office. He had briefly met Bunke, a young Argentine-German, when she was working as a translator in Berlin in 1960. Tania had been recruited by the Cuban secret service and trained in espionage for a year. Che spoke to for several hours about the pre-revolutionary situation in Latin America and finally told her the aim of her mission: to settle in Bolivia, where she was to establish relations within the armed forces, the local aristocracy, and the government. She was warned that under no circumstances should she make contact with the Bolivian left. She must wait for a direct line from Havana. Present at the conversation was a Cuban secret agent who would also be a key player in the future: the former revolutionary fighter José Monleón, known as Iván or Renan.

Tania left for Bolivia in April. She was just one piece in a complex jigsaw puzzle that Che was fitting together in his head, a jigsaw puzzle neither necessarily perfect nor possible to complete. Who was the man or woman who could play a similar role in Argentina? How would the armed movements in Peru and Argentina be linked in the future? What role was Che reserving for the Bolivian Young Communists? What role, for that matter, was he reserving for himself?

All bets were off when Masetti's guerrilla campaign was routed in April of 1964. It had been infiltrated by the Argentine gendarmes a month earlier. "Diego" was later wounded in an "accident." A camp was seized, with all its provisions and another four men. The guerrillas, starving, wandered a desertlike wilderness. "Antonio" was murdered, thrown from a high cliff. Another group was captured on April 18. Several days later, Hermes Peña and "Jorge" either died in combat or were captured and executed. Three fighters got lost and starved to death. The rest spread out and were picked up slowly by the police. Alberto Castellanos, who was among those captured, kept up his cover as a Peruvian student until he was freed in December 1967.

The Argentine novelist Rodolfo Walsh, a former colleague of Jorge Ricardo Masetti at Prensa Latina, said, "Masetti never turned up. He just vanished into the jungle, into the rain and into time. In some unknown spot the body of Commander Segundo holds a rusty gun. He was thirty-five years old when he died."

When did Che hear about the destruction of the guerrilla group in Salta? Why did he refuse to accept that his friend was dead? Over the following year, he interviewed dozens of people, sent envoys and messages, and organized fruitless investigations trying to find at least the body of Jorge Masetti, Commander Segundo.

When Che left for the United Nations at the end of 1964, the Argentine project had been canceled, Peru was afflicted by terrible repression, and the future of the MIR guerrilla campaign was uncertain. Che's Andean project seemed to be in tatters. The condition of the armed struggle elsewhere in Latin America was no better. Guerrillas in Venezuela had failed politically, there had been military coups d'état in Brazil and Bolivia, and the agrarian revolution had been confined to Merquetalia in Colombia.

The routes seemed to be closed off for the time being.

35.   The Rediscovery of Africa

During the tour of Africa at the end of 1964 and the beginning of 1965.

THE DAY HE LEFT FOR NEW YORK TO REPRESENT CUBA AT THE UNITED NATIONS, Commander Ernesto Guevara had no socks. His old pairs were full of holes and his ration book gave him no right to any more until the following month. It would never have occurred to him to request more: he was going to wear high boots instead. One of Che's guards passed the word, obtained some socks, and forced him to accept them. What they could do nothing to improve was his olive-drab uniform, which was a disaster. The trousers had been washed so often that they no longer matched the shirt.

Che was true to form in New York, where he was to be seen playing chess with the New York City police guarding the entrance to the Cuban delegation at 6 East Sixty-seventh Street. He moved around the city with only a small group of bodyguards, despite threats. A woman from an armed group of Cuban exiles had been arrested near the UN building at that time. She was freed when she said her aim was to kill Che. Several nights later, while in a movie house, Che was told the same woman was at the door. He joked with one of his companions that **it would be really romantic to die at the hands of a woman.** He walked out of the movie toward her, and his penetrating glance was supposedly enough to stop her—the glance, and the fact that his guards surrounded her.

Che addressed the United Nations on December 11. His speech was a great settling of accounts between the Cuban revolution and the United States and the Latin American dictatorships. It was perhaps his best-rounded speech, and one of the best expressions of the sixties revolutionary left.

After establishing that the winds of change were blowing everywhere, he complained that **U.S. imperialism has above all tried to pretend that peaceful coexistence is for the exclusive use of the great powers on earth.** He cited aggression against the kingdom of Cambodia, bombing in Vietnam, Turkish pressure on Cyprus, aggression against Panama, the imprisonment of Laura de Albizu Campos in Puerto Rico, maneuvers to delay independence in Guyana, apartheid in South Africa, neocolonial intervention in the Congo. He devoted a large part of his speech to Africa: **all free men in the world should come to avenge the crime in the Congo.** After joining in the call for nuclear disarmament, one of the conference's main issues, Che outlined U.S. aggression against Cuba, and the recent U.S. prohibition on the sale of medicines to that country. He proposed a peace plan for the Caribbean, which included dismantling the U.S. base in Cuba at Guantánamo, halting spy flights, attacks, and infiltration by saboteurs, stopping pirate launches from the U.S., and an end to the economic blockade. To give an idea of the scale of the problem, Che listed 1,323 acts of all types of aggression that had been launched so far that year from the base at Guantánamo.

Che described the United States' support for dictatorships in Latin America and its indirect intervention in Venezuela, Colombia, and Guatemala. Far from speaking the language of peaceful coexistence, Che offered a challenge and a threat: **Our example will bear fruit.**

His speech earned a schoolmasterish reply from U.S. Ambassador Adlai

Stevenson, and provoked the anger of the delegates from Costa Rica, Nicaragua, Panama, Venezuela, and Colombia.

Che returned to the podium several hours later, taking advantage of his right to counter the replies. Now he showed his mettle as a polemicist and gave brickbats to the other delegates. He accused the Costa Rican government of ignoring the existence in its country of a Cuban counterrevolutionary base whose commander who used it to smuggle whisky. He struck back at the Nicaraguan delegate:

> I did not quite understand his argument about accents, although I think he referred to Cuba, Argentina, and perhaps to the Soviet Union. In any case, I hope the Nicaraguan representative found no trace of an American accent in my speech, because that really would be dangerous. Indeed, something from Argentina may have found its way in. It's no secret I was born in Argentina. I am Cuban, and I am also Argentine. Furthermore, if I don't offend their most illustrious lordships of Latin America, I am a patriot of Latin America, too—of any country in Latin America or anywhere else—and, whenever necessary, I would be prepared to give my life for the liberation of any country in Latin America, without asking or demanding anything from anyone or exploiting anyone. And this temporary delegate to this assembly is not the only Cuban in that frame of mind. The entire Cuban people feel that way.

Che then turned his guns on Adlai Stevenson, who had withdrawn from the assembly. Che said that he had lied in denying the embargo on medicine, and said he was being a hypocrite on the issue of asylum for the invaders from the Bay of Pigs: They were going to give asylum to those they had armed. He reminded the audience of how Stevenson had insisted that the aircraft that attacked Cuba during the battle at Girón had taken off from Cuba, when they were really part of a CIA operation. He stuck the knife in: Come what may, we shall still be a little headache when we come to this assembly or any other, because we'll be calling things by their right names and calling the representatives of the United States "gendarmes of repression throughout the world."

His speech was not only solid and full of facts and figures, doubtless culled from memory, but also very personal, and for that reason very unusual in the United Nations.

On December 14, Che was interviewed for *Face the Nation* by Richard Hottelet, Tad Szulc, and Paul Niven. The show was billed as a "spontaneous and unrehearsed interview," open and without pre-program questionnaires. Che's performance was not brilliant; he was nervous and fell back on oft-repeated ideas:

We neither accept conditions nor impose them for reestablishing relations with the U.S. The best thing would be for the U.S. to forget about us. . . . Revolutions are not exported; they arise from the conditions of exploitation that the governments of Latin America inflict on their people.

Was he in favor of disarmament and of the missiles having been withdrawn? Of course. Why don't we inspect each other, and if you like we can dismantle all the atomic bases.

On isolation: We have many friends among the peoples of Latin America. On the Sino-Soviet dispute: We maintain that unity is necessary. On a peaceful road to socialism: That's very difficult, practically impossible in Latin America.

Crowds gathered to see Che and talk to him when he ate in the United Nations cafeteria. He walked around New York buying books. On December 16, as if in response to his speech, Congress passed an amendment to a foreign-aid law, requiring all those who received U.S. aid to join in the blockade of Cuba.

The next day, Che left New York for Algeria. On the way, he wrote to his father from Dublin: I am on the emerald isle of your ancestors. When the television people found out, they came to ask me about the Lynch family history, but, in case they were horse thieves or something, I kept mum.

In Algeria, Che met a symbolic figure in the African revolution: Josie Fanon, the widow of Frantz Fanon. Che said: Africa represents one of the most important battlegrounds, if not *the* most important. . . . There are great possibilities of success in Africa, but also great dangers. What place in his thoughts was occupied by the anticolonial revolution in Africa just then?

Che left Algeria on a whirlwind tour of the continent, as if he urgently needed to cover as much ground as possible, as fast as possible, as if the UN speech had been incidental, and Africa had been his real aim and obsession all along. Hopping from airport to airport, he struck up relations with new progressive leaders, held discussions with liberation-group leaders, spoke with students and journalists, visited guerrilla training camps, dams, wildlife preserves, parks, new factories, held talks with presidents of countries in the front line of the anticolonial struggle.

On December 16, he went to Mali and on January 2, 1965, to Brazzaville (capital of the former French Equatorial Africa), where he held talks with President Alphonse Massemba-Débat. He also held talks with the Angolan revolutionary leader Antônio Agostinho Neto and, under instructions from Fidel Castro, offered the fledgling revolution assistance in the form of Cuban instructors for the guerrillas.

Guevara arrived in Conakry, in the Republic of Guinea, on January 7, and by January 15 was in Ghana, where he held talks with President Kwame Nkrumah and attended a news conference, wearing a kente-cloth robe. Seven days later he was in Dahomey (now Benin); on January 24, he was in Algeria again. From there, to the surprise of interested observers, particularly the U.S. intelligence services, he departed for China, where he stayed from February 2 to February 5.

He was accompanied by Osmany Cienfuegos and Emilio Aragonés. The aim of the visit was to explain the Cuban position regarding the Sino-Soviet dispute. (They saw only Zhou Enlai and Liu Shaoqi; hearsay has it that Mao Zedong refused to receive them because some members of the delegation were very tense.) According to a translator, Che listened very calmly to arguments by Chinese officials, who accused the Cubans of having aligned themselves with the Soviet Union at a recent conference of Latin American Communist Parties, and thus of abandoning their erstwhile neutrality in the dispute. The meeting turned out to be useless and painful for Che, although he felt closer to the Chinese side.

He arrived in Paris on February 6, and stayed twenty-four hours before continuing with his African tour. He spent four hours in the Louvre, in the Greek and Egyptian rooms, and also took a special interest in El Greco, Rubens, and Leonardo da Vinci. He looked at the Mona Lisa awhile and got lost looking for the works of Hieronymus Bosch. In Paris, Che's friend Gustavo Roca again confirmed the deaths of Jorge Masetti and Hermes Peña.

Che was received in Dar es Salaam, the capital of Tanzania, by Pablo Rivalta, his old comrade-in-arms from the Las Villas campaign. Rivalta later recalled:

> He met President [Julius] Nyerere at a reception in the palace at Dar es Salaam. They spoke of aid to Tanzania. The talks even included a commitment to deliver a small textile factory and other items of support, mainly doctors and technicians. All this was discussed in a really informal visit. They also spoke of support for liberation movements. Nyerere agreed.

The most important talks Che held were not with presidents, however, but with revolutionary armed groups, particularly successors to Lumumba from the Congo who had set up a rear guard in Tanzania.

> **The visit to Dar es Salaam was particularly instructive. A number of "freedom fighters" live there, the majority quite pleasantly in hotels, and they have made a real profession out of their situation, a lucrative business at times and always comfortable. That was the setting for the talks, in which they generally requested military training in Cuba and financial support.**
>
> **I also met the Congolese fighters. From the very start we could tell there was an incredible variety of diverse tendencies and opinions, in contrast to the leaders of the Congolese revolution.**

Che proposed to Laurent Kabila, a rebel front commander, and then to Kabila's boss, Gaston Soumaliot, that training should take place in the Congo, and under combat conditions. Rivalta recalled: "Most of those present at the meeting did not like that. They didn't like it because what they were really after was to leave the Congo, rather than enter it." Che offered them **some thirty instructors**, a figure that would later grow to 130. Rivalta said:

> I spoke with Che about the group of Cubans proposed to support the armed struggle in the Congo, and even suggested that they be led by Víctor Dreke, as he was black and they had been asking for black fighters and also because we knew how he had fought in the Escambray campaign. I then thought of Efigenio Ameijeiras, who had already been in Algeria; Che also knew him from the Sierra Maestra, and was familiar with his bravery and daring. I proposed these two to Che and also proposed myself. Che didn't answer; he just smiled.

Che was not acting on his own initiative in offering the help of the Cuban brigade, but under orders from Fidel, who in turn was responding to requests from the National Council of the Cuban Revolution, which had previously asked for support. This was also the basis for talks that had been held in Brazzaville with Nyerere and Massemba-Débat, who sought backup and extraterritorial points of support. Apparently no one leaked the details of these agreements to U.S. intelligence, which was very concerned over Che's tour of Africa (they had not detected his interest in that continent before). As a CIA memorandum written a month later said there was no confirmation of Cuban arms shipments to Africa apart from those to Algeria in 1963.

After the formal talks, Che decided to sound out the "freedom fighters" by talking to them individually but the Cuban embassy mistakenly organized a full-scale meeting **attended by fifty or more of the various tendencies or movements in the country.** At this assembly, Che evaluated the requests for instructors and money in light of the Cuban experience:

> **A revolutionary soldier is made in war. . . . I proposed to them that their training should not take place in our faraway Cuba, but in their nearby Congo, where the fighting was going on, not just against a puppet like Tshombe, but against imperialism in its neocolonial form. . . . The reaction was more than chilly. Although the majority kept quiet, some asked to speak so as to severely rebuke me for my advice. . . . I tried to make them see that here it was not a question of fighting inside frontiers, but a war against the common master, who was just as much present in Mozambique as in Malawi, Rhodesia, or South Africa, the Congo or Angola, but no one saw it like that.**
> **They took their leave coldly and formally, and it was made clear to us just how long a road we needed to travel in Af-**

rica. . . . I decided to arrange the selection of a group of black Cubans and send them as volunteers, of course, to support the struggle in the Congo.

At the same time, Congolese prime minister Moïse Tshombe was holding talks with U.S. Senator Dodd in London. He was told how difficult it would be for the U.S. to provide support, much as the envoy would like them to, because groups of white mercenaries and soldiers from South Africa and Rhodesia were still operating under Tshombe's command. Tshombe agreed to withdraw them when their contracts expired. They discussed the possible alternative of recruiting to Tshombe's armed forces men from Senegal and Nigeria, and even French army veterans from Togo.

Meanwhile, Che was holding a conversation with Rivalta that seemed a little odd to the latter:

> He told me he was going to test how well I spoke Swahili. I thought little of it at the time. He commented that I had many servants and employees at the Embassy—I had recruited many people with a view to creating a cover and to penetrate—and he said he didn't like that. As soon as he left I cut the staff back by half.

Che was in Egypt on February 19, meeting with President Gamal Abdel Nasser. During their very brief conversation, Che, among other things, said, as if in passing, that it might have been interesting to enter the Congo to support the liberation movements.

He had thought of visiting the Sudan, but political conditions there were not good so the journey was canceled. On February 24, he was in Algeria for the third time this trip, to take part in the assembly for the Second Economic Seminar for Afro-Asian Solidarity. His speech was very polemical he caused a stir in the socialist bloc by saying that national liberation struggles should be paid for by the socialist countries. **We say that without the least desire to blackmail anyone or produce a sensation.** He pressed on: there should be no talk of mutual aid based on the principles of the theory of surplus value. **How can mutual benefit mean selling, at world market prices, raw materials that cost limitless sweat and suffering in backward countries—and buying, at world market prices, machinery made in large automated factories? Arms should come free: When faced with the ominous attack of U.S. imperialism on Vietnam or the Congo, we should respond by supplying these brother countries with all the means of defense they need and with our unconditional solidarity.**

Che was pleased with his speech, which he made his comrades in the delegation read, and which found a resounding echo among the African delegates. (However, the Cuban press did not print it in full. On that same day, Ernesto, his fifth child, was born in Havana.)

Meetings with African and Asian delegations meanwhile continued in Algiers, with Cuban ambassador Jorge Serguera and President Ahmed Ben Bella. He spoke of collaborating with the guerrillas in the Congo. Che was in Egypt again and sent a postcard to his aunt Beatriz on March 8: **From Thebes, the first capital of dreams, a greeting from this poet who writes no poetry and has become a worthy bureaucrat with a respectable paunch and such sedentary habits that he walks around gripped by longing for slippers and children.** It was on this trip that he first encountered camels, and no one could make him come down from these newly discovered quadrupeds, on which he rode around the pyramids.

This time Che had long talks with Nasser, in which he explicitly confessed that he was thinking of going to the Congo to join the struggle. Nasser was fascinated with Che Guevara; according to Nasser's biographer, Che told him there was no conflict between him and Fidel: **We made mistakes and it's possible that I was responsible. We nationalized 98 percent of everything we came across.** He spoke of the lack of cadres, and of others, who made themselves comfortable: **those who close the door to workers so as not to let the air-conditioning escape.** He also wondered: **What's the relationship between the party and the state? Between the revolution and the people? Relations have so far been determined by telepathy, but telepathy isn't good enough. . . . We're not happy with Stalinism, but we don't like the Soviet reaction to it.**

Throughout their talks in Nasser's house, the Egyptian president told Che to forget going to the Congo, that he would have no success there, that he was a white man and would be seen as such. And when they took their leave of each other, Che said he had given up that idea.

Throughout the journey, Che had been taking notes for an article he was to publish three months later in the Uruguayan magazine *Marcha,* entitled "Socialism and the Common Man in Cuba." The Uruguayan journalist Carlos María Gutiérrez later said that the text "took the form of a hidden good-bye." I think not. It seems rather to have been a roundup of some ideas that Che had been mulling over for years—his thoughts on art and literature. On the one hand, he dismissed socialist realism and rejected cultural straitjackets. On the other hand, he protested the lack of artistic creativity that would break with the anxieties of the past; such creativity should have been exercised by intellectuals, whose Original Sin lay in not being genuine revolutionaries and thus not able to empathize with the downtrodden and their struggles. Somewhat unjustly, Che dismissed the entire Cuban intelligentsia with the stroke of a pen, and became bogged down in a rigmarole in which it was not clear what he was asking from literature: freedom from anxiety, or new anxiety?

He went on to the subject of the New Man, the focal point of his obsessions. There could be no socialism, nor any point in attempting it, without a New Man. From there he took up the role of the cadre:

And it must be said quite sincerely that in a true revolution, to which everything is given, from which no material returns are expected, the task of the revolutionary vanguard is both

> magnificent and anxious. . . . In these conditions, a great dose of humanity is needed, a sense of justice and truth, if we are not to fall in the trap of extreme dogmatism, of cold scholasticism or isolation from the masses. Every day you have to fight so that that love for humanity can be transformed into concrete deeds, into acts that set an example, that mobilize.

He closed with one of his old ideas, and this is what Gutiérrez saw as a farewell: Proletarian internationalism is a duty, but it is also a revolutionary need. . . . Our sacrifice is conscientious, a quota to pay for the freedom we build.

The African tour ended on March 13, when Che left for Prague. His plane broke down at Shannon Airport in Ireland, and he was stranded there for days. He had long conversations with the Cuban poet Roberto Fernández Retamar, who was working then for the famous publisher Casa de las Americas, and was returning from Paris on the same plane. Che was stranded with no books or Cuban cigars (would he have smoked Camels or Lucky Strikes in those days?). They spoke of Frantz Fanon, whose book had acquired a new dimension for Che during the tour, and which he recommended to Fernández for publication. They also discussed an article by Régis Debray that had just appeared in *Les Temps Modernes,* "Castroism: The Long March of Latin America." Fernández had recently seen Debray in Paris, and found there was only one photograph in his Latin Quarter home: a photo of Che that Debray had taken. They talked about reprinting *Guerrilla Warfare,* which Che opposed: he wanted to update it and add other experiences and a prologue.

It's faggy that you went to Paris and not to Africa, Che told Fernández, immediately after confessing that when he was a young man what he would most liked to have done was study in Paris, but Africa, Africa was . . .

36. "My Modest Efforts Are Required Elsewhere"

In disguise for his clandestine trip to the Congo, April 1965

COMMANDER GUEVARA RETURNED TO HAVANA ON MARCH 14, 1965. He was about to turn thirty-seven and had a new namesake, less than a month old, whom he had not yet seen. Fidel Castro was waiting for him at the airport. Carlos Franqui wrote years later that Fidel accused Che on the spot of indiscipline, because of his Algiers speech setting Cuba against the Soviet Union. Franqui says that Che admitted the act but told Castro he had explicitly been expressing his own opinion rather than that of the Cuban government.

It is believed that besides rejoining his family in those first two days, Che also had several long conversations with Fidel. The Argentine lawyer Ricardo Rojo later said that a mutual friend told him the two met for forty hours. What happened during that long-drawn-out conversation? It seems clear that Che had made a firm decision to leave Cuba and throw himself into another revolutionary venture. The failure of Masetti's guerrilla campaign in Argentina, where the dictatorship had been replaced by a civilian régime, and the disaster in Peru, would seem to have closed off Latin America for the time being. Was he haunted by former Congo premier Patrice Lumumba? Despite his final talks with Egyptian president Nasser, did he believe his presence could be decisive in Africa?

The only record of their conversation is several short comments proffered by Fidel over the years. Once he said: "I told Che myself that we had to wait until the time was ripe"—that is, before beginning any undertaking in Latin America. But Che wanted to go. Did he feel the years piling up on him? Did he fear that he was no longer fit enough for a new guerrilla endeavor? Fidel himself suggested as much in a conversation with the Italian journalist Gianni Miná: "I think he was influenced by the passage of time. He knew he needed physical fitness for all that." And José Manuel Manresa seems to confirm the statement: "At the Industrialization Department [in 1961], when we got to the office that Oltuski had set up for us, Che leaned on a filing cabinet and said to me: **We'll stick this out for five years and then we'll be off. We can still fight a guerrilla war when we're five years older.** "

Those five years had turned out to be just four.

Fidel never could stop Che or restrain him. And Che may well have appealed to an old debt that Fidel had owed him since those far-off days in Mexico. "When he joined up with us in Mexico," Fidel said, "he asked for just one thing: **All I want after the revolution triumphs is to go and fight in Argentina, without restrictions or raisons d'état to hold me back.** And I made him that promise. No one knew, at first, whether we would win the war and who would stay alive."

Fidel accepted that he had to allow an eager Che to go to Africa. Guevara was ready to become involved in Latin America without any prior preparation. Fidel himself seemed to suggest as much: "So we made him responsible for the group that went to help the revolutionaries in what is now Zaire." On another occasion, Fidel said: "He was assigned other tasks that were to enrich his guerrilla experience."

A month later Che (saying **It was time to get involved in Africa**) set forth his key arguments for going to the Congo with Víctor Dreke, who was to be his second-in-command there, and Pablo Rivalta, the ambassador to Tanzania. Says Dreke,

> Why did we opt for the Congo? Why not Angola, Mozambique, or Guinea? Because the objective conditions seemed to be right in the Congo. The Stanleyville massacre had taken place shortly before. The situation was different from that in the Portuguese colonies, whose struggle seemed still to be in the making. The Congo had two features: Brazzaville had asked us for help, and the guerrillas had liberated an enormous patch of territory in the former Belgian Congo, with a lot of Chinese and Soviet arms. Even the geographical conditions were good.

Rivalta added: "The Congo could be a base—that is, a sort of detonator—for revolutionizing all the African countries. The combat and training, and the activation of the liberation movement in the Congo, would be helpful everywhere, and especially in South Africa."

If the ultimate aim was Third World revolution, there was a certain geopolitical logic to Che's improvised plans. On the other hand, the signs that Cuba was aligning with the Soviet Union in its breach with China could not have pleased him very much.

The fact is that his decision was a quick one. On March 16, just two days after his return to Havana, Che gave Gustavo Roca a letter for his mother, Celia, in which he said (according to Rojo) that he proposed to leave the revolutionary leadership in Cuba; he was going to cut sugar cane for thirty days and then work in a factory for five years to study it from the inside. (Che's letter did not reach Celia for another month.)

On that same day, Roberto Fernández Retamar passed by Che's ministry office to pick up an anthology of poetry that he had loaned Che at Shannon Airport. Manresa received him and told him in confidence that the commander had asked him to copy a poem before returning the book. "Which one?" Retamar asked with interest. It was "Farewell," by Pablo Neruda.

At the end of March, Che did some uncharacteristic things. He gave away personal belongings, loaned books to his friends, took roll after roll of photos, and wrote even more letters than usual. He went to just one public meeting, but held several in private with his colleagues. Raúl Maldonado was among those he saw; he had been asked to resign from the Ministry of Foreign Trade after being branded pro-Chinese. Maldonado recalled: "I went to see Che and found him stretched out on the floor doing exercises. He told me: **A revolutionary never resigns.** I didn't resign; I was fired."

At the Industry Ministry meeting on March 22, Che gave a talk about his African tour, focusing on African influence in everyday life in Cuba, on Cuban painting, music, and customs. He ended the meeting as he would any other. Then he announced that he would be away cutting cane in Camagüey for a while. Some cadres expressed concern at this, but Che dispelled their doubts: there were capable cadres at the ministry, he said, and things were running well, with no problems. The meeting ended at 11:30 A.M. Gravalosa saw him amble down the corridor, with his dog Muralla following happily along.

Foreign Minister Raúl Roa met him and left a final account:

> He was fingering the black beret with the shiny star on it as he savored the lingering delight of the aromatic smoke from his cigar. . . . He suddenly stood up, shook my hand in an expansive gesture and, by way of saying good-bye, he said, *I'm going to Oriente Province tomorrow to cut cane for a month.* "Hey, aren't you coming with us?" *No, not this time.* And in that uncomplicated way of his, with his characteristic walk and shallow breathing, he went off, greeting everyone he met on his way through the ministry garden.

He also met with one of his young cadres, Miguel Angel Figueras,

> to talk about the latest edition of the magazine Nuestra Industria Económica. I had sent numbers 13 and 14 to him in New York and Algeria. The last night we spoke was March 25–26. We were alone; the ministry staff had mobilized and gone to do voluntary work. He was very upset by what the imperialists had done in the Congo and complained at the way the Czechs and the Soviets had been selling arms to the liberation movements: *That's not socialism or anything like it; they should have given them away.* He asked me: *What have you got for edition number fifteen of the magazine? Run the article that appeared in Marcha—run Alberto Mora's piece where he hits at me and supports material incentives, run Mandel's article, and run the Argentine sociologist's article on human nature and the incentive problem.* And he said to me: *Ask so-and-so for a piece by one of Ford's vice presidents, explaining development methods for cadres.* It was an article by Iacocca. Then the Argentine went away, dammit, and I had the Party asking me: Who told you to run that piece?

Che saw Gravalosa for the last time when the latter was on guard duty outside the Ministry of Industry. Che came by with Esteban Cárdenas, Aleida, and Muralla. He had a machete for cutting cane and a backpack in the trunk. As he was saying good-bye, his driver put the radio on, a midnight show playing tangos. "Adíos muchachos" ("Good-bye, Boys") was playing. Che realized the theatrical potential of all that and asked it to be turned up, and so he went off to the words "twenty years is nothing," with a feverish look, the music floating in the air through the streets of Havana.

The Congo operation was set up in Emilio Aragonés's office, with backup from Manuel Piñeiro's team. The group that was in training—the one that was to accompany him—was discussed, as were the journeys to be organized, weaponry, camouflage, and cover. Aragonés pressed to go along, but Che offered a counterproposal, that Aragonés should set up his own operation: **You in one, I in the other.** Aragonés's final argument did not prevail: "You're a stubborn Argentine mule and you need a politician with you."

Víctor Dreke, the man who was to lead the column of Afro-Caribbean Cubans who were going "somewhere," was briefed in the training camp around March 28 or 29 by Osmany Cienfuegos, who was then minister of construction. Cienfuegos told him that a new chief was to take charge of the expedition, that he would go as second-in-command, that the new chief was called Ramón and "had experience." That same afternoon, Dreke and Cienfuegos met in a safe house in an area called El Laguito with José María Martínez Tamayo, the Interior Ministry captain who had previously been involved with Che in preparing some operations in Latin America, and who had given collateral support to Masetti.

Dreke:

> I heard Osmany talking to somebody. We were in a little patio and a comrade came out; he was white, with crew-cut hair and glasses.
> "Do you know him?"
> "Not even slightly. I haven't even seen this man in the newspapers."
> "Comrade Ramón," says Osmany.
> **You okay, Dreke?**
> "You don't know him yet?"
> The voice sounded familiar, but I couldn't place it. He had false teeth. We sat down at a small table.
> **Stop fucking around and just tell him.**
> "Don't you know Che, then?" Osmany said.
> When you're wounded, you feel an impact, something hot and like an electric shock. My heart jumped, and I jumped up.
> **Sit down, sit down,** said Che.
> It was him, all right, but now he spoke normally. Che told me we were about to leave. He asked me about the column, the training. He talked about the mission, to the Congo! He gave me a tiny little Makarov pistol.
> **Can you play chess? He can't either,** he said, complainingly, referring to Tamayo. . . . Then he kept on writing. The papers ended up crumpled on the floor.

Dreke did not return to the camp but stayed in the safe house where Carlos Coello, Che's adjutant, was staying, as were Che and Martínez Tamayo. The next day, Che kept busy writing and reading now and again, suddenly jumping up to do some push-ups. Fidel turned up with Osmany Cienfuegos on the night of March 31, then walked out with Che to have a talk. Che gave him the papers he had been writing—his farewell letter:

> **Fidel, I can remember so many things right now: when we met at María Antonia's house, when you asked me to come along, and the tension involved in the preparations. One day somebody came around asking who should be told in case of our death, and the real possibility struck us all. We later knew that that was how it is, that in a revolution you either win or die (if it's for real). A lot of comrades fell on the road to victory.**
> **Today, everything sounds less dramatic, as we are more**

mature, but the situation is the same. I feel I have fulfilled my duty to the Cuban revolution on its soil, and so I take my leave of you, of the comrades, of your people, who are now my people.

Che went on to say that he had a debt to Fidel, having thought at some point that they would not make it.

I have lived through some great days, and by your side I have felt proud to belong to our people in the darkest and brightest days of the Caribbean crisis. Seldom has a statesman shone brighter than you did then, and I am also proud to have followed you without hesitation, to have identified with your way of thinking and seeing, and to have appreciated the dangers and the ideals. My modest efforts are required elsewhere, in other parts of the world. I am able to do what is denied you because of your responsibility at the helm of Cuba, and the time has come for us to go our separate ways.

The letter was not without some drama, but Che's usual jesting tone was absent. He seemed to feel this farewell was for good.

Here, among the ones I love most, I leave behind my purest hopes as a builder . . . and I leave behind a people who took me in as a son; and that tears at a part of my spirit.

The tone was repeated:

I will say once again that the only way that Cuba can be held responsible for my actions is in its example. If my time should come under other skies, my last thought will be for this people, and especially for you.

He also left something of a will in the letter:

I have nothing material to leave my wife and children, and I am glad of it. I ask for nothing for them, as the state will give them enough to live on and be educated.

I could say much more to you and to our people, but I do not feel the need. Words cannot express what I would like them to, and there's no point in scribbling any more. On toward victory, always. Fatherland or death!

A revolutionary greeting.

Che

Fidel read the letter. It must have been a difficult moment, despite the control under which both usually kept their emotions. Che's companions, Dreke and Martínez, were watching from a few yards away. Fidel took them aside and told them that they had to look after Che carefully and protect him, without letting him know they were doing so.

Commander Ernesto Guevara left the safe house the next day. When he departed Cuba, he left behind three old uniforms hung in a closet, enough books to fill a library, a secondhand 1956 car, and a pile of papers, diaries, and notes. Of his few possessions, he was to recover only some books, which he sent for in the months to follow.

37

AT DAWN ON APRIL 2, CONSTRUCTION MINISTER OSMANY CIENFUEGOS, Camilo's brother, drove three very special passengers to the Havana airport: Víctor Dreke, who had a passport in the name of Roberto Suárez; José María Martínez Tamayo, who was traveling as Ricardo; and Ernesto Guevara, known as Ramón (Tamoyo and Guevara used false surnames). All three names happened to begin with R.

Jokes were cracked in the car. The newspaper headlines that morning reported that there were "20 eggs freely available" in the city—that is, they could be bought in addition to the ration quota. The usual lack of humor in the Cuban press triggered all sorts of jokes. In Latin America, you cannot go around saying that eggs ("balls") are freely available. The undercover Dr. Ramón, traveling as a translator and medic, would ask his contacts he met in the many airports they passed through over the next few days:

Did you know that balls are freely available in Cuba?

They arrived at Dar es Salaam on April 19, just two months after Che's last visit and just one month after his return to Cuba. He was not, however, the same man. He was once more a man of independent action, no longer a minister speaking in the name of a government and a revolution that had taken power, no longer subject to silence, diplomacy, and protocol, wanting as all these may have been in his case. He was a guerrilla; he was Ernesto on a motorbike again, not knowing what the future would bring, as he had not known on board the *Granma*. Eduardo Galeano, the Uruguayan journalist, said years later: "With the capacity for sacrifice of a Christian in the catacombs, Che had chosen a spot in the firing line once and for all, not allowing himself the benefit of the doubt or even the right to be tired."

Was it self-sacrifice that drew him to Africa, or was it freedom? It was doubtless a sort of freedom, the sort he outlined in his farewell letter:

> **I formally resign from my leadership posts in the party, from the ministry, and from my rank of commander, and I renounce my status as a Cuban. I have no legal ties with Cuba, only the sort that cannot be broken by relinquishing appointments.**

Ambassador Rivalta was waiting for them in the airport. He had received a coded wire telling him of the arrival of a group of Cubans on an important mission.

> When the aircraft arrived, I was waiting for the group and first saw Dreke come down, then Martínez Tamayo, then a man I thought I knew. A white man, mature, with glasses, a little overweight. I recognized the type from when I used to live underground. I said to myself: "This guy's come along as a bodyguard for Dreke and Martínez." And I stopped and I stared and stared again, and kept on staring, because his eyes really were unmistakable. With his eyes and that bit of brow, he was unmistakable. And I said, "Dammit, I know this man." But I couldn't place him. I couldn't quite place him.

He was introduced to Ramón, but Che could not help making a joke, having a laugh:

You don't know me?

Rivalta hesitated, then said no.

Potbelly, Che said to him, and threw in some more petty insults.

"No, no, comrade, I don't know you," Pablo said.

Are you still the same old shitkicker, then? Che asked, and now Rivalta reacted with tears in his eyes.

Shut up, damn you, don't make a fuss, it's me.

Rivalta said, years later: "I was happy—but terrified, too."

The group was put up in a hotel in the center of Dar es Salaam, and later in a house in the outskirts under tight security. Soon the fighters who had been trained in Pinar del Río began to arrive. They had been sent off from Havana by Fidel Castro himself: "When you get to the Congo you'll meet somebody who will command you as if he were I myself."

The volunteers in Che's column may have been Afro-Caribbeans, but they had only the vaguest idea of Africa itself. In their own words, it was a hodge-podge of "lots of monkeys, the jungle, zebras and elephants—herds of them—lots of cobras, ferocious Africans with those sinister-looking blowpipes Tarzan used."

The Cubans made contact with the highest-ranking representative they could find in Tanzania just then, Antoine Godefroi Chamaleso. The Congolese were talking about setting up a great army, opening up several fronts, and launching a major offensive. Che and Dreke were left with the impression that there was no unified command. To make matters worse, the front commanders for the Tanzanian border region were all abroad.

Under Che's supervision, Rivalta obtained a boat, but repairs had to be made and time was pressing.

We can start with ten men; we mustn't wait long, he told Dreke.

A day or two before leaving Dar es Salaam, Che grabbed a Swahili-French dictionary that he had been studying and gave the group new pseudonyms: Dreke was to be "Moja" (the number one in Swahili), Martínez Tamayo "M'bili" ("Two") and he himself "Tatu" ("Three")

At last, the boat was ready. Che gave his final instructions. He left four Cuban volunteers in Dar es Salaam to await the groups that had yet to arrive. He also left his Swahili dictionary behind, so that the fighters could keep naming the new arrivals. There was an awesome glee in Che's voice when he talked later about his feeling before the imminent departure: **We were already at war. It was knocking on the door.**

The group departed Dar es Salaam at dawn on April 23 in cars bought by the embassy: one Land Rover and three Mercedes-Benz. Che drove for a while, over bare earth and dirt tracks. It was a long and suffocating route, which crossed deserts and jungles. By nightfall, they arrived at Kigoma, a small town on the shores of Lake Tanganyika, the crossover and entry point to the Congo.

Their boat wasn't ready: engine trouble. Che got mad. **We have to get** a move on. **We're going in whatever we can.** A truck took them to the lakeshore, where there was a small motor launch with room for no more than a dozen and a half people. Dreke, looking back, said:

> It looked to me as if that boat was going to damn well sink. It was no more than thirty feet long. We were to go from Kigoma in Tanzania, across Lake Tanganyika, to Kibamba in the Congo. Tshombe's troops were constantly on the watch, patrolling the lake. The crossing could take six to seven hours, if we stuck to the shore to avoid the Belgian mercenaries.

The crossing was a difficult one. One engine broke down in the middle of the lake, and Che cursed at it to get it going again. It was raining, and flares suddenly appeared in the sky. Che insisted that they should sneak over the border rather than fight. **If we have a confrontation in the middle of the lake, we'll never get there.**

It was about six or seven in the morning when they landed in the Congo, near the small village of Kibamba.

38

The Wait

The base at Luluabourg in the mountains of the Congo, near Lake Tanganyika. Classes in mathematics for the guerrillas

I N THE DAWN'S EARLY LIGHT, A SMALL GROUP OF CONGOLESE FIGHTERS dressed in yellow uniforms met the Cubans with slogans and chants. This proved to be the only time the Cubans saw signs of martial bearing in the Congolese People's Liberation Army. Surprising soldiers with good infantry weaponry, who very solemnly provided us with a guard of honor.

A second meeting took place in the afternoon between some of the tribal chiefs.

Che held an odd conversation with one of the Congolese officers:

> Colonel Lambert . . . told me that they didn't worry about planes, as they had the dawa, a medicine that made them bulletproof:
>
> "They've hit me several times, and the bullets just dropped to the ground."
>
> I soon realized he was quite serious. This dawa is a potion of herbs and other magic ingredients; it is poured over the fighter, mystical signs are made, and, almost always, the forehead is marked with charcoal. The fighter is now protected from every type of enemy arms (although this also depends on the witch doctor's power), but he must not touch any object or woman that does not belong to him, or be afraid, or else he will be defenseless. The explanation in case of any failure is then simple: a dead man was scared, had stolen something, or had slept with someone else's woman. A wounded man was a scared man. And as dead men tell no tales, they can be found guilty of all three faults.
>
> The belief is so strong that no one goes into combat without performing the dawa ceremony. I always feared that this superstition would turn against us—that the Congolese would blame us for some failure in combat that left many dead; in conversation with commanders I sought several times to persuade them against it. It was impossible; dawa was a recognized article of faith. The most politically enlightened guerrillas say that it is a natural force; as dialectical materialists, they acknowledge the power of the dawa, whose secrets belong to the witch doctors of the jungle.

Che decided to let Chamaleso in on his true identity. He was flabbergasted. He kept on repeating "International scandal," and "Don't let anyone know, don't tell anyone." It really caused a huge fuss, and I feared the consequences. The Congolese leader wasted no time and, anxious over the responsibility, left that night for Tanzania to inform Kabila that Che Guevara was in the Congo. What was to be a long wait had just begun.

It was at the end of April that Che first proposed that the Congolese organize the training of about a hundred fighters, who would then go into combat a month later, when a second group would begin to train.

> **As always during that war, we received evasive answers.**
> **They asked me to put it in writing. I did, but no one knew**
> **where the paper ended up. We kept on insisting in going up**
> **and starting work at a base farther up the mountain. . . . But**
> **we couldn't go because the commander had not arrived; we**
> **had to wait because "We are in meetings."**

As the days went by Che became irritated, but there was no way out. He decided to go ahead and set up a permanent base on the mountain near Luluabourg. The Congolese, who had at first agreed, did not give the go-ahead. They were house-building for us, and that would take a few days— so they said. I patiently told them that we wanted to help.

Che held several conversations around that time with some of the local commanders, who painted a picture of tribal disputes and of infighting among chiefs. One of them, Olenga, promoted himself every time he took a town.

> **And so the days went by. I worked for a few days in the dis-**
> **pensary with Kumi and observed several alarming incidents.**
> **The sheer number of cases of venereal diseases!—mostly con-**
> **tracted in Kigoma.**
> **I was concerned that** [the prostitutes in Kigoma] **were ca-**
> **pable of infecting so many people. . . . Who paid these women?**
> **What were they paid with? How was the revolution's money**
> **being spent?**

And to make matters worse, the shipments of arms and vital military equipment were always arriving incomplete: field guns and machine guns lacked ammunition or spare parts; rifles came with the wrong ammunition and mines without detonators.

It was organized disaster. The soldiers were dumping the food and weapons supplies on the beach, mixing them up in a cheerful and fraternal chaos.

We had to do something to avoid complete idleness. Classes in French, Swahili, and general knowledge began. Our morale was still high, but the comrades began to murmur when they saw the days go by with no action. And the threat of fever, which afflicted almost all of us, was hanging over us.

All was quiet on the battlefronts, meanwhile; Che and Rafael Zerquera treated guerrillas whose bullet wounds were received in horseplay and bar fights rather than in combat.

Amid the chaos Che sang tangos out of tune and read books: *Das Kapital,* the selected works of José Martí, and Mehring's biography of Marx.

On May 8, eighteen Cubans, led by Santiago Terry and Congolese leader Leonard Mitoudidi, arrived at the Kibamba camp. Mitoudidi, a university activist and middle-ranking leader of the liberation movement, spoke good French and had been in charge of organizing arms supplies to guerrillas on the eastern front. Kabila sent word to Che, through Mitoudidi, that he should be discreet about his identity.

After a month of enforced idleness and participation in a nonexistent war, Che decided to move to Luluabourg. The new base was at the highest point in the mountain range, some three miles from Kibamba; the fog-shrouded peak lay at an altitude of almost 10,000 feet.

The Cubans' training had not fitted them for this effort; they had expected to be on the plains, and several fighters fainted from the altitude. Che himself had an asthma attack during the climb. They received an order to attack Albertville with two columns plus the Cubans, taking part [but the] order is absurd. We lack preparation and there are only thirty of us, ten of whom are ill or convalescing. However I explained the instructions to the men and told them to be prepared to go and fight, although I will try to change the plans, or at least delay them.

During a meeting, Che managed to convince Mitoudidi, who had returned and was acting as chief of staff on the front, that the proposal was very risky and that it was more important to reconnoiter the entire combat zone well and get to know the means at our disposal; the High Command did not have a clear picture of what was happening on each of the separate fronts.

Three expeditions set out to assess the situation. The fourth, in which Che was to take part, was postponed again and again, having to wait for gasoline, a boat, or the imminent arrival of Kabila, who never showed up. It was the first clear idea the Cubans had of the situation in which the revolutionary process stood in the Congo.

Dreke spent four days criss-crossing the Lulemba and Fizi zone, which bordered Lake Tanganyika; he discovered exaggerations: eighty men where there were supposed to be a thousand; "fronts" where there had been no fighting for some time. Apathy reigned. Eduardo Torres went to the troops at the Front de Force, and found that the rebels did not want to go near the Tshombe government's gendarmerie barracks.

Far worse, though, in Che's view, were the cadres: just hangers -on. They were never around when they were needed. The higher ranks spent their days drinking; they became incredibly drunk, not even bothering to hide the fact from the population. He concluded that a training camp needed to be set up, far away from tribal influence and revelry.

Freddy Ilanga was fourteen years old, spoke French, had a pistol, and was an officer. He recalled, "They told me, 'This is Che.' Just like that. 'Did you hear what I said?' and I was told to be quiet about it or I'd be shot. Who the fuck was this Che for them to threaten to shoot me, I said to myself." Several days later, Mitoudidi told Che that Freddy had been appointed his Swahili teacher. The classes began under a tree at the Luluabourg base. Freddy reported: "I didn't like him, because he had a penetrating look. He stared at you as if forcing you to say something."

The net day, Che happened to be repairing an anti-aircraft gun, and Freddy went off without giving him his lesson. He was discovered by Mitoudidi.

"What are you doing here?" Mitoudidi asked me,

I reported to Che: "Comrade Tatu, I have to be here with you, sleep where you do, eat where you do."

He asked me: **Does that bother you?**

"On the contrary."

You look bothered.

The next day I went with Tatu to climb the hill. The weather up there was balmy, and you had to go to a clearing, otherwise the sun didn't get through, and the ground was always damp. All I had was a bedspread.

In Freddy Ilanga's eyes, Che was not just a mysterious person, but a pretty strange one:

He wore an olive-drab uniform, not a yellow one, a black beret, a pistol, a canteen, boots like everyone else's, and no rank markings or cartridge belts. When he went out he took his gun, an M-2 with a couple of clips, his pockets always full of papers, binoculars and an altimeter. Every time he arrived he looked up our altitude. He carried a compass in a small case. At first he used to carry a backpack, until he had started having asthma attacks. One day when we were climbing, we took a break halfway up a hill and I saw him "click-clicking" this thing in his mouth, and I said. "Come on, you spray perfume in your mouth, Comrade?" And he said, **No, I suffer from an affliction called asthma.**

He always wrote at night, and that was when he smoked his pipe. He didn't get washed every day, oh no. It was quite a sight to see him go down to the river to bathe.

Che was quite taken by his teacher:

He was an intelligent boy, who had to initiate me into the mysteries of the language. We began very enthusiastically, with three hours of classes a day, but in fact, it was I who cut the teaching down to an hour a day, and not out of lack of time—which I had to spare, unfortunately—but out of a complete incompatibility between my character and languages. In that country, with its peculiarities, people speak Swahili along with their mother tongue, their own tribal dialect—so, to a certain extent, it turns out to be a conqueror's language or the symbol of a superior power.

Ilanga, though, ended up learning Spanish easily, beginning with the wide range of insults and raunchy expressions that the fighters taught him. Furthermore, Che soon gave him a Beretta.

During the first days at the Luluabourg base, about one month after arriving, Che paid tribute to the climate in the Congo by running a very high fever, although it didn't last long. However, he fell sick again a few days later. During that second bout of fever, one of the fighters had the ill-conceived idea of commenting, "If the commander stays that way he'll have to go." Hearing this, Che lost his temper and shouted: I'm not going, I'll die here first. And *it*'ll soon go, it's an illness, that's all.

Then came a message: "A Cuban minister's on his way up the hill with a pile of other Cubans."

> **That was so absurd that no one could believe it. Still, to get some exercise, I walked partway down the mountain and to my great surprise met Osmany Cienfuegos. After the hugs, the explanations: he had come for talks with the government of Tanzania and had asked permission to visit the comrades in the Congo. [He] brought me the saddest news of the whole war: telephone calls from Buenos Aires said that my mother was very ill, and the implication was that it was simply a question of time. Osmany had not been able to get any more calls.**

Celia de la Serna was probably in a coma by the time Osmany arrived in Luluabourg. She had been taken to the hospital on May 10, and became seriously ill on May 16, the day a very bad line to Havana was connected and Aleida was given word. She died on May 19 and the news was published in the Cuban press on May 21.

> **I had to spend a month in sad uncertainty, waiting for an outcome that I had guessed at, but with the hope that there had been some mistake in the news, until the confirmation of my mother's death reached me.**

The news came from the lake camp in a magazine received by Dr. Zerquera.

> I sent him a note begging him to come down because I wanted to talk to him. He turned up the next day and sat down in the hammock. I gave him the magazine, Bohemia. His reaction was to say that a friend had told him his mother was ill. He began to talk of his childhood. He wanted to drink tea; I asked him not to go. He didn't say either yes or no, but stayed anyway. We shared our meal and walked around singing tangos. He went away in the early morning.

Despite this stoic reaction, Celia's death must have come as a terrible blow. For so many years, the mother and her confidant had kept up a frail but permanent link, a relationship of love and complicity.

Celia never received the farewell letter Che had left for his parents in Havana. It was delivered to his father in October, when Che's absence was made public. And only after her death did Che receive his mother's reply to his news that he was leaving Cuba. The end of a long history of correspondence was full of lost messages and letters that crossed in the mail or failed to reach their destinations.

Another deeply upsetting piece of news also arrived at about that time: Che's friend Ahmed Ben Bella, president of Algeria, was overthrown in a military coup on June 15. His fall held up an arms shipment in Oran that was headed for the Congo operation.

Near the Luluabourg base were several villages where Rwandan migrants were living. Their greatest wealth consisted of their cows, with which the men bartered for wives and for life itself. This area would, in the course of the war, require us to partake of glorious beef—which even cured homesickness, almost. But the fact that the guerrilla groups supporting Lumumba were split along tribal lines and a fixed approach to war, as opposed to the guerrillas' tactic of constant movement, was driving Che to despair.

> The fighters were occupying what they call barriers over here. These barriers were in spots that were well chosen from a tactical point of view, on high hills which were not easily accessible. The men there, however, lived . . . trusting to the enemy's lack of activity, and depending on peasants for their supplies. The latter had to bring them their food and suffer frequent abuses and mistreatment. The People's Liberation Army was a parasitic army: it did no work or training, did not fight, and levied supplies and work from the population, and often very severely. [When it came to organizing the camp,] the Congolese fighters made the peasants transport their food and military equipment. [They were] bone idle when it came to fetching food from the base camp. If you gave people something to carry, they would say "Mimi apana motocari" ("I am not a truck") or "Mimi apana Cuban" ("I am not Cuban").

Mitoudidi, probably on Kabila's express orders, was waiting for the latter's arrival before ordering a sortie. Every day it was the same litany: Kabila didn't come today, but tomorrow without fail, or the day after. . . . If the order of the day was not changed, the Congolese revolution was irrevocably condemned to failure.

Mitoudidi meanwhile tried to impose some organization and bring the drinkers (90 to 95 percent of the men, according to Che) to heel. He froze the distribution of rifles, and demanded that heavy-gun operators gave him a demonstration before he handed ammunition over to them. But there was still too much left to do. And he was just one man. Even his assistants did not help him very much. . . . We confided a lot in each other.

With Freddy, Che began the ascent to the Luluabourg base on July 7, after taking his leave of Mitoudidi. Mitoudidi must have thought that Kabila would not cross over from Tanzania, being engaged in talks with Zhou Enlai in Dar es Salaam, so he set off shortly afterward with two Cubans in a boat to Ruandasi, four kilometers away, where he planned to attempt to reach the high command. A messenger caught Che and Freddy halfway up to tell them that Leonard Mitoudidi had drowned.

A strong wind was blowing and the waves were high; it would seem that he did fall in the water by accident—everything indicates that. From that moment on a strange chain of events took place, which I would not know whether to put down to stupidity, extraordinary superstition—the lake was home to all sorts of spirits—or something more serious. The fact is that Mitoudidi, who could swim a little, managed to get his boots off and stayed alive for ten to fifteen minutes, calling for help, according to several witnesses. People dived in to save him; one was his orderly, who also drowned. Commander François, who was traveling with him (I never knew whether he fell overboard at the same time or dived in to save Mitoudidi) also disappeared. They cut the motor when the accident happened, so the boat lost all its handling; then, when they started it again, some magic power seemed to prevent it from approaching Mitoudidi. Finally, while he continued to shout for help, the boat headed for the shore and the comrades saw him disappear shortly afterward. So a man lost his life in a stupid accident just as he was beginning to achieve some organization amid the terrible chaos at the Kibamba base. Mitoudidi was a young man, barely thirty.

Mitoudidi's death prompted Kabila to write another letter to Che in which he asked him to keep waiting. He sent him a new liaison officer, a certain Muteba, who vanished after a couple of conversations in which he suggested moving the base so as to exorcise Mitoudidi's ghost. So much for Che's suggestion that a couple of mixed Cuban-Angolan units be set up to train cadres and soldiers in combat and use the central base as a training camp.

The Front de Force front was manned by Rwandans rather than Congolese, which came as a surprise to the Cubans. The Rwandan exiles had a strong presence in the Congolese army. Their commander, Mudandi, turned up mid-June to tell Che that his proposals had been approved and they could begin ambushes.

He had studied in China and gave a very fair impression of being serious and firm, but in our first conversation he let slip a tale of a battle in which they had caused thirty-five enemy casualties. I asked him how many weapons they had taken as a result of those casualties, and he told me none, as they had attacked with bazookas and the weapons were blown to pieces. My diplomatic skills have never been abundant and I just told him that was a lie. He apologized, saying that he was not actually present during the battle, but his subordinates

had reported to him. . . . But as exaggeration was the norm in that region, saying outright that a lie is a lie is not the best way to set up fraternal friendship with any one.

Mudandi asked Che for fifty Cubans to attack Front de Force, also known as Force Bendera, where there was a hydroelectric plant on the banks of the Kimbi River. The place was not a minor objective; it was reckoned that a battalion of 500 to 700 men could be stationed there, including white mercenaries, and there was a small airfield. The guerrillas were given **the order to attack on June 25. I asked why that particular date and Mudandi could not answer. . . . He seemed to be a poor unfortunate entrusted with a task beyond his abilities . . . but [he] also [had] a large measure of duplicity.**

The plan drawn up by the Congolese leadership abroad was to attack Front de Force, trusting that surprise would bring success. This tactic risked the "foreign" forces—the Rwandans and Cubans—involved in the guerrilla war. Che had serious doubts about the plan: it was reported that the strong-hold had **trenches, natural defenses, and heavy artillery.** He also wished to take part personally in the operation and said so in a letter to Kabila: **I can assure you that as a man of action, I am impatient; this does not imply any criticism.** Kabila's reply came on June 17, confirming the attack but asking Che not to take part and to stay at the base.

39. Defeat at Front de Force

ON JUNE 19, 1965, CHE TOLD HIS COLUMN THE PLAN TO ATTACK FRONT de Force.

An analysis of the barracks was made the next day with the Rwandan officer Mudandi. Once again, Che objected to the operation and suggested attacking a less important barracks, but the Congolese refused. Che despaired at having to stay behind, but recognized his conflict: **What if I go and they throw us out, because this is their country?**

As if in ill omen, Che's hut burned down accidentally that day.

Among the thirty-nine Cubans, including three medics, who arrived at the camp on June 24, Che was pleasantly surprised to find men who had been his escorts in recent years, and before that his comrades in the Sierra Maestra and Escambray: Harry Villegas and Carlos Coello. They had been sent personally by Fidel, without Che's knowledge, to keep an eye on him and keep him safe.

The first news of the Front de Force attack came July 1, in a brief note from Dreke: "The attack began at five A.M. on June 29. Fatherland or death. Moja."

A second message arrived shortly after: "It's 7:30; things are going well, people are happy and behaving well." **But along with this note came alarming news of scores of dead, of Cubans dead and wounded, which made me think things were *not* going so well.**

No, everything was going badly. At five A.M., the Cubans had opened fire with a small cannon and a machine gun. The defenders were indeed surprised, but when they responded with mortar and machine-gun fire the Rwandans almost immediately began to desert. Dreke, in despair, said: "By then, only the Cubans were still firing. The Rwandans didn't know how to fire short bursts. They kept their trigger fingers down and soon used up all thirty rounds. We were fighting against a battalion of 500 to 600 men." **That was the tone of the operation. It began with spirit, but men had been lost in many positions before things got under way, and then people ran off pell-mell.**

Meanwhile, a second group, commanded by Pichardo, had entered the combat in an ill-chosen spot; they were discovered at the moment they were crossing the highway to take up positions. Four Cubans died, along with fourteen Rwandans. Before the combat began, all the fighters had been asked to leave behind any documents that could be used to identify them, but Pichardo's group went into combat with their rucksacks, so the government forces discovered a diary indicating that Cubans participated in the attack. One of the dead men was even wearing underwear with a label reading "Made in Cuba."

Dreke led an orderly retreat. Years later he would say: "We Cubans upset the balance of armed peace achieved by the Congolese. They were armed, but at home with their wives and children. They were not fighting." At the time, Dreke could not have had any idea of the terrible significance that result of the Cuban presence could have.

As the fighting took place at Front de Force, another Cuban-led column fought at Katenga with the same outcome, or worse.

> Of 160 men, sixty had deserted before the fighting began and many others did not fire so much as a shot. At the agreed time, the Congolese opened fire on the barracks—shooting into the air most of the time, because most of them closed their eyes and squeezed the triggers of their automatic rifles until the ammunition ran out. The enemy responded with accurate .60 mortar fire, which caused several casualties and an almost immediate disorderly retreat.

The outcome of the two engagements was greatly demoralizing for the native forces,

> but there was great dejection among the Cubans, too. Every one of our fighters had the sad experience of seeing troops going into battle break up the moment the fight began, dumping their priceless weapons anywhere so as to escape faster. They also saw the lack of comradeship among the fighters. The wounded were abandoned to their fate; terror took hold of the soldiers and . . . they dispersed without waiting for orders of any sort.
>
> In the days following the attack, a large number of soldiers deserted or asked to leave. Mundandi wrote me a long letter, full of heroic deeds as usual, in which he lamented the loss of his brother and said he had died after wiping out a truckload of soldiers. . . . He also mourned the loss of several of his best cadres and complained that the high command was in Kigoma while men were fighting and being sacrificed in the Congo. In passing he said that two-thirds of the enemy troops had been wiped out. . . . These letters were only the beginning of the disintegration that would eventually destroy the entire Liberation Army and drag the Cuban troops in its wake.

The fundamental problem Che now faced was to halt the dissolution of the defeated column and to improve the behavior of the Rwandan and Congolese guerrillas.

Kabila finally arrived, with an entourage that included his chief of staff, his foreign-affairs minister, and several mixed-race women from Guinea. He turned out to be cordial but aloof. Che asked that Kabila tell the Tanzanian government of the Cuban presence. He suggested instead a tour of the fronts, beginning with Kabimba; they could leave that same night. Finally, even the tour was postponed, and postponed again. Around July 11, five days after

Kabila arrived, he sent for me to tell me that he was leaving that night for Kigoma.

Che asked Kabila where he was headed, to the border with Tanzania or to Dar. Kabila replied that he would return the next day.

> **When the news of Kabila's departure broke, hearts sank among Cubans and Congolese alike. Changa, our brave "admiral" from the lake, was furious, and said: "Why did this man bring so many bottles of whisky, if he was only going to be here five days?"** . . .
>
> **The next day, the mood of the base, which had improved thanks to Kabila's presence and drive, began to darken. The soldiers in charge of the trenches said they were not going to work that day as the chief had gone away.**

Fortunately, Martínez Tamayo led twenty-five Cubans and twenty-six Rwandans in an ambush on a Congo Army truck on July 22. (Another fifty-seven men, claiming they were sick, were not available to fight.)

Zacharias, the Rwandan Commander, proposed cutting two fingers off everyone who had fired by accident. Martínez Tamayo tactfully prevented this. One Cuban who tried to stop a Rwandan from running got a bite in the hand for his trouble.

> **The farcical nature of the ambush did not stop there. There was beer and whisky in the truck. Martínez Tamayo tried to get the foodstuffs carried away and the rest destroyed, but it was impossible. All the Rwandan fighters were drunk inside a few hours, while the Cubans, who were forbidden to drink, looked on. The Cubans held a meeting and decided to return to base. Zacharias killed a peasant on his way back.**

Frankly depressed, Che later wrote: Five years is a very optimistic estimate for bringing the Congolese revolution to a successful conclusion if it is all to be based on developing these armed groups.

Work on fortifications at the lake stopped once Kabila left; several Congolese had deserted, and fighting broke out due to the substitute chiefs' lack of authority. In Che's words, the base had fallen into chaos. On one occasion there was a shameful episode in which a chief ran to take refuge in the Cuban hut: a soldier had asked for rice, then chased him with gun in hand when he refused to give him any. Che asked himself whether the presence of the Cuban column had been positive, and answered that it had, as the difficulties arose from the huge differences between them and the Congolese. Those would have to be turned to some advantage. He reiterated:

> **Our mission is to help win the war. By our example, [we must] show the differences, but without making the cadres hate**

us. . . . revolutionary comradeship at the grassroots level . . . We generally have more food and clothing than the comrades here, and must share it as much as possible, doing so selectively with those comrades who show their revolutionary mettle.

The next day, August 18, Che could take no more and left for Front de Force at dawn. At last, after four months of forced confinement, after a seemingly endless walk, across the plateau . . . I felt a little like an outlaw on the run but was determined not to return to the base for a long time.

I had no sooner arrived at Front de Force and laid down on the ground to enjoy my overwhelming fatigue when the comrades were complaining to me about the attitude of the Rwandans, especially Captain Zacharias, who used physical punishment on his men and who was doubtless capable of murdering anyone. Nonetheless, the Rwandans' welcome was cordial.

Che saw the Force power station at dawn. His meeting with the ambush party was a mixture of celebration and sorrow. Víctor Dreke recalled, "The comrades were overjoyed to see him arrive, with his beard, olive-drab uniform, .25 caliber Soviet pistol, M1 rifle, and beret. . . . He was full of ideas, in good health, only a little tired. We were greatly concerned over the reaction of the Congolese. . . . They had no idea who Che was. They only knew him as Ramón the medic, as Tatu-muganga, as they call doctors." **The peasants were quite friendly to us, and I felt obliged to return to my former profession of medicine, which was simplified in the circumstances to dispensing antimalarial tablets and giving penicillin injections for their common disease, gonorrhea.**
Villegas added,

A legend developed in short order. Wherever we went, we found we were known because of Dr. Tatu, a white medic. Although we had other medics, people came to Dr. Tatu to be treated. Che went back to doing what he did in the Sierra Maestra. That was how he quickly won the natives over.

40

An Omnipresent Ghost

CHE'S DISAPPEARANCE FROM CUBAN PUBLIC LIFE GAVE RISE TO A FLOOD of disinformation, ranging from speculative fantasies by unemployed journalists to smoke screens thrown up by the Cuban secret services, or by the CIA itself trying to flush him out. Absurdity played a prominent part in this dance of stories.

Originally the Cuban government had given the matter minimal attention; Che could be seen cutting cane in documentaries shown in Havana movie houses in April 1965. José Manuel Manresa confessed: "For a month and a half I was warding off all comers with 'Che's gone to cut cane.' " But the charade could not be kept up for long.

Rumors published in the Brazilian press years afterward located Che in mid-1965 in Colombia, Peru, Chile, Argentina, Brazil, Uruguay, and even a psychiatric clinic in Mexico City. Six news items in various newspapers around the world in 1965 said he had met with a violent death. Perhaps the most surprising item had him dead and buried in the basement of a factory in Las Vegas. There was no clear indication of how he had got there, who had killed him, or what the factory made.

According to a Cuban source, CIA-controlled radio stations said in their broadcasts to Asia that Che had been murdered by Fidel because of his pro-Chinese leanings, and in their Radio Free Europe broadcasts to Eastern Europe that he had been killed for his pro-Soviet leanings. There was even a leaflet circulated showing a photograph of Che's father carrying a banner asking Fidel to give back his son's body. Guevara Senior tried to publish a denial, but that did not make the news.

Around June 1965, while Che was in the Congo, a series of strange news items, known as "Memorandum R," made the rounds of security agencies close to the CIA and were leaked to the mass media. The items were said to have been written by a secretary with the initial "R," who worked at the Soviet Embassy in Havana, and to be based on supposedly reliable sources reporting that Che was locked away in the Calixto García Hospital in Havana, suffering from exhaustion and mental derangement. While afflicted by fevers whose origin was unknown, Che was said to see Camilo's ghost exhorting him to carry on the revolution in other parts of the world. The "memorandum" said Che was suffering from an attack of graphorrhea and wrote Fidel Castro delirious letters in which he proposed, among other things, to go to Zanzibar to work with the Chinese.

It was during those months that the French novelist and conservative journalist Jean Larteguy, writing in *Paris Match,* volunteered the theory that Che's disappearance was due to Fidel having murdered him.

Nonetheless, it seemed that Che was alive after all, because an Italian journalist had meanwhile interviewed him in Peru, although a CIA source, asked if Che had gone underground, replied, "Yes, six feet under." It would appear that there was a decided tendency throughout the disinformation operation to make the public believe that Fidel "got rid of" Che.

Newsweek carried a long series of rumors in its June 28 edition: he had committed suicide after being fired from the Industry Ministry; he was running guerrilla campaigns in Vietnam or Santo Domingo. One story said he had defected and sold Cuban secrets to the U.S. for $10 million. Fidel himself, intentionally or otherwise, gave rise to speculation with his answer to a journalist's question:

"When will the people know about Che?"

"Whenever Commander Guevara wishes."

When a popular uprising took place in the Dominican Republic, a story came out of Miami putting Che in that country. With remarkable precision it named names, dates, and places. He was supposed to have landed near Santo Domingo from a fishing boat out of Santiago de Cuba; the same source insisted he had been seen fighting on the streets of Santo Domingo and had died in an engagement there. When the U.S. Marines invaded the country, a U.S. radio station said that a Cuban minisubmarine with a crew of two, one of whom was Che, had landed on the island. It was also said that Cuban secret agents on a disinformation mission had hidden a report in the office of Antonio Imbert Barreras, one of the pro-U.S. military triumvirate in the Dominican Republic. According to the report, Che had died in a street in Ciudad Nueva while fighting under Camaño during the Dominican uprising.

Che's ghost was haunting the globe.

Intelligence reports exchanged among President Lyndon Johnson's advisers were headed with notes to the effect that they had another contribution to make to the growing story of the whereabouts of Che Guevara. The CIA itself was caught up in the version it attempted to spread—that a disagreement with Fidel had led to Che's ruin, and as a consequence he had been imprisoned or executed in Cuba. This was according to Victor Marchetti, a writer on CIA affairs, who simultaneously kept churning out new stories about Che's madness, and spreading rumors that he was in Latin America or waiting to go there.

Some of the Company's analysts began to gather information about the Cuban presence in the Congo, and one even suggested that Che might be there, but that notion was ruled out.

The news agency Agence France Presse transmitted the rumor that shots had been fired in an argument between Fidel and Che, and the latter had died. That story was seconded by a Trotskyist newspaper. The Peruvian *La Prensa* set the ball rolling on the rumor that Che had been eliminated by the Soviet Union for his pro-Chinese tendencies.

Under pressure from these rumors and a thousand more, on October 3 Fidel took to the podium during a public ceremony to form the Central Committee of what was to be the Cuban Communist Party. He held five sheets in his hand and a typewritten transcription. There was great tension in the theater. He began his speech:

> Someone on our Central Committee is missing, someone who has a very high degree of merit, of virtue. . . . [Because he has been missing] the enemy has been able to come up with a thousand guesses, has tried to con-

fuse people and sow discord and doubt. But since it was necessary to wait, we have patiently waited.

Fidel then began to read the farewell letter that Che had given him in April. Applause broke out at the end of the letter, Fidel tried to resume his speech, but the applause went on and on, as though it would never stop.

Fidel acknowledged years later that publishing Che's farewell letter "was an unavoidable political necessity."

41

The Pessimistic Optimist

EMILIO ARAGONÉS AND OSCAR FERNÁNDEZ MELL WERE IN THE CONGO because Fidel had given way to their requests to go as volunteers after the defeat at Front de Force and Che's letter describing the situation there.

Che feared at first that they had come to ask him to return to Cuba or to put pressure on him to leave the fighting. **I just couldn't think why the Party's organization secretary would leave his post to come to the Congo.** When he realized Aragonés and Fernández Mell were there as volunteers, he quickly enrolled them.

Aragonés was the 120th Cuban to arrive in the Congo. There were 107 fighters and four medics at that time, plus casualties; Changa, who was at Lake Tanganyika; and two who had returned to Cuba. **It could have been the core of a larger army, had conditions been otherwise.**

Reinforcements arrived: a group of Congolese students trained in China and Bulgaria. But they would be of no use in the fighting. The French-speaking sons of chieftains, they were versed in theory, did not want to go to the hills, had been educated with colonialist ideas, and brought with them the negative aspects of European culture. **They came back [from training] with a veneer of Marxism, full of their importance as "cadres" and frank eagerness to give orders—all of which translated into lack of discipline and even elitist conspiracies.**

With these forces, Che planned to reorganize the war.

Militarily, the guerrilla contingent was immobilized. While fruitless engagements continued, Che took the opportunity for widespread social action in the zone by working as a doctor and distributing vegetable seeds to the villages. He later decided to go to Lulemba to propose setting up more ambushes with Lambert and to look into the possibility of attacking the town, as it was defended by only fifty-three men, according to a captured payroll.

They reached the front line, a string of flea-infested huts by the side of the road, with no trenches or shelters; there were a couple of anti-aircraft guns and bazookas. **Trenches always were a headache as, out of some superstitious fear, the Congolese soldiers were reluctant to get into holes they had dug themselves and made no solid defenses for resisting attacks.** They were told Lambert was in Fizi with a sick daughter. He had not been in the camp for a month and a half, for one reason or another.

Che's reconnaissance expedition took him to the Fizi area, where

> **the important thing now was to organize the "show." General Maulana put on his combat gear, which consisted of a motorcycle helmet with a leopardskin on top and made him look quite ridiculous. Coello called him "The Cosmonaut." . . . A military parade was organized, which culminated in a speech by General Maulana. The ridiculous reached Chaplinesque proportions then; I felt like I was seeing a bad comic movie, boring and lacking substance, while the chiefs shouted,**

stamped the floor, and made about-turns. . . . That same night we returned to Fizi.

The enemy, who had thus far been quiescent, now began to make his presence felt. The bombing and machine-gunning of peasant villages were stepped up, along with the distribution, from planes, of leaflets in which the government of President Mobutu Sese Seko offered the peasants rewards for turning in the Cuban advisers and a fair deal for those who laid down their arms. Two hundred million dollars in U.S. aid for the government arrived, as did CIA advisers. These included Americans, Cubans who had fought at the Bay of Pigs, and Rhodesian and South African soldiers. The Agency used to say, "We brought our own animals."

A new Cuban mission arrived, led by the minister of health, José Ramón Machado Ventura. He gave Che a view of what was happening in the outside world.

> **The people from the Revolutionary Council had not been truthful—I suppose partly because that always happens in such cases, and partly because they had no knowledge at all of what was actually going on. . . . The fact is that they painted an idyllic picture, with military formations everywhere, forces in the jungle and continuous fighting . . .**

A key meeting with the Congolese leaders was finally held on October 5 on a hillside between Fizi and Baraka. Che did not go easy on them.

Having had direct experience with the war in the Congo, Aragonés and Fernández Mell argued with Che. Fernández Mell said: "We told him that in Cuba there had been a population against Batista but here, there were no people against anything." Aragonés added, "We didn't understand what the hell he was doing there."

There were also doubts in the rest of the Cuban guerrilla column; Che confronted them and countered the rumor that

> **the Cubans were in the Congo because Fidel was unaware of the real situation. . . . I could not demand their confidence in my leadership, but as a revolutionary I could demand that they respect my honesty. . . . I was not going to sacrifice anyone for my personal honor. If it was true that I had not communicated to Havana the opinion that all was lost, it was because I did not share it.**

The fact is, only personal loyalty to Che kept the group going. The romantic times had gone, when I could threaten insubordinates with sending them back to Cuba. If I did that now, I'd be lucky to be left with half the troops.

Che wrote a Fidel long letter:

> I received your letter, which gave me mixed feelings, as in the name of proletarian internationalism we are committing errors that may be very costly. Furthermore, I am personally worried that it may be thought I am suffering from the terrible ailment of unjustified pessimism, whether because of my lack of seriousness in writing or because you don't quite understand. . . . I will just tell you that here, according to those close to me, I have lost my reputation for being objective, by keeping up a groundless optimism when faced with the existing situation. I can assure you that if it were not for me, this beautiful dream would have collapsed totally in the midst of a general catastrophe.

He made it clear he needed cadres, not men—there are plenty of armed men, but we lack soldiers—and warned Fidel very seriously of the Congolese leaders' irresponsibility and unwillingness to fight, their lack of truthfulness, their distance from the real fighting, and the generally disastrous situation in the Congo. He warned that no money should be handed over to the Congolese, as it would not serve the struggle. We alone cannot liberate a country that does not want to fight; we have to create that fighting spirit and look for soldiers with Diogenes' lantern and the patience of Job, a task that becomes even more difficult the more these people fart around with everything they come across.

Strangely enough, the usually overoptimistic Che appeared a pessimist in Fidel's eyes.

In October, Prime Minister Moïse Tshombe fell victim to a military coup. The propaganda campaign offering peace to the rebels was stepped up. Joseph Kasavubu was named president; he met African heads of state several days later in Accra, the capital of Ghana, and made overtures to them to break the anticolonial front. He announced a reconciliation with the Brazzaville government in the Congo. The political trap to isolate the remains of Patrice Lumumba's followers, and with them Che's guerrillas, was laid.

Meeting with his fellow Cubans, Che

> asked who believed that victory was possible and only Dreke and Martínez Tamayo raised their hands. . . . I closed the meeting with the conviction that very few people shared my dream of making an army that would bring triumph to Congolese arms, although I was reasonably sure there were men prepared to sacrifice themselves even though they felt their sacrifice was useless.

The Congolese chiefs were campaigning against the Cubans, saying they were clowns. A peasant defended them: He told anyone who would listen that it was a disgrace to compare us with the Belgians. . . . He had never before seen a white man eating the same share of food in his mess tin as the rest of the fighters. The chiefs made fun of the Congolese in the Cuban group, because the foreigners made them work. There was also a rumor that mines that had wounded their men had been laid by the Cubans.

The fact, as despicable as it was, was that we had given the chiefs a really raw deal, [complaining of] their ignorance, their superstition, feeding their inferiority complex. We had hurt their sensibilities, maybe, by the painful fact that a white man was reproaching them, just as in the bad old days.

At that time, Congolese radio repeatedly reported the death of Che Guevara in the Congo. Had there been a leak? Was the report groundless propaganda? In any case, the news did not even make the international press.

Che went down to Lake Tanganyika on November 1. He was followed by Captain Sánchez Bartheley, a.k.a. Lawton, who brought a worrisome message for Che from Dar es Salaam. The Tanzanian government had summoned Cuban ambassador Pablo Rivalta and informed him that

> in view of the decision by African states regarding nonintervention in the internal affairs of other countries, they themselves, as well as the other governments that had so far been giving support to the Congolese Liberation Movement, would have to change the form of that support. That, in consequence, they were asking us to withdraw the forces we had sent as our contribution to that policy. That they acknowledged we had given more than many African states and that for now we would say nothing of our plans to the Congolese Liberation Movement until such time as we had withdrawn, that the president himself would call those leaders and tell them of the decision made by those African states. I have sent a report on the subject to Havana. We await your opinion.

That was the coup de grâce for a dying revolution. Due to the nature of the information, I said nothing to the Congolese comrades, and waited to see what would happen over the next few days. The reply from Havana, a cable from Fidel to Rivalta in Dar es Salaam, was retransmitted to the Congo shortly after:

> We must do everything except the absurd. If in Che's opinion our presence has become unjustifiable and useless, then we must think of withdrawal. You must act according to the objective situation and the spirit of our men. If you feel we must stay, we will try to send as many human and material resources as we can. We fear you will mistakenly assume that our attitude is defeatist or pessimist. If you decide to leave, Che may maintain current status quo, returning here or staying elsewhere. Will support any decision. Avoid risking our men's lives.

Another message arrived from Fidel via Dar es Salaam on November 4, saying that the government's mercenaries had yet to withdraw from the Congo. It concluded: "In this case it would mean betrayal to withdraw our revolutionary support to the Congolese, unless they request it or abandon the struggle." The lines of communication were crossed, but the messages coincided. Che sent a letter to Dar es Salaam for retransmission to Fidel, in which, after giving information on the state of the war, he wrote:

> **There was a time when a mass desertion by all the Congolese chiefs was spoken of. I had made the decision to stay behind, in that event, with about twenty hand-picked men (you don't get blood out of a stone), send the rest elsewhere, and continue to fight until all possibilities were exhausted; in that case I would decide whether to go to another front by land or avail myself of the sacred right to asylum. In view of the latest news my reaction was the same as Fidel's: we cannot leave. Furthermore, not a single Cuban should leave under the circumstances proposed. The Tanzanian leadership should be seriously spoken to about finalizing details.**
>
> **These are my propositions: that a high-level Cuban delegation, or Aragonés from here, or both, visit Tanzania. The proposal should be more or less this: Cuba offered support subject to approval by Tanzania; the latter accepted, and we came up with that support, with no conditions or time limits. We understand Tanzania's difficulties today, but do not agree to their proposals. Cuba does not renege on its promises and cannot flee shamefully, leaving brothers at the mercy of the mercenaries. We would abandon the struggle only if the Congolese themselves asked us to for some good reason or in overwhelming circumstances, but we will fight to prevent that.**

The military situation at the beginning of November seemed reasonably stable, but the rebel forces' disintegration proceeded swiftly. Rumors were everywhere that South African and Belgian mercenaries and government troops, with the support of the former Katanga gendarmerie, would push toward Lake Tanganyika. The government air force was bombing. Trenches had been dug and several ambushes set up—but again, deterioration was well advanced. Tensions between Cubans and Congolese troops had reached the breaking point at the Aly front. Martínez Tamayo had great trouble stopping the remaining Congolese from deserting, and demoralization was beginning to affect the Cubans who were talking of withdrawal.

The front's collapse was inevitable. The Rwandans were abandoning the Front de Force zone and dragging the Cubans behind them. At least they were departing in an orderly fashion, and regrouping with weapons in the Nganja zone. Mudandi sent this note to Che:

I am incapable of holding the position and ensuring its defense. . . . I beg you to understand me: I have decided to retreat; I am not abandoning the Cuban comrades. . . . I cannot expose all the Rwandan comrades to annihilation. . . . I have sought to support this revolution to be able to fight another in our country. If the Congolese will not fight, I prefer to die on our soil.

Faced with this situation, Che sent a telegram to Cuba: **Enemy pressure up and tentatively we are still blockading the lake. Urgent large amounts Congolese money in case cut off. Offensive sustained and advancing. Must move fast. Preparing to defend base.** The Cubans decided to evacuate women and children to Kigoma, and agreed to set up a secret base in Tanzania to be used in case they were cut off.

On the night of November 17, Che ordered a second withdrawal toward the inner circle of defense. Along with the troops, Congolese soldiers and compesinos with their women and children withdrew.

42. The Closing Days of That November

O N November 18, 1965, Chamaleso, speaking for the Congolese and their chief at the front, Ildefonse Masengo, said they were in favor of abandoning the struggle.

Rumors that the Congolese had decided to retreat multiplied in the camp, and chaos took hold. Che didn't give up. He spoke with his most trusted men and suggested the possibility of organizing an evacuation and then crossing the country with a small guerrilla band to link up with rebel forces led by Pierre Mulele in the north. This, however, would have involved a walk of over 600 miles through unknown territory, crossing virgin jungle, without guides and without even knowing what state Mulele was in, as they'd never been in contact with those forces.

Che insisted on staying in the Congo with a hard core of fighters. He explained months later:

> **My intention was to evacuate the sick, the weak, and all those not steady on their feet, and stay behind with a small group to continue the fight. With an eye to this objective I carried out a little test . . . which brought discouraging results among the comrade fighters: almost no one was prepared to keep on fighting. So it was left to me to decide.**

The next day, November 19, part of the Congolese contingent began to retreat toward Fizi. Che, out of contact with the launch that had left for Tanzania before the evacuation order was given, decided to order the camp and documents to be burned. But before any such order was given, someone set fire to the powder kegs.

> **While I waited for the stragglers, we watched the fireworks from the first hill on the Jungo road as the valuable powder charges burned and exploded. There were a lot of stragglers, and they seemed to have an age-old weariness and an alarming lack of vitality. There were practically no Congolese left in the groups.**

Toward three o'clock they made contact with Captain Lawton at the lakeside base in Tanzania, asking him to return to the Congo because there was to be an evacuation.

> **The expressions of all the comrades present changed when they heard the word "understood" from the lake, as if a magic wand had been waved in their faces. . . .**
>
> **All the chiefs were withdrawing; the peasants were more and more hostile toward us. But the idea of completely evacuating and departing the way we came, leaving behind defenseless peasants and men who were armed but also defenseless, given their meager fighting skills, defeated and feeling betrayed, hurt me deeply.**

**For me, staying in the Congo was not a sacrifice, and nei-
ther was the one or five years with which I had threatened my
people; it was part of the idea of a struggle I had completely
worked out in my head.**

**In fact, the idea of staying lingered until the dead of night;
perhaps I never made a decision, but became just another
fugitive.**

A message from Cuba arrived, telling Che it was madness to try to link up
with Mulele in the north of the Congo and that he must "seek any way possible to get out of there."

Víctor Dreke:

> The evacuation had to be effected amid a large number of Congolese
> guerrillas and civilians who had gathered there, fleeing the advancing
> Belgians, who were mopping up. It was an awesome spectacle, because
> among that whole crowd there were wounded and sick people, women,
> children, old people. We needed a few boats to get everybody out, but
> those boats didn't exist.

That evening, Che made another attempt to stay; he insisted on waiting
for a group of Cubans who had yet to regroup and were probably lost. That
caused a fierce clash among the Cuban commanders. Emilio Aragonés, whose
hat Che knocked off his head, during their argument, said that if dying was
the issue, he would be glad to sit beside Che on the pier after the others had
been evacuated, to argue about what the hell idealism really was. Che finally
gave in.

**For me the situation was decisive. Two men would be aban-
doned if they did not arrive within a few hours. . . . My troops
were a hodgepodge from which, I figured, up to twenty men
would follow me, and they'd have misgivings at that point.
And afterward, what would I do?**

**Our retreat was a flight, pure and simple. Worse, we were
accomplices in the deceit with which we left the people on
land. On the other hand, who was I now? I got the impression
that, after my farewell letter to Fidel, the comrades began to
see me as a man from other climes, like someone removed
from everyday problems in Cuba, and I did not feel like demanding the ultimate sacrifice of staying. I spent the last
hours that way, alone and perplexed.**

Toward two A.M., three of Lawton's launches appeared, preceded by flares
and bombing. The first thing they did was set up a gun in one of them.

**The evacuation was organized. The sick climbed aboard, then
all of Masengo's high command—forty men picked by him—
then all the Cubans. Then there began a painful, plaintive,**

and inglorious spectacle. I had to refuse men who begged to be taken. There wasn't a shred of grandeur in that retreat, nor a sign of rebellion.

Some eight Rwandans, who had stayed with the group to the end, boarded the launches. Che wanted to be the last to board but the Cuban officers, thinking it was a ploy to stay behind, refused to go aboard if he did not. He went in the first launch with José María Martínez Tamayo, Aragonés, and Fernández Mell.

Toward six in the morning, as the first houses in Kigoma became visible, Che spoke to the Cubans from his boat. Dreke reported that he said:

Comrades, the time has come to split up, for reasons you all know. I will not go ashore with you; we have to avoid any type of provocation. This battle we have waged has been a great experience. I hope that despite all the difficulties we have been through, if someday Fidel calls on you to go on another mission of this kind, some of you will answer, "Present." I also hope that if you're home by the twenty-fourth, when you're eating the suckling pig you so look forward to, you'll remember this humble people and the comrades we have left behind in the Congo. Maybe we'll meet again in Cuba, or some other part of the world.

A small launch approached the boats. Che boarded it, and with him Martínez Tamayo, Harry Villegas, and Carlos Coello; then he took his leave.

Dar es Salaam

VÍCTOR DREKE, WHO HAD BEEN SECOND-IN-COMMAND OF THE CUBAN expedition to the Congo, remembered Che's words as he went off at Lake Tanganyika: "Be seeing you, Moja. It was awful; people cried. You couldn't tell if they were happy or sad. I never saw Che again."

The Cuban soldiers recovered when they reached Kigoma. Erasmo Videaux recalled: "We shaved our heads, got rid of the filth. We were almost naked and barefoot. We disinfected ourselves—we were all full of lice. The fighters were happy to find medicine there. Morale just then was good. We felt we had put up a fight, that we weren't the guilty ones."

They were then taken to Dar es Salaam, from where they would leave in groups for Havana. A small group led by Oscar Fernández Mell stayed in Kigoma to try and find the three Cubans who had stayed in the Congo. (They succeeded two months later.)

Meanwhile, Ambassador Pablo Rivalta received orders to clear the top floor at the Cuban embassy in Dar es Salaam, to which only he and the cipher clerk had access. This was to be a refuge for Che, longhaired and defeated, thin from hunger and dysentery. His three right-hand men were with him: Harry Villegas, Carlos Coello, and Captain José María Martínez Tamayo.

It was food and literature that dragged Che out of his initial apathy and anguish. Several days after moving in, he began dictating notes, based on the diaries he had kept in the Congo, to the embassy cipher clerk, a man named Colman. The pace picked up little by little, and he wrote almost nonstop for three weeks.

The manuscript taking shape would be called "Reminiscences from the Revolutionary War (The Congo)." The dedication read "to Baasa and his fallen comrades, in an attempt to find some sense in the sacrifice." In the prologue, he wrote:

> This is a story of failure . . . but it is put into perspective by observations and criticism. I feel that, if the story has any value, it is in portraying experiences that may be of use to other revolutionary movements. Victory is a great source of positive experience, but defeat is all the more so, in my opinion—particularly in this case, when the actors and informants are foreigners who go to risk their lives in unknown territory, whose language is not their own, linked only by proletarian internationalism and introducing a modern war of liberation being waged by countries with a degree of international solidarity not practical since the civil war in Spain.

In that same prologue, Che said that he intended

> these notes [to] . . . be published a long time after they were dictated, when maybe the author [will] no longer be asked to answer for what is said here. Time will tell, and if the appearance of these remarks has any importance, the editors will be able to make the corrections they deem necessary, ap-

pealing to the relevant sources in order to clarify events or
opinions in the light of elapsed time.

Che was not to know that the manuscript would not be published for almost
thirty years, and even then not in its entirety.

He honed his capacity for self-criticism, as if the book were an exercise in
psychoanalysis, laying his feelings bare and judging himself more harshly than
in his Cuban *Reminiscences*. And in that self-criticism, he left the best portrait
of his personality that I have found:

It behooves me to make the most difficult analysis, that of my
personal actions. In extending my self-criticism as much as I
have been able, I came to the following conclusions: in my relations with the commanders of the revolution, I was hampered by the somewhat unusual way I entered the Congo and
was not capable of overcoming that obstacle. I was inconsistent in my reactions; I long maintained an attitude that could
be described as overly complacent. At times I was guilty of
very abrasive and hurtful outbursts, maybe due [to] some in-
nate characteristic of mine. The only people I doubtless maintained correct relations with were the peasants, as I am more
used to speaking in political language, giving direct explanations, and setting an example, and in those respects I think I
was successful. I did not learn Swahili quickly enough or well
enough. This defect was attributable above all to my knowing
French, which allowed me to communicate with the chiefs but
kept me away from the grassroots. I lacked the will to make
the required effort.

As for contact with my men, I think I made enough sacrifices so that no one could blame me for anything on personal
or physical grounds, but my two main weaknesses were allowed me in the Congo: tobacco, which I rarely lacked, and
reading, which was always abundant. The inconvenience of
having a pair of broken boots or no change of clothes, or eating the same rations as the troops, represents no sacrifice for
me. Above all, the fact that I withdrew to read set me apart
from the comrades, even without taking into account traits of
mine that make close relations difficult. I was harsh, but not
excessively, I think, not unfair. I used disciplinary methods
not practiced in a regular army, such as withdrawing food. It's
the only effective way I know in a guerrilla campaign. I tried
moral coercion at first, and failed. I tried to make my troops
have the same view of the situation as my own, and failed. . . .

I did not rouse myself to demand the maximum sacrifice at the
decisive moment. This was because of an internal psychological block. It would have been easy for me to stay in the
Congo. From the point of view of a fighter's amour-propre, it
was the thing to do. . . . When I thought about the decision, the

fact that I knew how easy it was for me to make the sacrifice weighed against me. I feel I ought to have overcome the stumbling block of that self-criticism inside me and imposed the final move on a few determined fighters. Only a few, but we should have stayed.

Finally, my farewell letter to Fidel weighed heavily in my relations with my staff. I could see that full well, although my perception is totally subjective. The letter made the comrades see me—as they had many years ago, when I began in the Sierra Maestra—as a foreigner among Cubans. Back then I had arrived among them, now I was leaving. There were things we no longer had in common, certain common longings that I had tacitly and explicitly renounced and that are most sacred for each man individually: his family, his home, his background. The letter that led to so much praise within and without Cuba cut me off from the fighters.

These psychological musings may seem uncalled-for in an analysis of a struggle on an almost continental scale. I still hold to my concept of a hardcore leader—I was the chief of a group of Cubans, no more than a company, and my task was to be their real chief, to lead them to the victory that would produce a genuine people's army. But my particular situation turned me at the same time into a soldier, a representative of a foreign power, an instructor of Cubans and Congolese, a high-flying political strategist in an unknown setting. And also into a Cato the Censor, repetitive and hard-hitting, in my relations with the revolutionary chiefs. By pulling so many strings I wound a Gordian knot I did not have the resolve to cut. Had I been a genuine soldier I would have been able to have more influence on the other aspects of my complex relations. I have told you about those moments of crisis when the leader, I myself, took care of my own safety—how, in extreme danger, I wasn't able to go beyond considerations of self.

This was the analysis of a man taking stock of himself for the next venture, of someone trying to stretch himself and find out how and when he broke, all the while expecting to dice with death the next time. Che was no longer utterly defeated. He had converted defeat into partial defeat; he could outlive his own at times exaggerated guilt complexes, his own brutal demands on himself.

He gave another explicit message in the prologue:

I have learned in the Congo. There were errors I will not commit again; maybe others will be repeated and I will commit new ones. I have come through with more faith than ever in guerrilla warfare, but we have failed. My responsibility is great. I will not forget the defeat or its hard-earned lessons.

With Rivalta and Fernández Mell, he went over the events. According to both men, after the first postmortem Che was convinced that in the short term the conditions were not conducive to resuming the war and that it would need to be done otherwise, if the struggle were to begin again. He began to recover physically. Although Che was tight-lipped and did not easily reveal his true moods, his small jokes and gestures told his men that he was still depressed. They went about bewildered and uneasy.

Che edited his typed manuscript and gave a copy to Fernández Mell at one of their meetings in Dar es Salaam, to pass on to Fidel and Aleida in Cuba.

Che was doubtless in constant contact with Havana during those months in Dar es Salaam. There is no record of any communiqués or of the letters he must have exchanged with Fidel. What we do know today is that Aleida, on the initiative of Rivalta himself, was able to travel secretly to Dar es Salaam via Cairo. Rivalta said that the couple were together for several days in the Cuban embassy, that they spoke about their children, and that Che was happy.

Rivalta himself also took charge of revamping Che's appearance: "I went out to the market and bought clippers, scissors, combs, and a razor. The haircut came out well—I graduated as a barber. When I finished, I put a cigar in his mouth." There is a photo that shows a rejuvenated and clean-shaven Che, looking playfully over the cigar. Eddy Suñol, a man from the Cuban Interior Ministry, traveled secretly from Havana to transform the character with false teeth and spectacles. Che was unrecognizable when he finished.

In February 1966, Che wrote to his daughter Hilda, now ten years old:

> You're already a woman, and I can't write to you as if to a child, telling you trifles and fibs. You must know that I'm still far away and will be apart from you for a long time, doing what I can to fight our enemies. Not that it's much, but I'm doing something, and you'll always be able to be proud of your father.

Shortly afterward, Che said good-bye to Aleida and left Tanzania for an unknown destination. His farewell appeared in a message he sent to the Tri-Continental Conference held in Havana in January.

> The fight goes on between the successors to Lumumba and Tshombe's old cronies in the Congo, a fight that seems to be going the latter's way at the moment, in favor of those who have pacified a large swathe of the country for their own benefit. But the war still looms.

44. Prague: The Cold, the Loneliness

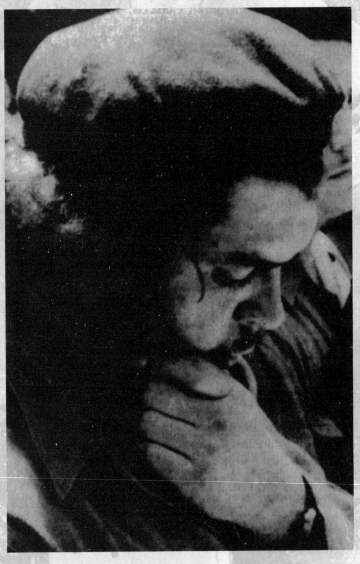

HE AUTHOR ONCE AGAIN WISHES HE HAD RECOURSE TO CHE'S OWN words. There is no way to approximate that narrative tone, that incredible sincerity, and that caustic sense of humor. Nonetheless, like so much other material, the diaries Che must have written after leaving Africa—the hypothetical "Prague diaries"—have not been made public, if they still exist. In addition, we must point out that Cuban historians avoid the image of a dejected and depressed Che like the plague. Little or nothing has been written about the "cold" period, between the end of March (or earlier) and July 1966. The only thing left therefore is to try to reconstruct that first "Prague spring" from loose and very different ends.

Che abandoned Africa and went to Europe, to a place where he was able to stay in complete secrecy. He was waiting for the oft-postponed Latin American operation to be reactivated; doubtless then the Andean project would be revived.

Oscar Fernández Mell, a doctor and Che's former comrade-in-arms, saw Che in March 1966 in Dar es Salaam and, as he himself was returning to Cuba, met Aleida in Cairo on her way to see her husband.

If Fernández Mell's memory serves, March was the month in which Che left the heat of defeat for the cold calculation of a new plan. (If Cuban historians Adys Cupull and Froilán González are correct, the turning point was a few months earlier.) March, then, was also the month that Captain Martínez Tamayo was sent by Che to Bolivia to revive the support network set up by young activists there. On one date or another, Ernesto Guevara, in disguise again, left Tanzania for Prague, via Cairo and Belgrade.

On behalf of Manuel Piñero, Ulises Estrada was entrusted with the mission, which was defined as "taking Che to a safe place until he decided what he was going to do." Their safe house was a small apartment in Prague. Its only furnishings were some beds and a kitchen table. There the days passed slowly. Che almost went mad when he ran out of books to read and was forced to concentrate on solving chess problems without an opponent.

Harry Villegas and Carlos Coello, his bodyguards and constant friendly shadows, were with him. The accounts of that period come from Villegas, who remembers spending part of their days walking through that wonderful city in the biting cold, as though possessed. At least the climate did not bring on Che's asthma. For reasons of security, they ate in restaurants as far from the city center as possible.

Secrecy was total. Che deeply mistrusted the Czechoslovaks and wanted to have nothing to do with their secret services. He used to say that if they found out, so would the CIA; therefore, the entire operation was strictly Cuban. Guevara frequently exchanged messages with Fidel. He escaped from his bodyguards one day to go to the cinema, where in an almost deserted theater he saw *The Tokyo Olympics*, a film he could understand although it was narrated in Czech.

Che sent Estrada back to Cuba because, as a large black man, he stood out in Prague. He was replaced by Juan Carretero, known by his alias, Ariel. Finally, when the Latin American operation began to take shape, Che sent to

Havana for Alberto Fernández Montes de Oca, "Pachungo," his old comrade from the battle for Santa Clara and at the Ministry of Industry.

During that spring and summer in Prague, Ernesto Guevara shaped the new project, taking elements from the original action in 1964 and adapting them to changes that had taken place in Latin America while he was in Africa. The original project had been temporarily postponed by when Jorge Ricardo Masetti was killed in Argentina, and the National Liberation Army (ELN) was wiped out in Peru. Basic was the concept of a "continental front" that had been suggested during Che's meeting with Josie Fanon in Algiers in 1964.

Where did Che find the energy to plunge into this scheme after his terrible experience in the Congo? After Che's death, the U.S. journalist I. F. Stone conjectured that when a revolution acquires temporal power,

> like the Church, it enters a state of sin. One can easily imagine how this slow erosion of pristine virtue must have troubled Che. He was not a Cuban, and could not have been satisfied with building freedom from Yanqui imperialism in one Latin American country only. He thought in continental terms. In a sense he was, like some early saint, taking refuge in the desert. Only there could the purity of the faith be safeguarded from the unregenerate revisionism of human nature.

There was something that escaped Stone, however. Latin America was not just a territory Guevara had read about in books when he was a child—some story from the works of Emilio Salgari, in which sword thrusts would dispatch the wretched with honor. The continent was no childish dreamland where someone like Captain Nemo appeared to right all wrongs. Latin America was absolutely real, as were its images: the extreme poverty of the slums of Caracas; the horrors of social inequality in Peru; the demagoguery of Bolivia; the high-handedness of the Colombian military; and the gangsterlike abuses of Central American governments. The cardboard-cutout dictators who ordered torture; the malnutrition, hunger, ignorance, and fear were real images etched on Che's mind during his travels as a young man. It was from those images that Che derived his steadfastness, his clear awareness that the need for a revolution in Latin America was more than just a moral need, and could not be ignored. What is more, in 1966 that revolution seemed possible, not just in the sense of being attainable, but also close and nearby in the most urgent and terrible sense.

In that new phase, the initial objective seems to have been Peru, with a base of support in Bolivia, and a second guerrilla flashpoint in Argentina in the immediate future. Villegas confirmed this: "The initial action that we had envisaged was not for Bolivia, but Peru, which is where the guerrilla war was being organized."

In April 1965, Héctor Béjar had reorganized a new front for the ELN and in June, Luis de la Puente Uceda's Revolutionary Left Movement (MIR) began to operate very actively on three guerrilla fronts after several months' political work in that zone. Shortly afterward, the ELN entered the action, led by Héctor Béjar, Guillermo "Paco" Lobatón, and Juan Pablo Chang.

The enormous momentum of the Peruvian guerrillas, who drew strength from the constant unrest in the countryside, had suffered a series of setbacks at the end of 1965, while Che was in Africa, that beheaded the movement. De la Puente died on October 23, while trying to break out of a siege of the Mesa Pelada camp, and the ELN's guerrilla army was torn apart when a guide betrayed it.

Che doubtless weighed the possibility of joining the guerrillas in Peru, but scrapped the idea because the Cuban government was convinced that the movement there had been infiltrated. Villegas later told the Peruvian guerrillas: "There are still many things to be cleared up, like the capture of 'Calixto' [Béjar had been captured], there was de la Puente's death, Lobatón had disappeared and Gadea [Hilda's brother, Che's ex-brother-in-law] taken prisoner. In our judgment, Che must not go there."

In the opinion of French intellectual Régis Debray, "Until mid-1966, it seems, Che did not effectively think of Bolivia except as a starting point for Peru." Specifically, by the time Che left Africa, he had apparently already dropped the Peruvian plan and begun to think of Bolivia as possibly something more than a rear base for an entry elsewhere.

In November 1964, the remains of the Bolivian revolution, which Che had seen at its birth, had collapsed amid a bloody military coup by Generals René Barrientos and Alfredo Ovando Candía. The aftermath was terrible repression, which hit the miners particularly hard. The union leader Juan Lechín was deported and part of the left outlawed. Although the military government acquired a legal gloss in 1965, when elections gave the presidency to Barrientos with Hernán Siles Suazo as vice president, political instability still prevailed.

Che had not only maintained direct and indirect links with the Bolivian Communist Party leadership before he left Cuba in 1964; he had also met Oscar Zamora, the leader of a radical dissident wing of the Party that favored armed struggle and was soon to begin an internecine dispute under the pretext of a split between pro-Chinese and pro-Soviet elements. This meeting and others had prompted the PCB to send its leader, Mario Monje Molina, to Cuba to protest that the Maoists in his party were preparing a guerrilla war that involved support for Oscar Zamora's group.

In April 1965, as Che was leaving Cuba for the Congo, the PCB had split and a tendency toward armed opposition to the military government was growing in both factions. In mid-1965, a group of twelve young Bolivian Communists studying in Havana asked "repeatedly" to be trained. Jorge Kolle Cueto, the second secretary of the PCB, was in Havana at the time; he agreed and even sent a new group of young people, with whom Che had previously had links in the support network for the Masetti and Puerto Maldonado operations: Roberto "Coco" Peredo, Luis "Ñato" Méndez, Rodolfo Saldaña, and Jorge Vázquez Viaña.

Talks on guerrilla activity in Bolivia, either to establish a rear base for guerrillas in Peru or to set up an active base, resumed in Havana in January 1966, while the Tri-Continental Congress was in session. Fidel personally discussed the situation with the PCB leader, and it is even said that Monje underwent brief training after the conference and was sworn in in front of a group of young Bolivians with a 9mm Browning pistol in his hands.

It would appear the collaboration agreements between the Cuban government and the PCB had their cost. The PCB was obsessed with excluding other left-wing groups, which it saw as rivals, and must have pressed successfully to exclude from the Tri-Continental Conference another left-wing delegation, which had arrived uninvited. In hindsight, Régis Debray called this decision regrettable, because it limited the support base for Che's project and made the Cubans hostages of Monje and the official PCB.

With Che out of the Congo and his manifest intention of beginning activities in Latin America, the work of "Tania," known in Bolivia as Laura Gutiérrez Bauer, assumed new importance. Tania had made connections with the local oligarchy during her time in Bolivia; she had married a Bolivian student, had thus gained resident status, and had twofold cover, as an archaeologist and a German teacher. She was on excellent terms with the Presidential Office of Information, and had even met President Barrientos. In January 1966, a Cuban secret service agent with the code name Mercy, disguised as a representative of an Argentine cosmetics firm, went to see whether Tania's cover was still intact and to offer to extend her training. Mercy trained Tania for two months in Bolivia and Brazil on a variety of matters, including countersurveillance, analyzing information, karate, and reading microdots. When he left, he repeated Che's orders that Tania stay in the shadows, away from the Bolivian left, and wait for a messenger to arrive from Cuba to activate her mission.

In March 1966, Captain Martínez Tamayo, who had been with Che in Prague, arrived in Bolivia. His presence there indicated that the Peruvian project had been temporarily set aside—or rather, adjusted to reality—and that Bolivia was now the focus of Che's guerrilla plans. How was it to be organized, under what conditions, and with which collaborators? Did Che think the conditions for armed struggle existed in Bolivia? Had the failed revolution of the fifties paved the way for a socialist revolution? No leftist movement in Bolivia had opted for an armed struggle against the military government. War was indeed being spoken of, but the lines had not been drawn. As Inti Peredo said years later, the PCB was always "on the edge of armed struggle," an edge they never stepped over.

It was Che Guevara's project, as Fidel put it: "We did not give him the mission. The idea, the plan, everything, were his alone." The project was never fully mapped out, either in Che's Bolivian diary or in conversations with the men who were later to accompany him there. Debray noted years later:

> Che's real plans were never set out in writing, as far as we know, and even less were they published. At no time did Che explicitly or systematically map them out with the group of guerrillas at Ñancahuazú. The plans were

everywhere and went without saying, were guessed at by the majority and envisaged by others, but known by very few.

From what we know today, and judging by Che's actions over the following months, sending Martínez Tamayo to Bolivia was the beginning of a plan to give some shape to a guerrilla operation in that country, in a struggle that was meant to spread throughout the continent in the second stage and take in the whole Andean range, with Argentina and Peru as joint battlegrounds. The idea was to set up a "mother front" in Bolivia that would operate as a battle line, and also offer armed training. It also seems evident that when the new columns were to separate and head for Peru and Argentina, Che meant to go to his homeland. This intention had been augmented by another military coup in Argentina, in which President Arturo Illia was thrown out of office by General Juan Carlos Onganía. The Argentine military seemed to be working in the spirit of Che's own project.

Martínez Tamayo's immediate tasks were to restore links with the remains of the Peruvian ELN, particularly with Juan Pablo Chang, to make contact with the Bolivian Communist Party, to set up the support network anew and include the "fellow travelers"—the Peredo brothers, Saldaña, Ñato, and Vázquez Viaña—and, above all, to set up a main base where the guerrillas could be trained. These assignments were soon accomplished and the group set to work. Martínez Tamayo bought a farm in Yungas, in the Beni region, not far from Caranavi northeast of La Paz. But it was found to be too close to a military base and was soon to be abandoned.

The man who had been present at Che's meeting with Tania two years previously in Cuba, José Monleón ("Iván," "Renan"), a Cuban secret service agent, left Havana in April to support the work in hand. Part of Piñeiro's group, he was to keep his distance from the Bolivian left and operate as a mole as long as the mission lasted, under cover as a prosperous tradesman. A Cuban source said, "Iván was trained in countersurveillance, obtaining and transmitting information, counterintelligence, visual observation, security measures, radio communication, and secret codes, encrypted and invisible writing."

Tania left Bolivia to get a better forged passport and receive additional training in Mexico and Prague. Did she meet Che there again? This is not likely, as Che's presence in Prague was a very delicate matter, top secret outside the small circle of fighters he knew (Pacho Montes de Oca, Martínez Tamayo, Carlos Coello, and Harry Villegas) and the men from the Interior Ministry (Ulises Estrada, Carretero, and José Luis) who worked at the embassy. Che himself was very careful not to reveal his presence.

Che's three agents—Tania, Monleón, and Martínez Tamayo—met in Bolivia in May. That same month, Fidel met Monje and gave him a vague idea of the operation. Did Monje leave with the impression that an essentially Bolivian operation in its first phase was being prepared? Monje returned and gave the green light for training a small group of Bolivian Young Communists headed by Inti Peredo, who went to Buenos Aires with eight other comrades.

Che began to pull strings from Prague, in the cold and loneliness. On July 10, Tania received the message that activated her; she began to obtain storage places, and safe houses for the coming fighters. Four days later, Villegas and Coello left Prague for Bolivia. Che was sending his righthand men to the battleground. They had to act jointly with Martínez Tamayo and start up the operation. A week later, Che himself left for Latin America.

45.   Burning His Boats

Training in the mountains of Pinar del Río, Cuba, for the guerrilla war in Bolivia

O N JULY 19, 1966, A MAN CALLED RAMÓN BENÍTEZ, CARRYING A PASSPORT identifying him as a citizen of the then placid Oriental Republic of Uruguay, traveled by train from Prague to Vienna. It was the beginning of a journey that was to take in more than the countryside. He had seat number 22 in car 121; seat 24, beside him, was occupied by a Cuban friend, Fernández Montes de Oca. Señor Benítez changed trains in Vienna, going to Geneva and then to Zurich. Turning formal logic on its head, he now flew to Moscow where, after changing his passport, he flew on to Havana. The man had gone halfway around the world to come home. Home?

The Che Guevara who returned had no place to call home. He had burned his boats. Havana was just a port of call on the way to a new exploit. One year and three months after having left for the African venture, he was returning to set up another guerrilla expedition, this time in Latin America. Fidel Castro wrote: "With his kind of sensitivity, it bothered him to return to Cuba after having left in such a final way. I persuaded him to come back because it was the most convenient and practical move for all his intents and purposes." And just what were those intents and purposes? They were to pick the men who were to go with him, to settle the details of the plan, and to begin training.

I have only one account of where Che stayed in Cuba for the following three months. Obliged to keep up the utmost secrecy, he was, it appears, somewhere between the Los Portales Cave (where he had set up his command post during the Cuban missile crisis) and La Palma, in Pinar del Río, near a small town called San Andrés de Taiguanabo. The exact location was on the slope of an almost inaccessible hill, in the abandoned residence of an American who had owned half the province before the revolution. The estate served as a sanatorium, thanks to the microclimate there, which helped keep Che's asthma away. "He was fat and stocky," the anonymous source said.

Fidel's many conversations with Guevara left the Cuban premier feeling that Che was unstoppable. Despite his many attempts to talk Che into letting other cadres set up the operation, then joining them at a later stage, Che was adamant. Fidel said, "He was impatient, really very impatient."

It was not hard for Che to find volunteers to go along with him on his forthcoming venture, of, for want of a better term, armed Latin-Americanism. The ideal of international solidarity—particularly solidarity with other Latin Americans—was very popular with many young revolutionaries in Cuba. There was also a desire to turn the clock back, to get away from the tough task of constructing socialism and return to the days of glory. Memory had filtered out the bad times and only the good ones lingered: the solidarity, the total commitment and—why not?—the heroism, too.

Over the previous years there had been Cubans asking Che to let them join him in revolutionary ventures, and it was public knowledge that many middle- and even high-ranking members of the Cuban revolutionary government had volunteered to take part in a Latin American revolution outside Cuba. Dariel Alarcón: "We expressed our willingness to go along, as we feared he would go off and fight without us. And not just me. A lot of us comrades felt the same." Che chose men after his own heart, men he had seen overcome fear, who were a little carefree about death—"handsome" men, in the Cuban meaning of the word, and a little crazy. He gave preference to fighters who met his political standards but also were furiously egalitarian, selfless, and stoic—everything he demanded, everything he himself was. He looked for the capacity to rise above exhaustion and hardship, to call on strong will when all else failed.

First, his old guard. There was his escort party: Carlos Coello and Harry Villegas, his countrymen, his everlasting friends, who were almost like children to him and had been with him since the Sierra Maestra. To them he added Leonardo Tamayo, the "little Indian" messenger who had flown across the Sierra on winged feet. Also there was Alberto Fernández Montes de Oca, who had gotten lost in the Mexican jungle one day, and in Santa Clara had led a squad ten yards ahead of his men while facing a tank. Montes de Oca was also an old comrade from the Sierra Escambray and the Industry Ministry, and had spent the last few months with Che in Prague.

Che chose the best of the guerrillas who had served under him in the Sierra Maestra and especially in the invasion: Eliseo Reyes, "San Luis"; Olo Pantoja, who was said to have undertaken a prior mission in Peru with Hugo Blanco while working with Ramiro in the Interior Ministry; Manuel Hernández, the best advance-guard captain in the Las Villas invasion.

From his recent African experience, Che drew on Dr. Octavio de la Pedraja ("Morogoro") and Israel Reyes Zayas, Manuel Piñeiro's former escort. There were other cadres from the revolutionary struggle whom Che would doubtless have liked to take with him: Captain Dariel Alarcón, an old Sierra Maestra hand; Antonio Sánchez Díaz, "Pinares," one of Camilo's lieutenants who had symbolically stepped into his former chief's shoes. "Antonio was really Camilo." Che unwittingly slipped into these nostalgic weaknesses.

Che included two important cadres from the postrevolutionary stage. Jesús Suárez Gayol, "Blondie," had first met Che when his feet were burned after he torched a radio station and later became his deputy at the Ministry of Industry, **one of the few who showed faith and enthusiasm.** Juan Vitalio "Vilo" Acuña was a Party Central Committee member whom Che had known since the first days in the Sierra Maestra and whose strong-willed nature and capacity for self-denial he admired enormously.

Che would, of course, also be accompanied by Captain José María Martínez Tamayo—"Papi," "M'bili," who had been with the operation from the start. At the latter's suggestion, his brother René Martínez Tamayo would also go. René, an asthmatic like Che, was an Interior Ministry lieutenant and escort to Manuel Piñeiro; who had just qualified as a shortwave radio operator.

Finally, there was Gustavo Machín Hoed, who had fought the revolution as part of the Directory and who wrote to Che asking for a chance to fight outside Cuba. His well-earned reputation for bravery preceded him. His political life after the revolution was split between the army and the civil service; he was a deputy minister of industry.

These were, as far as is known, the chosen fighters, all men with ample guerrilla experience. Almost all were of campesino stock, except for Pachungo, Blondie, and Gustavo Machín. If we are to be guided by their Cuban army or Interior Ministry positions, three of them—Machín, Acuña, and Pinares—held the rank of commander, the highest bestowed by the army. There were also two group captains, seven captains, two first lieutenants, and two lieutenants. It is very possible that Fidel himself, Raúl Castro, and Ramiro Valdés took part in the selection process, and it is also possible that that process began while Che was still in Prague.

Villegas and Coello arrived in Santa Cruz, Bolivia, on July 25, after leaving Che in Prague and journeying across Germany, Africa, and Brazil. Martínez Tamayo, the operations advance man, was there to receive them. Two other cadres took part in the preparations at that time. One I can identify only as "El Flaco" ("Skinny"); shortly afterward, he asked to leave the operation. The other, a Peruvian named Julio Dagnino Pacheco, was to be the liaison officer to his fellow countrymen from the ELN. Almost simultaneously, Coco Peredo and three other Bolivians returned home from Havana after training to operate in collaboration with the Bolivian Communist Party, in what was planned as a new operation in Argentina or Peru, with a base in Bolivia.

Villegas and Coello transmitted Che's latest instructions to Martínez Tamayo: Tania should remain unconnected with the group that was to prepare the guerrilla campaign. It would be necessary to acquire a farm in the northern part of the possible zone of operations. They told him the date of Che's possible arrival in Cuba, and the possible duration of the training period there. Martínez Tamayo's reply to Villegas was devastating: "In view of what he told us, we were going to have to start right away, as nothing had been done."

Villegas himself wrote in his diary that Martínez Tamayo's first talks with Bolivian party leader Mario Monje were very confused, that Monje in fact opposed the armed struggle, and that Tellería, the Bolivian Party's Central Committee member in charge of supplies, was very inefficient.

From then on, talks between the Cubans in Bolivia and Che's envoys took place at full speed, but without producing any clear plan or set of goals, maybe because of the ambiguity and many changes the project had undergone over the last several years.

From La Paz, Villegas and Coello transmitted a message to the ELN via Pacheco, the Peruvian, saying that the operation would "start first in Bolivia, then spread to Peru." The man seemed to agree and told Juan Pablo Chang, Che's old acquaintance, that the Peruvian ELN would send a group of twenty men to be trained and to take part in the Bolivian guerrilla campaign.

The next day, July 30, Martínez Tamayo and Villegas made contact with Moisés Guevara, a miners' leader who had been expelled from the PCB for pro-Chinese tendencies and had repeatedly requested weapons and money from Cuba to set up a guerrilla campaign. They proposed that he join the group now forming, but told him that there would be no money or weapons, as everything was "being centralized." Moisés Guevara accepted.

The Party's Monje was kept in the dark about the links with Moisés Guevara's group. He was laboring under the impression that Bolivia was to be no more than a rear-echelon base in some strange Cuban scheme. Monje was sounded out in another meeting:

"And what if Che were to come?"

"I would fight alongside him anywhere."

And so the meetings went on. The Peruvian ELN's reply was as complaisant as their envoy Pacheco had been. Why Bolivia, and not Peru, as the Cubans had said before? However, they offered six men to train and fight under the new proposal.

Again and again Che's men prodded Monje. They asked him for the twenty men he had promised. What twenty men? he answered. He ignored the promise and said the Central Committee did not favor the armed struggle, because the 32,000 votes the Communists had received in the previous year's elections were a victory for them. As Villegas said, "Martínez Tamayo had to breathe down these people's necks to get them to do something."

The Cuban team began to arrive; meanwhile, the search for a farm continued.

The meetings went on throughout August. Just when did they begin to talk of the fact that there would be fighting in Bolivia, that the base there would be armed, would be more than a base for actions in other countries?

Villegas's diary records conversations with Monje, Coco Peredo intervened to support the Cuban position. Monje counterproposed a variant of the guerrilla plan—an urban uprising in the Peruvian capital, followed by a withdrawal to the mountains: "an uprising that would have the impact of a punch and which, if it failed, would still serve to arouse the people's awareness." The Cubans explained to him that their plan was for a continentwide operation under Che's personal direction. Monje reiterated: "I will fight alongside Che anywhere." But the waffling continued.

Meanwhile, back in Cuba, the chosen men were called up abruptly. Dariel Alarcón and Manuel Hernández, who had taken guerrilla training courses with a view to helping a guerrilla campaign in a Latin American country, which they thought might be Venezuela or Colombia, received a call from Raúl Castro telling them to proceed immediately to the airport at Santiago de Cuba to get a plane for Havana. Alarcón, seeing a lone plane waiting just for them, thought they were "going to have us elegantly shot."

"What kind of shit have you been up to," Manuel asked, "for them to shoot the pair of us?"

The head of Raúl's escort party was waiting for them at the Havana airport. He drove them to the Armed Forces Ministry and took them directly to the minister's office there. They were the first to arrive, but soon their old comrades began to turn up: Pinares, Pantoja, San Luis, all old Sierra Maestra hands. Alarcón greeted them jokingly: "So, guys, you're here, too?" "Yeah, we're here. "Good. And for what?" "Who knows? But we're not leaving, not us nor the troubles here." No one knew the reason for meeting. Che, who reveled in slapstick, would have loved that preamble.

Raúl received them with a smile. Fears were allayed and cigars handed out. Pinares took three, "one for now and two for whenever." The defense minister told them that their requests to volunteer in an international mission had been granted. According to Tamayo, not all of the interviews were quite so friendly. Some were tête-á-têtes, and one of the men called up had declined the offer.

The group went off directly to San Francisco, a training camp where Che had had his command headquarters in 1960. Training began under Pinares.

At the beginning of September, Che had picked the Alto Beni zone, close to the border with Peru and Brazil, to set up his first guerrilla camp, and sent Pacho Fernández Montes de Oca to swap impressions with the group that was already in Bolivia. Meanwhile, a new character had entered the thickening plot. Fidel had been in contact for a year with a young Frenchman, Régis Debray, who had just finished writing *Castrismo: la larga marcha de América Latina (Castroism: The Long March of Latin America)*. The poet Roberto Fernández Retamar had recommended the work to Che, who had read it in French, brought it to Cuba for translation into Spanish, and heartily recommended it to Fidel. Debray was drawn into the project. He took part in the Tri-Continental Conference and wrote, with Fidel's backing, an essay called "Revolutión en la revolutión," ("Revolution Within Revolution,") which was to be a summary of official Cuban guerrilla thinking. Debray, who had just finished the work, agreed to collaborate with the Cubans. Alone in Havana, he received instructions from Fidel to establish links with Bolivian revolutionary groups to the left of the Communist Party and to sound them out about the possibility of guerrilla action. Debray would say years later that he "thought it was an important operation by the way Fidel spoke of it." Debray was also asked to undertake a political study of two Bolivian zones, Alto Beni and Chapare. Fidel gave Debray no further information, and the Frenchman did not know that he was working for a project directly involving Che.

Fernandez Montes de Oca arrived in La Paz via Santiago, Chile, on September 3, and met with the other two Cubans. To locate the camp in Alto Beni would conflict with preparatory work the young Bolivian Communists had done with the support of the Bolivian CP in the Camiri zone. Weapons, food, and clothing had already been gathered in Santa Cruz.

Martínez Tamayo was disgusted with the Alto Beni proposal and ventured the comment that "many nonsensical things were proposed by Che." He did not like the new relationship with Moisés Guevara's group, which he thought could bring trouble with the PCB people with whom they had been working. Pacho insisted that relations with the PCB were to take a back seat; they had to fall back on their own networks. They had to disencumber themselves of the Santa Cruz site and look for a new one in Alto Beni.

Villegas sent a report to Che on September 10, in which Martínez Tamayo's opinion prevailed. Following talks with Monje and having weighed the three zones, the Cuban group in La Paz rejected the proposal to act in the

Alto Beni or Chapare zone. They turned back to Santa Cruz–Camiri, the argument being that this was an uninhabited area close to the Andes, which was in line with Che's idea (according to Villegas) of establishing an "extreme rear-rear base from which to organize the guerrilla campaign, advance northward without any engagements, and gradually march toward a more central zone, using the western range of the Andes, which stretched to the Argentine frontier, as basically a communications route."

The report also said that relations with Moisés Guevara had placed the Cubans in a difficult position with the Bolivian CP. By that stage ten men were working with the Cubans under the direction of the Peredo brothers, Jorge Vázquez Viaña, and Rodolfo Saldaña. And the report presented a fait accompli: a farm had been bought in a very remote spot, close to the Ñancahuazú River, not far from the town of Lagunillas and the safe house in Santa Cruz Province where the military equipment was stored. The farm covered 3,000 acres "in a mountainous area with lush vegetation"; a pig ranch had been thrown in, along with two Bolivian farmhands who were Communist Party members. Coco Peredo was the one who made the purchase and was the officially named owner. Strangely enough, as early as September 11, one day after informing Che of the purchase, Villegas warned that a neighbor, Ciro Argañaraz, posed a certain risk; he was "extremely curious."

Pacho returned to Havana on September 12, while Martínez Tamayo went to visit another possible farm in the Alto Beni area. Although they had opted for the Ñancahuazú area, it appears that they had not totally dismissed the alternative; they were waiting for what Che would say. Meanwhile, Debray was undertaking a sociopolitical study of this zone as well as the Chapare region, to the north of Cochabamba. It would take him all of September, "under the worried and suspicious eye of the Bolivian CP." He and Martínez Tamayo did meet there, although Martínez Tamayo pretended not to know the Frenchman.

By mid-September the volunteers in Cuba were on their way to an unknown mission, under the command of an unknown chief. They climbed onto a tarpaulin-covered truck, still with an undisclosed destination, and were driven by a top-flight driver, Commander Tomasevich. Out of mild mischief, Pinares burned a hole in the tarpaulin with a cigar and began to observe the passing scene, describing it to the rest in detail as they went. He happened to know the route: they were moving across his home turf, Pinar del Río, in the east of the island.

When they arrived at the farm, the volunteers lined up in the garden some fifty yards from the house and Tomasevich warned them:

"You'll need to pluck up your courage, as you'll be going with somebody who's very conceited and very rude."

Pinares called the squad to attention. The minutes went by. Just as they were expecting someone in an olive-drab uniform to appear, an individual leaned out of the window who, in Alarcón's words, "was dressed in a Parisian-style suit and tie, holding a pair of eyeglasses in the air. He was balding, with a few straggly gray hairs. He was smoking a pipe." The man walked toward the group, stopping a couple of yards away, and ceremoniously greeted Tomasevich and shook his hand.

"Well, Doctor, this is the group you will be training." And Tomasevich began to introduce them, using their code names. The man looked right at them and said with a Spanish accent: **Well, Commander, I have to tell you something. They look like a real bunch of assholes to me.** He introduced himself to the group one by one, calling himself Ramón.

"What do you think of them now?" Tomasevich asked.

They're still the same bunch of assholes, he answered, looking them up and down. Then he spoke to Pinares: **I know you.**

"You couldn't possible know me."

Aren't you Commander Pinares? Aren't you the commander who spent the whole missile crisis driving around Pinar del Río in a battered old jeep spouting shit to all the campesinos around here?

The joke was so insulting that it sparked off guffaws in the group. San Luis grimaced, as if trying to guess who the person behind the disguise was. He even thought it might be one of Che's brothers, whom he'd never met, as he could detect an Argentine lilt behind the fake Spanish accent. It was Jesús Suárez Gayol who broke the spell and rushed forward to hug the stranger.

"Dammit, man, it's you, dammit, Che!"

Overcome with joy, they made him take off his glasses and put on an olive-drab tunic and a beret. Like millions of other Cubans, they had not heard anything about Che in a year and a half. San Luis began his first combat diary entry: "We were incredibly moved when we recognized him." They were proud, too, that they were going to fight with Commander Guevara.

Once they had calmed down, Che described the initial part of the operation without making any specific reference to any country. Alarcón recalled, "He warned that although we were not off to the slaughterhouse, the struggle would be long and harsh, under the most difficult conditions." Finally, Che insisted that he did not want anyone to be press-ganged into the operation, and made them confirm that they were indeed volunteers.

Régis Debray later analyzed the volunteers and their motives for joining. His was another point of view, just as relevant: "A high-ranking leader is not just a little red tsar lounging in a chair. Four Central Committee members, two deputy ministers, and two high-level officials left their families, cars, houses, and privileges behind to go with Che to an unknown jungle where some became skeletons in rags, their limbs swollen, drinking their own urine so as not to drop dead. No one forced them to go, and the television was not around to pick up their last words, their last thoughts."

————

In Bolivia, meanwhile, the comedy of errors continued. The three Cubans there met with Mario Monje on September 23. In the name of the Bolivian CP, he asked for explanations concerning Debray's connections with other left-wing groups, particularly Oscar Zamora's Marxist-Leninist Communist Party. The Cubans replied that they were not aware of Debray's mission, and disowned all knowledge of it. Monje told them that the Party had been working on a general uprising with the guerrilla campaign playing a secondary role. When the Cubans asked what had been done to further the uprising, he answered, "Nothing."

A second meeting took place on September 28, when Monje reiterated that his agreement with Fidel was confined to setting up a support base for a campaign to take place in the south, that Bolivia was to have second place in the overall plan. The Cubans replied that Bolivia had been made the main location, as the conditions there were right. The meeting ended on a sour note, Monje saying that he would not stand for being treated like a puppet.

Two days later, Villegas met with part of the Bolivian Young Communist group, who had been working more closely with them, to explain Monje's doubts. Rodolfo Saldaña and Coco Peredo said that they did not care about Monje's position, they would fight anyway. On October 4, a message from Che arrived in which he said that a breach would be a grave matter at the preparatory stage: **Maintain relations with Monje and avoid arguments.**

As this was going on, the deceptive peace and quiet at the training camp at San Andrés in Cuba were soon broken. Reality intruded: the key word "Bolivia" was spoken. The reaction was one of surprise.

Che began what turned out to be a brutal training program. Alarcón said, "It was so tough we didn't think we could keep up. We had thought we were fit, and Che said we had to start all over again." First he read them the rules: Officer privileges were over; they were all on the same level again. Guard duty was strictly shared; he would take the first watch. Whoever was on the final watch, which ended at five A.M., would be in charge of breakfast. Half an hour later was reveille, and target practice began at six on the dot. For anyone who did not improve, the journey was over. So shots rang out from the Fals, the Garands, the M1s, the Thompsons, and the Uzis, hundreds of rounds per session. On Saturdays and Sundays, the volunteers practiced firing bazookas and .30- and .50-caliber machine guns. Weapons were cleaned after firing practice, and then came a six-hour forced march carrying backpacks full of ammunition. From seven P.M. on, the group was split into two. Che and Gustavo Machín taught history, Spanish, and math classes to one or the other half of the group. This strict and crazy routine also required language classes beginning at nine P.M.: French and Quechua! Che took part in all the activities and in addition had to prepare his classes.

Cover identities and papers for the men turned up fifteen days later. One of the group became an Ecuadorean salesman, another a Uruguayan meat trader. Others had to learn the Colombian national anthem, the baseball teams of Panama, or the names of newspapers in Montevideo.

The long-suffering volunteers asked Che to suspend the general culture classes temporarily so they could devote the time to learning their covers. Che replied that that task could be completed in the men's free time. What free time? they wondered. After midnight, he replied calmly. Quite normal for a man who never slept.

The training produced results. Tamayo, Alarcón, Alfonso Zayas, and San Luis Reyes, the advance guard, managed to complete the march in one hour and fifty minutes. Che then put the rest under pressure, which earned the advance guard insults until they were all bored with hearing them. Fidel turned up at least once a week during the training. Che took advantage of one such visit to make him timekeeper for the march, along a fixed route up hill and down dale, over ravines and across rivers. Fidel gave his watch to the best marcher.

As a man who switched from stoicism and frugality to abuse, Che ate "like a horse" in those days—in his comrades' words, "as much as three men's rations," which made Vilo Acuña jealous because he was overweight and had to go on a diet. This weakened him dangerously, and he was to pay for it during the campaign.

Among the many anecdotes about the training at Pinar del Río is one that amuses me and that, although it has never been confirmed, has something characteristic of what is now known about Fidel and Che. Apparently, Guevara was having a heated argument with Ramiro Valdés one day, and was even hitting him, while Aleida March sat in a nearby car, at the foot of a hill where the men had been training. The men realized that Ramiro was being chewed out because Aleida had been brought along while the other comrades' wives had not. "Shit"s and "hell"s flew through the Cuban air.

Fidel arrived—opportunely, since Che could be dangerous when he flew off the handle.

He grabbed hold of Che and told him, "It's not Ramiro's fault, it's mine. We thought we'd give the rest of the men a day's leave to see their wives, but we didn't include you—that's why Aleida's here." Little by little, Che began to calm down. Fidel offered to take some of the comrades up the hill in his car. But his driving scared them, so they begged off. "That's okay; we'll follow you, Commander."

Guevara and Aleida shared a room in the camp that night, and Che could not make it up the hill the following day. The Cubans, with their usual respect and to show that his exhaustion was not worth making such a big deal of, just asked slyly, "Sleep well, Commander?"

Captain Martínez Tamayo came from Bolivia on October 5 to see Che. Among other things, he wanted to tell him he was not overjoyed about setting up a camp at the Ñancahuazú farm and would prefer to go to another region. Che became angry with him: the journey was useless and a security risk. Furthermore, the ranch well fulfilled their need for a remote base that would allow for a long training period, and that was near the Argentinian border.

As October wore on, Ernesto Guevara met his children for the last time, on the outskirts of Havana. Celia, the youngest, who was ill with a kidney infection, had visited Che along with Aleida. She had yet to turn four, and there was no danger that she would recognize him. Che turned up at the final meeting already disguised as his new cover, Adolfo Mena, a Uruguayan functionary working for the Organization of American States. His four youngest children, Aleida's children, were there. Hilda, who was ten years old then, was left out: "maybe they thought I might let slip to my friends or comrades that I had seen him, or that he was about to go."

Aleida Guevara, the oldest of the children there, then almost six, clearly recalled the meeting: "The man said hello to me. He said he was Spanish, his name was Ramón, and he was a good friend of my daddy."

"Hey, you don't sound Spanish, you sound Argentine," Aleida told the man. Everyone was startled: if the disguise could not fool a six-year-old, it was useless.

Che stayed calm. **Why Argentine?**

"It was just something I thought of," she replied.

Shortly before leaving, in October, Che received Debray's report ("the best I have written in my life") and could check it against Pacho's: maps, plans, political reports, lists of sympathizers. It was strikingly clear that other regions in Bolivia offered a better foundation for a guerrilla flashpoint, with a more socially aware campesino class; less isolation from the miners, one of the most radical political forces in Bolivian society; and a broader militant base among the left-wing parties. It seems evident, however, as Debray said, that "impatient as he was to return to guerrilla life . . . and busy with picking men for the campaign and in preparing future contacts, he gave only secondary importance to the initial location of the flashpoint."

But there was more to Che's decision. He accepted the base camp's location at Ñancahuazú, in a region where no prior political work had been done, because he saw it as a rearward base, rather than an operational base, and thus ascribed more importance to its isolation.

The final details were being arranged. The absence of a dozen and a half well-known Cuban military figures had been covered up by the Cuban secret services, which spread the rumor that they were in Vietnam. The training was drawing to a close, and had revealed some flaws in the selection process: Pinares turned out to be undisciplined and uncontrolled, although a pleasant person, while Vilo Acuña, overweight and sickly, had lasted as long as he did out of sheer willpower.

Martínez Tamayo returned to Bolivia on October 21, still smarting from the dressing down that Che had given him. (He admitted to Villegas that he was only participating in the operation out of loyalty to Che). He was instructed to make contact with all radical left-wing groups, even with former vice president Juan Lechín.

José Monleón, "Renán," got in touch with Villegas and Coello on October 10; through him, Tania reached Martínez Tamayo. Che's people linked up with a parallel network run from Havana by Manuel Piñeiro. The compartmentation that Che had initially wished for was slipping away; the Cubans were acting like an integrated group. Shortly beforehand, Villegas had met Monje, who told him that the Party's Central Committee had approved the idea that the road to power in Bolivia did entail armed struggle. Monje admitted, though, that he felt "that much of the support for armed struggle was just lip service and that they [his comrades, the PCB leaders] were incapable of physically taking part in one."

Yes or no? Nothing seemed to be clear. Shortly afterward, Monje left for Bulgaria via Cuba. He had one last confrontation with the Cubans, in which he asked them for economic aid for the trip and, sick of his shenanigans, they ignored him.

———

On October 22, the training was over. The combatants were granted leave to visit their families and say their farewells, although they were to keep their destination top secret. Manuel Hernández told his wife he was going to cut cane in Camagüey, but the farewell took longer than usual and he began to cry. Pinares is said to have taken his leave with his usual caustic humor: "Go and look for some other husband, because I won't be coming back from this one."

Che dressed up for his second departure from Cuba. He used the disguise he had already tried out in San Andrés. Maybe its most annoying aspects were the false teeth he used to alter his lower jawline and the eyeglass lenses, suited for nearsightedness, which forced him to walk carefully so as not to trip. On their last day, Fidel organized a meal with trustworthy members of the Cuban government and warned them that a visitor would be coming. The disguise worked; no one recognized him.

There is one last photo with Fidel: Che, in his final masquerade, dressed like a top-level bureaucrat, with an overcoat, tie, hat, square-framed eyeglasses. He can be seen looking at Fidel, who is holding a cigar and checking Che's passport. They are eight inches apart. Behind them is an open closet with no clothes or even clothes hangers in it. There is no record of either man's parting words, apart from a few brief phrases Fidel confessed to Italian journalist Gianni Miná: "We were not very fulsome, because we are men of few . . . He wasn't like that, I'm not like that, but we did feel very strongly."

Ernesto Guevara, on his way to being Che again, left Cuba on October 23, 1966.

46. "Today the Next Stage Begins"

Disguised as "Adolfo Mena," Uruguayan social researcher, as Fidel checks Che's passport

THERE EXISTS A PHOTOGRAPH OF A MAN LOOKING INTO A MIRROR IN A ROOM in the Hotel Copacabana in La Paz. The photograph was taken the day the man returned to the city after an absence of several years. It shows a man who had just spent the worst year of his life, and was nevertheless ready to try again. It was November 3, 1966, and Ernesto Guevara had arrived in the Bolivian capital for the second time in his life after thirteen years away, like a character dancing a tango with the tempo changed.

Was there some sort of reunion then—between 1953's Dr. Guevara, an adventurer wandering around Latin America, and 1966's Che, with the Cuban revolution and the African disaster behind him? The thirteen years separating them were short but momentous. The man taking his own photograph in the mirror was temporarily called Adolfo Mena; he was a Uruguayan agricultural researcher from the Organization of American States, holding identification issued by the National Information Directorate of the Bolivian president's office.

And there is another photograph, retouched in the CIA laboratories to make Che Guevara look clean-shaven. Doubtless this one had been in the hands of passport control at the airport through which Dr. Mena had just passed.

Che, pressed by the danger of traveling under cover, began operations the next day, without giving himself time to get his bearings or to familiarize himself with the political situation in Bolivia. He used Pacho Fernández Montes de Oca to arrange a meeting with Renán at a safe house that evening, and Renán gave him instructions about receiving the rest of the group and about arms transfers. Renán contacted Martínez Tamayo, who mistakenly told Harry Villegas and Carlos Coello that Che did not want to see them; what the message had really said was that Che did not want to see the whole group at once. Consequently, Che's two former escorts were afraid they were in for a hard time with their boss, whose temper they knew well, and spent a sleepless night.

Finally, Che contacted Tania and drafted her into the network organized to set up the column. Just when did he change his mind about keeping Tania apart from the guerrillas, using her as a spy whose job was to try and infiltrate Bolivian government circles? The fact is that from that moment on Tania was fully involved in the group's work and her compartmentation was over.

Curiously, the Argentinian secret services placed the homes of Guevara's relatives under surveillance at just that time; maybe they had been tipped off that Che was in the area. The CIA would admit a year later that it had received information from the Bolivian government that a guerrilla campaign was being organized. (The source of the information may have been the tentative recruitment under way among the members of the Communist Party and of Moisés Guevara's group.) But the North Americans attached no importance to the news. They had no respect for the Bolivian government's intelligence apparatus and saw the government as prone to distract public attention from more pressing domestic problems.

Che headed off with Pacho for Ñancahuazú in a jeep at 6:30 P.M. on November 5. He had been preceded by Martínez Tamayo and Coello, and was followed several hours later by Villegas and the Bolivian activist Jorge Vázquez Viaña. It took them a couple of days to cross Bolivia. They were met on November 7 by the rear echelon jeep.

Years later, I saw a short film by the Cuban filmsmaker Santiago Alvarez, *Ever On to Victory!*[*] Alvarez's zoom lens showed the Bolivian dirt roads going nowhere, in a wilderness that was the middle of nowhere. It was unbelievable. Che was entering the heart of Latin America, the hell that he knew so well.

They reached the Río Grande at four P.M. on November 7. Now that they were close to the farm, **we stopped the cars, taking just one the rest of the way so as not to attract the attention of a nearby owner** [Ciro Argañaraz], **who was making noises about our business being cocaine. A curious detail is that the ineffable Coello traveled as the group's chemist.**

During the second stage of the journey, with the four of them in the same jeep, Che revealed his identity to Vázquez Viaña, who was so startled he nearly drove over a precipice. In his first conversation with the Bolivian, whom he knew only from reports of missions he had controlled, Che told him: **We can't afford to dream of a revolution just in Bolivia, without having at least one revolution in an adjoining country, if not in all of Latin America. If that doesn't happen, this revolution will be crushed. I came here to stay and I will leave only if I'm dead or shooting my way across the border.**

It was clear from their talk that the young Communist was willing to follow Che, **but he seemed to be loyal to Monje, whom he respected and appeared to like. According to him, Rodolfo Saldaña feels the same way and so does Coco, but we have to get the party to fight. I asked him not to inform the party** [of my presence] **until Monje arrived—he was away in Bulgaria—and to ask Monje to help. He agreed on both counts.**

The group arrived at the farm after midnight. Che spent a few moments beginning his Bolivian diary, opening a notebook he had bought in Frankfurt. **Today the next stage begins.**

The first several days, Commander Guevara did not stay in the farmhouse, a two-room adobe structure with a corrugated-metal roof. They named it the Galvanized Metal House. Che camped out a hundred yards away, to evade any possible ambush. Three Communist Party workers—Apolinar Aquino, Aquino "Serapio" Tudela, and Antonio Domínguez—stayed in the house meanwhile, posing as farmhands.

Reconnaissance missions began. First Che and Coello followed the course of the Ñancahuazú River, but were not able to find its source. Pacho and Villegas made more progress than Che when they tried later on. These were peaceful days, in which they fought only the mosquitoes and ticks. **I removed six ticks today.**

[*]Translator's note: One of Che's legendary battle cries.

Che wrote the word "Ñancahuazú" several times in his diary, using five different spellings: Ñacahuaso, Ñacahuasu, Ñacahuazu, and Ñacahuazú, according to how it appeared in books or on maps, or how the locals pronounced it. The word means "Water entry" or "Water head," and is derived from the Guaraní word "Yakaguasú."

One thing was clear, however. A line dropped into Che's diary seems to provide the key to the type of project he had in mind: The region is, apparently, little visited. With appropriate discipline, we could stay here awhile. Nonetheless, Argañaraz's driver saw some of the Cubans on November 10. When Che found out, he angrily dressed them down, and decided to move into the jungle to set up a permanent base there. This is quickly getting worse. We have to see if at least we'll be able to get our men in. I'll be content with that.

In the second week of November, while waiting for the rest of the Cuban volunteers, Che began digging a tunnel in which they could store food as well as everything that might compromise us. and make it a food store at the same time. Pachungo's morale was low, as he missed his family, but Che felt as if he'd been born anew. A very telling sentence closed his diary entry for November 12: My hair has grown, albeit very sparsely; my gray hairs are turning blond and fading; my beard is growing. In a few months I'll be me again.

While the days were spent reconnoitering the Ñancahuazú and digging the tunnel, Che took time to read. He had on hand Benedetto Croce's *History as the Story of Liberty,* Trotsky's *The Age of Permanent Revolution* and *The History of the Russian Revolution,* and Paul Rivet's *The Origins of the American Man.*[*] He may also, surprisingly, have read General Charles de Gaulle's war memoirs or Winston Churchill's. Maybe he read something by Denis Diderot or laid into the maze of Georg Hegel's *The Phenomenology of the Spirit.*

The only concern was their bothersome neighbor Ciro Argañaraz, who loitered around the Galvanized Metal House. The boys from the house spoke to Argañaraz, from whom they bought some things, and he insisted again that they were building a cocaine factory.

Antonio Sánchez Díaz—"Pinares"—and Eliseo "San Luis" Reyes finally arrived on November 20. They were accompanied by Rodolfo Saldaña, from the original group of Bolivian Young Communists, who had just helped Tania bring arms to Ñancahuazú in a small jeep from which they had removed one of the seats. Che continued to probe the young Bolivians, since all he got from the party leaders were ambiguous statements. Saldaña made a good impression on me; he seems to be more determined to make a break with everything than Vázquez Viaña is. A couple of days before, Che had written to Fidel: This is all right. There are four of us in the shelter and it seems more can make it without difficulties. . . . There are signs that the best cadres will break with Monje if he does not make

---

[*]Translator's note: This book does not appear to have been translated into English.

his mind up. Since Monje would have to travel through Havana on his return from a conference of the Communist International bureaucracy in Bulgaria, Che suggested: **You should fill his head with the urge for glory, but don't give him any money or essentials unless absolutely necessary.**

Bolivian Communist Party leader Mario Monje seemed not to have realized yet that his ship was sinking. Several days earlier, on November 9, he'd bumped into Inti Peredo in Paris's Orly Airport. (Peredo was returning from training in Havana.) Monje told him, "I'll quit the secretaryship if the Party doesn't fight." That stance contradicted the events of two weeks earlier, when he had sent Inti's brother Coco to Havana with orders to suspend training. Five of the twelve Bolivians training there disobeyed Party discipline in order to continue.

While the Cubans were traveling to the camp, Jorge Vázquez Viaña stayed to work in the Galvanized Metal House. Che had asked Rodolfo Saldaña to find a farmer among his comrades who could improve their crop yields. He had also spoken with Rodolfo about constructing a mechanic's workshop, a shoemaker's, and a dispensary. Che was doubtless thinking of setting up a major rear base in Ñancahuazú, if they were not discovered and forced to move on to armed struggle. On November 21 he wrote: **We'll try to make this last as long as possible.**

The reconnaissance expeditions continued, each more extensive than the last, but the explorers always returned to the camp near the Galvanized Metal House, which now had a sentry post in the trees.

Coco Peredo, perhaps one of the most admired figures among the Bolivian Young Communists, arrived on November 27, accompanied by Vilo Acuña, Leonardo Tamayo, and a Bolivian medical student named Freddy Maimura. He returned shortly after with Captain Martínez Tamayo, Israel Zayas, Manuel Hernández, and Coco's brother, Inti Peredo. **Martínez Tamayo brought some inconvenient news. The Chinaman is in Bolivia and wants to send twenty men** [from the Peruvian ELN] **and see me. This is inconvenient, as it internationalizes the struggle before we can count on Monje. We agreed that Chang should go to Santa Cruz and be picked up there by Coco.** Che gathered the Bolivians together the day after to announce Chang's offer; **all agreed to accept them, but after actions had begun.**

Che continued to sound men out. *I had a preliminary talk with Inti, who felt that Monje would not fight. But he himself seemed determined to get going.* He was not the only one. Che later wrote in his monthly roundup for November that those participating in Martínez Tamayo's support network would **rise up come hell or high water.**

The group was in high spirits, Israel Reyes sang and cracked jokes. Coello too went around cracking jokes. To express his admiration, he used to say his "balls were groaning," and Che rebuked him.

In the November roundup just mentioned, Commander Guevara scribbled:

> The outlook is good in this isolated region: everything indicates we will be able to spend practically as much time here as we deem convenient. The plans are: wait for the rest of the people; raise the number of Bolivians to at least twenty; and begin to operate. We still have to discover Monje's reaction and that of Moisés Guevara's people.

Che was becoming Latin American without realizing it. In his diary entries, alongside the usual Cuban and the inevitable Argentine expressions, Mexican idioms reemerged from his memory. And popular Bolivian expressions began to appear.

On December 2, his old friend Juan Pablo Chang arrived,

> very effusive. We spent the day chatting. The essentials: he will go to Cuba and personally report on the situation; within two months, i.e., when we have begun to act, five Peruvians can join up. Two will come for now, a radio technician and a medic, who will be with us for some time. He asked for weapons and I agreed to give him a Bz as well as some Mausers and grenades, and to buy an M-1 for them. I also decided to give them support to send five Peruvians to set up a weapons relay in a region near Puno, on the other side of Lake Titicaca. He told me of his troubles in Peru, even of a daring plan to free Calixto [Héctor Béjar, the overall leader of the National Liberation Army in Peru, had been arrested and imprisoned in the San Quintín jail in Peru in 1966], which seems a little far-fetched to me. He thinks some guerrilla survivors are acting in the zone, but not to his certain knowledge. He left for La Paz as enthusiastic as when he arrived.

Coco accompanied Chang to La Paz with the mission of buttressing the urban network, which was still in diapers, and of getting in touch with Julio Dagnino, who was to maintain links with the Peruvian guerrillas, and with Inti's brother-in-law, Gonzalo López Muñoz, head of information at the president's office, who might have been able to serve as an unwitting informant.

Because Che had decided that the camp was to be self-sufficient, and as there was not much to be hunted, food began to run out during the second week in December. Work continued on organizing stores, now in camouflaged caves; also, a second, more isolated camp was set up, farther away from the farm and the Galvanized Metal House. In his diary, Inti Peredo described the first camp as a training base, apart from the caves, which were strategic. Régis Debray, who arrived there some weeks later, described the second camp as a rear base, with an arsenal, food and equipment storage, and a training camp.

The Cubans were meanwhile arriving in La Paz and were received by Tania. Those who did not know her were surprised to see a woman in charge of the operation, as Tania gave many orders, treated them familiarly, and struck them as being antagonistic. She behaved toward them as if they were old acquaintances. The safe house had just one real bed and two camp beds; true to the egalitarian Guevara spirit, they all ended up sleeping on the floor. Tania told the Cubans: "You can say you've slept with a woman." They were making too much noise, and she calmed them down good-naturedly. Dariel Alarcón later said that photographs did not do her justice, as her beauty was not photogenic.

The penultimate contingent of Cubans arrived at Ñancahuazú on December 11, brought by Coco Peredo and Martínez Tamayo. Among them were Gustavo Machín, René Martínez Tamayo, an unnamed medic, Octavio de la Concepción, Dariel Alarcón, and three Bolivians: Lorgio Vaca, Orlando Jiménez, and Ñato Méndez. Two of the Bolivians were of campesino stock and had worked at the farm in the Alto Beni region, the one that had been bought for the operation and was now being deactivated.

Che was doubtless content with the quality of the people in the new contingent. According to Villegas's diary, "Che thinks that not even Havana can produce a group like this." Dariel Alarcón took charge of the kitchen to celebrate: "Che had asked me to prepare a meal worthy of a reunion for several comrades. I think I made a good stew in record time. It was what we call 'oriental' style, using salted dried meat and parboiled sweet potatoes. And I made a good strong coffee, which I served first to Che, before putting the sugar in, to round off the meal."

Che instructed Coco Peredo and Martínez Tamayo to dismantle the safe house in La Paz, transfer the remaining weapons from the Alto Beni farm, and summon Monleón and Tania to the camp.

Inti told Che he had reservations about Lorgio Vaca, who had said he would take part in the armed operation with the Party's approval. So on December 12,

> **I spoke to the whole group, reading them the rulebook about the reality of war. I stressed [the need for] sole command and discipline and advised the Bolivians of the responsibility they took in breaking Party discipline to adopt another line.**
>
> **I made appointments: Vilo as military second-in-command, San Luis and Inti as commissars, Machín Hoed as head of operations, Villegas i/c services, Inti i/c finances, Ñato Méndez as quartermaster, and, for now, Octavio as medical officer.**

At that time, Che was concerned over the presence of a hunter known as the "man from Vallegrande," who was working for his curious neighbor, Ciro Argañaraz. The man was sniffing around, and the guerrillas thought he might be trying to find out more about the group, which was true. He had been sent by Argañaraz to locate the cocaine factory that Argañaraz thought his strange neighbors had, and of which he wanted a share. Che monitored the hunter's movements for several days and, possibly because of his constant presence, decided to move to the second camp, to be known as the Central Camp, in the thick of the jungle. We left in the morning—Villegas, Leonardo Tamayo, Coello, Machín Hoed, Octavio, René, Inti, and I, heavily laden. We made the trip in three hours.

Over the following days, they moved the electricity plant and dug new caves. In his mind, Che was building a big rearward camp along the lines of the El Hombrito and Minas del Frío camps of the Cuban revolution, but with the difference that there was not a sympathetic base of campesino support in Bolivia. Here there was just a solitary camp provided, as Mexican journalist Luis Suárez said some months later, with "vegetable walls and roofs."

The last two Cubans Che had been expecting, Olo Pantoja and Jesús Suárez Gayol, arrived on December 19, guided by Martínez Tamayo and Coco Peredo. In addition, Apolinar Aquino returned from his requested three-day leave, and Monleón came from La Paz. Che spent the night talking with Monleón, Coco, and Martínez Tamayo.

Che welcomed the two Cubans saying, **At last those who were lost are found,** but they could not speak with him then, as he was holding a private meeting with Monleón. They became the butt of jokes by the rest of the comrades, who said Che was going to "give them a hard time" for arriving late. He did not, but he had done it in the same kind of situation several times before, with all the Cuban cadres, and the episode gives a clear idea both of the respect Che commanded and of how his comrades and friends feared his outbursts.

Che's private talks with Monleón were somewhat odd. Che granted him permission to marry a Bolivian woman with whom he had fallen in love, the daughter of a politician who did business with President René Barrientos. Monleón's future father-in-law wanted to give him a job in an agricultural project in the Beni region. Che seemed to encourage this idea; he thought of Monleón more as a link in a future urban network than as part of a guerrilla uprising, and felt he could infiltrate circles of power and maintain secret communications with Havana, like Tania. Monleón's possible move to the Beni area must have appealed to Che, who had thought of setting up a second flashpoint there. Reportedly, these talks ended with a warning from Che: **But you must be careful and keep yourself in reserve for the future when you will have more extensive responsibilities.**

It seems evident that Che did not as yet have a clear idea about what features an urban support network for the guerrillas should have; rather, he was in a hurry to move on to training the group and finalizing relations with Mario Monje and the Bolivian Communist Party. Monje was due to arrive around that time, after he had failed to show up at a first appointment.

Work at the Central Camp continued until December 24, as did the small-scale reconnaissance missions, but without making contact with campesino groups, which gives a good idea of how uninhabited the area was. Che wrote in his diary on December 24: **Day spent in Christmas Eve celebrations. There were people who had to make two journeys to get here, and arrived late, but we all got together in the end and had a good time,** some a little too much. Vázquez Viaña said the Lagunillas man's trip had not come up with the goods, just a little, very rough sketch. The "Lagunillas man" was Mario Chávez, a Party member who had been stationed in the area six months previously by the Peredo brothers and had taken over the management of a small hotel in Lagunillas as cover. His mission, apart from gathering information, had been to help to draw a coherent map of the area.

On December 30, reconnaissance continued, as did the work of moving to the central camp (the place is very good), where an oven for baking bread and a small auditorium were being built. Finally, on December 31, the general secretary of the Bolivian Communist Party, Mario Monje, arrived at the first camp. Che was advised immediately. His reception was cordial, but strained. The question "What are you here for?" was left hanging in the air.

Coco Peredo had told Monje on the way that Che would hand over political leadership to him, but under no circumstances would he do so with military leadership of the future armed movement, which he was putting pressure on Monje to join. Inti applied more pressure when Monje arrived at the camp, telling him the war was about to begin and he should join up.

"We'll see, we'll see . . ." Monje replied.

Monje got a cool reception, among other things, because he did not even greet the guerrillas, Alarcón said. Tania, on the other hand, obtained a rapturous welcome, as she was a sort of fairy godmother bringing letters and gifts. Martínez Tamayo also came—to stay, along with a new recruit, Antonio Jiménez, known as "Holy Bread." Without beating about the bush, Che went off to talk alone with Monje. A photograph shows them sitting, one on a stone and the other on a tree trunk. Monje had had his hair recently cut and Che smoked a cigar. There was a jar of coffee or tea between them. The talks lasted several hours.

The idea that the Party should take on the project of an armed struggle under Che's military leadership was ruled out immediately. Monje offered in exchange that he would resign as Party leader, but would get the latter to at least stay neutral and would bring other cadres to the struggle. Che did not oppose this but said it was a terrible mistake, showing a vacillating and opportunistic attitude that allowed the Party's position to remain ambiguous—its former secretary general might be in the armed struggle, but the PCB as such would neither support nor condemn it.

Another of Monje's proposals was that he should handle relations with other South American parties, trying to draw them to support the liberation movements. Che was very skeptical; the idea, as he saw it, was condemned to failure. Asking Codovila (the very moderate Argentine Communist leader) to support Douglas Bravo [a Venezuelan guerrilla leader] was like asking him to condone an uprising in his own party.

The main bone of contention, however, was Monje's request to lead the political and military struggle. Che would not budge: *I was to be the mili-*

tary chief and I would brook no compromise on that. The Congo experience was weighing on Che at that time; he felt he could not fall into the same trap a second time in his life, subordinating himself to political leaders who had no intention of fighting. The discussion was getting nowhere, it was going in a vicious circle. Mario Monje argued that if the revolution was to take place in Argentina, then he would carry Che's baggage, but in Bolivia a Bolivian would have to lead. Che hit him with a potted history of Latin Americanism, the independence struggle of the former Spanish colonies, and the constant movement of revolutionaries beyond arbitrary borders. Monje insisted on his position, and suggested that Che be his adviser. Che answered that he was adviser to no one. In exchange for his own military leadership, he offered Monje formal leadership and even said that, for the sake of appearances in front of infiltrators, he would salute him every morning and ask for instructions. But he, Che, would have real leadership, and that was not negotiable. Neither would give way. Monje began to argue using hypothetical situations, but Che cut him off, saying: I'm already here and they'll only get me out over my dead body.

The talks continued. Monje attacked Moisés Guevara's group, accusing them of being untrustworthy opportunists. Che in turn accused Monje of being sectarian.

My impression is that after Coco told Monje of Che's decision not to give way on strategic issues, he dug his heels in on that point. For his arguments were inconsistent.

After several hours, the two men's differences seemed to be irreconcilable. Monje asked Che to allow him to consult with the Bolivian Party members who had joined the guerrilla group, so they moved to the new camp. There Monje met the Peredo brothers, Ñato Méndez, Freddy Maimura, Vázquez Viaña, Antonio Domínguez, and Lorgio Vaca, all of whom, one of the others reported, "gave him a stony stare." He argued that military leadership was owed to the Party, that the people would turn their backs on the guerrillas once they knew they were led by a foreigner. He offered them guarantees of amnesty if they abandoned the struggle—"Come with me now"—and even proffered the veiled threat that, although the Party would carry out no reprisals, the men would do well to leave with him.

Monje probably did not expect a sharp and unanimous reply. The young Bolivians lashed out; they insisted he stay, that the Party not desert them, that serving under Che was a privilege. The discussion became confused. Monje then returned to the idea that he once had offered to Martínez Tamayo and Villegas: the correct way to insurrection was via an urban uprising followed by a retreat to the hills. He said he would in any case resign the Party leadership and join the column as just another soldier, although he let slip the cryptic phrase, "I'm not here to turn into a Van Troi," [i.e., not self-serving] a Vietnamese leader very popular at that time.

Monje seemed overwhelmed. He ate with the men in the camp, but there was a cool atmosphere he must have resented. When Alarcón suggested that Méndez, a Bolivian, lend his plate to the party leader, Méndez replied: "Look,

GUEVARA, ALSO KNOWN AS CHE

comrade, I don't know where the hogs eat in your country, but in mine they eat off the ground."

The next morning, **Monje told me he was leaving and would tender his resignation to the Party leadership on January 8. According to him, his mission was over. He left as one going to the gallows.**

Che assembled the guerrillas and commented **on Monje's attitude, saying that we would unite with all those who wanted to make a revolution and that I saw difficult days of moral anguish ahead for the Bolivians.** San Luis made a good prophesy in his diary: "It's most likely that there'll be a split and that some people will join us." The loneliness had begun.

In his diary, Che noted pragmatically that **Monje's attitude may hold up developments, on the one hand, but may contribute on the other, by freeing me from political commitments.** The project had certainly been weakened by the withdrawal of the most important radical left-wing group in Bolivia, and the guerrillas would now have to set up an urban network independent of the one they had used hitherto.

Che was now pressed to see whether Moisés Guevara's group had made up its mind and if they could set up some sort of joint front. Meanwhile, he began to set up a support network in the cities, where he could count on Dr. Humberto Rhea—who, however, was in Cuba at the time—Rodolfo Saldaña, and Loyola Guzmán, the Young Communist leader, who was to be the movement's treasurer. Che also had available the Peruvian Dagnino who, could add the urban network to his tasks as liaison officer with the ELN. Monleón was also available, as part of a parallel network with links to Havana.

Che did not seem to be excessively worried. As in Cuba in 1958, he underestimated the importance of a broad, solid urban movement behind and beside the guerrilla movement. Reading between the lines in his diary shows him seemingly much more interested in the urgent need to begin battle-hardening the group by undertaking an extensive reconnaissance mission in the zone, and to make links with the Argentines in his continental scheme.

On December 10, Che had already decided to send Tania to Buenos Aires, to hold talks first with some Argentines and then later to bring a group of them to Ñancahuazú. Che's diary and papers name Ciro Bustos (a supervisor of Masetti's guerrillas); Jozami—Juan Gelman the poet, then linked to a dissident left-wing faction in the Argentine Communist Party; Jauregui from the press union, and Stamponi. Tania left on that mission on January 2, 1967.

It was time to wait again. Five-day reconnaissance missions scouted out the terrain; the other comrades worked on the second camp, digging caves, shelters, and hideouts and putting roofs on the basic installations. Che began to discover that he was surrounded by a barely inhabited jungle wilderness. Hardly any of the reconnaissance found signs of habitation. Che's reports were succinct and very exact. The immediate plan was taking shape in his head: **Vilo and the medico followed the Iquiri until they ran into an unscalable rock face; they found no people but did discover some traces of** them. Pinares, Manuel, and Dariel walked along the river bed until they came to an inaccessible outcrop.

Che held a first meeting with the group to nip tensions in the bud.

> I had a little outburst about the attributes of a guerrilla fighter and the need for more discipline, and explained that our mission was, above all, to form an exemplary hard core of steel. . . . I explained the importance of study, which was indispensable for the future. I then gathered together the higher ranks—Vilo, Pinares, Machín Hoed, Inti, San Luis, Villegas, the medico, "Ñato" Méndez, and Martínez Tamayo. . . .
>
> I explained why Vilo had been named second-in-command: it was because Pinares had made some of the same mistakes over and over again. . . . Unpleasant incidents are ruining our work.

Matters did not end there, however; the problems with Pinares continued. A week later Che noted in his diary: Vilo told me that Pinares had been very hurt by the reference to his mistakes in the meeting the other day. I must talk to him. And the next day:

> I spoke to Pinares; his complaint was that he had been criticized in front of the Bolivians. His argument had no foundation, apart from his emotional state; that was worthy of note. The rest was unimportant. He referred to unflattering phrases Machín Hoed had used with him, which I looked into and it seems there was no such episode, just a little gossip. Pinares has calmed down a little.

Being absorbed in small details, Che seems to have omitted from his diary the fact that there was no reply from Monje on January 8. Nor did he mention the landscape. Pacho, on the other hand, noted: "The view of the Andes is marvelous, and climbing the hills is stirring; you get very tired, the more so without enough to eat." Camp life had raised Coello's spirits: he went around singing Charles Aznavour's "Isabel" and answered complaints with, "I'm not mad. If you're mad, blame imperialism for the fact that you're here." He talked to his rifle while cleaning it: "Listen, I've cleaned you, but I don't want you to fire shots. After the war, I'll take you to the museum."

The reconnaissance continued. On January 11 the group began to study Quechua, taught by Aniceto Reinaga and Jiménez Tardío. Che wrote: It was "boro" day today, and we spent it removing fly larvae from Pinares, Lorgio Vaca, Villegas, Olo Pantoja, Octavio, and Vilo.* Villegas merely noted "a boring day" in his diary, while Pacho said: "I rescued a butterfly from a spider's web. We arrived at camp at 6:10. Che was teaching."

---

*Translator's note: The Spanish edition of Che's Bolivian diary notes that a *boro* is a fly that lays eggs on the spot where it bites.

Communications with Havana worked properly on the Havana–Ñanc-ahuazú route, but slowly along the return Ñancahuazú–La Paz–Havana route (known in code as Manila). Che reported on his talks with Monje to Fidel, and in reply received the news that Juan Pablo Chang, the Peruvian strongman, was shortly to arrive. On January 11, Che received a message from Fidel telling him that he had held talks with another Communist Party functionary, union leader Simón Reyes, who "agreed to provide us with support, but without saying what type. He knows how to get hold of good American boots. He can be used for that immediately. He'll be there in two weeks." Ten days later, Fidel told Che that the Communist Party's second secretary was about to arrive in Havana and that "we shall listen to his suggestions and be tough and active about them." Two weeks after that Fidel reported on the meeting with PCB second secretary Jorge Kolle and Simón Reyes:

> Kolle stated [that] Monje informed PCB secretariat [of the] domestic operation and this angle seemed to bring confusion. Kolle was told [about the] continental scale and strategic content [of the] operation. This cleared confusion and he agreed [it would be a] mistake for leadership [to] demand cooperation whose content is strategic and not domestic. Asked [to] talk to you [to] set [the] ground rules [for] their collaboration and participation in operation . . . made favorable impression on me. Think you will reach satisfactory agreement.

If this was Fidel's view in Havana, where he was trying to smooth relations between Che and the Bolivian Communist Party, it did not fit in with Che's ideas based on the information he was getting. Between Fidel's two messages, Coco returned to the camp with another three Bolivian recruits and told Che that not only had Monje not resigned the Party leadership, he had **spoken with three who came from Cuba and talked them out of joining in the guerrilla war. . . . If this hostile attitude prevails, we shall have only eleven Bolivians in our ranks.**

In his roundup for January, Che said:

> **As I expected, Monje was evasive at first and treacherous later. The Party is already taking up arms against us and I don't know where it'll end, but it won't stop us and maybe, in the long run, it'll be to the good (I'm almost sure of that). The most honest and combative people will be with us, even if they go through a more or less serious crisis of conscience.**

By breaking off almost all relations with the Bolivian Communists and ridding himself of any dependency on them, Che seemed to have relieved himself of a burden. Debray put it well, years later:

> Local politics concerned him little. Bolivian Communists? A bunch of chickens. The national left-wing leadership? A bunch of shortsighted

politicians. The tin miners? A workers' aristocracy that would cause problems for proletarian egalitarianism tomorrow. Bolivia itself was a point of departure, the first link in a chain.

Despite the lack of activity, life in the camp was not easy during the third week in January. Food, was scarce: the region lacked resources, there was no possibility of barter with the campesinos, and hunting was bringing less food in. Pacho reported: "I dream of food every night. It must be the scant diet, with no meat or milk." Disease made its appearance: **Machín Hoed has symptoms of malaria. . . . Manuel came down with a high fever that has all the signs of malaria. I felt my own body "griping" all day, but the disease did not break out.**

References appeared now and again in the guerrillas' diaries to wives and families, to memories. Villegas on January 18: "A thousand kisses, a million to Harry and Custi." Pacho, on January 1: "I spent the day thinking about Terry." San Luis, on January 10: "I am reading the *The Charterhouse of Parma* and remembering my beloved wife and Eliseíto." Che himself noted the birthdays of his wife, his brother, and his sisters. Dariel Alarcón wrote in his diary: "Homesickness really is a gloomy companion in the jungle."

Strange things involving Ciro Argañaraz had been happening. On January 18, Che had written:

> **Vázquez Viaña arrived in a heavy downpour to say that Argañaraz had spoken to Olo Pantoja, showing that he knew a lot and offering to collaborate with us in the cocaine trade or whatever . . . he knew something was up. I gave Vázquez Viaña instructions to compromise him without offering much, just to pay him for all he can carry in his jeep and to threaten him with death if he doesn't comply.**

The police arrived at the Galvanized Metal House the next day.

> **Lieutenant Fernández and four plainclothes policemen turned up in a rented jeep looking for a cocaine factory. They just searched the house and noticed several odd things, like paraffin, for our lamps, that had not been taken to the cave. They took Vázquez Viaña's pistol off him, but left him with his Mauser and his .22. They made a show of taking a .22 off Argañaraz, which they showed Vázquez Viaña, and went away warning us that they knew everything and we had to rely on them. Vázquez Viaña would be able to reclaim the pistol in Camiri, "without too much fuss, by speaking to me," said Lieutenant Fernández. He asked for the "Brazilian."**

In this situation, Che insisted that Vázquez Viaña threaten Argañaraz and his assistant to scare them. He also reorganized the second camp so as to avoid surprises:

> The plan was based on the rapid defense of a zone near the
> river; we expected to counterattack with some men from the
> advance guard along trails parallel to the river that would lead
> to the rear guard. After reconnoitering, we would move the
> camp closer to Argañaraz's house. If its cover's blown, we'll
> make our influence felt on this person before leaving the
> zone.

Tensions continued to mount in the last days of January. Meanwhile, Che
was managing to make iron discipline take hold in the camp. Vilo Acuña
slipped while crossing the Ñancahuazú River with a hundred corncobs in his
backpack and lost his rifle in the water. Dariel Alarcón reported: "We saw
Vilo come out of the water and stare at us with a face I wouldn't dare describe.
'I dropped my rifle . . . and if I appear with Che without the gun . . . I'll shoot
myself first!' So there was the whole group diving around for the rifle."

On January 26, some good news arrived at last: Barely had we begun
to work on the new cave when news came that [Moisés] Guevara
had arrived with Loyola Guzmán. The Young Communist leader was
twenty years old at the end of January when she met Che in Ñancahuzú. She
was greatly surprised when Coco Peredo told her who was waiting to meet her.
"News at that time said that Che was in Colombia." The first thing that unsettled her was that the commander had lost his Argentine accent.

Why are you wet? Because the river's deep or because you're
small?

He ordered her to take off her socks and dry off. And he renamed her
Ignacia.

"Why Ignacia?"

For St. Ignacio Loyola.

While Loyola was to be a key cadre, as part of Che's plan for a future urban
network, Moisés Guevara, the leader of a small Maoist group with whom
Martínez Tamayo and Villegas had been cultivating relations for several
months, was essential if PCB support disappeared.

> I told [Moisés] Guevara my conditions: he'll have to dissolve
> the group; there will be no ranks for anyone and no political
> organization yet and we have to avoid controversy over na-
> tional or international contradictions. He accepted it all with-
> out demur, and, after a cool beginning, relations with the
> other Bolivians became friendly.

Loyola insisted later that Che said several times that here there would be
neither pro-Soviets nor pro-Chinese.

> Loyola made a good impression on me. She's very young and
> gentle, but one can tell she's totally determined. She's about
> to be expelled from the Young Communists, but they're trying

to get her to resign instead. I gave the cadres instructions and other papers. I also gave her back the money she had spent which now runs to 70,000 pesos. We're running short of cash. Dr. Pareja will be named head of the network and Rodolfo [Saldaña] will join up within two weeks.

In his talk with Loyola, Che simply explained the key ideas behind setting up an urban network and gave her a radio transmitter, which was broken and would have to be fixed. In Moisés Guevara's case, Che arranged for the first group [to arrive] between February 4 and 14. He said he couldn't come sooner because of communications, and the men slipped away from him now because of carnival season.

With this small support and a fledging urban network being organized, Che decided to set off on an extensive reconnaissance mission within three days, as soon as Coco had returned from escorting the visitors away. It seems surprising that Che's priority was to test his men, though he knew that doing so could lead to problems with the curious police and eavesdropping by their neighbor Argañaraz, and without the PCB's participation the urban network was "still in diapers." Was Che in a hurry to begin the campaign? January 31 was the last day spent in the camp. A small group headed by Olo Pantoja stayed behind to wait for the recruits and guard the base. I spoke to the troops and gave them their final instructions as we left.

The aim of the extensive reconnaissance mission was to establish relations with the campesinos in the area and to try, in principle, to avoid fighting, unless it could be useful to teach the group adapt to the hardships of guerrilla life and reinforce training that was expected to be brutal. Pacho wrote in his diary:

> Tomorrow we leave and I'm choosing things to take on the hike. There's so much I don't know what to do; blanket, backpack, hammock, 15 lb. of food, rice, beans, corn, sugar, coffee, quinine, hash, soup, one can of milk, one of sausages, one of sardines, a change of clothes, dried meat, bullets, rifle, radio communications book, class notebook, pistol, canteen . . .

Che wrote: Now the real guerrilla stage begins and we can try out the troops. Time will tell what they can do and what the prospects are for a Bolivian revolution.

47. The Brutal Expedition

At the base at Ñancahuazú, Bolivia, December–January 1966

THE EXPEDITION SET OFF ON FEBRUARY 1, 1967. IT WAS SCHEDULED TO take twenty days and although the guerrillas were not seeking a confrontation, the possibility of a clash with the army was not ruled out, as Che told Inti Peredo. At the end of the first stage, Che wrote: People arrived somewhat tired but, in general, held up well. Vilo, in the rear guard, suffered from his weight and held up the whole group. Pacho Fernández Montes de Oca was happy: "I felt great today and broke all records so far, as I never lagged behind."

The troops marched in the rain and explored the terrain, since their maps were not accurate: This brook cannot be the Frías River, it just isn't on the map. Che went along trying to draw our own maps, correcting the ones they had with colored pencils, putting mountain ranges and rivers in the right place, and taking photographs.

The column began to feel the effects of fatigue on February 4, after marches of ten or twelve hours a day. We followed the Ñacahuasu, which was relatively easy but deadly on our boots; several comrades are now almost barefoot. The men are tired but all have responded very well. I have shed almost fifteen pounds and can walk easily, although the pain in my shoulders is unbearable at times. According to Inti, Che was too sanguine in his diary entry; he dismissed the problems of the reconnaissance too lightly. The trekking was turning out to be extremely tough, thanks to the jungle terrain and the constant downpour. Pacho noted: "The men are worn out. Leonardo Tamayo has fever, Alarcón swollen glands, and I can't eat."

And all this amid complete isolation. We have found no signs of people recently passing through along the river, but we must run into habitation sooner or later, according to the map. The map was unreliable and Che was constantly correcting it. Régis Debray later noted:

> The region between Ñancahuazú and Río Grande is almost completely deserted, and socially and economically inert in its rural areas, so much so that the jungle really is unexplored and uncharted in not a few places. All the available maps of the region were full of gaps, approximations, or mistaken locations.

On February 5, the guerrillas arrived at a wide river, several times wider than the Ñacahuasu and not fordable. We . . . found a true Río Grande ["Big River"], and a full one, too. The river was between eighty and a hundred yards wide at that point, and joined by other rivers, like the Rosita and the Ñancahuzú. Pacho wrote: "Che jumped for joy, and said to me: Pacho, we've reached the River Jordan. Baptize me."

Still they saw no evidence that anyone human was anywhere around. There are signs of life, but old ones, and the trails we followed vanished into thick undergrowth with no indication that they are being used. Che finally decreed a rest stop; they would try to cross the river the next day.

On February 6, a day of quiet and getting strength back, the patrols sent up and down the river found no place to ford. Some of the guerrillas tried to swim across but failed. Pacho noted: "I dived into the river four times; it was impossible to make way."

They tried again the next day with a very big and unwieldy raft made by Pinares. The advance guard crossed over in two trips; half the middle column and my clothes, but not my backpack, went on the third. Suárez Gayol's calculations about where he expected to land were wrong: the raft was carried far downstream and he couldn't get her back. She broke up and Vilo Acuña made another, which wasn't ready till 9:00 p.m., so the rest of the middle column did not cross until the next day.

On the other side of the river, the column found more of the same: solitude and hunger. They made their first contact on February 9, with a man named Honorato Rojas, a campesino who was to be a key player in the future. Che saw him the next day: The campesino is true to type, incapable of helping us, and also incapable of foreseeing the dangers we face. Thus he is potentially dangerous—our security is not important to him. The medic treated his children for worms, and another one for a kick from a mare, and we took our leave.

Che laid out his scenario that night: To begin with, I'm thinking of marching for another ten days toward Masicurí and making all the comrades look physically like soldiers. He did make it clear the aim was not to enter into combat: We will then try to make it over the Frías River to reconnoiter another route.

The guerrillas arrived at the Masicurí. In his diary, Pacho rejoiced: "I got washed with soap. It was great." From then on, the guerrillas had to hack their way through the jungle with machetes. They made occasional contact with campesinos, who supplied very little food. Even Che, despite his tremendous stamina, was beginning to show signs of exhaustion: I was terribly tired, as the humitas had not agreed with me and I had not eaten for a day.* They decided to rest on February 13 in the vicinity of a campesino's house. Pacho spoke from his guts in his diary entry: "I went off with Pinares to look for corn, our only food of any sort for days." Che maintained discipline; what little food there was, was to be eaten in marching order. He occupied place number 14.

That same day they decoded a message from Havana, which brought news of more talks with the Bolivian Communist Party. Second secretary Jorge Kolle repeated that he had not been informed of the continental scope of the project. That being the case, they were prepared to collaborate in a plan whose details they asked to discuss with me. The message announced that PCB leaders Kolle, Humberto Ramírez, and Simón

---

*Translator's note: *Humitas* resemble tamales.

Reyes would visit the group and that the Party would collaborate in whatever was decided. It also announced that Juan Lechín, who led a party with strong influence among the miners, and whom Che had met on his way through Bolivia in the fifties, was ready to join the armed struggle. Strangely enough, this news of a change that would extend the political front in which the guerrillas could operate was noted in Che's diary only with the stony phrase: **We'll see how we face this new conciliatory offensive.**

The days went by in more hacking away with machetes, scant contact with campesinos, and little food. Corn saved them from starvation. Pacho wrote: "Breakfast, maize soup. Lunch, nothing. Supper, a little maize."

On February 16, Che decided to cross the sierra, heading toward the Rosita River. A campesino had spoken to them of soldiers building a road there and said they had thirty rifles in their camp. Che looked into the possibility of entering combat with his men and concluded there was no point, as everything was planned for a first action in July, with the guerrillas trained and reinforced.

For the next several days it was the rain that afflicted the column most cruelly. They began their ascent in a torrential downpour that went on for eighteen hours. On February 18, Pacho wrote that they were "marching toward the Rosita River through steep mountains, with sheer drops on both sides." Che added: **Very bad news. The slope is covered with manmade embankments and is impossible to descend. There's no option but to turn back.** February 20: **Day of slow marching,** and other entries indicating the guerrillas' efforts to make some headway between fordable brooks and crags with no easy access.

February 22: **The whole day was spent climbing up very difficult slopes and through thick jungle. After all that . . . we're at the head of the brook that flows into the Masicurí River, but going southward.** February 23: **A grim day for me. I made it through sheer pluck, as I felt exhausted. We left at twelve, under a sun hot enough to crack stones; shortly afterward I got somewhat dizzy as we breasted the highest hill, and from then on I walked out of determination.** Pacho added: "Not a drop of water, thirsty and little food." The terrible march went on and on. On February 24: **A listless day and hard going. Little progress. No water, as the brook we've followed is dry.** February 25: **A bad day:** Che had to intervene in a clash between two men:

Pacho [who was in the advance guard] **called me to say he and Pinares had had an argument and Pinares had given him peremptory orders, threatening him with a machete and hitting him in the face with the handle. When Pacho turned and said he would go no further, Pinares threatened him again with the machete, jostled him, and tore his clothes. It was a serious incident, so I called Inti and San Luis, who confirmed that Pinares's temper made for bad feeling in the**

advance guard but also told me of some insubordination by Pacho.

It did not rain, it poured. Che had noted two days previously in his diary that he had heard Pinares tell a comrade to "go to hell" and had had to have words with him.

Che spoke with the two the next day. He felt that Pinares was overbearing but that Pacho had exaggerated and also took his time to report the machete incident. Che used the occasion to explain that tension arising from tiredness and hardships (which Inti described in his diary as "hellish") had to be kept under control. And he threatened harsh punishment for transgressors. According to San Luis's account, Che said:

> **Seven years of revolution had made their mark on some comrades, who had become used to having chauffeurs, secretaries, and other aides, to giving them orders and getting everything done for us. A relatively easy lifestyle sort of made us forget the rigors and sacrifices of the life we were now leading again.**

Pacho was particularly hurt when Che told him and Pinares they were a pair of "shitkickers."

The Río Grande looked threatening, Alarcón said: "When we stopped to look at the river, it awed and even frightened us a little. Already flowing along in it were bits of earth that it had torn up, with huge trees in the middle pointing skyward." A fatal accident occurred as they reached the river. Benjamín Coronado, one of the Bolivians trained in Cuba, slipped on the riverbank and drowned before they could rescue him. **We have now had our baptism of death on the banks of the Río Grande, and absurdly.**

On February 27, the guerrillas had no food, only tea. The last of the canned food was gone. Some of the newer recruits ate their iron rations. Several scouting parties looking for a way to ford the river found nothing, so the guerrillas built a raft where the Río Grande met the Rosita River. The raft was lost halfway across. They spent two days trying in vain to cross the river and finally walked on along the riverbank, without meeting their advance guard.

On March 3, the guerrillas ate just palm hearts and corozo palm. Pacho wrote: "One hell of a day." The next day they managed to kill two monkeys, a cockatoo, and a dove, which were shared out among the whole group. **People are in low spirits and are going physically downhill by the day. I have the beginnings of edema in my legs.** Pacho wrote: "Marching on and on, without food and exhausted under the rain, looking at the trees, looking for fruit, something to hunt, but nothing, nothing. I get dizzy and see stars. Only willpower keeps me upright."

The guerrillas' great enemy now was hunger. Palm hearts and birds caught by chance were barely enough to fool their stomachs. On March 7, Che wrote: **4 months. People are more and more discouraged, with the end of our provisions in sight, but not the end of the road.** They were looking for the Ñancahuazú River again.

Inti and Martínez Tamayo got lost on March 8. Dr. Pedraja Morogoro noted that Che was "skinny and certainly very weak, but making a great effort and hiding it from the rest." The lost men were found the next day, but there was bad news: the Ñancahuazú was five days' walk away, and Pinares had entered an oil drilling camp with the advance guard. The workers had seen their weapons.

Che had no way of knowing, although he guessed, that Pinares's error led Captain Silva, an army officer who was hunting in the region, to learn from the oil workers that armed men were in the zone. He thought they were drug traffickers, and informed his superiors. A Major Patiño of the Bolivian army questioned the oil workers and then ordered the captain to take a patrol to search for the men. After three days, Silva had not found them, but their presence had been detected. Almost at the same time, and again without Che's knowledge, a couple of volunteers that had arrived with Moisés Guevara, Vicente Rocabado and Pastor Barrera, deserted from the main camp.

Che's guerrillas advanced only two and a half to three miles per day over the following three days. On March 13, Che wrote: **People are very tired and again in low spirits. There's only one meal left. We walked some six kilometers, but to little effect.**

The invisible and still very faint circle closing in on the guerrillas acquired a new link when the police arrived at the Galvanized Metal House. They beat up Serapio—Aquino Tudela—in an attempt to discover who was roaming around the area, and they hoisted a flag on the roof to mark the spot in the middle of the jungle for helicopters. The police did not really know what they were looking for.

On March 14,

> **almost without our realizing it, we reached the Ñancahuazú. (I was-am tired, bowed down as if by sorrow.) The river is wild and no one's in the mood to cross it, but San Luis volunteered and got over comfortably, heading back to base at 15:20 sharp. I expect he'll get there in two days. We ate the last of our food—stewed corn with meat—and now we'll depend on hunting. At the time of writing we have a small bird, and I've heard three shots. The medic and Inti are the hunters. We heard parts of the speech in which Fidel railed against the Venezuelan Communists and the U.S.S.R.'s attitude toward its Latin American puppets.**

That same day, the police arrested Vicente Rocabado and Pastor Barreras when they tried to sell a rifle in Lagunillas. Rocabado, who had been fired from the Criminal Investigation Police for corruption, tried to curry favor with his former colleagues; he told more than he knew and a good deal of what he had heard. He identified the chief (Olo Pantoja) as "Antonio the Cuban"; he said the "big chief," whom he had never seen, was Che; he spoke of Argentines, Peruvians, and a Frenchman (Régis Debray) in the camp, described Tania's jeep in detail, named members of his group recruited by the miners' leader Moisés Guevara, and offered to guide the army to the Galvanized Metal House and the guerrilla base camp. He even claimed to have joined the guerrillas on an information-gathering mission to see if he might derive some benefit from it later.

Coco Peredo would later say angrily that "the Bolivian guerrillas recruited by Moisés Guevara . . . were picked up in brothels and bars and joined us for money." This was unfair, but it was true that Guevara had recruited very superficially, for of the dozen men who arrived at the camp, some were proven union activists. But mixed in with them were *lumpen* proletariat elements from the mining regions.

On March 15, the small middle column led by Che tried to cross the Ñancahuazú, and partly succeeded. The raft broke down again, dragging them half a mile downstream and leaving behind two guerrillas from Che's group and the rear guard on the other bank. Some of the group were suffering from foot ailments, and all the guerrillas were suffering from protein and fat deficiency because of the persistent lack of food.

From the beginning of the expedition, the guerrillas had marched with a horse they had found. When hunger began to gnaw at them, several men approached Che to propose eating the animal. On one occasion he threatened to leave two men without food if they raised the issue again. But on March 16, Che, who had grown fond of the horse and wanted to use it on the farm, made his decision: **We decided to eat the horse, as hunger was causing the men's bellies to swell alarmingly. Manuel Hernández, Inti, Leonardo Tamayo, and Gustavo Machín had several symptoms** [of malnutrition]. **I was extremely weak. We feasted on horsemeat from five p.m. onward. We'll probably pay for it tomorrow.**

At least the radio worked properly. A message from Havana confirmed that Régis Debray had arrived in Bolivia. Che thought he must already have been at the base camp, which was true: Tania had picked him up in La Paz at the end of February along with an Argentine, Ciro Roberto Bustos, and Coco Peredo had taken them to the camp on March 5. Fidel Castro had sent Debray directly to Bolivia this second time, telling him he was to meet Che on this trip, but his purpose was not made clear. Debray thought Fidel wanted him to help Che broaden the support base in the Bolivian left, among Maoist and Trotskyist groups with whom he had previously made contact following the friction with the Communists.

The guerrillas had another accident on March 17, when the raft overturned as the rear guard tried to cross the Ñancahuazú River. Lorgio Vaca— **until then, considered the best of the Bolivians in the rear guard, for** his seriousness, discipline, and enthusiasm—was drowned. By now Che must have been doubting the virtues of the region he had chosen. But, as Debray would later say, it was too late to "abandon it and head off to a better one."

Meanwhile, Captain Silva and his patrol arrived at Ciro Algañaraz's farm. In the course of a violent interrogation, in which Silva shoved a pistol in Argañaraz's mouth, he obtained the same information that the police had had for days, that there was a group of strange people, probably drug traffickers, a few miles away. The army deployed almost sixty men in the zone. Silva advanced toward the Galvanized Metal House with nine soldiers, but found nothing. Two Bolivians, Reinaga and Domínguez, watched the soldiers from ambush. Shots were fired at nightfall when Vázquez Viaña, who was returning to the camp, ran into another patrol and wounded a soldier. The army then arrested Salustio Choque, one of the Bolivian workers who looked after the farm.

The main camp got conflicting news of all these army movements. Che's advance guard, led by Pacho and Alarcón, had arrived a couple of days before the main body of guerrillas; then San Luis suddenly turned up, as Che had sent him ahead with news of their delay in crossing the river. Debray wrote: "San Luis had arrived suddenly, without warning, the day before, with a rifle but no backpack. A savage child, all skin and bone; no one heard him come. Others walk or hesitate but he, green behind the ears, slips through the jungle leaves like a cat."

While Che was making slow progress toward the main camp, ambush parties were set up around the second camp, now known as the Bear Camp, and Pacho set off with a patrol to look for the commander, but to no avail. Debray later noted that there was a sort of power vacuum—lax discipline and a feeling of chaos—in the camp headed by Olo Pantoja. Were they to fight the army or wait for Che?

Che kept up the pace on March 19, keeping a tight grip on his men, who were quarrelling over trifles because they were so fatigued. They met an advance guard at 5:30 P.M.

> We were met by the Peruvian medic, Restituto José Cabrera, who had come with Chang and the telegraph operator, Lucio Galván. They brought the news that Dariel Alarcón was waiting with food, that two of Moisés Guevara's men had deserted, and that the police had been to the farm. . . . Neither Olo Pantoja nor Coco were there. The latter had gone to Camiri to look for some more of Guevara's men, and Olo had left immediately with word of the desertion.

Che ordered Manuel Hernández to retrace his steps to search for the rear guard. By dawn, all who had set out on the expedition were together again.

As the guerrillas headed off for the camp the next day, Che heard the rest of the news—Salustio Choque's arrest, the army's presence at the Galvanized Metal House, the disappearance of Vázquez Viaña after he shot the soldier and the loss of the farm mule and a jeep (which Che, ever loyal, noted in that order). The column continued on its way. Debray saw them arrive:

> In the distance, a procession of hunchbacked beggars emerged from the night little by little, with the rigid slowness of blind men. The middle column, at last . . . And now, in the gray light of dawn, on the edge of the jungle, on this desolate savannah that stretches its hills and hollows as far as the eye can see, the khaki silhouettes drew near against the yellow-green brush, zigzagging among the sharp high grasses with their scattered rattan palms. They looked like sleepwalkers in Indian file, wearing harnesses or rather wobbling pack saddles, ragged and bent under the weight of their backpacks (which weighed at least thirty kilos each). Their rifles pointing horizontal, rifle-holders at right angles on their shoulders; the first light gathers and spreads. Their canteens are soon jangling, as are the pistols on their belts, the unbearable and noisy soot-black pots tied onto their backpacks, their mugs and machetes. As taciturn as a guerrilla may be, he sounds like a one-man band with all his hanging goods and chattels. Che was in the middle, his torso almost straight, with a backpack rising above his head, his M1 rifle vertical, his brown felt beret on his head, and the beginnings of a beard.

Sorry about the delay, he said, taking off his backpack with a wry smile. He stayed on his feet, wiping his face and catching his breath while the rest collapsed as they came in. **Time to cook,** Che said when he saw a four-legged carcass hanging by its paws. For twenty-four hours, and to everyone he saw, he kept shouting, **Come on, cooks, get a move on!**

"Can we light a fire, Commander, in broad daylight?"

Yes, under exceptional circumstances. But no one touches a bite until the rear guard gets here.

Che met Tania and Juan Pablo Chang, the Peruvian ELN leader, in the camp.

A climate of defeat prevailed. Shortly afterward, a recently recruited Bolivian medic arrived with a message for San Luis saying that Pinares and Olo Pantoja were at the water place and that he should go talk to them. I sent him back with the word that wars were won with bullets, that they should withdraw immediately to the camp and wait for me there. All this gives an impression of terrible chaos. They don't know what to do.

Che spoke with Chang while trying to reorganize his men:

He wants $5,000 a month for ten months, and Havana told him to talk it over with me. . . . I told him yes, in principle, as

long as he led a rebellion in six months. He's thinking of doing so with fifteen men led by him in the Ayacucho region. We also agreed he would receive five men now, and fifteen more sometime; they would be sent with their arms after being trained in combat. . . . He seemed very enthusiastic.

Combat

Reading from a seat in a treetop, the base at Ñancahuazú, 1966

LTHOUGH CHE MUST HAVE FELT THAT THE TIME TO FIGHT WAS NEAR, HE spent March 21, 1967, shaping up his multinational project, in the detached and painstaking manner that so used to fascinate his men. He made it clear to Debray (who brought news from home, a brief note from Aleida saying "I'm fine; I worry about the kids. Their grades are good.") that he would have preferred to have him abroad as an international liaison for the guerrillas, rather than here as a fighter or even as a liaison to the left wing in La Paz. Che suggested that before returning to Havana and Europe, Debray go to Brazil to link up with Carlos Marighella, who was training and organizing a breakaway group from the Brazilian Communist Party. Debray's chief task would be to set up a European support network. Che proposed to send letters via Debray to Jean-Paul Sartre and Bertrand Russell.

Che entrusted the Argentine Ciro Roberto Bustos with a fundamental mission in his country. He wanted him to get in touch with **Jozamy, Gelman and Stamponi's groups**, a broad spectrum of militants and "tendencies" ranging from revolutionary supporters of Perón to splinter groups from the Communist Party, all of which favored the armed struggle. There could be no delays. If these people accepted a role in the movement that was shaping up, **they should begin reconnaissance missions in the north and send me a report.**

On the evening of March 21, Che received a report from Olo Pantoja with news of desertions from the guerrilla group and the presence of the army. Debray described Che's reaction:

> Che's face fell. He was beside himself. He got up and shouted:
> **Just what is going on? What kind of shit is this? Am I surrounded by traitors or cowards? Ñato, I don't want one of your Bolivian assholes here, not one. Agreed? They're out, until things change. Got that?**
> "Yes, Commander."
> **Vilo, go to the rear guard, run to the camp. There we are and there we stay. Pinares and Olo Pantoja are to do nothing, dammit, I'll have words with them. Go now, right there. I'll reach you with my people tomorrow. See you tomorrow.**
> The outburst was a cold rage that erased the atmosphere of overall fraternity Che normally inspired; it was as if he wanted to shatter the communion he had with his comrades and reinforce his loneliness. An awed fear colored the respectful silence of the men who had fought under him in Cuba and elsewhere.

Che began the march the next day. Around noon, he gathered the guerrillas into a single group of forty-seven men, **counting visitors and all.** Five men were lying in ambush near the river and another three were out scouting to forestall any surprises.

Inti Peredo told Che about more problems that Pinares's attitude was causing. Che exploded: **I told Pinares he would be thrown out of** the guerrillas if this was true. He answered that he'd rather be shot.

Che said: You've insulted us, all of us, especially me. You're no longer in command of the advance guard. Manuel Hernández will take your place. Get out of here. Any more indiscipline and you're out.

"I'd rather be shot."

If that's what you want . . .

The meeting was explosive and stormy and did not go well. But Che took the opportunity to fix his strategy. If they were to withdraw just now, without giving battle, the army, with all the information the deserters must have given them, would go after them, fresh and with morale high. Better to wait for them and strike the first blow.

Che was right. At seven A.M. on March 23, San Luis and Dariel Alarcón led an ambush party, including six of the Bolivians, and routed an army column that was advancing along the river after arresting Serapio near the Galvanized Metal House. The shooting lasted just seven minutes, but seven soldiers were killed and four wounded, a major and a captain among them.

> We captured their operations plan, which consisted of advancing from both ends of the Ñancahuazú to meet in the middle. We quickly dispatched men to the other end and posted Pinares and almost all of the advance guard at the end of the maneuver route, the middle and part of the rear guard in defense, and Israel Reyes set up an ambush at the other end of the maneuver route. We'll spend the night like that and see if the famous Rangers turn up tomorrow.

The next day,

> I sent Inti to talk for the last time with the prisoners, take all useful clothing off them, and free them, except the two officers who were spoken to separately and left fully dressed. We gave the major until noon on the 27th to remove the dead and offered a truce throughout the Lagunillas area if he stuck around, but he said he was leaving the army. The captain said he had rejoined the army a year ago at the [Communist] Party's request and had a brother studying in Cuba. Furthermore, he gave the names of two other officers ready to collaborate.

Captain Silva's sympathies toward the guerrillas were later discovered and cost him a harsh interrogation and dismissal in Camiri.

Random air raids took place regularly over the following days, scaring the Bolivian rookies. Then the Bolivian air force began to use napalm. Pinares went on reconnaissance without finding anything in his zone. Inti recalled that Pinares was reacting to Che's criticism: "He strove to be the best.

He even made a point of carrying the heaviest backpack in tougher and tougher conditions, and his Garand, too."

Che then moved the ambush parties ahead and on March 25 took advantage of the relative calm to analyze the situation. **We've put our balls on the table; let's see who can stand it most,** Che said in Debray's account, with a "naturally sardonic ease and explicitness." He assembled most of the guerrillas in the middle of the jungle and went over the expedition and the fatal accidents, with his hands behind his back, as usual. **I analyzed the journey and exposed Pinares's faults, said I had demoted him and named Manuel Hernández as advance guard leader.**

Che continued to lash out at the group, especially at the four Bolivians (Julio Velazco, José Castillo, Eusebio Tapia, and Hugo Choque, all recruited by Moisés Guevara), whom he called the "hangover boys" for their lack of discipline and unwillingness to fight. He ordered them to surrender their arms, **telling them they will not eat if they don't work and will have no smoking rights. Their personal belongings will be divided among the neediest comrades.**

Debray heard

> a sarcastic baritone lashing out here and there. Why had Tania come with the visitors? More indiscipline. She was ordered to stay in the south to do liaison work. . . . *And you, René, have come here as a technician and can't even make the transmitter work* . . . . Tania, the only woman in the group, turned away with tears in her eyes. René did not answer. There was no more fuel to power the transmitter's motor. Che was unbending, with himself above all, much more than with his men and more with his men than with the enemy. If he wanted more and indeed mistreated himself less. . . . his only two personal privileges were not to have nighttime guard duty and, when they were away from camp, to carry a thermos of coffee in his knapsack.

Che also spoke of the duplicitous Bolivian Communist Party leadership, of how at the same time as they arranged a meeting with Fidel in Havana supposedly to agree to supporting the guerrillas, they expelled young activists for having joined the rebels. **Facts are what matter; words that don't fit the facts aren't important. I announced that classes would resume** (in the Quechua and French languages, and in culture and politics). Che also talked to the guerrillas one on one; he spent some time with Juan Pablo Chang, making it clear that Chang was there to train under combat conditions and then go to Peru. As things stood, the last thing Che wanted to do was internationalize the guerrilla group. **In the course of the meeting the group was named the Bolivian National Liberation Army. Minutes of the meeting will be made.** Pacho's diary curtly said: "I'm dead tired."

As Che was tightening discipline, the Bolivian army command was reacting to the ambush. Major Plata and Captain Silva were interrogated in Camiri, from where Silva was sent to La Paz to spend fourteen days in a dungeon under further interrogation. A couple of CIA agents turned up who were interested to know whether Silva had seen Che in the camp. He could not identify any of the photographs they showed him.

The CIA's presence was no accident. They had been alerted by the Bolivian military and the Interior Ministry, and had taken part in interrogating the deserters Rocabado and Barrera in Camiri. A certain Dr. González was one of the first interrogators; he was later identified by Cuban sources as Gustavo Villoldo Sampera, a Cuban exile. Other CIA agents, like Edward Fogler and station chief Tilton, took part in a later interrogation of Salustio, the farmworker arrested at the Galvanized Metal House.

The CIA's involvement was only one of the steps taken by the U.S. government. Only hours after the first armed clash in Bolivia, they responded to a request from the Bolivian government to U.S. Ambassador Douglas Henderson by offering aid from Panama to the Bolivian army in the form of C-rations, training, and arms.

On March 26, the guerrillas played hide-and-seek with the army. Two reconnaissance expeditions reported on troop movements but did not engage in combat. The next day, **the news broke and the airwaves were filled with bulletins, including a press conference by** [President] **Barrientos.** The military reports spoke of many nonexistent guerrilla casualties, but there was some most serious news: Tania had been identified, **with which two years of good, patient work are lost.** The deserters' statements, together with the discovery of a jeep in Camiri, had led to a police search of the house of the jeep's owner, Laura Gutiérrez Bauer. They were surprised to find photographs of her with President René Barrientos and General Alfredo Ovando. It took them a couple of days to make the connection between Laura and the Tania mentioned by the deserters.

The unmasking of Tania left a huge hole in La Paz, as Rodolfo Saldaña said years later: "I became very worried when I saw that Tania didn't return to camp. . . . Her presence was very important for the armed movement."

The army arrested Ciro Argañaraz and his helper, Rosario, the "man from Vallegrande," after the ambush. They ransacked the house and beat up the man from Vallegrande, in such a way as to make him appear to have committed suicide. They even stole the doors from the house. And Argañaraz, who had denounced the guerrillas to the police when he thought they were drug traffickers, was thrown in jail for nine months.

The army, which had, according to radio broadcasts, deployed 2,000 men in the guerrillas' area of operations, began to close in from a distance. The radio continued to broadcast disinformation, talking of ten to fifteen guerrilla casualties. What the radio did not say was that U.S. Army major Ralph W. Shelton, a guerrilla warfare expert with combat experience in Vietnam, had meanwhile arrived in Santa Cruz.

At the end of March, Che tried to obtain food and scout for exit routes from the zone; meanwhile his men were recovering from the terrible experience of the expedition. A guerrilla patrol made contact with Red Cross workers who were looking for the bodies from the first ambush, then with an army truck. Rather than shoot at it, the guerrillas asked the driver to withdraw. Che lay low for another three days. Debray said:

> He was angry and did not utter a word to anyone over the following days. He sat apart in a hammock, smoking a pipe under a plastic cover, reading, thinking, drinking maté, cleaning his rifle, and listening to Radio Havana by night on his transistor radio. Laconic orders. Absent, wrapped up in his thoughts. Tense atmosphere in the rest of the camp. Arguments, national sensibilities, wrangling over tactics to be used, all sharpened by exhaustion, hunger, lack of sleep, and the relentless onslaught of the jungle. Otherwise, he would have mingled with the troops, talking and joking with all of them. Che laid discipline bare, unadorned and with no personal attachments. Can there be charisma at a distance? *Absolutely not*, he told me good-naturedly, one night shortly afterward, when alone, in confidence, I asked him about his deference toward Fidel and his tyranny toward the rest.
>
> *You do what you can, given your disadvantages. I'm Argentine and lost among these tropical people. It's difficult for me to open up, and I don't have Fidel's gift for communicating. I'm left with silence. Every chief must be a myth to his men. When Fidel wants to play baseball, he convinces those around him that they're the ones who want to play and they follow him to the ball park. When I was in Cuba, and the others suggested playing ball, I'd say "Later" and go off to a corner to read. If people don't like me for that at first, at least they'll respect me for being different.*

Meanwhile, President Barrientos was meeting with his military high command to explain his decision to appeal to the U.S. government for military advice. Some nationalist officers were uneasy about the decision. Barrientos also sought advice from the German war criminal Klaus Barbie, then in hiding in Bolivia. Vice president and armed forces chief General Alfredo Ovando, who had just returned from a tour of Europe, took charge of requesting support, arms, and ammunition from the military in Argentina and Brazil. The army's situation in Camiri was bad. Major Rubén Sánchez led a patrol into the area and found "demoralization and fear among commanding officers and all those in the operations zone." However, the army occupied the Galvanized Metal House once and for all on November 30, so for the time being the guerrillas were ghosts that aroused fear.

Che centered his March 1967 summary on three points. He planned to stop training the Bolivian recruits, particularly those from Moisés Guevara's group, who have generally been of very poor quality (2 deserters, 1 "singing" prisoner, 3 shirkers, 2 malingerers). And he assessed the need to get moving before I had thought to, leaving a group on standby and hindered by four possible informants. The situation is not good, but now we enter another period of trial for the guerrillas, which will be good for them once they are over it.

The first U.S. aircraft carrying supplies, and probably napalm bombs, arrived in Santa Cruz on April 1, while Che was arranging new caves and keeping the entire column active (Pacho wrote: "We haven't slept for days") by sending the troops out on patrol or to set up ambushes.

The guerrillas marched off at night on April 3:

> **We walked slowly until we reached the bend in the shortcut at 6:30 and arrived at the edge of the farm at 8:30. When we came to where we had ambushed the army, all that was left of the seven dead were skeletons picked perfectly clean by birds of prey, which had done their duty most responsibly. I sent two men (Leonardo Tamayo and Ñato) to make contact with San Luis, and in the evening we went to Piroboy Ravine, where we slept after gorging ourselves on beef and corn. I spoke to Debray and Bustos and proposed three alternatives to them: to carry on with us, to strike out alone, or to take Gutiérrez and try their luck from there. They chose the third. We'll try our luck tomorrow.**

There was more hide-and-seek between the guerrillas and the army on April 4. They passed through a spot where 150 soldiers had lain in ambush. **We found military hardware, such as plates, canteens, even bullets and equipment. We confiscated it all.**

That same day, a patrol led by Major Sánchez followed Salustio's directions and advanced on the camps. Sánchez recalled:

> I went so quickly I was 200 meters from the central camp, according to Salustio's directions. Then the air force appeared and, taking us for guerrillas, began to bomb us. Once the bombing was over, I entered the camp. On the way in, all we noticed were large quarters for several men and individual posts, probably built for sentries. In the middle of the ravine, in the first camp, I found a sort of kitchen with the ashes still warm. In each of those three or four camps there were positions set in circles, not just a row, but many of them, so as we advanced uphill, I thought: I don't believe the guerrillas have gone to wage war in the conventional way. I found documents, lists of guerrillas, reports, sentry rosters, a set of papers with information, and most important, photographs in which Che appeared.

Much was to be said about one of these photographs.

The army allowed the press access to the camp four days later and journalists milled around the military remains. Héctor Pracht from the Chilean newspaper *El Mercurio* took note of the Dominican ammunition, the Argentine newspapers, and the American cans of milk, the vegetable patches, and a hen and chickens. **A Chilean journalist wrote a detailed account of our camp; he had found a photo of me, clean shaven and smoking a pipe. I'll have to look more deeply into how it was obtained.**

Che never did find out, but there were three apparently contradictory versions of how the photograph was found. A British journalist, Murray Sales, said that he found a photograph of Dr. Guevara and a copy of a speech by Vo Nguyen Giap among the rubbish carefully removed from the dormitories. The photograph of Guevara was of a younger man than the one he had seen in Cuba in 1964, and he thought it had been taken some years before in the Sierra Maestra.

The Mexican journalist Luis Suárez said another photograph of Che showed him sitting in a clearing similar to those at the campsite. This photo, in which he was bearded and had no pipe, was found by Ugalde, the Bolivian president's photographer. Specialists from the state oil corporation, Yacimientos Petrolíferos, filmed the campsite in search of the angle corresponding to the photograph to see if it was current, but one part of the jungle looked too much like every other for thousands of miles, so there was no conclusive proof that Che had been there.

The next day, Che continued to advance, setting up ambushes to protect his flank as he went. **I thought of leaving at dawn and going downstream, but soldiers were sighted bathing 300 meters from our position. We then decided to cross the river without leaving a trace and walk along the opposite bank until we reached our stream.** The day after that, the guerrillas broke the first cordon and captured a group of campesinos who had rounded up several lost cows. **We spent the night eating.**

Debray recalled:

> During the five minutes' rest there were for each hour's march he could drink one or two cups of a fairly muddy grog for himself. Otherwise everything was the same for everyone. He strung up and took down his hammock with no help, and in each meal demanded the same half-sardine or three morsels of meat, allotted to each man. He carried the same weight in his backpack and after his corn rations fell in a river he was crossing, he spent a whole day without eating, so as not to draw from any one else's rations. This rule of equality of mortification had become a creed and a touchstone for ideological examination:
>
> **You see this bun, Debray?** *It was after supper, at night, around the campfire. He was lying back on the ground.* **Suppose it weighs twenty grams. You could get two good slices from it, two hundred calories in each and no more. Suppose you're surrounded by ten hungry men and it all depends on you, what do you do?**
>
> "Draw lots for the two slices."
>
> **Why?**
>
> "It's better to have two comrades who can survive by eating a bit than ten who have none, eating ten times nothing."
>
> **Well, you're wrong, Debray. Each should have his crumbs and then whatever's God's will. The revolution has its principles, and there can always be two fewer bureaucrats.**
>
> "Do you think it's best for ten revolutionaries to meet their certain end under absolute equality of conditions?"

As long as morals are saved, then the revolution will be, too. If not, what's the point?

For the next three days the advance guard and the middle column advanced toward Pirirenda, with Vilo Acuña leading the rear guard. Pacho wrote in his diary: "The radio says Che is in Bolivia." It was a rumor with no clear basis, but was perhaps enough to spur a meeting at the Pentagon on April 9 attended by several generals, CIA director Richard Helms, and the U.S. president's adviser on national security and Latin American issues, Walter Rostow. Although they believed that they were on a wild-goose chase and Che was not in Bolivia, they decided to cooperate more closely with the Bolivian armed forces.

On April 10, the Peruvian medic in the column came to tell Che **that 15 soldiers were coming downstream. Inti had gone to tell San Luis in the ambush party. There was nothing to do but wait, and that's what we did. I sent Coello upstream so he could inform me of their progress.**

The rear guard, backed up by Inti and San Luis, was posted on both sides of the river when the patrol advanced along the banks looking for traces of the guerrillas. The guerrillas fired, killing one soldier and wounding three; they took six prisoners, but also suffered a major casualty, a severe blow to them. Jesús Suárez Gayol, "Blondie," Che's comrade for several years, was shot in the head during the brief exchange. **His Garand was jammed and a grenade, without its pin but unexploded, was by his side.**

The troops with which they had clashed were part of a larger patrol scouting the environs of the Ñancahuazú River. Major Rubén Sánchez, who had led the company that took the camp, recalled:

> At three P.M., two desperate soldiers who had escaped from the Iripiti zone appeared. Some of the officers were so shocked they could not even explain what had happened. I calmed one of the soldiers down and he told me that they had fought with the guerrillas at eleven A.M., that they had been ambushed. He could give me no details of distance or the number of guerrillas, because the soldiers were disoriented; they had fled as best they could and had a hard time reaching the camp. Lieutenant Saavedra was killed. I received instructions to advance from Colonel Rocha, then commander of No. 4 Division. It was already four P.M. and night was about to fall, so I set off as quickly as possible with the thirty-five soldiers I had, plus eighteen who had returned from the morning's ambush and were anxious to recover the officer's body.

Che guessed what the army's reaction would be. So, instead of resuming the march, he ordered the ambush party to advance, again under San Luis's command, **by about 500 meters, but now with the support of the entire advance guard. At first I had ordered a withdrawal, but it** seemed logical to leave the situation as it was. At about 1700 news came that the army was advancing in large numbers. There's nothing for it but to wait. I sent Harry Villegas to give me a clear idea of the situation.

Major Sánchez:

> Instead of drawing away from where they first ambushed us, they advanced two or three kilometers and set up another ambush. A Cessna was flying overhead to assist in the attack. As agreed, I gave the signal by firing a flare pistol. Then the fighting began. I was in third place although a commander should normally be in the middle or the rear guard, but I did so to rouse the very demoralized troops.

The soldiers advanced **along the river, but without great precautions, so they were taken completely by surprise.** Pacho opened fire. In Sánchez's account:

> Everybody around me was dead or wounded. Lieutenant Ayala, who was carrying a .60 mortar, was wounded in the chest. I was the only one still alive and unhurt. Then I dived to the left, looking for shelter, and found two other soldiers who were retreating. The guerrillas were demanding our surrender from in front. We took up positions and began to fire toward where they were shouting. Then another group appeared from behind and demanded that we surrender. I had one soldier shoot behind us while the other one and I kept shooting forward. Then the firing stopped. It became totally quiet. I felt a man's knee on my body; he grabbed my chin and twisted it. I later learned it was Maimura. The soldiers managed to shout: "Don't kill him, he's the major!" We surrendered. One tried to take away my revolver, but I took the bullets out and held on to it. "No one takes this revolver off me," I said. San Luis asked me: "How many men do you have? Where did you come from?" I told him:
>
> "You're wasting your time. I won't tell you a thing."
>
> Another guerrilla, who seemed to be Bolivian, said: "These soldiers are a bunch of thieves."
>
> "You're the thief, not I."
>
> It was then that San Luis shoved me downhill and I ended up by the river, near a guerrilla halfway up the bank with a carbine over his shoulder, smoking a cigarette. Some kept firing and others tried to withdraw through the area. The smoke was Inti. San Luis came down and said:
>
> "Major, order your troops to surrender."
>
> "I can't order my men to surrender, only to retreat."
>
> "Make them surrender or we'll kill them."
>
> "Kill me if you like," I told him, "but I won't order a surrender."
>
> San Luis went off and I stayed with Inti. He told me: "Major, please don't move from my side." But I could not obey: I had dead and wounded, one of them still floating in the water, and I had to rescue them. Inti saw me and said nothing. When I finished rescuing the wounded, I of course returned to his side.

"You're thieves and murderers," I told Inti. "Why do you kill my soldiers?"

Inti gave me a ring, from the lieutenant who had died that morning, and told me:

"Take this for his widow. We need the watches, so we won't give them back. We're neither thieves nor murderers. You call us that because you don't understand the meaning of our struggle."

Sánchez wrote: "They all spoke of a chief and I laughed. Well, they all seemed to be the high command, the way they talked. San Luis had been the most active one in the fighting, and Inti said he had been in command of the ambush, so the chief could be none other than Che."

Villegas sent Che a first report: *This time there are seven dead, five wounded, and a total of twenty-two prisoners.* The guerrillas had routed the army twice in one day. Che's band of ghosts had struck again. Journalist Luis Suárez got the defeated soldiers' version some months later: "The guerrillas are skinny, very pale and like wax."

Che drew close to observe the soldiers, but without letting himself be seen. He ordered Inti to sound Major Sánchez out about switching sides. Sánchez refused, but agreed to take with him an ELN press release, and kept his word. He took two copies, one of which he gave to military intelligence without mentioning the second. This he gave to a brother of his who was a journalist, and who in turn leaked it to the newspaper *Prensa Libre* in Cochabamba.

Not only did Sánchez keep his word but the guerrillas had made a great impression on him and his social convictions. Some years later he was a key figure in a left-wing military coup.

Che conducted a brief ceremony on April 12 to bury the first Cuban to die in the fighting, his friend Suárez Gayol.

I gathered all the fighters, except the four "hangover boys," to hold a small memorial service for Blondie and to mark the fact that the first blood shed was Cuban. I grappled with a tendency that had been made clear yesterday when Camba said he trusted Cubans less and less. . . . I made a new appeal for integration as the only way to develop our army, to increase its combat ability and battle-harden its fighters, but not increase numbers—which, on the contrary, have fallen in recent days.

Che also heard a protest from Tania, who had stayed behind in the camp during the fighting and now demanded to be allowed into the front line.

After stashing the booty away in a cave that Ñato had prepared very well, we left at 1400, at a slow pace, so slow we made almost no progress and had to sleep in a small water station shortly after

starting. Pacho wrote in his diary: "The dried salted meat is full of maggots. Even though it's rotten and I've got a bad stomach, I eat my fill of it."

The guerrillas turned full circle and returned to the main camp (Pacho later said: "We've messed around with the Guards' heads and are at the starting gate") and discovered that the army had not found their most important cave. Che wrote in his diary: **The Americans claim that their sending advisers is part of a long-standing plan and has nothing to do with the guerrillas. Maybe we're seeing the beginning of a new Vietnam.**

Che's first plan was to mobilize the guerrillas as a whole, **operate a little in the Muyupampa zone, and then retreat northward, if possible. Debray and Bustos would then be on their way towards Sucre-Cochabamba, depending on the circumstances.** With radio communication cut off and no links with the cities, Che wrote a coded message to Fidel, which he hoped to send by hand through Debray:

> **The farm has been discovered and the army pursued us; we've dealt the first blow, but we are cut off. . . . Tania is cut off here, as she contravened orders and was caught up in events. . . . We now have enough Glocontime; send no more. There is no news from the trio** [Monje, Kolle, Reyes]. **I do not trust them either, and they have expelled youth members who are with us. I can receive everything by radio but it is useless if they do not simultaneously communicate with La Paz, so we are cut off for now.**

He added that he wanted Debray to leave and organize a European solidarity network, while Bustos should do the same: **organize trips to the south and collect Argentines; he's also bottled up here.**

The guerrilla column was on the move again on April 16, after rejoining the rear guard, led by Vilo Acuña.

> **The advance guard left at 6:15 and we at 7:15, walking well until we reached the Ikira River, but Tania and Machín lagged behind. When their temperatures were taken, Tania's was over 39 [102.2] and Machín's 38 [100.4]. Furthermore, the delay kept us from marching as planned. We left them both, plus Dr. Cabrera and Serapio, one kilometer upstream from the Ikira, and went on our way, taking possession of a farmhouse called Bella Vista, or to be more exact, of four campesinos who sold us potatoes, a pig, and some corn. They're poor peasants and are very frightened by our presence here.**

Earlier, Bolivian soldiers had terrorized the locals with some far-fetched propaganda: "the guerrillas are Paraguayan; they rape women and hang men from trees or take them along to carry their backpacks; they steal animals and crops and set fire to houses. They have come to sow Paraguayan Communism in our land." The distressed campesinos wondered what all this "Paraguayan Communism" was and, to be on the safe side, avoided the guerrillas like the plague.

Despite Che's skepticism, and although he was never to know it, the guerrillas were striking a chord. The solemn faces of the isolated Bolivian campesinos revealed nothing, but the people did begin to be interested in the guerrillas and ask questions, even though the army had by now begun reprisals, kidnapping, torturing, and beating the peasants, destroying their crops, and offering rewards for information about the guerrillas.

On April 17, the Cuban newspaper *Granma* ran a banner headline saying: "Message to the Peoples of the World from Commander Ernesto Guevara via the Tri-Continental Conference." The text filled two full pages of the newspaper and was illustrated with photographs of Che cutting his beard from the time of his departure for Africa and from training in Pinar del Río. To those unaware of the inside story of the previous two years, these could have appeared to be current photographs of Che. Che's message kicked off with a remark by the nineteenth-century independence hero José Martí: "This is the hour of burning, and nothing but light will come from these fires." Che analyzed the social war that would inevitably arise in the Third World, and called for a tempering of differences in the left-wing: **To want to change things by words is an illusion; history will wipe them out or give them their true meaning.** He pointed out that the left should work steadfastly toward the objective: war on the empire, waged at its periphery. **All of our action is a war cry against imperialism.**

The document, which was to be the basis of Cuban proposals and of all the radical left at the end of the sixties, insisted on **creating one, two, three, many Vietnams.**

Che heard his own appeal from afar, by radio. He made no comment. An Italian journalist in Havana, Saverio Tutino, studied the text and realized, from references to the anniversary of the end of World War II, that it had been written in 1966; but he dug no deeper. Which references pertained to events after 1966 had been written into the text afterward? One sentence, doubtless added by the editors, gave a clue to Commander Guevara's situation: New wars will break out in these and other countries [referring to Guatemala and Venezuela], as has already happened in Bolivia. No one would then have read that into it.

Meanwhile, in the jungle, Che was looking for a way through to Muyapampa for Debray and Bustos. He was forced to leave a group in the rear guard with the sick, including Moisés Guevara, who had a digestive illness, and the hangover boys, under Vilo Acuña. He ordered this group **to show themselves in the area so as to keep the enemy from learning of our movement, and to wait for us for three days. At the end of that time, they were to stay in the zone, but not to precipitate any real** fighting, just wait until we come back. Che was not to be aware of the future consequences of this division.

On April 18, the guerrillas encountered some campesinos while on the march. There is a record of the following exchange:

Good evening.

"Good evening, sir."

Don't say "sir"; a "sir" is someone who humiliates and mistreats poor people.

"It's just that in these parts we say that to a gentleman."

Inti spoke with the campesinos, and his words stayed vivid years after. "We're not Paraguayans. Here there's Bolivian hunger and Bolivian poverty." Pacho's diary gave an insight into the group's situation: "We haven't slept for days. We walk by night, stand guard and cook by day."

The guerrillas captured a rather questionable character the next day, April 19. He was

> an English journalist called [George Andrew] **Roth, brought by some children from Lagunillas who were following our trail. His documents were in order, but there were suspicious aspects. His passport had "student" crossed out as his profession and "journalist" written over it (he claims to be a photographer really). He has a visa for Puerto Rico. . . . He said he had been in the camp and had been shown a diary by Israel Reyes recounting his travels and experiences. It's the same old story, indiscipline and irresponsibility running the show.**

Roth is still an enigma. Cuban sources insist that he had met with CIA agents in La Paz between April 8 and 16, before finding the guerrillas. Furthermore, they assert, Roth had agreed to enter the combat zone to see if Che was there and to spray chemicals on the guerrillas' clothing so they could be tracked by dogs later. Future history could not confirm this but did not eliminate suspicion, either. Che thought Roth could be used to provide additional news coverage of Debray and Bustos, and decided to send him away with them. Inti gave him an ELN communiqué addressed to the general public.

So as not to be identified, Che avoided the journalist and gave his final instructions to Ciro Bustos. As well as coordinating Argentine groups, Bustos had, in his own words, to

> make contact in La Paz and transmit a series of orders to the network regarding urgent tasks: moving, setting up caches of money and military equipment, and basically re-establishing contact with the guerrillas. There is an urgent need to draft new recruits, plan how to do that, and find new places to live and meet, etc. Also to inform Havana that the group was cut off as their transmitter was broken, and that the group was in a decidedly critical logistical and political situation.

The three journalists left the guerrillas at 11:45 A.M. as Che was preparing to take the town of Muyupampa, an idea he scrapped after he discovered that the soldiers there were on alert after a reconnaissance expedition. From that moment on, the guerrillas were to have no contact with anyone outside Bolivia.

The journalists were discovered shortly afterward by a police patrol, which identified them after recognizing Roth. Although they did not arrest the men, they did sound the alarm. The three were detained several hours later by the army and taken in a jeep to Muyupampa.

The guerrillas moved away from the zone, but some campesinos told them the next day that Debray and Bustos had been arrested. Che curtly noted: **Bad news for Ciro. Debray should be okay.** Several days later, he wrote: **They were victims of their own haste, impatience almost, to leave and my lack of strength to stop them, so communication with Cuba has been cut off and a plan for action in Argentina has been lost.**

The main group of guerrillas, cut off from the rear guard, spent two days moving toward Taperillas.

49. Intervention and Dead Friends

With Olo Pantoja during the last days of the campaign of Las Villas

N April 1, 1967, a C-130 Lockheed Hercules landed at Santa Cruz Airport, having taken off from a U.S. base in the Panama Canal Zone. It was the first part of an airlift that included light planes flying on to Camiri. The arrival of these first aircraft with food rations and napalm provoked a reaction by the Bolivian newspaper *Presencia* in mid-April that was echoed by the Cuban news agency Prensa Latina, reporting that fifty U.S. military advisers had arrived in Bolivia. Agence France Presse mentioned a more modest twenty-seven men, including the C-130 crew, four technicians assembling a helicopter, five U.S. Rangers, and several unidentified personnel. Agence France Presse's figure was the closest to reality. The U.S. government had opted to collaborate only in a small way with the Bolivian government, as they were convinced he was not in Bolivia.

On April 18, U.S. general William Tope traveled to Bolivia to review the local armed forces and the future military aid plan. Tope held a breakfast meeting with Ambassador Douglas Henderson (who had requested military intervention on previous occasions to protect U.S. companies affected by strikes), President René Barrientos, and three of his ministers. Tope summed up the meeting in a message to Washington, calling it cordial, but very frank and open. The U.S. representatives were not happy with what they learned. The only new information Barrientos had concerned the accidental finding of the guerrillas; the Americans also got the impression that Barrientos and his ministers thought the army defeats had had a major psychological impact on the rest of the country, particularly among other subversive groups.

Tope came away believing that the problem was not to change the troops in the field, but the attitude of those above, including Barrientos; the president was moving troops aimlessly and did not know how to pull the rabbit out of the hat. He had merely demanded supplies of matériel. Tope reported that the requests were for those eternal Bolivian panaceas, aircraft and automatic weapons (these to replace the army's aging Mausers). Tope answered that the aircraft would be of no use under the present combat conditions, while if soldiers threw down their arms, a Mauser was as good as an automatic; they would have to learn to use and maintain them. The U.S. mission concluded that the Bolivians had a huge problem, but that the U.S. was going to have great difficulty even in agreeing how to approach it, to say nothing of finding a solution. It was obvious that the U.S. had to take a practical approach, building on what they had to force improvements.

For the time being the U.S. government felt it had a minor problem on its hands as they thought the phantom they were hunting was not in Bolivia. Intelligence analysts heard the first rumors of Che's presence with interest, but the CIA leadership was very skeptical and thought the story amounted to another smoke screen thrown up by the Cuban government. The discovery of the Ñancahuazú camp and the photograph found there seemed to support the idea that Che was or had been in Bolivia, but the opinion of director Richard Helms and the CIA leadership prevailed: Che was not there now.

As part of its strategy, the Pentagon sent a Mobile Training Team (MTT) from Fort Gulick under the command of Major Ralph "Pappy" Shelton, who had been in the region some weeks earlier. He was accompanied by Captain Michael Leroy, recently returned from Saigon, another three officers, and twelve men, including Margarito Cruz, a Cuban exile who was to train a death squad. They set up base at La Esperanza, a deserted sugar mill fifty miles north of Santa Cruz. The Bolivian army reactivated the Manchego regiment to receive U.S. training, with 650 officers and men from other branches of the armed forces, including Colonel Gallardo and Major Miguel Ayoroa. The Pentagon also sent five P-51 planes and two H-19 helicopters. President Barrientos told Luis Suárez: "It's nothing special; military missions like this have been going on for fifteen years."

Meanwhile, Régis Debray, Ciro Bustos, and the journalist Roth began their ordeal. After being arrested, they were taken to city hall, where they met Hugo Delgadillo, a journalist from *Presencia,* who spoke to them for several minutes and took their photograph. The three insisted they were foreign correspondents, but the army saw through their covers thanks to statements from Salustio, the farmhand arrested at the Galvanized Metal House. They were interrogated and beaten there and then. Debray was taken by helicopter to the Choeti air force base near Camiri the day after. Bustos and Roth were taken by jeep.

Barrientos stated that the three journalists were dead. It was the easiest way to make the whole matter disappear. Che heard the news by radio. Delgadillo's photograph saved their lives, however. He had given the roll of film to a woman to keep the military from confiscating it, and she took it to Cochabamba. Having been photographed alive in custody, the three could not now be retroactively "killed in combat." But though the photograph's publication saved the three detainees' lives, it did not prevent them from being tortured. Two colonels interrogated Debray for the first three days insisting on one question: Was Che in Bolivia? They beat Debray, hit him with hammers, and sent him to a dummy firing squad. Salustio had identified him as a man who had borne arms with the guerrillas. Bustos's cover held up at first, because he had a forged passport identifying him as an Argentine journalist named Fructuoso. Debray lost consciousness under torture and was given up for dead. Major Rubén Sánchez, who was in Camiri, kept the soldiers from killing him. So far, both Debray and Bustos had denied that Che was in Bolivia, and Roth could say nothing as he knew nothing. A new team of interrogators—led by Colonel Federico Arana from military intelligence; Roberto Quintanilla, an adjutant from the Interior Ministry; and a CIA agent known, like his predecessor, as Dr. González and also as Gabriel García—changed the tone. Bustos divulged information he thought would not affect the guerrillas: he spoke of the central camp that had been discovered on April 4, of the presence of foreigners, and of the fact that Inti Peredo was the chief, as Che had told him to.

The guerrillas had only lost one man in combat, but had lost another two who had drowned, two who had deserted, and one who was captured by the army besides the arrests of Debray and Bustos. They were to suffer another blow at that time: Jorge Vázquez Viaña had been cut off from the main group after a chance clash with the army and could not be found. He wandered through the jungle for days until he ran into an army post near Taperillas and killed two soldiers, but was wounded and captured two days after that. Meanwhile, the main body of the guerrillas were advancing through the mountains, almost without food. Che wrote: **Much work is still needed to make this a combat force, although morale is very high.** He attempted to make contact over the following days with Vilo Acuña's rearguard group. On April 25, at about ten A.M., Che heard that a group of soldiers was approaching. Reports were contradictory, mentioning thirty to sixty men. Che personally took part in the ambush.

> **The vanguard soon appeared and, to our surprise, consisted of three German shepherds and their handler. The animals were uneasy, but I don't think they would have given us away. However, they continued to advance; I fired at the first dog and missed, and my M2 jammed when I was about to shoot the dog handler. Manuel Hernández killed another dog, as I later confirmed, and no one else fell into the ambush.**

Che was wrong; he had not missed. The army later reported the names of two dead dogs, Rayo ("Lightning") and Tempestad ("Storm"). The clash did not end there, however: more firing was heard on one of the flanks. San Luis had adopted the riskiest position possible, as ever, and was wounded while he faced machine-gun fire from the soldiers at the mouth of a cave.

> **They soon brought him, but he had lost blood and died when they began to transfuse plasma. A bullet had smashed his femur and the whole vascular and nervous network. He bled to death before we could act. We have lost our best man in the guerrilla group, one of its pillars, a comrade of mine since, when almost a child, he was No. 4 Column messenger, then in the invasion, and now on this new venture.**

Che recalled the Chilean poet Pablo Neruda, of his obscure death we can only say, for a hypothetical future that may become real: "Your little brave captain's body has spread its metallic shape out into the immense void."

San Luis's death was a terrible blow. Despite the guerrillas' successful ambushes of the army, they had now lost two key fighters—two cadres—and furthermore, they were surrounded:

> **We now have two natural exits blocked off and will have to "play mountaineering" as the Río Grande exit is not suitable, for the twin reason that it is a natural barrier and takes us farther from Vilo Acuña, of whom we have no news. At night we came to a fork in two waterways, the Ñacahuazú and the Río**

Grande, where we slept. Here we will wait for Coco and Camba to regroup our little column. The operation's outcome, on balance, has been very negative. San Luis is dead, but it's not just that. Despite all the shooting, the casualties we inflicted on the army can't be more than the two men and the dog we killed, as positions were neither studied nor prepared and the shooters could not see the enemy.

The guerrillas tried to leave the area to return to search for the rear guard, along almost inaccessible trails and with almost no food, and on very cold nights. The army was also in the dark. Reports from campesinos had allowed them to locate the rear guard, which they took for the main group, and then the guerrillas suddenly appeared elsewhere.

Che, who had adopted the new nom de guerre of Fernando after Debray and Bustos were arrested, led the group on long marches towards the Ñancahuazú toward the end of April, still trying to find food. A message from Havana told them that their actions had struck a chord among other political groups, including the Bolivian Communist Party.

On the other hand, our isolation is total. Disease has undermined some comrades' health and forced us to split up, which has made us much less effective. We have not yet made contact with Vilo Acuña, and the campesinos have yet to be organized at the grass roots.

Che saw the struggle beginning to outstrip national boundaries and become another Vietnam: **It seems certain the Americans will commit themselves heavily here. They're already sending helicopters and, it seems, Green Berets, although they haven't been seen hereabouts.** He closed on a frankly optimistic note after recording the total breakdown in communications between the cities and Havana: **To sum up, a month in which every problem has been solved as well as may be expected, considering a guerrilla group's occasional needs. Morale is good among all fighters, who have passed their preliminary guerrilla exams.**

When did Commander Guevara accept that the Andean project would be confined to Bolivian soil, at least at that stage?

On May 1, an unusual guest stood on the podium in Havana's Revolution Square: Che's seven-year-old daughter, Aliusha (Aleida), dressed in olive drab and smiling between Fidel and President Osvaldo Dorticós, while tugging at their trouser legs to point to the MIGs doing acrobatics in the air. Although he didn't know his daughter was the guest of honor, Che heard a speech by his old comrade from the Cuban guerrilla war, Juan Almeida, who cryptically dedicated a passage to him: **Almeida spoke in Havana, passing the man-**

tle to me and the famous Bolivian guerrillas. The speech was a bit long, but good. We have three days' acceptable food left. Ñato killed a bird with a sling today; we have entered the age of the bird. And three days later, Pacho Fernández Montes de Oca wrote in his diary: "Food, a sparrow hawk, two birds. I got a sparrow hawk's wing and noodles."

That same May 1 saw the publication of the guerrillas' first news release, smuggled out by Major Sánchez. The newspaper *Prensa Libre* sold out in Cochabamba to workers going to the May 1 parade, and was read over the radio as well. The military arrested the newspaper's editor for this. The guerrillas were not politically isolated despite their numbers, and were having a greater effect than it seemed on Bolivian society. Families demonstrated that same day in Trinidad, in the Beni region, against the taking of 160 conscripts to the guerrilla combat zone.

With scarcely any food and no water, Che's guerrillas searched for a way back to their former campsites. They finally arrived on May 7. Pacho wrote in his diary: "Our aim, to make contact with Vilo Acuña and prepare weapons." Che laconically noted the lack of food and that they had been in the zone for six months.

The next day, the guerrillas were collecting food they had left in the caves when the army's presence was detected again. Pacho and Olo Pantoja and others had ambushed and shot at unarmed soldiers gathering water. Shortly afterward, they captured another two soldiers who were gathering maize. The encounters did not stop there: **Everyone was tense when guards arrived, about 27 of them. They had seen something odd and the group led by Second Lieutenant Laredo advanced. He himself opened fire and was killed in the act, along with another two recruits.** On Laredo's body was a letter from his wife, asking him to bring back a guerrilla's scalp to decorate the living room. **Night was already falling, and our men advanced and captured six soldiers. The rest retreated.** The guerrillas had killed another three soldiers in this clash, wounded two, and taken eight prisoners.

Che ordered the march to get under way again at four A.M., after releasing the prisoners. He had passed a sleepless night because of an asthma attack. **The only food we had left was lard, I was famished and must have slept two hours, so I was only able to follow along at a slow, stumbling pace. The march was generally like that. We ate lard soup at the first watering hole. The men are weak and we have several cases of edema.**

At the beginning of the second week in May, Colonel Arana, Lieutenant Colonel Quintanilla, and "Dr. González" went back to interview Debray, Bustos, and Roth at the Manchego regimental headquarters in Santa Cruz, accompanied this time by General Arnaldo Saucedo. Bustos's cover was blown when the agents declared that his passport was false and he had been with the guerrillas as a fighter, not a journalist. The interrogators compared details provided by Debray, Bustos, and Roth with those given by the deserters, and confronted them with their own contradictions. "I had no option but to confess the undeniable," Bustos said years later, when he admitted his concession that the guerrillas were led by Che. That was part of a 20,000-word confession and a series of sketches of the fighters. Bustos argued years later that Che had given him permission to say he was there: **Well, if you see it's obvious, blurt it out right away. That way I can be me and put on my beret again.** Debray later confirmed Bustos's story in part. In that same round of interrogations he admitted that, as part of his journalistic work, he had interviewed Che in a guerrilla camp during the third week of March. The statements were conclusive, as far as the Bolivian army and the CIA's field agents were concerned, but Helms stuck to the idea that they were disinformation and that Che was probably dead. He argued about it with his head of undercover operations (euphemistically called the Joint Planning Board), Thomas Karamessines.

A memorandum from Walter Rostow to President Johnson summed up the situation, saying that the CIA had just received the first credible report that Che Guevara might be alive and operating in South America, but that they needed more information before concluding that Guevara was not dead, as the intelligence community, as time went by, had been more and more inclined to believe. Meanwhile, despite the director's doubts, the CIA sent a new group of advisers to the zone, extended its infrastructure there, and set in motion an aerial reconnaissance operation to produce reliable maps of the area. Four advisers were also attached to the Bolivian Interior Ministry under the direction of Minister Antonio Arguedas.

Not knowing that his presence in Bolivia had been discovered, Che led the guerrillas to Pirirenda in search of Vilo Acuña and the rear guard. Pacho wrote: "We're very weak and hungry. It's hard to keep walking, especially with machetes and weapons weighing us down. Only willpower and discipline keep us going." The lack of grassroots support and direct contact with the campesinos; poverty; the scanty settlement in the area; and the scarcity of game had condemned the guerrillas to permanent hunger.

While the guerrillas had been a disaster operationally, in strictly military terms they had been undefeated in six clashes with the Bolivian army. In view of this situation, on May 11, Colonel Rocha was relieved of his command of the 4th Division in Camiri. (He had confined himself to furiously repressing the campesinos in the area, subjecting them to torture, beatings, arbitrary arrests, and reprisals, even when they revealed the guerrillas' whereabouts.) Replacing him was Luis Antonio Reque Terán, while Colonel Zenteno Anaya took over from Colonel Roberto Vargas at 8th Division.

The guerrillas arrived at a campesino's house on May 12, bought a pig from him, and cooked it with maize. They paid for their gluttony the next day, **a day of belches, farts, vomiting, and diarrhea, a real organic concert. We stayed absolutely still trying to digest the pig. We have two cans of water. I was very ill until I vomited and got better.**

A day later, they arrived at Pirirenda Pond, a watery mirror surrounded by greenery, as Pacho would say in his diary, but Che was inured to scenery by now. He was more concerned with lapses in discipline arising from the lack of food:

> **Before leaving, I assembled the men and let fly at them over the problems we faced, basically, food, criticizing Dariel Alarcón for having eaten a can of food and denying it; Tamayo for eating salted, dried meat in secret, and Aniceto for his readiness to participate in anything to do with food and his reluctance to do anything else.**

Some hours later, an air raid took place two miles away.

The next day, May 15, Che wrote in his diary No news today. Pacho was more explicit: "He looks really bad. He gave away his meat ration last night." The day after, Che wrote:

> **I head a terrible attack of colic when we began the walk, with diarrhea and vomiting. They stopped it with Demerol and I lost all notion of anything as they carried me in a hammock. When I woke up I was relieved but covered in shit like a babe in arms. They lent me trousers, but with no water you can smell the shit a mile off. We spent the day there, dozing.**

Pacho concluded: "Almost all of us are ill; the Guards fired several times in the night. . . . The problem is to break out of the cordon and move to a place with water."

Army patrols had shot blindly at the guerrillas over the previous days. They broke out of the cordon to the southwest on the night of May 16, and received a report from Havana that night that their isolation was increasing. Renán had been recalled from La Paz as his entry permit had expired and he was ill. The urban network depended on Rodolfo Saldaña and some confused cadres who communicated with Havana but not with the guerrillas. The fighting had awakened the sympathies of the most radical opposition groups, but there was no way to turn that budding sympathy into practical support. Havana's message ended, oddly, with a report on the willingness of part of the PCB leadership to join the movement. Did Che then miss Celia Sánchez and her July 26 Movement network—the support groups in Havana and the urban mobilization against the Batista dictatorship, that he had so underestimated at the time?

The guerrillas wandered for a week, having scant contact with the campesinos and heading for the first campsite again while waiting to connect with the rear guard. Che heard Barrientos announce Debray's trial on the radio: he will ask Congress to restore the death penalty. To defend him, Debray hired Argentine attorney Ricardo Rojo, who thus made a reappearance in Che's life. Bustos was to stand trial also, while Roth was released on bail and vanished into thin air.

Vázquez Viana had meanwhile been holding out under violent interrogation after being arrested with a wounded leg. He was taken to the state oil corporation hospital in Camiri, where he asked to be operated on without anesthesia so as not to talk during surgery. He was then moved to the Choeti barracks. "Dr. González" questioned him there, who said Vazquez Viana had pretended to be a Panamanian journalist who had infiltrated the military security network, but was really an envoy from Havana. "González" seems to have convinced Jorge, to admit to Che's presence in Bolivia, because later a man from the Interior Ministry, Roberto Quintanilla, appeared in his cell and showed him a tape of the interrogation and threatened to make it public if Vázquez did not reveal what he knew about the urban network and the safe houses. In return he was offered a faked escape and a passage to Germany. Vázquez refused; the interrogation became tougher. Quintanilla broke both his arms and in a subsequent torture injured him severely. Hours later he was thrown out of a helicopter over the jungle; the news was broadcast that he had escaped. Che, who had reacted positively to the captured guerrilla's first public statements, believed that Vázquez really had escaped and would succeed in making contact with the urban networks to inform them of the guerrillas' situation: **He must now be rejoining them or going to La Paz to make contact.**

The guerrillas took the town of Caraguatarenda on May 28; they replenished their supplies (flour, sugar, sandals, tobacco, toothbrushes) and commissioned transportation. They spent the following days driving from farm to farm in oil corporation jeeps whose radiators were filled with both water and urine. On May 30, they ambushed a patrol from Colonel Calderón's regiment, whose rear guard was accompanied by journalist José Luis Alcázar. The soldiers fled, leaving three dead and one wounded man behind. The guerrillas encountered the army again, but with no results.

Che could not avoid some optimism in his monthly roundup: **From a military standpoint, three engagements, in which we inflicted casualties on the enemy but sustained none, as well as breakthroughs in Pirirenda and Caraguatarenda, constitute success. Dogs have been declared useless and retired from circulation.** After admitting that lack of contact with Havana and La Paz drove him to despair, he wrote that they had to be patient in the matter of the campesinos' joining up, that the Debray affair had given the guerrillas publicity, and that they were **gaining the moral high ground which, if well managed, is a guarantee of success. Whereas the army is still disorganized, and its techniques have not greatly improved.** Finally, Che stressed: **The trouble is the impossibility of making contact with Vilo Acuña, despite our pilgrimage over the mountain ranges. There are signs that he has headed north.**

Acuña's rear guard was hindered by illness in its ranks—among the sick was Gustavo Machín—and had been cut off from the campesinos by army repression. Julio Velazio's desertion at the end of May—he was murdered when he gave himself up to the army—forced the group to be constantly on the move while scouting around to see if they could make contact with the main body led by Che. Pinares who had been working like Hercules since Che's criticism, undertook lengthy foraging expeditions among the hills and plantations. On June 1 he decided to go out foraging again. Acuña heard gunfire two hours later and afterward discovered that the army had ambushed and killed Pinares and a Bolivian, Casildo Condori.

At the beginning of June, Che moved on, avoiding clashes with the army. A cold front made temperatures plunge at night. Food and water were scarce, and the guerrillas had to fill their canteens with salt water. Che did not lose his sense of humor, and told Pacho that **"with my skinny, bearded appearance, I looked like Saint Lazarus."** On June 6 they arrived at the Río Grande again and heard that new army patrols were in the area. Che spent the nights giving history classes and playing chess.

The sentries clashed with the army on June 10, while the main group was making a raft.

> **All the signs are that our men were walking without taking precautions and were sighted. The guards began shooting around as usual and Villegas [actually it was Pacho] and Coco gave their position away by firing willy-nilly. We decided to stay put and march off tomorrow. The situation is a little inconvenient; if they decide to attack all-out, in the best case we'd have to cross steep rocky mountains without water.**

Pacho and Coco's firing had killed one of Captain Rico Toro's troops, seriously wounded another, and lightly wounded a third. Rico claimed to have killed four guerrillas. The ambush produced no more results and Che advanced again, this time toward the Rosita River.

On June 13 Che wrote: **The fascinating thing is the political ferment in this country, the welter of pacts and counterpacts in the air. Rarely has is seemed so clear that guerrilla activity could act as a catalyst to revolution.** Messages from Havana were still arriving (although Fidel could not know whether the guerrillas were receiving them) and seemed to confirm that the guerrillas could have become a standard-bearer for opposition to the military government. Juan Lechín was in Chile, preparing to enter Bolivia, and even the moderate Víctor Paz Estenssoro was preparing military action in exile. Havana's messages included information on reorganization by the National Liberation Army in Peru, which had five men providing military training and a propaganda group at work in Lima.

On June 14, Che headed his diary entry with the name of his daughter, Celita—"Little Celia"—and a question mark by the number 4, wondering whether she was four years old. Just like that. The entry finished on a personal note: **I have turned 39 and the time is irrevocably coming when doubts will crop up about my future as a guerrilla. For now I'm sound.** Sound, that is, in his willpower and moral resources, but hungry and undermined by intestinal infections and asthma attacks—although, as his alter ego, a character in Julio Cortázar's short story "Reunion," remarks, "Asthma is my lover and has taught me to make the most of the night."

The guerrillas spent the following days marching along the banks of the Rosita without meeting any campesinos, using up their scant food supplies. They spent four days to make contact with a community of a whole dozen campesinos: **The inhabitants have to be chased before you can talk to them, as they're like little animals. They generally welcomed us, but Calixto, named mayor by a military commission that passed through a month a go, was reserved and reluctant to sell us some small things.**

The group was wary of three armed campesinos who purported to be tradesmen. Another campesino denounced them as a police lieutenant, a border guard, and a teacher searching for information about the guerrillas. **We considered killing them, but then I decided to turn them over to the army with a stern warning about the conduct of war.**

Che practiced dentistry again in this hamlet: **After two days of plentiful extractions in which I made Chaco famous under my name as Fernando Toothpuller, I closed my surgery and we set off in the afternoon, walking for over an hour.** The events were recorded by several photographs, including a series on Che's dental activities in front of a straw cabin with a suffering campesino a patient and three or four onlookers; an assistant held the patient down.

There was good news: **I rode a mule for the first time in this war.** Che had a mount again. A photograph shows him smiling, smoking a cigar, with the mule's head in the foreground.

When the guerrillas left the hamlet, they took a campesino with them, apparently as a prisoner. They traded him for Paulino Baigorria, aged twenty, who asked to join the guerrillas. **Paulino has promised to take my message to Cochabamba. He'll be given a letter for Coco's wife, a coded message for Havana, and four news releases.** In its fourth news release, the National Liberation Army denied news of Inti's death and added:

> As for the indications of the presence of supposed fighters from other Latin American countries, for security reasons and [in obedience to] our own code, that of revolutionary truth, we will give no figures, but just make clear that any citizen who accepts our minimal program conducive to the liberation of Bolivia will be accepted in our ranks with the same rights and duties as the Bolivian fighters who, naturally, constitute the overwhelming majority of out movement.

Che's message to Havana sent greetings "from the Bolivian mountains" to be read on July 26.

Paulino was captured by the army and tortured in Santa Cruz, then taken to La Paz and jailed after refusing to say who the messages were for.

On June 24, the feast of St. John the Baptist, Che heard on the radio about a massacre in the mining zone. The miners, one of the few organized groups in Bolivian society and whom Che had had occasion to admire in his first Latin America journey in the fifties, had always resisted the military junta and faced continual repression. They had even had their wages cut by 40 percent two years previously. At about that time the then-underground Union Federation of Bolivian Mine Workers (FSTMB) held a congress. The Catavi miners had previously decided to donate a day's wages and a batch of medicines to the guerrillas; this decision was ratified by the congress. After the St. John's Day celebrations, the army attacked miners' camps with the obvious aim of setting an example to other labor unions if they supported the guerrillas. At the Siglo XX mine, the soldiers fired on defenseless men, women, and children, killing eighty-seven in what was to be known as the St. John's Massacre. Che followed the events as reported on Argentine radio, unable to act because he could not mobilize toward the area of conflict, could not contact the urban organization, could not evaluate the situation, and did not wish to dispense with a single man, betting everything on the guerrillas' capacity to expand their military strength. Several days later the government accused the guerrillas of having instigated the miners' so-called uprising.

Che had been suffering from asthma attacks since June 23. **The asthma is a serious threat and there are few medicines in reserve.** He had controlled his asthma over recent years in Cuba, but now was suffering from the loss of part of the guerrillas' stock of medicines when the army took the camps. The attacks got worse at the end of June. **My asthma is on the increase and will not let me sleep well.** When he could not sleep at night and gasped for air, he would throw himself on a tree trunk to try to raise his chest, or have Tamayo and Carlos Coello give him massages. During one of these, Tamayo asked him:

"Come on, isn't asthma a psychological problem?"

Yes, I know it's a psychological problem, so I use the little inhaler. If I throw the inhaler away because the asthma is psychological, I get more asthma.

On June 26 the guerrillas killed four soldiers in an ambush, but this time, instead of running off, the Bolivian army advanced and outflanked the guerrillas, wounding two before Che gave the order to retreat. **Villegas was wounded in one leg and Coello in his stomach. We quickly took them to the house to operate on them with what we had. Villegas had a superficial wound and his lack of mobility would just be a headache; Coello's liver was smashed and his intestine perforated.** Che left Dr. de la Pedraja in charge of the operation, as he refused to operate on his comrades and confined himself to lighting the surgical field. Halfway through the operation, while the medic was stitching Coello's colon, Tamayo realized Coello was dead.

In him I lost a comrade from whom I had been inseparable all these years, whose loyalty was proven and whose absence I now feel as that of a child. He asked them to give me his watch

when he was hit, and as they didn't take it off to treat him, it was taken to be given to René who gave it to me. His asking showed he wanted it to be given to the son he never knew, as I had previously done with other dead comrades' watches. I'll wear it throughout the war. We carried his body on an animal to bury it far away.

The group went away with nine horses. Che had lost three men, vital comrades: Suárez Gayol, San Luis, and now Coello, and he did not yet know that Pinares and Vázquez Viana were dead, too. A black day for me.

The guerrillas kept moving in search of the rear guard over the following days. On June 29,

I talked with the troops, now made up of 24 men. Once more I gave an example of the Chinaman as an exemplary man. I also explained the meaning of losses and the personal loss that Coello was for me; I considered him almost as a son. I criticized the lack of self-discipline and the slowness of the march and promised to give some more ideas so that in future ambushes what had happened would not happen again, useless losses of life due to not following procedure.

Toward the end of June, Walter Rostow informed Johnson of events in Bolivia. Rostow correctly surmised that the guerrillas had been discovered while they were still training, but the Bolivian army's severe weaknesses had also been exposed. Rostow described the lack of coordinated command, leadership ability, training, and discipline among the Bolivian armed forces. He also pointed out that U.S. advisers were training a Bolivian regiment and that both the U.S. and Argentine governments were contributing matériel. But this did not seem to be enough for the Bolivian government, whose ambassador in Washington, Julio Sanjinés, pressed the U.S. to help prepare a search-and-destroy mission against the guerrillas.

In his monthly summary for June, Che cited as problems the gradual loss of men, each of whom is a serious setback, although the army does not know it, and the lack of contact with the rear guard. (Though Che did not know it, Acuña's group was again trying to reach them, leaving the zone they were in once or twice a week on reconnaissance expeditions toward the Yuque River, apparently another previously agreed-on rendezvous.) Curiously, Che had lost the ability to take a more political view of the situation; he saw no great problems in the guerrillas' inability to link up with the growing social movement against the military junta. Che saw the importance of military action by his small group of twenty-four men (with Villegas wounded and mobility reduced) from the standpoint he had learned in guerrilla warfare.

In this project, which began in other political circumstances arose from impossibilities and disagreements, was born prematurely, and lost its urban and international links at the start, everything pointed toward disaster.

Nonetheless, Che's men had defeated the army ten times thus far and their legend grew like wildfire; we are now invincible supermen.

Our most urgent task is to reestablish contact with La Paz, and to obtain new supplies of military medical equipment and recruit 50–100 men from the city. Che thought of urban reinforcements because the lack of peasant recruits can still be felt. It's a vicious circle: to obtain the necessary recruits, we need to take permanent action in a populated zone, and to do that we need more men. There was a final note of concern: The army's military work is still nil, but it is working with the campesinos—a fact we should not ignore, as it turns all the members of a community into informants, either out of fear or because they have been deceived about our aims.

A message received from Havana several days later seemed to give Che an answer, although he must have felt very frustrated at not being able to transmit his comments. Rodolfo told him via a go-between who went back and forth to Cuba that a second front might open. Havana also confirmed that a group of Bolivian students was being trained. This good news was offset by the disaster in communications links. After Monleón had left La Paz, not only did La Paz not have contact with Che, it had none with Havana.

Bolivia's Vice President Ovando meanwhile decided to step up pressure for more U.S. aid by making public the information that Che was in Bolivia; he backed this up with a news statement by Debray that he had interviewed Che in Ñancahuazú in March. Furthermore, [Ovando] said that the army was facing perfectly trained guerrillas, whose Vietcong commanders had defeated crack U.S. regiments. An Associated Press wire from that time reported, in rebuttal, that Che had died in Cuba and that information about his presence in Bolivia was intended to rouse guerrillas. The wire might have aimed to force the Cuban government to confirm Che's whereabouts. Ovando's remarks were followed by General Barrientos, who held a press conference in which he admitted my presence but said I would be liquidated in a few days. He spouted the usual stream of nonsense, calling us rats and snakes and repeating his stated intention to punish Debray.

Che's hard core had moved further during the first days of July, while Villegas's leg slowly healed and their commander had asthma attacks. Che planned a daring action on July 6, sending a group led by Coco Peredo and Pacho to take the town of Samaipata.

Martínez Tamayo, Coco, Pacho, Aniceto, Mario Gutiérrez, and Juan Pablo Chang, the Chinaman, were commissioned for the action. They stopped a truck coming from Santa Cruz, nothing happened, but another came up behind and stopped out of solidarity so they had to hold it up, too. Then the tussling began, with a lady traveling in the truck who did not want her daughter to get down; then a third truck stopped to see what was happening and since now the road was blocked, a fourth one

stopped too—because of everyone's confusion. Things were sorted out and the four vehicles stayed to one side and a driver spoke about a rest stop when the army questioned him. The men left in a truck, got to Samaipatia, captured two militiamen and then Lieutenant Vacaflor, in charge of the post, and a sergeant whom they made tell them the password, and took the post with ten men in a lightning action.

Coco killed a soldier during the fight. There was an accidental power cut, which the army later thought was due to collaboration by locals. The captured soldiers were left naked one kilometer from the town. **The action took place under the eyes of the whole town and the many travelers there, so news of it will spread like wildfire.**

A photograph taken of Che near Samaipatia showed him kneeling, surrounded by campesinos while he studied something. The new cap on his head made him look like a nineteenth-century Russian revolutionary, but it wasn't the right thing; Guevara iconography demands a beret.

As far as supplies go, the action was a failure. El Chino stopped Pacho and Mario Gutiérrez from plundering but he didn't buy anything useful, and none of the medicine I need. But they did get some indispensible things for the guerrillas. By 2 we were already walking back with the booty. According to Pacho's diary, Che forgot to say he had been quite happy munching cookies and drinking Pepsi-Cola.

In the following days, while the press was criticizing the inefficiency of the military cordon, there was a report of a Vietcong colonel among the guerrillas. Juan Pablo Chang, a Peruvian of remote Chinese ancestry, never knew what he had been turned into.

50. The Massacre of the Rear Guard

Part of the proof of Che's presence in Bolivia produced by the Bolivian minister during a press conference in Washington, D.C., September 22, 1967. The photo was taken in November 1966 during a river crossing on the way to Camiri.

CHE'S GUERRILLAS MOVED SLOWLY DURING THE SECOND WEEK OF JULY 1967. But beneath this apparent calm lay the fact that the army was able to clearly trace their southward route.

For Commander Guevara the main enemy was illness. **My asthma is getting worse,** he wrote on July 7, and the next day he added: **I injected myself several times and ended up using a 1 to 900 adrenaline solution prepared for eyedrops. If Paulino hasn't accomplished his mission, we will have to return to Ñacahuazú to look for medicines for my asthma.**

The trial of Ciro Bustos and Régis Debray had meanwhile begun. The Bolivian government's intention to condemn them at all costs caused friction with some army officers, like Major Rubén Sánchez, who agreed to take the stand as a witness for the defense. Minister of War Alfredo Ovando summoned him and the following conversation took place:

" 'I hope you testify conveniently.'

" 'What does "conveniently" mean?' I asked. 'I will tell the truth: I have not seen Debray fighting.'

" 'Go and see President Barrientos.'

"The President clutched his head:

" 'You will make the armed forces look bad.'

" 'I am the only one who can salvage the Armed Forces' honor,' I answered Barrientos, 'because this trial is a travesty in which all the officers are lying and I am going to tell the truth.' "

Che commented on Debray and Bustos's opening statements in the trial: **They are not good; first of all, they've confessed to the guerrillas' intercontinental aims, which they did not have to do.**

The guerrillas were meanwhile traveling in an uninhabited area they had not previously reconnoitered; Che was seriously ill with asthma, and they faced the risk that the few campesinos they saw might report them to the army, motivated by the reward of "50 million pesos for whoever catches the guerrilla Ernesto Che Guevara, dead or alive, preferably alive."

Flyers such as this, and Barrientos's statements that Che was leading the guerrillas, caused friction between the Bolivian president and U.S. Ambassador Henderson, who insisted that the evidence of Che's presence was disinformation and that if Che had somehow been in Bolivia, he would have left by now. Barrientos publicly contradicted the ambassador, telling the press that the guerrilla problem might well last some time.

The Bolivian president was also under pressure from the small parties making up the governing coalition. Che commented on July 14: **The PRA and the PSB have withdrawn their opposition to revolution and the campesinos are warning Barrientos against an alliance with the Falange. The government is quickly falling apart. Shame not to have 100 more men right now.**

Under these circumstances the government declared the start of Operation Cynthia (named for Barrientos's daughter), intended to liquidate the guerrillas within hours. The plan was for No. 4 Division, which was operating between the Ñancahuazú area and the Río Grande, to surround the guerrillas, but they failed. The cordon closed in on thin air, having chased shadows and taken camps to no avail.

The government's crisis worsened:

> **The political news is of a huge crisis, with no end in sight. For now, farmworkers' unions in Cochabamba have formed a political party "of Christian inspiration" which supports Barrientos, and the latter has asked that they "let [him] govern for four years." He is almost pleading. Siles Salinas threatened the opposition, saying our rise to power would cost all of them their heads, and called for national unity, declaring that the country was on a war footing. It seems like pleading on the one hand and demagoguery on the other; maybe they're preparing a replacement.**

Che was right. On July 17, Barrientos, backed up by two small parties, the PSD and the PRA, announced the dissolution of the cabinet. It seemed he wanted to make way for a broader coalition.

The guerrillas returned to the area where they had buried Carlos Coello on July 27. Some campesinos they encountered warned them that the army had passed through a week before. One of the last photos of Che was taken in the hamlet of Tejería. As ever, he had an animal by his side. Che and a mule; he's holding the bridle and smoking a huge cigar, looking at the camera, with the brim of his cap almost covering his eyes, and the mule, very serious, in profile. Despite his smile, he was not well; he had stopped eating. **The asthma hit me hard and the miserable tranquilizers are running out.** A Radio Havana broadcast restored his sense of humor: **Raúl refuted the Czechoslovaks' criticism of the article on the Vietnams. These friends call me a latter-day Bakunin, and lament the blood that's been shed and that would be shed if there were another 3 or 4 Vietnams.**

Another message informed him that Cuba had yet to send another operating agent to La Paz, although a replacement for Renán was being prepared, a "Cuban who fought in the Sierra, with a good record." Rodolfo Saldaña in La Paz had given up preparing a second flashpoint at the Cubans' request, and it had been suggested that he concentrate on getting in touch with Che. In Havana, meanwhile, the group of Bolivians receiving military training now numbered twenty-three from several left-wing Bolivian groups, including the Communist Party.

On July 26, the anniversary of the Moncada raid, Che, still plagued by asthma, gave the group a small talk on the meaning of the Cuban revolution: **rebellion against oligarchies and against revolutionary dogma.** He did not know that his southward route had been traced by the army, which had airlifted the Trinidad Company to the zone. Che ambushed some soldiers hours later: **It happened like this: 8 soldiers appeared on the crest,** walking south, following a little old trail, and then turned back, firing mortar rockets and waving a rag. They returned shortly afterward and the eight were ambushed, suffering four casualties. We withdrew without taking their weapons and equipment, as salvage was difficult. We went off downstream. There was another ambush just after we crossed a little canyon, the horses advanced as far as the trail went.

At 4:30 A.M. three days later, Che having passed a sleepless night due to his asthma, soldiers from the Trinidad Regiment clashed with the guerrillas again. When de la Pedraja was making coffee, he said he could see the light of a lantern coming across the river. Manuel Hernández, who was awake, ready for the changeover in sentry duty, went with de la Pedraja to stop the walkers. Halt, who goes there? It was the Trinidad patrol.

> **The shoot-out there and then. Manuel Hernández immediately took an M-1 and a cartridge belt from a wounded man, and also brought news that there were 21 men on the way to Abapó and 150 in Moroco. There were other army casualties not well tallied amid the chaos that reigned. It took a long time to load the horses and Restituto got lost with an ax and a mortar he had taken from the enemy. It was now almost 6, and even more time was wasted because some packs were dropped. The end result is that in the latest clashes we have been under fire from the soldier boys, who have gotten braver.**
>
> **I hurried the men and went with Villegas, again under fire, through the river canyon where the trail ends and we finally made a stand. I sent Manuel Hernández with Coco and Mario Gutiérrez to take the lead while I spurred the horses.**

Che's horse slipped and fell as they were fording a river, but Coco, Mario Gutiérrez, and Manuel Hernández formed a line of defense to keep the army fire from concentrating on him. The soldiers shouted: "We got him!"

Twelve men stayed to cover the retreat as the guerrillas spent hours climbing from position to position. In one of the final stretches, Martínez Tamayo, Raúl Quispaya, Pacho Fernández Montes de Oca, Simón Cuba, Jaime Arana, and Aniceto Reinaga were fired on; Raúl was hit by a bullet in the mouth and died instantly, while Martínez Tamayo and Pacho were wounded. The latter two kept the army at bay for two hours.

> **After a tough march through the mountains they came to the river and rejoined us. Pacho was on horseback, but Martínez Tamayo could not ride and had had to be slung in a hammock. I sent Manuel Hernández, Francisco Huanca, [David] Adriazola, Coco, and Aniceto to guard the opening of the first brook, on the right bank, while we treated the wounded. Pacho had a superficial wound that cut across his thighs and the skin of his scrotum, but Martínez Tamayo was very seriously**

> wounded and our last batch of plasma had been lost with Simón's backpack. Martínez Tamayo died at 2200 and we buried him near the river in a well-hidden spot, so the Guards don't find him.

The army had lost three dead and five wounded in the clash. The guerrillas, meanwhile, lost their damaged radio transmitter and the tape recorder with which they recorded and decoded transmissions from Havana. From now on, they would have great difficulty translating messages from Havana, and would have to depend more and more on commercial radio for news of the outside world. They also lost eleven backpacks, medicines, and books (one by Trotsky and another by Debray, with handwritten notes by Che).

The guerrillas retreated, wiping away their tracks as they went. Che's analysis of the two comrades he had lost was as dry as usual:

> Of our dead, it is almost impossible to catalogue the introspective Raúl. He was not much of a fighter or worker, but you could tell he was always interested in political problems, although he never asked questions. Martínez Tamayo was the most undisciplined of the Cubans and the least disposed to day-to-day sacrifices, but an extraordinary fighter and an old comrade-in-arms, from Masetti's initial failure, to the Congo, and now here. It is a loss we feel for its quality. There are 22 of us, among them two wounded, Pacho and Villegas, and I, with my asthma going full-tilt.

Che was also very cool in his monthly roundup for July, but again referred to isolation as, rather than a political problem, a problem of organizing the La Paz–Havana network. Strangely enough, just then the three most important left-wing groups in Bolivia (the PCB, the pro-Chinese Communists led by Zamora, and the Trotskyist POR led by Lora) declared their support for the guerrillas, despite their differences, and agreed that their members could join up on an individual basis, in the enthusiasm of the guerrillas' military success and the junta's repressive backlash.

It was true that from outside, the legend of the guerrillas acquires continental dimensions: Onganía closes borders* and Peru goes on alert. But those outside did not see the group's weaknesses, the casualties, the isolated rear guard, the failure to recruit campesinos.

Che also evaluated the maturity of the group of fighters (The guerrillas' morale and combat experience improve with each clash; Orlando Jiménez and Jaime Arana are still weak) and the army's inadequacies: they still cannot hit the mark, but there are units that seem more combative.

But now there was a new priority, besides reestablishing contact with the outside world and recruiting fighters: the need to return to the caves in the old

---

*Organía, Argentina's military dictator at the time, had closed the Argentine-Bolivian border.

bases to replenish drugs and equipment lost in the last clash, as well as asthma medicine. **The asthma sounded bad to me and I've used the last anti-asthma injection. I only have ten days' worth of tablets.**

With the wounded getting better, Che wrote in his diary on August 3: **We are making slow progress. There is no news. Pacho is recovering well. I, on the other hand, am in a bad way. The day and night were hard for me and I can see no way out in the short term. I tried an intravenous injection of novocaine, to no effect.** Pacho: "Che has stopped eating, just a jar of corn, as the horse is bad for his illness, which gets worse by the day, despite the injections." Two days later, Che wrote: **My asthma was implacable. Despite my opposition to our separating, I had to send a group ahead. Dariel Alarcón and Mario Gutiérrez volunteered.**

To make matters worse, the horse threw Che the next day as they were climbing a hill; he lay on the ground, tangled in the stirrups and in the throes of a bad asthma attack. Despite the danger he could not postpone a decision. August 7: **My asthma is unchanged but the medicine is running out. I will make a decision tomorrow about sending a group to the Ñancahuazú River. It was exactly nine months ago today, on our arrival, that the guerrilla group was formed. Of the first six, two are dead** [Martínez Tamayo and Coello], **one missing** [Vázquez Viaña, who was dead, although Che did not know it] **and two wounded** [Pacho and Villegas]. **And then there's me, with an asthma I cannot stop.** The normally stoic Che must have been in a really bad way.

President Lyndon Johnson received a CIA memorandum at about that time, evaluating the guerrillas' situation. It asserted that there were a hundred fighters, mostly Bolivians and some Cubans, who were well trained and disciplined, better led, and better equipped than the poorly trained and organized Bolivian army. Skepticism still prevailed on the crucial issue of Che's presence, because while this was attested to by sources the CIA analysts considered of questionable credibility (Debray and Bustos), they had obtained no conclusive information that Che was in Bolivia. The CIA leadership still thought that Che had died in Cuba.

The memorandum showed that the U.S. government was irritated with its Bolivian allies, particularly President Barrientos, whose sole strategy was to obtain more U.S. firepower. The U.S. analysts were critical, too, of the Bolivian armed forces, which were inept and aggressive toward civilians terrorizing the townspeople, molesting women, and in general making an unfavorable impression, unlike the well-disciplined guerrillas. The report concluded that nothing on the horizon could lead to the conclusion that the guerrilla problem would end soon.

A new group of CIA agents had landed at the airport in La Paz the week before, led by Félix Rodríguez, a Cuban exile who had fought in the dirty war against Cuba and in Vietnam. They were to work directly with Bolivian military intelligence, operating with Bolivian uniforms and documentation.

Che held a session of criticism with his men on August 8:

I gathered every one together and unleashed the following outburst: We are in a difficult situation. Pacho is recovering but I am a human wreck and the episode with the little mare [in an act of despair he had stabbed his mount in the neck] **shows that I have lost control at times. This will change, but the situation must be borne by all of us and whoever doesn't feel capable of overcoming it must say so. It's one of those times for making big decisions. This type of struggle gives us the opportunity to become revolutionaries, the highest rung on the human ladder, but will also allow us to graduate as men. Those who cannot attain either of those two states must say so and leave the struggle.**

All the Cubans and some Bolivians decided to stick it out to the end.

Some of the men became bogged down in petty criticism and Che intervened again.

I closed the discussion by saying that two things of a very different order were under debate here: one was whether or not people were willing to continue the struggle, and the other concerned the group's internal squabbles and problems that detracted from the magnitude of the major decisions.

At that time the guerrillas were slowly hacking their way through jungle mountain ranges, killing their horses for food. Over the radio they heard news that one of Vilo Acuña's guerrilla fighters, Antonio Jiménez, had been killed as he broke out of a military cordon. After Antonio's death graffiti supporting him appeared all over his hometown, Tarata, and the result was serious repression. The guerrillas were attracting more sympathy but could not capitalize on it: their political zone of influence was a long way from their geographical zone of action.

Finally, on August 13, Che agreed under heavy pressure from Inti and Pacho to send a group to Ñancahuazú to look for medicines in one of the caves. **Pacho is improving fast, while my asthma is getting worse. I have been on 3 tablets a day since yesterday. The foot I injured is almost better.**

Something Che could not know, which affected the circumstances of his decision to send a patrol, was that two men had deserted from Vilo Acuña's group at the end of July. Hugo Silva and Eusebio Tapia were captured by the army and sent to Lagunillas for questioning by the army and the CIA. They were tortured at the hands of Colonel Reque Terán, and between August 10 and 11 Silva led a Captain Saravia to the four caves containing the guerrillas supply caches. The army found ammunition, medicines, and very important documents and photographs. The news was mistakenly leaked by the military and published by the newspaper *Presencia,* then broadcast by radio, and heard by Che, days later.

> **A black day . . . The nightly news told of how the cave where the patrol was headed was taken, and the description was so precise that it could not be doubted. I am now condemned to suffering from asthma indefinitely. They also took all sorts of documents and photographs of ours. It's the toughest blow they have dealt us. Some one talked.**

To the material losses was added the enormous risk to the men who had gone to search for the medicines.

Among the items captured by the army were photographs; a manuscript by Che about Latin American economics and politics; and Che's passport, film, and, of course, asthma medicine. The photo in "Benítez's" passport matched the one previously discovered. More proof that Che was in Bolivia.

Che had another riding accident on August 16: **The mule threw me clear out of the saddle when a branch poked it, but I was okay. The foot is getting better.** They arrived at the Rosita River. Food was scarce and they were afraid to hunt in case the sound of shooting tipped off the army. The marches were grueling. On August 19, Pacho wrote: "The bullet entry and exit wounds have healed; the wound between my thighs has yet to heal. My balls are almost okay."

A week later, the guerrillas finally ambushed the army after sighting soldiers several times, but Olo Pantoja, in his haste, shot too soon, which gave the enemy a chance to react.

> **Inti and Coco went after them but they took cover and held them off. While I watched the chase, I saw how bullets from our side were getting close to Coco and Inti, so I ran out and found that Lucio Galván was firing on them, because Olo Pantoja had not told him where they were. I was so furious I lost control and really lit into Olo.**

The army did not follow the retreating guerrillas, but that was not their main concern: they had nothing to eat or drink. Che wrote on August 27:

> **The day was spent desperately seeking a way out; the outcome is not yet clear. We are close to the Río Grande and have already passed Yumao, but there are no new fords, according to reports; we could continue along [the] Manuel Hernández' rock face, but the mules won't make it. There is the possibility of crossing a little mountain range and then continuing towards the Río Grande–Masicurí River, but we won't know till tomorrow whether it is feasible.**

Pacho added: "We don't eat. No water."

Fortunately the group led by Dariel Alarcón returned from its search for medicines.

> Their odyssey was a long one, as there are soldiers in Vargas and Yumao and they almost clashed with them. Then they followed some troops who went down the Saladillo and up the Ñancahuazú, and found that Congrí Brook had three climbing routes made by the soldiers. Bear cave, where they arrived on the 18th, is an antiguerrilla camp which has some 150 soldiers; they were almost caught there, but managed to return without being seen.

The guerrillas' thirst was now worse than their hunger, a fact despairingly echoed in Che's diary on August 29:

> A tough and very anxious day. The hackers advanced little and went the wrong way on one occasion, thinking they were headed for Masicurí. We camped at an altitude of 1,600 meters, in a relatively damp spot with canes whose pith relieves thirst. Some comrades—Jaime Arana, Eustaquio and Chang—are wilting from lack of water.

Pacho wrote: "We cooked six jars of beans from our reserve and made broth from rotten maggoty mare's meat."

The next day, August 30, Che wrote: The situation is becoming desperate. The hackers are fainting; Manuel and Adriazola were drinking their urine, as did Chang, with the terrible effect of diarrhea and cramps. Fortunately Tamayo and Alarcón found water at the bottom of a ravine.

In his August summary, Che wrote:

> It was doubtless the worst month we have had so far in the war. The loss of all the caves with their documents and medicines was a tough blow, especially psychologically. The loss of two men at the month's end, and the following march on horseflesh (crossing the San Marcos mountain range again) demoralized the men and saw the first case of [proposed] quitting, by Orlando Jiménez—which would be a net gain, but not under these circumstances. The lack of contact with the outside world and with Joaquín, and the fact that prisoners taken from his group have talked, also demoralized the men somewhat. My illness sowed the seeds of doubt in some. And all this was reflected in our only engagement, in which we should have caused the enemy several casualties but wounded only one. On the other hand, the difficult march in

the mountains made some of the men's negative traits come to light.

Our morale and revolutionary spirit are at a low point.

Che was not to know that the situation was to became even worse.

An event with very serious repercussions for the guerrillas' survival occurred on August 31. A patrol led by Captain Mario Vargas Salinas had surrounded Honorato Rojas's house, waiting for him to return from the guerrilla campaign. The campesino had been recruited by the army as a guide, had confessed to his contacts with Che in March, and had agreed to collaborate with the army. In a desperate attempt to rejoin Che, Vilo Acuña's group decided to go to Honorato's house in search of news. Gustavo Machín led a reconnaissance expedition to the house, and Honorato agreed to guide them to a nearby ford. But while the guerrillas were talking to Honorato, two soldiers were on sentry duty inside his house—which the guerrillas did not enter because Honorato's dogs were barking fiercely.

The army was alerted within hours and Captain Vargas prepared an ambush with Honorato. The campesino, wearing a white shirt, led the guerrillas to a ford across the Río Grande, where he left them to return home. Che and his guerrillas were only twenty-five miles away just then.

At about 5:30 A.M. the guerrillas appeared at the Yeso ford. Vargas described the scene: "The one who entered the water was a tall, stocky, dark man carrying a backpack, as they all did, and a weapon I could not make out. They came to the ford, Tania included. Just then the first one entered the water." Honorato Rojas had left the scene. The guerrilla column, nine strong, was led by Israel Reyes, with a submachine gun in his left hand and a machete in his right. He crouched, drank from the river, and then signaled his comrades to follow him. The shooting suddenly started. Only Israel was able to react; he shot a soldier dead. Vilo Acuña, Gustavo Machín Hoed, and Moisés Guevara dropped into the flowing river, dead. Freddy Maimura, the medic, was dragged off by the current when he tried to save Tania after seeing her wounded. José Castillo surrendered and was taken prisoner.

Maimura dragged Tania's body onto the riverbank. Some sources say he was captured shortly after, others that he wandered the jungle paths for days before being captured by the army and murdered. Castillo was taken to Vallegrande, where he was interrogated by military intelligence and the CIA.

On September 1, Che advanced along the brook leading to Honorato Rojas's house in search of the rear guard. As night fell the guerrillas discovered that **the house was empty, but had had several sheds added for the army; these were now abandoned. We found flour, lard, and goats. We slaughtered two goats, which made for a feast with the flour, although we spent the night waiting for them to cook.**

Just twenty-four hours had passed since Vilo Acuña was ambushed.

51

"Clear Out and Look for More Suitable Zones"

O N SEPTEMBER 2, 1967, CHE HEARD OVER THE RADIO THAT THE REAR guard had been annihilated. He doubted the truth of the report for three days, although the various radio stations gave more details with each broadcast. He then made no more mention of the issue until his September roundup, which included a note written as if he did not quite want to believe it:

> On the other hand, some reports of dead in the other group appear to be true; they must now be given up as liquidated, although it is possible that a splinter group is wandering and shunning contact with the army, as the report of 7 dead in one fell swoop may be false, or at least exaggerated.

When Che finally accepted what had really happened, he realized he had to leave the area with the remainder of the guerrilla group. On the first day of the march, September 2, the group moved northwest after clashing with a lone soldier. On Sunday, September 3, the advance guard came upon a landowner's house where forty soldiers were billeted; a confused clash arose in which our men killed at least one soldier, the one with a dog. The soldiers reacted and surrounded them [the guerrillas] but then withdrew after the shouting. We couldn't seize so much as a grain of rice.

The guerrillas continued to advance, trying to leave the zone. Wherever they went, they found traces or random reports from the campesinos' of the army's passing. Che wrote on September 4: Remember that not to sustain casualties is basic; caution is recommended.

The guerrillas managed to decipher a message from Havana on September 5, five days after receiving it. It included comments for Che on the outcome of the OLAS, a large convention of the Latin American left held in Cuba to reactivate the proposal to wage a continental guerrilla war. Che's proposals had met with majority approval despite opposition from the most pro-Moscow Communists there (the Bolivian delegation was a crock of shit. Aldo Flores from the PCB pretended to speak as a representative of the ELN. The ELN had to say he was lying). A final note in the message reported that a Dr. Lozano, a member of the Bolivian urban network, had had his house searched.

On September 6, the guerrillas encountered the army again, and again with a patrol led by dog-handlers. Che was without them for several hours while the eight men lay in ambush. However, Manuel Hernández cut across country with all his men to regroup. The army had passed by without seeing them and without the guerrillas realizing their presence.

Che advanced slowly through the jungle. He had the feeling that they were in the midst of a large body of troops.

> The air force is not looking for us around here, even though they've found the camp and the radio has reported that I'm the leader of the group. The question is, Are they scared? Not very

likely. Do they think we can't escape through the mountains? With our previous experience, which they know about, I don't think that's it. Do they want to let us through, to wait for us in some strategic spot? That's possible. Do they think we will insist on staying in the Masicurí zone to gather supplies? That is also possible.

Commercial radio was still the guerrillas' only contact with the outside world; the news occasionally provoked outbursts from the commander:

A Budapest daily criticizes Che Guevara as a pathetic and seemingly irresponsible character, and praises the Chilean Communist Party's Marxist stance, which was demonstrated in the practical measures they adopted. How I would love to take power, if only to unmask cowards and lackeys of all stripes and wipe their noses in their own crap.

Two days later, his anger was directed toward Cuban radio: **Radio Havana said the OLAS had received a message of support from the ELN. Telepathic miracles shall never cease!**

The guerrillas advanced up the Río Grande under terrible conditions. Che lost his shoes swimming across. (Ñato Méndez made him some sandals.) They lost pack mules and weapons; Dr. Octavio de la Pedraja was in very poor health, and Che was still suffering from asthma. There were nights he could not sleep. **I forgot to make note of an event: today, for the first time in about six months, I had a bath. Six months is a record, which several are now achieving.** The guerrillas squabbled over trivia over food, over who was refusing to pull his weight. They moved along exhausted, climbing less and less accessible slopes and crossing streams. One day, Olo Pantoja saw five men advancing along a trail. He told Che.

It proved to be a hallucination, a dangerous thing for the men's morale as they immediately began to talk of psychosis. I spoke to Olo and it was obvious that he wasn't normal. He was brimming with tears but denied anything was wrong and said he was just suffering from lack of sleep, as he has been an adjutant for five days after falling asleep at his post and then denying it.

In September, contradicting all his previous statements, President René Barrientos accepted the U.S. version of events, saying on the radio that Che was dead and news of his presence in Bolivia was just propaganda. That same day, however, the Bolivian army offered a reward of over $4,000 for information leading to the capture of Che, dead or alive. Douglas Henderson scoffed at this bungling, but the same ambiguity was present in the upper echelons of the CIA and among Lyndon Johnson's advisers, who still doubted whether Che was alive and acting in Bolivia.

Those who had no doubts were the CIA's field agents led by Félix Rodríguez, who had interviewed José Chávez and studied Israel Reyes's diary, which was found after the rear guard was ambushed at the Yeso ford. These new leads allowed the agents to clear up the differences between Vilo Acuña's former group, the recently massacred rear guard, and the main body of the guerrilla group, led by Che. They now knew who they were looking for and how big the group might have been.

The radio brought Che terrible news on September 15. "Ignacia" Loyola Guzmán, the ELN treasurer and a key cadre in the urban network, had been identified thanks to photographs found in the caves at a guerrilla camp. Arrested in La Paz, she tried to commit suicide by throwing herself out of a window in the Government Palace. Her arrest prompted student demonstrations, protests by teachers, and manifestos from intellectuals. The relatives of several guerrillas were then arrested or harassed. Antonio Arguedas, the Interior Ministry official advised by the CIA, was behind the operation. The urban network was rendered practically inoperative, with just Rodolfo Saldaña in charge. He received a visit from a Cuban agent code-named Natasha, but could not make contact with the guerrillas.

On September 19, Che wrote in his diary: **A sign of the times: my ink has run out.** Two days later, after nighttime marches climbing up mountains, Che saw that his altimeter had gone off the end of its scale at 6,730 feet. **People are very scared and try to make themselves scarce when we appear. We've lost a lot of time because of our limited mobility.** It took them four and a half hours to cover the last seven miles of that day's march. The next day, September 21, they arrived at the town of Alto Seco, some twenty miles south of Valle Grande; they were welcomed by furiously barking dogs, which calmed down when the guerrillas took no notice of them. Alto Seco was a **one-horse town with 50 houses,** at an altitude of some **1,900 meters. The townspeople welcomed us with a well-seasoned mixture of fear and curiosity.**

Inti Peredo and Che gave a talk in the schoolhouse to a group of campesinos who listened to them in silence. Years later, one of them recalled that Che said: **Tomorrow the military will come and they will know you exist and how you live. They will build a school and a health clinic; they'll improve the road to Valle Grande, make the telephone work, and look for water for you.** "Che spoke the truth. They did build the school and the health clinic, and the phone was fixed. But everything is worse now. The phone doesn't work, the health clinic has no doctor and no medicine, and the road is in ruins."

When interrogated by the police, the peasants assured them that there in the guerrilla group were two black men who spoke Portuguese, and that Che looked ill and exhausted.

On September 24, the guerrillas arrived at a ranch called Loma Larga. Che had a **bad liver, and was vomiting, and the men are worn out with pointless marches.** The campesinos fled on seeing them, as frightening rumors had preceded them, but the news was that the army had not been in the zone. Two days later, they came to the town of Abra de Pichaco, which was having a fair. A campesino later recounted: "Don Che came on a mule, and he was followed by other animals loaded with food. He was with us three hours. He drank *chicha* but didn't want to dance, because he said he was tired. As he was leaving we told him not to go to La Higuera, but over the mountain instead, but he seemed to mistrust us and went downhill, along the Yuro ravine."

> When we came to La Higuera, everything changed. All the men had disappeared, and there was only the odd woman. Coco went to the telegraph operator's house, as there was a telephone there, and brought back a bulletin from the deputy governor of Vallegrande to the sheriff saying they had reports that guerrillas were in the area and that any news should be sent to Valle Grande, where they would pay expenses. The man had fled.

Ninfa Arteaga, the telegraph operator's wife, said: "They were hungry and weak when they came. They ate a lot and told me they would never forget us. . . . The medic was from the Beni region. He spoke so sweetly to us, about how things would be if the guerrillas won. He said there would be doctors and medicines. What's more, I know people. You get to know whether they're good or bad."

As they were leaving town, the advance guard was ambushed by the army's Galindo battalion. Dariel Alarcón, who was at the head, stopped to remove a stone from his shoe and thus saved himself from the first burst of fire, which mowed down Manuel Hernández along with Mario Gutiérrez Ardaya and Coco Peredo. Alarcón tried to rescue Coco by slinging him over his shoulder, but a bullet hit Coco's body and wounded Dariel.

Che took set up a line of defense in the town. A few moments later Dariel Alarcón arrived, wounded, then Aniceto and Francisco Huanca, with his foot in a bad state. Two Bolivian fighters, Antonio Domínguez and Orlando "Camba" Jiménez, had disappeared in the clash.

> The rear guard advanced along the road and I followed them . . . taking the two mules. Those behind were fired on from very close by. They lagged behind and Inti lost contact. After waiting half an hour for him in a small ambush party and receiving more fire from the hill, we decided to leave him, but he soon caught up with us.
>
> Inti then discovered that his brother was dead. "I didn't see him die. Neither did I shed a tear; that's the way I am, I find it hard to cry." Our casualties have been extensive this time. The greatest loss is that of Coco, but Manuel Hernández and Mario Gutiérrez were magnificent fighters, and the human value of the three is incalculable. Antonio Domínguez painted well.

Domínguez, who had fled, knew which way the guerrillas intended to follow, so Che had to modify his plans, but the army troops surrounding them blocked every route. The night after the skirmish, Che assembled the survivors and offered the Bolivians the chance to quit the column, but none accepted. Alarcón said that Che told the Cubans: We represent the prestige of the Cuban revolution and we will defend that prestige to the last man and the last bullet.

Was he assuming that defeat was inevitable, and preparing to take it to its ultimate consequences? It was not the first time he had been in a no-win situation, and doubtless he was not a man to give in to adversity, but he had lost a dozen of his friends over the last two months; he had been completely cut off, unable to fall back on the almost totally destroyed urban networks and the distant rear echelon in Havana. He could not even count on one solid point of support among the campesinos. But if deeds speak for a man, then Che did not speak of defeat: he said he was not prepared to surrender, not even to withdraw.

Meanwhile, rumors preceding the ambush had prompted the Bolivian army command to mobilize the ranger battalion that had been training at the La Esperanza base and dispatch it to the Vallegrande area. Details of who the dead were and information from deserters confirmed that Che and his group were in the area, that Commander Guevara was ill, and that the group was weak. This allowed the army to devise its strategy.

On September 28, Che wrote: A day of distress, which at one point seemed to be our last. Every time they tried to find a way out of the canyon, they found soldiers. At ten A.M., a group of forty-six men,

> taking ages to go past. Another group appeared at 12, this time with 77 men. And, to make matters worse, a shot was then heard and the soldiers took up positions. The officer ordered them to descend the ravine, which seemed to them to be where we were. In any case, in the end, they reported by radio he seemed to be satisfied and resumed the march. Our shelter has now no defense from attack from above and the chances of escape would be remote if they caught us.

Pacho wrote in his diary: "The sound of opening sardine cans, careful as we tried to be, seemed like a terrible racket to us."

They spent three days pent up in the ravine; their scouts could find no way out. Chilean radio reported that Che was trapped in a canyon in the Bolivian jungle. They saw more patrols pass by on the third day and finally, at ten P.M. on September 30, with both their medic and Alarcón in a bad state, they managed to get out of the rat trap. Che admitted to Pacho that it was like dying and being born all over again.

In his September roundup, Che wrote:

> The most important task is to get out of here and look for more suitable areas, then for contacts, even though the entire ap-

paratus in La Paz has been smashed . . . they dealt us a severe blow. Morale among the remaining men has been very good, and my only remaining doubts concern Simón Cuba, who may take the chance to escape in some clash if he is not warned.

Pacho wrote: "Only the sound of Che's voice makes the men walk." Driven by this man who seemed tireless and undeterred, the guerrillas arrived at a new campsite in a **sparse stand of trees.** Here Che gave them a break: I **decided to stay another day, as the spot is good and has a guaranteed retreat, given that we can see all enemy troop movements.**

For the next two days, they advanced by night to avoid the surrounding troops. They had almost no water and suffered from enormous tension.

52

The Yuro Ravine

CHE'S LAST BATTLE IN BOLIVIA TENDS TO LIVE ON IN THE MEMORY OF THE surviving guerrillas in a cruel, indelible, fixed way, playing over and over in their minds and always nagging them with the same question: Might things have turned out otherwise?

On October 4, 1967, Che led his forlorn band as fast as caution allowed, scaling and descending mountains, without water to drink. He still had a chance to laugh at the military in his diary: The radio broadcast . . . a comment that if forces from No. 4 capture me, I will be tried in Camiri, and if No. 8 does, in Santa Cruz.

The next day they advanced by night along a cattle trail. Dariel and Pacho went on ahead to search for water.

> When the reconnaissance was over, they saw six soldiers arrive at a house, apparently stopping on their way elsewhere. We left at nightfall with the men worn out by lack of water, and Lucio Galván carrying on and crying from thirst. After a very bad trail studded with frequent stops, we arrived at dawn at a clump of trees where we could hear dogs barking nearby. We could see a high and very bare rock face very close by.

On October 6, the seventeen-man guerrilla group led by Che found water and decided to pitch a temporary camp. Pacho wrote in his diary: "I'm beginning to lose track of the days. We march at any time of day or night, mainly by night, and man our posts and ambushes by day. I can't tell where one day ends and the other begins."

Life magazine published an extensive feature that same day: "Bolivian Pictures of Missing Che Guevara." The photographs—the ones found in the caves; an army officer had sold them to the magazine—produced a worldwide sensation that enhanced Che's legend. Juan Pablo Chang could be seen in the foreground of one, and Che in the background smoking a cigar. Another photograph clearly showed Che at a campsite on a hill, sitting on the grass surrounded by a dozen fighters, including Carlos Coello, Pacho Fernández Montes de Oca, and Olo Pantoja.

Che wrote on October 7:

> We spent the 11-month anniversary of our guerrilla venture rustically, with no complications until 12:30, when an old woman brought her goats to graze in the canyon where we had pitched camp and we had to detain her. The woman gave us no credible news of the soldiers, answering every question by saying she doesn't know, that she hasn't been here for a while.

Inti Peredo, Aniceto Reinaga, and Francisco Huanca took her home. The woman feigned deafness, then she said she spoke no Spanish, then she said she did not want the guerrillas to come in. It was sad to see.

At dusk the group mobilized again in the moonlight; the march was very tiring and we left many traces behind in the canyon where we were. There were no houses nearby, but there were potato patches watered by ditches branching out from one brook. In the dark they saw a light, but could not tell where it came from. Years later it transpired that the light came from a campesino picking potatoes, who saw the guerrillas go by. They were walking very slowly because Juan Pablo Chang was exhausted and he had dropped his glasses, without which he could not see. The medic, too, was a physical wreck. The radio reported that the army had the guerrillas surrounded between Río Grande and the Acero River, which this time was true. Dariel Alarcón recalled years later: "It seemed that everything piled up, the months of training, the hunger, the nakedness, the illnesses, the thirst, the isolation and now knowing we had been detected by Radio Bemba [the bush telegraph]. The army was saying on the radio that it was just a matter of hours before we were annihilated."

A crag suddenly loomed in the guerrillas' path. They wanted to stop. At the crest of the crag there was a five-foot gap that they would have to jump across; below that was a pit full of freezing water. Alarcón recalled: "And Che was staring at us. No one wanted to be the first to try to scale that crag. A man is a man, not a cat. Then he said he would climb the crag and began to climb, clawing at the rock face." At 2 we stopped to rest; it was useless to try and continue.

At 4:30 A.M. the group was on foot after just a couple of hours' rest. They advanced along another ravine called the Yuro, but which Che and the other Cubans called the Yuro.

At 5:30 A.M. on October 8, Che ordered three reconnaissance details, one on the left flank with Dariel Alarcón and Pacho, another ahead with Tamayo and Ñato Méndez, and the third on the right, with David Adriazola and Aniceto. Alarcón: "I was in the reconnaissance detail . . . and Pacho said to me: 'Look, there's a man!' and I saw a man spring up from the ground, like a sentry. We saw another man further ahead, and just then the sun started to come up. When we saw there were several men getting up, we climbed down."

Che, who had been hoping to ambush the soldiers and break out of the cordon, now scrapped that plan and ordered the three reconnaissance details to withdraw. Inti Peredo recalled: "We could not turn back; the road we had covered was very exposed and made us easy prey. Neither could we advance, as that meant walking right into the soldiers' positions. Che made the only decision that fit the circumstances: he gave the order to take cover in a small canyon beside us and take positions. It was about 8:30 A.M. The seventeen of us sat in the middle and on both sides of the canyon waiting. Che's great question, and ours, was whether the army had spotted us."

The rangers had been tracking a much broader area, but had not spotted the guerrillas, who they thought were somewhere within the cordon set up following the skirmish on October 1.

At dawn on October 8, Pedro Peña, the campesino who had seen the guerrillas when they passed his potato patch, turned up to report them to Second Lieutenant Carlos Pérez who was camping in the vicinity.

Two platoons from A Company of the ranger battalion advanced toward the ravine, accompanied by a mortar and machine-gun section, after informing Captain Gary Prado, who rendezvoused with them where the Yuro met the Tusca Ravine. Prado set up his command post and ordered the rangers to take the heights looking over the ravine.

Che, not knowing how many men he was facing, decided to withdraw the guerrillas to the bottom of the ravine to wait for nightfall so they could climb the crag face and break out of the cordon.

Toward 11:30 A.M., Che sent Aniceto Reinaga and Ñato Méndez to relieve Leonardo Tamayo and Harry Villegas, who were keeping watch at one end of the ravine. Alarcón recalled: "Aniceto, complying with orders, cut across the ravine but, as his curiosity was aroused when he heard the soldiers talking above, he kept walking and stuck his head above the edge of the ravine. I could see him from my position but could not warn him—I couldn't say anything to him as they would have spotted us." A soldier then caught sight of Aniceto and killed him with two shots to his head. Alarcón and Inti's group opened fire and wounded a soldier. "Then three soldiers and a sergeant came to help them and we also hit them." Prado informed La Higuera that his men had entered action and requested a helicopter to pick up the wounded.

The crest of the crag to the guerrillas' left had been fixed as a rendezvous, but they could not climb it because the army controlled access. Dariel Alarcón, Inti Peredo, and David Adriazola returned the army's fire from where they were lying in ambush, and the army began to launch grenades at the bottom of the ravine, where Che's group was. "We only fired from our spot when we were fired on, so as not to give ourselves away and to save ammunition. We took several soldiers out of action."

The firing continued for three hours. Sometime after two o'clock that afternoon, Che must have ordered Francisco Huanca to withdraw with the men who were in the worst physical condition—the Peruvian medic, Octavio de la Pedraja; Lucio Galván; and Jaime Arana. He kept the rangers at bay with the rest of the group (Pacho, Simón Cuba, Juan Pablo Chang, Olo Pantoja, and René Martínez Tamayo). Prado stationed Sergeant Bernardino Huanca's platoon into the ravine and ordered the machine gun and mortars to be aimed at where the two ravines met, where they expected the group to try to escape.

From his vantage point, Alarcón watched Che's group start moving. He and his comrades thought they had broken through the cordon. Villegas and Tamayo were at another high spot in the ravine.

Just then Che was wounded in the right calf, about four inches above the ankle. The burst of fire also smashed the breech of his M2 carbine and made a hole in his beret. He was forced to retreat into the ravine, and his group split up. Villegas recalled: "You have to imagine what those places are like: very sheer terrain, full of zigzags and hills joined together so that although we were only 300, 400, or 500 meters apart, you couldn't really see what was happening from one position to the next."

The sixteen guerrillas left alive were facing about a hundred rangers.

53

Capture

The last photo of the living Che, October 8, 1967, in the village of La Higuera, the town where he was captured. CIA agent Félix Rodriguez is on his left, in a Bolivian Ranger's uniform. Che has a bullet wound in his left leg. He was murdered inside the schoolhouse there.

Toward 2:30 p.m., on October 8, 1967, three startled soldiers from B Company of the rangers—who had not previously taken a direct combat role, because they were manning a mortar—saw a guerrilla fighter appear just a few yards from them, on the brow of a hill. He had a gun strapped to a bandolier and was struggling to drag, or almost carry, another guerrilla fighter, who had a leg wounded and was fighting for breath.

Simón Cuba (of whom Che had said a week earlier that he **may take the chance to escape in some clash**) was about to reach the top of a very steep climb of some sixty meters, during which he had borne practically all of Commander Guevara's weight. Che, wounded in his right leg and suffering from a severe asthma attack, could barely move. He was still holding his M2, though it had been rendered useless in his last encounter.

Corporal Balboa and Privates Encinas and Choque let them make way, and then Balboa shouted for them to surrender. Simón had no time to raise his rifle as the three soldiers took aim at him. It is said that he shouted, "This is Commander Guevara, show some respect, dammit!"

The soldiers were unsettled and humbled, and one reportedly went so far as to say, "Please take a seat, sir." Then, recovering from their initial shock, they relieved their prisoners of their weapons: Simón's rifle, Che's wrecked M2, and a Solingen steel dagger.

The story of Che's capture has been told as many times as it has been mistold. There have been those who lied to steal a piece of the action and those who lied for political reasons. There have been those who turned a half-memory into a whole one and ended up believing in it. Finally, there have been those who timidly offered a bit here and a piece there over the next twenty-five years. Curiously, it has been the smallest details that have obscured the final version, particularly the Bolivian guerrilla war leader's 9mm Walther PPK pistol, the story of which has also been cloaked in mystery.

Pacho Fernández Montes de Oca, in his diary entry for October 1, a week before the events described here, had written: "Fernando [Che] asked me for a cigarette and to load a pistol magazine for him. He had hold of the pistol as if he meant to kill himself before being taken prisoner. I feel the same way."

Dariel Alarcón would muse years later, "In the heat of the battle, Che obviously lost the magazine that Pacho had prepared for him, or else some other unknown prevented him from making a decision that nobody who knew of his extraordinary courage, proven many times, and his disregard for death, could have doubted."

Fidel Castro himself, in his introduction to Che's Bolivian diary, related: "It has been proven that Che fought on while wounded, until the barrel of his M2 rifle was smashed by a shot that rendered it totally useless. There was no magazine in the pistol he was carrying. These incredible circumstances explain why they were able to take him alive."

The account of Che's capture that was offered a year later by Antonio Arguedas confirmed that the pistol's magazine was missing. According to the military, however, in its inventory of Che's personal belongings as well as the account given by the head of military intelligence, Colonel Saucedo, the pistol was said to be loaded.

Was the Bolivian military lying, as it did in so many other respects in its accounts of Che's capture and death? Was Commander Guevara willing to commit suicide rather than be captured? Was the magazine lost in battle? Did he use up the bullets in his pistol after his rifle was smashed? Or did he simply not have time to react when he was taken prisoner, overwhelmed as he was by an asthma attack and surprised by the unexpected appearance of three soldiers? There is no way to tell.

Beyond these minor mysteries, the sources do agree that Che's first contact with his captors was a brief conversation with the corporal:

What's your name?

"Corporal N. Balboa Huayllas."

What a great name that would be for a guerrilla commander. He then handed out some Astoria cigarettes to the soldiers who had arrested him.

Captain Gary Prado Salmon, the commander of the nearby military post, would later say (referring to himself in the third person):

> . . . advising his company commander, who was fifteen yards away:
> "There's two of them, Captain, we've caught them."
> Captain Prado observed the guerrilla fighters and asked: "Who are you?—addressing himself first to Willy (Simón Cuba)—who answered "Willy" . . . and then the other one. . . . *I'm Che Guevara.* Taking out a copy of Bustos's drawings, the officer compared his features with the sketch and asked him to stretch out his left hand, on the back of which he clearly saw a scar that had been cited as a distinguishing mark.

One of the rangers would later say that Che spoke "proudly, without lowering his head, and looked the captain straight in the eye." Years later, Gary Prado described the impression his enemy had stamped on him forever: "Che had an imposing look about him, clear eyes, a mane of hair that was almost red, and a thick, heavy beard. He wore a black beret, a filthy military uniform, and a blue jacket with a hood; he was almost bare-chested, as his tunic had no buttons left on it."

Prado used a U.S. World War II surplus GRC9 transceiver to contact his second-in-command at the nearby town of Abra de Picacho, Lieutenant Toti Aguilera, who in turn contacted the division headquarters at Vallegrande. The message to "Saturno"—Colonel Zenteno—went out at 2:15: "Three guerrillas dead and two seriously wounded. Troops maintain Ramón captured; but we have yet to confirm it. We have two dead and four wounded."

Prado reports: "Once back at the command post, I issued some orders. We were under the shade of a small tree, at the edge of a ravine, but ten meters above it and sheltered by a small hollow. I ordered the prisoners to be bound hand and foot using their own belts, with their hands behind them." He says that Che told him:

Don't worry, Captain. It's all over now.

"For you, yes, but there are still some good fighters out there, and I don't want to run any risks."

It's useless, we've failed.

Lieutenant Aguilera returned Prado's call, telling him that Vallegrande was requesting confirmation of the capture. The colonels who had been waging this war miles away from the battlefield could not bring themselves to believe it. At 3:30 P.M., Prado sent another radio message: "Ramón's capture confirmed. Awaiting orders. He is injured."

Half an hour later, Colonel Andrés Selich left Vallegrande in a helicopter headed for La Higuera, the closest town to the Yuro ravine. About 4:30 P.M., the helicopter flew over the ravine and drew fire from the guerrillas who were still fighting.

Two planes loaded with napalm were also approaching the combat zone, but Prado requested them not to bomb the zone because the fighting was at very close quarters, with guerrillas and rangers shadowing each other's moves both down in the Yuro Ravine and the one next to it. A few minutes later, a platoon of rangers clashed with Olo Pantoja and René Martínez Tamayo. Three soldiers were wounded, one of whom died shortly afterward. The guerrillas were attacked with hand grenades and killed. That was the official version.

At five P.M., a curt wire went from Vallegrande to the army command in La Paz: "We confirm Ramón captured." They had waited two and a half hours before bothering to inform the high command.

At around that time, one of the three guerrilla groups, which was fighting at the top part of the ravine (Inti Peredo, Harry Villegas, Dariel Alarcón, Ñato Méndez, Leonardo Tamayo, David Adriazola), managed to avoid the Bolivian soldiers and rendezvous at the spot previously agreed on with Che. On the way, they found some flour dumped on the ground, which worried them: Che would never have let such a thing happen. Later, his trampled mess tin turned up. Inti Peredo later said, "I recognized it because it was an aluminum dish. We met nobody at the rendezvous, although we did recognize Che's footprints—his sandals left different tracks behind than the others' and were thus easy to identify. But the trail was lost further on."

Alarcón completed the picture:

> We saw Che get out and escape the cordon, so we thought he was out of danger. It would have been about three in the afternoon that we saw him begin the retreat, so we said, "He's out of danger now," but what we didn't see was that he was going back to rescue Willy [Simón Cuba] and Chang. . . . The fighting would have finished at around five in the afternoon.

So where was Che? Gunfire could still be heard. Another group,—the sick, led by Francisco Huanca—had managed to get through, accompanied by the medic Morogoro de la Pedraja and the Peruvians Restituto Cabrera and

Lucio Galván. Pacho, on his own, managed to hole up in a cave at the bottom of the ravine.

It was getting dark. Captain Prado decided to withdraw to La Higuera with his most valued prize, Commander Guevara.

A strange procession, a wake, got under way. Almost a hundred frightened soldiers carried the bodies of their comrades-in-arms, and of Olo Pantoja and René Martinez Tamayo, on improvised stretchers. Che and Simón were tied up and led by two other soldiers, surrounded by a substantial "security detail."

La Higuera was a mile and a half away; en route, the procession found a few wounded soldiers who were being evacuated, and whom Che offered to treat. Captain Prado refused and blamed Che for their condition. That's war, Che said, laconically. The captain offered him some light Pacific cigarettes, but he would accept only a dark Astoria, from one of the soldiers.

It must have been around seven o'clock at night. The soldiers were under orders not to speak to the guerrilla fighters. In any case, Che did not speak again for the rest of the journey. Maybe he remembered what he had written when he visited Bolivia for the first time: Life here is worth little; they take it or leave it without the least fuss.

54. Eighteen Hours in La Higuera

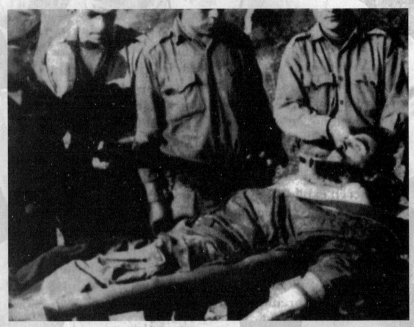

Che's body, still in La Higuera, surrounded by Bolivian Rangers.

TOWARD 7:30 P.M., ERNESTO GUEVARA ENTERED LA HIGUERA FOR THE second time in his life, but now as a defeated man. This destitute hamlet, with no more than thirty adobe houses and some 500 inhabitants, owed its name—"The Fig Tree"—to the fact that the place once teemed with now long-gone figs. Remote, accessible only by a bridle path impassable for vehicles, La Higuera is a place where folklore has it that only the stones are eternal.

Some frightened peasants had gathered at the edge of the town. Twenty years after Che's death, one old lady would tell how she saw him pass in procession in front of her house in La Higuera, and that they then flew him away, up in the sky . . . in a helicopter, she would finally say, as if accepting an explanation given her many times that seemed outlandish to her, compared to the fact that he flew off into the heavens.

Rangers major Ayoroa and Colonel Selich, who had arrived by helicopter in midafternoon, were waiting. The prisoners and the guerrillas' dead were taken to the schoolhouse, an adobe building with a tiled roof and just two open rooms separated by a partition. Simón Cuba was locked up in one room with the bodies of Olo and René, and Che was in the other. He had been untied and given an aspirin for the pain from the wound in his leg.

Juan Pablo Chang, who had a face wound, was also detained. Was he caught at the same time as the others, or afterward?

At 8:30 P.M., Gary Prado transmitted the same message he had been sending all afternoon, again and again, but by telegraph this time: "Papa wounded." He and Selich then went over the miserable belongings in Che's rucksack: twelve rolls of film, a couple of dozen maps, corrected by Che in colored pencil, a portable radio, two small code books, two notepads with copies of messages received, and a pair of notebooks—diaries, maybe?—full of Che's small, rapid handwriting.

Colonel Selich requested instructions from 8th Division headquarters over the phone. They answered him ten minutes later: "Prisoners must be kept alive until orders received from above." Another message arrived from Vallegrande an hour later: "Keep Fernando alive until I arrive by helicopter first thing tomorrow. Col. Zenteno."

In La Higuera, meanwhile, the three commanding officers were trying to interrogate Che, but did not get anything out of him, as he refused to talk to them. Prado recalled that Selich said to Che: "How about us shaving you first?" and tugged at Che's beard. Che slapped him. According to the telegraph operator at La Higuera, Selich went further when Che refused to answer questions—he threatened to kill him and took two pipes and a watch from him.

The town was in a state of alert and expecting an attack from the surviving guerrillas at any time. Two concentric barriers of guards, plus a lookout, had been placed around the schoolhouse.

By 10:10 at night, "Saturno" at 8th Division in Vallegrande was telegraphing the army's high command (Generals Ovando and Lafuente) in La Paz using a proposed code devised for use when dealing with the prickly issue of

Che's capture. The code was: "Fernando (Che): 500. Alive: 600, [send] former only by Morse, the rest by radio. Dead: 700."

Saturno's message read: "Good evening. Last report ratifies we hold 500. Request strict instructions whether 600 or 700."

The high command replied: "Must be kept 600. Red alert. There are leaks."

The high command was deliberating in La Paz. The initial message had been received by General Lafuente Soto, the army commander; Vázquez Sempertegui, the army chief of staff; and Lieutenant Colonel Arana Serrudo, of military intelligence. Argentine writer Jorge Gallardo provided a memorable description of these three characters: Lafuente was a squat individual, with a face like an orangutan, a bushy beard, and the nickname Chkampu ("Fungus-Face" in Quechua); Vázquez, the perpetrator of the miners' massacre, was stocky and had a cynical smile; Arana was deformed, with a very long, thick neck on a contrasting body, and very dark.

They went to look for the war minister, General Alfredo Ovando, in the small office he used in the Miraflores military fortress. On receiving the three, he sent for General Juan José Torres, the armed forces chief of staff, who occupied the office opposite the conference room annexed to Ovando's office. In this conference room, the five met. They may have consulted some other high-ranking officers, such as air force Commander León Kolle Cueto—who, strangely enough, was the brother of the Bolivian Communist Party chief, Jorge Kolle.

There is no record of what was discussed in that room, only of the decision. Having reached their agreement, the generals consulted President Barrientos, who approved.

At 11:30 that night, the armed forces high command sent the following message in Morse to Colonel Zenteno in Vallegrande: "President orders Fernando 700."

Che Guevara had been sentenced to death.

———

Those eighteen hours in La Higuera are enough to drive even the most cold-blooded biographer to despair, to say nothing of the hot-blooded ones. Ernesto Guevara had thus far spent his life leaving behind a flood of papers in which he recorded his impressions, his accounts of events, and his most intimate feelings in diaries, letters, articles, interviews, speeches, and minutes. He had lived surrounded by narrators, witnesses, and friendly voices who talked and talked about him. Now, for the first time, the biographer will have to rely only on unfriendly witnesses, many of whom had axes to grind and a vested interest in distorting events and constructing a false account. What we know today has been put together from dribs and drabs over thirty years; it is the product of journalistic persistence and of testimony given belatedly as apologias, often false, for long-ago actions. La Higuera is a morass of words that only leaves room for questions:

Did he know they were going to kill him?

How did he now rate Simón Cuba, of whom he spoken so many times in his diary?

Did he take a roll call of those guerrillas who were alive, those who were detained, and those who were dead? Pacho Montes de Oca and Pombo were with Inti Peredo, Dariel Alarcón, David Adriazola, Ñato Méndez, and Leonardo Tamayo; Francisco Huanca and Octavio de la Pedraja had escaped with the wounded. Would they have seen him taken prisoner? Would they try something?

Did Che spend his time thinking about Aleida and his children? Or did he think about the dead, the other dead who had paved the way: René Ramos Latour and Geonel Rodríguez, Camilo Cienfuegos and Ricardo Masetti, Eliseo "San Luis" Reyes, Manuel, Vilo Acuña, and Tania? The list was endless.

Did his wound hurt him? He had never failed to treat a prisoner, and they had given him nothing but an aspirin for a bullet wound.

Did he go over his defeat, the last link in a chain that stretched back a long way: the Puerto Maldonnado group, the one in Salta, and now his, Che's, guerrilla war?

What did the future have in store for him? Fifty years in jail? A bullet in the nape of his neck? This was not the first time he had been beaten, but who knew if it would be the last?

His diary was meanwhile in the telegraph house, a few yards from where they were holding him prisoner. There had been other military defeats, but for the first time in his life, Ernesto Guevara was a man without pen and paper, a man essentially defeated because he could not tell things his way.

The first change of guard in La Higuera had taken place an hour and a half earlier. Che was lying slumped on the floor, and his leg wound had stopped bleeding. One of the guards on duty in the room would tell, years later:

> One thing I saw, and it seemed to me like an affront to the guerrilla fighter, was Carlos Pérez Gutiérrez come in, grab him by the head, and spit in his face. Che did not put up with that—he spat back and kicked him so that he doubled up, too. I don't know where he kicked him, but I saw Carlos Pérez Gutiérrez laid out on the floor, with Eduardo Huerta and another officer holding Che down.

A short while later, a medical orderly washed Che's leg with disinfectant, and that was the extent of the treatment he was given. Ninfa Arteaga, the telegraph man's wife, offered to take food to the prisoners. The guards' second-in-command refused, and Ninfa said, "If they won't let me feed him, then I won't feed anybody." Her daughter, Élida, took some food to a "blind" guerrilla fighter (Juan Pablo Chang?). Che's last supper was to be a bowl of peanut soup.

Lieutenant Toti Aguilera entered the room: "Mr. Guevara, you are now in my charge." Che asked him for a cigarette. Aguilera asked whether he was a doctor, to which Che replied that he was, and said he was a dentist, too, that he had pulled some teeth in his time.

The lieutenant walked around the room, trying to get a conversation going, but ended up walking off. There was no way of talking to the legend lying there, wounded and reserved, with that awkward distance that Che always kept even with those close to him, and how much more so with strangers, and with enemies.

Later on, several soldiers entered the room. They asked about all sorts of things, hesitantly, in fits and starts. Did they have religion in Cuba? Was it true that the Cubans wanted to exchange some tractors for him? Did you kill my friend? Insults were flung. A sergeant major reportedly said to Che, as he saw him huddled up in a corner of the room:

"Are you thinking of the immortality of the donkey?"—a Spanish idiom meaning something like "sweet nothings."

Che, who had always loved donkeys, smiled and answered: **No, Lieutenant, I'm thinking about the immortality of the revolution so feared by those you serve.**

Toward 11:30 P.M., a couple of soldiers remained alone with Che, without no noncoms or officers present. Che talked with them and asked them where they were from. Both were from mining families; one was the son of a miner. They thought that they could probably escape with him. One of them went out of the room to see how the land lay. The town was still in a state of alert, with three cordons of guards, the third one from another regiment. The soldiers told Che this. They say he replied: **Don't worry, I'm sure I won't be a prisoner for long, because a lot of countries are going to claim me, so there's no need to worry yourselves too much. I don't think anything whatever will happen to me.**

One of the guerrilla groups still at large had meanwhile managed to slip through the army's net. Inti Peredo recalled: "On that tense and agitated night, we had not the faintest idea of what had happened, and asked ourselves in hushed tones whether some other comrade, besides Aniceto, had died in the encounter." At dawn, they went down to the ravine again; after a short wait, they mobilized at the second rendezvous, a few miles from La Higuera. Alarcón: "We made our way to the second rendezvous, close to the El Naranjal River. We had to head for La Higuera again, and . . . daybreak caught us close to the little village."

It was dawn, October 9. Wires were on their way from the U.S. embassy to Washington, D.C., and Ambassador Henderson informed the State Department that Che was among the prisoners and was seriously ill or wounded. Lyndon Johnson's advisers on Latin American affairs, using CIA sources, reported that Barrientos was holding Che and that he wished to check his fingerprints.

In La Higuera, the guards were relieved as day broke, to the sound of helicopter rotor blades. The helicopter carried Colonel Zenteno, Saturno, who had been accompanied from Vallegrande by CIA agent Félix Rodríguez. The two made their way to the telegraph house where the documents found in Che's knapsack were being kept.

Under Major Ayoroa's command, the rangers were meanwhile combing the ravines to search for survivors. The official version, from Captain Prado:

> This operation began on the morning of the ninth, carefully turning over every yard of land. A company located the caves where Chang and Pacho were holed up; upon being asked to surrender, they opened fire and killed a soldier. This occasioned a rapid response by the rangers, who silenced them with hand grenades and machine guns.

Curiously, in another part of his account, Prado said that his soldiers reported the presence of *one* guerrilla fighter in the cave, not two. Why, if there were two men in the ravine, had the surviving guerrillas not seen them the night before? Why did Pacho's diary have no entry for October 8?

In La Higuera, the colonel and the CIA man went in to see Che. One soldier told, years later, of how "one of the commanders argued loudly with Che, and this commander had somebody by his side, a journalist maybe, who was recording things with a kind of big tape recorder slung against his chest."

According to Rodríguez, things were friendlier. They took Che out of the schoolroom and asked for permission to take a photograph. Félix stood beside the guerrilla fighter while Major Niño de Guzmán, the helicopter pilot, snapped the CIA man's Pentax. We have the photograph: Che's hair was a tousled mane; there is a certain look of grim desolation on his face, his eyes drooping with exhaustion, and his hands are together, as if they were bound.

Another two photographs were taken by soldiers that morning; both are very similar, with Che avoiding the camera.

Zenteno went up to the Yuro Ravine to supervise operations under way, while Rodríguez sent a coded message with his portable RS48. Selich, who observed him, was very precise: "He was carrying a long-range radio transmitter, which he set up at once and used to transmit a coded message of about sixty-five groups. [After that,] he immediately set up a camera on a sunlit table, on a frame with four telescopic legs, and began to take photographs." Of particular interest to Rodríguez were Che's two diaries, the code book, and his address book with addresses of people all over the world.

Rodríguez remarked, as he was photographing the code book: "There's only two of these in the world, one in Fidel Castro's hands, and this." Selich went back to Vallegrande in the helicopter with the two wounded soldiers and, at half-past eleven, Zenteno returned to La Higuera with an escort and Major Ayoroa. They found the CIA agent in full swing; Zenteno barely commented, assuring him that the U.S. agents would be given copies of the photographs in La Paz. "No one objected to the photographs being taken; no one took exception," Major Ayoroa would later recall.

From the loneliness of the schoolroom, Che asked his captors to let him speak to the schoolteacher, Julia Cortez.

Ah, you're the teacher. Did you know that the e in "sé" has an accent in "ya sé leer?" he said, pointing to the chalkboard. By the way, they don't have schools like this in Cuba. This would be like a prison for us. How can peasants' children study in a place like this? It's anti-pedagogical.

"Ours is a poor country."

But the government officials and the generals drive Mercedes cars and have a host of other things. . . . Don't they? That's what we're fighting against.

"You've come a long way to fight in Bolivia."

I'm a revolutionary and I've been in all sorts of places.

"You've come to kill our soldiers."

Look: in war, it's either win or lose.

Just when did Colonel Zenteno transmit the presidential order to kill Che? Did Félix Rodríguez try to convince the Bolivians not to kill him, arguing that Che was more useful alive and defeated than dead at that time? The CIA man said in his memoirs that he did so, but Zenteno's statements make no mention of the matter.

Rodríguez also claims that he spoke with Che for an hour and a half, and that Che even asked him to transmit a message to Fidel, saying that the Latin American revolution would triumph, and to tell his wife to remarry and be happy.

But the hour and a half was really no more than fifteen minutes, and other military sources agree that Che recognized Rodríguez as a *gusano,* a Cuban turncoat, working for the CIA; Che called him a mercenary and after that their conversation became no more than a shouting match.

The fact is that at 11:45 A.M., Zenteno picked up Che's diary and rifle and left with Rodríguez in the helicopter that had just touched down.

At midday, Che asked permission to speak to the schoolteacher again, but she did not want to: she was scared.

Meanwhile, the surviving guerrilla fighters were some 500 or 600 meters from town, waiting for nightfall in order to make a move. Alarcón recalled:

> It was there we realized that Che was in captivity. . . . We heard the news on a little radio we had, which had an earphone. . . . We thought it was disinformation spread by the army. But at about ten in the morning, they were already saying that Che was dead and . . . were speaking of a photograph he had had in his wallet, of his wife and children. When the three of us Cubans heard that, we stared at one another while we silently shed tears. . . . That did it; for us, Che really had died in combat. It never crossed our minds that we had him there, alive, a bit more than 500 meters away.

At mid-morning, Ayoroa asked for volunteer executioners. Sergeant Major Mario Terán asked to be allowed to kill Che, one soldier recalled: "His argument was that three buddies called Mario from B Company had been killed, and that in their honor, he should be given the right to kill Che." He was half drunk. Sergeant Bernardino Huanca offered to kill Che's comrades.

Just after one in the afternoon, Terán, a short man not more than five feet, two inches tall, stocky, weighing 145 pounds, went into the schoolroom where Che was held. Terán held an M2 rifle, which Sergeant Major Pérez had lent him. Huanca was meanwhile riddling Chang and Simón with bullets in the room next door.

Che was sitting on a bench, with his wrists tied together, his back against the wall. Terán hesitated, said something, and Che answered:

Why bother? You've come to kill me.

Terán turned as if to leave, then let off his first burst of fire in response to the words that almost thirty years later would be attributed to Che: **Shoot, you coward, you're going to kill a man.** As Terán tells it:

> When I got there, Che was sitting on the bench. When he saw me, he said: *you've come to kill me.* I couldn't bring myself to shoot, and the man said to me: *Take it easy, you're going to kill a man.* I then took a step back, toward the doorway, closed my eyes, and fired the first burst. Che fell to the floor with his legs smashed, writhing, and began to gush blood. I got my nerve back and shot a second burst and hit him in the arm, his shoulder, and his heart.

A short while later, Sergeant Major Carlos Pérez entered the room and fired a shot into the body. His was not to be the only postmortem bullet: Private Cabrero also shot Che's body, to avenge the death of his friend Manuel Morales.

The various witnesses seem to agree on the time of Che's death: around 1:10 P.M., Sunday, October 9, 1967.°

The teacher screamed at the killers.

A Dominican priest from a nearby parish had tried to get to La Higuera in time to speak to Ernesto Guevara. Father Roger Schiller recalled:

> When I found out that Che was being held in La Higuera, I got a horse and made my way there. I wanted to hear his confession. I know he would have said, "I'm a lost cause." I wanted to say to him: "You're not a lost cause. God still believes in you."
>
> On the way, I met a peasant. "Don't rush, Father," he said to me, "They've already done away with him."

At around four P.M., Captain Prado came back to the town, from the latest foray into the nearby ravines. On his way into La Higuera, Major Ayoroa informed him that Che had been executed, at which he frowned in disgust: he

°The army tried to change the date of Che's death to create a version of Che being killed in combat. The anniversary was "celebrated" for years on October 8 because of this disinformation.

had taken Che alive. Preparations were being made to transport the body by helicopter. Prado tied Che's jaw with a handkerchief, so that his face would not be distorted.

A street photographer took pictures of the soldiers surrounding the body, which lies on a stretcher. They look like photographs from a Sunday outing, with only the smiles missing. One of the photos shows Prado, Father Schiller, and Doña Ninfa, the telegraph man's wife, beside the body.

The priest entered the schoolhouse, but did not know what to do, so he picked up the rifle shells and kept them, and then washed the bloodstains away. He wanted to wash away some of the sin of a man having been killed in a school.

Mario Terán was promised a watch and a trip to West Point to take part in a course qualifying him as a sergeant major, but neither promise was kept.

The helicopter took off with the body tied to one of its skids.

55. The Missing Body

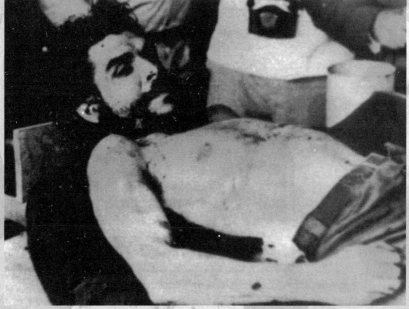

Che's body in the Malta hospital in Villegrande, Bolivia. At a press conference held by the Bolivian military, they announced that he had received ten bullet wounds in combat, and that his death was caused by a confrontation with the Rangers in the Churo ravine.

VALLEGRANDE 765 KILOMETERS—475 MILES—SOUTHEAST OF LA PAZ, 8th Division headquarters, ten a.m. on October 10, 1967. Uruguayan journalist Ernesto González Bermejo provided a description of the scene:

> A town like so many others, with its main square, a dried-up fountain, a bust in somebody-or-other's memory, and some quarries. The town hall, with the clock forever stopped at ten past five on who-knows-what day, Julio Durán's drugstore, the Montesclaros grocery, Doña Eva's store, which doubles as a boardinghouse, and the church, of course, which is called, maybe a little pretentiously, a cathedral.

The Bolivian military, anxious to show off their triumphs, called a press conference. Cynically, they not only did not wait for Che's body to cool; they announced his death while he was still alive, although they were the only ones to know it at the time. René Barrientos made the announcement at ten A.M., speaking off the record to a group of journalists in La Paz; Colonel Zenteno did likewise at one P.M. in a press conference at 8th Division headquarters. Colonel Zenteno declared that Che had died in a clash with the army in the vicinity of La Higuera, some twenty-odd miles from Vallegrande: "The engagement lasted four hours . . . but Guevara, wounded in the groin and lungs, died at the beginning . . ."

The army chief, General Alfredo Ovando, arrived at Vallegrande at 1:50, accompanied by General Lafuente and Rear Admiral Ugartechea. They visited the mess where the bodies of those who had died in the recent operations were laid out. Ovando looked tense and stiff, as if hiding his nervousness. This was a strange kind of victory, which made the victors more scared than triumphant.

Three hours later, at exactly five o'clock in the afternoon, the helicopter landed at the airport, a body tied to one of its skids. The transport operation seemed to be under the command of a man wearing military fatigues, but with no insignia of rank, which attracted the journalists' attention and made them decide he was a CIA agent. Some of them took his picture—he was "Dr. González." His colleague Félix Rodríguez was also present. The journalists approached the agents and asked where they were from: Cuba? Puerto Rico? "From nowhere," they said, in English.

Rodríguez then shouted to his colleague: "Let's get the hell out of here."

A campesino who had turned up at the airport saw the body carried past: "He looked like he was in one piece. It was like he wasn't dead. He was laid out on the stretcher with his eyes open, looking at us, as if he was still alive." The body was taken in a closed Chevrolet pickup, amid a huge entourage of soldiers, to the San José de Malta Hospital, where it was placed on a slab in the hospital laundry.

A nurse, Susana Osinaga, undressed the body: "He was wearing a jacket, his pants, a black beret with something sewn into it—I don't know whether it was green or red: a little naval star—three socks on each foot, some brown ones, some striped ones, and some blue ones." Two doctors took part in the proceedings, as did Colonel Selich, who would not leave the body.

The second press conference was held in the hospital laundry, where the body was exhibited and which some would see as a hyperrealist version of Rembrandt's painting *Dr. Tulp's Anatomy Lesson.* Alberto Zuazo, the UPI correspondent, reported:

> The slightly watery transparency of those expressive green eyes, as well as a sort of enigmatic smile that was faintly traced on his face, gave the impression that there was life in that body. I think that more than one of us out of the score of journalists who went to Vallegrande that October 10, 1967, was just waiting for Che to speak to us.

There followed the photographs of a military man showing the gunshot wounds, photographs that would then be published around the world.

The military were mistaken again if they thought they could exorcise Che's spirit by trying to show that he was dead beyond any doubt, by bringing to bear the rationality of stark photographs of a corpse, the false proof of reason. The horrible photos of his face, the strange calm of a rest after a year of terrible hunger, asthma attacks, fevers, upsets, doubts, became, thanks to the technical wizardry of wire services, the province of millions around the globe. In keeping with the terrible Christian tradition of venerating tortured Christs and saints riddled with wounds, the image inevitably evoked a lot: death, redemption, and resurrection.

Drawn by these ghosts, the Vallegrande campesinos paraded in front of the body, in single file, amid an awesome silence. When the army tried to control access, an avalanche of people broke through the cordon of soldiers. That night, candles for Che were lit for the first time in the small holdings around the little town. A saint was being born, a secular saint of the poor.

At 5:30 P.M. the high-ranking officers had their pictures taken with the body, and Ovando put the words *"I'm Che; I'm worth more alive than dead,"* into Che's mouth at his capture. Ovando later repeated a variation on the same theme: *"I'm Che, and I've failed."* This marked the beginning of a long stream of disinformation. An army officer showed Che's diary to the journalists and "quoted" a remark supposedly written in it: *"I never thought Bolivian soldiers could be so tough."*

Lyndon Johnson first learned of Che's death at 6:10 P.M. in a memorandum, from Walter Rostow, describing the report in *Presencia* of Che's capture, and Barrientos's ten A.M. statement that Che was dead. The CIA later came up with a far more accurate firsthand account.

Havana at first reacted cautiously. Fidel later admitted that he had slowly begun to accept that Che was dead under the weight of the photos that were flowing in, but still awaited more exact confirmation: this was not the first time the press had killed Che in some part of the world or other. What he could not say was that his uncertainty arose from the fact that communications with the guerrillas had been lost several months earlier and that even contacts with the remains of the urban network were nil.

The autopsy was performed later that evening, by the hospital director and an intern—Abraham Baptista and José Martínez Casso, respectively—under the watchful eye of Toto Quintanilla (the intelligence chief at the Interior Ministry) and "Dr. González" from the CIA. The subsequent report was inevitably full of ambiguity. The death certificate itself read: "death caused by multiple bullet wounds in the thorax and limbs." And the autopsy report listed nine bullet wounds: two in the legs, one in the middle third of the right leg, the other in the middle third of the left thigh; two around the clavicles; two in the ribs; one in the pectoral muscle. The cause of death was attributed to "wounds to the thorax and the consequent hemorrhage."

However, an army officer, in the sight of the journalists, counted ten wounds. The "extra" one, in Che's throat, was not mentioned in the autopsy. The discrepancy went unnoticed at first, as did the fact that the chest wounds were fatal. For that reason, had the autopsy been correct, Che could not have been taken alive—albeit seriously injured—and still have been alive in La Higuera, as per the second press conference. Much less could he have spoken with his captors. The Bolivian army's sloppiness was beginning to make itself evident; whereas they had reached agreement on killing him, they could not get their stories straight as to how he died.

The military had another matter pending: what to do with the body. A telegram had arrived at ten A.M. from the armed forces chief of staff, General Juan José Torres: "Guevara's remains must be incinerated immediately and ashes kept apart." But the body could not be disposed of without having first been positively identified. Even more dangerous than Che's grave would be his ghost. Ovando suggested that his head and hands be cut off and preserved for the sake of a later positive identification. CIA man Rodríguez tried to convince Ovando that the hands would be enough, enabling the fingerprints to be checked afterward, and that the Bolivian government would look like some barbaric tribe in the eyes of the world if they were to cut his head off.

Another operation was to be carried on at the hospital. The tension and the butchering of the corpse were too much for one of the doctors, Martínez Casso, who got drunk. Dr. Baptista was the one who cut the hands off at the wrist and inserted them into a flask of formaldehyde. A wax death mask was made, too, but according to Susana Osinaga, "They ruined his face when they made the wax mask from it."

In the early hours of October 11, toward three A.M., Colonel Zenteno and Lieutenant Colonel Selich, who were in charge of the operation, gave Captain Vargas Salinas, the man who had ambushed Vilo Acuña's guerrilla group a month before, the order to dispose of Che's body and those of Alberto Fernández Montes de Oca, Orlando Pantoja, Simón Cuba, Aniceto Reinaga, Juan Pablo Chang, and René Martínez Tamayo, seven in all. Under no circumstances was Che to have an identifiable grave: there was to be no place in Bolivia for people to offer their respects for the dead man and his comrades. The original idea, of incineration, had been rejected when one of the doctors explained how difficult it would be without a proper crematory oven.

Despite the precautions, an old man working opposite the Malta Hospital managed to see the operation taking place in the dark. He described it to the journalist Guy Guglietta ten years later:

> "They put his body in the old laundry and took it out later, along with the others. They took it away that night in a big army truck. They tossed the corpses in the truck and off they went."
> "Where did the truck go?"
> "Who can say?"

Another journalist, Erwin Chacón from *Presencia,* who had not been invited to the party Ovando threw for the military at the Vallegrande mess, did have a vague idea, however. He had spent the night watching outside the Malta Hospital and followed the trail as far as the nearby Pando barracks, where the tracks left by the truck disappeared. Chacón also knew that Selich and Vargas were the men who had to do the dirty work, to get rid of Che's body.

The bodies were taken, then, by truck to the Pando regimental barracks in Vallegrande, where four tanks of fuel were waiting with which the burial detail was to burn them despite the doctors' warnings. By daybreak on October 11, however, Captain Vargas opted for a secret burial. The burial squad took advantage of some building work under way beside an airstrip near the regimental barracks; they tossed the bodies into a ditch and covered them with dirt using a wheelbarrow.

As far as the public was concerned, the story was that the body had disappeared. From that moment on, the Bolivian army engaged in a spate of contradictory and ludicrous statements regarding the final resting place of Che's body. While Torres was saying that it had been incinerated, Ovando spoke of a secret burial, which forced Torres to recapitulate and say that it had first been incinerated, and then buried.

Lyndon Johnson received a memorandum from Walt Rostow at 6:15 P.M. on October 13, saying that he was being told to ask Corey Olivier if it was true that the Bolivians cremated the body of Che Guevara, and that the CIA had told the State Department that this was the case.

The next day, three Argentine police inspectors checked the handwriting in the diaries and took fingerprints from Che's preserved hands. Comparison with old documents provided a positive identification.

Meanwhile, Che's brother Roberto flew to Santa Cruz along with a group of journalists, to pick up his brother's body ("We flew to Bolivia, on a press plane, as I had no money") but got only evasive answers and contradictory information from the military.

Rumors concerning the missing body ranged from the plausible to the outré. The Mexican journalist José Natividad Rosales held that Che was buried in a glass-topped coffin in the La Esperanza barracks, where the green berets had been trained. Another rumor making the rounds had it that the body had been incinerated and the ashes scattered from a helicopter over the jungle. Alternatively, it was walled up in Vallegrande city hall. Two months after Guevara's death, journalist Michelle Ray picked up yet another version: the body was being kept on ice down in the cellars of someplace or other in La Paz.

How had Che died? Where was his body?

An Interpress wire report released October 11 and 12 and based on a conversation with forensic expert Martínez Casso, was the first to cast doubts on the official version of the death. He hesitantly pointed out that that the time of death was between eleven A.M. and noon that same Monday, October 9, so if the clashes had taken place on the eighth . . .

On Sunday, October 15, Captain Gary Prado, whom a journallist had accused of killing Che, granted an interview to the UPI correspondent and gave an account that was ambiguous but cleared him of any part in the death: when captured, Che was alive, and it was as a living man that he had been handed over in La Higuera. Was he wounded? Seriously? That subject wasn't mentioned.

On October 15, in his first appearance on Cuban television to confirm Che's death, Fidel Castro accused the Bolivian military of having executed Che. He based the accusation on the contradictions between the autopsy report and the many statements to the effect that Che was wounded, but not seriously, when he was captured. A Bolivian government cable on October 17 upheld their armed forces' version of events: "Che Guevara died hours after being taken alive . . . due to the wounds he had sustained." But *Time* magazine, doubtless on the basis of information leaked by the U.S. government, confirmed Fidel's assessment that very day: the Bolivian military had ordered Che's execution, after he had been captured alive though wounded. A few days later, British journalist Richard Gott, writing for Chile's *Punto Final*, revealed that the news had been leaked to the paper (probably from Pappy Shelton himself, at the Santa Cruz golf club) as early as October 8 that Che had been captured.

Not until four months later, on February 5, 1968, did the first account appear that contained full details of how Che had been captured on October 8 and killed the day after at the La Higuera schoolhouse. The report, by French journalist Michelle Ray, was published by the U.S. magazine *Ramparts* and entitled "In Cold Blood: How the CIA Executed Che."

As time went by, the true picture began to appear through the fog of disinformation. But discovering the whereabouts of Che, Pacho, Chang, Olo, René, Aniceto, and Simón's bodies was to be more difficult. At the end of the eighties, Cuban researchers Adys Cupull and Froilán González picked up rumors about two possible locations of a mass grave: "a plot at the foot of the dormitory in the Pando barracks, or beside a landing strip at the Vallegrande airport. The sites are 200 meters apart." However, the first to break the official silence, which had kept the graves' location under wraps for years, was Major Saucedo Parada of Bolivian military intelligence. He would later confess to several key elements of information that the author has gathered.

And twenty-eight years were to go by before one of the burial detail, the then Captain Vargas Salinas, now a retired general, decided to speak up once and for all. In November 1995, Vargas Salinas attested that he, along with Major Flores, had taken part in the burial. Vargas told how, at dawn on October 11, 1967, they used a tractor to dig a ditch beside the airstrip, threw in the bodies of Che and his comrades, and then covered the grave over so as to leave no traces.

The revelation produced an uproar. The Bolivian army wavered and contradicted itself; the mayor of Vallegrande sought to have the airport's surroundings declared a "historical heritage" site, in order to foster tourism in that town forsaken by all gods. Bolivian President Gonzalo Sánchez offered to mount a search so that Che could receive a "Christian" burial. . . .

In November and December 1995, teams managed by Argentine experts, and advised by a Cuban forensic scientist, began to excavate the site. A search based on information provided by local residents revealed a second mass grave, at Cañada del Arroyo, which contained the bodies of Huanca's group and the wounded who were with him, one that had been killed later at Cajones. At the time of going to press, however, the search for Che's body was still on. . . .

56.   Commander Guevara's Many Watches

The CIA official "Dr. González" climbing into a jeep at the airport in
Vallegrande.

T IS SOMEWHAT SURPRISING THAT A MAN WHO IN LIFE SHOWED SUCH DE-tachment from material possessions should have left such a trail of belongings behind in death—things that he lived with, things that belonged to him . . . and things that may have belonged to him.

In Cuba, Che's belongings are venerated as the secular equivalent of saintly relics. In the entrance to the offices of *Verde Olivo*, there is a small display case containing the camera that Che loaned the staff in 1960, and later gave to them. It's an ordinary 35-millimeter Exacta. Visitors invariably stop in front of the display and then raise their eyes to a photo of a smiling Che.

Lina González, an old campesino woman from the Cuban village Lomas del Pedrero, showed journalist Mariano Rodríguez "the stool, the table, and the little cup where he sat and drank coffee."

In Cabaiguán, Cuba, there is a municipal museum dedicated to Che, where visitors can see the plaster cast he had on his fractured left arm during the final days of the battle of Santa Clara. How did it get there? Is it real? As it happens, the cast went with him all the way to the triumphant entry into Havana, and there are photographs that show his arm still in plaster in the La Cabaña fortress. How did the cast find its way back to Cabaiguán?

Several years ago in Cuba, an exhibition of objects related to with the guerrilla campaign in Bolivia was held in the Museum of the Revolution, but "Tania's" jeep was not Tania's, nor did the socks—"thin ones, like those used in Cuban Army dress uniforms"—belong to Che. A survivor of the Bolivian guerrilla campaign told me indignantly: "Che wore thick stockings, bought in France, and those socks [in the exhibit] were nice and new, whereas Che's were torn and stiff, because he never used to wash his feet."

Just like splinters from the True Cross, or good luck charms, Che's belongings inspire a quasi-religious quest among friend and foe alike, a friendly veneration, an unscrupulous traffic and a whole host of ridiculous frauds.

The trade in Che's scant possessions got under way immediately after his capture, between La Higuera (where, as the poet Enrique Lihn said, Che "has set up his posthumous headquarters"), Vallegrande, and La Paz. A mentality that was a combination of looting lust, war booty collecting, and fetishism, which made first the military and then the nearby civilians steal anything they could lay their hands on that had once belonged to Che. U.S. dollars, Bolivian pesos, and Canadian dollars were shared out in La Higuera, behind the backs of the commanding officers. Che's Parker pen found its way into the hands of a sergeant major, who ended up trading it with a journalist for a set of photos. The man who picked up by Che's marriage ring turned his hand to making copies of it, which he was still selling years later. The wrecked M2 rifle landed in Colonel Zenteno's hands; the word is that he gave it to General Alfredo Ovando, to score some brownie points. One of Che's pipes was filched by Colonel Selich, the other by Sergeant Bernardino Huanca. No one, meanwhile, wanted Che's sandals, which were pieces of leather cobbled together with bits of string to replace his lost boots.

Nothing, however, came to have as many simultaneous owners as Che's watch.

When he was captured, Commander Guevara was wearing two Rolex Perpetual Oysters, his own and the one that had belonged to his assistant, Carlos Coello, who gave it to Che moments before he died. The soldiers who captured him took both of them. Che told Captain Prado about this during the latter's first visit to the schoolhouse in La Higuera. Prado summoned the soldiers and retrieved the two watches.

"Here's your watches. Hang on to them, nobody will take them off you."

Che answered that he preferred that they be held in safekeeping for him; if anything should happen to him, he wanted them given to "my folks." Prado asked Che to point out which was his, so he marked the back of one with an "X," using a small stone. Prado hung on to Che's watch, and gave Carlos Coello's to Major Ayoroa.

That was as far as the official version went, but Cortez, the telegraph operator at La Higuera, saw Colonel Selich take Che's watch off his wrist while the prisoner's hands were tied. CIA agent Félix Rodríguez told how he obtained Che's watch by tricking a soldier who had taken it off him; Rodriguez said he placed it on his wrist as the helicopter took off from the town of La Higuera, but in his account the Rolex Perpetual Oyster has turned into a GT Master. The journalist Luis Suárez, meanwhile, maintained that Sergeant Bernardino Huanca came by Che's Rolex by stripping it from his body.

Others attribute ownership to General Alfredo Ovando; in another version, the most fantastic, the watch covers thousands of miles, from the corpse to the doctor who performed the autopsy, and from the doctor to his son, who handed it over to settle a bar debt in the Mexican city of Puebla.

57. The Slippery Diaries

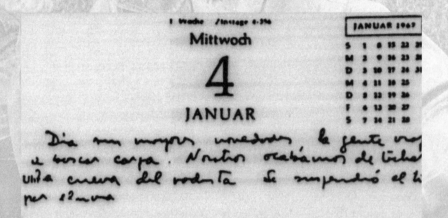

Part of a page from Che's Bolivian diaries

O F ALL THE BOOTY TAKEN FROM THE GUERRILLA FIGHTERS AFTER THE battle at the Yuro Ravine, quite apart from the fetishistic obsessions of officers and soldiers, there was a pile of notebooks and diaries that turned out to be mouth-watering spoils of war for the military. Two items were particularly valuable: a reddish spiral-bound 5 1/2" x 7" notepad with "1967" written on the cover, and a brown diary bought in Frankfurt. The first one contained Commander Guevara's diary for November and December 1966, with messages between Che's guerrilla group and Havana written on the back of each sheet, and the second was a diary for 1967, with entries up to October 7. The haul also included an address book of contacts across the world, two small codebooks, and a green notebook in which he had copied down poems by Pablo Neruda and Nicolás Guillén. Captain Gary Prado had marked one of the diaries picked up in the ravine itself with the words "found in backpack."

The two diaries' existence was first made public by General Alfredo Ovando, who showed them to reporters at a news conference given at the Santa Teresita Hotel in La Paz on October 10, 1967.

The diaries passed through many hands in those early days: from Prado, who marked where they were found, to Colonel Zenteno in La Higuera, to Félix Rodríguez, who photographed them, to military intelligence in Vallegrande, to Ovando, who leafed through them at his billet in the Central Bank, to his adjutant, Lieutenant Olmos, who in turn handed them over to 8th Division command for a press conference and who, when he went to reclaim them, found that they had ended up in the hands of a CIA agent known as Garcia. The agent was asked for them on the plane journey back to La Paz, and a Captain Pamo received them there and then. Ovando later handed them over to military intelligence, who placed them in a safe.

The CIA's photographic copy came to Washington in the course of the next few days. A memo from Walt Rostow to President Johnson, dated October 11, 1967, alludes to the diaries' existence; Rostow says that as of that morning, he was 99 percent sure that Che Guevara was dead and that "these" had to get to Washington that day or the next.

A week later, the two central figures in the Bolivian dictatorship unleashed a blitz of statements and maneuvers involving Commander Guevara's diaries, beginning with an October 16 ANSA cable in which the Bolivian army told the world that it intended to "sell the diaries to make good the losses caused by the guerrillas." General Ovando announced on November 7 that the diaries would be sold to the highest bidder. President René Barrientos, just to be different, announced that they had just been sold to a U.S. publishing consortium.

Throughout November, the Bolivian armed forces attempted to close a sale, weighing offers from Doubleday in the U.S. and Magnum, an imprint of the French publisher Paris Match. The latter offer was actually a lure cast by a French journalist in order to obtain more information. Sums were spoken of ("they started at around $20,000 and reached $400,000") which seemed somewhat exaggerated in 1967. A presidential decree, issued November 22, authorized the armed forces to avail themselves of Che's belongings and documents.

Several Cuban researchers have insisted that the publishing project was not serious, that it was simply an attempt to authenticate a distorted version of the diaries that was being created by the CIA. Adys Cupull and Froilán González maintain that technicians and calligraphers at the Agency's La Paz station were at work producing distortions, omissions, and alterations in order to establish a new version of the diaries that would be useful in a hot war against Cuba. Doubtless the Agency would have found it very useful to have available a version that allowed them to present a scenario involving a faceoff between Che and Fidel, to heighten tensions between Cuba and the Soviet bloc, or to tarnish Che's prestige by insinuating that he was a despotic adventurer or a dreamer, and thereby to increase tensions between Guevarism and the various Latin American Communist parties. An operation of such extent, however, would have required a credible version of the diaries, one that would fit in as much as possible with Che's character and his previous writing.

Whether or not the CIA was revising the diaries, two U.S. journalists were acting as intermediaries between the Bolivian military and U.S. publishing houses. The two, characterized by Fidel Castro as "journalists with CIA links," were Andrew St. George and Juan de Onís, from the *New York Times*. They had photocopies of the diaries, but under the condition that they not publish them. The negotiations reached a halt when Doubleday withdrew, arguing that Aleida March could dispute the publication rights.

Meanwhile, an unexpected development occurred at the end of January 1968. Out of the blue a mysterious individual entered the Santiago, Chile, bureau of Prensa Latina, the Cuban press agency, and said, like a magician pulling a rabbit out of a hat:

"I am here on behalf of Antonio Arguedas. He wants to hand Che's diaries over to Cuba."

The Bolivian interior minister-as-emissary insisted that his boss was annoyed by U.S. interference in his country. A group of journalists headed by Hernán Uribe got together to evaluate this unusual situation and decided they had nothing to lose; they gave the go-ahead to Arguedas's representative and sent a message to the Cuban deputy minister of the interior, Manuel Piñeiro. Shortly afterward, the Bolivian came back to Santiago with some microfilm hidden inside a record of folk music. Mario Díaz Barrientos, known as the Dwarf, was chosen to be the courier, and went to Havana via Mexico, accompanied—unknown to him—by agents from the Cuban Interior Ministry.

Fidel Castro later said:

> Although there was not the least doubt as to the authenticity of the document itself, all the photocopies were subjected to a rigorous examination

in order not only to establish that authenticity but also to discover any alteration, small as it may have been. The information was checked against a diary from one of the surviving guerrilla fighters.

The task of deciphering the handwriting was undertaken by Aleida March, who was helped by his former secretary José Manuel Manresa and three Cuban survivors of the guerrilla campaign in Bolivia, Dariel Alarcón, Leonardo Tamayo, and Harry Villegas.

The Cubans had just one lingering doubt, which Fidel referred to in his foreword to the book:

> As this diary contains repeated mentions of the Cuban revolution and its relations with the guerrilla movement, some may interpret our publication as an act of provocation, which would provide arguments to the enemies of the revolution, the Yankee imperialists and their allies, the Latin American oligarchs, to redouble their plans to blockade, isolate, and commit acts of aggression against Cuba.

This objection was made absurd by the fact that copies of the diaries were already in the hands of Barrientos and the CIA.

Work on the diaries was kept under wraps. After several months of transcription and authentication, the book was handed over to the Osvaldo Sánchez press on Saturday, June 22, 1968. Technical-school students helped preparing the million-copy print run; by 11:45 A.M. on Sunday, June 30, *Diario del Che en Bolivia (Che in Boliva: His Diary)* was ready. The next day, copies were available in Havana bookstores, free of charge; almost simultaneously, the book was released by *Punto Final* in Chile; Masperó in France; Ruedo Ibérico, also in France, for distribution in Franco's Spain; Siglo XXI in Mexico; Feltrinelli in Italy; Trinkot in West Germany; and *Ramparts* magazine in the U.S. Strangely enough, the list included no publishing houses or magazines in Eastern Europe, which gives some idea of the strained relationship between unreal European socialism and the Cuban revolution, and of the mutual dislike between the East European bureaucrats and Che. In a wire commenting on the Havana edition, the Czech news agency CTK even expressed doubts of the diaries' authenticity.

The Havana bookstores were swamped; there are photographs showing the amazing crowds. A high school teacher, Israel Díaz, was the first to receive a copy at the bookstore on the corner of L Avenue and 27th Street; he had been in line since four A.M. Within weeks the diaries had millions of readers around the world, and subsequent reprints would number in the hundreds of thousands.

The Czechs were not the only ones to cast doubt on the Cuban version; surprisingly, Andrew St. George had misgivings too, although despite he must have known the diaries were genuine. He held that the authentic version would be published in the United States by Stein & Day, and that the original he saw had contained criticisms of Fidel Castro.

The Cuban president's reply was not long in coming. On July 3, 1968, he made the following statement on network television: "Nobody in his right mind could imagine that someone would publish a faked version of a book that is also in someone else's hands, especially when that someone else is an enemy."

The Cuban edition did, however, have its faults: thirteen days were missing, which, while they may not have contained earth-shattering information, did contain clues as to how the text ended up in Cuban hands. Several days after Fidel's statement, someone—either a friendly nationalist or the Bolivian military—leaked Che's diaries to the La Paz daily *Presencia* and the radio network *Nueva América*, which made public the complete version on July 11 and 12. If ever there had been an attempt to manipulate the diaries, it was now ruled out.

The leak produced a national scandal in Bolivia, and an investigation ensued. General Ovando summoned the press to his office in order to exculpate the armed forces; he showed them the diaries in a shoe box, inside a safe. On July 19, Barrientos announced a new investigation. That same day, Antonio Arguedas and his brother disappeared; they surfaced in Chile, requesting political asylum.

Arguedas turned out to be an odd character—to put it mildly. A forty-year-old lawyer and former air force major, he was also a former Communist Party member, a former member of the left wing of the MNR, *and* a former CIA agent. Having undergone so many sea changes in his political life, he had no credibility whatever. He had been accused of masterminding the repression meted out to the urban cadres of Che's guerrilla campaign, and of turning a blind eye to torture and murder. Nonetheless, during his exile he declared his admiration of Fidel Castro and said that he wanted to hold, in his hands, the gun left behind by "his friend" Coco Peredo. Were these statements to be believed? A few months later, he said of his motives: "My main aim is to prevent U.S. imperialism from substituting a forgery for Che Guevara's diary or distorting it." Fidel Castro confirmed several days later that Arguedas had been the source of the leak, and that he had turned over the diaries with no strings attached.

Another chapter in the odd tale then took place. Arguedas moved his exile once again, to London this time, where he was interrogated by the CIA and the British secret service before moving on to New York (!) and Lima. He finally returned to La Paz, where he faced trial but was released on bail—thanks, seemingly, to insinuations that he would reveal connections between the CIA and the Bolivian government, cited in over 134 documents that he had in his possession. Later on, Arguedas's house was blown up, he was shot at, and he ended up seeking asylum at the Mexican embassy in La Paz.

Fast forward to the 1980s: the diary scandal erupted anew when Sotheby's announced that it would soon auction off Che's original diaries; the anticipated price was £250,000. How did the diaries get to Sotheby's? The Bolivian government ordered an investigation, and the trail quickly led to former dictator Luis García Meza, who had sold the diaries to "a Brazilian," who had in turn sold them to Sotheby's or was doing so by using a British gallery as middleman. In June 1984, in the face of a series of lawsuits by the Bolivian government, Sotheby's canceled the sale.

58.   Che's "Curse"

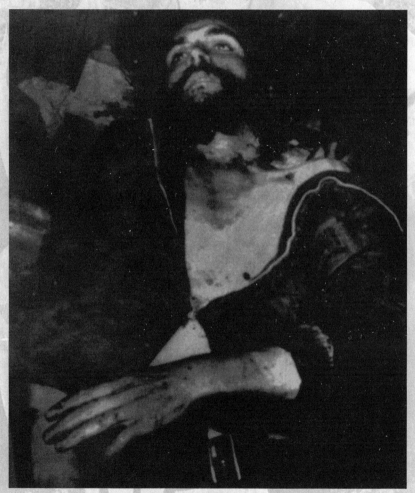

The body, October 9, 1967

OVER THE FIRST FIFTEEN YEARS AFTER CHE'S DEATH, IN A WHOLE SERIES of amazing coincidences, most of those who had had something to do with his capture, the assassination order, and the disappearance of his body died unnatural deaths. They had strange fatal accidents in helicopters or cars, were executed by successors to the guerrilla campaign, mowed down by phantom left-wing guerrillas or the most Neanderthal of right-wing groups—or were beaten to death by their own former comrades-in-arms. Others were deported, fell ill, or were shot. A relentless wave of violence hit nearly all the main players, one by one, doubtless because the people concerned lived in troubled times and by their wits.

But it was also as if Che's ghost had returned to haunt his killers and settle accounts with them. It is hardly surprising, then, that this surfeit of fatalities gave rise to the legend of "Che's curse." Rumor or popular wisdom claimed that he had arranged this slew of accidents, attacks, and illnesses from the beyond. Another totally unfounded rumor blamed the Cuban secret services for an international revenge operation. Strangely enough, those who proposed the first hypothesis were less delighted with it than a Cuban writer to whom the author spoke, who gave a knowing smile and hinted at "our services . . ." with a certain satisfied tone in his voice.

Let us take stock:

Honorato Rojas became a public figure in the wake of a photograph of Vice President Hernán Siles Suazo congratulating him for having informed on the guerrillas and enabling led Tania and Joaquín's group to be ambushed at the El Yeso ford. The photo was pathetic: Honorato dressed as a ranger, in a beret too big for him, his year-and-a-half-old daughter in his arms.

The re-formed National Liberation Army executed him with two shots in the head on July 14, 1969. At the time, he was living on a twelve-acre ranch that President René Barrientos had given him, a few miles from Santa Cruz.

Barrientos himself was to the second to fall. On April 29, 1969, less than a year after he had confirmed the order to execute Che, he died when his helicopter burst into flames and crashed near the town of Arque. The accident has never been fully explained. Rumor has it that his former comrade-in-arms, General Alfredo Ovando, was behind the crash which took place at a time when Barrientos was planning a palace coup to rid himself of domestic and foreign opponents. What is certain is that Ovando himself was later evicted from the presidential palace, which he had reached after a military coup against Barrientos's successor, another general called Rogelio Miranda.

Jorge Gallardo, a writer who was in close contact with the military high command that took part in Juan José Torres's progressive coup some years after the events, related that "three years after Che's death, popular superstition had it that he would take with him to his grave those responsible for his death." Two Cuban historians who traveled around the part of southern Bolivia where Che's guerrillas had operated, noted:

> A chain letter stemming from those beliefs began to circulate among the Bolivian military and their relatives. It said that Barrientos's death had

been divine punishment and that a cruel fate awaited all those guilty of Che's murder. In order to save themselves, the letter recommended, they should say three "Our Father"s and three "Hail, Mary"s. The letter had to be copied out nine times and sent to as many people again.

Perhaps not enough copies of the chain letter were made, or perhaps the events that followed were random, but in any case, shortly after Barrientos's death another fatality helped perpetuate the rumor. On October 10, 1970, a day after the third anniversary of Che's death, Lieutenant Huerta, who had been the commanding officer when Che was taken prisoner, was killed in a car crash.

The next link in the chain was the murder of Lieutenant Colonel Selich, one of the few high-ranking military officers who had spoken to Che in the La Higuera schoolhouse, and who tried to mistreat him. Selich became interior minister during the dictatorship of Hugo Banzer; he was beaten to death at the beginning of the seventies during an "interrogation session" by military security agents who had caught him plotting another in the sequence of coups that make up Bolivian history.

In April 1971, Colonel Roberto Quintanilla, who as chief of intelligence at the Interior Ministry witnessed the amputation of Che's hands and who years later was the killed Inti Peredo, was executed in Hamburg by a member of the ELN, Mónica Earlt. Posing as a German citizen who wanted a visa, Mónica entered the Bolivian consulate, asked to see Colonel Quintanilla, shot him twice in the chest, and left unharmed without being apprehended.

Che's "curse" did not always bring death to the military foes of the guerrilla operation; at times it took a different course. Félix Rodríguez, the CIA man who identified Che and photographed his diary, began to suffer from asthma when he returned to Miami, even though asthma usually begins during childhood and he had never suffered from it before: "When I got back to Miami . . . I ended up with an asthma attack. I had all sorts of allergy tests done, and none were positive. They concluded that it was either something psychological or Che's curse, as I had attacks in dry as well as damp weather, cold as well as hot."

Major Juan Ayoroa, whose Rangers had participated in the last stages of the campaign against Che and in his capture and murder, was exiled by Banzer's government at the end of September 1972.

General Juan José Torres, who was chief of staff at the Bolivian army during the Che campaign and seconded the execution order, came to power years later but was unseated by a far-right military coup. He was killed with three shots to the head by the far-right group Triple-A in Buenos Aires on February 12, 1976.

A couple of months after that, it was the turn of General Joaquín Zenteno Anaya, who as commander of the 8th Division had relayed the order to execute Che. In May 1976, he was shot down in Paris, where he was serving as Bolivian ambassador, by a short-lived group calling itself the Che Guevara Internationalist Brigade, which after that operation never acted again. Zenteno was shot three times at point-blank range with a 7.65-caliber pistol in front of his office door. He had been publicly accused of harboring old Nazis, such as Klaus Barbie, who were hiding in Bolivia.

Gary Prado Salmón, the army captain who had captured Che, was shot in early 1981 during a confrontation at a Santa Cruz oil field occupied by a fascist group. Both his lungs were punctured and an injury to his spinal column left him paralyzed. Strangely enough, the shot was accidental and came from one of his own men, whose name was never revealed.

Twenty years after the events, former interior minister Antonio Arguedas was serving an eight-year sentence in a Bolivian jail for having kidnapped a salesman. It may be recalled from the preceding chapter that this was not his first misadventure.

Little is known about the fate of Sergeant Major Mario Terán, although some newspaper reports suggest that he has taken to wandering drunk around the streets of Cochabamba, that Che haunts him in his nightmares, and that, like Sergeant Bernardino Huanca, he has needed frequent psychiatric treatment.

59.   Images and Ghosts

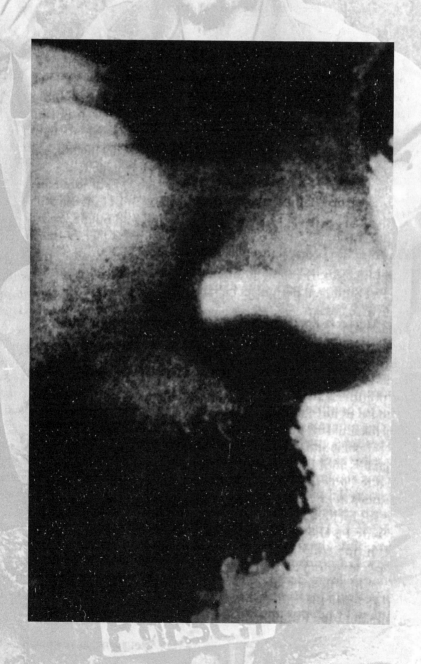

THE ARGENTINE POET PACO URONDO, WHO DIED YEARS LATER AT THE hands of the Argentine military, wrote when he heard of Che's death:

It will rain without stopping for a week, and the unbelieving, or those who are not superstitious, will think it is just a coincidence, that what is happening is somewhat exceptional but pure chance. Friends come along wetter each time and now this shitty weather has gone on longer than ever. But this time the guesses will not be done à la Buenos Aires; people will not speak of the damp and the calamities that plague them—no, not even about their livers: this time they will guess some other way; there is no peace, just silence.

Celia, Che's fourth daughter, was born in 1963, during her father's next-to-last year at the Cuban Industry Ministry, a year and a half before he left for the Congo, and can only see her father through other people's memories. She has tried many times to read the Bolivian diary, but has not been able to bring herself to do so.

Fidel Castro says he has often seen Che in his dreams in recent years. He confessed to Italian journalist Gianni Miná that Che speaks to him and "tells me things."

Ana María, Che's sister, told a Spanish journalist at the beginning of the seventies: "At times I feel that someone is looking at me but beyond me, as if I were somehow he, and I feel as if I am no one and I do not know what to do. I have had to learn to live with these events."

This is not unusual. We all know the strange and amazing way that dead people leave a huge void, a gaping hole in the lives of those who survive them. Ernesto Guevara has acquired a magical aura over all these years, however; it has not been dimmed by his death, and has touched many people who never knew him.

After the guerrilla campaign passed near the town of La Higuera, whose school sheltered Che in last hours and then as a corpse, the town was devastated by a terrible drought. Plants and animals died and the peasants were forced to emigrate. Popular wisdom, hushed rumors, and folk tales had it that the weather was a divine punishment for allowing Che to die at the hands of the soldiers.

In La Higuera, locks of hair and bloodstained scraps of Che's pants are exhibited like a saint's relics. In Lagunillas, a street photographer has had a good business of selling photos of Che's corpse, and many of the town's inhabitants have made it a point to place a photograph of the dead Che on top of the stone slab in the laundry at the Malta Hospital, the photo of a secular Christ.

The peasants of Cochabamba have evolved a litany, a strange kind of prayer: "Little soul of Che, by your leave please work the miracle that will make my cow well again. Grant me that wish, little soul of Che."

The Vallegrande nurse who stripped Che's corpse admits: "At times I dream about Che and I see him as if he were alive, and he tells me that he's going to take me away from the wretchedness in which I live."

The La Higuera schoolhouse was torn down and a health clinic built in its place. The clinic never opened, and no doctors or medicines ever appeared. Eventually another school was built. The Uruguayan journalist Ernesto González Bermejo visited it in 1971:

"What do you know about Che?" he asked a campesino boy when the teacher wasn't paying attention.

"That's him there," the child answered, pointing to a portrait of Simón Bolívar.

Francisco Rivas, a sixty-year-old campesino who lived near La Higuera and had fourteen children, said: "I didn't realize it then. Now I know that I have lost a lot."

In a church in Matanzas, Cuba, Ernesto Guevara can be found in an altarpiece, one of a heavenly host; at another church, in the Mexican state of Tamaulipas, he shares the corner of a mural with the devil.

Che's death left thousands of men and women dumbstruck, disconcerted, astonished, unsettled. After eleven short years on the political scene—and without meaning to—Che had become a living symbol of the much postponed, much betrayed Latin American revolution; the only thing of which we may be sure is that such stuff as dreams are made of never dies. Nonetheless, Ernesto Guevara had died in Bolivia. The Uruguayan poet Benedetti wrote:

> *There we are*
> *shaken*
> *enraged*
> *though death might be*
> *another foreseeable absurdity*

In Santa Clara there is a twenty-one-foot bronze statue of Che by Jose Delarra, the same person who gave a porcelain sculpture of Che's face to a Cuban astronaut, so that Che could travel to the stratosphere. The statue is a stocky, almost fat Che Guevara, who has a Santa Claus–like beard and does not smile. That's the trouble with statues: bronze reproduces the smile badly.

I interviewed Dariel Alarcón at his home on the outskirts of Havana. He is a witty, smiling man, but toward the end of the interview, when he remembered that Inti Peredo, Harry Villegas, Leonardo Tamayo, and he might have been able to rescue Che that October afternoon, a shadow fell across the room. It is one of those things a person cannot live with.

I spoke with Che's former secretary, José Manuel Manresa, in the dark, as there was a power cut in the Havana district in which he lives. At times he broke down, and he wore his emotions on his sleeve.

"You Guevara men, the ones who lived alongside Che, give the impression of being marked, branded, with a Z on your foreheads like Zorro used to make."

"We were poor benighted souls who were going who-knows-where in life and just waiting to meet a man like Che."

There was a long silence; then a sob could be heard. One did not know what to ask next.

That sense that they have been abandoned, that Che has gone without them, kills them. Joel Iglesias entered a severe crisis that drove him to drink; Alberto Mora committed suicide. Díaz Argüelles could never forgive Che for having taken his bosom pal Gustavo Machín rather than him, and did not forgive Che even when he himself died years later in Angola facing South African armored cars, in an epic event not at all unworthy of Che himself. Efigenio Ameijeiras wavers between saying he could have kept Che's enthusiasm at bay, and feeling pain at not having been there to keep it at bay. For many years Víctor Dreke wondered what he had done wrong in Africa for Che not to have taken him to Bolivia. And although the answer is "Nothing," the question gnaws at him. The Acevedo brothers ask themselves the same question, as does Che's friend Oscar Fernández Mell, as does Emilio Aragonés, who was struck by a terrible illness that nearly killed him when he returned from Africa. As does Ulises Estrada, whom Che sent away in Prague because he was very visible. As does Orlando Borrego, his deputy at the ministry of industry. As does Enrique Oltuski, who has yet to write the book that will say that they did not agree on so many things . . . And when I speak to them I could bet my head and not risk losing it, by wagering that in Cuba today, almost thirty years after his death, there are almost a hundred men and women who would have sold their souls to the devil in exchange for being able to die with Che in Bolivia.

I was to find one last photograph of Che. In Theo Bruns's house in Hamburg is a poster with the caption "Comrades: I have a poster of all of you at home. Che." I was thankful for a respite, and for the return of the biting wit that was so much his in life.

My neighbor and friend Juan Gelman wrote some time ago:

> But
> the serious thing is that Che
> really did enter into death
> and wanders thereabouts, they say
> beautiful
> with stones under his arms
> I am from a country where now
> Guevara must die other deaths
> each of which will atone for his death now
> he who laughed is dust and food for worms now
> may he who cried think of this
> and may he who forgot forget or remember.

Memories.

There is a memory. Out of thousands of photos, posters, T-shirts, tapes, records, videos, postcards, portraits, magazines, books, phrases, accounts—all ghosts haunting an industrial society that does not know where to put its myths in the sobriety of memory—Che is watching over us. He is our secular saint. Despite all the paraphernalia, he comes back. Thirty years after his death, his image cuts across generations, his myth hovers over neoliberalism's delusions of grandeur. Irreverent, a joker, stubborn, morally stubborn, unforgettable.

NOTES

1. Little Guevara: Childhood Is Fate

Sources

The best source for this period is doubtless the memoir by Ernesto's father, Ernesto Guevara Lynch, *Mi hijo el Che*, which has to be read with the same detachment as all reverential material on Che's life. Full of anecdotes that sometimes don't make sense chronologically, it may be complemented by interviews Guevara gave to Mariano Rodríguez Herrera ("El niño de las sierras de Altagracia") and Mario Mencia.

Adys Cupull and Froilán González's book *Ernestito vivo y presente* is especially helpful and, despite some simplistic photograph captions and a reverential tone, has the virtue of being an exhaustive compilation of accounts and previously unknown photographs.

Che would doubtless have been very wary of so much reverence toward his childhood, a matter of which he spoke little. The only quotation I have used from material he wrote later is from a letter to the writer Lisandro Otero, dated June 23, 1963, which was by no means self-flattering, and which is in some editions of his collected works.

There are some interviews with Che's mother which touch on his childhood and his youth. The best is doubtless the one conducted by Julia Constela, "Cuando Ernesto Guevara aún no era el Che."

The account by Che's sister Ana María is from "Hablan el padre y la hermana del Che," published in the Peruvian magazine *ABC*. The account by Che's brother Juan Martín is from "Mi hermano el Che," by Luis Adrián Betancourt. The account by his brother Roberto is from the above-mentioned book by Cupull and González. His cousin "La Negrita," Carmen Córdoba de la Serna, gives her account in "Ernesto y los poemas del amor," an interview with Cupull and González published in the Cuban magazine *Verde Olivo*.

The Guevara and Lynch family trees can be found in the appendix to the Spanish edition of *Mi hijo el Che*.

A good collection of accounts by childhood friends may be found in a report by Mariano Rodríguez Herrera: "El niño de las sierras de Altagracia."

There is an excellent and lucid account of Che's stay in Córdoba by his then neighbor Dolores Moyano Martín, "A memoir of the Young Guevara." I have also used Alberto Granados's memoirs, "El Che y yo," in the essay collection *Guevara para hoy*. The fascinating perspectives of Che's "Republican" friends, the children of Spanish exiles, Fernando Barral and José Aguilar, can be found in their articles "Che estudiante" and "La niñez del Che," respectively.

Portions of this chapter draw on Che's birth certificate; on the *Atlas histórico, biográfico y militar de Ernesto Guevara;* on an interview with Raúl Maldonado, who was later to be a close collaborator; on JGS's biography in the Mexican magazine *Sucesos;* on an article by Mariano Rodríguez Herrera, "Un joven llamado Ernesto"; and on "Che, niñez, adolescencia, juventud" by Aldo Isidrón and Fulvio Fuentes. I have also relied on notes for a biography of Che by Aldo Isidrón himself. The references to his teenage notebooks are in María del Carmen Ariet, *Che, pensamiento político*.

The Philosophical Dictionary

There are seven notebooks; the fourth has been lost. María del Carmen Ariet, who was an assistant to Che's widow, Aleida March, had access to these still unpublished documents, which are closed to most historians, and commented on them in her book.

A couple of pages are reproduced in *Ernestito vivo y presente*. Che seems to have made entries until 1955, when he was twenty-seven and in Mexico.

2.   Remembrance of Leading Players Past

Sources

In *Mi hijo el Che*, Che's father uses Che's first notebook, as a source for the bicycle journey across Argentina. Young Ernesto's impression of his first contact with medicine is from a speech to Cuban Ministry of Health workers in 1960. References in Che's book *Notas de viaje* and works by Alberto Granado, *Con el Che por Sudamérica* and in "El Che y yo." Granado was also interviewed by Aldo Isidrón in "Un viaje en moto de Argentina a Venezuela."

For Che's correspondence and relations with Tita Infante, see *Cálida presencia: Su amistad con Tita Infante* and Tita's account, "Evocación a un año de la muerte del Che" in the epilogue to *Aquí va un soldado de América*.

Accounts by Ana María, Carlos Figueroa, and Juan Martín are from *Ernestito*, by Cupull and González.

Che's university grades appear in an appendix to the Spanish edition of *Mi hijo el Che*. Also interesting are works by Constantín and Elmar May. *Che Guevara*, Daniel James. *Che Guevara, una biografía* and Aida Cárdenas, "Médico y Soldado," as well the one quoted by Dolores Moyano and the report "Hablan el padre y la hermana del Che."

The Family Breakup

If this episode took place, it was ignored by Ernesto Guevara Lynch, whose book has become the official version. Daniel James, quoted in turn by Elmar May, says the parents broke up over economic disputes and Ernesto Senior's infidelity, and that Che's father opened an office on Paraguay Street, where he slept, although he did visit the family home. I have found no other basis for this story, which he dates to 1949.

Ernesto's letters over the next three years were indistinguishably addressed to his father, his mother, or both, which suggests they were living together. It is true, however, that Ernesto was somewhat reserved with his father, while for his mother he had limitless affection. Could this be explained by the parents' split?

3.   The Discovery of Latin America

Sources

Che wrote a long account of his first journey across Latin America in his book *Notas de Viaje*, which covers the first stretch, up to his departure from the lepers' hospital in Huambo. I have also relied on his article on Macchu Pichu in the Panamanian magazine *Siete*, reprinted by the Cuban publishers Casa de las Américas, on fragments of his diary in his father's book *Mi hijo el Che*, and on the letter to Tita Infante from Lima in *Ernestito . . .* by Cupull and González, where he gives news of the first part of the journey.

Another slant is given by Alberto Granados in his book *Con el Che en Sudamérica* and his article "Un largo viaje en moto de Argentina a Venezuela."

Guevara Senior's interesting accounts appear in interviews by Mencia ("Así era mi hijo el Che") and Mariano Rodríguez ("Cuando el Che comenzó a recorrer nuestra América").

Che's stay in Panamá is well documented in the essay collection *Testimonios sobre el Che*, edited by Marta Rojas.

Other information comes from articles by Sanjuana Martínez, "Unidad de Latinoamérica y necesidad de armas, apuntes de su diario juvenil"; José Aguilar, "La niñez del Che"; Aldo Isidrón, "Che Guevara, apuntes para una biografía"; Dolores Moyano, "The Making of a Revolutionary: A

Memoir of Young Guevara"; "Mambo Tango navega el Amazonas," and a biographical article about Che by JGS, published in the Mexican magazine *Sucesos*.

On the Diary

The writer Jorge Castañeda drew my attention in conversation to the discrepancies between the version of the diary given by Ernesto Senior in *Mi hijo el Che* and that in *Notas de viaje*. Where he saw criminal signs of censorship, I just saw something Ernesto often did—i.e., rewriting a text. He always thought of his diaries as material for rewriting. That was what he did with the war diary entries that reappeared as *Pasajes de la guerra revolucionaria*, and his *Pasajes de la guerra revolucionaria (Congo).** I understand *Notas de viaje* as a reworking of the diary (just as Che says, "more than a year after those notes") in which he incidentally loses the day-to-day sequence that must have been in the original. Once more, the fact that not all of Che's written work has come to light produces confusion.

4. In Through the Out Door

Sources

Material from this chapter is from Ernesto's *Notas de viaje*, from the historiography *Un hombre bravo*, from *Ernestito* by Adys Cupull and Froilán González, from his father's book *Mi hijo el Che*, and from Dolores Moyano's above-mentioned article.

5. America or Bust

Sources

Ernesto's family correspondence and Calica Ferrer's diary entries can be found in *Aquí va un soldado de América*. The notes on his second journey, his diary note-

books, have yet to be published. The only source for these is some fragments published in María del Carmen Ariet's *Che, pensamiento político*.

Important sources are the article "Los primeros cubanos que conocieron al Che," by Mencía; Tita Infante's letters in *Cálida presencia*, Marta Rojas's article "Ernesto, médico en el Perú," and an article by Aldo Isidrón, "Presencia de Ernesto Guevara en Panamá." Ricardo Rojo's book, *Mi amigo el Che* is vague about dates and manipulates details, but is very interesting as its perspective differs from more traditional versions.

Also useful are Hilda Gadea's *Che Guevara, años decisivos*; the historiography *Un hombre bravo*; the *Atlas histórico, biográfico y militar de Ernesto Guevara*; Aldo Isidrón's "Che Guevara, apuntes para una biografía"; and Eduardo Galeano's *Violencia y enajenación*.

6. Guatemala: The Moment of Truth

Sources

The best information is in *Che Guevara, años decisivos* by Hilda Gadea, which, unlike Ernesto's family correspondence in *Aquí va un soldado de América* and his letters to Tita Infante in *Cálida presencia*, offers a very detailed view of those months. Some quotations from his unpublished diary appear in María del Carmen Ariet's book.

Stephen Schlesinger and Stephen Kinzer's book *Bitter Fruit: The CIA in Guatemala* is maybe the best review of the coup and the political world that Che found in Guatemala.

On Ñico López and relations with Cuban exiles, see Mario Mencía's article "Los primeros cubanos que conocieron al Che," and "Símbolo de valor y fidelidad" by Verónica Alvarez and Sergio Ravelo.

---

*Translator's note: In the main text, the former is referred to by its English title, *Reminiscences from the Revolutionary War.*

Minor details are from Ricardo Rojo's book and articles by Aldo Isidrón: "Aquel joven argentino de ideas profundas," "Fue una noche de junio cuando conocí al Che" by Clara Mayo, and "Un chico argentino muy atractivo llamado Ernesto," "Así era mi hijo Ernesto," and "Así empezó la historia del guerrillero heroico" by Clara Mayo.

For Alfonso Bauer's recollections, see Mencia's in three parts: an article "Por última vez," in the magazine *Bohemia*, Bauer's piece in *Casa de las Américas*, and the interview by Aldo Isidrón, "Alfonso Bauer Paz y Ernesto Guevara."

The Southward Train?

It is not clear whether Ernesto was able to go beyond his good intentions to fight in the last days of Jacobo Arbenz's government. There is the following account in Romero's memoirs, although he does not make it clear if Ernesto accompanied them on that journey: "One day, we were going by train to the front; an army sergeant at Zacapa told us that we had to go back to the capital, as the treachery had already happened.

Thinking of Guatemala

There are several references in Hilda Gadea's memoirs to Ernesto Guevara talking about Guatemala in later years and all of them have the same question. "Shouldn't we have fought?"

On May 1, 1955, in Mexico, Ernesto had a chance to directly ask the PGT secretary Fortuny. He was not satisfied with the man's ambiguous reply.

The Turning Point

Dolores Moyano believes that Guatemala turned Ernesto from a skeptic into an activist. This opinion is shared by many authors, who see Guatemala as a political turning point for him, a radical redefinition. One only has to observe Guevara's political wavering in Mexico to realize that

this analysis is not exactly accurate, although the coup doubtless made a deep impression.

The Article

The sources are contradictory. Ernesto wrote it either "underneath falling bombs," as Dalmau said, or in the Argentine Embassy. Hilda Gadea said Ernesto dictated it to her. If so, it was written before the counterrevolutionaries won. Entitled "Yo vi la caída de Jacobo Arbenz," it was more than a dozen pages long, according to several accounts. A number of copies were made; one was sent to Argentina, but the rest seem to be lost. The article ended with the line "The fight begins now."

7. Ports of Call

Sources

Che's viewpoint and many of his anecdotes come from his 1954–56 correspondence with his father, his mother, and his aunt Beatriz (compiled by Ernesto Senior in *Aquí va un soldado de América*); his letters to Tita Infante are in *Cálida presencia*. The draft outline of the book on the role of the doctor in Latin America is in the archive belonging to Che's widow Aleida March, to which Cuban historian María del Carmen Ariet had access. These references are from del Carmen's book *Che: pensamiento político*.

The text with the most information about Che's twenty-six months in Mexico is *Che Guevara, años decisivos*, by Hilda Gadea, which contains a few errors although it recounts the events from her perspective—not necessarily that of Ernesto Guevara—and often contradicts his family correspondence.

The poems not published in Guevara's lifetime may be found in the epilogue to Hilda Gadea's book and in an edition of *Bohemia*.

Ernesto's impressions of his friendship with Julio Roberto Cáceres appear in the chapter "El Patojo" in his book *Paisajes de la guerra revolucionaria.* There are also brief passages on his stay in Mexico in "Proyecciones sociales del ejército rebelde," and in the article "Una revolución que comienza."

The wedding certificate of Ernesto Guevara de la Serna and Hilda Gadea Acosta, dated August 18, 1955, is in the Tepotzotlán courthouse. and in Guevara's statement to the Procuraduría General de la República (Mexican Federal Attorney General's Office) dated June 27, 1956, four sheets, typewritten.

Four texts by Mexican authors provide some small elements of context and information on Che's stay in Mexico: José Natividad Rosales, "¿Qué hizo el Che en México?"; Alberto Bremauntz, *México y la revolución cubana socialista;* JGS's biography in the magazine *Sucesos;* and "Un personaje de leyenda," in a special edition of the magazine *Alarma.*

There are some interesting fragments in Roberto Rojo's book *Mi amigo el Che,* although they are biased toward the account the author wishes to give of himself and Che. Particularly interesting is Rojo's account of a conversation with Fidel Castro in Mexico City. It could not have taken place: Fidel was on tour in the United States at the time of Rojo's second trip to Mexico City.

The interviews with Mario Mencia, Alfonso Bauer, and Myrna Torres were published in the magazine *Bohemia,* as were their articles "Así empezó la historia del guerrillero heroico" and "Los primeros cubanos que conocieron al Che," which provide important pieces of information.

The best sources of information on Che as a doctor are Marta Rojas's compilation *Testimonios sobre el Che* and her account "Ernesto, médico en México." In an interview with me in Havana in September 1995, Marta corrected several details and gave me tips that were helpful when I came to write this chapter.

The most complete versions of the Cuban exiles' experience of Mexico and the invasion preparations that culminated in the voyage of the *Granma* are in *De Tuxpan a La Plata* (including two dozen interesting photos) and in *Cuba, revolución en la memoria* by Minerva Salado, which along with eyewitness accounts by Commanders Juan Almeida *(Exilio),* Universo Sánchez (unpublished interview by Luis Adrián Betancourt) and Efigenio Almeijeiras *(1956, un año tremendo)* provide very detailed background. I wrote an article on the same issue in 1995—"El verano y el otoño del 56"—which was published as a prologue to the war diaries of Raúl Castro and Che Guevara in the Sierra Maestra. Corrections by Cuban historian Alvarez Tabío were essential.

The most exact description of the training at the ranch in Chalco and the military preparation for the expedition may be found in Colonel Bayo's book *Mi aporte a la revolución cubana;* in documents kept in the Che museum in the La Cabaña fortress; and in José Aguilar's interview with García Dávila.

During this period, Fidel Castro published four interesting articles in *Bohemia* that set out his viewpoint: "Sirvo a Cuba" (Nov. 20, 1955); "Carta sobre Trujillo" (Aug. 26, 1955); "El Movimiento 26 de Julio" (Mar. 19, 1955); and "El Movimiento 26 de Julio y la conspiración militar" (May 15, 1956) in Aldabonazo. These, along with "Manifiesto 1 del 26 de Julio al pueblo de Cuba," Tad Szulc's biography *Fidel,* Lionel Martin's book *El Joven Fidel,* and Fidel's replies in his extensive interview with Gianni Minà, give a clear idea of the July 26 Movement's political leader at that time and of his early relationship with Che. A careful, detailed account of Fidel's time in Mexico appears in Mencia's article "El exilio turbulento."

The July 26 Movement "Mexican support network" is described in detail by Minerva Salado in *Cuba, revolución en la memoria,* and in Ander Landáburu's interview with Vanegas. An extensive conversation between the author and Antonio del Conde, aka "El Cuate" (November 1995), was very useful.

Che's fleeting contacts with Arnoldo Orfila and Raúl Roa are in their respective texts, "Recordando al Che" and "Che," published in a Casa de las Américas special edition, Jan.–Feb. 1968.

Some odds and ends that round out this chapter are from Masetti's interview with Che in *Los que ríen y los que lloran;* María Cristina Mojena's account of Camilo Cienfuegos ("Camilo era mucho Camilo"); Eduardo Galeano's report "El Che Guevara" in *Violencia y enajenación;* and María del Carmen Ariet's article "Hasta vencer o morir" in the magazine *Moncada.*

Interviews of Hilda Guevara Gadea by Yurina Fernández Noa and Román Orozco are interesting. To determine the exact state of the Guevara-Gadea marriage when Che left Mexico City, I had a long conversation with Hilda in Havana in February 1995.

Che's contacts with Soviet citizens are described in Luis Miranda's article and Lavretsky's biography. For events in Argentina in April and May 1955 and the military coup, which are entered into briefly here, the best book the author has found is *La caída de Perón,* by Julio Godio.

Jorge Castañeda lent me the manuscript of his 1995 interview with Gutiérrez Barrios. Also see Surí, "Nadie se cansa de pelear"; Cupull and González, *Un hombre bravo,* which provides a chronological account with much information; Carlos Franqui, *Vida, aventuras y desventuras de un hombre llamado Castro;* and Portuondo, *La clandestinidad tuvo un nombre, David.*

Also useful were Guevara's Agencia Latina press pass and more than two dozen photos of the time from the archives of Cuban magazines and the Mexico City newspaper *El Universal.*

Meeting Fidel

Cuban historians and journalists have been very imprecise as to when Che met Fidel.

Fidel arrived in Mérida on July 7, 1955; there he changed planes and flew on Mexicana flight 566 to Veracruz. Salado dates the meeting in September, while others set it in August, Massari in November, and Hilda Gadea at the beginning of July. Fidel speaks of "July or August." It was

doubtless in the second week of July, because by the third week they had already met and taken part in the ceremony at the Boy Heroes monument.

The Traitor

Cuban history has drawn a veil over the identity of the traitor within the ranks of the July 26 Movement in Mexico. Antonio del Conde said years later that it was Rafael del Pino. Lavretsky gave more precise details, saying the traitor had accepted $15,000 from the Cuban embassy in Mexico to betray the rebels. Bayo later accused Ricardo Bonachea, who had quit the movement some weeks earlier. Minerva Salado's book cites evidence that Miguel A. Sánchez, "The Korean," who took part in the training but did not sail with the *Granma,* had links with the Cuban embassy.

Patojo's Fate in Mexico

Che: El Patojo spent his time working as a journalist, studying physics at the University of Mexico, quitting and resuming his studies without making much progress, earning his living in several places with different jobs, but never asking for anything. I still can't tell whether that sensitive and introverted boy was incredibly shy, or too proud to acknowledge some weaknesses and his most personal problems, and approach his friends to ask for the help he needed. From "El Patojo," in *Paisajes.*

About the Poem

Che never gave his poem "Come, Blazing Prophet of Dawn" to Fidel. According to one source, he gave it to Hilda in the Miguel Schultz jail; according to another, it turned up in the suitcase he gave Hilda when he left Mexico: "He left me his suitcase, which had his book of poems in it." What is clear is that Che did not think the poem was any good and never intended it to be anything more than a memoir.

Years later, Leonel Soto, editor of *Verde Olivo,* published the poem and Che sent him an angry note warning him not to publish anything without permission, especially **those awful verses** (see Pardo and Kutbischkova). Che felt his poetry was something private. On another occasion, when Pardo threatened to publish another poem or read one on the radio, Che jokingly threatened him with the firing squad.

8. *Granma* Takes On Water

Sources

Che gave only a brief account in *Una revolución que comienza.* His diaries from this period are still unpublished, although entries from the following days suggest that they must have been brief. The most detailed accounts are perhaps the ones by Faustino Pérez, *El Granma era invencible como el espíritu de sus combatientes,* and Juan Almeida, *Desembarco.*

A very complete anthology under the same title as Faustino Pérez's, *El Granma era invencible . . . ,* contains accounts of the *Granma* and the first days of the revolution published over twenty years in the magazine *Verde Olivo,* which also contains government army's communiqués regarding the search for the *Granma* in the Gulf of Mexico. Of especial interest are accounts by Norberto Collado, "Una travesía heroica"; Calixto García, "Yo fui el número 15"; Leonardo Roque "Rescate en medio del mar"; and the account jointly penned by Efigenio Ameijeiras and René Rodríguez, "Con los fusiles, los uniformes y las balas." Ameijeiras returns to the same theme in his article "Miedo a las ballenas" and in one chapter of his book *1956, Un año tremendo.*

Other useful accounts of the expedition are those of Guillén Zelaya, who was interviewed by Estela Guerra for *Moncada* magazine; Jesús Montané, "Testimonios sobre el Che"; and Chuchú Reyes (interviewed by Alfredo Reyes), "El maquinista del Granma."

Fidel refers several times to the seven-day voyage; perhaps the most detailed account is in a speech he gave on March 13, 1991. An article and two books on the *Granma* are especially interesting: "*Granma:* Recuento en el XX aniversario," published in the magazine *El Oficial; Granma, rumbo a la libertad,* published by Gente Nueva; and an anthology edited by Pedro Alvarez Tabío, *La epopeya del Granma* (with the same text as a special edition of the magazine *Bohemia,* but a different format).

The texts of the telegrams sent from Mexico are in Yolanda Portuondo's book *30 de noviembre* and N. Sarabia's article "La Mujer . . ."

Food on Board the *Granma*

Two thousand oranges, forty-eight cans of condensed milk, four hams, a box of eggs, 100 slabs of chocolate, and 100 pounds of bread, which had to be shared by eighty-two men throughout the voyage.

About the Uprising in Santiago

Frank País had planned a series of shock and diversionary actions and had also ordered that no sabotage take place between Manzanillo and Pilón, to avoid drawing troops into the potential landing site.

The objectives included taking the police station, attacking the maritime police, surrounding the Moncada barracks, taking the Quintero post and organizing a breakout of political prisoners, and capturing weapons. At a later stage the urban guerrillas planned to take the airport and join the rebels who had landed. The idea of a general strike was scrapped because the July 26 Movement had not sufficiently linked itself to the labor movement.

Frank País had agreed with Fidel Castro in October 1956 that the uprising should occur five days after the *Granma* set sail. The wire with the news of the sailing arrived at eleven A.M. on October 27, so not only was the uprising not postponed, it was put forward a day, as the organizers thought the news of the landing might have been censored. In Santiago, 200 men took part and the olive-drab uniforms of the July 26 Movement were seen on the streets for the first time. The army heard the night before that an uprising was to take place, but did not know where or when.

The M26 shock groups controlled the city for two hours, but the army and police rallied and counterattacked at nightfall. The prison breakout was successful, the attack on the police station relatively so; the attempt to surround the Moncada failed. There were still snipers on the rooftops on December 1, but the movement had gone underground.

The best account of the November 30 uprising with which I am familiar is *30 de noviembre* by Yolanda Portuondo, which compiles testimony from most of the leading players who survived the revolution. *La clandestinidad tuvo un nombre, David,* by the same author, provides an interesting account of the movement's leader, Frank País. Other sources: *Una revolución que comienza;* the articles by Benítez and Valdés, "Vivencias de una heroica hazaña" and the interview with Vilma Espín, "Reflejos de una época"; Castor Amador's "El desembarco del *Granma* y el 30 de noviembre," and an unsigned article in *Verde Olivo,* "30 de noviembre."

The Fate of the *Granma*

The yacht survived over the years under the care of a Sergeant Pantoja and the watchful eyes of friends and relatives of helmsman Collado, who was detailed by Camilo Cienfuegos to rescue the yacht when he got out of the Isla de Pinos jail after the revolution took power. Collado told Fidel the yacht was ready when he entered Havana on January 8, 1959.

After the little boat gave its name to a newspaper and a Cuban province and became a source of national pride equaled only by one other yacht (Ernest Hemingway's, at the San Francisco de Paula ranch), its exhibition as a museum piece prompted the same question again and again among the public: How did eighty-two men manage to spend seven days there?

Efigenio Ameijeras: "Some time ago, eighty-two Pioneers [comparable to Boy Scouts] stormed the yacht *Granma* to emulate the eighty-two expeditionaries. Surprisingly, they did not fit, no matter how much they pushed and shoved. Some boys had to go on the roof. Imagine what it was like to sail on that yacht, overloaded and riding with the waterline well below the surface."

9. The Disaster

Sources

Che devoted "Algería de Pío," part of what later became his *Paisajes de la guerra revolucionaria,* to this first clash with Batista's army. He also described the episode in a couple of pages in the article "Una revolución que comienza." Che's diary and Raúl Castro's appear in *La conquista de la esperanza.*

An excellent description of the area may be found in the article by Reyes Trejo and Lisanka, "Escenarios de la Lucha." Several of those who took part have offered their accounts, some of which have noteworthy literary quality: Efigenio Ameijeiras in *1956, Un año tremendo;* Juan Almeida in *Desembarco.* Two interviews with Universo Sánchez have been helpful: one by Luis Adrián Betancourt, and another published by Erasmo Dumpierre in *Bohemia* magazine. See also the jointly written accounts by Guillermo García, Fajardo, and Ponce, recorded by Carlos Franqui in *Cuba, el libro de los doce;* Faustino Pérez, in *El Granma era invencible como el espíritu de sus combatientes;* and René Rodríguez's article "Con los fusiles, los uniformes y las balas." Ameijeiras's and Crespo's accounts are in *Che sierra adentro* by Escobar and Guerra.

The rebels' first contacts with campesinos are described in articles by Benítez, "La colaboración campesina," and Reyes Trejo's "Belic: se inicia el camino hacia la liberación." Army dispatches and the official announcement over UPI that Fidel was dead appear in "Sucedió hace veinte años" by Rolando Pérez Betancourt and in Franqui's diary, which points to a variation on the theme of disinformation: "Among the most noteworthy chiefs who died in the attack at Castro's side were his brother Raúl and Juan Manuel Márquez."

The *Bohemia* special edition "XX aniversario" (edited by Alvarez Tabío), along with including many accounts by those who took part, describes the fate of most of the invaders and provides military information, maps, and sketches, as well as a priceless set of photos from that time and the years following.

Casualties

Strangely enough, the ambush at Alegría de Pío did not result in many casualties on the rebel side—just two dead and, probably, another wounded and then taken prisoner and murdered by the military. But over the following days another eighteen rebels were captured and murdered, and seventeen more taken prisoner.

The Remark

The remark "No one surrenders here, dammit!" ("Before I met Camilo, I knew him by a symbolic exclamation") attributed by Che to Camilo Cienfuegos and later incorporated into the mythology of the Cuban revolution, was later discovered to have been said by Juan Almeida, who never dared to correct Che and consequently kept very quiet.

Diaries

Fidel: "It was Che's habit as a guerrilla fighter to carefully note down his observations every day in a diary. On long marches through harsh and difficult terrain, in the middle of damp forests, when the ranks of men, their backs bent double by backpacks, stopped to rest awhile, or received the order to halt and make camp at the end of a tiring march, Che . . . could be seen taking out a book and taking notes in his small and almost illegible doctor's scrawl" ("A Neces-

sary Introduction," in Che's Bolivian diary). Che kept a diary throughout the Cuban revolution. Only the diaries from the first months of the campaign have been published.

10.   No Place to Go

Sources

One of Che's *Paisajes de la guerra revolucionaria* "A la deriva," describes this period. Che's diary entries are available in "La conquista de la esperanza," in an article, "Camilo," which he wrote in 1964, and in "Una revolución que comienza."

Che's account should be read in tandem with Almeida's account in "Desembarco." Two other articles by Mariano Rodríguez are also useful: "Che en Cinco Palmas" and "Hablan el padre y la hermana del Che." See also the text of the letter in "Mi hijo el Che" by Ernesto Guevara, Sr.

Celia and the Campesino Network

Cuban historians have generally underestimated the network of agrarian activists set up in the foothills of the Sierra Maestra by Celia Sánchez. From their accounts, it would appear that the wandering rebels just happened to meet the key campesinos, who offered them food, shelter, and (above all) guides. Che himself did not attach much importance to the network, although it was a key factor.

From January 1956 onward, Celia Sánchez, daughter of a middle-class doctor, began, under the tutelage of Frank País, to prepare political activity in the east of Cuba in expectation of Fidel Castro's return at the head of an army. She had a thorough knowledge of the rural areas in the municipality of Niquera, as she had grown up in Pilón, a small village between Santiago and Manzanillo.

With the help of Crescencio Pérez, Celia built up a network that included a fledgling campesino militia and some caches of food, gasoline, and ammunition.

Pérez had resisted evictions ordered by rural bosses and carried out by the Rural Guards.

For Celia Sánchez's network, see "Celia," a special issue of *Moncada* magazine; "El otro Ignacio" by Mariano Rodríguez Herrera, a very interesting feature on the mentality and anecdotes by one of Crescencio's sons who joined the guerrillas; "En espera del desembarco," by Alvarez Tabío; Crescencio's own testimony in *El libro de los 12* by Carlos Franqui, and José Mayo's article "El primer Apoyo."

Camilo and Food

Che: **Camilo was hungry and wanted to eat—he did not care how or where, he just wanted to eat. We had real trouble with him, because he was forever wanting to enter campesino huts to ask for something and twice, after following the great glutton's advice, we nearly fell into the hands of the army. A dozen of our comrades had been murdered there. On the ninth day of the march, gluttony won out. We went to a campesino hut, ate and all got sick. Among the sick, of course, was Camilo, who had eaten a whole kid by himself. At that time I was more of a medic than a soldier, so I put him on a diet and ordered him to rest in the hut for a day** (from *Paisajes de la guerra revolucionaria*).

Efigenio Ameijeiras said that it was not hard to eat a kid in those days, but what about putting away a whole cauldron of rice and chicken, as Camilo did?

11. River Plate Resurrection

Sources

Che's *Paisajes de la guerra revolucionaria* includes chapters that pertain to the first stage of fighting in the Sierra Maes-

tra: "Combate de La Plata," "Combate del Arroyo del Infierno," "Ataque aéreo," "Sorpresa de Altos de Espinosa," and "Fin de un traidor." See also "Una revolución que comienza," Che's war diary in *La conquista de la esperanza,* and the article "Camilo Cienfuegos."

The legend of the twelve men, which has a hackneyed evangelic ring to it, comes from *El libro de los 12* by Carlos Franqui. Even Che used it, in *Guerra de guerrillas*° ("Twelve men were able to set up the hard core of the army that was formed").

Franqui's *Diario de la revolución cubana* is essential for this stage, as is *Che sierra adentro* by Froilán Escobar and Félix Guerra.

Also of use are the following. Faustino Pérez's piece in *Testimonios sobre el Che;* "Dibujó con flores su sonrisa en el mar," by Efigenio Ameijeras; "El amanecer victorioso de la Plata," by José Afront, and Mariano Rodríguez's articles, based on Sergio Pérez's testimony: "Llanos del infierno, la primera emboscada guerrillera," "Che en Cinco Palmas," "Por la ruta de Fidel en la Sierra Maestra," and "La Plata, gran sorpresa de Batista."

The author's interview with Dariel Alarcón was essential.

The Repression of the Campesinos

The campesino whom the rebels saw go by, tied up by Basol, and whom they did not free so as not give themselves away, came to a terrible end. Che: **We thought that campesino was out of danger, as he was not in the barracks and in the line of fire when we attacked. But the next day, when they found out about the attack and its outcome, he was cruelly murdered in El Macío** (*Paisajes de la guerra revolucionaria*).

Wounded

Che: **Our attitude toward the wounded always contrasted with the army's. They not only murdered ours**

*Translator's note: This book is referred to by its English title, *Guerrilla Warfare,* in the main text.

but abandoned theirs. That difference made itself felt over time and was one of the reasons for our victory. Despite my reluctance—as a medic I felt the need to keep reserves for our men—Fidel ordered us to hand over all available medicine to the prisoners to treat their wounded, and that is what we did (*Paisajes de la guerra revolucionaria*).

Julio Zenón Acosta

Che: Julio Zenón Acosta was another great support at that time. He was tireless, he knew the country, and he always helped a comrade down on his luck or a city comrade who did not yet have the strength to get out of the mire. He was the one who brought water from a faraway watering hole, who could make a fire quickly, who found the Jamaican rosewood needed to light a fire on a rainy day (*Paisajes de la guerra revolucionaria*).

Juan Almeida: "He was, all in all, the one-man band of that time. A strong, tough black man, forty or forty-five years old" (*La Sierra*).

Matthews

See Matthews's articles in the *New York Times*, Feb. 24, 25, and 26, 1957. On this theme, see also Universo Sánchez in *Testimonios sobre el Che,* the interview with Fajardo in *El libro de los 12,* and the faithful recapitulation of Matthews's interview in *La conquista de la esperanza.*

Herbert Matthews paid for his scoop with interest. After the Cuban revolutionaries took power, and particularly after Fidel Castro took a leftward turn in 1960, Matthews was harassed by Senate inquiries, visits from the FBI, and pressure from far-right groups. For another account of Cold War insanity, see the chapter "Cuba and the [N.Y.] Times" in his book *A World in Revolution.*

Camilo Again

Che: We used to clash over matters of discipline, over problems caused by the guerrillas different points of view, and different attitudes. Camilo was a very unruly and very temperamental guerrilla in those days (*Paisajes de la guerra revolucionaria*).

12. Execution

Sources

Che gave several accounts of this stage, all of them collected in *Paisajes de la guerra revolucionaria.* See the chapters "Días amargos," "El Refuerzo," "Adquiriendo el temple," "Una entrevista famosa," "Jornadas de marcha" and "Llegan las armas." Bits and pieces of the story also appear in *Guerra de guerrillas* and *Una revolución que comienza.*

The account of Eutimio's death is from Luis Adrián Betancourt's unpublished interview with Universo Sánchez.

Efigenio Ameijeiras's account of March 1957, which appears in Carlos Franqui's in *Cuba, el libro de los 12,* is excellent. Also of interest are Robert Taber's *M26: Biography of a Revolution* and Joel Iglesias's article "Experiencias y vivencias junto al Che." There are fragments of the author's interview of Dariel Alarcón, José Lupiañez's "Entre versos y fusiles sobre el primer refuerzo," the book *Cinco Picos* by Froilán Escobar and Félix Guerra, Crespo's account in "Luchar junto al Che," and the book *The Winds of December* by Dorschner and Fabricio.

The Raid on the National Palace and the Humboldt Crime

See Berta Bonne, *Menelao, su lucha y acción;* Julio García Oliveras, *José Antonio;* Faure Chomón's account in *El libro de los 12;* and *Sangre y pillaje* by Enrique de la Ossa. Carlos Franqui's *Diario . . .* devotes a good few pages to the issue, with some interesting eyewitness accounts.

Also of interest is Franqui's April 1957 letter (confiscated along with the *Revolución* printing press a little after the raid) to Frank País, in which he describes the political climate among the revolutionary forces at that time. The points of agreement with the Directorio in jail: "They're like us apart from certain differences: the role of Havana, which they overestimate and we underestimate; they favor striking on high and fighting in the Sierra, and they share our concern over Fidel's dominance." The differences with the PSP: "They criticize sabotage and guerrilla warfare. They say we're playing into the hands of the terrorists in the régime. They say the M26 has coup tendencies, likes daredevilry, and is petit bourgeois. They don't understand the nature of tyranny and don't believe a revolution is possible."

Debray: Tried and True

"Che's character did not contradict his myth but he was someone different and more complex. An incorruptible seeker of justice, idealistic hero, and romantic adventurer? Certainly, but one doesn't need rosewater to be romantic or believe that idealists in action behave like the Sisters of Charity? A revolutionary, as I have said before, is moved above all by feelings of love, but he [Che] used to hide his personal tenderness like a fault. In the heart of the Cuban leadership, he was not inclined toward indulgence, and in the brutal dilemmas of 'revolutionary justice' (arrests or executions of suspects or others), he inclined more toward Robespierre than Danton—and, of course, never toward Fabre d'Eglantine. As opposed to Fidel. Myth, however, has assigned them the opposite roles, and nothing can be done about myths" *(Les masques)*.

The "Cowboy Kid"

Che: The "Cowboy Kid" and another comrade ran into us one day and said they had been looking for us for over a month. He said he was from Camagüey Province, from Morón, and, as always in such cases, we began to question him and give him some rudimentary political training, which was frequently my lot. The Cowboy Kid had no political ideas and seemed nothing more than a healthy, jolly boy who saw everything as a great adventure. He was barefoot, so Celia Sánchez lent him some extra shoes she had. They were factory-made or Mexican style, hand-tooled, and they were the only shoes that were any good for the short Cowboy Kid. With his new shoes and a big straw hat, he looked like a Mexican cowboy and that's how he got his nickname. . . .

The Cowboy Kid was a terrible liar—and he probably never said anything without embellishing the truth for that he made it practically unrecognizable; but in his actions . . . the Cowboy Kid demonstrated that the difference between fact and fantasy were not clear-cut and on the battlefield he displayed the same harebrained behavior he dreamed up when he wasn't fighting.

I once happened to question the Cowboy Kid after one of the nighttime reading groups we held in the column, some time after he joined. He began to tell me about his life and idly began to make a tally with a pencil. When he finished, after many riveting anecdotes, we asked how old he was. He was a little over twenty then, but the tally of his deeds made him look as if he had started five years before he was born *(Paisajes de la guerra revolucionaria)*.

Andrew St. George

Che: At that time, he showed only one of his faces, the least ugly one, that of a Yanqui journalist. Besides that, he worked for the FBI. As I was the only one in the column who spoke French (no one spoke English back then) I had to see to him and, honestly, he didn't look to me like the dangerous character who turned up in a later interview no longer constrained by his undercover work. *(Paisajes de la guerra revolucionaria).*

Jim Noel, then the CIA station chief in Havana, told Dorschner and Fabricio that St. George collaborated with one of his men.

13. Scratching the Dirt

Sources

Four sections in Che's *Paisajes de la guerra revolucionaria* deal with the subject of this chapter: "El combate del Uvero," "Cuidando heridos," "De regreso," and "Se gesta una traición," as does part of *Una revolución que comienza.* Che's war diaries from this period have not been published.

Fidel's account of the clash at El Uvero is in Carlos Franqui's *Diario de la revolución.* The best eyewitness account is in *Che, sierra adentro* by Escobar and Guerra, which includes accounts by Crescencio Pérez, Efigenio Ameijeiras, Edelfín Mendoza, Joel Iglesias, and Alfonso Zayas. Of special interest are the article "El ataque a El Uvero" and the book *La sierra,* both by Juan Almeida; "Dos ángulos del Uvero" ("Two Aspects of El Uvero": those of Escalona and army lieutenant Carreras), by Alfredo Reyes Trejo; "Manuel Acuña Cuenta del Uvero," in the *Verde Olivo* anthology about the history of No. 1 Column; *Un médico en la sierra,* by Julio Martínez Páez; and *Cinco Picos* by Guerra and Escobar.

For the wandering column, see a new chapter in *Che, sierra adentro* that includes eyewitness accounts by Alejandro Oñate and the campesinos Polo Torres, Juana González, and Isidora Moracén.

The following articles are interesting: "Así lo cuenta David" by Manuel González Bello, which gives the foreman's tale; "Yo soy el oscuro teniente" by Luis Báez, with an account by army lieutenant Pedro Carreras; "Uvero: Mayo amanece con disparos de fusil," by Mariano Rodríguez; and "Mis vivencias con el Che," by Joel Iglesias.

Army Casualties

Che: Out of sheer statistical curiosity I kept a tally of all the enemy dead claimed by our side during the fighting and it turned out to be larger than the whole group we had faced. Each man's fantasy embellished his own feats. This and other, similar experiences made us realize that figures had to be clearly confirmed by several people. We even went so far as to demand articles of each dead man's clothing to confirm a kill; concern for truth was always crucial to the rebel army, and we tried to imbue our comrades with deep respect for it and the need to put it before any fleeting advantage *(Paisajes de la guerra revolucionaria).*

Batista and Che

Che found Lieutenant Pedro Pascual Carrera lying wounded as he entered the bullet-ridden El Uvero barracks. Carrera thought the rebels would kill him. Che explained that they were not murderers and respected the wounded, and he was indeed the last to treat him. Carrera saved Cilleros from being taken to Santiago; later, he himself saw Batista and told the dictator, "There was one man there, the one who did all the talking. He was a leader, who treated me properly although we had inflicted several casualties on them. He doesn't speak like we do, and he's a medic. Batista interrupted me and exclaimed: 'That's Che, a Communist renegade!' I said immediately that I was sure they would hand back the comrades of mine they had captured.

"Tabernilla interrupted: 'Shut your mouth, shitkicker, you're only spouting propaganda for those bandits. . . . Our comrades must be dead by now.' My men turned up three days later, safe and sound."

Che on Chibás and Pazos

Che: They were two totally different characters. Raúl Chibás merely basked in the glory of his brother, who really was the symbol of an era in Cuba, but he had none of his brother's merits. He was neither eloquent nor wise, nor intelligent, either. It was precisely his mediocrity that made him a leading light in the orthodox Party. He spoke little and wanted to get away from the Sierra as soon as possible.

Felipe Pazos was his own man, respected as a great economist; what's more, he had a reputation for honesty earned by not raiding the public purse in an administration as riddled with crime and larceny as was that of Prío Socarrás when he headed the Banco Nacional. It was a great merit, you may think, to have remained untainted by those days. It may be a merit for an official to pursue his career while remaining blind to the great problems that beset his country, but how can one conceive of a revolutionary who did not denounce that era's incredible abuses every day? Felipe Pazos did manage not to do so, and after Batista's palace coup he eased his way out of the Banco Nacional leadership, taking with him his honesty, his intelligence, and his great prestige as a gifted economist. He was vainglorious enough to think he could come up to the Sierra and take over—as his little machiavellian brain saw it, he was the one to take the country's reins. He may already have thought of defecting to the movement, or he may have considered it afterward, but his behavior was never quite candid *(Paisajes de la guerra revolucionaria)*.

14. Commander

Sources

Che included several sketches relating to this period in his *Paisajes de la guerra revolucionaria:* "El ataque a Bueycito," "Lucha contra el bandidaje," "Pino del Agua

1," "El cachorro asesinado," "Altos de Conrado," "Lidia y Clodomira," "Se gesta una traición," "El combate de Mar Verde," and "Alto de Escudero." Also essential reading are the communiqués between Che and Fidel, which appear in Carlos Franqui's *Diario de la revolución cubana* and were published in several newspapers and magazines.

Frank País's death: see Alvarez Tabío's "El más extraordinario de nuestros combatientes" and Yolanda Portuondo's *Sus últimos treinta días.* The Cienfuegos uprising is covered in Franqui's *Diario de la revolución cubana* and in Prendes's *Piloto de guerra.*

Interesting details for this chapter come from the eyewitness accounts by Guile Pardo, Harry Villegas, and Zoila Rodríguez in *Entre Nosotros,* by Cupull and González, and from my interviews with Leonardo Tamayo and René Pacheco.

Among memoirs by fighters, "En la guerra revolucionaria junto al Che," by Joel Iglesias is very helpful, as are "El Che que yo conocí," by Rogelio Acevedo; *Descamisado* (an excellent account of everyday guerrilla life) and "El hombre que me hizo guerrillero," by Enrique Acevedo; "Dibujó con flores su sonrisa en el mar," by Ameijeiras, and "La Sierra Maestra y más allá," by Juan Almeida.

Mariano Rodríguez's unpublished, untitled book is essential, as is Helio Vitier's article "Che en Buey Arriba" and Sergio Giral's film *Un relato del jefe de la Columna 4.*

A remarkable inside account of the enormous campesino guerrilla support network is contained in Sergio Bacallao's biographical sketches, compiled by Betancourt. *El Dorado,* by Orestes Adán, may be consulted for the urban network.

For the ins and outs, maneuvers and conflicts of the movement in exile, see Llerena, *La revolución insospechada.*

Bits and pieces from journalists: "Guevara," by Walsh; "Ernesto Che Guevara, fundador del Cubano Libre," by Sarabia; and *Los que luchan y los que lloran,* by Masetti.

Also see "El castrismo," by Debray; "El Che Guevara, un hombre através de sus anécdotas," by Ana Núñez; "Era muy humano . . . ," by Javier Rodríguez; "Alto de Escudero," by Roland Castillo; "Lidia y Clodomira" by Lázaro Torres; "Castro comienza la revolución," by Meneses; "El armero del Che," by Zúñiga; and Carlos María Gutiérrez's article "Una madrugada de febrero."

Roberto Rodríguez's Suicide

Che: Roberto Rodríguez was disarmed for insubordination. He was very unruly, so his squad lieutenant disarmed him as a disciplinary matter. Roberto Rodríguez snatched a revolver from a comrade and killed himself. We had a minor incident, because I opposed our giving him military honors, while the fighters felt he was another man killed in action and I argued that suicide under our circumstances was a repugnant act, regardless of his fine qualities as a comrade. After an attempt at insubordination, the men held a wake over the comrade's body, but without honors.

A day or two beforehand he had told me part of his life story, and one could tell he was an overly sensitive boy who was making a huge effort to adapt to the hard life of a guerrilla, and also to military discipline, things that clashed with his physical weakness and his rebellious instincts (from *Paisajes de la guerra revolucionaria*).

The Murdered Puppy

Che: Everything would have been just fine were it not for the new mascot, a little hunting dog a few weeks old. Despite Félix's repeated attempts to entice the puppy into returning to our center of operations, a house where the cooks stayed, he tagged along with the column. Crossing the slopes in that part of the Sierra Maestra is very difficult because there are no trails. We crossed a difficult spot where a lot of old fallen trees were covered by undergrowth; the going was very tough. We leaped from tree trunk to bush, trying not to lose contact with our guests. The column marched in silence, as usual in such conditions, without so much as a broken branch to stand out from with the bush's usual murmur. The quiet was soon shattered by the little dog's alarmed and despairing yelps. He had fallen behind and was barking like mad to call for help from his masters. Someone fetched the little thing and off we went, but while we were resting in a hollow with a sentry watching enemy troop movements, the dog began to howl like fury again. He was no longer content with calling; he was scared he would be left behind, and began to bark in desperation.

I can remember my strict orders: "Félix, that dog must not bark anymore. You settle the matter. Hang it. It mustn't bark again." Félix looked at me with expressionless eyes. Among the exhausted men were the dog and he. He slowly fetched a rope, tied it around the animal's neck, and began to strangle it. The dog's friendly tail-wagging soon gave way to death throes, and then faded away to a low moan that mocked the iron grip choking him. I don't know how long it took, but ages seemed to pass before it was over. After a last spasm, the dog stopped struggling. He remained still, emaciated, with his head bent back over some hillside branches.

We marched on without even commenting on the incident. Sánchez Mosquera's men had stolen a bit of a march on us, and we heard shots after a while. We quickly climbed down the slope, seeking the best route through the brush to the rear guard. We knew that Camilo had fired at the enemy. It took us quite some time to find the last house before the climb. We went along very stealthily, expecting to bump into the enemy at any moment, all in a state of tense expectation. The shooting had been heavy, but did not last long. The last house was abandoned also. Not even a trace of the soldiery. Two scouts climbed up the "Cojo" slope and came back with the news: "There's a grave up there. We dug it up and found a little helmet." They brought along some papers found in a dead man's pockets. There had been a battle with one fatality. The dead man was one of theirs, but that was all we knew.

We went back slowly, discouraged. Two reconnaissance trips showed many traces of troops passing on both sides of the Sierra Maestra slopes, but no more. We went back slowly along the valley.

At nightfall, we came to a house, which was also empty. It was on the Mar Verde farm, and we managed to rest there. A hog was soon cooked with yucca and the meal was ready. Someone struck up a tune with a guitar—the campesino houses used to be abandoned suddenly with all their belongings inside.

I don't know if the tune was sentimental, or whether it was the night or the fatigue, but what happened was that Félix, who ate sitting on he floor, gave a dog a bone. A dog from the house came and tamely took it. Félix put his hand on its head. The dog looked at him. Félix looked back at it and we exchanged a guilty glance. We were suddenly quiet. There was an unseen pang of feeling between us. There with the rest of them, with his tame and naughty but reproachful look, the murdered puppy was looking at us through the eyes of another dog (from *Paisajes de la guerra revolucionaria*).

15. Controversy

Sources

Che devoted several of his *Paisajes* to this part of the war: "Lidia y Clodomira," "Un año de lucha armada," and "Pino del Agua 2." It is also described in some brief

passages in the article "Una revolución que comienza," and a speech at Minas del Frío after the revolution took power.

The best, and best-documented, history of Radio Rebelde is *7RR* by Ricardo Martínez, based on interviews with all involved except for Carlos Franqui, who later took charge of broadcasting but whose role was played down after the rift. See Franqui's *Diario de la revolución cubana.*

Also see *Con la adarga al brazo,* by Mariano Rodríguez; *La Batalla de Pino del Agua,* by Castillo Bernal; "Recuerdos del Che," by Harry Villegas; "En la guerra revolucionaria junto al Che," by Joel Iglesias; *El armero del Che* by Ramos Zúñiga; "Che, innovador técnico," by Alexis Schlachter; "La primera armería de la guerra," by Hugo Chinea; "Entre nosotros," by Zoila Rodríguez; "Sin darle tregua al enemigo," an interview with Pablo Rivalta by Juana Carrasco; "El Che en lo suyo," by Carlos María Gutiérrez; "Castro comienza la revolución," by Enrique Meneses; "La primera escuela del ejército rebelde," by Nydia Sarabia; "Ernesto Guevara, fundador del Cubano Libre," by Escobar and Guerra, and two of their books: *El fuego que enciende los fusiles* and *Che sierra adentro.*

Che's Account of the July 26 Movement Leadership

In the preparation stage, up till Fidel left for Mexico, the national leadership was composed of Fidel himself, Raúl, Faustino Pérez, Pedro Miret, Ñico López, Armando Hart, Pepe Suárez, Pedro Aguilera, Luis Bonito, Jesús Montané, Melba Hernández and Haydée Santamaría, if my information is not mistaken, as my personal participation at that stage was very brief and remaining documentation is poor.

Later, when we were in Mexico, Pepe Suárez, Pedro Aguilera, and Luis Bonito drifted apart from the leadership because of some incompatibility or other, while Mario Hidalgo, Aldo Santamaría, Carlos Franqui, Gustavo Arcos, and Frank País joined its ranks.

Of all the comrades I have named, only Fidel and Raúl came to the Sierra to stay during the first year. Faustino Pérez, who was on board the *Granma,* took charge of actions in the cities. Pedro Miret was arrested hours before we left Mexico and stayed there until the next year, when he arrived in Cuba with an arms shipment. Ñico López was killed hours after the landing. Armando Hart was taken prisoner at the end of the year we are looking at (or the beginning of the one following). Jesús Montané was captured after the *Granma* landed. Mario Hidalgo, Melba Hernández, and Haydée Santamaría were active in the cities. Aldo Santamaría and Carlos Franqui joined the struggle in the Sierra the next year, but were not there in 1957. Gustavo Arcos stayed in Mexico arranging political contacts and supplies there. Frank País, in charge of actions in Santiago, was killed in July 1957.

Those who joined up in the Sierra afterward were Celia Sánchez, who stayed with us throughout 1958; Vilma Espín, who worked in Santiago and ended the war in Raúl Castro's column; Marcelo Fernández, the Movement's coordinator, who replaced Faustino after the April 9 strike and was only with us for a few weeks, as his job was in the towns; René Ramos Latour, who commanded the militias on the Plains, came up to the Sierra after the failed April 9 strike and died fighting heroically as a commander in the second year of the struggle; and David Salvador, a labor movement leader.

Also, some of the Sierra fighters, like Almeida, joined up later.

As can be seen, the comrades from the Plains made up the majority and their political extraction, which had not been influenced by the process of gradual revolutionary maturity, inclined them toward a certain "civic" activism and away from the "leader" figure they feared in Fidel, as well as from the "militarist" element represented by those of us in the Sierra. The differences were already apparent, but were not then wide enough to spur the violence that marked the second year of the war. (from *Paisajes de la guerra revolucionaria*).

16. The Sierra and the Plains

Sources

There are two accounts of this period in Che's *Paisajes de la guerra revolucionaria:* "Interludio" and "Una reunión decisiva." The April strike is mentioned in "Notas para el estudio de la ideología de la revolución cubana" and in Che's prologue to the book *El partido marxista-leninista,* as well as in *Una revolución que comienza.*

Franqui devotes an important chapter of his *Diario de la revolución cubana* to the April strike, as does Rodríguez Loeches in "La Sierra y el llano." Ameijeiras's essay in *Más allá de nosotros* are essential, as are Mirta Rodríguez Calderón's interview of Faustino Pérez in "Semillas de fuego" and her "Anverso y reverso de una página de lucha."

Other useful sources for this chapter are Sergio Bacallao's *Relatos históricos, Che sierra adentro* by Guerra and Escobar, Milagros Escobar's article "Guerrilleros," Yolanda Portuondo's book *El sacerdote comandante,* Guerra's "Camilo Cienfuegos, un tránsito fulgurante," Masetti's *Los que luchan y los que lloran,* and *Camilo, señor de la vanguardia* by William Gálvez.

17. The Offensive

Sources

Che wrote only a few lines on this period, in the "Interludio" chapter of *Paisajes* and in *Una revolución que comienza.* Some of his communiqués with Fidel are in Betancourt's archive. Other sources are his letter to Sergia Cordoví and his speech at Minas el Frío.

The best sources for reconstructing this period, which has yet to be studied in depth by Cuban historians, are chapters 14 and 15 in Franqui's *Diario*, Ameijeiras's "Las guerras no se ganan en el último combate" ("Wars Are Not Won in the Last Battle"; ironically, Ameijeiras was not around for these battles: he was commanding a column on the second front), and a half-dozen articles by veterans in the anthology *El alma de la revolución.*

There is an interesting account from Batista's army's standpoint in "La batalla del Jigüe" by José Quevedo, who commanded No. 18 Battalion. There is also an account by Evelio Lafarté, a recent recruit to the guerrilla ranks, in Mariano Rodríguez's *Abriendo senderos.*

The author was able to consult a recording of Fidel's very detailed report on Radio Rebelde on the 18th and 19th. It also included a recording of his speech on the twentieth anniversary of Che's death.

For personal anecdotes, see Julio Martínez Páez's book *Un médico en la Sierra* and Juan Almeida's *La Sierra Maestra y más allá,* as well as Villegas and Lafarté's accounts in "Entre Nosotros" by Cupull and González. No one describes the feeling of chaos among the guerrilla foot soldiers better than Enrique Acevedo in *Descamisado.*

For the People's Socialist Party, I consulted "Cómo vi surgir en la sierra nuestro ejército rebelde," by Carlos Rafael Rodríguez, and books by Draper, Thomas, and Darushenko. I also interviewed Jorge Risquet.

Also of interest are Ramiro Abreu's book *En el último año de aquella república,* which provides the most concentrated view of the period; *7RR* by Ricardo Martínez, with special emphasis on Radio Rebelde; the interview with Reyes Trejo de la O in "Recuerdos del Che"; Josefina Ortega's interview of the Del Río brothers; *Che sierra adentro,* by Escobar and Guerra; *Camilo,*

señor de la vanguardia, by William Gálvez, and *Camilo Cienfuegos, cronología de un héroe.*

A Spy's View of Che

"Elegant, brilliant, much more intelligent than Fidel. Either Che is a Communist, or in my two years of studying Communists I've never seen one. His headquarters has all the luxuries of the city: a paraffin refrigerator, a paraffin stove, special food, Uppmann cigars, Coca-Cola, wine, and a wide variety of maté. He sleeps in a comfortable bed. . . . Che loves authority. . . . Unlike Fidel, Che is physically a weak man. . . . Castro walks miles a day. Che never walks; he goes by jeep or mule. Castro is a very brave man. Che is not very brave, but is a good actor and is a past master at boasting. He pretends to read while his house is being strafed" (Richard Tullis, Batista spy who infiltrated the guerrillas. LAB archive).

The Soup Collectivization

Evelio Laferté: "We spent the night in Minas del Infierno. We were soaked with rain and the Spaniard in Minas del Infierno made supper. He had a turkey, I think. He grabbed its feet, wings, and giblets and made a broth into which he threw some rice. He made a fricassee for what he called the high-ranking officers. Che saw that as he was passing through the kitchen and said to him:

"Come on, Spaniard, what are you making here?

" 'A broth for the boys who are wet from the rain.'

"And Che asks:

And what's this fricassee, Spaniard?

" 'That's for you officers.'

"Everyone knows what happened next. Che grabbed the pot with the fricassee in it and threw the lot into the cauldron with the broth and swore four or five times at the Spaniard. "Brown-nosing," "ass-licking" in Mexico, adulacion, being servile in

Spain, was a great sin in Che's book and the word was his favorite one for chewing the men out."

The Communists

Carlos Rafael Rodríguez, the leading member of the PSP Central Committee, had arrived in the Sierra during the offensive, a little after July 21, to pledge his party's support to Fidel.

It was another of the PSP's contradictory moves, and probably arose from divisions within its upper circles. After keeping up its harsh political criticism of the July 26 Movement for the first year of the rebellion, the PSP ordered some cadres (for example, Acosta and Rivalta) to join the struggle in February 1958 and led the agrarian cadres to collaborate with the guerrillas in Oriente Province. In June, however, a month before that, the party wrote a manifesto calling on its members to leave the armed struggle.

Carlos Rafael met Fidel at the battle for Santo Domingo on July 26. Fidel told him to accompany him to the battleground and must have loved the way he threw himself on the ground when the bullets rang out. There is no record of the matters discussed at this meeting, but when Carlos Rafael returned to Havana in August, he began to mobilize the PSP networks in Camagüey and Las Villas to support the rebel army's forthcoming push toward the west of the island.

18. The Invasion

Fuentes

Two texts of Che's about the invasion are known: his letter reports to Fidel (Sept. 8–13 and Oct. 23, 1956) which appear in most editions of *Paisajes de la guerra revolucionaria* under the collective title "Sobre la invasión"; and a large part of *Una revolución que comienza*. Also useful are notes that Che sent to Camilo while their two columns were marching in tandem, the letter he sent to Faure Chomón on arriving in the Escambray Mountains, part of his speech at the School of Mining in 1963, a note to Angel Salgado from September 9, 1958, and the minutes of a Ministry of Industry board meeting held on December 5, 1964.

The most complete review of the invasion and No. 8 Column, for its precision and detail, is *De la Sierra Maestra al Escambray*, by Joel Iglesias. Iglesias provides additional material in his interview by Alfredo Reyes Trejo, "Mis vivencias junto al Che," and in his articles "En la guerra revolucionaria" and "La emboscada de cuatro compañeros."

Fidel's orders to Che and Camilo in Franqui's *Diario* and Martínez's *7RR* contain an interesting report on the Invasion along with other material.

There is a document about No. 8 Column and the invasion that was drawn up by the history department at the Revolutionary Armed Forces and has the virtue of having been reviewed by most of the cadres who actually took part. I was able to read it and compare it with my own version thanks to the kindness of one of those cadres. I was also able to interview four invaders: Leonardo Tamayo, Oscar Fernández Mell, Pablo Rivalta, and Jesús Parra.

The most interesting personal account is doubtless the one given by the then teenager Enrique Acevedo, in his book *Descamisado* and his article "Los últimos días en la Sierra Maestra." Unfortunately, he takes the story only as far as the clash at La Federal, where he was wounded. His brother and platoon chief at that time, Rogelio Acevedo, contributes even more in his articles "La Federal" and "El Che que yo conocí." Besides the latter, Fernández Mell's very precise articles "La sierra, la invasión, Las Villas" and "De las Mercedes a Gavilanes" are useful, as are Pablo Rivalta's remarks in his interview by Juana Carrasco; Leonardo Tamayo's interview by Katia Valdés and his article "Luchar junto al Che"; Harry Villegas's "Recuerdos del Che"; Alfonso Zayas's interview by Luis Pavón, "Cumpliendo la misión del jefe"; and Eliseo

Reyes's "Desde las Mercedes hasta Las Villas."

I consulted three contemporary accounts: by Emilio Surí about Eliseo "San Luis" Reyes, "El mejor hombre de la guerrilla"; by Larry Morales about the Cowboy Kid, "El jefe del pelotón suicida"; and a very precise military account by Colonel Alberto Ferrera, "El comandante Ernesto Guevara y la invasión de Las Villas."

Among general accounts the only ones worth mentioning, as they provide some small details, are Aldo Isidrón's "La victoriosa marcha hacia el Escambray, brillante proeza militar y revolucionaria" and "La invasión," both in *Bohemia* magazine; and Mariano Rodríguez's article "La invasión, epopeya de gigantes."

Mariano Rodríguez's articles published in *Bohemia* in 1982 are useful for an understanding of the geography of the zones covered. On the papers found by the army in the backpacks left behind in La Federal, see "Circular del mayor general Díaz Tamayo Sept. 30, 1958," and the booklet distributed by the army in *Gente*, "Desaliento y comunismo dentro del 26 de julio."

For an account of the invasion from Camilo's viewpoint, see his report to Fidel and in William Gálvez's *Camilo, señor de la vanguardia*, Guillermo Alvarez's book *Hablar de Camilo*, and Alvarez's article "Operación caja de tabaco."

The Directory's wait in "Cuando el Che llegó al Escambray" and "Che en el Escambray" by Faure Chomón, Betancourt's interview of Chomón, and Casañas's article "Che, una de sus proezas militares."

See also "Entre nosotros" by Zoila Rodríguez and the article "Invasión" in *Bohemia*.

How Many Were They? How Many Could Read?

Sources do not agree on the number of invaders; they cite 142 or 144, and the number waxed and waned as the days went by. Precision is also lacking as to their degree of literacy. Che said 90 percent were illiterate; others lower the figure to 52 percent, although most who were taught to read and write learned to do so at a most rudimentary level—like Joel Rodríguez or Edilberto del Río (dubbed "Illiteratic" by Che back in the Sierra Maestra). Edilberto del Río: "Once Che sent me to fetch a book, and I didn't know how to read so I gave it to him upside down and I told him: 'Che, I don't know what this says, it's written in English' and Che replied, Illiteratic, it's upside down.And from that moment on he gave me the nickname Illiteratic."

A Woman's Fate

Zoila Rodríguez and Che did not see each other again until after the revolution, when Che returned to Las Mercedes some months before leaving Cuba. "We held a conversation," said Zoila.

The Invasion Cadres

Very little is known about Mark Herman and very little of that recorded about this enigmatic character, who faded from the scene toward the end of the Cuban revolution. His name appears variously as Mark Herman or Herman Mark. He is said to have fought and been wounded at Guadalcanal in World War II. An instructor for Che's recruits in the early months of 1958, he appears to have been a disagreeable character who went by the book and was not well liked by the men. But Che must have trusted him greatly, to have given him an important post during the invasion.

Manuel Hernández Osorio was born March 17, 1931, in Diamante, a neighborhood in the outskirts of Santa Rita, in Oriente Province. He was born to a Spanish campesino and a woman of mixed race whose father owned a little store. As a teenager he was always on horseback, his enormous energy concealed in the figure of a skinny, gangling youth. He had worked as a machete cutter; later he wheeled a cart in the Charco Redondo mines, where he founded a July 26 Movement chapter and stole dynamite. He decided to take up arms and, with some others, went to look for the rebels in the Sierra. His friends gave up; he persisted and was found by a patrol who said, to test him, that they were from Batista's army.

"Tough luck, because I've come to join up with Fidel Castro."

The March 13 Revolutionary Directory

After the failed attack on the National Palace and the cadres dissolving, the Directorio was rebuilt. There was a landing in Nuevitas, and an armed front was set up in Las Villas. Actions resumed in Havana.

Besides the sources already mentioned, see "Historia del II Frente Nacional del Escambray," "13 de marzo, asalto al Palacio Nacional," Guillermo García's in Sexto's work "El pacto reiterado," "Bandidismo en el Escambray" by Crespo and "Segundo Frente Nacional del Escambray, negación del ejército rebelde."

19. More Hills, More Problems

Sources

Che fortunately left many written accounts of this period. There are fragments of "Un pecado de la revolución," which are usually published as an appendix to *Paisajes de la guerra revolucionaria* and to *Una revolución que comienza*. He also sent many notes to Faure Chomón and Fidel Castro, many of which are reproduced in Rosado's work. Details of Batista's November–December offensive are in Franqui's *Diario*.

I have already drawn on much of the material for *La batalla del Che, Santa Clara*.

The radio interview with Camilo and the one by Radio Rebelde can be found in their entirety in *Días de combate;* extracts appear in *Diciembre del 58* and Franqui's *Diario*.

Faure Chomón's memoirs are essential; he drew on them for his articles "Cuando el Che llegó al Escambray" and "Che en el Escambray," and especially for the unpublished interview by Betancourt.

For Enrique Oltuski's view, I relied on my interview with him in February 1995, on a long interview in Gálvez's book *Camilo, señor de la vanguardia* and Oltuski's article "Gente del llano." For Bordón's viewpoint, I used an interview by Isidrón, "Che, ejemplo de moral revolucionaria, audacia y modestia," as well as the eyewitness account drawn on by Gálvez.

Observations by campesinos in the area are from an interview by Navarro with someone who wished to remain anonymous; from "Por la ruta invasora del Che. De Gavilanes al Pedrero," by Mariano Rodríguez; and from "El Pedrero en el camino del Che, reportaje en dos tiempos," by Juan Sánchez.

For Che's relations with Aleida March, see Nydia Sarabia's article "La mujer villaclareña en la lucha patria" and Castellanos's and Villegas's memoirs in Cupull and González's book *Entre nosotros*.

The best overall view appears in Fernández Mell's works and in the article "Estrategia del Che en Las Villas" by Enrique Buznego and Luis Rosado.

The battle at Güinía de Miranda can be reconstructed on the basis of eyewitness accounts by Parra, Figueredo, and Argudín in "Güinía de Miranda," by Rosado; "Güinía de Miranda, primera victoria de la columna 8 en el frente de Las Villas," by Isidrón, and "La campaña del Che en Las Villas," by Fernández Mell.

On the El Pedrero pact and relations between Che and the Directory, see Faure Chomón's above-mentioned works, my October-November-December 1991 interview with Víctor Dreke for the book *El año en que estuvimos en ninguna parte,* the article "El pacto reiterado," by Luis Sextor, and the book *Bajando del Escambray* by Enrique Rodríguez. For a Front II viewpoint, see "10 de noviembre, Escambray heroico" by Max Lesnik.

On Tirso's photo sessions in the Escambray mountains, see "Che y una vieja cámara," by Clara Velia, and "Fotos a Tirso," by González Bello. The best pictures from this stage of the war are in a *Cuba Internacional* article called "Guerra en el Escambray."

For Camilo's presence with Che in the counteroffensive, see Gálvez, *Camilo, señor de la vanguardia.* Ricardo Martínez's book *7RR* describes the No. 8 Column radio station. For the Caballete de Casa base, Juana Carrasco's interview of Pablo Rivalta, and Abreu's book.

Also see "Sobre la invasión," by Joel Iglesias; "El Vaquerito y el pelotón suicida," by Leonardo Tamayo, and *Cuba, la lucha por la libertad,* by Hugh Thomas.

Víctor Bordón

Bordón was a sugar worker who took up arms at the end of 1956 to avoid repression; he had not been included in the July 26 Movement's planned uprising in Las Villas. After the failed April strike, the new provincial coordinator, Enrique Oltuski, set up the guerrilla campaign in the Escambray Mountains, with a vague undefined relationship to Front II (military subordination, but a presence in Front II's high command). Bordón had suffered all sorts of hardships; his guerrillas had been harassed by Front II, which even attacked one of their camps to take arms from them and then kept him prisoner for four days at the beginning of October when he went to protest. A threat by Camilo when he arrived in Las Villas freed him.

Front II

An objective view of Front II is extremely difficult to put together. Guevara fans, particularly those close to the Directorio, paint a bleak picture, ignoring the better aspects of the group run by Eloy Gutiérrez Menoyo. Tension between the latter and Fidel went back to their university days; in the Sierra days, Gutiérrez called Che and Fidel "Ñángaras," uncomplimentary slang for Communists.

Front II's military actions were not outstanding; the group's official history reports no more than a few skirmishes with the army, in Río Negro, Charco Azul, and La Diana.

Enrique Oltuski: "They always felt they owned Las Villas Province, and they always thought they would dominate it when the time came in the revolution. They expected to be a force to reckon with when the revolution triumphed."

Che does not mention his relations with Gutiérrez during the Las Villas period, although there are records of several meetings between them—for example, the Placetas operation, on which Gutiérrez accompanied him, and another occasion on which they shook hands, as reported in a special edition of *Bohemia* at the end of the war.

José Ramón Herrera told me that Che bent over backward to maintain good relations with Front II. Once, a hundred Remingtons, which Nazario Sargent had landed on the coast and which were meant for Front II, ended up in Che's hands. Che gave them to Gutiérrez: **They're not ours,** he said.

Enrique Oltuski

The police dismembered the regional leadership of the July 26 Movement in las Villas at the end of 1957, using information they had extracted under torture. All the key cadres were arrested. The Havana leadership commissioned Enrique Oltuski to rebuild the organization in Las Villas.

Oltuski, the son of Ukrainian immigrants, had studied engineering in the U.S. and was a member of a José Martí–leaning fraternity. "My conscience pricked me even when I returned from the U.S. My comrades were fighting and dying in Cuba, while I was living well in the U.S. Every day I used to say I had to go back to Cuba, so one day I got up and went. When I got back I wasn't a member of the M26, but the MNR, directed by Professor García Bárcenas." Oltuski joined the M26 when the MNR merged with it, and helped draft a political program.

He organized the April strike in Las Villas. "The movement suffered a terrible blow when the strike failed, especially when many members quit."

The PSP in Las Villas

Taurino Terraza: "I took up arms under the Party's orders in 1958, with the Directorio 'He's okay, he's a good cook, but he's a Communist.' In October I told Faure that Che was approaching and that the Party had ordered me to go and work as a scout for him. I went to hand over my rifle to Faure, and he said, 'Keep it. We and they are all the same. We'll all go and welcome Che.' "

Oltuski: "There was a conflict with the PSP. I felt that Communist ideas were very advanced for that time in Cuba and that the Communists were authoritarian and sectarian. Furthermore, they did not support the revolution. I approached the Communists in Las Villas, but the PSP did not support the armed struggle, which I still felt was the only way to beat Batista."

Alberto Fernández Montes de Oca

Called Pacho or Pachungo by his family. Born 1933 in San Luis, Oriente Province. Moved to Santiago when four years old. As a boy, worked in a café owned by his parents in a working-class neighborhood full of prostitutes, while studying in a teacher training college where he made contact with Frank País and Tey's group. He graduated but did not find work as a teacher, because he was on a political blacklist. Next he studied journalism, but did not graduate, then emigrated to the U.S. in 1956 and survived without work but refused to accept help from his family. Back in Cuba, he was brutally beaten by the police in a student demonstration and imprisoned in 1957. He left for Mexico, took part in an expedition that was shipwrecked, survived because he was a good swimmer, wandered around Mexican jungles where he lived on monkey meat, and was arrested. He emigrated to the U.S. again, then arrived in Cuba in late 1957 disguised as an insurance salesman. His brother Orlando had just been murdered. He worked with the M26 in Santa Clara and went up to the Escambray Mountains in November 1958. See Alfredo Reyes, "Capitán Alberto Fernández

Montes de Oca," and Mariano Rodríguez, "Abriendo senderos" and "El escalón más alto."

20. The Lightning Campaign

Sources

Che left few known written accounts of this period: his report on the battle for Fomento, a message to the Placetas Red Cross, and parts of *Una revolución que comienza.*

I have cannibalized my book *Santa Clara, la batalla del Che* for this chapter and incorporated fresh material, such as *The Winds of December* by Dorschner and Fabricio, Alberto Castellano's eyewitness account in *Entre nosotros,* and my interview of Colonel José Ramón Herrera.

Also see "La batalla de Santa Clara," by Rolando Cubela; "Diciembre de fuego," by Aldo Isidrón; the book *Las Villas,* edited by Lisandro Otero; "Se inicia la lucha en el Escambray," by René Rodríguez; "Saber al Che frente a nosotros," by Julio Martí; "Fomento, 100 fusiles para la fuerza de la libertad," by Carlota Guillot; "Diciembre de fuego," by Elena Otero; "El Vaquerito," by Larry Morales; "Luchar junto el Che," by Victoriana Quintana and Freddy Torres; "Las Villas bajo las balas," by José Lorenzo Fuentes; "Corrió la noticia; el Che está herido," by Isidrón; "Desde la Sierra Maestra hasta Las Villas," by René Rodríguez; "La debacle del tren blindado," by Caridad Miranda; "Zafarrancho en Santa Clara, la batalla final," by Mario Kuchilán; "La batalla de Santa Clara," by Núñez Jiménez; "Placetas, un pueblo que forjó su liberación," by Eduardo Martín and Benito Cuadrado; "Diciembre del 58," by Buznego, Castillo, and Alvarez; "El cerco de Santa Clara," by Augusto Benítez; "La campaña del Che en Las Villas," by Fernández Mell; and "El mejor hombre de la guerrilla," by Surí.

My interviews of Pablo Rivalta in 1987 and of Aleida March in February 1988 were essential.

Plots

Among the many plots being hatched by the military during the last months of the dictatorship to offer Batista an easy way out, one had an effect on the battle for Santa Clara. Colonel Rosell, acting under the name of Cantillo, made contact with "Echamendía" (Israel Suárez de la Paz), a member of the Havana underground who was in Santa Clara. Echamendía took a message to Che from Río Chaviano asking for a cease-fire, incidentally telling Che about the armored train. See *The Winds of December.*

21. The Mau Mau in Santa Clara

Sources

Although it was doubtless Che's most important military feat and he would have found it one of the most exciting to write about, he never did write up the episode for his *Paisajes de la guerra revolucionaria.* This was probably due to lack of time. Only a part of *Una revolución que comienza* deals with Santa Clara. When she agreed to review my account of the battle of Santa Clara, Aleida March told me that under pressure of events Che had written nothing in those days, so there was no record of them in his war diaries. Some notes about his military ideas come from *Guerra de guerrillas.*

Again, as for the previous chapter, I have cannibalized my book *La batalla del Che, Santa Clara,* especially chapters 10 through 15.

Descamisado, by Enrique Acevedo, is an excellent account of the events; there is a feeling of chaos in the battle that only he has been able to convey. Accounts by his brother Rogelio Acevedo, Pedro de la Hoz's interview with him and his extensive account in Dorschner and Fabricio's *The Winds of December* are also first-rate.

Fernández Mell has written a pair of fascinating accounts, "La batalla de Santa Clara" and "La campaña del Che en Las Villas." He expanded on these in an interview

with me in Havana. Núñez Jiménez produced three very important accounts: "El tren blindado," "El Che y un instante de la rendición de Santa Clara," and "Santa Clara, la batalla final."

Also see "Con el Che en la batalla de Santa Clara," by Rodríguez de la Vega; "Tres relatos inéditos," an interview of Lolita Rosell by M. A. Capote; "La batalla de Santa Clara," by José Lorenzo Fuentes; "En zafarrancho. Santa Clara, la batalla final," by Mario Kuchilán; "Antes de la gran batalla," by Arístides Sotonavarro; "Desde la Sierra Maestra hasta Las Villas," by Rodríguez Zaldívar; "El capitán descalzo habla de su amigo el Vaquerito," by Nelson García and Osvaldo Rodríguez; "Diciembre de fuego. Santa Clara 1958. Semblanza de una batalla," by Aldo Isidrón; "Batalla victoriosa," by Luis Rosado; "El tren blindado," (including an eyewitness account by Ramón Pardo), by Orlando Contreras; "Che, arquitecto de una victoria," by Luis Adrián Betancourt; my interview of Pablo Rivalta; Leonardo Tamayo's eyewitness account in "Che Guevara, facetas de un jefe militar," by Katia Valdés; "Víctor Dreke habla sobre el combate en el escuadrón 31," by Víctor Dreke; and "Consecuente con sus principios," by Teresa Valdés.

22. Day One of the Revolution

Sources

Che left very little by way of a written account of the first and last day of the revolution. See *Una revolución que comienza* and "Un pecado de la revolución," in *Paisajes de la guerra revolucionaria.*

The most interesting material is from Enrique Oltuski's article "El día de la victoria," which complements the interview he granted me; and from "La batalla de Santa Clara," by Fernández Mell, which was reviewed by Che. Núñez Jiménez's three accounts must also be considered: "La batalla de Santa Clara," "El Che y un instante de la rendición de Santa Clara," and "Santa Clara, la batalla final."

Other important sources were the interview with M. A. Capote; *The Winds of December*, by Dorschner and Fabricio; my interview with José Ramón Herrera; and the conversation with Mustelier that appears in the short film *Viento del Pueblo* by Orlando Rojas.

Also see the AP wire datelined Dec. 31, Havana; "Cómo se enteró Fidel de la caída de Batista," by Pardo Llada; "Esto fue lo que ocurrió en Columbia después de la caída del régimen," by Villaronda; "Cámara de torturas en Santa Clara," by Samuel Feijó; "Prisión y muerte de Joaquín Casillas," "Después de la victoria: primeras horas en la capital"; "Camilo de Yaguajay a Columbia," by Iván Colás; *7RR*, by Ricardo Martínez; *En el último año de aquella república*, by Ramiro Abreu.

Victory Was Won Not Only in Las Villas

Following history from Che's point of view may give the false impression that everything was at stake in Santa Clara, whereas it is evident that although the engagement was decisive, the main combat took place in Oriente Province, where Fidel Castro was encircling Santiago for a final attack on December 31, after the battle for Baffo ended on December 30.

Che Goes to La Cabaña

Some historians believe that Fidel sent Che to La Cabaña rather than Columbia, where the most important garrison in Havana was based, so as to sideline him; in this view, Fidel distrusted Che's radical stance. Carlos Franqui: "What reason did Fidel have to send him to La Cabaña, a secondary position?" *(Diario de la revolución).*

Two of the most obvious reasons would seem to have been, first, Che's nationality—he did not know Havana; and second, Camilo's column was fresher.

Firing Squads in Santa Clara

Che owned up to signing twelve death warrants in Santa Clara, although the journalist he told this to, Piñeiro from *Prensa Libre,* could find only six cases in making his own tally. José Ramón Herrera, in an interview he granted me, spoke of fourteen deaths, but said that his memory could be failing him as he could never reach that number when he tried to make a list. Captain Suárez Gayol ("Blondie") told me in an interview that the executions were a matter of "social cleansing" and added to the list I compiled the name of one Capetillo. Police Chief Rojas's name does not appear on the list, because he was very summarily tried and shot after Che had left the town.

23. The Long January of 1959

Sources

In some of his articles, Che wrote separate notes on the first month of the revolution; these may be found in "Un pecado de la revolución," "Notas para el estudio de la ideología de la revolución cubana," "Guerra y población campesina." Che's talk "Proyecciones sociales del ejército rebelde" appears in every edition of his works.

A visit to the La Cabaña museum is important, not only for the documentation but because there are parts of the environment of the fighting that are preserved as they were in Che's day.

For the arrival of the columns, see Franqui's *Diario* and Colás's article "Che, de Santa Clara a La Cabaña." There certainly are discrepancies over the time Che's column entered La Cabaña. While Martínez Páez says it was at 1:30, Castellanos, Che's driver at the time, places it between two and four, and Núñez Jiménez at four.

Of use are "El Che que conoce al pueblo" in *Juventud rebelde* and *Un hombre bravo* by Cupull and González, although the first is inaccurate as it often gives the articles' date of publication as the date the events took place.

For an overall view, see *Cuba, la lucha por la libertad,* by Hugh Thomas, and *La toma del poder* by Toledo Bastard.

Vitally important were my interviews with José Manuel Manresa, Fernández Mell, Vilaseca, and Hilda Guevara.

Cuban press reports from this period are very interesting, particularly "Entró primero la columna de Ameijeiras"; "Che Guevara habla para Prensa Libre. Lo que interesa ahora es defender la libertad de Cuba"; and "Fue asaltante en el Moncada y vino con Fidel en el *Granma*" (interview with Ramiro Valdés), all three by Sergio Piñeiro; "El directorio aspira a ver a una patria nueva" (interview with Faure Chomón), by Heli Montoto; "La entrada del presidente Urrutia en palacio"; "Habla el comandante Guevara"; "Los fusilamientos y los maldonados," by JCM; and "Las ejecuciones en Cuba," by Jules Dubois.

Also see "Un gran muerto invencible," by Guillén; "Che y Pinares hablan de Camilo"; *En marcha con Fidel*, by Núñez Jiménez; "Fidel y el Che," by Santiago Aroca; *Mi hijo el Che*, by Ernesto Guevara Lynch; "El embajador Smith, servidor del déspota"; *La Sierra Maestra y más allá; The Fourth Floor*, by Earl Smith; *World in Revolution*, by Herbert Matthews; *The Black Beret: The Life and Meaning of Ernesto Che Guevara*, by Harris; *Che Guevara, años decisivos*, by Hilda Gadea; "Osvaldo Sánchez," by J. C. Fernández; *Retrato de familia con Fidel*, by Carlos Franqui; "Crónica de un periodista soviético en Cuba," by Vasili Chichkov; "Tiene la palabra el Che Guevara," by Julio Martí; "Diario de sesiones del senado de Chile, séptima sesión," Oct. 18, 1967; "Prensa Latina, un desafío" and interview with Borrego in *Entre nosotros*.

U.S. attempts to create a third option neither pro Batista nor pro Castro, are well reported in *The Winds of December*, by Dorschner and Fabricio and *The Fourth Floor*, by Smith.

24. The Battle for Agrarian Reform

Sources

Various editions of Che's works relating to this period contain much correspondence. His reflections on "Year 1" also appear in *Una revolución que comienza* and several important articles, speeches, and television appearances: "¿Qué es un guerrillero?"; "Discurso en El Pedrero" (speech); the epilogue of *Guerra de guerrillas;* the October 28, 1964, memorial speech for Camilo Cienfuegos; Che's television appearance on March 20, 1960; the open letter to Franqui concerning Che's convalescence in Tarará; and his comments on the agrarian reform in a letter to Ernesto Sábato, April 12, 1960.

A copy of the *Official Gazette* of February 7, 1960, declaring Che Cuban is in the La Cabaña museum, as is a medical certificate diagnosing his condition. His original office may be seen in the same museum. His military file is reprinted in Teresa Valdés's article "Al lado de cada rebelde un maestro."

Cupull and González's account "22 años de cronología" are useful for context.

On the lengthy debate over agrarian reform, see *Cuba, la lucha por la libertad*, by Hugh Thomas; *En marcha con Fidel*, by Núñez Jiménez; *Los guerrilleros en el poder*, by K. S. Karol; *Cuba, Socialism and Development*, by René Dumont; *Anatomía de una revolución*, by Leo Huberman and Paul Sweezy; *Retrato de familia con Fidel*, by Carlos Franqui.

On Prensa Latina and *Verde Olivo:* "Prensa Latina, un desafío"; *Guevara*, by Rodolfo Walsh; "Faltaba papel y tinta pero salía," by Elsa Blaquier; "Así se cumplen las órdenes."

On Che's relations with his daughter Hilda, see the interview with her by Román Orozco, "Mi padre tenía un gran sentido del humor," and Roberto Travieso, "Mi papá el Che."

Some elements from articles: "Sentirlo

más cercano," by Marta Gómez Ferrals; "Un gran muerto invencible," by Nicolás Guillén; "Con el Che por Sudamérica," by Aldo Isidrón; "Cariño de buenos hermanos," by Mariano Rodríguez; "Mi compañero de los aires," by Casilda Pereira; "Llegaron los barbuditos, avisen al Che," by Roberto de los Reyes; and *El Che que yo conocí*, by José Pardo.

Of great use were my interviews of Jorge Risquet, Raúl Maldonado, and Oscar Fernández Mell.

The Famous "Siquitrilla"

Risquet: "Camilo's term came from an article by the journalist about hunters aiming at a little bone in the necks of "la siquitrilla," a little native bird, and in the ranchers' association's delivery of 5,000 heifers hoping only for inconsequential land reform. Comparable to our using a cannon to swat a fly.

25. "You Cannot Dream in the Shade of a Pyramid"

Sources

Che gave a not very consequential account of the tour in a series of articles published in *Verde Olivo* over the following months: "La República Arabe Unida, un ejemplo," "La India, país de grandes contrastes," "Recupérase Japón de la tragedia atómica," "Indonesia y la sólida unidad de su pueblo," "Intercambio comercial con Ceilán y Pakistán," and "Yugoeslavia, un pueblo que lucha por sus ideales." After he returned, Che gave a roundup of the tour on the television program *Comentarios económicos* on September 14 and in a news conference published in *Verde Olivo* the same day. The letter from India is part of the collection of Ernesto Guevara's letters that his father considered publishing in *Mi hijo el Che* but left for a possible third volume of correspondence after the revolution triumphed. It has only been accidentally published in González Acosta's book.

There are two lengthy accounts by people who accompanied Che: José Pardo Llega's, in *El Che que yo conocí*, and Salvador Vilaseca's, in an interview with me.

Odds and ends of information are drawn from articles "El primer embajador," by Reynaldo Lugo, and "Fidel y el Che," by Santiago Aroca; in the book *Prensa Latina, un desafío;* and in my interview with Raúl Maldonado.

For Che's relations with Nasser, see the account by Mohamed Heikal based on Nasser's papers. Context from Thomas and Abreu's books.

2.6.   Return

Sources

A dozen of Che's speeches from this period appear in various editions of his works, including the three speeches given at universities in Oriente Province, Las Villas, and Havana; the farewell speech in Abrantes and Jorge Villa; and the speech at the National Palace rally on October 26. Che also wrote two helpful articles— "América desde el balcón afroasiático" and "Tareas industriales de la revolución en años venideros"—and made two television appearances, the second, about the fledgling industrialization department, on October 20, 1960. His "Palabras del Che a la policía" are excluded from most editions of his works, but appear in a leaflet edited by the Interior Ministry.

Once more, Franqui's *Retrato de familia con Fidel* is essential reading. For Camilo's death, see "Apareció para siempre" and Che's own prologue to *Guerra de guerrillas*.

On the beginning of voluntary work: "Conmemoran aniversario 30 del primer trabajo voluntario," by Felipa Suárez, "Che Guevara iniciando el trabajo voluntario en Cuba," by Rubén Castillo, and Martí's interview of Eliseo de la Campa. Very important for finalizing details were my interviews with Salvador Vilaseca, Raúl Maldonado, and Valdés Gravalosa.

27. "Every Time a Guevara Starts a Business, It Goes Bust"

Sources

Besides writing *Guerra de guerrillas*, Che wrote many articles in this period. The series of nineteen, "Sin bala en el directo" (Random Shots), on international affairs was published April 10–August 14, 1960, written under pressure with a certain sense of humor, using everyday language and in a pedagogical vein: "El payaso macabro y otras alevosías," "El más poderoso enemigo y otras boberías," "El desarme continental y otras claudicaciones," "No seas bobo compadre y otras advertencias," "La democracia representativa surcoreana y otras mentiras," "Cacareo, los votos argentinos y otros rinocerontes," "El salto de rana, los organismos internacionales y otras genuflexiones," "Los dos grandes peligros, los aviones piratas y otras violaciones," "Estambul, Puerto Rico, Caimanera y otras bases de discusión," "Ydígoras, Somoza y otras pruebas de amistad," "El plan Marshall, el plan Eisenhower y otros planes," "Nixon, Eisenhower y otros toques de atención," "El café, el petróleo, el algodón y otras cuotas," "La acusación ante la OEA, las Naciones Unidas y otras fintas," "Beltrán, Frondizi y otras razones de pesos," "Las bases de submarinos, las de cohetes y otros engendros," "La corte de los milagros y otros motes de la OEA," "Para muestra basta un botón y otras historias breves," "Había una vez un central azucarero y otras leyendas populares."

The series "Consejos al combatiente" began on May 8, 1960, with "La disciplina de fuego en el combate" and ended fifteen articles later with "La artillería de bolsillo III" on October 22. These articles do not appear in the latest edition of Che's selected works, although a compilation was being prepared by the publishers of *Verde Olivo* at the time of writing.

An interesting correspondence from 1959–60 may be found in several editions of the works. The letter "Emplaza Guevara to Conrado Rodríguez" is in *Revolución*, as is a letter wishing his parents a happy new year. The article "Cuba, su economía, su comercio exterior, su significado en el mundo actual," written at the end of 1964, refers to his chairmanship of the central bank.

The transcripts of three television appearances were most helpful: on the economics and planning series, April 15, 1961; on the Home University series *Soberanía política e independencia económica,* on March 20, 1960, and on *Ante la prensa,* October 20, 1960. The February 4, 1960 letter is not in Che's collected works, but appears in a leaflet. Important speeches discussed in this chapter are the one to textile workers on February 7, 1960, and the one on May 20, at the opening of an industrial exhibition.

Essential for depicting Che's activities as central bank chairman were interviews with Salvador Vilaseca, Raúl Maldonado, Valdés Gravalosa, and Enrique Oltuski; Edward Boorstein's book *The Economic Transformation of Cuba;* "La revolución entró en el banco," by Susana Lee; "Che ministro, Che funcionario," by Angela Soto; "Reportaje a un billete"; "Aquella visita a una agencia bancaria," by María Isabel Morales; the booklet "La presencia del Che en el Banco Nacional de Cuba y la selección del 26 de noviembre como Día del Economista"; "El recuerdo y sus propias palabras"; "Su incurable pasión creadora" by Sara Más.

There are many reports on the photographs of Che's: "Una foto recorre el mundo," by Alberto Korda; "El regalo de la foto del Che"; "Entrevista con un reportero gráfico," by Gabriel Molina; "La efigie simbólica del Che," by Angela Capote; "Visa europea para una imagen nuestra," by Toni Piñera; "Treinta años de la foto más famosa del mundo," by René Ascuy; "En cargo de la conciencia," by Alina Perera and Eduardo Jiménez; and "Che en el recuerdo de dos fotógrafos," by Santiago Cardosa.

Some elements in this chapter come from Jean-Paul Sartre's *Huracán sobre el azúcar* and "Vengan temprano a medianoche, me dijo el director del Banco Nacional"; Castellanos's memoirs, in *Entre nosotros;* "Yo soy el niño de la foto," by Gerardo Hernández; "A Preview of History?"

by James Higgins; "Un extraordinario formador de cuadros," by Joaquín Oramas; "Periódico de la palabra," by José Pardo; "Che, la ventana encendida," by Luis Pavón; "Un montón de memorias," by Fernández Retamar; "The Legacy of Che Guevara," by I. F. Stone; and the documentary *Una foto que recorrió el mundo.*

On Che's first contacts with Soviet officials, see "Mis recuerdos de Cuba," by Anastas Mikoyan; "Ernesto Che Guevara"; "Las relaciones cubano-soviéticas en la revolución: historia y documentos," by Luis Miranda; "Cuba, el camino de la revolución," by Oleg Darushenkov; and "Mis encuentros con Che Guevara," by Nikolai Kudin.

Also useful were my interview with Fernández Mell; Guerra's book *Barro y cenizas;* "El futuro de la economía cubana," by Leo Huberman and Paul Sweezy; the interview with Raúl León in *Entre nosotros;* and "The Castro Regime in Cuba," U.S. State Department, NSF, Country File, Gordon Chase file vol. A, LBJ Library, *City, State.*

For some minor elements, I drew on "Un montón de elementos," by Fernández Retamar; *En Cuba,* by Ernesto Cardenal; *Los guerrilleros en el poder,* by K. S. Karol; "The Castro Regime in Cuba," U.S. State Department, NSF, Country File, Gordon Chase file vol. A, LBJ Library, and the films *Historias de la revolución,* by Tomás Gutiérrez Alea, and *Che,* by Enrique Pineda.

The Spade Factory Bought on the Tour

Che: And it is worth going to see the spade factory to get an idea of what should not be done in development policy. . . . The factory is a press that turns a metal sheet into a lunch pail, and makes it look like that. Yes, it's no more than a press, it's no spade factory, nevertheless it already has all the awesome features of a factory, with its office, its specially tiled bathroom for the most distinguished workers, and four offices and four bathrooms for four groups of workers spread out in the same area.

28. Factories and Deodorants

Sources

Che gave an account of the journey in "Comparecencia televisada acerca de la firma del acuerdo entre los países socialistas" and several speeches in the period immediately following, among them his speech to the militias in Cabañas, Pinar del Río. His article "Un pecado de la revolución," should also be consulted, as should his contribution to the bimonthly Ministry of Industry board meeting, July 14, 1962.

The tour may be followed in detail in Cupull and González's history *Un hombre bravo;* in Lavretsky's biography, *Ernesto Che Guevara;* in Llompart's interview in *Entre nosotros;* and in the article "Lo que el Che vio en la URSS," by Mario G. del Cueto. My interview with Raúl Maldonado was essential.

29. Girón Beach

Sources

Several of Che's speeches cover this period: those to the national convention of technical advisory committees; to outstanding workers; to the national sugar workers' convention in Santa Clara; to the militias in Pinar del Río; and at a memorial ceremony for Guiteras. Also useful were a couple of Che's articles: "Contra el burocratismo" and "Cuba, excepción histórica o vanguardia en la lucha anticolonialista."

My interview of Enrique Oltuski provided essential information, as did Oltuski's article "¿Qué puedo decir?" Of importance are Edward Boorstein's book *The Economic Transformation of Cuba;* Orlando Borrego's leaflet "El estilo de trabajo del Che"; "Che, la ventana encendida" by Luis Pavón, and Pavon's prologue to *Días de combate;* the anthology of works on or by Che *Che: El recuerdo y sus propias palabras.* Also see CIA, Intelligence Memorandum, Directorate of Intelligence, "Cuba: Delay and Misdirection of the Industrial Production Program," November 1965.

Again, vitally important to me were interviews granted by Manresa, Gravalosa, and Maldonado, as were references by Acevedo in *Entre nosotros;* "Un día conocí al Che," by Tania Peña; "El alucinante viaje del yo al nosotros," by Eduardo Galeano; and *Mi amigo el Che,* by Ricardo Rojo.

Works on Girón–Bay of Pigs are abundant. Perhaps the most interesting is Peter Wyden's *Bay of Pigs,* along with an unpublished manuscript by Cuban novelist Juan Carlos Rodríguez, "La batalla inevitable," which he allowed me to read. Exciting eyewitness accounts include "Girón en la memoria," by Víctor Casaus; "Girón, la batalla más corta," by Efigenio Ameijeiras; "La batalla de Girón," by Quintín Pino Machado; "Diario de Girón," by Gabriel Molina; and "Amanecer en Girón," by Rafael del Pino. The best documentary history, including many eyewitness accounts from the Cuban side, appears in four volumes published by Ediciones R, edited by Lisandro Otero: *Playa Girón: derrota del imperialismo.* Concerning accounts by captured counterrevolutionaries, see "Historia de una agresión" and *El interrogatorio de La Habana,* by Hans Magnus Enzensberger. Recent CIA documents have been partially compiled in *Playa Girón, la gran conjura. Relatos de Girón,* by José Manuel Marrero, combines narrative with eyewitness accounts.

30. No Time to Get Tired

Sources

Che delivered many speeches and gave news conferences or made television appearances between April 1961 and April 1962. For this chapter, the following are essential: "Discurso de la graduación de las escuelas populares de estadística y dibu-

jantes mecánicos," "Conferencia en el ciclo Economía y Planificación de la Universidad Popular," "Discurso en la V sesión plenaria CIES, Punta del Este, 8 agosto," "Conferencia de prensa en Montevideo, 9 de agosto," "Intervención en la reunión del CIES, 16 agosto, 1961," "Discurso en la Universidad Nacional de Montevideo," "Comparecencia televisada en Cuba sobre la reunión de Punta del Este, 23 agosto 1961," "Discurso en la Primera Reunión Nacional de Producción, 27 agosto, 1961," "Discurso clausura en la Primera Asamblea de producción de la Gran Habana, 24 septiembre, 1961," "Charla a los trabajadores del Ministerio de Industria," "Discurso en la inauguración de la planta de Sulfometales Patricio Lumumba, 29 octubre, 1961," "Discurso en la conmemoración del 27 de noviembre de 1871," "Conferencia del curso de adiestramiento del Ministerio de Industria," "Intervención en TV del 27 de enero del 62." And see Che's articles "Discusión colectiva: decisón y responsabilidad única" and "Tareas ministeriales en años venideros." Also useful were Ministry of Industry board minutes from January 20 and March 10, 1962; abstract of the "Primera reunión nacional de producción" and "Intervención sobre el ausentismo y los males del trabajo"; the prologue to "El partido marxista-leninista," and minutes of the February 22, 1962, bimonthly meeting of the Ministry of Industry board.

Of great importance are interviews with Dumont in "Cuba Socialist and Development," K. S. Karol, in "Los guerrilleros en el poder," and Leo Huberman in "Cuba and the U.S.A.," with Juan Gelman, as well as "Che y el desarrollo de la economía cubana" by Carlos Rafael Rodríguez; "El pensamiento económico del Che" by Tablada; Borrego in "Entre nosotros" and CIA, Intelligence Memorandum, Directorate of Intelligence, "Cuba: Delay and Misdirection of the Industrial Production Program," November 1965.

Essential for Ministry of Industry activities were my interview of Valdés Gravalosa; Edward Boornstein's "The Economic Transformation of Cuba"; Angela Soto's article "Che comandante, Che ministro"; and chronologies by Cupull and González and in the magazine *Juventud Rebelde (Rebel Youth)*.

Also of interest were "Un constructor llamado Che," by Ciro Bianchi; "El Che entusiasta y consumado ajedrecista," by Ricardo Agancino; "El Che entusiasta ajedrecista" by José Barreras; "Su incurable pasión creadora," by Sara Mas; "El comandante Guevara en Punta del Este," by Manuel Galich; "Telefoto exclusiva," by Carlos María Gutiérrez; "Amigo, sus recuerdos del Che," by Eráclides Barrero; "Mi amigo el Che," by Ricardo Rojo (the only account of his meeting with Frondizi); "Los dos interlocutores eran muy distintos por su origen"; "Che, ejemplo de moral," by Aldo Isidrón; "Che ajedrecista," by Carlos Palacio; Martí's interview of Eliseo de la Campa; *L'ottobre cubano*, by Saverio Tuttino; and *Cuba no es una isla*, by Sol Arguedas. Also see "Operación Mongoose: una guerra interminable," "Antecedentes, estructura e ideología del partido Comunista de Cuba" by Hans Magnus Enzensberger; and "Resultado final de campaña."

Aircraft and Initiation Rites

Che had flown in a glider in his youth, in 1947. He flew solo for the first time at the end of 1959. It was traditional in Cuba to initiate a pilot flying solo for the first time: colleagues would dip him in a barrel of water, then throw dirt and pour oil on him. Che's comrades were terrified of him, however. He later confessed that he was hurt by their failure to subject him to the rite.

31. The Urge to Shoot Down Planes

Sources

Che wrote several articles during this period: "La influencia de la revolución cubana en América Latina"; "Táctica y estrategia de la revolución latinoamericana";

"Tareas industriales de la revolución en los años venideros"; and "El cuadro, columna vertebral de la revolución." He also made several key speeches: "El Che con las delegaciones fraternales extranjeras"; "En el aniversario de las organizaciones"; and "En el teatro América reunión sobre emulación en acto de la CTC." Also important are the minutes of a Ministry of Industry board meeting held July 14, 1962, and of the bimonthly meeting held September 28, 1962.

The missile crisis has been extensively dealt with in *The Cuban Missile Crisis, 1962*, edited by Laurence Chang and Peter Kornbluth; "L'occhio del barracuda," by Saverio Tutino; *Retrato de familia con Fidel*, by Carlos Franqui; *Fidel, un retrato crítico*, by Tad Szulc.

See also "Cuba en octubre," in *La senda de la guerrilla*, by Adolfo Gilly.

Che's participation in the crisis may be documented in "Cuando el Che estuvo en San Andrés de Ciaguanabo," by Julio Martí; "Cuando cantan los ruiseñores," and "Una cueva con historia," by Luis Ubeda.

Of great help in drafting this chapter were my interviews of Leonardo Tamayo, Miguel Figueras, Heras León, and Enrique de la Ossa, as well as the interview of Rogelio Acevedo in *Entre nosotros*.

Also see "¿Qué puedo decir?" by Enrique Oltuski; "La huella imborrable del guerrillero de América," by Rolando Montalbán; *Con la adarga al brazo*, by Mariano Rodríguez; Hilda Gadea, K. S. Karol, *Black Beret*, by Resnick and *KGB vs. CIA*, by David C. Martin.

32. "Even Che Couldn't Always Be like Che"

Sources

Original material by Che from this period: "Discurso en la Escuela de Minas del Frío"; letters to Lisandro Otero and Ezequiel Vieta; the prologue to "El partido marxista-leninista . . ." "Informe al consejo de ministros 1963," *Paisajes de la guerra revolucionaria* and his interruption at the Ministry of Industry board meeting, October 12, 1963.

Very interesting are Che's letter to Franqui, and Franqui's reply "Carta de Che a Redacción y una aclaración nuestra."

Franqui's *Retrato de familia con Fidel* was essential, as were my interviews with Miguel Figueras, Gravalosa, Jorge Risquet, Enrique de la Ossa, and Oscar Fernández Mell, and a February 1995 letter from Lázaro Buría. Also see "Che ministro, Che funcionario," by Angela Soto, and "Che, una nueva batalla," by Gerónimo Alvarez.

Anecdotes about Che's visits to factories are from "Con los creadores de la riqueza," by Ernesto Montero; "Esos refrescos que saben a jarabe de Tolú," by Guillermo Lagarde; "Cinco temas breves," by Siquitrilla; the documentary *Constructor cada día compañero*, by Pedro Chaskel; "Che en Gibara," by Pedro Ortiz; "Lecciones para no olvidar" Liset García.

On Che's passion for chess, see "Pasión por el deporte," by Severo Nieto; "Ajedrecista fuerte," by Adolfo Fernández; "El Che y el ajedrez," by Eleazar Jiménez; "El Che entusiasta y consumado ajedrecista," by Ricardo Agancino; and "El Che entusiasta ajedrecista," by José Luis Barreras.

Also see "Nuestra industria"; "Mi llamada es," by Ezequiel Vieta; *En Cuba*, by Ernesto Cardenal; "¿Qué puedo decir?" by Enrique Oltuski; "Un ejemplo de virtudes revolucionarias," by Alfonso Purón; "Cuba's First Venture in Africa: Algeria, 1961–65," by Piero Gleijeses; "En la brecha," by Gregorio Ortega; Rodolfo Walsh's foreword to *Los que luchan y los que lloran*, by Ricardo Masetti; "Un trabajador incansable," by Teresa Valdés; "Implications of Cuba's Renewed Campaign of Incitation to Violent Revolution in Latin America," addressed to Bowdler, NSF, Country File, Gordon Chase file, vol. A, LBJ Library.

Controversy

Those interested in the long controversy over surplus value theory and its implications in the agrarian-industrial management model for Cuba may consult "En torno a la cuestión de funcionamiento de la ley del valor en la economía cubana en los actuales momentos," by Alberto Mora, and "Sobre el concepto de valor: contestando algunas afirmaciones sobre el tema," by Ernesto Guevara.

The controversy has been divided into two parts for the sake of chronology; the second part is in chapter 33. Apart from original material, the controversy has been discussed in "El pensamiento del Che Guevara," by Michael Lowy; in vol. 2, chapter 7 of *Pensar al Che*, with contributions by Carlos Tablada, Pérez-Rolo, and Orlando Borrego; by Tablada himself, in "El pensamiento económico de Ernesto Che Guevara." The third part of José Arico's anthology *El socialismo y el hombre nuevo* includes a foreword by E. Mandel. Also helpful were no. 5 of the pamphlet series Pasado y Presente; chapter 3 of Roberto Massari's book *Che Guevara, grandeza y riesgo de la utopia;* Mandel's article "El debate económico en Cuba durante el período 1963–64," published in *Partisans* and which is included in *El socialismo y el hombre nuevo*. Also see Sergio de Santis's article "Debate sobre la gestión socialista en Cuba," in *Cuba, una revolución en marcha.*

33. 1964: In the Revolution's Basement

Sources

Che maintained some interesting correspondence during 1964; it is compiled in several editions of his works. There are also records of his speeches: "En la entrega de certificados de trabajo comunista," "En la asmablea de emulación del Ministerio de Industria," "En homenjae a Camilo Cienfuegos," "En la conmemoración del 30 de noviembre"; the March 20, 1964, speech in Geneva; the May 9, 1964, Ministry of Industry speech, and the August 2, 1964, speech at the Patrice Lumumba management school. Essential are Che's "Tareas fundamentales para 1965" and the Ministry of Industry board minutes from February

22, September 12, and December 5, 1964; the minutes of the April 20, 1964, ordinary meeting; "Informe de la Empresa Consolidada de los Silicatos," July 20, 1964; "Informe de la Empresa Consolidada de Equipos Eléctricos," May 11, 1964; "Informe de la Empresa Consolidada de Tenerías," August 8, 1964.

Two interviews are useful: the one by the Popular de Montevideo in Moscow, and "Tiene la palabra el Che Guevara."

The controversy may be followed up in Che's "Sobre el sistema presupuestario de financiamiento"; "Desarrollo y funciones del banco socialista en Cuba," by Fernández Font; "La banca, el crédito y el socialismo"; "Formas y métodos de la planificación socialista y nivel de desarrollo de las fuerzas productivas," by Charles Bettelheim; "Las categorías mercantiles en el período de transición," by Ernest Mandel; "La planificación socialista, su significado," by Che; "Características del funcionamiento de la empresa autofinanciada," by Juan Infante; and "Sobre el método de análisis de los sistemas de financiamiento," by Luis Alvarez Rom.

Of great use to me were interviews with Vilaseca and Hilda Guevara, as well as those Che granted to Travieso and Román Orozco.

Also important in reconstructing this period are "Lecciones para no olvidar" by Liset García; "El día en que el Che inauguró la fábrica de bujías," by Luis Lara; "Un constructor llamado Che," by Ciro Bianchi; "La última entrevista del Che en Moscú," by Igor Nemira; "El alucinante viaje del yo al nosotros" by Eduardo Galeano; "Che y los comités de calidad," by Carlos Tablada; "Entre la coexistencia y la revolución," by Adolfo Gilly; "El Che" and "Lleras fue amigo del Che," by Carlos Lleras Restrepo; "¿Qué puedo decir?" by Enrique Oltuski; and the documentary Hasta la victoria siempre, directed by Santiago Alvarez.

On Guanahacabibes: my interview with Gravalosa; "Che ministro, Che funcionario," by Angela Soto; "Un día sin ver el eucalipto," by Cazalis; "Lecciones para no olvidar," by Orlando Borrego; Francisco Martínez Pérez in Entre nosotros.

"Proceso al sectarismo," by Janette Habel and Fidel Castro, includes Fidel's lengthy speech at the trial. The February 26 State Department Intelligence Directorate memorandum is of interest on the same issue.

Also see Retrato de familia con Fidel, by Franqui; Che Guevara, grandeza y riesgo de la utopía, by Roberto Massari; "Castroism, Theory and Practice."

34. Latin America Again

Sources

Quotations from Che are from his letter to Ernesto Sábato, from his articles "Táctica y estrategia de la revolución Latinoamericana" and "La influencia de la revolución cubana en América Latina," and from his speech in honor of outstanding workers, August 21, 1962.

The meaning of "liberación": see Jorge Castañeda's interview of Ulises Estrada. Unfortunately, Commander Manuel Piñeiro, better known by his nickname "Barbarroja" ("Redbeard") has granted no interviews and written no (known) accounts of this period.

For links with future Sandinistas, particularly Carlos Fonseca, see two works by Tomás Borge: Carlos, el amanecer ya no es una tentación and La paciente impaciencia, and Iosu Perales's book Querido Che. The Sandinistas-to-be received $20,000 from Che, which they used to set up guerrilla campaigns in Río Coco and Bocay. One group was trained in mortar fire by Cuban militias, and Borge recalls that Fonseca "made friends with Commander Guevara" and, oddly enough, with Tamara Burke, a.k.a. Tania. The links went back to 1959 and continued until 1963.

for the first Peruvian guerrilla campaign and Bolivian collaboration, see Jesús Lara's book Guerrillero Inti Peredo. Béjar's account is from Humberto Vázquez-Viaña's work Antecedentes de la guerrilla del Che en Bolivia. It is interesting to see what Fidel has to say in his "Necessary Introduction" to Che's Bolivian diary.

For Hugo Blanco's exciting story, see his own book "Hugo Blanco y la rebelión campesina" by Víctor Villanueva, "Cuzco, Tierra y muerte" by Hugo Neira and the pentalogy by Peruvian novelist Manuel Scorza, probably one of the most interesting sagas of Latin America: *Redoble por Rancas, Historia de Garabombo el invisible, El jinete insomne, Cantar de Agapito Robles,* and *La tumba del relámpago.*

Fidel's speech on the twentieth anniversary of Che's death confirmed that Che was much more than a collaborator with the EGP, and referred to the project as one of the "first efforts undertaken by him."

On Martínez Tamayo's presence in Bolivia and his support network, see "Antecedentes, preparativos y principales acciones de la guerrilla del Che en Bolivia," by Alina Martínez, and Lídice Valenzuela's interview with Rodolfo Saldaña.

On Masetti's guerrilla campaign, "El castroismo . . . ," by Régis Debray, is interesting, as is the open letter to Ricardo Rojo by two of the survivors, Méndez and Jouvé, published in "El Che y los argentinos." See also "Los guerrilleros de Salta" by Frontini and above all Ricardo Walsh's foreword to *Los que luchan y los que lloran* by Ricardo Masetti himself. On his training in Africa, and Algerian support for the operation, see "Cuba's First Venture in Africa: Algeria, 1961–65," by Piero Gleijeses.

The book *Mártires del periodismo* gives Ricardo Masetti's date of death as April 21, 1964, with no backup source; this is probably the date he disappeared. On the presence of Cubans in Masetti's guerrilla campaign, Sánchez Salazar's book and my interview with Oscar Fernández Mell were helpful, as was the interview Juan Gelman gave me in Mexico City. Of interest is a fictionalized account of the EGP, doubtless based on firsthand evidence, from the third part of *Los guerrilleros* by Iverna Codina. Che's search for Masetti's body as recounted in *La senda de la guerrilla,* by Adolfo Gilly.

Essential for Tania's entrance on the scene is the above-mentioned interview with Ulises Estrada, her companion, who by the way says that Tania and Che met twice, once at the beginning of her training and again at the end. Also see Marta Rojas and Mirta Rodríguez Calderón's book *Tania, la guerrillera inolvidable.*

Iván-Renán's identity was provided to the author by one of his colleagues. The author tried several times to make contact with him but failed. Oddly, Miguel Bonasso identified him as Andrés Barahona López in an article published by *Proceso* magazine in Mexico.

Martínez Tamayo

It is said this man, with a tough Galician face was born the day the lions came to town, in Mayarí, in 1938. He had to quit school at an early age to drive tractors. He took up arms in 1957 after stealing a shotgun from his grandfather, fought with Raúl Castro in Front II, and worked for the secret services.

He had already completed an important mission in Guatemala in the midst of the missile crisis. He was a generous character, capable of giving away everything he had to whoever needed it. He had uncommon physical strength. He did not like school and went only as far as fourth grade. He grew flowers all his life; knowledgeable about roses, he grew them at home. He had learned to fly aircraft after the revolution triumphed. (See *Ellos lucharon con el Che* and *Con la adarga al brazo,* both by Mariano Rodríguez, and "Capitán José María Martínez Tamayo" by Alfredo Reyes Trejo.)

Víctor Dreke: "Captain José María Martínez Tamayo was a strong, affectionate white man of few words, who loved Che like hell and idolized him. He got on well with the comrades, was daring, and took personal risks. He didn't like to speak about his own affairs. He preferred underground intelligence struggles. But he was not a bad guerrilla fighter."

Onï Tania

The black book on Tania seems to have been a fabrication. James, an East German agent who defected, claimed to recognize her and said she had worked with the East Germans in controlling foreigners. On top of this there are intimations that she was Che's lover (there is no foundation for this or for claims that she also worked for the KGB, as a natural extension of her work for the East German secret service). In any event, it is obvious that Tania had just one allegiance when she was recruited by the Cuban secret services and later by Che.

A pathetic smear campaign was mounted after Tania's death, based on small details about Vilo Acuña's guerrilla campaign: that it was her fault the group was slow, that she was pregnant, that she had cancer of the uterus, etc.

Accounts that back up the smear campaign appear in "La verdadera historia de cómo murió El Che Guevara," by Andrew St. George; *Che Guevara, una biografía,* by Daniel James; *Yo tengo siete vidas,* by Frederik Hetmann; and *Che Guevara* by Elmar May.

On Argentina

Leonardo Tamayo: "Che had Argentina on his mind even though he made many cutting comments about his native land and his compatriots. Che used to say: 'The last country in Latin America to be liberated will be Argentina. In Argentina, although there are poor people, campesinos eat good steaks and the struggle is among extreme poverty. It takes a crane to get those Argentines out of their homes.' "

35. The Rediscovery of Africa

Sources

Che left an account of part of his African tour: the manuscript "Pasajes de la guerra revolucionaria en África" ("Reminiscences of the Revolutionary War in Africa"). His series of articles "Socialismo y el hombre en Cuba" is essential reading, as are his speeches (and the replies to them) at the United Nations, and to the Second Seminar on Afro-Asian Solidarity in Algiers. Also see his interview on *Face the Nation* and his meeting with Josie Fannon.

Mohammed Heikal's book *Los recuerdos de El Cairo* is very interesting, but with the caveat that it offers memories of memories—i.e., Heikal's recollections of what Nasser told him about Guevara.

Of vital importance are the interview with Rivalta in "El año en que estuvimos en ninguna parte"; Jorge Castañeda's interview with Emilio Aragonés; "Antecedentes de la guerrilla del Che en Bolivia," by Humberto Vázquez Viaña; "L'occhio del barracuda," by Tuttino; and "Aquel poema" and "Un montón de memorias," by Fernández Retamar.

Some facts are provided by issue no. 13 of *Nuestra Industria* (June 1965); see the articles "Luis Miranda se refiere al Che" and "Para combatir el imperialismo o ir de vacaciones a la Luna." Also consulted: *Los hombres de la historia: Che Guevara* and "Los motivos del Che," both by Carlos María Guetiérrez, as well as Piero Gleijeses's essay on the Cubans in Africa.

U.S. sources from the memorandum on Senator Dodd's talk with Tshombe in the Savoy Hotel, Jan. 31, 1965, and by Thomas Hughes from the Department of Intelligence to the Secretary of State, Jan. 5, 1965, as well as the report "Cuba en África."

The Group That Was to Go to Africa

In January 1965, while Che was still on tour, Víctor Dreke, the former Directorio leader who had fought alongside Che at Santa Clara and was now fighting a counterinsurgency campaign in Las Villas, was asked if he wished to volunteer for a mission outside Cuba. When he agreed, he was asked to recruit a platoon of Afro-Caribbean soldiers with combat experience. Three groups gathered in Havana: Dreke's; a second, composed of men from Oriente Province, commanded by Captain Santiago Terry; and a third, from Pinar del Río, commanded by Berthelemy. Dreke was to command the column.

Training began in the hills of Candelaria, Pinar del Río, where revolutionaries from other parts of Latin America had been trained before. The column was put together on February 2. When the lights were turned on in the barracks, someone exclaimed: "Holy shit, aren't there some blacks here! They got all the blacks in Cuba together and brought them here!" Training was intense: target practice, long hikes, pole vaulting and obstacle courses, 75mm artillery, bazookas, laying and disarming mines, Molotov cocktails, and, above all, irregular warfare. Fidel himself visited and took part in the training.

The group was finally informed that their mission would be in Africa, and the reading material they were given included texts by Patrice Lumumba. The column was ready in less than forty-five days.

36. "My Modest Efforts Are Required Elsewhere"

Sources

Che's farewell letter appears in all editions of his works.

Of great importance were interviews granted me by Maldonado, Valdés Gravalosa, Vilaseca, Figueras, and Manresa; Castañeda's interview with Aragonés; and the interview with Dreke in *El año en que . . .*

Quotations of Fidel come from the interview with Gianni Minà, "Habla Fidel" and from his speeches on the formation of the Cuban Communist Party Central Committee and on the twentieth anniversary of Che's death.

Also see "Che" by Raúl Roa, "Los motivos del Che" by Carlos María Gutiérrez and *Mi amigo el Che* by Rojo.

Che's Party Cadres

The composition of the Cuban Communist Party Central Committee was announced on October 1; oddly, three government ministers close to Che were excluded: Sugar Minister Borrego; Alvarez Rom in Finance; and Arturo Guzmán, who had replaced Che at Industry.

Vilaseca had been relieved of his chairmanship of the central bank in June and appointed rector of the University of Havana.

The CIA drafted a special report on November 5, 1965, concerning the new Central Committee members, saying that those close to Guevara had been relegated to the sidelines and that Che's "discredited" economic viewpoint had no exponents on the Central Committee. But the 100-strong Central Committee did include several cadres wholly identified with Che: San Luis, Dreke, Zayas, José Ramón Silva, Fernández Mell, Vilo Acuña, and Acevedo. Also, Che's economic guidelines remained in place for another couple of years. Raúl Maldonado, who had had to resign as deputy minister, gave a version of events more in line with reality: "The three ministers were excluded for political reasons: they had pro-Chinese leanings rather than being pro-Soviet." On the same issue, see "La renuncia del Che," by Adolfo Gilly, in *Arauco,* October 1965.

Alberto Mora's Suicide

Raúl Maldonado: "It has been said that his suicide was a direct result of his ousting from Foreign Trade and the controversy with Che. That's not so. Mora was young and a little unstable; he drank and . . . took to partying and there was some infidelity. He went crazy, cruised the bars playing saxophone in a combo. He was a young man who had no childhood. Dorticós pulled him up and he was sent home, on his own. Che brought him back to Industry, where he was Che's adviser, and he ran a consolidated industry in 1964. Bettelheim awarded Mora a scholarship and he went, remarried now, to Paris. He was settling down. He was brought back to Cuba again because of a bureaucratic policy to cut down on the number of Cubans abroad, as there had been too many defections. He had a handicapped daughter from his new marriage, and his wife left him. He was in a mess and he shot himself."

37. Tatu, Number 3

Sources

Practically all the material in this chapter is from *El año en que estuvimos en ninguna parte,* co-written by me, Froilán Escobar, and Félix Guerra. That book is based on Che's own unpublished manuscript "Pasajes de la guerra revolucionaria en Africa" and interviews with Víctor Dreke, Ambassador Pablo Rivalta, Freddy Ilanga, Dr. Rafael Zerquera, and Sergeant Eduardo Torres, undertaken in 1991–92.

Departing from Guevara's practice, in narrating the Congo episode I have used the real names or common nicknames of the Cuban fighters involved, rather than the noms de guerre Che used in his diaries and his reports.

To enable the reader to compare this with other accounts, here is a list of those noms de guerre:

In the Congo, Che will be "Tatu" or "Ramón"; Dreke, "Mota"; Eduardo Torres, "Nane"; Martínez Tamayo, "Ricardo," "Papi," or "M'bili"; Dr. Rafael Zerquera, "Kumi"; Norberto Pichardo, "Inne"; Santiago Terry, "Aly"; Crisógenes Vinajeras, "Ansurene"; Israel Reyes, "Azi"; Arcadio Benítez, "Dogna"; Erasmo Videaux, "Kisua"; Catalino Olachea, "Mafu"; Octavio de la Concepción de la Pedreja, "Morogoro"; Harry Villegas, "Pombo"; Carlos Coello, "Tuma"; Víctor Shueb, "Ziwa"; Roberto Sánchez Barthelemy, "Changa."

The Terrain

Che: The geographical terrain we ended up living in is hallmarked by the great basin that fills Lake Tanganyika, some 35 square kilometers in area and with an average width of approximately 50 kilometers. It separates Tanzania and Brundi from the Congo. There is a mountain range on each side of the basin, one belonging to Tanzania-Burundi, the other to the Congo. The latter has an average altitude of 1,500 meters above sea level (the lake is at 700 meters) and stretches from the vicinity of Albertville in the south, where it occupies the battleground, to beyond Bakuville in the north, seemingly in hills that descend into tropical jungle. The width of the system varies but we can estimate an average of 20 or 30 kilometers for the zone. There are two higher, steeper, and rockier ranges, one to the east and the other to the west, which border a wavy plateau, suitable for agriculture in its valleys and for raising cattle, an occupation preferred by the Rwandan tribal herdsmen, who have traditionally practiced it. To the west, the mountain plunges into a plain 700 meters high, which is part of the Congo River basin. It is like a savannah, with tropical tress, shrubs, and some natural meadows that break the continuous mountain scenery. The hills close to the mountains are not steep, either, but farther west, to the Kabambare zone, it is closed in an with entirely tropical features.

The mountains emerge from the lake and give the entire terrain a haphazard look. There are little plateaus suitable for landing boats and billeting invading troops, but very difficult to defend if the heights are not taken. Land communication routes are cut off to the south at Kabimba, where one of our positions was; to the west the mountains line the route to Albertville and Lulimba-Fizi; and from the latter it goes toward Bukavu, via Muenga, a trunk road and another skirting the coast via Barake and Uvira to get to that point. The road goes through the mountains after Lulimba and is suitable for guerrilla ambushes—as also, albeit to a lesser extent, is the part that crosses the Congo River plain.

It rains frequently, daily from October to May, and almost not at all, on average, between June and September, although odd showers begin in the latter month. It rains year-round in the mountains, but infrequently in the dry months.

38. The Wait

Sources

The essential sources, as for previous chapters, are from *El año en que . . .* , the primary sources for which were "Pasajes de la guerra revolucionaria en Africa," by Che himself and my interviews with Dreke, Ilanga, Zerquera, and Rivalta; see also interviews with Videaux, Torres, Benítez, and "Kahama" and Emilio Mena's war diary, "Informe en relación . . ."

The Letter from Celia de la Serna

The letter from Che's mother is reproduced in Rojo's book. One of my Cuban sources suggested the letter might be a forgery; I do not think so.

Celia: "Do my letters sound odd to you? I don't know if we've lost the natural way of talking we used to have, or whether we never did have it and have always spoken in that slightly ironic tone that is practiced by those of us who lived on both banks of the River Plate, and that became even more remote because of our own family code. The fact is that I have always been worried over abandoning that ironic tone to be direct. It seems that that is when my letters are not understood and become odd and enigmatic. In that diplomatic tone adopted in our correspondence, I, too, have to read and interpret the hidden meanings between lines. I read your last letter as I read the news published in *La Prensa* or *La Nación* in Buenos Aires, sifting out, or trying to sift out, the real meaning of each phrase and the extent of each one. The result is a welter of confusion and unease and even more alarm. . . . I won't use diplomatic language. I'll be very direct. When there are so many good cutters among the population in Cuba, and so few heads capable of organization, it seems really crazy to me that you all go off to cut cane for a month, as your main activity. Doing so as voluntary work at times normally set aside for rest or leisure, like Saturdays or Sundays, is quite another matter. It is also another matter when the point is mainly to show forthrightly the advantage of machines to cut cane and the need to use them—when the flow of foreign currency into Cuba depends on the tonnage of sugar obtained. A month is a long time. There will be reasons for it unknown to me. Speaking of your personal case now, if after that month you devote yourself to running a firm, work done with some success by Castellanos and Villegas—then, I feel, madness will have reached absurd proportions, especially if this work is to be done for five years to obtain a real position. As I saw you strive not to be absent so much as one day from your ministry, when I saw your trip abroad was going on too long, my first question was: will Ernesto still be industry minister when he gets back to Cuba? Who has been found right or gotten ahead in the dispute over the motives that must lie behind incentives? These questions are only half-answered. If you're going to run a firm, you have quit being a minister. Depending on who is named in your place, we'll see if the matter has been resolved wisely. In any case, spending five years running a factory is too great a waste of your talents. And this is not a mother talking, but an old lady who aspires to see the whole world converted to socialism. She thinks that if you do as you have said, then you will not well serve world socialism. If for some reason the doors are closed to you in Cuba, then there is a certain Mr. Ben Bella in Algeria who would be grateful to have you organize the economy there or advise him on it, and a Mr. Nkrumah in Ghana who would feel the same way. Yes, you'll always be a foreigner. That seems to be your destiny forever."

39. Defeat at Front de Force

Sources

To the sources cited for Chapters 37 and 38, add Juana Carrasco's "El combate de Forces Bendera" and "Tatu, un guerrillero africano" (interview with Víctor Dreke). And see "Proyecto de informe al acto central por la conmemoración del XX aniversario de la formación, salida y cumplimiento de misión internacionalista de la Columna 1 en el Congo-Leopoldville"; *The CIA and the Cult of Intelligence*, by Marchetti and Marks, and *The CIA: A Forgotten History*, by Blum.

The Cuban's First Shots

It is not clear whether an ambush of a launch from Santiago Terry's group, or the June 19 action against Canberra aircraft, prompted the fatal bombing and strafing of the lakeside ranch known as Kisosi. The shots were from 12.7mm machine guns posted above the Kibamba base, and the aircraft did not return fire.

The Aircraft That Bombed Them

Marchetti: "The CIA supplied money and weapons to (Tshombe's) Mobutu and Cyril Adoula's cause. In 1964 the CIA imported its own mercenaries to the Congo. The B26s piloted by Cuban veterans of the Bay of Pigs thoroughly bombed the insurgents. When the CIA intervened in 1964, the veteran Cuban pilots who intervened had been contracted by a company called Caramar (Caribbean Marine Aero Corporation, also CIA-owned.) Weapons and military equipment were supplied by various "private" arms dealers. The biggest in the United States was the International Armament Corp. (Interarmco), based in Alexandria, Virginia. A journalist reporting from Tucson, Arizona, in 1966 wrote that he saw over 100 B26 aircraft with devices prepared for installing machineguns and bombs." The CIA reported that they were aircraft for a company that searched for an extinguished forest fires, Intermountain. In reality, they were headed for the Congo and Southeast Asia.

The researcher William Blum added that the CIA pilots undertook bombing missions against the insurgents, but there were problems because some Cubans refused to bomb civilians.

As for previous chapters, refer to *El año en que . . .* ; also see Harry Villegas's account in "Entre Nosotros" and the author's interview with Fernández Mell.

Debray briefly mentions this period in *Les masques* but is very inaccurate: "In the Congo, to better integrate his group of white internationalists with the black fighters, who went barefoot in the jungle, he ordered them to remove their footwear, setting the example himself. All to respect local customs and put everyone on an equal and quickly bloody footing."

Withdrawal with Military Bearing

Dreke: "Che was very careful with the men: **We have to get them to fight, to dig trenches in a war of positions. We have to run, but elegantly. You stop, two shots, you stop, you run. That doesn't mean you don't withdraw, you just have to know how.** He jokingly showed how, walking along. **What I don't want is dropping guns and running.**

"We used to say, as a joke, 'Commander, I withdrew, but with military bearing.' "

40. An Omnipresent Ghost

Sources

On the outpouring of disinformation, books by Hetmann, May, and Larteguy, and K. S. Karol's *Los guerrilleros en el poder* are important, as is *Un hombre bravo*, by Cupull and González.

Also see my interview with Manresa, and the August 10, 1965, report from the director of intelligence and research at the U.S. State Department.

Che's letter appears in all editions of his works. The way Fidel read it is in Enrique Pineda's documentary *Che* and ICAIC (Cuban Film Committee) newsreel No. 278. Some denied the farewell letter's authenticity although it is doubtless genuine, Siquitrilla said in exile that Che could never have written such a thing. Some authors, for example Elmar May, insist that the original was never produced, only the typewritten version. Che, on the other hand, does mention the letter in "Pasajes de la guerra revolucionaria en Africa" after it was made public by Fidel, without having been changed.

Other sources for this chapter include Hetmann, *Yo tengo siete vidas; Los guerrilleros,* by Larteguy; the anonymous biography *Che Guevara* published by Planeta Agostini; Gilly's article "Cuba, entre la coexistencia y la revolución"; and the July 9, 1967, report in *O Estado de São Paulo.* See also the U.S. memorandum to W. G. Bowdler, Sept. 26, 1966.

41. The Pessimistic Optimist

Sources

To Che's manuscript and the above-mentioned interviews contained in *El año en que . . .* must be added Jorge Castañeda's interview with Emilio Aragonés and the author's interview with Fernández Mell. Blum's book *The CIA: A Forgotten History* provides interesting information.

Money

Che stated explicitly in his letter to Fidel that the Congolese leaders should not be given money: **The money business is what pains me most, as I insisted on it so much. In my worst spendthrift arrogance, after whining a lot, I had promised to fund a front, the most important one, on condition that I would direct the fighting and form a mixed column under my direct command. . . .**

For that I calculated, though it hurt me deeply, $5,000 per month. I now find that twenty times that sum is given to the sightseers, in one go, to live well in the world's capitals. . . . Not one cent (of the money) finds its way to a wretched front—where the peasants suffer every hardship imaginable, including pillage by their own defenders—or to the poor devils stuck in Sudan.

Hunger

Hunger is a theme common to all accounts by the Cuban fighters. Videaux said: "You burn up more than you eat. Men feel like wolves, they think they could eat anything they see. . . . We would have eaten a lion if we could."

Marco Antonio Herrera, a.k.a. Genge: "It was no longer so easy to catch the much reviled monkeys to eat. They hid because of the bombing. We lived on yuca [cassava] and yuca leaves."

Aragonés said that when they caught a deer it was shared among thirty. Che and he asked for a small piece to be roasted on the embers instead of being used in a stew with yuca; they were merrily eating their meat from a stick when one of the Africans asked: "Is that good?" Che gave him his, and Aragonés had no option but to do the same ("That lousy bastard, instead of saying, 'I already ate mine . . .' "). Aragonés slimmed down from 250 pounds to 100-and-some. When he returned to Cuba, he suffered from a severe kidney infection, which was caused by protein deficiency and had him at death's door.

42. The Closing Days of That November

Sources

See the sources for previous chapters, and also "L'ascension de Mobutu" and Godley's Feb. 4, 1966, intelligence memorandum to the Secretary of State, "The Situation in the Congo."

43.   Dar es Salaam

Sources

The most important sources were "Pasajes de la guerra revolucionaria en Africa," my interviews with Fernández Mell and Pablo Rivalta, and Castañeda's interview with Aragonés.

Of some use is U.S. documentation from the 1965 State Department file on the situation in the Congo.

44.   Prague: The Cold, the Loneliness

Sources

This chapter was assembled like a jigsaw puzzle from scraps of information, the most notable sources being Irene Izquierdo's interview of Harry Villegas in "Bolivia fue el Moncada de América"; *Antecedentes de la guerrilla del Che en Bolivia*, by Humberto Vázquez Viaña; *La guerrilla del Che*, by Debray; "El Che en Africa, los meses de tinieblas," by Gabriel García Márquez; *Guerrillero Inti Peredo*, by Jesús Lara; *La CIA contra el Che*, by Cupull and González; *Tania, la guerrillera inolvidable*, by Marta Rojas and Mirta Rodríguez Calderón; my interview with Fernández Mell; and Jorge Castañeda's interview with Ulises Estrada.

Also *Guerrillas vs. the Bolivian Metaphor*, by F. A. Dwight and B. Heath.

45.   Burning His Boats

Sources

For this period, see diaries by Harry Villegas, "San Luis," and Israel Reyes. Dariel Alarcón, a.k.a. Benigno in the Bolivian campaign, has left several accounts of the training, for example, "Diálogo con Benigno" and the interview by Elsa Blaquier,

"Mucho gusto, Ramón." He described the training in great detail during his interview with me, and I compared his notes with Leonardo Tamayo's in a second interview. There is other material from survivors: "Su ejemplo inmortal" by Harry Villegas and María Garcés; *Materiales sobre la guerrilla de Ñancahuazú*, edited by María Garcés; "Héroes inmortales de nuestra América."

Aleida March recounts the family farewell in "El último encuentro del Che con su familia" by Héctor Danilo Rodríguez; Hilda Guevara mentions it in "Han hecho del Che un mito . . .," by Campa.

Régis Debray has written several volumes on the Bolivian guerrilla campaign. For the preparation, my sources were *La guerrilla del Che* and an interview granted me.

Cupull and González offer interesting perspectives. See also Fidel's interview with Minà and his speech on the twentieth anniversary of Che's death. On Che's comrades in Bolivia, see "Capitán José María Martínez Tamayo," by Reyes Trejo; *Ellos lucharon con el Che* and *Abriendo senderos*, by Mariano Rodríguez Herrera; and "La guerrilla boliviana" by Betancourt.

Also see *Tania, la guerrillera inolvidable*, by Marta Rojas and Mirta Rodríguez Calderón; *La guerrilla inmolada*, by Gary Prado; *Vida, aventuras y desastres de un hombre llamado Castro*, by Franqui; "Los motivos del Che," by Carlos María Gutiérrez; "Murió el Che Guevara," by Alcázar and Chacón; and *Che Guevara, una biografía*, by Daniel James.

The story of Aleida and Che has its origin in an anonymous source. In an interview with the author, Leonardo Tamayo insisted it could not be true, as Aleida was constantly at the house where they were billeted in the last weeks before the departure.

Nicknames

Unlike other accounts, mine are real names or common nicknames in narrating the Bolivian campaign, rather than the noms de guerre that appear in diaries by Che and several of his comrades and in communiqués from the guerrillas. The equivalents used in Che's Bolivian diary are as follows.

Che used the name "Ramón at first, later replacing it with "Fernando." Alberto Fernández Montes de Oca remained "Pacho" or "Pachungo." Commander Vilo Acuña was "Joaquín"; Eliseo "San Luis" Reyes was also called Rolando. Manuel Hernández was "Miguel"; Deputy Minister Suárez Gayol, "Blondie"; Orlando "Olo" Pantoja, "Antonio"; José María Martínez Tamayo, "M'bili," "Papi," and "Ricardo"; his brother René, "Arturo"; Harry Villegas, "Pombo," as in Africa; Gustavo Machín Hoed, "Alejandro"; Antonio "Pinares" Sánchez, "Marcos"; Leonardo Tamayo, "Urbano"; Carlos Coello, "Tuma" or "Tumaini," as in Africa; Dariel Alarcón, "Benigno"; Israel Reyes, "Braulio."

Another Account of the Farewell

Tomás Borge describes another moment prior to the departure in a similar tone, when at the end of the training "Che sat on a tree trunk next to Fidel (and) they sat next to each other for over an hour, without saying a word. They didn't end up saying anything either. Che just draped his hand over Fidel's back, Fidel's over Che's, and they slapped each other heartily."

The Difficulties of Excessive Traveling

Plotting Che's journey from Cuba to Bolivia is a jigsaw puzzle worthy of a fanatic in such matters.

He very probably left Cuba on October 23, 1966 (although some insist he left on October 19, which is not very likely as the training ended on October 22), traveling from Havana to Moscow with a Cuban passport in the name of a National Agrarian Reform Institute official called Luis Hernández Galván.

The next day, October 24, in Moscow, he exchanged that passport for one identifying him as a Uruguayan citizen, Ramón Benítez; he used it to go to Prague, where

he changed his passport name to Adolfo Mena, then traveled by train to Vienna on October 25.

To remove evidence of the forged passports, two pages were removed from the Passport Department register at the Uruguayan Foreign Ministry. The same photograph was used for both "Benítez" and "Mena," but with slight differences: one was born in 1920, the other in 1921, but on the same date, June 25.

The sources go crazy when it comes to following the trail from Vienna. The passports have false stamps indicating transit through Madrid before the departure from Cuba (October 9 and 19). It seems Che went via Frankfurt, where he bought the first diary, or via Paris (or by train from Vienna to Frankfurt and then to Paris) and arrived in Sao Paulo on November 1. If so, then Che and Pacho wandered around Europe for five days of which there is no record. Some sources insist that for one stage of the journey both Che and Pacho posed as Spanish cattle dealers (a trade that could not have interested Che in the least).

The Mena cover crops up again in São Paulo. Che was detained there by customs, who demanded a vaccination certificate (**It is necessary to foresee that Uruguayan vaccination certificates need a stamp; I had to get another one there in São Paulo**, Che told Havana at the beginning of November). Tamayo said: "Che told us that that happened at about nine A.M. and they let him go at about four P.M. the same day, on condition he turned up the day after with his papers in order. Che told us that worried him a little, as the other Latin Americans were traveling under the same conditions and the authorities took no notice of them. He said: **It seemed they had found me out.**"

Che requested a tourist card for Bolivia on November 3 and went to La Paz as Mena once more. Neither passport records his entry into Bolivia, however. He later said: **I have made a great discovery: now we know that if we dress some-**

one up as an elephant, he will still get here. (See Israel Reyes's diary; Tamayo interview; Alarcón interview; Che's message to Havana, no date (around November 1966); Pacho's diary; Tamayo interview by Minà, in *Un continente desaparecido; Un hombre bravo*, by Cupull and González; *La guerrilla del Che*, by Debray; and "Fantasma del Che rondó por Brasil antes de por Ñancahuazú," by René Villegas. In *Che Guevara, una biografía*, James analyzed the passports, as did Gary Prado in *La guerrilla inmolada*).

"Revolución en la revolución"

Debray's book was published in January 1967 by Cuadernos de Casa, Havana. Che could well have read the proofs of a final copy in September or October 1966. He had a copy in Bolivia, and doubtless Vilo Acuña carried a copy in his backpack.

46. "Today the Next Stage Begins"

Sources

The backbone of the story told in this chapter is Che's Bolivian diary, the diaries by Villegas ("Pombo"), Eliseo Reyes ("San Luis") and Pacho Montes de Oca, and the books *Mi campaña con el Che*, by Inti Peredo; *Les masques*, by Régis Debray; and *La guerrilla del Che* by Dariel Alarcón (with Mariano Rodríguez). Also helpful were my interviews with Alarcón and Leonardo Tamayo.

Che's communiqués to Fidel, and Havana's to Che, appear in scattered sources: the Mexico City Siglo XXI edition of Che's diary; articles by Vacaflor; James's *Che Guevara, una biografía;* and notes to books by various Bolivian soldiers (Gary Prado, Diego Martínez Estévez, Arnaldo Saucedo Parada, Mario Vargas Salinas); they have never been placed in chronological order and compared with Che's diary.

Of particular importance are the books *De Ñancahuazú a La Higuera*, by Cupull and González, and *Tania, la guerrillera inolvidable,* by Marta Rojas and Mirta Rodríguez Calderón, which may be supplemented by Lídice Valenzuela's article "Tania la guerrillera."

The best review of the conversation between Che and Monje is from González and Sánchez Salazar's book, which includes a later account by Kolle. The photograph of their meeting is from Luis Hernández Serrano's article "La selva en la Mochila."

Of great interest are Lara's *Guerrillero Inti Peredo;* Ana María Radaelli's article "Del oriente al altiplano"; Valenzuela's interview with Rodolfo Saldaña and that of Alberto Zuazo's with Loyola Guzmán.

The list of books that Che was reading is in his own hand, in the article "La canallada."

Some elements of this chapter are taken from Santiago Alvarez's short film *Hasta la victoria siempre* for ICAIC, from the article "Hablan la hermana . . . ," and from Diana Iznaga's article "Che Guevara y la literatura de testimonio."

For the CIA's knowledge of the guerrilla organization, see the CIA Directory of Intelligence, Intelligence Memorandum: "The Bolivian Guerrilla Movement: An Interim Assessment."

Journeys and Nationalities

The Cubans who accompanied Che left in pairs between the end of October and mid-November 1966, and took several days to arrive, due to their intricate travel arrangements.

Israel Reyes: "I left my house on Thursday, October 25, and left Havana October 29 and that was where my second adventure began. I was traveling to Bolivia under my own name, Israel Reyes, with a Panamanian passport and $26,000 in my pocket, $1,000 for my expenses and $25,000 for Ramón. My itinerary was Moscow-Prague-Frankfurt-Chile-Bolivia."

Israel Reyes, Vilo Acuña, and Eliseo Reyes traveled as Panamanians, Tamayo as a Mexican, Manuel Hernández as a Spaniard, and de la Pedraja, Suárez Gayol, and Olo Pantoja as Ecuadorians. James was fascinated by the way the Cuban secret services managed to produce twenty-one impeccable Ecuadorean, Panamanian, Colombian, Peruvian, Uruguayan, and Bolivian passports, and he didn't even know about the Spanish ones.

Pseudonyms

Again, I have used real names or common nicknames for the Peruvian and Bolivian guerrillas instead of the noms de guerre that appear in diaries by Che and several of his colleagues, as well as in communiqués. By the same token, real names or nicknames replace noms de guerre in quotes from diaries by Che and others. Equivalents used in the Bolivian diaries are as follows:

Guido Peredo will be known as Inti; Jorge Vázquez Viaña as "Loro"; Rodolfo Saldaña will appear under his own name; Roberto Peredo as "Coco"; Lorgio Vaca Marchetti, "Carlos"; Orlando Jiménez Bazán, "Camba"; Julio Méndez Korne, "El Ñato"; David Adriazola, "Darío"; Jaime Arana, "Chapaco" or "Luis"; Mario Gutiérrez Ardaya, "Julio"; Freddy Maimura, "Ernesto the medic." The following will use their own names: Raúl Quispaya, Salustio Choque, Benjamín Coronado.

Among the campesinos whom the Bolivian Communist Party had looking after the farm and who fought alongside the guerrillas, Apolinar Aquino will keep his own name; Aquino Tudela will be Serapio, and Antonio Domínguez "León."

In Moisés Guevara's group: Simón Cuba will be "Willi" or "Willy"; Casildo Condori, "Víctor"; José Castillo, "Paco"; Hugo Choque, "Chingolo"; Julio Velazco, "Pepe"; Francisco Huanca, "Pablo"; Antonio Jiménez, "Pan Divino" or "Pedro." Under their own names: Pastor Barrera, Vicente Rocabado, Walter Arancibia, Aniceto Reinaga, and Eusebio Tapia.

Among the Peruvian guerrillas, Juan Pablo Chang will be "El Chino," ("the Chinese Man"); Lucio Edilberto Galván Hidalgo, "Eustaquio"; Restituto José Cabrera, "the Medic" or "El Negro" ("the Black Man").

Manila

In the various Bolivian diaries, communications from Cuba come from "Manila." This refers to a communications center near Havana, on the outskirts of a small town called Punta Brava, near San Antonio de los Baños. There were wide wooden disposable boats near the entrance, and windowless underground bunkers almost a mile from the entrance, with 50,000-watt transmitters. There were thirty-five to forty transmitters and receivers working 24 hours a day (Lionel Remigio, "Manila: centro de contacto").

A Suicidal Commander?

In the view of some authors, Che was seeking his own death in Bolivia.

Debray: "Ramón is alone with himself. He will soon offer himself to death, resigned, with his asthma, his unbearable back and neck pains, and in the depths of his soul, a bucolic calm" (*Les masques*).

Carlos María Gutiérrez: "Convinced of his isolation and lack of prospects, he decided to launch the guerrilla war in Bolivia and close it with his own immolation" (*Los hombres de la historia: Che Guevara*).

And Dolores Moyano refers to the Bolivian venture using the words: "Hara-kiri, seppuku."

It would seem evident there was no such thing.

47. The Brutal Expedition

Sources

Essential were diaries by Che, Pacho, Harry Villegas, and San Luis, and parts of de la Pedraja's diary read out the Camiri trial and quoted by Phillip Labreveux in *Bolivia bajo el Che*.

Also essential were my interviews with Alarcón and Debray, and their books *La guerrilla del Che* and *Les masques*.

Captain Silva's account is from "De

Ñancahuasú a La Higuera" by Cupull and González. Coco Peredo's remark is quoted in Vargas Salinas, *El Che, mito y realidad.*

Pastor and Rocabado's trial statements at Camiri are very interesting.

Also see Cupull and González, *La CIA contra el Che;* James, *Che Guevara, una biografía;* and Gary Prado, *La guerrilla inmolada.*

Some authors present the later finding of the caves and documents as a result of "willful" negligence by Tania. In James's view, the jeep Tania left in Camiri had traceable documentation in it—among other things, four notebooks with addresses of members of the urban network and contacts outside Bolivia—that "attracted the attention of the authorities." James attributes the police presence at the farm to this. He also deduces from Tania's negligence that she was under Soviet orders to remain at the camp. But in an interview with me, Régis Debray agreed that there was little foundation for these beliefs.

48.   Combat

Sources

Diaries by Che and Pacho Montes de Oca are again essential, along with accounts by Inti Peredo, San Luis Reyes, and Harry Villegas.

Dariel Alarcón's unpublished account, "Che y la guerrilla de Ñancahuazú" (jointly written with Mariano Rodríguez), is very interesting, as are Debray's accounts in *La guerrilla del Che* and *Les masques* and my interviews of both men.

U.S. intervention may be followed in Cupull and González, *La CIA contra el Che* and "De Ñancahuacú a la Higuera"; Andrew St. George's report; Alcázar's book, *Ñancahuasú, la guerrilla del Che en Bolivia;* Hernández Serrano's report, quoted in Phillip Agee, *Diario de la CIA;* Interior Minister Arguedas's account, in statements to news agency EFE during his trial in Bo-

livia, Blum's *The CIA: A Forgotten History;* and documentation from the U.S. State Department Directorate of Intelligence and Research.

Messages exchanged between Fidel and Che appear in appendices to Che's diaries and in Vacaflor's article.

For other interesting accounts see Luis Suárez's *Entre el fusil y la palabra;* the report in *Granma,* April 17, 1967; Murray Sales' report "Las guerrillas . . ."; Valenzuela's interview with Rodolfo Saldaña; my interview of Juan Gelman; and with Bustos in "Las revelaciones de Ciro Bustos," *Punto Final* magazine.

About the Argentines

Of all aspects of the operation, the weakest link appears to be the Argentine connection. Luis Faustino Stamponi was in Havana at the time and did not know Che wanted his support until a year and a half later, when he read the diaries. Gelman's identity is still a matter for confusion. The Argentine poet, who at that time was active in a small revolutionary group, was told that Che was looking for him and then, contradictorily, that actually the person meant was Alfredo Hellman, a Young Communist leader from Mendoza. Tania had lost contact with "Black Jáuregui's" group, and Jozami—Juan Gelman—was in Bolivia, but did not make contact with Che.

"Braulio's" Diary

Adys Cupull and Froilán González rightly insist that Israel Reyes's diary did not fall into the hands of the army and the CIA in April 1967, but five months later when Vargas Salinas and his patrol killed Reyes, that Roth's account "I Was Arrested with Debray" (based on this supposed diary) was fabricated, that in fact Israel Reyes's name was obtained from a scrap of paper addressed to Blondie, and that Reyes was thus identified with a passport in the name of one Israel Reyes Tapia, who had entered the country and disappeared.

49. Intervention and Dead Friends

Sources

In addition to diaries by Che and other guerrillas mentioned in previous chapters, of great help were my interview with Leonardo Tamayo, Katia Valdés's interview with Tamayo (published as "Che Guevara, facetas de un jefe militar"); Mariano Rodríguez Herrera's "Los que cayeron con honor serán los inmortales"; and Vásquez Díaz's *Bolivia a la hora del Che.*

For my account of U.S. support for the Bolivian army, see memos from Bowdler to Rostow; Blum, *The CIA: A Forgotten History;* Marchetti and Marks, *The CIA and the Cult of Intelligence;* Colonel Joaquín Zenteno's statement at Arguedas's trial; "La CIA en Bolivia," in *Marcha;* and Jay Mallin, *Ernesto "Che" Guevara.*

It is interesting to compare Busto's two accounts. First, the copy of his statements in Martínez Estévez's *Ñancahuazú* and second, his statements in *Punto Final* magazine. "Las revelaciones de Ciro Bustos," as well as Roth's article "*I Was Arrested with Debray.*"

Also see Alcázar, *Ñacahuasú, la guerrilla del Che en Bolivia;* Cupull and González, *La CIA contra el Che;* James, *Che Guevara, una biografía;* Luis Suárez, *Entre el fusil y la palabra;* Prado, *La Guerrilla Inmolado* and the unattributed article "Debray en peligro." The May 1 photographs from Havana are by Roberto Salas.

Abandoning Them to Their Fate

Some authors have toyed with the idea that Havana, and Fidel in particular, decided not to continue to support "Che's adventure" and therefore made no serious attempt to reestablish contact. In his latest book, Dariel Alarcón in particular insists on this version of events (which he did not do when he and I spent over six hours discussing the matter). It seems evident that once the guerrillas were cut off from the urban networks and communication with Havana was lost, there was little the Cuban government could have done short of an outright intervention. The only shadow of a doubt is produced by the sudden departure of Monleón ("Iván"-"Renán") because "his cover was blown," and the fact that his replacement, by "a Cuban fighter from the Sierra," never took place. This episode will remain unclear so long as Monleón and his chief, Commander Piñeiro, do not provide their versions of events.

50. The Massacre of the Rear Guard

Sources

Again, the indispensable sources were diaries by Che, Montes de Oca, and Villegas, as well as my interviews with Leonardo Tamayo and Dariel Alarcón, and Alarcón's unpublished book (co-written with Mariano Rodríguez) "Che y la guerrilla de Ñancahuazú." Some information comes from the interview with Villegas in *Che, teoría y acción,* by Villegas et al.

For massacre of the rear guard, see Mario Vargas Salinas, *El Che, mito y realidad;* González Bermejo's two articles compiled in "El escalón más alto;" Mariano Rodríguez Herrera, "Los que cayeron con honor serán los inmorteles"; Marta Rojas and Mirta Rodriguez Calderón, *Tania, la guerrillera inolvidable;* and Cupull and González, *De Ñancahuasú a La Higuera.* For the U.S. version of events see Intelligence Information Cable, NSF Country File, Bolivia, C8, Vol. 4: cables (LBJ Library).

Also see Vásquez Díaz, *Bolivia a la hora del Che;* Betsy Zavala, UPI cable, July 15, 1967; Gary Prado, *La guerrilla inmolada;* and Julio Cortázar, "Reunión," *Todos los fuegos el fuego.*

For the CIA's version, see "The Bolivian Guerrilla Movement: An Interim Assessment."

The Yeso Ford?

Adys Cupull and Froilán González believe the ambush at the Yeso ford really took place at the ford in Puerto Mauricio, on the Río Grande, in No. 4 Division's zone, but the army changed the locale in its account because the ambush was undertaken by troops from No. 8 Division. Che made fun of the territoriality when he heard an earlier report on the radio about where his trial would be held.

Incidentally, Vilo Acuña was incorrectly identified for the first few days after his death. The CIA and Bolivian military intelligence thought he was Cuban Major Antonio E. Lusson, a member of the Central Committee.

51. "Clear Out and Look for More Suitable Zones"

Sources

Again, I relied extensively on diaries by Che, Montes de Oca, and Villegas, as well as on interviews with Leonardo Tamayo and Dariel Alarcón, and on the latter's article "La Quebrada del Yuro."

Of great interest are Mariano Rodríguez Herrera's article on Coco Peredo, "Miguel, Coco, Julio: inmortales soldados de la libertad americana"; Félix Rodríguez and John Weisman, *Shadow Warrior: The CIA Hero of a Hundred Unknown Battles;* Gary Prado, *La guerrilla inmolada;* and the unpublished manuscript by Emilio Surí and Manuel González Bello, "Los últimos días del Che."

Interesting information is are provided by Cupull and González, book *De Ñancahuazú a La Higuera;* Araoz, "Hablan los testigos de la muerte del Che"; the unsigned article "Debray reitera su apoyo a la guerrilla," in *Punto Final;* and "Quebrada del Yuro" in Villegas et al., *Che, teoría y acción.*

Information about official U.S. sources in cables received by the State Department Intelligence Division.

"Léon's" Diary

In *El Che, mito y realidad,* Captain Mario Vargas Salinas quotes a diary entry by one of the Bolivian guerrillas, "León" (Antonio Domínguez), which gives an eyewitness account of the guerrillas' isolation: "What is happening in our camp now? Why does doubt gnaw away at the guerrillas? We have come from far away to fight to the end. It should be said we will come out of this victorious or dead. The Cubans seem to believe we are afraid and accuse us of being cowards. That's not true, and we've proved it when there was occasion to. It so happens we have to be more practical and meet reality head-on. I am a little ill—maybe we all are, from hardship and lack of food—but as for the people understanding our good intentions and the comrades from the cities rallying to our aid, no one believes that anymore."

This diary's authenticity has not been proved.

The Rangers' Mobilization to La Esperanza

They received the order to go to Vallegrande on September 25 (Prado, *La guerrilla inmolada*) and the ambush took place on September 26. This makes Félix Rodríguez's claim unbelievable, that the mobilization took place because he had concluded that the casualties indicated they had ambushed Che's group.

52. The Yuro Ravine

Sources

Some information comes from diaries by Che and Montes de Oca. The most complete account of the engagement is from two collective interviews with Alarcón, Villegas, and Tamayo: "El combate de la quebrada del Yuro," in *Verde Olivo,* and "La quebrada del Yuro, recuerdos de un combate," in *Tricontinental.* Tamayo went into detail in February 1995 interview with me, which, together with Inti Peredo's diary, fills out the guerrillas' view of the action.

Dariel Alarcón has given several other accounts, all consistent, but there is fresh information in his unpublished book "Che y la guerrilla de Ñancahuazú," written with Mariano Rodríguez Herrera, and in an interview he gave Rodriguez Herrera for *Juventud Rebelde*, as well as in the interview he granted me in February 1995 and in Rodríguez Herrera's "El día que cayó el Che."

For the Bolivian army's viewpoint, I consulted Diego Martínez Estévez, *Ñancahuazú; Saucedo Parada, No disparen;* and above all, Captain Gary Prado, *La guerrilla inmolada*. Alcázar's book *Ñacahuasú, la guerrilla del Che en Bolivia* has a version more critical of the army.

José Luis Morales's article "No sabíamos que el Che estaba vivo y preso," is interesting. Some information comes from the two accounts given by Fidel in October 1967, in his appearance before the press and during Che's funeral ceremony.

The geographical description of the area draws on González Bermejo's article "Che, su paso por la tierra," and on the Cupull and González, *De Ñancahuazú a La Higuera*. Also see "Bolivian pictures of missing Che Guevara."

The Betrayal

The survivors thought for a long time that they had been given away by the old woman they saw that day, to whom they gave fifty pesos to keep quiet. Dariel Alarcón said the true story became clearer when General Torres took power in Bolivia: the son of the mayor of La Higuera had seen them while he was watering his potato patch and had run to town to give them away.

Che's October 7 diary entry mentions that the old woman was with a little girl. Twenty years later, Cuban journalist found out who the little girl was: the granddaughter (not the daughter—Che was wrong) of the old lady, Epifania.

When he asked her her name, she replied: "No, because a lot of journalists have come here, and then things change."

According to González Bermejo, her name was Florencia Cabritas, and the daughter's, Alejita.

Old Florencia said: "I saw them turn up that afternoon, bearded, with their weapons, and I was scared. I didn't want to talk. Then I told them more or less where they were. I didn't know who that Che was" (Marta Rojas in "El Che Guevara bajo el cielo de la Higuera"; Orlando Oramas León in "La Higuera, donde la muerte devino redención"; and Ernesto González Bermejo in "Che, su paso por la tierra").

53. Capture

Sources

The first account of Che's capture was given by Captain Gary Prado in his book *La guerrilla del Che*, which offers two versions—a cold one, and a more personal one written in the first person.

Arnaldo Saucedo Parada's *No disparen* provides some more information, as well as army radio messages; it puts Prado's version into perspective and calls some aspects of it into doubt.

Another account, which includes a number of inaccuracies, is by Arguedas; it is based on an account by a soldier he met in jail, who took part in the operation.

Among Bolivian journalists, the one who undertook the most thorough investigation, talking to rangers from the rank and file and taking advantage of his status as a war correspondent, was José Luis Alcázar. His account was published as *Ñacahuasu, la guerrilla del Che en Bolivia*, and as an article, co-written with Edwin Chacón, "Murió el Che Guevara."

Inti Peredo's account is from his memoirs, *Mi campaña con el Che;* Dariel Alarcón's is from the unpublished manuscript he wrote with Mariano Rodríguez Herrera, "Che y la guerrilla de Ñancahuazú," as well as from my interview with him in 1995.

"Don't Shoot . . ."

The cry attributed to Che, with variations ("Don't shoot any more, dammit! I'm Che, and I'm worth more alive than dead!"), is cited in many sources—e.g., Gonzalo de Bethencourt in "Muerte y sepulcro del Che," the Spanish *Reader's Digest* article "La muerte del Che," and Daniel James's biography. However, it does not appear in any firsthand account. It originated in General Ovando's news conference several days after Che's capture and death.

Juan Pablo Chang

In many accounts, a third man, wounded in the face and with blood blinding him, appears alongside the miner Simón Cuba and Che. This is Juan Pablo Chang, who disappears in most official accounts, to magically reappear as a corpse in the schoolhouse at La Higuera. An anonymous soldier: "he held up a wounded man with his right arm, and with his left, another man whose face was covered in blood." See "The Order of Execution" in the notes to chapter 57.

54. Eighteen Hours in La Higuera

Sources

The first written accounts of Che's murder are essential: Michelle Ray, "In Cold Blood: How the CIA Executed Che"; and Fidel Castro's public speeches, October 15 and 18, and "Un introducción necesaria" to Che's Bolivian diary. Also important is Arguedas's account which aside from mistakenly identifying the killer as Sergeant Huanca, includes many facts consistent with other accounts. Arguedas's most exact ac-

count was one he gave in a private talk in Cuba, of which I have a typewritten version in my possession. Also see *Ñacahuasu, la guerrilla del Che en Bolivia*, by the Bolivian journalist José Luis Alcázar.

In subsequent years, accounts have appeared by Colonel Saucedo *(No disparen)*; by Captain Gary Prado *(La guerrilla inmolada)*; and by César Peña, interviewing Colonel Roque Terán ("Cómo fusilamos al Che," which includes a confession by Sergeant Mario Terán). Finally, an essential source is the accounts by two soldiers who wished to remain anonymous; they have been published in a book edited by Carlos Soria Galvarro, and barely distributed outside Bolivia: *El Che en Bolivia*.

Of great interest are works by Cuban journalists Adys Cupull and Froilán González—*La CIA contra el Che* and "De Ñancahuazú a La Higuera" (although Cupull and González insist, with no grounds for doing so, that the CIA was behind the death warrant)—and an excellent account by the Uruguayan journalist Ernesto González Bermejo, "Che, su paso por la tierra."

On the conclave of generals who ordered the killing, Jorge Gallardo Lozada's book *De Torres a Banzer* is essential reading, as is a UPI cable dated June 12, 1978: "Revela Alfredo Ovando que las fuerzas armadas bolivianas dieron la orden de asesinar al comandante Ernesto Che Guevara."

Félix Rodríguez's account is from his book *Shadow Warrior*, and from interviews by Jane Bussey ("CIA Veteran at Peace with Killing of Rebel El Che") and Carlos Puig ("Sentí por un momento que ya no lo odiaba").

There are interesting minutes by Zenteno, Selich, and Ayoroa of the Bolivian armed forces' internal meetings during the investigation concerning the disappearance of Che's diary.

The two U.S. memos referred to are: Bowdler to Rostow, Oct. 9, 1967, and Ambassador Henderson's telegram to the State Department, of the same date. Also of interest are accounts by Gustavo Sánchez ("El

Gran rebelde"), Alcázar and Baldivia (*Bolivia, otra lección para América*), Gonzalo de Bethencourt ("Muerte y sepulcro del Che"), Enrique Araoz ("Hablan los testigos de la muerte del Che") and Eduardo Paz Rada ("Cómo murió Guevara").

The photographs of Che after his capture appear in Félix Rodríguez, *Shadow Warrior,* and Arnaldo Saucedo Parada, *No disparen.* The first photo of La Higuera is from *Life* magazine.

The Sentence

The most precise account of how Che's death warrant was issued is Jorge Gallardo Lozada's, in *De Torres a Banzer;* it is doubtless based on information from the book's leading player, General Torres. Whether from caution or reticence, Gallardo omits to mention what Torres' stance was, and then without any basis says rhetorically that the CIA gave the order.

Arguedas convincingly argues that Torres was one of those who voted in favor of the murder, which would explain the coolness Fidel Castro's government repeatedly showed the progressive government briefly led by Torres years later.

Colonel Reque Terán said years afterward that Ovando, Barrientos, and Torres made the decision. Betancourt added another officer, Belmonte Ardiles, to the list. Vacaflor also added that one of the officers consulted, Air Force Commander León Kolle Cueto (brother of the Communist Party leader), voted against.

Ovando said ten years later that the killing of Guevara "was ordered" (Ovando did not say by whom) and did not originate with him, when he was head of the armed forces. See Alcázar and Baldivia, *Bolivia, otra lección para América.*

The U.S. government was kept in the dark. Two days later, Walter Rostow sent President Johnson a memorandum saying that the latest information they had was that Che Guevara was being held alive and that after a brief interrogation to establish his identity, General Ovando had ordered him to be shot. Rostow said he saw this as stupidity, but understandable from the Bolivians' point of view, given the problems that French Communists and Castro's courier, Régis Debray, had caused them.

The Order of Execution

In the labyrinth of small contradictions and poor, misplaced, or willfully misleading memories, chaos reigns regarding details— e.g., the exact time the helicopter carrying Zenteno and Félix Rodríguez arrived in La Higuera. Prado put the time at nine A.M., Selich at 6:15 A.M.; Saucedo says it *left* at seven A.M., and Zenteno himself says they arrived at 7:30 A.M.

The execution order arrived in La Higuera orally from Colonel Zenteno, who had received it the night before in Vallegrande. It is possible that there was a confirmation order, as Colonel Reque Terán said in an interview years later, but Zenteno doubtless transmitted it to Selich and Ayoroa on the morning of October 9, 1967.

Although he says in his memoirs that he received the order and transmitted it to the Bolivians and then personally transported Che's body, it would seem obvious, as Captain Prado affirms, that neither Félix Rodríguez nor Colonel Zenteno was in La Higuera when Che was killed, as the helicopter left the hamlet at 11:45 A.M.

However, it does seem evident that Rodríguez's instructions were to keep Che alive so as to take him to Panama for prolonged questioning, and that the U.S. intelligence services had nothing to do with killing Che.

Was liquor present? Were the soldiers drunk? Accounts picked up by the Spanish reporter Betancourt and by Alcázar, as well as by the French journalist Michelle Ray, say they were, and all seem to confirm that Terán needed a drink to steel his nerves. Prado dismisses the story, though, saying there was not enough liquor in this wretched hamlet for 150 soldiers.

The Mystery of Chang and Pacho

The telegraph operator's wife spoke of a blinded guerrilla; he is also mentioned in Arguedas's account, and one of the anonymous soldiers interviewed by Carlos Soria Galvarro for *El Che en Bolivia* insisted two guerrillas, one of whom was blinded, were killed in the adjacent room. Why, then, do the sources who admit to the killing of Che and Simón Cuba deny that of Chang?

This is only one of the many small mysteries surrounding the death of Che. Why is there no entry for October 8 in Pacho's diary, if he did not die until October 9? Did Prado make up the clash on October 9 to justify his not being in La Higuera when the killings took place? Could Pacho have died in combat on October 8 and not been recorded as dead until his body was found on October 9? According to Prado, Chang and Pacho were together in one of the caves. I have opted for this version, on the ground that the Bolivian army consistently made up nonexistent clashes throughout the guerrilla war and the month following whenever it had executions to deny.

Major Rubén Sánchez

Years later, Sánchez said: "They were going to post me to the zone where Che had been captured, but my wife was about to have an operation and I could not go. I could tell you I was lucky, or I don't know. If I'd been there, they would not have killed Che the way they did, or they would have killed us both."

55. The Missing Body

Sources

Michelle Ray's article "In Cold Blood," in *Ramparts,* is very interesting, as are pieces by other journalists who were on the scene at that time: Richard, Gott, "Yo vi el cadáver del Che en Vallegrande"; Ana María Radaelli, "Del oriente al altiplano";

Alberto Zuazo, "20 años después sigue siendo un misterio que pasó con el cadáver del Che Guevara"; José Luis Alcázar and Edwin Chacón, "Murió el Che Guevara." Also essential were, e.g., General Ovando's statements to agencies AP and AFP on October 9, 1967, and the *El Diario* (La Paz) report "Conmocíon popular por ver el Cadáver del Che." Roberto Guevara's statements are from "Che y los argentinos."

Also see Fidel Castro's two abovementioned speeches; González Bermejo, "Che, su paso por la tierra"; James, *Che Guevara, una biografía;* Félix Rodríguez, *Shadow Warrior;* Cupull and González, "De Ñancahuazú a La Higuera" and *La CIA contra el Che;* Marta Rojas, "La muerte del Che en la prensa internacional" and "El Che Guevara bajo el cielo de la Higuera"; Guy Guglietta, UPI cable, October 9, 1977.

John Berger's "The legendary Che Guevara is dead" is one of two sources for the analogy with Rembrandt's painting

The Anatomy Lesson of Dr. Tulp

On the recent project to find Che's body, see articles from the Mexico City daily *La Jornada* throughout November and December 1995 ("Descubren los restos de tres guerrilleros"; "Exigirán la entrega de los restos del Che sus familiares"; "Los restos del Che, incinerados y enterrados en Vallegrande, Bolivia"; "Militares bolivianos buscan ya los restos del Che"; "Ordena Sánchez de Lozada que sean localizados los restos del Che Guevara"; "Ordenan a Mario Vargas localizar los restos del Che"), article by Jon Lee Anderson in the *New York Times*: "Where Is Che Guevara Buried? A Bolivian Tells" and Miguel Bonasso's interview of Luis Fondebrider on the television program *Ernesto Che Guevara, el regreso de un mito.*

The Odyssey of the Survivors

For two weeks after Che was killed, the rangers tried to surround the two surviving guerrilla groups: Inti Peredo's group and the group of sick fighters. A ranger patrol captured and then shot the second group (De la Pedraja, Huanca, Lucio Galván and Jaime Arana) on October 12, 1967, in a place called Cajones. Inti's group, which included three Cubans (Villegas, Alarcón, and Tamayo) skirmished several times with the army, inflicting casualties, and finally managed to break out of the cordon, but El Ñato was killed in the process. Inti re-established contact with the Communist Party network and while he was returning upcountry, the three Cubans, with two new guides, crossed the border to Chile in mid-February 1968. They then arrived back in Havana after a long journey.

Inti Peredo took up arms again after reorganizing the ELN and died under torture in 1969, having been captured on being stunned by a grenade in a clash with the army. Alarcón himself returned to Bolivia in 1968 for the second operation by the ELN. Surrounded by troops from the Sucre regiment and the National Police in a bank in La Paz, he ran out shouting "Homeland or death!" and tried to commit suicide by shooting himself in the head. His life was miraculously saved when the attempt failed and he was freed under an amnesty decreed by General Torres's régime. David Adriazola died in a clash with police near Lagunillas in April 1968.

The survivors' odyssey is recorded in great detail in Inti Peredo's diary *Mi campaña con el Che* and in Mariano Rodríguez and Dariel Alarcón's *Les survivants du Che.* Military dispatches concerning the efforts to locate the guerrillas may be found in Gary Prado, *La guerrilla inmolada,* and Diego Martínez Estévez, *Ñancahuazú.* Gianni Minà's interview with Tamayo and Villegas in Minà's *Un continente desaparecido* is interesting, and the same naturally goes for Alcázar's follow-up of the story in *Ñacahuasu, la guerrilla del Che en Bolivia.* For the U.S. version of events, see NSF Country File, Bolivia, C8, Vol. 4, cables (LBJ Library).

56. Commander Guevara's Many Watches

Sources

The story of the Bolivian soldiers' pillage may be followed by reviewing Cupull and González, "De Ñancahuazú a la Higuera"; Hernán Uribe, *Operación Tía Victoria;* Enrique Araoz, "Hablan los testigos de la muerte del Che"; Prado, *La guerrilla inmolada;* Luis Suárez, *Entre el fusil y la palabra;* Félix Rodríguez, *Shadow Warrior;* and the anonymous soldiers in Carlos Soria Galvarro, ed., *El Che en Bolivia.* I heard the story of the bar in Puebla from my friend Fritz Glockner. Enrique Lihn's remark is from "Elegía a Ernesto Guevara."

While finishing these notes, I discovered that the unpublished book "Los últimos dias del Che" by my friend Emilio Surí and Manuel González Bello mentions that Che had four watches in his backpack in mid-September.

57. The Slippery Diaries

Sources

On the travels of Che's diaries, see Cupull and González, *La CIA contra el Che;* Michelle Ray, "In Cold Blood"; and, above all the internal investigation by the Bolivian military, whose minutes I have read through and which are quoted in part in Marcha, "La CIA en Bolivia." For the information President Johnson received concerning the diary, see NSF Country File, Bolivia, C8, Vol. 4, cables (LBJ Library).

Sources for the leak of Che's diaries to the Cuban government: Hernán Uribe, *Operación Tía Victoria;* Fidel Castro's "Una introducción necesaria"; and my interview of Manuel Manresa, Che's former secretary, in February 1995. For Arguedas's statement and his spectacular jailbreak, see his trial statements, published by the

Uruguayan magazine *Marcha,* and two articles, José Natividad Rosales, "En exclusiva mundial Antonio Arguedas revela a *Siempre* como y por qué entregó a Fidel Castro el diario del Che" and "El Caso Arguedas," in *Bohemia* magazine. On the trials and tribulations of the diaries in the eighties, see *Newsweek,* June 18, 1984; Prensa Latina cable, Aug. 6, 1984, and two articles by "El diario del Che fue robado por una banda de nazis y traficantes de drogas" and "Encuentran páginas perdidas del diario del Che Guevara." The days missing from in the original worldwide edition of the diaries were January 4, 5, 8, and 9, February 8 and 9, March 14, April 4 and 5, June 9 and 10, and July 4 and 5.

The Forgery Operation

Fidel Castro hinted at the possibility of forgery in the prologue to the diary when he wrote: "From a revolutionary standpoint the publication of Che's Bolivian diary allows for no alternative. Che's diary ended up in the hands of Barrientos, who immediately handed a copy to the CIA, to the Pentagon, and to the administration. Journalists with links to the CIA had access to the document in Bolivia itself and took photostatic copies of it, albeit with the commitment to abstain from publishing it, for the time being" ("Una introductión necesaria").

In *La CIA contra el Che,* Cupull and González assert that CIA calligraphers working on the top floor of the U.S. embassy were preparing a smear operation based on the diaries, and planning alterations and omissions. Their assertion is not supported by any other data.

St. George's assertions that the diary published in Cuba was not the genuine article suggest the conclusion that a false version probably *was* being worked on.

Hands and Mask

In May 1969, Arguedas, who was back in La Paz and sought by the police, told lawyer Víctor Zannier (a.k.a. El Mamut:

"The Mammoth"), before taking refuge in the Mexican embassy, that Che's hands were in a jar of formaldehyde which, together with his death mask, was in a wooden urn. Zannier later put them in a backpack and after many trials and tribulations, took them to Cuba.

During a speech on July 26, 1970, Fidel Castro asked the audience for quiet and then announced that Arguedas had sent not only Che's diaries to Cuba, but also his death mask and embalmed hands. When he asked whether these should be buried or preserved, the crowd replied, "Preserve them! Preserve them!" Castro said they would be buried beneath the statue of José Martí with olive-drab uniform sleeves with Commander's stripes on them (interview with Marta Rojas; Homero Campa, "Complicado itinerario de las manos del Che antes de llegar a La Habana en 1970").

58. Che's "Curse"

Sources

Mariano Baptista Gumucio has taken the trouble to compile several of the cases mentioned in this chapter in *¿La venganza del Che?* For the rest, see Gallardo, *De Torres a Bánzer;* Luis Suárez, *Entre el fusil y la palabra;* and Cupull and González, *La CIA contra el Che;* also, Zeballos, "20 años después el cadáver del Che es aún un misterio." For Rodríguez's asthma, see his interview with Carlos Puig, "Sentí por un momento que ya no lo odiaba," Prado's case is from Sebastián Gómez, "¿Vacío de poder militar?" For Ayoroa's deportation, see Gregorio Selser, *Bolivia. El cuartelazo de los cocadólares.* A letter by José Luis Alcázar published in the Mexico City daily *Excélsior,* clarifies important points, as does his book, co-written with José Baldivia, *Bolivia, otra lección para América.*

59.   Images and Ghosts

Sources

Poems by Benedetti and Gelman in a special issue of *Casa de las Américas*.

Other information is from Cupull and González, "De Ñancahuasú a La Higuera. Etapa de combate"; González Bermejo, "Che, su paso por la tierra"; the unsigned article "Hablan el padre y la hermana del Che"; Diego Martínez Estévez, *Ñancahuazú: Apuntes para la historia militar de Bolivia;* José Natividad Rosales, "En exclusiva mundial Antonio Arguedas revela a Siempre como y por qué entregó a Fidel Castro el diario del Che"; Héctor Danilo, "El último encuentro del Che con su familia"; Sergio Berrocal, AFP wire, Dec. 8, 1987; and Enrique Araoz "Hablan los testigos de la muerte del Che."

The Films

Hollywood tried to bask in a little of Che's magic and totally botched the effort. In 1968, 20th Century–Fox shot *Che!*, directed by Richard Fleisher, with Omar Sharif in the title role and Jack Palance as Fidel Castro. Filming took place in Puerto Rico. The weapons and even the cigars used were a disaster. The stereotypes that emerged from the film would ring false with any Latin American viewer—a fanatical, monastic, and humorless Che next to an alcoholic Fidel. The story was plagued with continual errors from Wilson and Bartlet's screenplay or from the way it was produced. In the restive Latin America of the late sixties, the film was taken as another product of the hot war between the empire and popular uprising. Molotov cocktails were thrown at theaters showing the film in Santiago, Chile, and in Venezuela, and it was sabotaged throughout the length and breadth of the continent despite Sharif's declared and somewhat naive admiration for the character he was playing. The film can now be found gathering dust on the shelves of any video store.

Paolo Heusch's Italian version of Che's story, with Paco Rabal playing the part of Che, met with a similar fate. ("Exclusive interview with Omar Sharif"; Gregorio Ortega, "Ladridos desde la cuneta.")

Bibliography

Bibliographies

"Bibliografía del comandante Ernesto Che Guevara." In *Revista de la Biblioteca Nacional José Martí* (Havana: Biblioteca Nacional José Martí, Reference Department), July–December 1967.

Bonich Fernández, Georgina, ed. *Ernesto Che Guevara, estudio bibliográfico.* Havana: Centro de Información Científica y Técnica, Universidad de La Habana, 1975.

———, ed. *Ernesto (Che) Guevara, bibliografía.* Havana: Coordinación de Información Científica y Técnica, Universidad de La Habana, 1985.

——— and Hilda Maidique Patricio. *Ernesto (Che) Guevara, estudio bibliográfico.* Havana: Centro de Información Científica y Técnica, Universidad de La Habana [University of Havana Scientific and Technical Information Center], 1975.

Cozean, Jon D. *Cuban Guerrilla Training Centers and Radio Havana: A Selected Bibliography.* Washington, D.C.: Center for Research in Social Systems, American University, 1968.

García Carranza, Araceli, and Georgina Bonich Fernández, eds. *Bibliografía cubana del comandante Che Guevara.* Havana: Ministerio de Cultura, 1987.

Para leer al Che. Havana: Verde Olivo, Imprenta de la Dirección Política de las FAR [Political Office Publications of the Revolutionary Armed Forces], 1988.

Pérez, Louis A., Jr. "Armed Struggle and Guerrilla Warfare in Latin America." In *A Bibliography of Cuban Sources, 1959–1979. Revista Interamericana de Bibliografía,* No. 4 (1983).

Salgado Moya, Clara, Juan R. Vázquez, Clara de la Torre, and Reina Morales, eds. "La insurrección armada; Camilo y Che en Las Villas, bibliografía." In *Revista de la Biblioteca Nacional José Martí* (Havana: Biblioteca Nacional José Martí, Reference Department), September–December 1987.

Anthologies

Pensamiento crítico, Havana: October 1967.

El Che en la revolución cubana (seven volumes). Havana: Ediciones del Ministerio del Azúcar, 1969.

Escritos y discursos (nine volumes). Havana: Editorial de Ciencias Sociales, 1977.

Obras escogidas (two volumes). Havana: Casa de las Américas, 1970.

Gómez Moreno, Gerardo, René Castellanos, et al., eds. *El hombre y la economía en el pensamiento del Che.* Havana: Editora Política, 1988.

Educación y Hombre Nuevo. Havana: Editora Política, 1989.

Other Works and Articles by Che

Guevara, Ernesto "Che." *Aclaración de algunos términos.* Typewritten manuscript with handwritten notes in Che's own hand, concerning terms used in "Pasajes de la guerra en Africa."

———. "Ante la agresion económica, si nos quitan la cuota perderán sus inversiones en nuestra patria," in *Verde Olivo,* No. 17, 1969.

———. "Camilo," in *Granma,* October 25, 1967.

———. "Carta de despedida del Che" (farewell letter to Carlos Rafael Rodríguez), in *Miami Herald,* December 11, 1983.

———. "El Che con las delegaciones fraternales extranjeras" (summary of speech at Ministry of Industry to foreign workers' delegations, May Day ceremony), in *Bohemia,* May 11, 1962.

———. "Diario de Bolivia," in special number of *Bohemia* magazine, 1968. The 1987 Editora Política edition contains the missing pages plus notes by Adys Cupull and Froilán González.

———. "Discurso del Che en Santa Clara," in *Revolución,* December 29, 1959.

———. "Discurso en el palacio presidencial," in *Granma,* October 26, 1967.

———. "Discurso pronunciado por el comandante Che Guevara en asamblea de obreros portuarios, 6 January 1962," in *Granma,* October 8, 1968.

———. "El divulgador de las teorías revolucionarias debe antes que nada mostrar su ejemplo," in *Verde Olivo,* No. 31, 1960,

———. *Escritos económicos.* Bettelheim, Charles, et al., eds. Córdoba, Argentina: Cuadernos de Pasado y Presente, Edicionos Pasado y Presente, 1969.

———. "La escuela de Minas del Frío" (speech delivered April 3, 1963), in *Opina,* February 1989.

———. *El gobierno revolucionario ha destruido los lazos coloniales en lo económico y lo político.* Santiago, Cuba: Gobierno Provincial de Oriente, 1960.

———. "Guerra y población campesina," in *Revolución,* January 14, 1959.

———. "La idea de la defensa de la revolución no puede desligarse de la idea de trabajo," in *Bohemia,* October 1, 1961.

———. "La influencia de la revolución cubana en América Latina" (address

to members of the State Security Directorate) pamphlet, no publisher, May 18, 1962.

———. Letter to Fidel Castro, January 6, 1958. Photocopy in author's possession.

———. Letter to Angel Salgado, September 9, 1958.

———. "No habrá desempleados en 62," in *Verde Olivo,* September 1960.

———. *Notas de viaje.* Santiago, Chile: Centro Latinoamericano Che Guevara, 1993.

———. "Palabras del Che a la policía," Editorial San Luis, n.d.

———. "Pasajes de la guerra revolucionaria (Congo)." Typewritten manuscript with handwritten notes in Che's own hand, p. 7 and 160, from appendix.

———. "Poemas," in Hilda Gadea, *Che Guevara, años decisivos* (Mexico City: Aguilar, 1972), and in *Bohemia,* June 10, 1988.

———. "Que el hombre sienta la necesidad de hacer trabajo voluntario." Typewritten manuscript, minutes of Ministry of Industry board meeting, December 5, 1964.

———. "¿Qué es un guerrillero?" in *Revolución,* February 19, 1959.

———. "Triunfo con Cuba o muero allá" (previously unpublished letter), in *Crisis* (Buenos Aires) No. 5, September 1973.

———. "Los últimos días, dos documentos," in *Granma,* December 21, 1968.

———, Raúl Castro, and others. *La conquista de la esperanza* (previously unpublished diaries by Cuban guerrillas). Mexico City: Mortiz, 1995.

Books and Articles

22 años de Revolución, cronología. Havana: Editora Política, 1983.

Abdrial, Alberto. "La fe que me inculcaste," in *El Mundo* (Madrid), October 1967.

Abreu, Carlos, and Carlota Guillot. *Sancti

Spiritus, apuntes para una cronología. Havana: Editora Política, 1986.

Abreu, Luis: *Algunas consideraciones acerca del pensamiento económico-militar del Che,* no publisher, n.d.

Abreu, Ramiro. *En el último año de aquella república.* Havana: Editorial de Ciencias Sociales, 1984.

———, Ricardo Alarcón, Carmen Almodóvar, José Bell Lara et al. *Pensar al Che.* Vol. I: *Desafíos de la lucha por el poder político.* Vol. II: *Los retos de la transición socialista.* Havana: CEE–Editorial José Martí, 1989.

Acevedo, Enrique. *Descamisado.* Havana: Editorial Cultura Popular, 1993.

———. "Jefe en toda su dimensión," in *Verde Olivo,* October 10, 1985.

———. "Los últimos días en la Sierra Maestra," in *Verde Olivo,* April 1989.

Acevedo, Rogelio. "Apuntes de la invasión," in *Verde Olivo,* September 1, 1983.

———. "Audacia, audacia y más audacia," in *El Oficial,* November–December 1978.

———. "El Che que yo conocí," in *Verde Olivo,* June 1988.

———. "La Federal," in *Días de combate.*

———. "Si sobresaliente fue el Che como guerrillero, aún más brilló su extraordinario talento en la hermosa obra de construir la nueva sociedad," in *Granma,* December 30, 1988.

Acosta, Bruno. *Ernesto Che Guevera y la disciplina militar consciente.* Paper presented at Scientific Conference on the Military Thinking of Commander Ernesto "Che" Guevara. No publisher, n.d.

Acta de Matrimonio (Wedding Certificate), Ernesto Guevara de la Serna and Hilda Gadea Acosta, Tepozotlán courthouse, document, August 18, 1955.

Acuña, Manuel. "Manuel Acuña cuenta del Uvero," in *Juventud Rebelde,* May 27, 1987.

Adán, Orestes. *El Dorado.* Havana: Letras Cubanas, 1986.

Adoum, Jorge Enrique. "El Che sin nosotros," in *OCLAE,* February 1968.

Afont Robaina, José M. "El amanecer victorioso de la Plata," in *Verde Olivo,* January 15, 1987.

Agacino, Ricardo. "El Che un entusiasta y consumado ajedrecista," in *Cuba Internacional,* September 1987.

Agee, Phillip. *Diario de la CIA.* Laia: Barcelona, 1978 (originally published London: Stonehill and Penguin Books, 1975).

Agüero, Luis, Antonio Benítez, Reynaldo González, et al. *Che comandante.* Mexico City: Diógenes, 1969.

Aguilar, José. "La niñez de Che," in *Granma,* October 16, 1967.

Aguilar, José. "82 hombres y una sola causa" (interview with Arsenio García Dávila) in *Verde Olivo,* December 6, 1964.

Aguilera, Armando R. "Creo en tí, Fidel, creo en la Revolución," in *Bohemia,* January 18, 1959.

Aguilera Morales, Roger. "El cantor de la tropa del Che," in *Verde Olivo,* November 1989.

Aguirre, Manuel Agustín. *El Che Guevara. Aspectos políticos y económicos de su pensamiento.* Bogotá, Colombia: Editorial La Oveja Negra, 1970.

Aguirre Bayley, Miguel. *Ernesto Che Guevara, arquetipo de la solidaridad revolucionaria.* De la Puerta, 1988.

Aiguesvives, E. "Un lector infatigable," in *Verde Olivo,* October 15, 1987.

Alarcón, Dariel. "Héroes inmortales de nuestra América," in *Bohemia,* August 26, 1977.

——— and Mariano Rodríguez Herrera. "Che y la guerrilla de Ñancahuazú," unpublished manuscript.

——— and Mariano Rodríguez Herrera. *Les survivants du Che.* Paris: Editions du Rocher, 1995.

———, Harry Villegas, and Leonardo Tamayo: "El combate de la quebrada del Yuro," in *Verde Olivo,* October 19, 1969.

Alarcón, Dariel, Harry Villegas, and Leonardo Tamayo. "La quebrada del Yuro, recuerdos de un combate," in *Tricontinental,* July–October 1970; also published in *Bohemia* and *Granma,* October 8, 1969.

Alcázar, José Luis. *Ñacahuasu, la guerrilla del Che en Bolivia.* Mexico City: Era, 1969.

——— and José Baldivia. *Bolivia, otra lección para América.* Mexico City: Era, 1973.

——— and Edwin Chacón. "Murió el Che Guevara," in *Presencia* (La Paz), October 10, 1967.

Allende, Salvador. Senate speech, reported in *Diario de sesiones de la República de Chile,* October 18, 1967.

Alles, Agustín: "Criminal bombardeo en Santa Clara," in *Bohemia,* January 11, 1959.

El alma de la revolución. Vol. I: *Principales acciones combativas del primer frente José Martí.* Vol. II: *Segundo Frente oriental Frank País.* Vol. III: *Otros frentes y columnas.* Havana: Editora Verde Olivo, 1991, 1992.

Almeida, Juan. "Un capitán, jefe de la vanguardia," in *Verde Olivo,* February 1988.

———. *Desembarco.* Havana: Editorial de Ciencias Sociales, 1988.

———. *Exilio.* Havana: Editorial de Ciencias Sociales, 1987.

———. *La sierra.* Havana: Editora Política, 1989.

———. *La sierra maestra y más allá.* Havana: Editora Política, 1995.

———. *La única ciudadana.* Havana: Editorial de Ciencias Sociales, 1987.

Alonso, Armando. "Una anécdota en la fundición," in *Juventud Rebelde,* October 7, 1968.

Alonso, Mercedes. "¿Quién ha dicho que el marxismo no tiene alma?" in *Granma,* May 25, 1987.

——— and Rafael Rodríguez Cala. *Reencuentro.* Havana: Ediciones Verde Olivo, 1993.

Althusser, Louis. "Ante la muerte de Ernesto Che Guevara," in *Casa de las Américas,* January–March 1993.

Alvarez, Gerónimo. *Che: una nueva batalla.* Havana: Editorial Pablo de la Torriente, 1994.

Alvarez, Verónica, and Sergio Ravelo. "Ñico López: Símbolo de valor y fidelidad," in *Bohemia,* October 2, 1987.

Alvarez García, John, ed. *Che Guevara.* Medellín, Colombia: Antorcha Monserrate, 1968.

Alvarez Palomares, Alodia. "Allí comienza el Che," in *Verde Olivo,* January 29, 1987.

Alvarez Rom, Luis. "Sobre el método de análisis de los sistemas de financiamiento," in *Cuba Socialista,* No. 35, 1964.

Alvarez Tabío, Pedro. "En espera del desembarco," in *Bohemia,* December 26, 1986.

———. "El más extraordinario de nuestros combatientes," in *Bohemia,* July 26, 1985.

———, ed. *La epopeya del Granma.* Havana: Oficina de Publicaciones del Consejo de Estado, 1986.

——— and Otto Hernández. *El combate del Uvero.* Havana: Gente Nueva, 1980.

Amador, Castor. "El desembarco del Granma y el 30 de noviembre," in *Verde Olivo,* November 30, 1969.

Amaya, Juana. "La pequeña hazaña que dejó valiosas experiencias guerrilleras," in *Trabajadores,* August 28, 1982.

Ameijeiras, Efigenio. "La batalla más corta," parts 1 and 2, in *Bohemia,* July 7 and 14, 1989.

———. "Capitán Habana," in *Verde Olivo,* December–January 1988–89.

———. "Dibujó con flores su sonrisa en el mar," in *Verde Olivo,* October 1989.

———. "Encuentro con Fidel en Puriales de Vicana," in *Somos Jóvenes,* January 1986.

———. "Las guerras no se ganan en el último combate," in *Bohemia,* July 15, 1988.

———. *Más allá de nosotros.* Santiago, Cuba: Editorial Oriente, 1984.

———. "Miedo a las ballenas," in *Verde Olivo,* September 1988.

——— and René Rodríguez. "Con los fusiles, los uniformes y las balas," in *Verde Olivo,* December 2, 1962.

Anderson, Perry, and Robin Blackburn. "Che and Debray in Bolivia," in *Ramparts,* October 1967.

Aragonés, Emilio. Transcript of interview with Jorge Castañeda, February 10, 1995.

Araoz, Enrique. "Hablan los testigos de la muerte del Che," in *Cambio 16* (Madrid), October 19, 1987.

Arcocha, Juan. *Candle in the Wind.* New York: L. Stuart, 1967.

———. *Fidel Castro en rompecabezas.* Madrid: Ediciones R, 1973.

Arguedas, Antonio. Untitled booklet on the capture and death of Ernesto "Che" Guevara, Universidad Técnica de Oruro, n.d. Photocopy in author's possession.

Ariet, María del Carmen. *Che, pensamiento político.* Havana: Editora Política, 1988.

———. "Hasta vencer o morir," in *Moncada,* October 1987.

Arguedas, Antonio. Typewritten transcript of statement in private meeting with Fidel Castro in Havana regarding the death of Ernesto "Che" Guevara and the subsequent hand-over of the Bolivia diary to Cuba.

Arguedas, Sol. *Cuba no es una isla.* Mexico City: Era, 1961.

———. "¿Dónde está el Che Guevara?" in *Cuadernos Americanos,* May–June 1966.

Aroca, Santiago. "Fidel y el Che," in *El Mundo* (Madrid), October 4, 1992.

Arostegui, María Begoña, and Gladys Blanco. *Un desafío al monopolio de la intriga.* Havana: Editora Política, 1981.

"Arribaron a Cuba los cinco guerrilleros que lucharon en Bolivia junto al Che," press cutting in possession of Luis Adrián Betancourt.

Arrufat, Berta, et al. *Vigencia del pensamiento ético del Che para el trabajo político y de partido en el Minit.*
Havana: Instituto Superior Minit, n.d.

Ascuy, René. "Treinta años de la foto más famosa del mundo," in *Juventud Rebelde,* March 30, 1990.

Asociación Nacional de Economistas de Cuba (Cuban National Association of Economists). *La presencia del Che en el Banco Nacional de Cuba y la selección del 26 de noviembre como Día del economista.* Pamphlet, no publisher, n.d.

Avila, Bienvenido. "Tres guías hablan de la invasión," in *Sierra Maestra,* October 8, 1972.

"Aviones piloteados por yankis son utilizados en bombardeos contra las áreas guerrilleras en Bolivia," in *Granma,* April 17, 1967.

Aznares, Juan J. "Buscando al Che," in *El País* (Madrid), January 22, 1996.

Bacallao, Sergio. "Relatos históricos de hechos ocurridos en la sierra maestra desde mediados de junio de 1957," unpublished manuscript.

Baez, H. Vitier. "Che en Buey arriba," in *Verde Olivo,* June 1988.

Baez, Luis. "Yo soy el oscuro teniente . . . ," in *Bohemia,* May 26, 1978.

Baptista Gumucio, Mariano. *¿La venganza del Che?* La Paz: Editorial e Imprenta Artística, 1988.

——— with Ted Córdoba Claure, Sergio Almaraz, and Simón Reyes. *Guerrilleros y generales sobre Bolivia.* Buenos Aires: Editorial Jorge Alvarez, 1968.

Barquín, Ramón. *Las luchas guerrilleras en Cuba. De la colonia a la Sierra Maestra.* Madrid: Editorial Playor, photocopy in author's possession.

Barral, Fernando. "Che estudiante," in *Bohemia,* June 13, 1969.

Barrera, Orlando. *Sancti Spíritus, sinópsis histórica.* Santiago, Cuba: Editorial Oriente, 1966.

Barreras, José Luis. "El Che, ajedrecista entusiasta," in *Cuba Internacional,* October 1963.

Barreras Ferrán, Ramón. "15 de diciembre de 1958," in *Vanguardia* (Santa Clara, Cuba), December 15, 1978.

———. "19 de diciembre de 1958," *Vanguardia* (Santa Clara, Cuba), December 19, 1978.

Barrero Pérez, Eráclides. "Amigo, sus recuerdos del Che," in *Trabajadores,* October 15, 1985.

Barreto, Jesús. "Camarada Tatu," in *Moncada,* October 1987.

Barrientos Ortuño, René. *El Che Guevara, el intervencionismo, un pueblo libre y heroico.* La Paz: Editorial del Estado, 1967.

"Batalla de Santa Clara," in *Granma,* December 27, 1967.

Batista, Fulgencio. *Paradojas.* Mexico City: Botas, 1963.

Bauer Paiz, Alfonso. "Testimonio sobre Ernesto," in *Casa de las Américas,* September–October 1977.

Bayo, Eliseo. "El mejor alumno," in *El Mundo* (Madrid), October 19, 1967.

———. *Mi aporte a la revolución cubana.* Havana: Imprenta del Ejército Rebelde, 1960.

Bedregal, Guillermo. *Los militares en Bolivia.* Mexico City: Extemporáneos, 1971.

Béjar Rivera, Héctor. *Perú 1965, una experiencia libertadora en América.* Mexico City: Siglo XXI, 1969.

Bellinghausen, Herman. "Fiesta en la selva en memoria del Che," in *La Jornada* (Mexico City), October 11, 1994.

Benítez, Augusto. "El cerco de Santa Clara," in *Bohemia,* December 9, 1983.

———. "La colaboración campesina," in *Bohemia,* December 26, 1986.

——— and Katia Valdés. "Reflejos de una época" (interview with Vilma Espín), in *Bohemia,* November 21, 1986.

——— and Katia Valdés. "Vivencias de una heroica hazaña," in *Bohemia,* November 21, 1986

Benítez, José A. "Bolivia: Dinamita y revolución," in *Bohemia,* October 6, 1967.

Benedetti, Mario. "Consternados, rabiosos," in *Casa de las Américas* (Havana), January–February 1968.

Berger, John. "The Legendary Che Guevara Is Dead," in *New Statesman* (London), August 28, 1992.

Bergquist, Laura. "2:30 A.M. Interview with Che Guevara," in *Look,* November 8, 1960.

Berrocal, Sergio. AFP cable, December 8, 1987.

Beruvides, Esteban M., Arsenio Parodi, and Ilario Morfa Vilariño. *Cuba y sus mártires.* Coral Gables, Florida: privately published, 1993.

Betancourt, Luis Adrián. "Apareció para siempre," in *Moncada,* October 6, 1984.

———. "Así murió el criminal. Ultimo minuto de Casillas Lumpuy," in *Bohemia,* January 18–25, 1959.

———. "Batista, capítulo final," in *Verde Olivo,* December 1988–January 1989.

———. "Campaña del Che," in *Bohemia,* January 19, 1968.

———. "La campaña en Las Villas," in *Bohemia,* October 7, 1968.

———. "Che, arquitecto de una victoria," in *Bohemia,* October 20, 1967.

———. "Habla el comandante Guevara," *Bohemia,* January 11, 1959.

———. "Un hombre hecho en los fuegos," in *Moncada,* October 1987.

———. Interview with Sergio Bacallao. Unpublished manuscript.

———. Interview with Faure Chomón, July 19, 1987. Unpublished typewritten manuscript.

———. Interview with Universo Sánchez. Unpublished typewritten manuscript.

———. "Mi hermano el Che," in *Moncada,* October 1987.

———. "Pasión y muerte de Joaquín Casillas," in *Bohemia,* January 11, 1959.

———. "XXII aniversario del asalto al cuartel Moncada. Santa Clara, ciudad 16," in *Bohemia,* July 25, 1975.

Betancourt, Raymundo. "La guerrilla boliviana," mimeographed, no place of publication.

Bethencourt, Gonzalo. "Muerte y sepulcro del Che," in *Pueblo* (Madrid), May 14, 1969.

Bettelheim, Charles. "Formas y métodos de

la planificación socialista y nivel de desarrollo de las fuerzas productivas," in *Cuba Socialista,* No. 32, 1964.

Bianchi Ross, Ciro. "Un constructor llamado Che," in *Cuba,* press cutting, in author's possession.

———. "Tiempo del Che," in *Cuba,* October 1982.

Blaquier, Elsa. "Así se cumplen las órdenes," in *Verde Olivo,* October 1989.

———. "Faltaba papel y tinta, pero salía," (interview with Luis Pavón) in *Verde Olivo,* April 1989.

———. "Mucho gusto, Ramón," in *Verde Olivo,* June 1988.

Blum, William. *The CIA: A Forgotten History.* New Jersey: Zed Books Ltd., 1986.

"Bolivia: Former Dictator Sentenced to 30-Year Prison Term," in *Notisur,* April 30, 1993.

"Bolivian Pictures of Missing Che Guevara," in *Life,* October 6, 1967.

Bonache, Ramón, and Marta S. Martin. *The Cuban Insurrection.* New Brunswick, N.J.: Transaction Books, 1974.

Bonne, Berta. *Menelao, su lucha y acción.* Santiago, Cuba: Editorial Oriente, 1987.

Boorstein, Edward. *The Economic Transformation of Cuba.* New York: Modern Reading, 1968.

Borge, Tomás. *Carlos, el amanecer ya no es una tentación.* Managua: Editorial Nueva Nicaragua, 1982

———. *La paciente impaciencia.* Managua: Editorial Vanguardia, 1989.

Bornot, Thelma, Enzo Infante, Magaly Chacón, Oscar de los Reyes, and Andrés Castillo Bernal. *De Tuxpan a la Plata.* Havana: Sección de Historia de las Fuerzas Armadas Revolucionarias, 1979.

Borrego Díaz, Orlando. *El estilo de trabajo del Che.* Havana: Asociación Nacional de Economistas de Cuba, March 1988.

Bouder, Rosa Ileana. *El Vaquerito.* Havana: Editorial Gente Nueva, 1983.

Breccia, Alberto, with Enrique Breccia and Héctor Osterheld. *Che.* Vitoria: Ikusager ediciones, 1987.

Bremauntz, Alberto. *México y la revolución socialista cubana.* Morelia, Mexico: Privately published, 1966.

Brugioni, Dino A. *Eyeball to Eyeball: The Cuban Missile Crisis.* New York: Random House, 1991.

Buría, Lázaro. Letter to the author, February 17, 1995.

Bussey, Jane. "CIA Veteran at Peace with Killing of Rebel El Che," in *Miami Herald,* October 9, 1992.

Buznego Rodriguez, Enrique, Andrés Castillo, Verónica Alvarez, et al. *Diciembre del 58.* Havana: Editorial de Ciencias Sociales, 1977.

Buznego Rodríguez, Enrique, and Luis Rosado Eiro. "Estrategia del Che en las Villas," in *Granma,* January 2, 1983.

Cabrera, Migdalia, ed. "La batalla de Santa Clara," no publisher, n.d.

Cabrera, P. E. "En la cueva de los Portales," in *Verde Olivo,* clipping in possession of Luis Adrián Betancourt.

Cabrera Alvarez, Guillermo. *Hablar de Camilo.* Havana: Instituto Cubano del Libro, 1970.

———. "Operación caja de tabaco," in *Bohemia,* October 23, 1979.

Calzadilla, Iraida. "La huella imborrable del guerrillero de América," in *Trabajadores,* September 21, 1982.

Campa, Homero. "Complicado itinerario de las manos del Che antes de llegar a La Habana en 1970," in *Proceso* (Mexico City), December 17, 1995.

———. "Han hecho del Che un mito para venerar, no un ejemplo a seguir: Hilda Guevara," in *Proceso* (Mexico City), October 25, 1993.

"La canallada," in *Zeta* (Venezuela), July 11, 1984.

Cantón Navarro, José. "Che, un modelo también para los que escriben historia," in *Cuba Socialista,* March–April 1989.

Cantor, Jay. *La muerte de Che Guevara.* Barcelona: Grijalbo, 1985.

Capote, Angela. "La efigie simbólica del Che," in *Tribuna*, March 7, 1990.

Capote, María Helena. "Tres relatos inéditos," in *Opina*, December 1988.

Cardenal, Ernesto. *En Cuba*. Mexico City: Era, 1977.

Cárdenas, Aida. "Médico y soldado," in *Bohemia*, October 25, 1974.

Cardosa, Santiago. "Che en el recuerdo de dos fotógrafos," in *Granma*, July 3, 1988.

Carrasco, Juana. "El Che hacía las portadas," in *Verde Olivo*, May 89.

———. "El combate de Forces Bendera," in *Verde Olivo*, June 90.

———. "Pablo Rivalta: Sin darle tregua al enemigo," in *Verde Olivo*, August 1988.

———. "Tatu, un guerrillero africano" (interview with Víctor Dreke), in *Verde Olivo*, June 1988, and *Cuba*, February 1989.

Carrillo, Justo. *A Cuba le tocó perder*. Miami: Ediciones Universal, 1993.

"Carta del Che a revolución y una aclaración nuestra," in *Revolución*, December 29, 1962.

Casal Guerra, Jesús. "Aquella madrugada amaneció más temprano," in *Verde Olivo*, December 27, 1984.

Casaus, Víctor. *Girón en la memoria*. Havana: Casa de las Américas, 1970.

"El caso Arguedas, una fuga sensacional," in *Bohemia*, August 2, 1968.

Castañeda, Jorge. "El Che es el último superviviente de la utopía naufragada," in *Proceso* (Mexico City), December 17, 1995.

———. Interview of Ulises Estrada, February 9, 1995.

Castelló, Humberto. "Segundo Frente Nacional del Escambray, negación del ejército rebelde," in *Verde Olivo*, February 19, 1961.

Castillo, Rolando. "Alto de Escudero," in *Sierra Maestra*, October 7, 1973.

Castillo Bernal, Andrés. *La batalla de Pino del Agua*. Havana: Editora Política, 1993.

Castillo Ramos, Rubén. "Che Guevara, iniciando el trabajo voluntario en Cuba," in *Bohemia*, October 18, 1985.

———. "Junto al Che en la sierra," (interview with Arístides Guerra) in *Bohemia*, November 21, 1969.

Castro, Fidel. "Carta sobre Trujillo," in *Bohemia*, August 26, 1955.

———. "Comparecencia de Fidel ante la prensa para informar sobre la muerte del Che," *Bohemia*, October 15, 1967.

———. "El diario del Che en Bolivia. Una introducción necesaria." *Bohemia*, special issue

———. "Discurso del 13 de Marzo del 91," in *Granma*, March 16, 1991.

———. "Discurso pronunciado el 8 de October de 1987 en el XX aniversario de la caída del Che en combate," in *Cuba Socialista*, November–December 1987.

———. "Discurso pronunciado en el acto de presentación del comité central del PCC" (October 3, 1965), in *Bohemia*, October 8, 1965.

Castro, Fidel. *Discurso pronunciado en La Concepción para dar inicio a las actividades de la Brigada Invasora de Maquinarias* (October 30, 1967). Havana: Instituto del Libro, 1967.

———. "Discurso pronunciado en la Plaza de la Revolución, en la velada solemne en memoria del Che, 18 de octubre del 67," in *El Mundo* (Madrid), October 19, 1967, and *Bohemia*, special issue.

———. "Discurso pronunciado en Santiago de Cuba el 1 de enero del 89," in *Granma*, January 3, 1989.

———. "La juventud del mundo ve en el Che todo un símbolo," in *OCLAE*, November 1977.

———. "Las manos del Che," in *Bohemia*, July 31, 1970.

Castro, Fidel. Messages to Che from February 16 and June 1958, photocopies of five typewritten originals.

———. "El movimiento 26 de julio," in *Bohemia*, March 19, 1955.

———. "El movimiento 26 de julio y la conspiracion militar" in *Aldabonazo*, May 15, 1956

———. "Sirvo a Cuba," in *Bohemia*, November 20, 1955.

———, Haydée Santamaría, Vilma Espín, et al. *Dice la palma*. Havana: Letras Cubanas, 1980.

Castro, Raúl. "Discurso en la inauguración del Congreso campesino en armas," in *Bohemia,* September 16, 1988.

———. "Un testimonio de la gratitud de todo un pueblo," in *Bohemia,* October 13, 1978.

"Castro's Brain," in *Time,* August 8, 1960.

Cato, Susana. "Operación Tía Victoria relata la burla a la CIA and la llegada del diario del Che a Cuba," in *Proceso* (Mexico City), April 13, 1987.

Cazañas, José. "Che, una de sus proezas militares," in *Verde Olivo,* October 7, 1973.

———. "Radio Rebelde. Su combate invisible y poderoso," in *Verde Olivo,* February 88.

Cazes Camarero, Pedro Luis. *El Che y la generación del 70.* Buenos Aires: Dialéctica, 1989.

"Celia," in *Moncada,* special issue, May 1990.

Cerecedo, Francisco. *Ernesto Che Guevara, protagonista de la historia.* Madrid: Ibérico Europea de Ediciones, 1968.

Cernadas Lamadrid, Juan Carlos, and Ricardo Halac. *El Che Guevara.* Buenos Aires: Editorial Perfil, 1968.

César, Antonieta. "Che: la tentación de un beso," in *Trabajadores,* September 5, 1994

Chang, Arturo. "Aquel hermoso amanecer de la liberación," in *Trabajadores,* December 23, 1983.

Chavez, Armando. *El pensamiento ético del Che.* Havana: Editora Política, 1983.

———. "Tan cubano como el que más," in *Moncada,* October 1987.

Che. Havana: Ediciones Cuba, 1973.

"Che, avance incontenible," in *Vanguardia,* December 23, 1967.

"Che Comandante," in *Cine Cubano,* No. 47, 1967.

"El Che como militar," in *El Oficial,* October 1972.

"Che. El recuerdo y sus propias palabras," in *Juventud Rebelde,* May 12, 1988.

"Che en Bolivia" (photographs), in *Granma,* October 8, 1968.

"El Che en el Escambray" (interview with Faure Chomón), *Bohemia,* October 1967.

Che Guevara. Barcelona: Planeta Agostini, 1996.

"El Che que conoce el pueblo" (chronology 1959–1965), in *Juventud Rebelde,* October 16, 1967.

"Che y Pinares hablan de Camilo," in *Verde Olivo,* October 27, 1974.

Chichkov, Vasili. "Crónica de un periodista soviético en Cuba," in *Verde Olivo,* January 5, 1984.

Chinea, Hugo. "La primera armería de la guerra," in *Cuba Internacional,* June 1972.

Chomé, Jules. *L'ascension de Mobutu.* Brussels: Editions Complexe, 1974.

Chomón, Faure. "Che en el Escambray," in *Bohemia,* special issue, October 20, 1967.

———. "Cuando el Che llegó al Escambray," in *Verde Olivo,* December 1, 1965.

———. "Santa Clara, la batalla final," in *Combatiente,* December 15, 1969.

"La CIA en Bolivia," in *Marcha,* 25 April 25, and May 2, 1969.

Ciechanower, Mauricio. "Con el padre del Che Guevara," in *Plural* (Mexico City), July 1984.

Cienfuegos, Camilo. Messages to Che, April 24, 1958.

Cienfuegos, Camilo. "Informe de la invasión" (pages from campaign diary) in *Días de Combate.* Havana: Instituto del libro, 1970. Another version in *La Sierra y el llano.* Havana: Casa de Las Américas, 1969.

Colás, Iván. "Che, de Santa Clara a la Cabaña," in *Juventud Rebelde,* January 3, 1990.

Collado, Norberto. "Una travesía heroica," in *Verde Olivo,* December 1, 1963.

Collier, Daniel M., Jr. "Guevara's Last Words," in *The New York Times,* December 10, 1995.

"Combatientes de la patria," in *Verde Olivo;* four parts: December 24, 1972; May

20, 1973, July 2, and November 22, 1974.

Villegas, Harry "San Luis" Reyes. *Días de Bolivia*. Caracas: Ediciones Bárbara, 1970.

"Como murió el Che," *Sucesos Para Todos*, February 17, 1968.

"Composición de la columna #8 Ciro Redondo," in *Verde Olivo*, August 25, 1963.

"Concurso de la vida del Vaquerito," in *Verde Olivo*, June 12, 1960.

"Conmoción popular por ver el cadáver del Che," in *El Diario* (La Paz), October 10, 1967.

Constantin, Elio. "Por las huellas del Che en su 45 aniversario. Su paso por la escuela primaria, la secundaria y la universidad," in *Granma*, June 14, 1973.

Constela, Julia. "Cuando Ernesto Guevara aún no era el Che" (interview with Celia de la Serna), *Bohemia*, August 27, 1961.

Conte Agüero, Luis. *Paredón*. Miami: Colonial Press, 1962.

Contreras, Orlando. "El tren blindado," in *Verde Olivo*, January 5, 1964.

Cormier, Jean, with Alberto Granado and Hilda Guevara. *Che Guevara*. Paris: Editions du Rocher, 1995.

"Corte suprema de justicia firmó sentencia contra Luis Garcia Meza," in *Presencia* (La Paz), April 16, 1993.

CRISP, eds. *Congo 1965: Political Documents of a Developing Nation*. Princeton, N.J.: Princeton University Press, 1967.

Cruz Díaz, Rigoberto. *Chicharrones, la sierra chiquita*. Santiago, Cuba: Editorial Oriente, 1982.

"Cuba's New Banker," in *U.S. News & World Report*, December 7, 1959.

Cubela, Rolando. "La batalla de Santa Clara," in *Bohemia*, July 22, 1963.

———. "Che, su campaña en las Villas," in *Verde Olivo*, December 3, 1961.

Cupull, Adys, and Froilán González. *Cálida presencia. Su amistad con Tita Infante*. Santiago, Cuba: Editorial Oriente, 1995.

———. *La CIA contra el Che*. Havana: Editora Política, 1992.

———. *De Ñancahuasú a La Higuera*. Havana: Editora Política, 1989.

———. "De Ñancahuasú a La Higuera. Etapa de combate," in *Moncada*, May 1989.

———. "Desde Ñancahuasú a La Higuera," in *Moncada*, October 1987.

———. *Ernestito vivo y presente*. Havana: Editora Política, 1989.

———. "Ernesto y los poemas de amor," in *Verde Olivo*, September 1989.

———. *Un hombre bravo*. Havana: Editorial Capitán San Luis, 1994.

———. "La Higuera," in *Moncada*, October 1987.

———. "Ninfa Arteaga. Nunca podré olvidar como el Che me miró," in *Bohemia*, November 13, 1987.

———. "Nunca podré olvidar su mirada," in *Moncada*, October 1987.

Dalton, Roque. "Combatiendo la libertad de América Latina ha muerto nuestro comandante Ernesto Guevara," in *Casa de las Américas* January–February 1968.

———. *"Revolución en la revolución" y la crítica de derecha*. Havana: Cuadernos Casa de Las Américas, 1970.

Daniel, Jean. "Un reportaje al Che Guevara en Argelia," in *L'Express* July 15, 1963 (manuscript translation in author's possession).

Darushenkov, Oleg. *Cuba, el camino de la revolución*, 3rd ed. (expanded). Moscow: Progress Publishers, 1984.

Davis, Thomas M., Jr., and Gary Prado Salmon. "The Defeat of Che Guevara: Military Response to Guerrilla Challenge in Bolivia," in *Hispanic American Historical Review*, November 1991.

Debray, Régis. "Ante la muerte de Ernesto Che Guevara," in *Islas* (Santa Clara, Cuba), January–March 1968.

———. "Un arcángel sin espada," in *El País* (Madrid), October 4, 1992.

———. "Bolivia: Nota para un análisis de la situación política," in *Oclae*, April 1970.

———. "El castrismo, la larga marcha de América Latina," in *Marcha* (Montevideo), July 1967; also in *Ensayos sobre América Latina.* Mexico City: Era, 1969.

———. *La crítica de las armas.* Mexico City: Siglo XXI Editores, 1975

———. *Diario de un pequeño burgués entre dos fuegos y cuatro muros.* Caracas: Monteavila Editores, 1978.

———. "Las dos muertes del Che" (trans. Mercedes Torres, MRE cable services), in *Le Nouvel Observateur* (Paris), October 10, 1975.

———. *Escritos en la prisión.* Mexico City: Siglo XXI Editores, 1972.

———. *La guerrilla del Che.* Mexico City: Siglo XXI Editores, 1975.

———. *Loues saient nos seigneurs le Che.* Paris: Gallimard, 1996.

———. *Las pruebas de fuego.* Mexico City: Siglo XXI Editores, 1975.

"Debray en peligro," in *Bohemia,* January 6, 1968.

"Debray reitera su apoyo a la guerrilla," in *Punto Final* (Santiago, Chile), October 24, 1967.

De la Fuente, Inmaculada. "Del poster al olvido," in *El País* (Madrid), October 4, 1992.

"De la guerrilla rural a la guerrilla urbana," in *Presencia* (La Paz), December 6, 1990.

De la Hoz, Pedro. "Cada santaclareño fue un combatiente," in *Verde Olivo,* April 6, 1981.

———. "Cuando Walcott cantó al Che," in *Granma,* October 13, 1992.

De la Ossa, Enrique. *Sangre y pillaje.* Havana: Editorial Pablo de la Torriente, 1990.

"De la tiranía a la libertad," (Noticuba news agency dispatch), in *Revolución,* January 14, 1959.

Del Cueto, Mario G. "Lo que vio el Che en la URSS," in *Bohemia,* December 11, 1960.

Delgado, Carlos Jesús. "La concepción de la guerra revolucionaria de guerrillas de Ernesto Che Guevara," in *Casa de las Américas,* July–August 1987.

De los Reyes Gavilanes, Roberto. "Llegaron los barbuditos, avisen al Che," in *Tribuna,* November 26, 1989.

Del Pino, Rafael. *Amanecer en Girón.* Havana: Edición de las Fuerzas Armadas Revolucionarias, 1969.

Departamento de consulta y referencia de la Biblioteca José Martí. *Tiempo de Che, primer ensayo de cronología.* Barcelona: Anagrama, 1976.

"Descubren los restos de tres guerrilleros," in *La Jornada* (Mexico City), December 14, 1995.

Desnoes, Edmundo. "Aniversario," in *Casa de las Américas,* January–February 1968.

———. "El tren blindado," in *Cuba,* August 1965.

"Despachos cablegráficos sobre los acontecimientos de Bolivia," in *Granma,* October 18, 1967.

"Después de la victoria primeras horas en la capital," *Bohemia,* January 11, 1959.

Deutscher, Isaac. *Rusia, China y Occidente.* Mexico City: Era, 1974.

De Vos, Pierre. *Vida y muerte de Lumumba.* Mexico City: Era, 1962.

Días de combate. Havana: Instituto Cubano del Libro, 1970.

Díaz Castro, Tania. "Del Moncada al triunfo," in *Bohemia,* July 26, 1968.

Díaz González, Anel. *El pensamiento militar del Che y su vigencia en la exploración.* Scientific Conference on the Military Thinking of Commander Ernesto "Che" Guevara, undated, no place of publication.

Díaz Loyola, Jesús. "La hija menor del Che," in *Bohemia,* October 7, 1988.

Díaz Martínez. *Camilo, por los montes surcados.* Santiago, Cuba: Editorial Oriente, 1989.

Díaz Tamayo. "Circular del mayor general del 30 septiembre 1958," unpublished manuscript.

Dickens, Beverley. *Paths to Pacifism.* New York: Exposition Press, 1972.

"Un dictador clandestino," *Presencia* (La Paz), March 1, 1989.

Dieterich, Heinz, "Diarios inéditos de la guerrilla cubana," in *Proceso* (Mexico City), February 20, 1995.

Díez Acosta, Tomás. "Las comunicaciones

en la guerrilla," in *Verde Olivo,* March 6 and 13, 1986.

———. "El vestuario en las montañas," in *Verde Olivo,* March 27, 1986.

Dirección de Propaganda y Agitación de la Dirección Política central de las FAR. *Preparación Política de sargentos, soldados y marineros.* Havana: 1987.

Dolgoff, Sam. *The Cuban Revolution.* Montreal: Black Rose Books, 1976.

Dolset, Juan. "Che en la ciencia y la técnica. Sueños hechos realidad de un revolucionario," in *Juventud Rebelde,* May 12, 1988.

Dolutsky, Ivan. "En torno a un artículo sobre el Che," in *América Latina* (Moscow), October 1987.

"¿Dónde está el Che?" in *Newsweek,* June 28, 1965.

Dopico Asensio, Adrián. "Treinta aniversario de la liberación de Trinidad," unpublished manuscript.

Dorschner, John, and Roberto Fabricio. *The Winds of December.* New York: Coward, McCann & Geoghegan, 1980.

"Dos expertos argentinos en leprología recorren sudamérica en motocicleta," in *Diario Austral,* February 19, 1952.

"Los dos interlocutores eran muy distintos por su origen," in *Bohemia,* August 13, 1961.

Douglas, María Eulalia. "Hasta la victoria siempre," in *Opina,* December 1987.

Dreke, Victor. "La toma del escuadrón 31," in *Bohemia,* December 28, 1973.

———. "Víctor Dreke habla sobre el combate en el escuadrón 31," in *Vanguardia* (Santa Clara, Cuba), December 27, 1978.

Dubois, Jules. "Las ejecuciones en Cuba," in *Bohemia,* February 1, 1959.

Dubois, Jules. *Fidel Castro: Rebel, Liberator or Dictator.* Indianapolis: New Bobbs-Merrill Co., 1959.

Dumont, René. *Cuba, Socialism and Development.* New York: Grove Press, 1970.

Dumpierre, Erasmo. "De alegría de Pío al Purial de Vicana. Relatos del comandante Universo Sánchez," in *Bohemia,* December 25, 1970.

Ebon, Martin. *Che: Making of a Legend.* New York: Universe Books, 1969.

Echegaray, Patricio. *Debates y búsquedas actuales para la construcción de una alternativa política revolucionaria en América Latina y el Caribe.* Paper delivered at International Seminar, June 12–14, 1992, Rosario, Argentina. Rosario, Argentina: no publisher, 1992.

"El embajador Smith, servidor del déspota," in *Bohemia,* January 11, 1959.

"Emplaza Guevara a Conrado Rodríguez," in *Revolución,* January 8, 1960.

"La entrada del presidente Urrutia en palacio," *Bohemia,* January 11, 1959.

Entralgo, Armando, ed. *Africa.* Vol. 4: *Religión.* Havana: Editorial Ciencias Sociales, 1979.

"Entró primero la columna Ameijeiras," in *El Mundo* January 5, 1959.

Enzensberger, Hans Magnus. *El interrogatorio de la Habana.* Barcelona: Anagrama, 1973.

Equipo de investigación y redacción del Centro de estudios de historia militar de las Fuerzas Armadas Revolucionarias. *13 de marzo 1957, Asalto al Palacio Presidencial.* Havana: Editora Política, 1982.

"Ernesto," in *Juventud Rebelde,* June 13, 1975.

El Escalón más alto (selection of articles published in *Verde Olivo* on Che's guerrilla campaign in Bolivia). Havana: Ediciones Verde Olivo, 1993.

Escobar, Milagros. "Guerrilleros y amigos," in *Juventud Rebelde,* May 12, 1988.

Escobar, Froilán, and Félix Guerra. *Che, Sierra adentro.* Havana: Uneac, 1982; first published in *Cuba* magazine, May–June 1970.

———. *Cinco Picos.* Havana: Editora Abril, 1988.

———. Interviews of Pablo Rivalta, December 1991 and January 1992.

Espinosa, Reinaldo, and Guillermo Grau. *Atlas histórico, biográfico y militar,*

Ernesto Guevara, Vol. I. Havana: Editorial Pueblo y Educación, 1990.

"Esta revolución ha traspuesto los límites de Cuba," in *Verde Olivo,* September 14, 1959.

"Estampas de un libertador," in *Bohemia,* undated.

Estrada Juárez, Adela. "Club Che Guevara, apoyar a los que luchan y sufren," in *Bastión,* November 23, 1989.

"Exigirán la entrega de los restos del Che sus familiares," in *La Jornada* (Mexico City), December 16, 1995.

"Falleció Ernesto Guevara Lynch, padre del Che," in *Granma,* April 4, 1987.

Fava, Athos. "Che y los argentinos," in *Tricontinental,* June 1987.

Fazio, Carlos. "Castro relata su primer encuentro con el Che, en Mexico," in *Proceso* (Mexico City), December 12, 1988.

"La fe del Che en Fidel," in *Opina,* February 1989.

Feria, Manuel de. "Santo Domingo, antes y 20 años después," in *Vanguardia,* December 29, 1978.

Fermoselle, Rafael. *Cuban Leadership After Castro.* Miami: North-South Center, University of Miami, 1992.

Fernández, Adolfo. "Ajedrecista fuerte," in *Moncada,* October 1982.

Fernández, Juan Carlos. "Che nació en Vallegrande," in *Moncada,* October 1987.

———. "La hazaña de Joaquín," in *Moncada,* October 1987.

———. "Imágenes de la guerrilla," in *Moncada,* October 1987.

———. "Osvaldo Sánchez," in *Moncada,* December 1975.

Fernández, Tony. "La batalla de Santa Clara," in *El Oficial,* November 1967.

———. "La batalla de Santa Clara," in *Granma,* December 28, 1974.

———. "La campaña del Che en Las Villas," *Granma,* December 21, 1967.

Fernández Font, Marcelo. "Desarrollo y funciones del banco socialista en Cuba," in *Cuba Socialista,* No. 30, 1964.

Fernández Mell, Oscar. "La batalla de Santa Clara," in *El Oficial,* May 1967.

———. "La campaña del Che en Las Villas," *Granma,* December 21, 1967.

Fernández Mell, Oscar. "De las Mercedes a Gavilanes," in *Verde Olivo,* August 25, 1963.

Fernández Mell, Oscar. "La sierra, la invasión, Las Villas," *Granma,* November 29, 1967.

Fernández Montes de Oca, Alberto. *El diario de Pacho.* Santa Cruz, Bolivia: Editorial Punto y Coma, 1987.

Fernández Noa, Yurina. "Testimonio de Hilda Guevara," in *El Habanero,* October 25, 1988.

Fernández Retamar, Roberto. "Un montón de memorias," in *Cuba Internacional,* August 1965.

Fernández Retamar, Roberto. "Aquel poema," in *Casa de las Américas,* January–February 1968.

———. *Para leer al Che.* Havana: Letras Cubanas, 1979.

Ferrera, Alberto. "El comandante Ernesto Guevara y la invasión de Las Villas." Pamphlet, Booklet, undated no place of publication, Scientific Conference on the Military Thinking of Commander Ernesto 'Che' Guevara.

———. "Principales características de la invasión de la columna 8 Ciro redondo a las Villas," in *El Oficial,* April 1978.

Figueras, Miguel Alejandro. "Aspectos y problemas del desarrollo económico cubano," in *Nuestra Industria* No. 9, October 1964.

Flores, Marcelo, et al. *Ernesto Guevara, nomade del' utopia.* Milan: Manifestolibri, 1993.

Fonseca, Rubén. "La primera escuela del ejército rebelde," in *Verde Olivo,* December 3, 1981.

Fontaine, André. "La revancha del Che," in *Cambio 16* (Madrid) September 19, 1983.

Franqui, Carlos. *Cuba, el libro de los 12.* Mexico City: Era, 1966.

———. *Diario de la revolución cubana.* Barcelona: R. Torres, 1976.

———. *Retrato de familia con Fidel.* Barcelona: Seix Barral, 1981.

———. *Vida, aventuras y desastres de un*

hombre llamado Castro. Barcelona: Planeta, 1988.

Freemantle, Brian. *CIA.* London: Michael Joseph, 1983.

Frías, Angel. "La Federal y cuatro compañeros," in *Verde Olivo,* September 4, 1963.

Fuentes, Fulvio, and Aldo Isidrón del Valle. "Che, niñez, adolescencia, juventud," in *Bohemia,* October 1967.

Fuentes, José Lorenzo. "La batalla de Santa Clara," *Bohemia,* December 30, 1958.

———. "Las Villas bajo las balas," in *Bohemia,* July 26, 1968.

———. "Tres momentos con el Che," in *Gaceta de Cuba,* September–October 1967.

Fuentes, Norberto. "La batalla del Che," in *Cuba Internacional,* October 1977.

Gadea, Hilda. "A Ernesto Che Guevara," in *Casa de las Américas,* January–February 1968.

———. *Che Guevara, años decisivos.* Mexico City: Aguilar, 1972.

Galeano, Eduardo. "El Che Guevara," in *Violencia y enajenación.* Mexico City: Editorial Nuestro Tiempo, 1971.

———. "Ernesto 'Che' Guevara: el alucinante viaje del yo al nosotros," *La Jornada* (Mexico City), September 21, 1987.

———. *Memoria del Fuego.* Vol. III: *El siglo del viento.* Madrid: Siglo XXI, 1986.

Galich, Manuel. "El comandante Guevara en Punta del Este, 1961," in *Vida Universitaria,* October 1967.

Gallardo Lozada, Jorge. *De Torres a Banzer.* Buenos Aires: Ediciones Periferia, 1972.

Gálvez, William. *Camilo, señor de la vanguardia.* Havana: Editorial Ciencias Sociales, 1979.

———. "Recuerdos del combate de Yaguajay," in *Juventud Rebelde,* December 26, 1988.

Gambini, Hugo, with J. Algañaraz and Leda Orellano. *El Che Guevara.* Buenos Aires: Paidós, 1968.

Garcés, María, ed. *Materiales sobre la guerrilla de Ñancahuazú.* Quito: Editorial El Mañana, 1986.

García, Calixto. "Yo fui el número 15," in *Verde Olivo,* December 1, 1963.

García, Nelson, and Osvaldo Rodríguez. "El capitán descalzo habla de su amigo el Vaquerito," in *Juventud Rebelde,* December 28, 1983.

García, Walterio. "El ejemplo de Camilo y el Che" (interview of Rogelio Acevedo), in *Juventud Rebelde,* November 16, 1965.

García Márquez, Gabriel. "El Che en Africa, los meses de tinieblas," in *Alternativa* (Colombia), October 10, 1996.

García Oliveras, Julio. *José Antonio.* Havana: Editorial Abril, 1988.

Gavi, Philippe. *Che Guevara.* Paris: Editions Universitaires, 1970.

Gelman, Juan. "Conversaciones," in *Casa de las Américas* (Havana), January–February 1968.

Geyer, Georgie Anne. *Guerrilla Prince: The Untold Story of Fidel Castro.* Boston: Little, Brown, 1991.

Gianturco, Corrado. *La revolución congoleña.* Barcelona: Bruguera, 1972.

Giáp, Vo Nguyên. *Guerra del pueblo, ejército del pueblo. Dien Bien Fu.* With foreword by Ernesto "Che" Guevara. Mexico City: Ediciones Era, 1971.

Gilly, Adolfo. "Cuba, entre la coexistencia y la revolución," *Monthly Review* Selections in Spanish, November 1964.

———. *La senda de la guerrilla.* Mexico City: Nueva Imagen, 1986.

Gleijeses, Piero. "Cuba's first venture in Africa: Algeria, 1961–1963." Unpublished manuscript.

Goldar, Ernesto. "John William Cooke: de Perón al Che Guevara," in *Todo Es Historia,* June 1991.

Gómez, Orlando: "Caballete de Casa en la memoria," in *Granma,* October 29, 1975.

Gómez, Sebastián. "¿Vacío de poder militar?" in *Caretas,* June 25, 1981.

Gómez Ferrals, Marta. "Sentirlo más cercano," in *Cuba Internacional,* September 1987.

González, Froilán. "Ernesto y los poemas de amor," in *Verde Olivo,* September 1989.

———. "Esa foto de Ernestito," in *Verde Olivo,* June 1989.

———. "Mi primo Ernestito," in *Verde Olivo,* July 1989.

González, Gloria, María Carolina Villazón, and M. A. Fernández. *Santa Clara, tres asaltos en el camino hacia la victoria.* Havana: Editora Política, 1985.

González, Luis, and Gustavo Sánchez Salazar. *The Great Rebel: Che Guevara in Bolivia.* New York: Grove Press, 1969.

González, Mike. "The Culture of the Heroic Guerrilla: The Impact of Cuba in the Sixties," in *Bulletin of Latin American Research,* December 1984.

González, Nelson. *Ideas del comandante Ernesto Che Guevara acerca del ataque a columnas en movimiento.* No place of publication; no publisher, n.d.

González Acosta, Alejandro. *Che escritor.* Guadalajara, Mexico: Diógenes/Universidad de Guadalajara, 1989.

González Bello, Manuel. "Así lo cuenta David," in *Bohemia,* October 29, 1978.

———. "Fotos a Tirso," in *Bohemia,* July 5, 1985.

González Bermejo, Ernesto. "Che, su paso por la tierra," in *Verde Olivo,* August 1, 1971.

———. "Odisea en la selva," in *Verde Olivo,* July 25, 1971.

———. "¿Quién es Rubén Sánchez?" *Juventud Rebelde,* September 5, 1971.

———. "El vado de la traición," *Verde Olivo,* July 4, 1971.

González Cabrera, Heidy. "Rostros más allá de la memoria," in *Mujeres,* October 1983.

González Guerrero, Roger. "Con el escudo y los laureles," in *Bohemia,* 1989. Clipping in the possession of Luis Adrián Betancourt.

González-Mata, Louis Manuel. *Las muertes del "Che" Guevara.* Barcelona: Argos Vergara, 1980.

González Rojas, Mori. *Reflexiones sobre el pensamiento del comandante Ernesto Che Guevara acerca de las comunicaciones.* Scientific Conference on the Military Thinking of Commander Ernesto 'Che' Guevara, undated.

Gorrín, Leonel. *El pensamiento pedagógico-militar del comandante Ernesto Che Guevara acerca de la preparación del hombre para las acciones combatives,* Scientific Conference on the Military Thinking of Commander Ernesto 'Che' Guevara, undated.

Gott, Richard. "Yo vi el cadáver del Che en Vallegrande," in *Punto Final* (Santiago, Chile), October 21, 1967.

Granado, Alberto. "Un largo viaje en moto de Argentina a Venezuela," in *Granma,* October 16, 1967.

———. *Con el Che por Sudamérica.* Havana: Letras Cubanas, 1986.

El Granma era invencible como el espíritu de sus combatientes. Introduction by Faustino Pérez. Havana: Colección Verde Olivo, 1988.

Gre, Jaime. "Entrevista a miembros del ELN en el Jigüe," Prensa Latina special service, mimeographed bulletin, n.d.

Guayasamín. Oswaldo. "Raúl Castro. "Che, es Granma vamos," in *America Latina* (Moscow), No. 2, February 1988.

"Guerra en el Escambray," in *Cuba Internacional,* August 1963.

"La guerra en las Villas," in *Prensa Libre,* January 6, 1959.

Guerra Alemán, José. *Barro y cenizas.* Madrid: Fomento Editorial, 1971.

Guerra, Estela. "Soldado de la revolución," in *Moncada,* October 1987.

Guerra, Félix. "Brindis por el futuro," manuscript in author's possession.

———. "Camilo Cienfuegos. Un tránsito fulgurante," manuscript author's possession.

———. "Un guerrillero y su fusil de tigre," in *Bohemia,* December 2, 1988.

———. "Médico y combatiente," in *Bohemia,* June 10, 1988.

——— and Froilán Escobar. *El fuego que*

enciende los fusiles. Havana: Uneac, 1988.

"Guevara Out of Cuba or Just Out of Favor," in *U.S. News & World Report,* October 18, 1965.

Guevara Lynch, Ernesto. *Aquí va un soldado de América.* Mexico City: Planeta, 1987.

———. *Mi hijo el Che.* Barcelona: Planeta, 1981.

———. "Mi hijo el Che," in *Cuba Internacional,* September 1987.

Granma, rumbo a la libertad. Havana: Gente Nueva, 1983.

Guevara sconosciuto. Rome: Datanews, 1995.

Guglietta, Guy. UPI cable, October 9, 1977.

Guillén, Nicolás. "Un gran muerto invencible," in *El Mundo,* October 16, 1967.

Guillot, Carlota. "Fomento. 100 fusiles para la fuerza de la libertad," in *Vanguardia,* December 19, 1978.

———. "Sancti Spiritus: una ciudad tomada por su propia población," in *Vanguardia,* December 23, 1978.

Gumucio, Mariano. *La venganza del Che.* La Paz: Editorial e Imprenta Artística, 1988.

Gustin. "Debray espera liberación," in *El Mercurio* (Santiago, Chile), December 11, 1970.

Gutiérrez, Carlos María. "El Che en lo suyo," in *Bohemia,* December 15, 1967.

———. *Los hombres de la historia. Che Guevara.* Buenos Aires: Centro Editor de América Latina, 1970.

———. "Una madrugada de febrero," in *Casa de las Américas* (Havana), January–February 1968.

———. "Los motivos del Che," in *Casa de las Américas* (Havana), May–June 1969.

———. "Telefoto exclusiva," in *Casa de las Américas* (Havana), May–June 1968.

Gutiérrez Barrios, Fernando. Interview of Jorge Castañeda, July 18, 1995.

Habel, Janette, and Fidel Castro. *Proceso al sectarismo.* Buenos Aires: Jorge Alvarez, 1965.

"Habla el comandante Guevara," in *Bohemia,* January 11, 1959

"Hablan el padre y la hermana del Che," in *ABC* (Lima), November 15, 1979.

Hafkemeier, Jorg. "No es fácil ser el padre del Che pero trato de seguir su ejemplo," in *Proceso,* April 13, 1987.

Harnecker, Marta. *Che vigencia y convocatoria.* San Salvador: Sistema Venceremos, 1989.

Harrington, Edwin. *Así fue la revolución cubana.* Mexico City: Grupo Editorial, 1976.

Harris, Richard L. *Death of a Revolutionary: Che Guevara's Last Mission.* New York: Norton, 1970.

Hart Dávalos, Armando. "Sobre el Che Guevara," in *Casa de las Américas* (Havana), March–April 1988.

Heikal, Mohamed. *Los documentos de El Cairo.* Mexico City: Lasser Press, 1972.

Hernández, Gerardo. "Yo soy el niño de la foto," in *Granma,* November 5, 1988.

Hernández, Jesús. "Un gesto de solidaridad," in *Moncada,* October 1987.

Hernández Artigas, J. "Columna 8, Ciro Redondo. Los soldados de la revolución," in *Revolución,* January 14, 1959.

Hernández Pérez, Jesús. "Un gesto de solidaridad," in *Moncada,* October 1987.

Hernández Serrano, Luis. "Como la CIA obtuvo una foto del Che sin barba," in *Juventud Rebelde,* February 20, 1994.

———. "La selva en la mochila," in *Juventud Rebelde,* April 10, 1994.

Hetmann, Frederik. *Yo tengo siete vidas.* Salamanca: Lónguez Ediciones, 1982

Higgins, James. "A Preview of History," in *Monthly Review,* September 1971.

Hinojosa, Oscar. "Murió convencido de la revolución continental, narra el que lo capturó," in *Proceso,* April 20, 1987.

"Historia del II Frente Nacional del Escambray," in *Combate,* February 1, 1961.

Historia de una agresión. Havana: Ediciones Venceremos, 1962.

Huberman, Leo. "Cuba and the U.S." (interview with Che Guevara) in *Monthly Review,* September 1961.

——— and Paul M. Sweezy. *Anatomía de una revolución*. Buenos Aires: Palestra, 1961.

——— and Paul M. Sweezy. "El futuro de la economía cubana," in *Monthly Review*, Selections in Spanish, May 1964.

Hutten, Mark. AFP bulletin, October 6, 1976.

Iborra Sánchez, Oscar. "Episodios de la revolución. El puente que dividió la isla en dos," in *Carteles*, June 1959.

———. "Primer aniversario. Fomento, el primer municipio libre de Cuba," in *Carteles*, December 27, 1959.

———. "Yo soy el hombre más odiado por Pedraza" (interview with Victor Bordón), in *Carteles*, September 1959.

Iglesias, Joel. "Che el combatiente," in *Oclae*, October 9–15, 1972.

———. *De la Sierra Maestra al Escambray*. Havana: Letras Cubanas, 1979.

———. "Emboscada en Cuatro Compañeros," in *Cuba Internacional*, October 1977.

———. "En la guerra revolucionaria junto al Che" (also entitled "Mis vivencias con el Che" and "Junto al Che,") in *Verde Olivo*, October 1974 or *Tricontinental*, July–October 1970.

"Inaugurada escuela con el nombre del Che," in *Granma*, August 2, 1990.

Inclán Lavastida, Fernando. *Apuntes biográficos de J. M. Márquez*. Havana: Comisión de Orientación revolucionaria del CC del PCC (Revolutionary Orientation Commission of the Cuban Communist Party Central Committee), 1972.

Infante, Juan. "Características del funcionamiento de la empresa autofinanciada," in *Cuba Socialista*, No. 34, 1964.

"Informaciones recibidas sobre la muerte del comandante Guevara," in *Juventud Rebelde*, October 17, 1969.

"Invasión," in *Bohemia*, January 11, 1959

Isidrón del Valle, Aldo. "Anuncia Guevara el inminente colapso de la tiranía," in *Vanguardia*, December 23, 1967.

———. "Aquel diciembre de victorias," *Bohemia*, December 28, 1973.

———. "La batalla de Santa Clara," *Granma*, December 19, 1965.

———. "Che, avance incontenible," *Vanguardia*, December 23, 1967.

———. "Che, ejemplo de moral revolucionaria, audacia y modestia" (interview with Víctor Bordón), in *Granma*, October 8, 1977.

———. "Che en Guatemala y México" (interview with Dalmau and Darío López), *Granma*, October 17, 1967.

———. "Che Guevara: apuntes para una biografía," in *Islas*, January–March 1968.

———. "Che y Camilo rechazan la ofensiva," in *Vanguardia*, December 22, 1967.

———. "Che y el segundo Frente del Escambray," in *Vanguardia*, December 19, 1967.

———. "Con el Che por Sudamérica" (interview of Alberto Granado), in *Cuba Internacional*, September 1987.

———. "Corrió la noticia, Che está herido," in *Juventud Rebelde*, December 27, 1973.

———. "Diciembre de fuego. Santa Clara. Semblanza de una batalla," Unpublished manuscript.

———. "Esos instantes que un revolucionario jamás olvida," in *Granma*, January 16, 1977.

———. "Güinía de Miranda, primera victoria de la columna 8 en el Frente de Las Villas," in *Granma*, October 26, 1978.

———. "Impresiones de un corresponsal de guerra," in *Granma*, January 23, 1977.

———. "Un largo viaje en moto de Argentina a Venezuela," in *Granma*, October 16, 1967.

———. "Santa Clara, semblanza de una batalla," in *Granma*, December 30, 1977.

———. "Vaquerito. Jugó con la muerte una y mil veces por la libertad," in *Granma*, December 30, 1970.

———. "La victoriosa marcha hacia el Escambray, brillante proeza militar y revolucionaria," in *Granma*, September 17, 1978.

Ivanov, Oleg. "La concepción de revolución en Ernesto Che Guevara," in *América Latina,* (Moscow), September 9, 1988.

Iznaga, Diana. "Che Guevara y la literatura de Testimonio," in *Revista de la Universidad de La Habana* (Havana), No. 232.

Izquierdo, Irene. "Bolivia fue el Moncada de América," in *Tribuna,* October 1994.

J.A. "Apellidarse Guevara puede ser una tragedia," *Blanco y Negro* (Madrid), December 12, 1979.

JCM. "Los fusilamientos y los Maldonados," in *Revolución,* January 14, 1959.

JGS. "Ernesto Guevara, el Che, vida y hazañas," in *Sucesos Para Todos* (Mexico City), July 27; August 3, 10, 17, 24, and 31; and September 7, 14, 21, and 28, 1968.

James, Daniel. *Che Guevara, una biografía.* Mexico City: Diana, 1971, originally published New York: Stein & Day, 1971.

———. *Cuba, el primer satélite soviético en América.* Mexico City: Libreros Mexicanos Unidos, 1962.

Jardón, Edmundo. "El ejército puede tomar el poder," *El Universal* (Mexico City), October 2, 1995.

Jérez, Jaime. *Che Guevara, el hombre y la leyenda.* Madrid: Círculo de Amigos de la Historia, 1972.

Jiménez, Eleazar. "El Che y el ajedrez," in *Bohemia,* October 20, 1967.

Jiménez Losantos, Federico. "La horrible aparición de los hijos del Che," in *Firmas Press,* March 18, 1989.

Junta de Coordinación Revolucionaria del Cono Sur. *Che Guevara.* Oakland, Cal.: Resistance Publications, n.d.

Kahama. "Diario," unpublished manuscript.

Karol, Claudia. *El Che y los argentinos.* Buenos Aires: Dialéctica, 1988.

Karol, K. S. *Los guerrilleros en el poder.* Barcelona: Seix Barral, 1972.

Klare, Michael. *War Without End.* New York: Knopf, 1972.

Koningsberger, Hans. *The Future of Che Guevara.* New York: Doubleday, 1971.

Korda, Alberto. "Una foto recorre el mundo," in *Cuba Internacional,* September 1987.

Koutzii, Flávio, and José Corrêa Leite. *Che 20 anos depois. Ensaios e testemunhos.* São Paulo: Busca Vida, 1987.

Kuchilán, Mario. "En zafarrancho. Santa Clara, la batalla final," in *Bohemia,* October 12, 1968.

Kudin, Nikolai. "Mis encuentros con Che Guevara," in *Novedades de Moscú* (Moscow), No. 40, 1968.

Kuteischikova, Vera, and Lev Ospovat. "La literatura en la vida de un revolucionario," in *Casa de las Américas* (Havana), September–October 1977.

La Rosa, Lesmes. "La campaña de Las Villas," in *Verde Olivo,* January 6, 1974.

———. "Los ingenieros que soñó el Che," in *Verde Olivo,* May 7, 1987.

Labreveux, Phillip. *Bolivia bajo el Che.* Buenos Aires: Colección Replanteo, 1968.

Lagarde, Guillermo. "Esos refrescos que saben a jarabe de Tolú," in *Juventud Rebelde,* October 7, 1968.

Landáburu, Ander. "Yo preparé al Che Guevara" (interview with Vanegas), in *Cambio 16,* November 23, 1987.

Lara, Jesús. *Guerrillero Inti Peredo.* Mexico City: Diógenes, 1979.

Lara, Luis. "El día en que el Che inauguró la fábrica de Bujías," in *Juventud Rebelde,* October 8, 1968.

Larteguy, Jean. *Los guerrilleros.* Mexico City: Diana, 1969.

Lauzán, Raúl Simón, Rafael Fernández Domínguez, et al. *Ideas del comandante Ernesto Che Guevara sobre la moral del combatiente revolucionario.* Scientific Conference on the Military Thinking of Commander Ernesto 'Che' Guevara, undated.

Lavretsky. *Ernesto Che Guevara.* Moscow: Progress Publishers, 1975.

Lebedinsky, Mauricio. *Cuba y el Che.* Buenos Aires: Dialéctica, 1988.

"Lecciones para no olvidar," in *Militante Comunista,* June 1988.

Lechuga, Carlos. *In the Eye of the Storm.* Ocean Press, 1995.

Lee, Susana. "La revolución entró en el banco," in *Juventud Rebelde,* November 26, 1979.

León, Laureano. "El Che, sus ideas sobre el control económico y la contabilidad," in *Bohemia,* June 10, 1988.

Lesnik, Max. "10 de noviembre: Escambray heroico," in *Bohemia,* November 22, 1959.

Letter, "to Comrade Lawton from his comrades in No. 1 Column," November 6, 1985, manuscript.

Lihn, Enrique. *Escrito en Cuba.* Mexico City: Era, 1969.

López, Miguel Angel. *Las acciones del enemigo aéreo y las enseñanzas del Che.* Scientific Conference on the Military Thinking of Commander Ernesto 'Che' Guevara, undated.

López Fresquet, Rufo. *My 14 Months with Castro.* Cleveland: World Publishing Co., 1966.

López García, Delia Luisa. "Ernesto Che Guevara: aspectos de su pensamiento económico," in *Economía y Desarrollo,* November–December 1985.

Lora, Guillermo. *Autopsia del gorilismo.* La Paz: Ediciones Masas, 1984.

Lorenz, Marita, and Ted Schwarz. *Marita.* Mexico City: Planeta, 1995.

Löwy, Michael. *El pensamiento del Che.* Mexico City: Siglo XXI, 1971.

Lugo, Reynaldo. "Dos hermanos," in *Moncada,* October 1987.

———. "¡Este es mi hijo!" in *Moncada,* October 1987.

———. "El primer embajador," in *Moncada,* October 1987.

———. "Rolando, oficio de revolucionario," *Moncada,* October 1987.

Luis, Roger Ricardo. "La historia de Román García," in *Granma,* October 7, 1989.

———. "El hombre que me hizo guerrillero," in *Granma,* October 1992

"Luis Garcia Meza, acusado de robo de diario del Che," in *Presencia* (La Paz), January 11, 1989.

"Luis Miranda se refiere al Che," in *Bohemia,* January 29, 1989.

Lumumba, Patricio. *Libertad para el Congo.* Havana: Ediciones Venceremos, 1964.

Lupiañez Reinlein, José. "Entre versos y fusiles," in *Verde Olivo,* March 1987.

Luque Escalona, Roberto. *Yo, mejor de todos.* Miami: Ediciones Universal, 1994.

Llamazares, Julio. "En busca del Che," press clipping.

Lleras Restrepo, Carlos. "Me encontré en la vida con el Che," in *Nueva Frontera,* No place of publication, no publisher: n.d.

"Lleras fue amigo del Che Guevara," in *El País* (Madrid), April 12, 1977.

Llerena, Mario. *The Unsuspected Revolution.* Ithaca, N.Y.: Cornell University Press, 1978. Spanish edition: *La revolución insospechada.* Buenos Aires: Editorial Universitaria de Buenos Aires, 1981.

Llobet Tabolara, Cayetano. "Guerrilla y clase (el caso boliviano)," in *Cuadernos* (Centro de Estudios Latinoamericanos, Mexico City).

Maestre Alfonso, Juan. *El Che y Latinoamérica.* Madrid: Akal, 1979.

Mallin, Jay. *Ernesto "Che" Guevara: Modern Revolutionary, Guerrilla Theorist.* Charlottesville, N.Y.: SamHar Press, 1973.

Mandel, Ernest. "Las categorías mercantiles en el período de transición," in *Nuestra Industria,* June 1964.

———. *El socialismo y el hombre nuevo.* Mexico City: Siglo XXI, 1974.

"Manifiesto 1 del 26 de Julio al pueblo de Cuba," printed manuscript, Mexico City: December 10, 1956.

"Mapa del itinerario de la invasión," in *Granma,* October 16, 1967.

Marchetti, Victor, and Marks, John D. *The CIA and the Cult of Intelligence.* New York: Dell Publishing Co.,1983.

Marrero, Damia. "Che, mi compañero en la mina," in *Verde Olivo,* September 1988.

Marrero, José Manuel. *Relatos de Girón.* Havana: Editorial Letras Cubanas, Havana, 1982.

Martí, Julio. "El Che piloto aviador," in *Moncada,* May 1978.

———. "Donde cantan los ruiseñores," *Moncada*, October 1987.

———. Interview of Leonardo Tamayo, unpublished manuscript.

———. "Mambo-Tango navega el Amazonas," in *Moncada*, October 1982.

———. "Saber al Che frente a nosotros" (interview of Reynaldo Pérez Valencia), in *Moncada*, October 1982.

———. "Tiene la palabra el Che Guevara," in *Moncada*, October 1986.

Martin, David C. *KGB vs. CIA.* Barcelona: Planeta, 1980 (Originally published as *Wilderness of Mirrors.* New York: Harper & Row, 1980.)

Martín, Eduardo, and Benito Cuadrado. "Placetas un pueblo que forjó su liberación," in *Vanguardia*, December 23, 1978.

Martin, Lionel. *El joven Fidel.* Barcelona: Grijalbo, 1982. (Originally published as *The Early Fidel.* Secaucus, N.J.: Lyle Stuart 1978).

Martínez, Ricardo. "Como si fuesen dos columnas guerrilleras," in *Moncada*, October 1987.

———. "Los órganos de la seguridad del estado: 30 años de arduas y complejas misiones" (interview with Abrahantes), in *Granma*, March 25, 1989.

———. *7RR. La historia de Radio Rebelde.* Havana: Editorial de Ciencias Sociales, 1978.

Martínez, Sanjuana. "A los 23 años, montado en una motocicleta y en 'aventones' el Che Guevara cruzó Sudamérica y encontró su vocación," in *Proceso* (Mexico City), October 25, 1993.

———. "Desde que leí el diario juvenil de mi padre, el Che Guevara, intento ser mejor: Aleida," in *Proceso* (Mexico City), October 25, 1993.

Martínez Estévez, Diego. *Ñancahuazú: Apuntes para la historia militar de Bolivia.* La Paz: privately printed, 1989.

Martínez Estrada, Ezequiel. "Che Guevara, capitán del pueblo," in *Casa de las Américas* (Havana), No. 33, 1965.

Martínez Heredia, Fernando. *Che, el socialismo y el comunismo.* Havana: Casa del Las Américas, 1989.

Martínez Páez, Julio. *Un médico en la sierra.* Havana: Editorial Gente Nueva, 1990.

———. "Los médicos guerrilleros," in *Granma*, November 25, 1967.

Martínez Triay, Alina. "Antecedentes, preparativos y principales acciones de la guerrilla del Che en Bolivia," in *El Militante Comunista*, October 1982.

Martínez U., Haroldo; Martínez U., Hugo. *Che. Antecedentes biográficos del comandante Ernesto "Che" Guevara.* Santiago, Chile: Talleres de Editorial Prensa Latinoamericana, 1968.

Marx, Gary. "Even Dead Guevara Sparks Trouble," in *Chicago Tribune,* May 17, 1992.

Más, Sara. "El Che no pudo conocerlos pero sí imaginarlos," in *Granma*, June 18, 1988.

———. "Su incurable pasión creadora," in *Granma*, October 30, 1992.

Massari, Roberto. *Che Guevara, grandeza y riesgo de la utopía.* Tafalla, Spain: Txalaparta, 1993.

Masetti, Ricardo. "Che en Guatemala," in *Granma*, October 17, 1967.

———. *Los que luchan y los que lloran.* With foreword by Rodolfo Walsh. Montevideo: Punto Sur, 1987.

Massip, José. "Che en el cine," in *Cine Cubano* 1947, 1967.

Matthews, Herbert L. *The Cuban Story.* New York: George Braziller, 1961.

———. *Revolution in Cuba: An Essay in Understanding.* New York: Scribners, 1975.

———. *A World in Revolution.* New York, Scribners, 1971.

May, Elmar. *Che Guevara.* Mexico City: Extemporáneos, 1975.

Mayo, José. "El primer apoyo," in *Verde Olivo*, December 3, 1978.

Mena, Emilio. "Informe en relación a la columna comandada por el comandante Moya" [in the Congo], unpublished manuscript.

Mena, Marcel. "Cinco meses después me

ha llegado la noticia de su muerte," in *Oclae,* August–September 1970.

Mencia, Mario. "Así empezó la historia del guerrillero heroico," in *Bohemia,* October 10, 1975.

———. "Así era mi hijo Ernesto," in *Bohemia,* October 8, 1976.

———. "Bolivia, 30 meses de historia y una interrogación" in *Oclae,* December 1967.

———. "Un chico argentino muy atractivo llamado Ernesto" (interview with Mirna Torres) in *Bohemia,* October 14, 1977.

———. "Cuando uno pasa con sed y bebe agua de la fuente," in *Granma,* June 9, 1972.

———. "Entrevista tras un rostro. Por última vez" (interview with Alfonso Bauer), *Bohemia,* October 28, 1977.

———. "Los primeros cubanos que conocieron al Che," in *Bohemia,* October 7, 1987.

Méndez Capote, Renée. *Che, comandante del alba.* Havana: Gente Nueva, 1977.

Meneses, Enrique. *Castro comienza la revolución.* Madrid: Espasa Calpe, 1995.

———. "Con Fidel en la sierra," in *El País Semanal* (Madrid), January 7, 1979.

Meneses, Orlando. "Hacia donde sople el viento," in *El Mundo,* October 16, 1967.

Mesa, Aida. "Israel Reyes Zayas," *Bohemia,* August 30, 1974.

———. "Juan Pablo Chang Navarro," in *Bohemia,* October 4, 1974.

———. "Manuel Hernández Osorio," in *Bohemia,* September 27, 1974.

Mesa Lago, Carmelo. *Cuba in the Seventies: Pragmatism and Institutionalization.* Albuquerque: University of New Mexico Press, 1974.

———, and June Belkin. *Cuba en Africa.* Mexico City: Editorial Kosmos, 1982.

Michaels, Albert. "Che Guevara, His Life: Myth and Reality." In James Wilkie and Albert L. Wallace-Michaels, *Two Essays on Latin American Political Myths: Octavio Paz and Che Guevara.* Buffalo, N.Y.: Council on International Studies, State University of New York at Buffalo, 1981.

Mikoyan, Anastas. *Mikoyan in Cuba.* New York: Crosscurrent Press, 1960.

———. "Mis recuerdos de Cuba," in *Prisma* (Havana), June 1978.

Mikoian, Sergo Anastasovich. "Encuentros con Che Guevara," in *América Latina,* (Moscow), 1974, number one.

"Militares bolivianos buscan ya los restos del Che," in *La Jornada* (Mexico City), November 24, 1995.

Miná, Gianni. *Un continente desparecido.* Milan: Sperling & Kupfer, 1995.

Miná, Gianni. *Fidel.* Mexico City: Edivisión, 1991.

———. *Habla Fidel.* Mexico City: Edivisión, 1988.

Mir, Pedro. "Una escala en mi diario donde aparece la gloria," in *Casa de las Américas* (Havana), March–April 1968.

Miranda, Caridad. "La debacle del tren blindado," in *Moncada,* December 1983.

Miranda, Luis. "Las relaciones cubano-soviéticas en la revolución: historia y documentos," in *URSS,* January 1989.

Mironov, Vladimir. "Ernesto Che Guevara: hombre-revolución," in *América Latina* (Moscow), Nos. 3 and 4, 1986.

Mojena, María Cristina. "Camilo era mucho Camilo" (interview with Pablo Díaz), in *Verde Olivo,* October 1989.

Molina, Gabriel. *Diario de Girón.* Havana: Editora Política, 1984.

———. "Entrevista con un reportero gráfico," in *Fototécnica,* July–September 1982.

Montané, Jesús, Faustino Pérez, Universo Sánchez, et al. "Testimonios sobre el Che," in *Militante Comunista,* October 1982.

Montaner, Carlos Alberto. *Informe secreto sobre la revolución cubana.* Barcelona: Sedmay, 1976.

Montero Acuña, Ernesto. "Con los creadores de la riqueza," in *Trabajadores,* June 13, 1987.

Montoto, Heli. "El directorio aspira a ver

una patria nueva" (interview with Faure Chomón), in *Prensa Libre,* January 6, 1959.

Montoya, Pedro. "El mito del Che," *El Mundo* (Madrid), October 4, 1992.

Mora, Alberto. "En torno a la cuestión del funcionamiento de la ley del valor en la economía cubana en los actuales momentos," in *Comercio Exterior,* June 1963.

Morales, Alberto, and Fabián Ríos. *Comandante Che Guevara.* Buenos Aires: Editora América Latina, 1968.

Morales, José Luis. "No sabíamos que el Che vivía y estaba preso," in *Interviú* (Madrid), October 14, 1987.

Morales, Larry. *El jefe del pelotón suicida.* Havana: UNEAC, 1979.

Morales, María Isabel. "Aquella visita a una agencia bancaria," in *Juventud Rebelde,* October 30, 1992.

Moreno, José Antonio. *Che Guevara on Guerrilla Warfare: Doctrine, Practice and Evaluation.* Latin American Studies Occasional Papers, No. 3. Pittsburgh: Center for Latin American Studies, University of Pittsburgh, 1970.

Moyano Martín, Dolores. "From El Cid to El Che: The Hero and the Mystique of Liberation in Latin America," in *The World and I* (Washington, D.C.), February 1988.

———. "The Making of a Revolutionary: A Memoir of Young Guevara," in *The New York Times Magazine,* August 18, 1968.

"Murió Che Guevara," in *El Diario* (La Paz), October 10, 1967.

Muñoz Unsaín, Alfredo, and Bertrand Rosenthal. "La guerrilla secreta del doctor Tatu," AFP cable, October 5, 1987.

"El museo de la Revolución," in *Bohemia,* April 23, 1974.

"Mystery Man Guevara, Bearded or Beardless," in *U.S. News & World Report,* May 1, 1967.

Naón, Jesús. "Cuando el Che estuvo en San Andrés de Caiguanabo," in *Granma,* April 16, 1967.

Navarro, Noel. "Los días de nuestra angustia," in *Bohemia,* October 20, 1967.

Navarro, Osvaldo. *El caballo de Mayaguara.* Havana: Editora Política, 1987.

———. "Con el Che terminé la guerra," unpublished manuscript.

Nemira, Igor. "La última entrevista del Che en Moscú," in *Bohemia,* October 26, 1973.

"A New Old Che Guevara Interview," in *Hispanic American Historical Review,* August 1966.

Nieto, Severo. "Che deportista," in *Verde Olivo,* June 21, 1984.

———. "Pasión por el deporte," in *Prisma,* April 1987.

Nieves Portuondo, Alfredo. "El Che vuelve a volar," in *Verde Olivo,* June 1988.

Nillo, Carlos. *Reflexiones sobre la artillería y el pensamiento militar del Che.* Scientific Conference on the Military Thinking of Commander Ernesto 'Che' Guevara, undated.

Nkrumah, Kwame. *Challenge of Congo.* New York: International Publishers, 1967.

"Notas de una gesta: En sus hombres," in *Verde Olivo,* October 1988.

Noval, Liborio. "La historia de Román García," in *Granma,* October 7, 1989.

"Nuestras estancias junto al Che," in *Juventud Rebelde,* October 8, 1968

Núñez, Carlos. "Un diálogo con Régis Debray," in *Casa de Las Américas* (Havana), July–August 1968.

———. "Régis Debray, culpable de ser revolucionario," in *Tricontinental,* November 1967.

Núñez Jiménez, Antonio. "El Che y un instante de la rendición de Santa Clara," in *Casa de las Américas,* January–February 1968.

———. *En marcha con Fidel.* Havana: Letras Cubanas, 1982.

———. "Santa Clara, la batalla final" in *Combatiente,* January 1, 1968.

———. "El tren blindado," in *Bohemia,* October 8, 1971.

Núñez Machín, Ana. "El Che Guevara, un hombre através de sus anécdotas," in *Bohemia,* October 1987.

————. *De los héroes a los niños.* Havana: Editorial Gente Nueva, 1985.

Oficina de Publicaciones del Consejo de Estado. "Guisa, preludio de la victoria," in *Granma* supplement, November 30, 1988.

Oliva, Enrique. "El embajador de Bolivia en París fue muerto a tiros," in *Clarín* (Buenos Aires), May 12, 1976.

Oltuski, Enrique. "El día de la victoria," in *Islas,* October–December 1968.

————. "Gente del Llano," in *Casa de las Américas* (Havana), No. 40, 1967.

————. "¿Qué puedo decir?" in *Casa de las Américas* (Havana), January–February 1968.

"Operacion Mongoose una guerra interminable," in *Cuadernos de Estudios,* Havana: Centro de Estudios Para Asuntos de Seguridad, December 1964.

Oramas, Joaquín. "Un extraordinario formador de cuadros," in *Granma,* September 19, 1992.

Oramas León, Orlando. "La Higuera, donde la muerte devino redención," in *Granma,* October 7, 1969.

"Ordena Sánchez de Lozada que sean localizados los restos del Che Guevara," in *La Jornada* (Mexico City), November 23, 1995.

"Ordenan a Mario Vargas localizar los restos del Che," *La Jornada* (Mexico City), November 25, 1995.

Orestes, Raúl. "Una emisora histórica," in *Opina,* February 1989.

Orfila, Arnaldo. "Recordando al Che," in *Casa de las Américas* (Havana), January–February 1968.

Orozco, Román. "Mi padre tenía un gran sentido del humor" (interview with Hilda Guevara), *Cambio 16* (Madrid), September 26, 1992.

Ortega, Benjamín. *El Che Guevara. Reacción de la prensa del Continente americano con motivo de su muerte, octubre–noviembre 1967.* CIDOC Dossier No. 30. Cuernavaca, Mexico: Centro Intercultural de Documentación, 1968.

Ortega, Gregorio. *En la brecha.* Havana: Editora Política, 1985.

————. "Ladridos desde la cuneta," in *Granma,* October 15, 1968.

————. *Santo Domingo, 1965.* Havana: Ediciones Venceremos, 1965.

Ortega, Josefina. "Al Che le debo la vida," in *Juventud Rebelde,* October 4, 1987.

————. "La batalla de Santa Clara," in *Juventud Rebelde,* December 29, 1983.

Ortiz, Pedro. "Che en Gibara," in *Ahora* (Holguín, Cuba), May 1, 1988.

Otero, Elena. "Diciembre de fuego," in *Granma,* December 30, 1966.

Otero, Lisandro. "La entrada del presidente Urrutia en el palacio," in *Bohemia,* January 11, 1959.

————. *Las Villas.* Havana: Ediciones Venceremos, 1965.

————, ed. *Playa Girón: derrota del imperialismo.* Havana: Ediciones R, 1962.

P.M. "El honor que se merece," in *Cuba,* December 1987.

Pagés, Raisa. "Los reclamos obreros conquistados," *Granma,* December 19, 1983.

"Palabras del Che en la TV de EEUU," in *Bohemia,* December 18, 1964.

Palacio, Carlos. "Che ajedrecista," in *El Mundo,* October 16, 1967.

Palmero, Otto, and Luz María Martínez. "Donde la libertad llegó de golpe," in *Vanguardia,* December 24, 1978.

"Para combatir al imperialismo o ir de vacaciones a la luna," in *Juventud Rebelde,* May 12, 1988.

Pardo Llada, José. *El Che que yo conocí.* Medellín, Colombia: Hedout, 1971. Also included in *Fidel y el Che.* Barcelona: Plaza y Janés, 1988.

————. "Cómo se enteró Fidel de la caída de Batista," in *Bohemia,* January 11, 1959.

————. "Periódico de la palabra," radio script, November 25, 1959.

Pavón, Luis. "Che, la ventana encendida," in *Verde Olivo,* October 8, 1987.

————. "Cumpliendo la misión del comandante en jefe" (interview of Alfonso Zayas), in *Verde Olivo,* August 1963.

————. Epilogue to new publication of Che's article "Lidia y Clodomira" in

Cuba, undated clipping provided by the author.

———. "Faltaba papel y tinta, pero salía," in *Verde Olivo,* May 1989.

Paz Rada, Eduardo. "Cómo murió Guevara," AFP cable, October 3, 1987.

Pellecer, Carlos Manuel. *Caballeros sin esperanza.* Guatemala: Editorial del Ejército, 1973.

Pentón, Jorge. *La ética del pensamiento del Che como fundamento de la actividad revolucionaria.* Havana: Instituto Superior del Minint, n.d.

"Pensamiento de valor permanente," in *Bohemia,* October 5, 1979.

Peña, César. "Cómo fusilamos al Che: general Reque Terán," in *El Universal* (Mexico City), October 8 and 9, 1978.

Peña, Tania. "Un día conocí al Che," in *Granma,* September 3, 1988.

Perales, Iosu. *Querido Che.* Madrid: Editorial Revolución, 1987.

Peredo, Inti. *Mi campaña con el Che.* Mexico City: Diógenes, 1971.

———. "Che, hombre del siglo XXI," in *Revista Che Guevara,* October–December 1977.

Pereira, Casilda. "Mi compañero de los aires," in *Moncada,* October 1982.

Perera, Alina, and Eduardo Jiménez. "Encargo de conciencia," *Juventud Rebelde,* June 13, 1993.

Pérez, Faustino. "Un revés que se convirtió en victoria," in *Bohemia,* October 1967.

———. "Yo vine en el Granma," in *Bohemia,* January 11, 1959.

Pérez Betancourt, Rolando. *Sucedió hace 20 años.* Havana: Editorial de Ciencias Sociales, 1978.

Pérez Galdós, Victor. *Un hombre que actúa como piensa.* Havana: Editora Política, 1987.

Pérez Tarrau, Gabriel. *Camilo Cienfuegos, cronología de un héroe.* Havana: Comisión Nacional de Estudios Históricos, UJC, 1989.

"Un personaje de leyenda, el Che Guevara," special number of *Alarma* (Mexico City), May 30, 1968.

Petinaud, Jorge. "Arturo: el más joven de los cubanos," in *Moncada,* January 1978.

Pino Machado, Quintín. *La batalla de Girón.* Havana: Editorial de Ciencias Sociales, 1983.

Pino Puebla, Alfredo. "La batalla de Santa Clara," in *Bohemia,* December 27, 1959.

Piñeiro, Sergio. "Che Guevara habla para Prensa Libre. Lo que interesa ahora es defender la libertad de Cuba," in *Prensa Libre,* January 6, 1959.

———. "Fue asaltante en el Moncada y vino con Fidel en el Granma" (interview with Ramiro Valdés), *Prensa Libre,* January 6, 1959.

Piñera, Toni. "Visa europea para una imagen nuestra," in *Granma,* February 15, 1990.

Pita Rodríguez, Francisco. "Cayó junto al Che en la quebrada del Yuro," in *Bohemia,* March 6, 1981.

Playa Girón, la gran conjura. Havana: Editorial San Luis, 1991.

Poemas al Che. Barcelona: Los Libros de la Frontera, 1976.

Pogolotti, Graciela. "Apuntes para el Che escritor," in *Casa de las Américas* (Havana), No. 46, January–February 1968.

Ponciano, Roberto. "Caballete de Casa: el primer campamento del Che en Las Villas," in *Juventud Rebelde,* June 12, 1968.

"Por el robo del diario del 'Che': Comisión de justicia abrió proceso contra Garcia Meza," in *Presencia* (La Paz), November 24, 1988.

"Por sustracción de diarios del Che: Congreso ordenó detención formal del ex-General Luis Garcia Meza," in *Presencia* (La Paz), January 13, 1989.

Portuondo, Nieves. "El Che vuelve a volar," in *Verde Olivo,* June 1988.

Portuondo, Yolanda. *La clandestinidad tuvo un nombre, David.* Havana: Editora Política, 1988.

———. *Frank, sus últimos treinta días.* Havana: Letras Cubanas, 1986.

———. *Guillermo Sardiñas. El sacerdote comandante.* Havana: Editorial Cultura Popular, 1987.

————. *30 de November.* Santiago, Cuba: Editorial Oriente, 1986.

Prado, Gary. "Félix Rodríguez es un mercenario fantasioso," in *Presencia* (La Paz), October 19, 1989.

————. *La guerrilla inmolada.* Santa Cruz, Bolivia: Punto y Coma, 1987. Also published as *Cómo capturé al Che.* Barcelona: Ediciones B, 1987.

Prendes, Alvaro. *Prólogo para una batalla.* Havana: Editorial Letras Cubanas, 1988.

Prida, Eduardo, and Rita María Estenoz. "Che, un maestro" (interview with Universo Sánchez), in *SEP* (Mexican Education Ministry magazine), July–August 1984.

Prieto, Martín. "Che," in *Cambio 16* (Madrid), October 26, 1992.

————. "El último de los enigmas," in *Cambio 16* (Madrid), October 16, 1992.

"Principales combates en que participó el Che en la Sierra Maestra y en Las Villas," in *Moncada*, October 1967.

"Prisión y muerte de Joaquín Casillas," in *Bohemia*, January 11, 1959.

"Proyecto de informe al acto central por la conmemoración del XX aniversario, de la formación, salida y cumplimiento de misión internacionalista de la Columna 1 en el Congo-Leopoldville" ("Draft Report on Principal Ceremony to Commemorate the 20th Anniversary of the Formation, Departure, and Accomplishment of the Internationalist Mission by No. 1 Column to the Congo-Leopoldville"). Unpublished manuscript.

Puig, Carlos. "Sentí por un momento que ya no lo odiaba" (interview with Félix Rodríguez), in *Proceso* (Mexico City), October 12, 1992.

Purón, Alfonso. "Un ejemplo de virtudes revolucionarias," in *Moncada*, October 1982.

Quevedo, José. *El último semestre.* Havana: Uneac, 1982.

Quintana, Mirella. "Pachungo en la guerrilla del Che," in *Verde Olivo*, September 30, 1982.

Quintana, Victoria, and Freddy Torres. "Luchar junto al Che" (interview with Leonardo Tamayo), in *Moncada*, October 1969.

Radaelli, Ana María. "Del oriente al altiplano," in *Cuba Internacional*, September 1987.

Ramírez, Anibal F. "Santa Clara, una batalla decisiva," in *Verde Olivo*, December 1978.

Ramos Pichaco, José. "Che y la misión en el Congo. El doctor Tatu," in *Vanguardia*, October 8, 1991.

Ramos Pichaco, José. "Che y la misión en el Congo (Final). Feliz desenlace del incierto rescate," in *Vanguardia*, December 1, 1989.

Ramos Pichaco, José. "Che y la misión en el Congo. Si repites ese nombre te fusilo," in *Vanguardia*, June 13, 1991.

Ramos Pichaco, José. "Che y la misión en el Congo." Part I: "Tatu, aquel hombre desconocido"; Part II: Yo ho me voy, primero me muero aquí." In *Vanguardia*, November 29 and 30, 1989.

Ramos Zúñiga, Antonio. *El armero del Che.* Havana: Universidad de Havana, 1985.

Rauber, María Isabel. *La guerra de guerrillas, cuestiones político-ideológicas de la estrategia del Che.* Scientific Conference on the Military Thinking of Commander Ernesto 'Che' Guevara, undated.

Ray, Michelle. "In Cold Blood: How the CIA Executed Che," in *Ramparts*, February 5, 1968.

"El recuerdo y sus propias palabras," in *Juventud Rebelde*, May 12, 1988.

"Red dictator back of Castro," in *U.S. News & World Report*, June 18, 1960.

Reed, David. "Los últimos días del Che Guevara," in *Selecciones del Readers Digest* (Spanish edition), clip, undated.

"El regalo de la foto del Che," in *Reforma* (Mexico City), December 23, 1995.

Remigio, Lionel. "Manila: centro de contacto," in *Ideal*, December 11, 1981.

"Repercusión mundial por la muerte del comandante Ernesto Guevara," in *Granma*, October 18, 1967.

"Reportaje a un billete," in *Bohemia,* October 16, 1970.

Magda Resnick. *The Black Beret: The Life and Meaning of Ernesto Che Guevara.* New York: Ballantine Books, 1969.

"Los restos del Che, incinerados y enterrados en Vallegrande, Bolivia," in *La Jornada* (Mexico City), November 22, 1995.

"Revela Alfredo Ovando que las fuerzas armadas bolivianas dieron la orden de asesinar al comandante Ernesto Che Guevara," UPI cable, June 12, 1978.

"Revelan localización de la tumba del Che Guevara," in *Novedades* (Mexico City), November 16, 1995.

"Las revelaciones de Ciro Bustos," in *Punto Final* (Santiago, Chile), February 2, 1971.

"Revista argentina acusa a la CIA," Prensa Latina, December 12, 1967.

Una revolución que comienza (anthology of reports from the magazine *Santiago*). Santiago, Cuba: Editorial Oriente, 1983.

Rey Yero, Luis. "Trinidad, 20 años de revolución triunfante," in *Vanguardia,* December 29, 1978.

Reyes Rodríguez, Eliseo. "Desde las Mercedes hacia Las Villas," in *Verde Olivo,* May 4, 1969.

———. "Diario." In *Compañeros del Che, diarios de Bolivia.* Caracas: Barbara, 1970.

Reyes Trejo, Alfredo. "Capitán Alberto Fernández Montes de Oca," in *Verde Olivo,* October 9, 1977.

Reyes Trejo, Alfredo. "Capitán Jesús Suárez Gayol," in *Verde Olivo,* May 8, 1982.

———. "Capitán José María Martínez Tamayo," in *Verde Olivo,* August 5, 1982.

———. "Capitán Orlando Pantoja Tamayo," in *Verde Olivo,* October 9, 1977.

———. "Cuba. Diciembre 1958," in *Verde Olivo,* December 31, 1966.

———. "Gustavo Machín Hoed," in *Verde Olivo,* August 28, 1977.

———. "El maquinista del *Granma*" (interview with Jesús "Chuchú" Reyes), in *Verde Olivo,* November 30, 1975.

———. "Mis vivencias con el Che" (interview with Joel Iglesias), in *Verde Olivo,* October 13, 1974.

———. "Primer capitán Manuel Hernández Osorio," in *Verde Olivo,* September 25, 1977.

———. "Recuerdos del Che" (interview with Commander Vicente de la O), in *Verde Olivo,* October 5, 1969.

Rivalta, Pablo. "Notas varias sobre la operación Omega." unpublished manuscript.

Rivas, Jesús, and Miguel Naón. "El Vaquerito," in *Granma,* December 30, 1967.

Roa, Raúl. "Che," in *Moncada,* October 1982; first published in *Casa de las Américas* (Havana), January–February 1968.

Roca, Blas. "Las calumnias troskistas no pueden manchar la revolución cubana," in *Cuba Socialista,* April 1966.

Rodda, José, and Luis Borges. *La exploración en el pensamiento militar del comandante Ernesto Che Guevara.* Scientific Conference on the Military Thinking of Commander Ernesto 'Che' Guevara, undated.

Rodríguez, Augusto. "Constructor del partido Comunista de Cuba," in *Bohemia,* October 3, 1980.

Rodríguez, Carlos Rafael. "Sobre la contribución del Che al desarrollo de la economía cubana," in *Cuba Socialista,* May–June 1988.

Rodríguez, Félix I., and John Weisman. *Shadow Warrior: The CIA Hero of a Hundred Unknown Battles.* New York: Simon & Schuster, 1989.

Rodríguez, Héctor Danilo. "El ultimo encuentro del Che con su familia," in *Granma,* October 25, 1987.

Rodríguez, Horacio Daniel. *Che Guevara, ¿aventura o revolución?* Barcelona: Plaza y Janés, 1968.

Rodríguez, Javier. "Era muy humano, con un enorme, con un terrible concepto del deber," in *Bohemia,* October 10, 1967.

———. "Las mujeres que se alzaron en el Escambray," in *Bohemia,* August 9, 1968.

Rodríguez, José Alejandro. "La bala que lo va a matar a uno nunca se oye" (interview with Paulino Gutiérrez), in *Trabajadores,* December 29, 1983.

———. "Santa Clara, la batalla que descarriló para siempre al ejército batistiano," in *Trabajadores,* December 31, 1983.

——— and Magda Resnick. "El Che hoy," in *Juventud Rebelde,* June 11, 1985.

Rodriguez, René. "Revolucionarios de cuerpo entero," *Verde Olivo,* June 13, 1985

Rodríguez Calderón, Mirta. "Anverso y reverso de una página de lucha," in *Granma,* April 14, 1988.

———. "De estrellas en las frentes," in *Bohemia,* August 19, 1988.

———. "Semillas de fuego" (interview with Faustino Pérez), in *Granma,* April 9, 1988.

Rodríguez Cordoví, Angel. "Rodeada la ciudad fue tomada palmo a palmo," *El Mundo,* January 6, 1959.

Rodríguez Cruz, René. "Se inicia la lucha en el Escambray," in *Bohemia,* December 25, 1964.

Rodríguez de la Vega, Adolfo. "Con Che en la batalla de Santa Clara," in *Granma,* December 1967.

Rodríguez Herrera, Mariano. *Abriendo senderos.* Havana: Gente Nueva, 1977.

———. "Acto Nacional por el XXX aniversario de la apertura del Frente Norte de Las Villas," in *Bohemia,* October 13, 1978.

———. "Antonio, Pachungo, Arturo, El Médico, el escalón más alto," in *Bohemia,* October 14, 1977.

———. "Las aventuras de Jacinto," in *Juventud Rebelde,* May 30, 1987.

———. "Bolivia, 10 aniversario," in *Bohemia,* August 26, 1977.

———. "Cariño de buenos hermanos," in *Juventud Rebelde,* May 12, 1988.

———. "Che, bandera flameando al viento de las libertades," in *Juventud Rebelde,* October 7, 1987.

———. "Che en Cinco Palmas," in *Juventud Rebelde,* December 21–28, 1987.

———. "Che, Fidel, una historia que ya cumple 20 años," in *Bohemia,* March 19, 1982.

———. "¿Cómo estás, muchachón?" in *Bohemia,* June 1982.

———. *Con al adarga al brazo.* Havana: Comisión Nacional de Historia UJC, 1973.

———. "Cuando el Che comenzó a recorrer nuestra América," in *Bohemia,* June 14, 1974.

———. *Ellos lucharon con el Che.* Mexico City: Prelasa, 1982.

———. "En Pinar de Pinares," in *Bohemia,* June 10, 1977.

———. "La invasión, epopeya de gigantes," in *Bohemia,* May 26, 1988.

———. "Jesús Suárez Gayol: la estrella que ilumina y mata," in *Bohemia,* April 8, 1977.

———. "José María Martínez Tamayo," in *Bohemia,* July 29, 1977.

———. "Un joven llamado Ernesto," in *Juventud Rebelde,* June 10, 1987.

———. "La Plata, la gran sorpresa de Batista," in *Juventud Rebelde,* January 17, 1988.

———. "Los que cayeron con honor serán los inmortales," *Juventud Rebelde,* August 30, 1987.

———. "Llanos del infierno, la primera emboscada guerrillera," in *Juventud Rebelde,* January 22, 1987.

———. "Miguel, Coco, Julio: inmortales soldados de la libertad americana," in *Bohemia,* September 30, 1977.

———. "El niño de las sierras de Altagracia." In *Testimonios sobre el Che.* Havana: Editorial Pablo, 1990.

———. *El otro Ignacio.* Havana: Editora Política, 1989.

———. "Palma Mocha, un combate sangriento y poco conocido," in *Juventud Rebelde,* August 19, 1987.

———. "Un poco de esta historia," in *Caimán Barbudo,* October 1969.

———. "Por la ruta de Fidel en la Sierra Maestra," in *Juventud Rebelde,* December 25, 1987.

——. "Por la ruta invasora del Che. De Gavilanes al Pedrero," in *Bohemia,* October 8, 1982.

——. "Por la ruta invasora del Che. De la Jagua a la Sierpe," in *Bohemia,* October 1, 1982.

——. "Por la ruta invasora del Che. El Jíbaro, la partida, el combate en La Federal," in *Bohemia,* September 24, 1982.

——. "Uvero, mayo amaneció con diparos de fusiles," in *Juventud Rebelde,* in May 27, 1987.

—— and Dariel Alarcón. "El día que cayó el Che," in *Cuba Internacional,* July 1981.

Rodríguez Loeches, Enrique. *Bajando el Escambray.* Havana: Letras Cubanas, 1982.

Rodríguez Ruiz, Hornedo. *Mando de las fuerzas guerrilleras de acuerdo con la concepción del comandante Ernesto Che Guevara.* Scientific Conference on the Military Thinking of Commander Ernesto 'Che' Guevara, undated.

Rodríguez Zaldivar, Rodolfo. "Desde la Sierra Maestra hasta las Villas" (interview with "San Luis"), in *Bohemia,* January 11, 1959.

Rojas, Manuel. "Comandante Che Guevara," in *Casa de las Américas* (Havana), January–February 1968.

Rojas, Marta. "El Che Guevara bajo el cielo de La Higuera," in *Granma,* October 11, 1987.

——. "¡Che vive!" in *Granma,* December 12, 1987.

——. "Ernesto, médico en México," in *Granma,* June 4, 1989.

——. "La muerte del Che en la prensa internacional," in *Granma,* October 8, 1990.

——, ed. *Testimonios sobre el Che.* Havana: Editorial Pablo de la Torriente, 1990.

—— and Mirta Rodríguez Calderón. *Tania, la guerrillera inolvidable.* Havana: Instituto Cubano del Libro, 1974.

Rojo, Ricardo. *Mi amigo el Che.* Buenos Aires: Editorial Jorge Alvarez, 1968.

Rojo del Río, Manuel. *La historia cambió en la sierra.* San José: Editorial Texto, 1981.

Roque, Leonardo. "Rescate en medio del mar," *Verde Olivo,* December 1, 1963.

Rosado Eiró, Luis. "Batalla victoriosa: Santa Clara," in *Verde Olivo,* December 29, 1983.

——. "Estrategia del Che en Las Villas," in *Granma,* October 18, 1981.

——. "Güinía de Miranda," in *Verde Olivo,* October 29, 1987.

——. "Una proeza militar: la batalla de Santa Clara," in *Granma.* special supplement, December 1988.

——. "Rasgos del pensamiento militar del comandante Ernesto Che Guevara," in *El Oficial,* October 1982.

Rosales, José Natividad. "En exclusiva mundial Antonio Arguedas revela a *Siempre* como y por qué entregó a Fidel Castro el diario del Che," in *Siempre* (Mexico City), July 2, 1969.

——. *¿Qué hizo el Che en México?* Mexico City: Editorial Posada, 1973.

Rosendi, Estreberto. "Cabaiguán: tradición revolucionaria y desarrollo," in *Vanguardia,* December 22, 1978.

Roth, Andrew. "I Was Arrested with Debray," in *Evergreen,* February 1968.

Rothschuch, Guillermo. *Che Guevara, poeta y guerrillero.* Managua: 1980.

Ruiz, Fernando. Untitled EFE cable, October 8, 1987.

Ruiz, Jaime. *El Che no murió en Bolivia.* Lima: Santa Magdalena, 1970.

Sáenz, Tirso W., and Emilio García Capote. "Ernesto 'Che' Guevara y el progreso científico-técnico en Cuba," in *Interciencia,* January–February 1983.

St. George, Andrew. "Secrets of the Che Guevara diaries," in *Sunday Telegraph* [London] July 1, 14, 21, and 28, 1968.

——. "La verdadera historia de como murió el Che Guevara," in *Visión,* April 25, 1969.

Salado, Minerva. *Cuba, revolución en la memoria.* Mexico City: Instituto Politécnico Nacional, 1994.

Saldivar, Dasso. "El Che en el mito" (interview with Roberto Guevara), in *Alternativa* (Colombia), January 30, 1971.

Salgado, Enrique. *Radiografía del Che.* Barcelona: Dopesa, 1970.

Sánchez, Antonio ("Pinares"). "El Che y Pinares hablan de Camilo," in *Verde Olivo,* October 27, 1974.

Sánchez, Juan. "El Pedrero en el camino. Reportaje en dos tiempos," in *Bohemia,* October 3, 1969.

Sánchez Vázquez, Adolfo. "El socialismo y el Che," in *Casa de las Américas* (Havana), January–February 1968.

Santamaría, Haydée. Foreword to special issue of *Casa de las Américas* (Havana), January–February 1968.

———. "Vamos a caminar por casa," in *Casa de las Américas* (Havana), January–February 1981.

Sanz Fals, Enrique. "La expedición de Nuevitas," in *Granma,* February 10, 1988.

Sarabia, Nydia. "Ernesto Guevara, fundador del cubano libre," in *Bohemia,* October 20, 1967.

———. "La mujer villareña en la lucha patria," in *Bohemia,* July 26, 1968.

Sarmiento, Raúl. "Un episodio en la batalla de Santa Clara, el combate del escuadrón 31," in *Vanguardia,* December 28, 1980.

Sartre, Jean-Paul. *Huracán sobre el azúcar.* Havana: Ediciones Prometeo, 1960.

———. "Vengan temprano, a medianoche, me dijo el director del Banco Nacional," in *Revolución,* August 3, 1960.

Saucedo Parada, Arnaldo. *No disparen: soy el Che.* Santa Cruz de la Sierra, Bolivia: Talleras Gráficos de Editorial Oriente, 1988.

Sauvage, Léo. *Che Guevara: The Failure of a Revolutionary.* N.J.: Prentice-Hall, 1973.

Scauzillo, Robert James. "Ernesto Che Guevara: A *Historiography*," in *Latin American Research Review,* Summer 1970.

Scheer, Ribert, and Maurice Zeitlin. *Cuba: an American Tragedy.* Harmondsworth, 1964.

Schlachter, Alexis. "Che, innovador técnico," in *Granma,* October 10, 1989.

Schlesinger, Stephen and Stephen Kinzer. *Fruta amarga, la CIA en Guatemala.* Mexico City: Siglo XXI, 1982. Originally published as *Bitter Fruit: The Untold Story of the American Coup in Guatemala.* New York: Anchor/Doubleday, 1983.

Sección de Historia de las Fuerzas Armadas Revolucionarias. "Granma. Recuento en el XX aniversario," in *El Oficial,* November–December 1976.

Selser, Gregorio. *CIA, de Dulles a Raborn.* No place of publication: Ediciones de Política Americana, n.d.

———. *La CIA en Bolivia.* No place of publication: Ediciones de Política Americana, n.d.

———. *Bolivia. El cuartelazo de los cocadólares.* Mexico City: Mex-sur Editorial, 1982.

Sexto, Luis. "El pacto reiterado," in *Bohemia,* December 2, 1988.

Silva, José R., Alfonso Zayas, and Rogelio Acevedo. "Che, un gran jefe," in *Juventud Rebelde,* October 20, 1967.

Sinclair, Andrew. *Che Guevara.* Barcelona: Editorial Grijalbo, 1972. (Originally published, under the same title, New York: Viking Press, 1970.)

"Siquitrilla" ("Cinco temas breves," in *Diario de la Tarde,* November 11, 1964.

Smith, Earl T. *The Fourth Floor.* New York: Random House, 1962.

Solano, Rafael. "Con el capitán descalzo: guía del Che en la Sierra," in *Granma,* October 22, 1986.

Sondern, F. "Sinister Man Behind Fidel Castro," in *Reader's Digest,* September 1960.

Soria Galvarro, Carlos, ed. *El Che en Bolivia, documentos y testimonios.* La Paz: CEDOIN, 1992.

Sorrentino, Lamberti. *Che Guevara è morto a Cuba?* Milan: Palazzi, 1971.

Sosa, José, José A. Rodríguez de Armas et al. *Algunas consideraciones acerca de las concepciones del comandante Ernesto Che Guevara sobre la guerra como fenómeno político-social.* Scientific Conference on the Military

Thinking of Commander Ernesto 'Che' Guevara, undated.

Soto, Angela. "Che ministro, Che funcionario," in *Juventud Rebelde,* October 7, 1968.

Soto Acosta, Jesús. *Che, una vida y un ejemplo.* Havana: Comisión de Asuntos Históricos de la UJC, 1968.

Sotonavarro, Arístides. "Antes de la gran batalla," in *Moncada,* September 1975.

———. "Che, el valor insuperable del ejemplo," in *Moncada,* October 1977.

———. "Tavito, médico de la guerrilla," in *Moncada,* October 1982.

A Standard Swahili-English Dictionary. Oxford: Oxford University Press, 1963.

Stanton, John. "Un rebelde en busca de una causa," in *Life en Español,* October 21, 1968.

Stone, I. F. "The Legacy of Che Guevara," in *Ramparts,* undated clipping.

Special Consultative Committee on Security. *Study of the "Diary of 'Che' Guevara in Bolivia."* Washington, D.C.: Pan American Union, 1968.

Suárez, Andrés. *Castroism and Communism.* Cambridge, Mass.: MIT Press, 1967.

Suárez, Felipa. "Conmemorarán aniversario 30 del primer trabajo voluntario," in *Granma,* November 23, 1989.

Suárez, Luis. *Entre el fusil y la palabra.* Mexico City: Universidad Nacional Autónoma de México, 1980.

———. "Tania la guerrillera," in *Siempre,* Mexico City, undated press clipping.

Suárez, Rogelio, Valentín Purón, Francisco Machado. *Conferencia científica sobre el pensamiento político del Che.* Escuela Nacional de tropa Guardafronteras del MININT, Cuba, undated.

Suárez Pérez. *Ideas del comandante Ernesto Che Guevara acerca del trabajo político educativo en el ejército revolucionario.* Scientific Conference on the Military Thinking of Commander Ernesto "Che" Guevara, undated.

Suárez Pérez. *Algunas concepciones del Che acerca de la guerra popular.* Scientific Conference on the Military Thinking of Commander Ernesto "Che" Guevara, undated.

Surí, Emilio. *El mejor hombre de la guerrilla.* Havana: Letras Cubanas, 1980.

——— and Manuel González Bello. "Los últimos días del Che." Unpublished manuscript.

Sweezy, Paul M. "La planificación económica," in *Monthly Review,* Selections in Spanish, November 1965.

Szulc, Tad. *Fidel, un retrato crítico.* Barcelona: Grijalbo, 1987.

———. "Shadowy Power Behind Castro," in *The New York Times Magazine,* June 19, 1960.

Tabares del Real, José. "El Che, revolución y economía," in *Bohemia,* October 17, 1986.

Taber, Robert. *M26, Biography of a Revolution.* New York: Lyle Stuart, 1961.

Tablada, Carlos. "Acerca del pensamiento económico del comandante Ernesto Che Guevara de la Serna," in *Cuba Internacional,* September 1987.

———. "Che y el control. La contabilidadad y la disciplina financiera," in *Bohemia,* October 2, 1987.

———. "Che y los comités de calidad," *Juventud Rebelde,* October 7, 1987.

———. "Las cualidades de un dirigente revolucionario," in *El Oficial,* May 1988.

———. "El pensamiento económico de Ernesto Che Guevara," in *Casa de las Américas* (Havana), July–August 1987.

Taibo, Paco Ignacio II. "La batalla del Che, Santa Clara," in *Verde Olivo,* December 1988–January 1989.

———. *La batalla del Che, Santa Clara.* Mexico City: Planeta, 1989.

———. "En la línea de fuego," in *Juventud Rebelde,* December 30, 1988.

———. "Estaciones de paso, el Che Guevara en México," in *El Universal,* January 2–11, 1996.

———. "Hoy sabemos," series of three reports in *Reforma* (Mexico City), December 1995.

————, with Froilán Escobar and Félix Guerra. *El año en que estuvimos en ninguna parte.* Mexico City: Mortiz, 1994.

Tamayo, Leonardo. "Luchar junto al Che," in *Moncada,* December 1970.

Tamayo, Leonardo. "El Vaquerito y el pelotón suicida," in *Verde Olivo,* January 5, 1964.

Tavora, Arakim. *Onde está Guevara?* Rio Janeiro: Editora do Reporter, 1966.

Thomas, Hugh. *Cuba, la lucha por la libertad.* Barcelona: Grijalbo, 1973 (Originally published as *Cuba, or the Pursuit of Freedom.* London: Eyre and Spottiswoode, 1971).

Toledo Batard, Tomás. *La toma del poder.* Havana: Editora Política, 1989.

"La toma del tren blindado," Santa Clara, Cuba: Political Orientation Directorate (DOR) of the Villa Clara branch of the Cuban Communist Party, July 1986.

Torres Hernández, Lázaro. "Lidia y Clodmira. Dos heroínas de la sierra y el llano," in *Bohemia,* October 1978.

Torriente, Loló de la. "Después de la gran batalla de Santa Clara," in *Carteles,* November 9, 1959.

————. "Memoria y experiencia de un guerrillero," in *Bohemia,* June 10, 1988.

Totti, Giani. "El Che ha vencido," in *Casa de las Américas* (Havana), January–February 1968.

"Traducido al polaco el diario del Che en Bolivia," in *Granma,* December 31, 1969

Travieso, Roberto. "Mi papá el Che" (interview with Hilda Guevara) in *Verde Olivo,* June 1988.

Tullis, Richard. "Informe a la seguridad batistiana" ("Report to Batista's Security Forces"), manuscript, July 1958.

Tutino, Saverio. "La hechura de Guevara," in *Casa de las Américas* (Havana), January–February 1968.

————. *L'occhio del barracuda.* Milan: Feltrinelli, 1995.

————. *L'ottobre cubano.* Milan: 1968.

Ubeda, Luis. "Una cueva con historia," in *Juventud Rebelde,* June 1988.

Uribe, Hernán. *Operación Tía Victoria.* Mexico City: Editorial Villicaña, 1987.

Urondo, Francisco. "Descarga," in *Casa de las Américas* (Havana), January–February 1968.

————. *Todos los poemas.* Buenos Aires: La Flor, 1972.

Urrutia Lleó, Manuel. *Fidel Castro and Company.* New York: Praeger, 1964.

Vacaflor, Humberto. "El diario del Che fue robado por una banda de nazis y traficantes de drogas," news agency cable, July 11, 1984.

————. "Encuentran páginas perdidas del diario del Che Guevara," in *Miami Herald,* June 14, 1984, and *L'Espresso* (Paris), June 24, 1984.

————. "29 años después aún duele a los campesinos la muerte del Che," in *Proceso,* October 12, 1987.

Valdés, Katia. "Che Guevara, facetas de un jefe militar" (interview with Leonardo Tamayo), in *Verde Olivo,* October 12, 1980.

————. "Hombre que inspira amor," in *Bohemia,* August 7, 1987.

Valdés, Ramiro. "Discurso," in *Bohemia,* October 20, 1978.

Valdés, Teresa. "Al lado de cada rebelde un maestro," in *Moncada,* October 1982

————. "Consecuente con sus principios," in *Moncada,* October 1987.

————. "De su espontanea sencillez," in *Moncada,* October 1982

————. "Donde surgió la victoria," in *Moncada,* October 1987.

————. "Recuerdos de una combatiente" (interview with Zobeida Rodríguez), in *Moncada,* October 1969.

————. "Sí, comandante," in *Moncada,* October 1987.

————. "Trabajador incansable," in *Moncada,* August 1987.

Valdés Figueroa, Juan. "Sus primeras medallas en combate," in *Verde Olivo,* March 22, 1981.

Valdivieso, Jaime. "Presencia del Che Guevara," in *Casa de las Américas* (Havana), September–October 1977.

Valenzuela, Lídice. "Tania la guerrillera," in *Cuba*, undated clipping in possession of Luis Adrián Betancourt.

Vargas Salinas, Mario. *El Che, mito y realidad*. La Paz: Editorial Los Amigos del libro, 1988.

Varlin, Thomas. "La mort de Che Guevara. Les problems du choix d'un théatre de opérations en Bolivie," in *Herodote* No. 5, 1977.

Vásquez Díaz, Ruben. *Bolivia a la hora del Che*. Mexico City: Siglo XXI, 1968.

Vázquez Auld, José Enrique, and Antonio Jesús Acero. *La campaña de Las Villas. Batalla de Santa Clara*. Scientific Conference on the Military Thinking of Commander Ernesto "Che" Guevara, undated.

Vázquez Viaña, Humberto. *Antecedentes de la guerrilla del Che en Bolivia*. Research Paper Series No. 46. Stockholm: University of Stockholm, Institute of Latin American Studies, 1986.

Vega Díaz, José, and René Ruano. "Cabairién, presencia en la historia," in *Vanguardia*, December 26, 1978.

Velázquez, José Sergio. "La batalla de Santa Clara," in *El Mundo Dominical*, September 20, 1962.

Velis, Clara. "Che y una vieja cámara," in *Opina*, November 1, 1987.

Vicente, Walfredo. "Comedido y sobrio llamaba a las cosas por su nombre," in *El Mundo*, October 18, 1967.

———. "De la Sierra Maestra a La Cabaña," in *El Mundo*, January 30, 1959.

Vilela, J. F. "Aquí dejo lo más puro de mis esperanzas de constructor," in *Bohemia*, October 11, 1974.

Villares, Ricardo. "Voluntad pulida con delectación de artista," in *Bohemia*, June 10, 1977.

Villaronda, Guillermo. "Esto fue lo que ocurrió en Columbia después de la caída del régimen," in *Bohemia*, January 11, 1959.

Villegas, Harry. "Recuerdos de Che," in *Verde Olivo*, October 10, 1971.

———, et al. *Che, teoría y acción*. Mexico City: Extemporáneos, 1972.

Villegas, René. "Fantasma del Che rondó por Brasil antes de por Ñancahuazú," Reuters cable, October 7, 1988.

Virtue, John. "Cuba Today," UPI cable, November 26, 1965.

Vitale, Luis. *Che, una pasión latinoamericana*. Buenos Aires: Ediciones al Frente, 1987.

Vitier, Helio. "Che en Buey arriba," in *Verde Olivo*, June 1988.

Vuskovic, Pedro, and Belarmino Elgueta. *Che Guevara en el presente de América Latina*. Havana: Casa de las Américas, 1987.

Walsh, Rodolfo. "Guevara," in *Casa de las Américas* (Havana), January–February 1968.

Winocur, Marcos. *Historia social de la revolución cubana*. Mexico City: Universidad Nacional Autónoma de México, 1989.

Wollaston, Nicholas. *Red Rumba*. London: 1962.

Wright Mills, C. *Escucha yanqui*. Mexico City: Fondo de Cultura Económica, 1961.

Wyden, Peter. *Bay of Pigs*. New York: Simon & Schuster, 1979.

Xiqués, Delfín. "El Vaquerito, simpatía, valor, inteligencia," in *Granma*, December 30, 1976.

Young, Crawford, and Turner, Thomas. *The Rise and Decline of the Zairian State*. Wisconsin: University of Wisconsin Press, 1985.

Yu, Winifred. "A Revolutionary Glamour," in *American Photographer*, May 1989.

Zavala, Betsy. UPI cable, July 15, 1967.

Zavaleta, René. "A diez años de la muerte del Che," in *Proceso* (Mexico City), October 3, 1977.

Zayas, Alfonso. "Cumpliendo la misión del comandante en jefe," in *Verde Olivo*, August 26, 1963.

———. "Nuestra estancia junto al Che," in *Verde Olivo*, October 8, 1968.

———. "Para poder conocerlo de verdad se necesitan unos cuantos años," in *Juventud Rebelde*, October 8, 1971.

Zeballos, Juan Javier. "20 años después el

cadáver del Che es aún un misterio," Reuters cable, October 7, 1987.

Zuazo, Alberto. "No hablar, no especular, recuerda la única boliviana en la guerrilla del Che," press clipping in possession of Luis Adrián Betancourt archive.

———. "20 años después sigue siendo un misterio que pasó con el cadáver del Che Guevara," UPI cable, October 3, 1987.

Zúñiga, Francisco. "Johnson planeó la muerte del Che," in *Sucesos para Todos* (Mexico City), undated clipping.

Early February 1964. Intelligence Information cable, NSF, Country File, Intelligence, Vol. 1.

December 30, 1963. "Implications of Cuba's Renewed Campaign of Incitation to Violent Revolution in Latin America," intelligence memorandum, NSF, Country File, Gordon Chase file, vol. "State Department."

January 5, 1965. Thomas Hughes, U.S. State Dept. Directorate of Intelligence and Research memo to secretary, inr. reports c24.

January 31, 1965. Memorandum of conversation, Savoy Hotel, London, Prime Minister Tshombe and U.S. Senator Dodd, NSF, Country File, Congo, Vol. XII.

February 26, 1965. Thomas Hughes, U.S. State Dept. Directorate of Intelligence and Research, memo.

August 10, 1965. Director of Intelligence and Research. U.S. State Dept. Memo.

November 5, 1965. CIA, Office of Current Intelligence. Special report: "The Cuban Communist Party." W. Bowdler file. Vol. 1, NSF, Country File, Cuba.

February 4, 1966. Godley to Sec. State, Intelligence Memorandum, "The Situation in the Congo," NSF, Country file, Congo, Vol. XII.

October 9, 1967. Memo from Bowdler to Rostow, NSF, Country File, Bolivia. C8, Vol. 4: Memos.

October 9, 1967. Telegram from Henderson to Sec. State. NSF Country File, Bolivia. C8, Vol. 4: Memos.

September 26, 1966. NSF, Country File, Cuba, W. G. Bowdler file, Vol. 2.

CIA. Directorate of Intelligence. Intelligence Memorandum: "The Bolivian Guerrilla Movement: An Interim assessment."

"Cuba in Africa." U.S. State Dept. Director of Intelligence and Research. NSF, Country File, Cuba, Vol. V.

F. A. Dwight, B. Heath. "Guerrillas vs. the Bolivian Metaphor," NSF, Country File, Bolivia. C8, Vol. 4: Memos.

"Intelligence Handbook on Cuba." CIA Directorate of Intelligence, January 1, 1965. NSF Country File, Cuba. Intelligence, Vol. 2.

"Havana's Response to the Death of President Kennedy and Comment on the New Administration." Foreign Broadcast Information Service, report on Cuba propaganda No. 12, Dec. 31, 1963. NSF, Country File, Gordon Chase file, vol. A.

Hughes, Thomas, U.S. Dept. of State Director of Intelligence and Research. Memoranda to Secretary of State, January 5, February 26, and May 15, 1965. Inr. reports c24.

NSF memo, Bowdler to Rostow. Country File, Bolivia. C8, Vol. 4: Memos.

CIA. Directorate of Intelligence. Intelligence Memorandum. "The Bolivian Guerrilla Movement: An Interim Assessment." NSF Country File, Bolivia. C8, Vol. 4: Memos.

NSF Country File, Bolivia. C8, Vol. 4: Cables.

"The Castro Regime in Cuba." NSF, Country File, Gordon Chase file, Vol. A.

"The Cuban Communist Party." CIA, Office of Current Intelligence. Special report. W. Bowdler file. Vol. 1. NSF Country Cuba.

"The Fall of Che Guevara and the Changing Face of the Cuban Revolution." CIA Intelligence Memorandum, October 18, 1965. W. G. Bowdler file, Vol. 1.

"The Trial of Marcos Rodriguez: Exposure

of Factionalism in the Cuban Party."
Foreign Broadcast Information Service, report on Cuba propaganda No. 15. NSF, Country File, Gordon Chase file, Vol. A.

Interviews by the Author, Froilán Escobar, and Félix Guerra for *El año en que estuvimos en ninguna parte*

Victor Dreke (Moja), October, November, December 1991

Arcadio Benito Hernández Betancourt (Dogna), November 1991

Herrera, September 1991

Marco Antonio Garrido (Genge), October 1991

Ernest Ilanga (Ulanga), March, April, June 1991

Alexis Tunjiba Selemani, November 1991

Erasmo Videaux (Kisna), February 1992

Interviews by the Author for This Book

Dariel Alarcón, February 1995

Régis Debray, May 3, 1995

Enrique de la Ossa, February 1995

Antonio del Conde (El Cuate), December 6, 1995

Oscar Fernández Mell, October 1995

Miguel Alejandro Figueras, February 1995

Juan Gelman, May 1995

Hilda Guevara Gadea, February 1995

Eduardo Heras, February 1995

José Ramón Herrera, October 1995

Raúl Maldonado, March 17, 1996

Manuel Manresa, February 1995

Aleida March, 1988

Enrique Oltuski, January 1995

René Pacheco, February 1995

Jorge Risquet, October 1995

Rafael Santiago (Kumi), February 1992

Leonardo Tamayo, February 1995

Eduardo Torres (Nane), November 1991

Jaime Valdés Gravalosa, February 1995

Salvador Vilaseca Forné, February 13, 1995

Palacio Zerquera, March 1992

Films, Documentaries, Television Programs

Che. Directed by Enrique Pineda for ICRT (Cuban Radio and Television Institute), 1967, b/w, 16mm, 29 min.

Che! Fictional feature-length film directed by Richard Fleisher for 20th Century–Fox, script by Wilson and Bartlet, starring Jack Palance (Fidel Castro) and Omar Sharif (Che), 1969.

Che comandante amigo. Documentary directed by Bernabé Hernández for ICAIC (Cuban Cinema Institute), 1977, color, 35mm, 17 min.

El Che Guevara. Fictional feature-length film directed by Paolo Heusch, with Paco Rabal in the role of Che.

Che, hoy y siempre. Documentary directed by Pedro Chaskel for ICAIC (Cuban Cinema Institute), 1982, color, 35mm, 11 min.

Constructor cada día, compañero. documentary directed by Pedro Chaskel for ICAIC (Cuban Cinema Institute), 1982, color, 35mm, 25 min.

Cuando pienso en el Che. Video documentary directed by Gianni Minà produced by Oficina de Publicaciones del Consejo de Estado, Havana, Cuba, 46 min.

Ernesto "Che" Guevara. Program hosted by Miguel Bonasso, Canal 40, Mexico City, March 1996.

Ernesto Che Guevara, le journal de Bolivie. Documentary directed by Richard Dindo, color, 35mm produced by Ciné Manufacture SA, París, 1994.

Ernesto Che Guevara. Hombre, compañero, amigo . . . Video documentary directed by Roberto Massari for Eme Edizioni, Editorial Abril, Etabeta, Roma-Havana, 1993, 90 min.

Una foto recorre el mundo. Documentary directed by Pedro Chaskel for ICAIC

(Cuban Cinema Institute), 1981, color, 35mm, 13 min.

Hasta la victoria siempre. Documentary directed by Santiago Alvarez for ICAIC (Cuban Cinema Institute), 1967, b/w, 35mm, 35 min.

El llamado de la hora. Documentary directed by Manuel Herrera for ICAIC (Cuban Cinema Institute), 1969, b/w, 35mm, 35 min.

Mi hijo el Che. Documentary directed by Fernando Birri for ICAIC (Cuban Cinema Institute), 1985, color, 35mm, 70 min.

Un relato sobre la columna cuatro. Documentary directed by Sergio Giral for ICAIC (Cuban Cinema Institute), 1972, b/w, 35mm, 45 min.

Viento del pueblo. Documentary directed by Orlando Rojas for ICAIC (Cuban Cinema Institute), 1979, color, 35mm, 17 min.

INDEX

and Guevara's diaries, 575–77, 597, 641
interviews, 109–10, 343
and "invasion" march, 180, 181
July 26th Movement, 54–55, 61, 63–66, 76
landing in Cuba, 87, 95
La Plata barracks incident, 100–103
mentioned, 31, 54, 226, 361, 382, 462
optimism, 98
Pino del Agua attack, 156–58
political program, 128
and Sardiñas, 139
Second Havana Declaration, 346
on sectarianism, 347–48
and/on Soviet missiles, 353, 355, 358
and Soviet Union, 297–98
taking of power, 263, 264, 266–67
Castro, Raúl
appointment as armed forces minister, 290
Granma expedition, 83, 86
and Matos, 290, 291
mentioned, 53–54, 55, 56, 58, 66, 95, 99,
107, 115, 121, 135, 155, 159, 263, 264,
275, 278, 279, 324, 334, 346, 348, 353,
361, 388, 462, 463, 464, 529
in Mexico, 68, 69, 70
at Pino del Agua, 157
Castro y Figueroa, Joaquín, 2
Castro y Figueroa, Pedro, 2
Cazalis, Severo (Siquitrilla), 372, 378, 379
Central Intelligence Agency. *See* CIA
Centralization, 380
Ceylon, 285
Chacón, Erwin, 567
Chamaleso, Antoine Godefroi, 416, 419, 444
Chang, Juan Pablo, 455, 457, 475, 476, 483,
495, 500, 525, 526, 535, 545, 546, 547,
552, 555, 559, 561, 566, 568, 637
Chávez, José, 540
Chávez, Mario, 479
Chávez, Ñuflo, 29
Chaviano, Ríos, 225, 233
Chess, 14, 341, 352, 370
Chibás, Raúl, 128, 601–2
Chichina. *See* Ferreyra, María del Carmen
Chichkov, Vasili, 269–70
China, 313–14, 388, 402
"Chinaman Chang", 140
Chomón, Faure, 205, 206, 208, 214, 228, 229,
234, 235, 247, 256, 261, 347, 382, 383
Choque, Hugo, 500
Choque, Salustio, 494, 495, 501, 503, 514
CIA (Central Intelligence Agency)
acts of sabotage, 343
and Bay of Pigs invasion, 325, 326
and Cuban exiles, 302
in Guatemala, 38, 43

and Guevara's diaries, 574, 575, 576
and Guevara's disappearance, 434
involvement in Bolivia, 501, 513, 518, 532,
558, 560
involvement in Congo, 627
Cienfuegos, Camilo
death, 291–92, 386, 557
and Guevara, 164–65
Guevara on, 300, 598, 599
at Guevara's wedding, 279
hunger, 598
mentioned, 74, 93, 102, 104, 177, 180, 186,
190–91, 192, 195, 216, 217, 225, 230, 234,
235, 244, 253, 256, 257, 259, 261, 262,
263–64, 273, 275, 278, 290, 304, 383
in Pino del Agua, 156–57
in Sierra Maestra, 115, 140, 147, 172–73,
174
wounding, 157, 158
Cienfuegos, Osmany, 291, 346, 402, 411, 415,
423
Cienfuegos (Cuba), 136
Cigars, 151
Cilleros (guerrilla), 124
Coco. *See* Peredo, Roberto
Codovila (Argentinian Communist), 479
Coello, Carlos, 320, 411, 428, 446, 448, 453,
457, 458, 461, 462, 469, 472, 473, 475,
478, 482, 505, 523–24, 529, 532, 545, 572
Cola, 339, 366
Colina, Orestes, 246
Collado, Norberto, 62, 81
Condori, Casildo, 521
Congo, 402–4, 405, 409, 417, 419–31, 437–50,
480, 627, 628
Coronado, Benjamin, 491
Cortez, Julia, 559
Costa Rica, 400
Cowboy Kid. *See* Rodríguez, Roberto
Crespo, Luis, 86, 87, 102, 104, 113, 115, 116,
128
Cruz, Margarito, 514
Cuba
anti-guerrilla offensive, 170–78
army casualties, 601
army surrender, 251–57
Bay of Pigs incident, 324–27
economic/industrial conditions, 288–89,
303–5, 309, 323–24, 329–32, 334,
338–40, 342, 345–46, 349, 352, 354–55,
361–62, 366, 367–68, 371–72, 377, 380,
383, 385
foreign aid to, 313–15
quality of products, 356, 372, 383–84
rationing, 336, 337, 338, 347, 349
revolutionaries' landing in, 86–96

hard to believe this all
actually happened :

Che all over place
from sugar cane fields
to lectures in Uruguay
to E~~soda~~ cola-factories
to the press

published a lot, spoke a lot
remarried - Aleida March - more kids

• won against U.S/LatAm dictatorships
shot himself

"learn from mistakes"
↳ industrialization
self-sufficiency

Pan-LatAmism → Identity
address U.N.
Africa & P. 401- black Cubans

P. 400

great quotes

always w/ people